# THE WORLD'S GREATEST STORY

*The Epic of the Jewish People in Biblical Times*

JOAN COMAY

*with drawings by Edward Bawden*

HOLT, RINEHART AND WINSTON
NEW YORK

*In memory of Yochanan*

The Scripture quotations in this publication are from
the Revised Standard Version of the Bible, copyright
1946, 1952, © 1971, 1973 by the Division of
Christian Education of the National Council of the
Churches of Christ in the U.S.A., and used by
permission.

**Library of Congress Cataloging in Publication
Data**

Comay, Joan.
  The world's greatest story.

  Includes index.
  1. Bible. O.T. – History of Biblical events.
2. Bible.   O.T. – Introduction.  I. Title.
BS1197.C53    220.9.5    78–2035
ISBN 0–03–019861–5

First Edition

Designed by Humphrey Stone and Sheila Sherwen
for George Weidenfeld and Nicolson Limited, 11 St.
John's Hill, London SW11

Printed in Great Britain
10 9 8 7 6 5 4 3 2 1

# CONTENTS

PART TWO

THE BOOKS OF LAW, POETRY,
WISDOM AND PROPHECY

# INTRODUCTION

### *The Nature of the Old Testament*

THE OLD TESTAMENT IS NOT A SINGLE or unified work. It is an anthology of the sacred literature of the Hebrew people, composed, edited, revised and compiled over a period of more than a thousand years, up to the third century BC. Its contents cover an extraordinary range: theology, history, law, prophecy, legends and folk-tales, proverbs and poetry.

Two centuries ago, it was regarded as heresy to doubt that every word in the Bible was a direct revelation from God, to be read in its most literal sense. Many of the devout, both Christians and Jews, believe that today. Darwin's *The Origin of Species*, published in 1859, stirred up fierce controversy. It is now generally accepted that the first man-like creatures evolved millions of years ago, and that the latest stage in the process, 'Homo sapiens', emerged at least 150,000 years ago already equipped with language, religion and tools. Even then, compared to the geological age of the earth itself, the story of man is but a few moments. To a modern mind, the account of the Creation in the Book of Genesis, is a striking parable.

When one comes to the historical narrative of the Old Testament, archaeological evidence bears out the general background of events, and sometimes confirms specific details. For instance, Assyrian and Babylonian inscriptions discovered in Mesopotamia describe campaigns and battles that are referred to in the Bible, and mention by name some Hebrew kings, like Ahab, Jehu and Hezekiah.

However, in assessing the exact degree of accuracy in the historical books, two factors must be kept in mind. Firstly, as a work written and rewritten over many centuries, the Old Testament blends together different ideas and ways of life at different periods in the Hebrew national saga. This lengthy process produced a certain amount of textual confusion, divergencies, repetition and obscurity. There are passages that still perplex scholars two thousand years later. Moreover, not all the original records have survived. In the biblical account of the monarchy, there are constant references to palace annals that either no longer exist or have not been found.

The second, and more basic factor, is the spirit in which generations of unknown biblical scribes approached their task. They did not purport to be 'objective' historians in the modern sense. Their overriding theme was a theological one. A single and invisible Deity was in control of all human affairs. A special covenant defined the relations between God and his chosen people. Whatever happened to that small people, for good or ill, derived from its observance or non-observance of its covenant obligations. If imperial powers trampled upon the nation, if it was afflicted by epidemic or drought, these were signs of divine displeasure. The record of each king was weighed in the scales of the religious code, for the rulers and the ruled were alike subject to God's law.

This special angle of vision dominates the Old Testament. It explains why the Hebrews felt no urge to idealize or deify their forefathers and their national heroes. They are depicted as fallible and sometimes erring mortals. Jacob, who became Israel, and fathered the Twelve Tribes, could trick his old, blind father out of a blessing that should have gone to his brother Esau. David, the founder of Hebrew statehood and its greatest king, could have an illicit affair with the wife of one of his army officers, and conspire to have him killed. It is this unsparing candour in portraying its characters that makes the Old Testament so intensely human a document.

## The Books of the Old Testament

*The Hebrew Bible* THE HEBREW OLD TESTAMENT BECAME DIVIDED into three sections: the Law (Torah, Pentateuch or Five Books of Moses); the Prophets; and the Writings. The Bible is known in Hebrew as the *Tanach*, from the initial letters of these three sections.

The Torah is the oldest section, and the first to be canonized (i.e. accepted as sacred scriptures) about 400 BC. Modern textual analysis distinguishes between four earlier written sources that were combined into the Torah as it now exists: the 'J' Document, compiled in the southern kingdom of Judah in the tenth century BC; the 'T' Document compiled in the northern kingdom of Israel in the ninth to the eighth centuries BC; the Book of Deuteronomy ('D' Document), dating from the eighth century BC; and the revisions introduced by the post-exilic priestly writers (the 'P' Document).

The second section, the Prophets, was finally edited and canonized by about 200 BC. It comprises two groups of books. The Former Prophets are the books of Joshua, Judges, Samuel and Kings, covering the historical period from the Conquest in the thirteenth century BC to the destruction of Jerusalem and the end of the First Temple in the sixth century BC. The Latter Prophets are the books that record the utterances of the individual preachers in the classical period of prophesy, from Amos in the eighth century BC to Malachi in the fourth century BC. The three 'major' prophets – Isaiah, Jeremiah and Ezekiel – each form a separate book. The twelve 'minor' prophets are in the Hebrew Bible brought together in a single Book of the Twelve.

The third section, the Writings, contains a miscellaneous list of works produced between the fourth and second centuries BC, though many of them are based on earlier traditions. Their selection and order was only settled about 90 AD, when a Rabbinical Council at Jamnia finalized the canon of the Old Testament. This step was prompted by the destruction of Jerusalem by the Romans in 70 AD, an event that brought the Second Temple period of Jewish statehood to an end.

Included in the Writings is the book of Chronicles, written about the fourth century AD. It is a revision, for didactic religious purposes, of much of the material in the earlier books, especially the historical narratives in Samuel and Kings. The books of Ezra and Nehemiah are generally regarded as a continuation of Chronicles; they bring forward the national history to the period of the return.

The books are listed below in the order in which they appear in the Hebrew Bible, with their abbreviations and their Hebrew names, where these are not the same as in English.

### The Law (*Torah*)
#### Hebrew

| | | |
|---|---|---|
| Genesis | (Gen.) | *Bereishit* |
| Exodus | (Exod.) | *Shemot* |
| Leviticus | (Lev.) | *Vayikrah* |
| Numbers | (Num.) | *Bamidbar* |
| Deuteronomy | (Deut.) | *Devarim* |

### The Prophets (*Nevi'im*)
#### The Former Prophets:

| | | |
|---|---|---|
| Joshua | (Josh.) | |
| Judges | (Judg.) | *Shoftim* |
| 1 Samuel | (1 Sam.) | *Shmuel Alef* |
| 2 Samuel | (2 Sam.) | *Shmuel Bet* |
| 1 Kings | (1 Kgs.) | *Melachim Alef* |
| 2 Kings | (2 Kgs.) | *Melachim Bet* |

#### The Latter Prophets:

| | |
|---|---|
| Isaiah | (Isa.) |
| Jeremiah | (Jer.) |
| Ezekiel | (Ezek.) |

#### The Twelve Minor Prophets:

| | |
|---|---|
| Hosea | (Hos.) |
| Joel | (Joel) |
| Amos | (Amos) |
| Obadiah | (Obad.) |
| Jonah | (Jonah) |
| Micah | (Mic.) |
| Nahum | (Nahum) |
| Habakkuk | (Hab.) |
| Zephania | (Zeph.) |
| Haggai | (Hag.) |
| Zechariah | (Zech.) |
| Malachi | (Mal.) |

LEFT The Nash Papyrus, a second-century BC fragment in square Hebrew script containing part of the Ten Commandments and the Shema prayer. It was the oldest biblical text known before the discovery of the Dead Sea Scrolls and was acquired from an Egyptian dealer and published in 1903.

RIGHT Page from the Peshitta, the fifth-century Syrian Bible, relating the story of Jacob.

### The Writings (*Ketuvim*)

| | | |
|---|---|---|
| Psalms | (Ps.) | *Tehillim* |
| Proverbs | (Prov.) | *Mishlei* |
| Job | (Job) | |
| Song of Songs | (S. of S.) | *Shir-ha-Shirim* |
| Ruth | (Ruth) | |
| Lamentations | (Lam.) | *Eichah* |
| Ecclesiastes | (Ec.) | *Kohelet* |
| Esther | (Esther) | |
| Daniel | (Dan.) | |
| Ezra | (Ezra) | |
| Nehemiah | (Neh.) | |
| 1 Chronicles | (1 Chr.) | *Divrei-ha-Yamim Alef* |
| 2 Chronicles | (2 Chr.) | *Divrei-ha-Yamim Bet* |

Traditionally, the Hebrew Old Testament is regarded as comprising twenty-four Books. In making up this number, Samuel, Kings, the Book of the Twelve Minor Prophets, Ezra, Nehemiah and Chronicles are each counted as one Book.

The oldest extant edition of the Old Testament in Hebrew is that of the Masoretic (traditional) Text, written in Tiberias in the ninth century AD. When the Isaiah Scroll, discovered as one of the Dead Sea Scrolls in 1947, was compared with the Book of Isaiah in the Masoretic Text, the differences were found to be negligible, although a thousand years separate the two texts.

The first translation of the Old Testament from the Hebrew was a Greek version produced in Alexandria, Egypt, in the third century BC for the use of the large and affluent Jewish community there. It was called the Septuagint, a Greek word meaning the Version of the Seventy, because that number of sages was said to have been brought from Jerusalem for the work. The Greek Bible continued to be amplified, and became the Old Testament generally used in the early Christian Church. The oldest full text to survive dates from the fourth century AD. It included fifteen additional Jewish works written in the second and first centuries that do not

*Greek, Latin, and Protestant Bibles*

appear in the Hebrew Bible. These writings later became known as the Apocrypha.

In the fourth century AD St Jerome produced in Bethlehem a Latin translation known as the Vulgate. St Jerome, working directly from the Hebrew text, wished to exclude the Apocrypha, but was overruled by the Church in respect of most of the stories.

On the authority of Martin Luther, the Protestant Bible reverted to the Hebrew canon. The Apocrypha were printed in a separate section in Luther's German translation (1534), as a collection of writings that were not part of the Scriptures but 'good and useful for reading'.

*English Translations*

The first English translations appeared a century-and-a-half before the Reformation. It was that of Wycliffe, about 1382. The Authorised Version (AV), or King James Bible, was published in 1611, and had a profound impact on the literature and thought of the English-speaking world. By the late nineteenth century the Authorised Version lagged behind the archaeology and biblical research that were throwing fresh light on the Scriptures. Furthermore, its lofty seventeenth-century style became more and more removed from current speech. A Revised Version (RV) was published in 1885. A Revised Standard Version (RSV) was later produced in the United States, and the Old Testament part of it appeared in 1952. The RSV has been used in the present work for quotations and the spelling of names.

Recent translations into modern English include the New English Bible, the Jerusalem Bible (Catholic) and the Good News Bible.

The order and arrangement of the books in Christian Bibles differ in certain respects from those in the Hebrew Bible. Moreover, there is no division into the three sections of Law, Prophets and Writings. The authoritative translation of the Hebrew Bible into the English language is that of the Jewish Publication Society of America.

PART ONE

# THE CHILDREN
# OF ISRAEL

# I

# IN THE BEGINNING

The
Creation:
The First
Version

'IN THE BEGINNING GOD CREATED THE heavens and the earth.'

These are the opening words of the Old Testament. They launch the majestic account of the Creation that appears in the first chapter of the Book of Genesis. In the course of six days the world emerges out of dark and watery chaos. First comes light, separated from darkness; they are called Day and Night. The heavens follow, dividing the waters below from those above. The lower waters are drawn together as the seas, and the earth is exposed. Vegetation springs forth, including fruit trees bearing seed. In the firmament of the heavens the sun, the moon and the stars are placed to give light upon the earth, to separate the day from the night and to regulate the seasons. In the seas swarms of living creatures come forth, and birds fly across the sky. On the sixth day the earth brings forth 'cattle and creeping things and beasts of the earth according to their kinds'. (Gen. 1:24).

Finally the human species appears: 'Then God said, "Let us make man in our image, after our likeness; and let them have dominion over the fish of the sea, and over the birds of the air, and over the cattle, and over all the earth, and over every creeping thing that creeps upon the earth". . . . male and female he created them. And God blessed them, and God said to them, "Be fruitful and multiply, and fill the earth and subdue it;"' (Gen. 1:26–28).

On the seventh day God rests from the work of creation, and therefore blesses and hallows that day. (This is the biblical reason for keeping the Sabbath as a holy day of rest.)

The
Creation:
The Second
Version

In the second chapter of Genesis there follows without any pause a different version of the Creation. It is more ancient and primitive in origin, and more vivid and detailed in style. Here God is known in the Hebrew text as Yahveh (Jehovah) instead of Elohim as in the first chapter. In this version, there is in the beginning a barren, dry wasteland instead of a watery chaos. The process of creation is not divided into successive days. After the Lord has made the earth and the heavens, man is the first form of life to be created, not the last: 'then the Lord God formed man of dust from the ground, and breathed into his nostrils the breath of life; and man became a living being.' (Gen. 2:7). [It is significant that in the Hebrew text the word used for Man, *adám*, is from the same root as the word for soil, *adamah*.]

God plants a garden in Eden, in the east, and there he puts the man. In the garden grows every tree that is pleasant to the sight and good for food. In their midst stands the tree of life and the tree of the knowledge of good and evil. A river flows out of Eden and divides into four rivers – Pishon, Gihon, Tigris and Euphrates – that between them water the known world of the ancient Near East. The man is told to tend the Garden of Eden, and permitted to eat freely of its fruits except for the tree of the knowledge of good and evil.

All the beasts and the birds are then formed out of earth, and each is brought to the man to be given its name (a symbolic act marking his dominion over them). But the man himself is still alone, without 'a helper fit for him' (Gen. 2:18); so the Lord causes him to fall into a deep sleep, removes one of his ribs and makes it into a woman. The man says: 'This at last is bone of my bones and flesh of my flesh. Therefore a man leaves his father and his mother and cleaves to his wife, and they become one flesh.' (Gen. 2:23,4). Adam's mate is called Woman (in Hebrew, *ishah*) because she was taken out of a male human being (in Hebrew, *ish*).

*The Temptation and the Fall*

Of all the creatures in the Garden of Eden, the craftiest is the serpent. It tempts the woman to ignore God's prohibition and to eat the forbidden fruit. (This fruit later became depicted in art and literature as an apple.) The woman not only eats the fruit but gives some to the man. They immediately become aware that they are naked, and make themselves coverings of fig leaves.

Towards evening, when they hear the sound of the Lord walking in the Garden, the man and the woman hide themselves. The Lord calls out to them and when Adam explains they cannot appear as they are ashamed of their nakedness, it becomes clear that they have eaten the forbidden fruit. The man blames the woman, she blames the serpent, and the Lord pronounces a curse on all three. The serpent will have to crawl upon his belly in the dust, and there will always be enmity between snakes and human beings. Women will bear their children in pain, and will be ruled by their husbands. Men will have to gain their bread from the soil by hard toil 'till you return to the ground, for out of it you were taken; you are dust and to dust you shall return'. (Gen. 3:19).

Having clothed the man and the woman in skins, the Lord expels them from the Garden of Eden. The way back is barred by cherubim (winged angels) and a flaming sword, to prevent them from eating the fruit of the tree of life as well, and thereby becoming immortal. Adam names his wife Eve 'because she was the mother of all living'. (The Hebrew word for Eve, *Chava*, means giver of life.)

*Creation Myths Elsewhere*

Certain elements in Genesis may have been derived from creation myths in other ancient Near Eastern religions – notably that of Babylonia. In particular, there are parallels with the ritual song called *Enuma Elish* chanted by the priests in the Babylonian New Year festival in the spring. It describes the victory of the god over the dragon of chaos, and the act of creation that follows. The idea that the first man was shaped out of earth or clay, and had life breathed into him, is common to many primitive peoples in various parts of the world. But whatever the similarities, among no other ancient people was there so powerful and dramatic a parable of the beginning of the world, and the evolution of life within it. The second Genesis account was in its time unique to the Hebrew faith, in that a single universal God was shown to be the Creator of all that existed.

The story of Adam and Eve, their temptation and fall, and the curse laid upon them, has served down the ages as a striking symbol of the human condition: paradise is lost through human weakness; men must struggle to wrest a living; women must bear children in pain; and the grave awaits each mortal being. Man clings to the dream-memory of an idyllic garden at the beginning of things, a place of abundance without labour, of security without strife. It is as well that the dream remains unattainable. Adam and Eve were flung into a real world of toil and suffering – but a world also of challenge, creative achievement and the restless quest for knowledge. To a twentieth-century mind, the paradise pictured in Genesis is the ultimate social welfare state, and its price might well be ultimate tedium.

The undying moral of the Genesis story is that all men are kin, for Adam and Eve are their common ancestors; and all men are equal, for they are created in the image of God.

Eve bore two sons, first Cain and then Abel. Cain became a tiller of the soil and Abel a shepherd. When they sacrificed the first fruits of

Eve tempting Adam. Woodcut by the sixteenth-century German artist Hans Burgkmair the Elder.

*Cain and Abel* their fields and flocks to the Lord, Abel's offering was accepted but not that of Cain. This rejection enraged Cain. He persuaded Abel to come into the field with him and there killed him. When the Lord asked him what had happened to Abel, he replied 'I do not know; am I my brother's keeper?' (Gen. 4:9). The Lord decreed Cain's punishment: his fields would no longer be fruitful, since Abel's blood had been spilt there; and Cain himself was doomed to become a fugitive across the earth. Cain protested that anyone who came across him would kill him, so God put a protective mark on him. Cain journeyed to the land of Nod, east of the Garden of Eden, where he settled down and married.

This brief story – apparently an incomplete fragment of a legend dating back to much earlier times – raises unexplained questions. To start with, no reason is given why the Lord should have rejected Cain's sacrifice. The shedding of Abel's blood in the field may possibly echo the primitive practice of human sacrifice as a means to secure the fertility of the crops. It is not made clear why Cain should have been condemned to be an outcast and then safeguarded by a special mark, the nature of which remains obscure. The circumstances of the story indicate that it took place at a time of widespread human settlement – otherwise why should Cain be afraid that he might be killed by strangers, and how could he marry? Yet, according to Genesis, the human family was still confined to Adam and Eve and one surviving son. Though there are no answers to these problems in the story, the clash between Cain and Abel clearly represents the age-old Near Eastern conflict between 'the desert and the sown' – the farmer cultivating his fields and the nomad shepherd in search of grazing and water for his flocks and herds.

*Adam's Descendants* A genealogical table gives Cain's descendants for the next seven generations. Economic and cultural progress is indicated. Cain builds a city and names it after his first son Enoch. Among his descendants are Jabal, ancestor of the nomad herdsmen; Jubal, father of harp and pipe music; and Tubal-cain, a master worker in bronze and iron.

Adam and Eve have another son, Seth. Eight generations of his descendants are listed, up to Noah, the hero of the Flood story. The life-span of Adam, Seth and most of the latter's descendants is given as over nine hundred years.

The oldest was Methuselah, who became a father at the age of one hundred and eighty-seven and died at nine hundred and sixty-nine. Noah was the grandson of Methuselah.

No explanation is offered in the text for the extraordinary ages attributed to the ten biblical fathers of mankind before the Flood. Here again, the Mesopotamian background of early Hebrew folk-lore becomes relevant. It cannot be mere coincidence that surviving records of the ancient Sumerian kingdom of Larsa (close to Abraham's birthplace of Ur) give a list of ten legendary kings before the Flood, and that each reigned between 10,000 and 60,000 years.

The belief in an earlier time when men lived much longer may derive from the human preoccupation in all ages with the mystery of death, and the longing for the divine attribute of immortality. The point is clearly made in Genesis:

Then the LORD God said, 'Behold, the man has become like one of us, knowing good and evil; and now, lest he put forth his hand and take also of the tree of life, and eat, and live for ever' – therefore the LORD God sent him forth from the garden of Eden. . . . (Gen. 3:22–23).

When Adam was told 'You are dust, and to dust you shall return,' no age limit was suggested. After the Flood, the Lord declared: 'My spirit shall not abide in man for ever, for he is flesh, but his days shall be a hundred and twenty years.' (Gen. 6:3) (To this day Jews wish each other long life 'up to a hundred and twenty years'.)

Actually the biblical life-span was reduced in stages. Compared to the pre-Flood ages (900–1000 years) Noah and his descendants were said to have lived between two hundred and six hundred years, and the Patriarchs between one hundred and two hundred years. Only with the monarchy does the biblical story enter into verifiable history, and does the length of life become the normal and transitory span of the psalmist:

The years of our life are threescore and ten,
 or even by reason of strength fourscore;
yet their span is but toil and trouble;
 they are soon gone, and we fly away.
(Ps. 90:10)

God despaired of what he had created, since the earth had become corrupt and filled with

*The Flood* violence. For that reason God decided to destroy life on earth by means of a great flood. However, Noah and his family would be saved, for 'Noah was a righteous man, blameless in his generation; Noah walked with God.' (Gen. 6:9). With him there would be preserved a pair of each species of animal, bird and creeping thing. On the Lord's instructions, Noah built a wooden ark with three decks and a roof. The ark measured 440 feet in length, 73 feet in breadth, and 44 feet in height – the equivalent of a ship of 43,000-ton displacement. It was covered with pitch inside and outside to make it waterproof.

On the appointed day Noah was shut into the ark with his wife, his three sons Shem, Ham and Japheth and their wives, and all the living things 'two and two ... male and female of all flesh'. (Gen. 7:15,16). Noah was six hundred years old at this time. Then, 'all the fountains of the great deep burst forth, and the windows of the heavens were opened. And rain fell upon the earth forty days and forty nights.' (Gen. 7:11–12). The water rose above the tops of the highest mountains and every living creature was drowned except for the occupants of the ark. After five months, the vessel came to rest on the top of a peak in the mountains of Ararat (a region in Armenia). Noah opened the window and released a raven that flew out over the water without returning. He then freed a dove that came back. Seven days later the dove was sent out again, and returned with a freshly plucked olive leaf in its beak, so Noah knew that somewhere land had re-emerged from the receding water. The dove went out again and this time it did not return. When the ground was dry, Noah led his family and the animals out of the ark. He built an altar and sacrificed burnt offerings in gratitude to the Lord.

Where did Noah get an animal or animals to sacrifice? He would not have touched the pairs of beasts taken on board for future reproduction.

The answer may lie in another tradition also included in the text. According to this version, the number of each kind of ritually clean animal (suitable for food or sacrifice) brought into the ark was seven pairs, not one pair. Moreover, the confinement in the ark lasted nearly a year, so some animals must have been born on board.

God made a covenant with Noah that there would not be another deluge, and that life would return to normal: 'While the earth remains, seedtime and harvest, cold and heat, summer and winter, day and night, shall not cease.' (Gen. 8:22). Man and all the living things that had been in the ark would be fruitful and multiply. A rainbow appeared as a sign of the covenant.

Noah started tilling the soil again after the flood. He planted a vineyard, then got drunk on the wine he made. Ham saw his father lying naked in a drunken stupor, and instead of doing something about it, he went and told his two brothers what he had seen. Shem and Japheth walked backward into the tent carrying between them a cloak, which they used to cover their father's nakedness without themselves setting eyes on it. When Noah aroused himself and learned what had happened, he cursed Ham's son Canaan, whose descendants would be slaves to those of Shem and Japheth.

*Mesopotamian* The flood story in Genesis has parallels in *Flood Stories* ancient Mesopotamian myths about the destruction of mankind by a deluge. The flat, alluvial plain (now Iraq) watered by the Tigris and Euphrates rivers at times suffered catastrophic inundations. One example of massive destruction from flood-waters was revealed in the excavation of the ancient city of Ur, near the head of the Persian Gulf, from where the patriarch Abraham started on his westward migration.

The most notable Mesopotamian flood story appears in the great Babylonian epic of Gilgamesh, inscribed on clay tablets discovered over a century ago in the ruins of Nineveh. This Babylonian account was itself derived from earlier Sumerian sources. In the epic an ancestor of Gilgamesh is warned in a dream that the gods have decreed that life on earth will be destroyed by flood. He builds a huge wooden ark lined with pitch and brings into it his family and the seed of all living creatures. As the waters recede and the ark comes to rest on a mountain top, he sends out in turn a dove, a swallow and a raven to look for dry land. On emerging from the ark, he offers a sacrifice to the gods.

The Mesopotamian flood stories also concern the theme of death and immortality. Gilgamesh seeks his ancestor, the Noah-hero of the deluge, to learn the secret of the eternal life afterwards bestowed upon the ancestor by the gods. Gilgamesh learns that the gift of immortality will never be repeated for any mortal being:

Gilgamesh, whither rovest thou?
The life thou pursuest thou shalt not find.

Alhie hanzt Nemrot den turn pawen ze Babelonia mit grozzer maisterschaft

The Tower of Babel. A painting from a World History in German (1385).

When the gods created mankind,
Death for mankind they set aside,
Life in their own hands retaining.

He is therefore urged to make the best of life while it lasts:

Thou, Gilgamesh, let full be thy belly,
Make thou merry by day and by night.
Hold a feast each day,
And dance and play day and night!
Let thy garments be sparkling fresh,
Thy head be washed; bathe in pure water.
Pay heed to the little one that holds
    on to thy hand.
Let thy spouse delight in thy bosom,
As is (a woman's) role.

This moving passage, with its hedonistic philosophy, was to find a startling echo in the words of Ecclesiastes two millenia later:

For the living know that they will die, but the dead know nothing, and they have no more reward . . . Go, eat your bread with enjoyment, and drink your wine with a merry heart . . . let your garments be always white; let not oil be lacking on your head. Enjoy life with the wife whom you love. . . . (Ec. 9:5,7–9).

Whatever the common elements between the Genesis account and that in the epic of Gilgamesh, they are on very different spiritual planes. In the Babylonian story the flood has no moral purpose at all, but springs from the whims and squabbles of the pagan gods. As against that, the stern, just God of Noah is concerned only with purging the earth of corruption and violence, and providing a fresh start for mankind and all other forms of life.

*The Table of the Nations* The flood story in Genesis is followed by the Table of the Nations. The peoples of the ancient Near East are divided into three groups, each descended from one of Noah's sons.

Ham is deemed to be the father of Egypt and other nations adjacent to Egypt: Libya (Put) to the west, Nubia (Cush) to the south and Canaan to the northeast. From Shem come the Hebrews, the Aramean nations to the north and east of Canaan, and the peoples of Mesopotamia and the Arabian Peninsula. To Japheth are attributed the countries in the mountainous belt of Asia Minor extending from the Caspian Sea westward to the Mediterranean coast, together with islands such as Cyprus.

For modern scholars, these three overlapping groups do not clearly correspond to divisions of either race or language, but are seen rather as geographical regions. The Hamites inhabited a southern area under Egyptian influence; the descendants of Japheth, a northern belt of peoples of Indo-European stock; and the Shemites (or Semites) a middle region including Arabia and most of the Fertile Crescent.

Although bracketed with the descendants of Ham in the Table of the Nations, the Canaanites, like the Hebrews, belonged to the Semitic language group. The term Semite first came into use at the end of the eighteenth century AD, and is employed by scholars today in a linguistic rather than in a racial context. However, in everyday language the Jews and the Arabs are still referred to as 'Semitic cousins' though the term anti-semitism is confined to anti-Jewish prejudice.

*The Tower of Babel* At that time, '. . . the whole earth had one language and few words' (Gen. 11:1). Men from the east settled in the Mesopotamian plain of Shinar, where they started building a city. Using burnt bricks with bitumen as mortar, they set out to erect a tower 'with its top in the heavens'. Perturbed at the power these men might be able to achieve, the Lord confused their language so that they could no longer understand each other, and he scattered them everywhere. As a result the ambitious building project came to a halt. The city was called Babel because the Lord confused (in Hebrew, *balal*) the tongues of men.

The 'land of Shinar' is the fertile plain between the Tigris and Euphrates rivers. Babel (more precisely, Bavel) is the Hebrew form of the name Babylon – the city on the Euphrates that became a dominant centre of power and culture in the life of the ancient Near East. The tower of Babel is presumed to be a reference to the great 'ziggurat' in Babylon, that carried on its top platform a temple to Marduk, the chief Babylonian deity. He was also known as Bel. The word Babel means in the Babylonian language the gateway (*bab*) of Bel.

To the small peoples of the region, including the Israelites, Babylonia was a ruthless empire swallowing up other states within its reach. The brief story of the tower of Babel predicts divine action to break up the concentrated population and power represented by the city of Babylon.

Archaeological evidence confirms that the great ziggurat of Babylon, like other public buildings in that city, was constructed of burnt bricks mortared with bitumen, as stated in Genesis.

# 2

# THE PATRIARCHS

## Abraham

HE WAS THE FIRST OF THE BIBLICAL patriarchs and the ancestor of the Hebrew nation. Abraham (first called Abram) was descended from Noah's son Shem. With his father Terah, his wife Sarah (first called Sarai) and his nephew Lot, he left his native city of Ur, near the head of the Persian Gulf, and migrated up the Euphrates Valley to Haran in northern Syria. Here the family settled and here Terah died. Their migration was probably part of a general movement of nomadic tribes in the region, about the eighteenth century BC.

*Abraham in Canaan* The Lord appeared to Abraham and told him to leave for 'the land that I will show you. And I will make of you a great nation . . .' (Gen. 12:1,2). Travelling slowly southwards with his family, servants, flocks and herds, Abraham came into Canaan, built an altar at Shechem (modern Nablus) and another near Bethel, a little north of the site of Jerusalem. The Lord again appeared to him and said, 'To your descendants I will give this land' (Gen. 12:7).

Driven by famine, Abraham and his party moved across the barren Negev and the Sinai desert into Egypt, the granary of the area. Sarah was a beautiful woman, and fearing he might be killed by those who desired her, Abraham passed her off as his sister. The Egyptian Pharoah took her into his own household, rewarding her 'brother' with servants and livestock. Pharoah learnt the truth when his court was stricken by plague, and he promptly restored Sarah to her husband, bidding them leave at once.

*The Rescue of Lot* Back in the Judean hills, Abraham and Lot found that the grazing was insufficient for their extensive herds, causing friction between their herdsmen. Abraham proposed that they should separate. He continued to live in the plain of Mamre, in the Hebron hills, while Lot moved eastward into the Jordan valley. Lot pitched his tents at Sodom, one of five cities standing in a green, well-watered plain at the lower end of the Dead Sea. The area had come under Mesopotamian control, but the five cities rebelled against their overlord, the king of Elam. He advanced upon them with three allied kings, ravaged Sodom and the nearby city of Gomorrah and carried off a vast amount of booty and a number of captives. Among them was Lot. A man

25

LEFT Samson grappling with the lion. From an illuminated manuscript Hebrew Bible produced in 1310.

ABOVE 'The Covenant.' From a hand-etched illustrated Passover Haggadah by the contemporary Israeli artist Yaakov Boussidan.

who had escaped brought Abraham the news of his nephew's fate. Gathering together three hundred and eighteen men from his household and servants, he set off in hot pursuit. He caught up with and routed the raiding force at Dan in the northeastern corner of the country, and pursued them to the vicinity of Damascus. Lot and the other captives were rescued and regained their possessions.

On Abraham's way back Melchizedek the priest-king of Salem (probably Jerusalem), brought him bread and wine and blessed him. Abraham donated to Melchizedek a tenth of the regained goods. When the king of Sodom came to meet Abraham in the King's Valley near Jerusalem, he proposed that the patriarch keep the rest of the recaptured property as a reward for returning the captives. Abraham declined, saying that he did not want as much as 'a thread or a sandal-thong' for himself. On this dignified note ended the only martial exploit in Abraham's peaceful life.

*God's Covenant with Abraham* The Lord made a solemn covenant with Abraham, promising that his descendants would be as numerous as the stars, and would be given the whole land of Canaan. Abraham demurred that he was childless, but nevertheless expressed his faith in the Lord's promise. The covenant was sealed with an ancient ritual. Animals were sacrificed and cut into halves facing each other. In a vision, Abraham saw a 'smoking fire pot and a flaming torch passed between these pieces' (Gen. 15:17). As a physical reminder of the covenant, Abraham was later instructed by the Lord that he and all the males in his household should be circumcised; this ceremony was thereafter to be carried out with every new-born male infant when he was eight days old. (The *brit millah* – Covenant of the Circumcision – is religiously observed by Jews to this day.) The covenant was also marked by an alteration in the original names of the couple. Abram (exalted father) became Abraham (father of a multitude); while Sarai (meaning unknown) became Sarah (princess).

*The Births of Ishmael and Isaac* The tragedy of Sarah's life was that she was barren. She made a suggestion that fitted in with the social customs of the period, by offering Abraham her maid Hagar, an Egyptian slave. When Hagar became pregnant, and was contemptuous of her mistress, Sarah could not contain her jealousy. The maidservant fled from Sarah's harsh treatment but was persuaded by an angel of the Lord to return. She bore Abraham a son who was named Ishmael (God heard).

When Abraham was ninety-one years old and Sarah ninety, the Lord made known to him that Sarah would bear a son. The statement was confirmed by three strangers, angels in disguise, who visited Abraham's home at Mamre and received his hospitality. Listening to them from inside the tent, Sarah laughed sceptically. In due time, however, a child was born and they called him Isaac, which in Hebrew means 'laughed'.

Sensitive about giving birth in her old age, Sarah was stung by the mockery of Hagar and her son Ishmael, then thirteen years of age, and demanded that Abraham cast them out. The kindly Abraham shrank from doing so, but the Lord reassured him that no harm would come to them and Ishmael also would be the ancestor of a great nation.

Abraham then provided Hagar with a supply of bread and water and she left with the boy. They wandered in the desert until the last drop of their water was gone. Unable to watch her son die of thirst, Hagar left him under a bush and sat down weeping a little distance away. Suddenly she saw a miraculous water-well, and they were saved. They settled in that part of the Sinai desert known as the Wilderness of Paran. Ishmael grew up to become a noted archer, and 'a wild ass of a man, his hand against every man and every man's hand against him' (Gen. 16:12). His mother obtained a wife for him from Egypt, her native land, and he had twelve sons who became heads of tribes (a biblical parallel with the twelve sons of Jacob). By tradition, Ishmael came to be regarded as ancestor of the nomad bedouin tribes in the southern desert. The Arabs maintain that they are descended from Abraham through Ishmael.

*The Destruction of Sodom and Gomorrah* The Lord revealed to Abraham that he intended to destroy the cities of Sodom and Gomorrah because of their immoral ways. Abraham's humanity made him intercede for them. Surely, he pleaded, the Lord would not wish to destroy the righteous with the wicked. Supposing there were fifty good men in Sodom – or forty – or thirty – or twenty – or ten? The Lord promised to spare the city if there were only ten. Even that number could not be found, as Abraham sadly understood when he looked from the hills towards Sodom and Gomorrah and saw the cloud of smoke arising from the destroyed cities.

The Angel appearing to Hagar in the desert. A seventeenth-century Dutch painting
of the School of Rembrandt.

ABOVE Noah's Ark. From a fourteenth-century
French illuminated manuscript.

RIGHT Noah harvesting his vineyard after the flood.
A Byzantine wall painting from Yugoslavia, dated 1350.

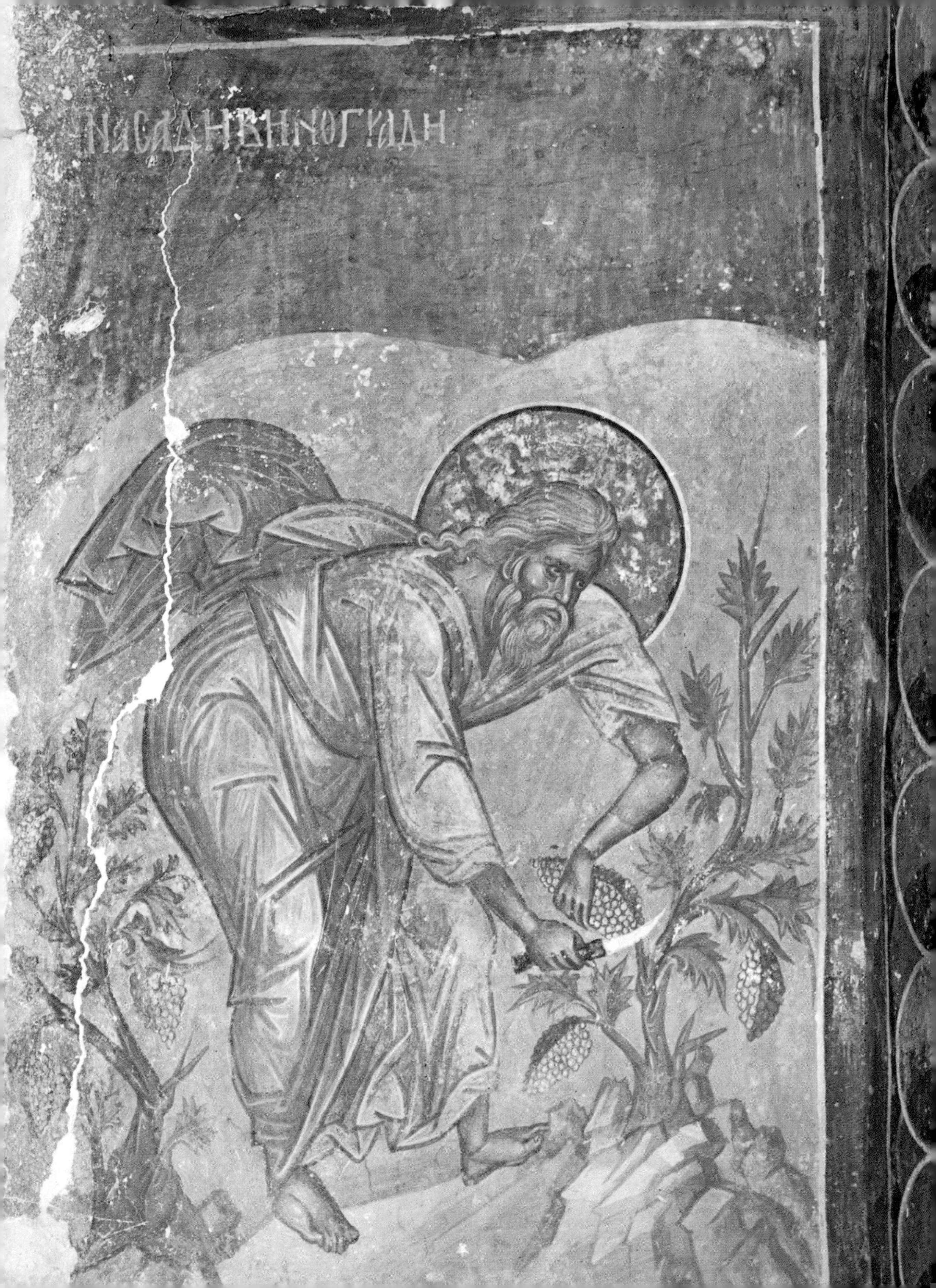

Before that happened, two angels in the guise of men came to Sodom, and were invited by Lot to eat and spend the night in his home. A mob of men gathered before his door and demanded that the strangers be handed over to them for carnal purposes. (Sodom became such a legend for sexual perversion that its name survives in the word sodomy). Lot came out to speak with them, shutting the door of the house behind him. The rigid laws of oriental hospitality bound him to protect the guest under his roof at any price. Driven desperate by the threats of the crowd, he even went to the length of offering to hand over his two virgin daughters as a substitute. He was saved by the two angels who pulled him through the door and slammed it shut, striking the men outside temporarily blind.

The angels then disclosed to Lot that the doom of the city was imminent, and insisted that he and his family should escape at once. On no account should they look back. Lot's two prospective sons-in-law derided the whole idea and stayed behind. Under cover of darkness Lot set out with his wife and daughters towards the town of Zoar, a little further to the south. When dawn broke, Lot's wife could not restrain her curiosity and looked back. In punishment she was turned into a pillar of salt.

Lot and his daughters took refuge in a mountain cave. Believing that no one was left alive on earth, the young women decided that there was only one way left to preserve the human race. On two successive nights they made their father drunk on wine, and had intercourse with him in turn. As a result of these incestuous acts they became pregnant. The elder bore a son and called him Moab; he was the legendary ancestor of the Moabites that later inhabited the high tableland to the east of the Dead Sea. The younger daughter also gave birth to a son, and called him Ben-ammi; the Ammonites who later established a kingdom in Trans-jordan were regarded as his descendants.

The story of the destruction of Sodom and Gomorrah by fire and brimstone may have originated in an actual volcanic upheaval in that area, about the time of Abraham or a little earlier. The Dead Sea, thirteen hundred feet below sea level, lies in the deepest trough on the earth's surface. It is conjectured that the plain on which the five cities stood in the story of Lot may have subsided and been inundated, and that it now forms the southern portion of the Dead Sea. The cliffs of salt and limestone at modern Sodom are eroded into odd shapes, and one projecting column of salt is by local legend reputed to have been Lot's wife.

*Abraham and Abimelech*

Abraham reverted to a semi-nomad way of life, and moved with his flocks and herds out of the hill country into the arid spaces of the Negev in the south. He reached the territory of Abimelech, king of Gerar (near Gaza), where he and Sarah again pretended that they were brother and sister, as they had done years before in Egypt. Struck by her beauty Abimelech had her brought to his residence, but hurriedly restored her to her husband when the truth was revealed to him in a dream. Abimelech proposed to Abraham that they should swear a pact of friendship between them and their descendants, and this was done at a well of water which had been disputed between their retainers. Abraham confirmed the covenant by handing seven ewe lambs to Abimelech. The place was named Beersheba, which could mean either the Well of the Swearing or the Well of the Seven. Abraham planted a tamarisk tree and settled there for some time.

*The Sacrifice of Isaac*

Abraham's faith was put to an agonizing test. He was instructed by the Lord to take his beloved son Isaac to a distant hill in the land of Moriah (later identified with the site of the Temple of Jerusalem). There he was to sacrifice the boy as a burnt-offering. The following morning Abraham set out with Isaac and two young servants, with a load of wood carried on the back of an ass. On the third day, Abraham saw from a distance the hilltop on which the sacrifice was to be made. He left the servants and the ass to await his return, and walked on holding the knife and the fire, with Isaac carrying the firewood on his back. Along the way the puzzled boy asked his father, 'Behold, the fire and the wood; but where is the lamb for a burnt offering?' (Gen. 22:7). Abraham replied evasively that the Lord would see to that. On arrival at the spot, he built a rough altar, arranged the wood on it, bound Isaac and stretched him out on the wood. As he grasped the knife, the angel of the Lord called out to him: 'Do not lay your hand on the lad or do anything to him; for now I know that you fear God' (Gen. 22:12). Suddenly Abraham noticed a ram nearby with its horns caught in a bush. The animal was quickly substituted for the boy and sacrificed. The two then turned back to the place where the servants

ABOVE An Angel stops Abraham from sacrificing
Isaac. A thirteenth-century tapestry
from Halberstadt, Germany.

OVERLEAF Abraham dismissing Hagar and their
son Ishmael. A painting by Rembrandt van
Ryn (1640).

were waiting, and the party returned to Beer-sheba.

The account of the averted sacrifice is known in Hebrew as the *Akedah*, the Binding (of Isaac). It may well symbolize the rejection by the Hebrew faith of the abominable pagan practice of child sacrifice. However, on the human level, it is a terse and mysterious story that defies understanding.

Over the fate of Sodom and Gomorrah, Abraham argued with God and insisted on divine justice and compassion. Yet, without hesitation or protest he accepts God's command to sacrifice the son miraculously born to Sarah and himself in their old age. He does not even remind God of the solemn promise that Isaac's descendants would be a great nation. And why should Isaac meekly collaborate in his own slaughter, letting himself be bound and stretched out on the altar, without trying to resist? After all, he was old enough and strong enough to carry the load of firewood on his back up the steep hill.

The scholars of later ages groped with little success to find in the story a hidden message for their own times. Christian theologians sought an analogy between the intended sacrifice of Isaac and the crucifixion of Jesus; but one death was averted and the other consummated. The Hebrew spirit is an affirmation of life that cannot be expressed through death. Jewish sages found in the *Akedah* a profound and mystic premonition of the survival of their people through centuries of persecution and pogroms. That would, however, be an unbearable parable for our time; there was no last-minute reprieve for Hitler's sacrificial victims! The *Akedah* remains a deeply moving episode fraught with unresolved questions.

*The Cave of Machpelah* At the age of one hundred and twenty-seven, Sarah died at Kiriath-arba (Hebron). After the mourning period, Abraham approached the elders of the city, who were sitting in front of the gate. Referring to himself humbly as 'a stranger and a sojourner among you' he asked their help in acquiring a suitable burying place. With a flourish of oriental courtesy, they replied: 'you are a mighty prince among us. Bury your dead in the choicest of our sepulchres' (Gen. 23:6). Abraham disclosed that what he had in mind was the cave of Machpelah in a field belonging to one of the elders present. Ephron the Hittite. After some negotiation, Abraham purchased the field,

together with the cave, for four hundred shekels of silver, weighed out in the presence of the elders as witnesses. This transaction is the first contract of sale recorded in the Bible. Abraham buried Sarah in the cave, which became the family tomb. In due course he himself, his son Isaac and daughter-in-law Rebekah, his grandson Jacob and Jacob's first wife Leah, were also interred. There is a tradition that Joseph too was buried there.

*Isaac's marriage to Rebekah* The aging Abraham decided the time had come to find a wife for Isaac. He sent for his trusted servant Eliezer and made him swear that Isaac would not be married to a local Canaanite girl, but to one of his own kin. She was to be brought by Eliezer from the area of Haran in northern Mesopotamia, where the family had settled before Abraham migrated to Canaan. By an ancient form of oath, the servant placed his hand under Abraham's thigh when he accepted the assignment. What was he to do, Eliezer asked, if the girl refused to leave her parents and come with him? Was he then to take Isaac to the family in Haran and leave him there? Abraham replied that on no account was Isaac to leave Canaan, the land that had been promised to his descendants by the Lord. If the girl would not come, Eliezer would be released from his oath.

With a string of ten camels loaded with provisions and costly gifts, Eliezer set out on his six-hundred-mile journey. At dusk one day he halted at a well outside the town of Nahor near Haran. Among the young women who came to draw water from the well was the comely Rebekah, whose father Bethuel was Abraham's nephew. At Eliezer's request she lowered the full jar from her shoulder and gave him water to drink. She then filled the trough for his camels as well.

Eliezer was delighted to learn her identity, as it meant he had reached his destination. He gave her a gold ring and two gold bracelets as gifts, and asked whether her father could provide him and his men with food and shelter for the night, as well as straw for the camels. When Rebekah returned home and told about her strange encounter at the well, her brother Laban went out to fetch Eliezer and his party.

The servant explained why he had come. He felt sure he had been guided to Rebekah by the Lord, and he stressed his master's wealth, to which Isaac was the heir. Rebekah's father gave his consent to the match, and when the girl was brought in, she agreed to go. Eliezer gave her the rich clothes and ornaments he had brought for her, together with gifts for other members of the family. On the following day Rebekah took leave of her parents and brother and set out with her maids on the long camel trek to an unknown land and husband.

Isaac was living at that time in the Negev, the southern desert. Towards evening he was strolling alone outside his encampment, when he saw a party approaching on camels and went towards it. When Eliezer told Rebekah who the man was, she modestly veiled herself and alighted to greet him. She then became his wife.

*The Death of Abraham*  In his last years Abraham took another wife, Keturah, about whose background nothing is known. They had six sons. Before his death Abraham gave them gifts and sent them eastward, leaving Isaac as his undisputed heir. Keturah's children were the legendary ancestors of six Arab desert tribes to the south and east of the Land of Israel.

Abraham died at the age of one hundred and seventy-five and was buried by his two sons Ishmael and Isaac in the cave of Machpelah next to his wife Sarah, with whom he had set out from Ur in Mesopotamia so long ago.

For Jews, the story of Abraham is of seminal importance. It marks the beginning of their identity as a people, the first divine charter to the Land of Israel, and the commitment to a single God.

As the legendary ancestor of the Arabs through Ishmael, Abraham is more revered by Muslims than any other character in the Bible. The Koran calls him El Khalil, the Friend of God, and the Cave of Machpelah at Hebron, where he was buried, is a holy place for Islam as well as for Judaism. The Jaffa Gate in the Old City of Jerusalem is inscribed with an Arabic verse from the Koran: 'There is no God but God, and Abraham is beloved of Him.'

## Isaac

ISAAC WAS FORTY YEARS OLD WHEN HE married Rebekah, He loved her dearly, and unlike the other patriarchs never took any other wife or concubine. It was tragic for the couple that Rebekah remained childless. After their incessant prayers to the Lord, she became pregnant with twins when they had been married twenty years. She suffered greatly because 'The children struggled together within her' (Gen. 25:22). The Lord told her:

> Two nations are in your womb,
>   and two peoples, born of you,
>     shall be divided;
>   the one shall be stronger than the other,
>   the elder shall serve the younger.
>             (Gen. 25:23)

*The Birth of Esau and Jacob*  The first twin to be born was Esau, red all over and matted with hair. (His name means shaggy.) He was followed by Jacob, clutching Esau's heel. (His name is derived from the Hebrew word for heel, or the word for supplanting.)

When the boys grew up, Esau became a skilled hunter and the favourite of his father, who loved to eat the game Esau brought in. Jacob was of a quiet disposition and remained close to the family tents. Rebekah loved him more than she did her other son. One day Esau came back famished from a hunting trip and found Jacob cooking a soup of red lentils. In exchange for a bowl of the soup, Jacob obtained a promise that Esau's birthright as the first-born of the twins would go to him.

*Isaac in the Negev*  Driven by famine, Isaac started moving towards the Nile valley, as his father Abraham had done. He reached Gerar, in the southwestern corner of Canaan, where his father's friend Abimelech was the king. The Lord told him not to go any further and reaffirmed the covenant made with Abraham that his descendants would become masters of the Promised Land.

As his father had done, Isaac claimed that his wife was his sister, fearing that he might be killed on her account. Abimelech saw them together; he realized they were married and forbade his people to molest them.

Isaac became affluent from a succession of good harvests and the increase of his flocks and herds. His water supply was ensured by reopening wells originally dug by his father. Water was precious in that arid area, and Isaac's right to the wells was hotly disputed by local herdsmen. Isaac was urged by Abimelech to move further away. He once more settled at Beersheba where he dug a new well and found fresh water. The whole of Isaac's adult life seems to have been spent in the northern and western Negev.

LEFT The two angels descending into the doomed
city of Sodom to warn Lot. A painting by the
nineteenth-century French Symbolist Gustave Moreau.

ABOVE Salt encrustations in the water
at Sodom, at the southern end of the Dead Sea,
1300 feet below sea level.

At the age of forty Esau married two 'Hittite' women. These Canaanite daughters-in-law 'made life bitter for Isaac and Rebekah' (Gen. 26:35). To placate his parents, Esau later took a third wife; she was the daughter of Ishmael, and therefore his half-cousin.

*The Stolen Birthright*  When Isaac was old, ailing and practically blind, he asked Esau to go hunting and to prepare for him the savoury venison dish he loved. He would then give him the paternal blessing due to the first-born. Rebekah overheard this conversation and decided to obtain Isaac's blessing for Jacob instead. Jacob was to impersonate his brother. He demurred saying 'my brother Esau is a hairy man, and I am a smooth man' (Gen. 27:11). Rebekah dismissed his qualms. She told him to choose two succulent kids from the flock. From their meat she prepared a dish that tasted like venison. She then dressed Jacob in Esau's clothes, covered his hands and neck with strips of the fleece from the kids, and sent him in to his father with the food. Suspicious because he did not expect Esau back so soon, Isaac felt the hands that served him with the food and said, 'The voice is Jacob's voice, but the hands are the hands of Esau' (Gen. 27:22). Esau's garments smelling of the fields satisfied the blind old man. After he had eaten and drunk wine he blessed his son, promising him wealth, status, and authority over the family and the surrounding peoples.

No sooner had Jacob left than Esau came in with his own dish of venison, to claim his father's blessing. Learning what had happened, he gave a cry of rage and grief. Isaac regretted he could not retract the solemn blessing given by mistake to Jacob. Esau implored him tearfully to bless him as well. Isaac stretched out his hand saying:

> Behold, away from the fatness of
>   the earth shall your dwelling be,
> and away from the dew of heaven on high.
> By your sword you shall live,
>   and you shall serve your brother;
> but when you break loose
>   you shall break his yoke from your neck.
>
> (Gen. 27:39–40)

(This utterance implied that Esau's descendants would inhabit the harsh desert country of Edom to the south and east of the Dead Sea; Edom would be subject to the Israelite kingdom and later would become independent.)

## Jacob

THE ANGRY ESAU THREATENED THAT AFTER their father had passed away he would kill his brother Jacob in order to wipe out the wrong done to him. Rebekah thought it prudent to send Jacob away. She persuaded Isaac that the young man should travel to her brother Laban in Haran and there find a wife, as had been done in her own case.

*Jacob's Dream*  Setting out from Beersheba on his solitary journey, Jacob trudged northwards through the Hebron hills and past the Jebusite city of Jerusalem. One evening he lay down to sleep on the ground with his head propped up on a stone. The place was near the edge of the Judean escarpment looking down into the Jordan Valley. In a dream he saw a ladder mounting up to heaven, with angels passing up and down it. From its top the Lord addressed Jacob, repeating to him the promise that had been made to his grandfather Abraham and his father Isaac. On his awakening the awestruck Jacob anointed with oil the top of the stone on which his head had rested, and named the spot Bethel (the House of God).

*Jacob Marries Leah and Rachel*  Near his destination of Haran, Jacob reached a well covered by a large stone that was rolled away when water was drawn. Three shepherds were waiting there with their flocks. He asked them whether they knew his uncle Laban. They replied that the young woman approaching with her sheep was Laban's daughter Rachel. Jacob helped her water the sheep, then introduced himself to her and kissed her with tears of emotion. She told her father, who came out to welcome his sister's son into his home.

For Jacob, it was love at first sight. He soon asked permission from Laban to marry Rachel, his younger daughter. Laban agreed, provided Jacob first worked for him for seven years, in lieu of the usual bride price. When that long period had passed (seeming to the lovelorn Jacob 'but a few days'), Laban invited everyone to the wedding feast. By the light of the following morning Jacob was shocked to find that his bride was not Rachel, but her plain elder sister Leah. Laban justified the deception to the angry Jacob by saying, 'It is not so done in our country, to give the younger before the first-born' (Gen. 29:26). He added that when the week set aside for celebrating the marriage was over, Jacob could marry Rachel as well – provided that he then worked another seven years for Laban.

RIGHT Jacob at Bethel: showing The Dream and Pouring Oil upon the Altar. An illumination from a Chronicle of World History in German (1360).

A village well in Haran, Syria – a scene that has changed little since
Jacob met Rachel watering her father's sheep at a similar well.

*Jacob's Children* Ironically, it was the unwanted Leah and not the beloved Rachel who produced sons for Jacob. They were at first four in number: Reuben, Simeon, Levi and Judah. Rachel then resorted to the traditional way of having children by proxy, by giving her maid Bilhah to Jacob as a concubine. Bilhah had two sons, Dan and Naphtali. Since Leah thought she had passed the child-bearing age, she also gave Jacob her maid Zilpah, who gave birth to Gad and Asher. Leah's fertility was renewed and she had three more children: Issachar, Zevulun and a daughter, Dinah. At last Rachel also became pregnant, and gave birth to Joseph. In the years that Jacob remained in the land of Haran with Laban, he thus became the father of eleven sons and one daughter.

*The Striped and Spotted Sheep* After the birth of Joseph, Jacob told Laban that he longed to return to his own country with his wives and children. Laban admitted that under Jacob's care his flocks had greatly increased and he had become wealthy. He offered to pay Jacob wages if he would continue to serve him. But Jacob was adamant. All he wanted as a reward for all the years of service was to pick out for himself from the herds the striped and speckled goats and sheep and all the black lambs. Laban agreed; but he at once arranged for his own sons to collect the animals marked in the way Jacob had stipulated and to move with them to a grazing area three days journey away.

Jacob took resourceful measures to counter this deceit. He set up peeled wands at the watering troughs where the animals bred, a visual device that produced a great number of striped and spotted offspring. He selected the most vigorous of them to augment his own flocks, leaving the weaker animals for Laban.

By now Jacob had been with his uncle for twenty years. He had become affluent in his own right, with a large household and a great number of servants. When the Lord confirmed to him that the time had come to return to the Promised Land, Leah and Rachel supported the move. Knowing that Jacob's wealth had aroused the resentment of Laban and his sons, they asserted that whatever Jacob had acquired from Laban would in any case have been part of their family inheritance.

Anxious to avoid a conflict with his father-in-law, Jacob waited until Laban and his sons were away shearing sheep elsewhere before he set out on his southward journey, with all his household and his animals. Unknown to him, Rachel had also taken with her the sacred images from her father's home. In due course, Jacob's caravan reached the hills overlooking Gilead in northern Trans-jordan, where they pitched their tents. It was here that Laban and his kinsmen caught up with them, after a seven-day pursuit. Laban bitterly upbraided Jacob for taking away his daughters and grandchildren behind his back, and even stealing his household images. Jacob hotly denied this last charge, and challenged Laban to search through the tents for the images. They were not found because Rachel hid them in the saddle of her camel, sat down upon the saddle and pretended she could not rise in her father's presence because she was suffering her monthly period.

*Return to the Promised Land*

Laban and Jacob decided to make peace with each other. A sacred pillar was erected, with a cairn of stones around it, marking a boundary which neither would cross with intent to harm the other. The cairn was called Galeed, the heap of the witness. (In later generations the border between the Aramean [Syrian] and Israelite peoples was regarded as dating from the agreement between Jacob and Laban, who is referred to throughout the story as 'the Aramean'.) Reconciliation was celebrated that night by a feast. The following morning Laban blessed his daughters and their children, and turned back to his own land.

Continuing his journey, Jacob came into Gilead, a broken, wooded region east of the Jordan valley. He reached the deep gorge of the river Jabbok, that rises from a spring near modern Amman and flows into the Jordan river. From here Jacob sent messengers to his brother Esau, who had settled in Mount Seir southeast of the Dead Sea, to announce that he had returned from Haran and wanted a reconciliation. The messengers returned and reported that Esau was coming up to meet him accompanied by four hundred men. Jacob feared that Esau might still be seeking vengeance for the wrong done to him twenty years earlier, concerning the blessing from their father Isaac. Jacob called on the Lord to protect him in this ominous encounter; at the same time, he took his own careful precautions. All his flocks and possessions were divided into two separate groups, so that if Esau and his men attacked one of them, the other might escape. Before the meeting Esau was to be appeased with a substantial gift of livestock, sent ahead in several batches, with spaces between them, as a softening-up process. For this gift, Jacob selected 'two hundred she-goats and twenty he-goats, two hundred ewes and twenty rams, thirty milch camels and their colts, forty cows and ten bulls, twenty she-asses and ten he-asses' (Gen. 32:14,15). This impressive tally showed how wealthy Jacob had become, and also how guilty and fearful he felt about his twin brother.

*Jacob Wrestles with the Angel*

That night Jacob's family, retainers and animals crossed the shallow ford of the Jabbok, while he remained behind alone. Here he was attacked in the darkness by a mysterious stranger, with whom he had to wrestle all night. Towards dawn his adversary tried desperately to free himself and struck Jacob in the thigh, putting his hip out of joint. (That is the biblical reason given for the taboo on eating a particular sinew in the thigh of an animal [Gen. 32:32].) Jacob hung on to the stranger and refused to let him go until he had obtained a blessing. The other, an angel in disguise, replied: 'Your name shall no more be called Jacob but Israel, for you have striven with God and with men, and have prevailed' (Gen. 32:28). The name Israel means 'one who has striven with the Lord'. The stranger refused to disclose his own name and vanished as the dawn was breaking. Jacob named the place Penuel, meaning God's face. With the oblique rays of the rising sun upon him, he limped painfully across the ford and up the steep opposite slope, to join the rest of his company on the upland above.

The tale of Jacob wrestling with the angel at the Jabbok ford is perplexing and obscure, and is thought to be an ancient legend that survived in fragmentary form. Its origin may have been related to the river gods in the folklore of many ancient peoples, who have to be propitiated or overcome before the water can be crossed. The significance of this Genesis passage is the change of Jacob's name to Israel, on the eve of his return to Canaan. It marks a turning point in the biblical narrative where the story of the individual patriarchs starts broadening into the history of an emerging nation, the Children of Israel.

*The Meeting with Esau*

At the meeting between the brothers, the manly Esau behaved with a warmth and family sentiment that showed Jacob's nervousness and precautions to have been unjustified. Jacob had arranged his womenfolk in the reverse order of their importance in his eyes: first the two concubines and their children, next Leah and her children, and at the back Rachel and her son Joseph. As Esau drew near, Jacob went forward and bowed down seven times to the ground. 'But Esau ran to meet him, and embraced him, and fell on his neck and kissed him, and they wept' (Gen. 33:4). The women and children were then brought forward and introduced in turn to their kinsman. Esau declined to accept the livestock, saying simply 'I have enough, my brother; keep what you have for yourself' (Gen. 33:9). But Jacob insisted on making the gift.

Esau proposed that Jacob travel behind him to his home territory in the land of Edom. Jacob did not want to refuse outright, for fear he might offend his brother and mar their emotional reunion. He pleaded that he could only move slowly, as his children were worn out by the long journey and his animals had to suckle their newly-born offspring. Esau, he proposed, should go ahead while he would follow at his own pace. After Esau and his men had disappeared southward on their way back to Mount Seir, Jacob resumed his own journey westward along the Jabbok river. He spent some time resting at Succoth, on the plateau, then descended to the Jordan valley, crossed the river into Canaan and pitched his tents on the outskirts of Shechem, the main town in the Samarian hills. Here he bought a piece of land from Hamor, the leading man of the city, and erected an altar to the Lord. The site later became the traditional burial place of his son Joseph.

*The Rape of Dinah*

Jacob's only daughter Dinah became friendly with other young women in the town. She was seen by Hamor's son and heir Shechem, who seized and raped her. Hamor ceremoniously visited Jacob to express regret and ask permission for his son to marry Dinah. The young man accompanied him, declared his love for Dinah and offered to provide any marriage gift Jacob might wish. Hamor went further: he proposed that his people and Jacob's should intermarry and unite.

Dinah's brothers concealed their rage at the dishonour inflicted on the family. They pretended that the merger would be acceptable, provided Hamor, Shechem and the other men of the city were circumcised, according to Hebrew custom. Hamor persuaded the others to agree to this condition, pointing out that they would in due course acquire a share in Jacob's extensive possessions. Three days after the painful operation, when the men of Shechem were still incapacitated by it, they were attacked and killed by two of Dinah's brothers, Simeon and Levi, who then despoiled the town.

Jacob was dismayed at this bloody reprisal, and feared that the surrounding populace would be aroused against them. He decided to move further south at once. Before the departure, he had all his household purify themselves in the sight of the Lord by changing their garments and by giving up all idolatrous images and amulets, which he buried under an oak tree near Shechem.

*The Deaths of Rachel and Isaac*  At that time Jacob's father Isaac was still alive in Hebron, aged one hundred and eighty. When Jacob was approaching Bethlehem on his way to Hebron, his beloved wife Rachel gave birth to an infant son and died in childbirth. Jacob buried her at that spot. A tomb reputed to be hers can still be visited at the side of the road just outside Bethlehem. The dying Rachel had named the infant Ben-oni (son of my sorrow) but Jacob changed it to Benjamin (son of the right hand). He was Jacob's twelfth son and the only one actually to be born in the Promised Land.

Isaac died soon after, and was buried in the cave of Machpelah in Hebron by his two sons Jacob and Esau. That was the last time the twin brothers met each other.

*Judah and Tamar*  The background to the following story about Judah, a son of Jacob and Leah, is based on the custom of levirate marriage. When a man dies leaving his widow childless, an unmarried brother is obliged to wed her; the first-born son of this union is then regarded as carrying on the name and inheritance of the deceased. (The story also illustrates how common it was at that time for Israelite men to marry local Canaanite women.)

Judah had a Canaanite wife who bore him three sons – Er, Onan and Shelah. The eldest son married Tamar, who may also have been a Canaanite, but he died young without children. Judah, then arranged for the second son Onan to marry her. He did so unwillingly, and in having intercourse with her 'he spilled the semen on the ground'. In this way he avoided having a son by Tamar that would be regarded as the offspring of his elder brother. (Hence the name 'onanism' given to interrupted coitus.) When Onan also died, Judah was unwilling to expose the youngest son Shelah to the risk of yet another unfortunate marriage. He got rid of Tamar by telling her to go back to her father's house and to wait until the boy was grown up.

Learning that Judah had lost his own wife, the frustrated Tamar waited for him at the gate of a nearby town, and pretended to be a prostitute wearing the customary veil of her calling. Judah was enticed into sleeping with her. He promised to send her a kid from his flock as payment, and meanwhile agreed to leave with her his signet ring, cord and staff as a pledge. When Tamar, who had resumed her widow's garb, became pregnant, she was condemned to be burned to death for immorality. But she was absolved when she produced the pledge and proved that her father-in-law Judah was the father of her child. He admitted that he had failed in his family obligation towards her by not giving her to his third son in marriage. Tamar gave birth to twins, one of whom, Perez, was the ancestor of king David.

## Joseph and his Brothers

THE LAST PART OF THE BOOK OF GENESIS IS devoted to the romantic story of Joseph, the Israelite boy who rose to be the most powerful man at the court of the Egyptian Pharaoh. It reads like a short novel of superb craftsmanship and human interest.

*The Young Joseph*  When the story opens, Joseph is a handsome and intelligent youth of seventeen – Jacob's eleventh son and the elder of the two born to Rachel, who had been the great love of his life. Joseph was spoilt by his father and detested by his older half-brothers. The symbol of his pampered status was the long-sleeved striped robe (translated in the King James Bible as the 'coat of many colours') that had been specially ordered for him by his father. It was a garment usually worn by the upper classes, in contrast to the short, sleeveless tunics that were the working clothes of his brothers in the field. Joseph became even more unpopular with them because he carried tales about them to his father, and because he recounted to them dreams that underlined his own superiority. In one such dream they were sheaves of wheat that bowed down to a sheaf that represented Joseph. In another dream the sun, the moon and eleven stars bowed down to him; this was too much even for his indulgent father, who asked him sarcastically, 'Shall I and your

*Joseph sold into Slavery*

mother and your brothers indeed come to bow ourselves to the ground before you?' (Gen. 37:10).

When his brothers had been away from home for some time with the flocks, Jacob sent Joseph to find them and bring back news. He found them at Dothan, a broad valley north of Shechem that was traversed by the main caravan route from Damascus to Egypt. When they saw him in the distance they conspired to do away with him, throw his body into an empty cistern and tell their father he had been killed by a wild animal. Hoping to rescue him afterwards, the eldest brother Reuben persuaded them to leave Joseph alive in the cistern, after taking his robe from him. In Reuben's temporary absence, the others hauled Joseph up again and sold him for twenty shekels of silver to a passing caravan of Midianite merchants, carrying balm and other spices from Gilead to Egypt. When Reuben returned he was horrified to find Joseph had disappeared. The brothers stained Joseph's garment with the blood of a goat, and brought it back to their father. Jacob, believing the youth had been killed by a wild beast, was plunged into deep grief.

*Potiphar's Wife*

In Egypt, the merchants sold Joseph as a slave to Potiphar, the captain of the palace guards. Joseph's charm and ability secured him quick advancement in the household of his important master, and he was eventually put in charge of all Potiphar's affairs. Unfortunately his good looks aroused the passion of Potiphar's wife, who tried hard to seduce him. Joseph resisted her advances, pleading that he could not betray his master's trust nor sin against God. One day, when she was alone with him in the house she grabbed hold of him, but he tore loose and fled, leaving his garment clutched in her hand. Vindictive at being spurned, she told her husband that Joseph had tried to rape her, and produced the garment as evidence. The angry Potiphar had Joseph thrown into the palace jail.

In this sudden adversity, Joseph won over the jailer, who made him the trusty over the other prisoners. Among them were the chief butler and the chief baker at the palace, who had offended their royal master. Each of them had a disturbing dream and Joseph undertook to interpret them. (Dreams were an accepted means of foretelling the future.) The chief butler had dreamt that he served Pharaoh wine from grapes grown on three branches of a vine; this meant, Joseph said, that

in three days he would be restored to his post. In the baker's dream, the birds came down and ate the food for Pharaoh he was carrying in three baskets on his head; Joseph sadly told him that in three days he would be hanged from a tree, and that carrion birds would eat the flesh from his bones. Both predictions came true. The butler had promised Joseph to intercede with Pharaoh on his behalf, but did not bother to do so once he was restored to grace.

*The Fat Years and the Lean Years*

Two years later, Pharaoh had two similar dreams during one night. In the first dream, seven thin cows ate up seven fat ones on the bank of the Nile. In the second, seven blighted ears of corn swallowed up seven full, plump ears. The following day all the leading wise men and magicians in Egypt were summoned to the palace, but failed to produce any plausible explanation for the disturbing dreams. At that point the chief butler recalled the young Hebrew slave in the prison who had shown such remarkable skill in dream interpretation. Joseph was hurriedly brought out of the dungeon, shaved, dressed in fresh clothes, and brought before the ruler.

Joseph declared that the double dream showed this to be a divine message: seven fat years of bountiful harvest in Egypt would be wiped out by seven lean years of famine. Joseph then proposed a practical policy. A fifth of the grain in the good years should be stored away as a reserve for the bad period; 'a man discreet and wise' should be appointed to carry out this programme, with all the necessary power. Pharaoh was so impressed by Joseph that he promptly chose him for the task. He handed Joseph the royal signet ring, and let him ride in the chariot behind the royal one. At the age of thirty, after thirteen years as a slave in Egypt, Joseph found himself the second most important man in the leading Near Eastern power of the time. Pharaoh arranged for him to marry Asenath, daughter of the high priest of the temple at On, and she bore him two sons, Manasseh and Ephraim.

During the seven years of plenty, Joseph had storehouses built in all the Egyptian cities and filled them with grain collected by his overseers from the surrounding farmlands. These huge food reserves became available during the prolonged famine that followed. There was even a surplus for sale to other hunger-stricken countries in the region, including Canaan.

Joseph's brothers show his bloodstained 'coat of many colours'
to their father Jacob. A painting by the nineteenth-century
English artist Ford Madox Brown (1867).

*Joseph's Brothers in Egypt*

Jacob sent his sons to Egypt to buy grain, keeping only the youngest, Benjamin, at home with him. The brothers arrived at the palace and bowed down humbly before the powerful chief minister who controlled the whole food supply in Egypt. Joseph recognized them, but did not reveal his own identity. Instead, he spoke harshly to them and accused them of being spies. In trying to clear themselves, they told him about their family background, mentioning their aged father Jacob, the youngest boy Benjamin who had been left at home, and the brother who had been lost many years before. Joseph was overcome with longing to see his young brother Benjamin. He threw the brothers into jail for three days, then said he would release them and let them return home with wheat for the family, provided they came back with Jacob's youngest son to confirm their story. Meanwhile, one of them would have to be left behind as a hostage.

The agitated brothers discussed the situation in their own language, unaware that Joseph, who had addressed them through an interpreter, could understand what they said. He turned aside and wept when he heard Reuben, the eldest, suggest that they were now paying the penalty for the sin they had committed against the young Joseph. Simeon, the second eldest, was bound and imprisoned as a hostage. The others loaded up their asses with the grain and started on the long journey back. At the first night's halt they were even more perplexed and worried when one sack was opened to feed the animals, and the money paid for it was found inside. They could not know that Joseph had ordered this to be done as a gesture to his brethren. At their journey's end, they found a similar amount of money concealed in each sack.

*The Reunion*

The report of what had befallen his sons in Egypt came as a tragic blow to Jacob. He could not bring himself to let Benjamin be taken off, but was persuaded to do so when their stock of food was again depleted. He told his sons that all the purchase money found in the sacks had to be returned to the high official with whom they had dealt in Egypt, together with a gift of 'a little balm and a little honey, gum, myrrh, pistachio nuts, and almonds' (Gen. 43:11).

This time Joseph received the brothers graciously, asked after their father, and sent them to his home as guests for the midday meal. Simeon was released and joined them. On his arrival, Joseph received the gifts they had brought, and Benjamin was presented to him. Joseph had to withdraw to hide his emotion. To their surprise, the eleven brothers were seated at the table in the precise order of their seniority. The Egyptian guests were served at a separate table – they would not 'eat bread with the Hebrews'. Joseph sat apart as befitted his rank, and had choice morsels from his own dishes served to the Israelite group, especially to Benjamin.

The brothers set out for home in good spirits with the fresh supplies of wheat they had bought. But their troubles were not yet over. Unable to be parted so soon from Benjamin, Joseph resorted to strategem. Once more the purchase money was hidden in the sacks. What was worse, Joseph's silver divining cup was put into Benjamin's bag. Joseph's steward, sent to pursue the brothers, accused them of theft and hauled them back. Feigning anger, Joseph demanded that Benjamin be left behind to serve as his slave. The distraught brothers pleaded that the loss of Benjamin would drive their father to his grave, 'as his life is bound up in the lad's life' (Gen. 44:30). In a moving speech, Judah offered himself as a substitute for Benjamin.

Joseph could no longer restrain his feelings. Sending everyone else out of the room, he remained alone with his brothers and revealed to them who he really was. He did not hold it against them for having sold him into slavery, for that had been God's way of bringing him to his present position, so that he would be able to help his family in distress and preserve their future destiny. As there would be another five years before the famine ended, he urged them to bring their father Jacob and all their families and possessions to Egypt. They could settle in the land of Goshen, the northeast corner of the fertile Nile delta, where Joseph would take care of them.

Pharaoh was delighted to hear of Joseph's family reunion. He approved of the proposed move from Canaan to Egypt and himself provided wagons as transport for the women and children. Joseph added a plentiful supply of provisions loaded on asses.

*The Land of Goshen*

Jacob was overwhelmed at the story his sons brought back from Egypt this time. He exclaimed 'It is enough; Joseph my son is still alive; I will go and see him before I die' (Gen. 45:28). With his children and grandchildren, seventy souls in all, he set out on his last migration. Joseph came to meet them in Goshen, and the aged patriarch could hardly believe that the resplendent viceroy he now embraced was the same son for whose tragic death he had grieved all these years. First five of the sons, and then Jacob himself, were brought to the royal court by Joseph and presented to Pharaoh, on whom Jacob bestowed a patriarchal blessing.

Joseph utilized the famine years to carry out sweeping agrarian reforms in Egypt. In exchange for an assured distribution of food and seed, the peasants surrendered to Pharaoh's ownership first their livestock and then their land holdings. Under the centralized feudal system Joseph developed, the cultivators became tenant-serfs on the royal estates, keeping four-fifths of the crops for themselves and handing over one-fifth to the estate. Temple lands were exempted from the one-fifth tax, as the priesthood was subsidized from state revenues.

There is evidence from Egyptian records that a feudalistic system of such a kind was introduced between 1700 and 1500 BC. This was during the period when Egypt, as well as Syria and Canaan, were ruled by the Hyksos, a people of Semitic language who had invaded Egypt from Canaan about 1720 BC. If the unnamed Pharaoh of the Joseph story was one of the Hyksos dynasty, it would explain the sweeping powers given to a non-Egyptian Semite like Joseph, and the benevolent treatment of Jacob and his clan, a group of nomadic immigrants from Canaan.

Jacob lived for another seventeen years in Goshen and reached the age of one hundred and forty-seven. When he heard that his father's health was failing, Joseph went to see him, bringing his own two sons, Manasseh and Ephraim. The dying Jacob rallied his strength enough to sit up in bed and embrace the boys, declaring that they would be regarded as equal in status to his own sons. In blessing them, Jacob brushed aside Joseph's objections and placed his right hand on the head of the younger, and his left hand on the head of the elder, indicating that in the future the tribe of Ephraim would be more important than the tribe of Manasseh.

*Jacob's Blessing* Jacob summoned all his sons to his bedside, and said, 'Gather yourselves together, that I may tell you what shall befall you in days to come' (Gen. 49:1). The blessing of Jacob that follows is in the form of a long poem. It is obviously of much later date, since it reflects circumstances relating to the different tribes after the Conquest and Settlement, four to five centuries after the time of Jacob.

The blessing refers to each of the sons in turn:

Reuben, you are my first-born,
my might, and the first fruits of my strength,
pre-eminent in pride and pre-eminent in power.
Unstable as water, you shall not have pre-eminence
because you went up to your father's bed;
then you defiled it – you went up to my couch!

(The tribe descended from Reuben, the eldest son, remained in southern Jordan and in due course disappeared.)

Simeon and Levi are brothers;
weapons of violence are their swords.
O my soul, come not into their council;
O my spirit, be not joined to their company;
for in their anger they slay men,
and in their wantonness they hamstring oxen.
Cursed be their anger, for it is fierce;
and their wrath, for it is cruel!
I will divide them in Jacob
and scatter them in Israel.

(Simeon and Levi are described as violent, because of their murderous attack on the city of Shechem, when Jacob first returned from Haran. The tribe of Simeon settled in the southern desert and became absorbed into Judah. The tribe of Levi never acquired territory of its own, but became a priestly community scattered among the other tribes.)

Judah, your brothers shall praise you;
your hand shall be on the neck of your enemies;
your father's sons shall bow down before you.
Judah is a lion's whelp;
from the prey, my son, you have gone up.

He stooped down, he crouched as a lion,
    and as a lioness; who dares rouse him up?
The sceptre shall not depart from Judah,
    nor the ruler's staff from between his feet,
until he comes to whom it belongs;
    and to him shall be the obedience
    of the peoples.
Binding his foal to the vine
    and his ass's colt to the choice vine,
he washes his garments in wine
    and his vesture in the blood of grapes;
his eyes shall be red with wine,
    and his teeth white with milk.

(The emphasis in this passage is on the royal Davidic dynasty drawn from the tribe of Judah – hence the reference to the sceptre and the ruler's staff.)

Zebulun shall dwell at the shore of
    the sea;
    he shall become a haven for ships,
    and his border shall be at Sidon.

(The tribe of Zebulun did not actually manage to occupy the coastal area but settled a little inland in the valley of Jezreel (or Esdraelon); it had close relations with the Phoenician coastal cities of Sidon and Tyre.)

Issachar is a strong ass,
    crouching between the sheepfolds;
    he saw that a resting place was good,
    and that the land was pleasant;
so he bowed his shoulder to bear,
    and became a slave at forced labour.

(The tribe of Issachar settled in the eastern part of the Jezreel valley, at the price of subjection to the Philistines.)

Dan shall judge his people
    as one of the tribes of Israel.
Dan shall be a serpent in the way,
    a viper by the path,
    that bites the horse's heels
      so that his rider falls backward.
I wait for thy salvation, O Lord.

(The reference to Dan is a play on the name, which means judge in Hebrew. The serpent biting the horse's heels is an allusion to the struggle of the small tribe of Dan to survive in the Judean foothills against the pressure of its powerful Philistine neighbours.)

Raiders shall raid Gad,
    but he shall raid at their heels.

(The tribe of Gad, like that of Reuben, settled in Trans-jordan and was constantly repelling desert raiders.)

Asher's food shall be rich,
    and he shall yield royal dainties.

(The tribe of Asher occupied part of the fertile farming area along the coastal plain of Acre, between Mount Carmel and the Ladder of Tyre.)

Naphtali is a hind let loose,
    that bears comely fawns.

(Naphtali was a tribe of hardy hillmen in the Galilee highlands; their freedom and vigour is compared to 'a hind let loose'.)

Joseph is a fruitful bough,
    a fruitful bough by a spring;
    his branches run over the wall.
The archers fiercely attacked him,
    shot at him, and harassed him
    sorely;
    yet his bow remained unmoved,
    his arms were made agile
by the hands of the Mighty One of
    Jacob
    (by the name of the Shepherd,
    the Rock of Israel),
by the God of your father who will
    help you,
by God Almighty who will bless you
with blessings of heaven above,
blessings of the deep that couches
    beneath,
blessings of the breasts and of the womb,
The blessings of your father
    are mighty beyond the blessings of
    the eternal mountains,
    the bounties of the everlasting hills;
may they be on the head of Joseph,
    and on the brow of him who was
    separate from his brothers.

(Joseph's descendants, the tribes of Manasseh and Ephraim, were blessed with strength and prosperity, and between them held the central region of the country on both sides of the Jordan. Ephraim led the coalition of northern tribes that eventually seceded from Judah and set up the separate kingdom of Israel.)

Benjamin is a ravenous wolf,
in the morning devouring the prey,
and at even dividing the spoil.

(The men of the small tribe of Benjamin occupied the hill terrain north of Jerusalem, and were renowned as warriors, especially as skilled archers. Saul, the first Hebrew king, was a Benjaminite.)

*The Deaths of Jacob and Joseph*

Joseph had promised his father that he would be buried in the ancestral tomb, the Cave of Machpelah at Hebron. Joseph had Jacob's body embalmed, decreed a period of public mourning usually reserved for members of the royal household, and then led the funeral caravan across the desert. It was accompanied by all Jacob's sons and a number of Egyptian dignitaries as a mark of respect. The family then returned to Egypt. Joseph's brothers were fearful that he would take vengeance on them with the restraining influence of their father removed. They came and bowed down to him, but he reassured them by saying, 'Fear not, for am I in the place of God?' (Gen. 50:19).

Joseph died at the age of one hundred and ten, after obtaining a solemn promise from his brethren that at the time appointed by God his remains would be carried to the Promised Land. Meanwhile, his body was mummified by Egyptian physicians, and preserved in a coffin.

# 3

# THE EXODUS

## *Moses*

THE FOUR CENTURIES AFTER JACOB and Joseph are a blank in the biblical record, except for the single statement that 'the descendants of Israel were fruitful and increased greatly; they multiplied and grew exceedingly strong; so that the land was filled with them' (Ex. 1:7). Then there came a change in their fortunes with the rise of 'a new king over Egypt, who did not know Joseph' (Ex. 1:8).

*The Oppression in Egypt*     This unnamed ruler decided that the Israelite community had become too large and established, and might constitute a security risk on Egypt's eastern border in time of war. He started to oppress them. His task-masters rounded up the men to work as slaves in the building of two 'store-cities', Pithom and Raamses, and the overseers 'made their lives bitter with hard service' (Ex. 1:14).

The Hyksos kings that had ruled Egypt in Joseph's time had been expelled in the middle of the seventeenth century BC. The Eighteenth Dynasty that succeeded them made Egypt the dominant power in the Near East with an empire extending into western Asia as far as the Euphrates river. However, by the fourteenth century BC Egypt's might had declined, and it had lost control of its Asian provinces, including Canaan. The Pharaoh 'who did not know Joseph' was almost certainly Seti I (1305–1290 BC), of the Nineteenth Dynasty. The new regime under Seti I, and his successor Rameses II (1290–1224 BC), strove to regain the lost empire. But an Egyptian drive into Canaan and Syria was blocked by the Hittite empire, pushing south from Asia Minor.

The energies and resources of Egypt were diverted into massive building projects. They were started by Seti I and developed during the long and prosperous reign of Rameses II. Their programme concentrated on the eastern Nile Delta in which the province of Goshen lay, where the Israelites were settled. The royal capital was moved from Thebes in Upper Egypt to the site of the old Hyksos capital in the Delta, which was rebuilt and named after Rameses. This new city, renowned for its beauty, was the 'Raamses' mentioned in the Exodus story. Pithom, the other city on which the Israelites were put to work, was located further south near Lake Timsah (now part of the Suez Canal).

In a period of revived Egyptian chauvinism, a foreign element like the Israelites in Goshen would be disliked and distrusted, as appears from Pharaoh's remarks about them. Hence they were exploited as a pool of slave labour close to the new cities being constructed in that area.

But the oppression did not stop there. Determined to cut down their numbers, Pharaoh decreed that all male infants had to be killed at birth. Hebrew midwives were ordered to carry out this savage measure. But they evaded doing so, giving as an excuse that the vigorous Israelite women had their babies before the midwives reached them. The decree then went out that the male babies should be thrown into the Nile.

*The Infant Moses* At this perilous time, a son was born to Amram, of the priestly house of Levi, and his wife Jochebed. His mother kept the infant hidden for three months, then had to contrive some other way of saving him. She put him in a basket woven of bullrushes and sealed with pitch, and concealed him among the reeds at the river's edge. An older child, Miriam, was posted a short distance away to see who would discover the infant, in the hope that he would be adopted into an Egyptian home.

The basket was spotted by Pharaoh's daughter, who had come to bathe in the river. One of her maids fetched it for her, and when she saw the wailing baby in it, she understood at once that 'This is one of the Hebrews' children' (Ex. 2:6). Taking pity on it, she decided to keep it. At this moment Miriam came up to the princess and offered to find a Hebrew woman to nurse the child. Pharaoh's daughter agreed. Miriam ran off to fetch Jochebed, who was hired to take care of her own infant. When he was weaned, his mother took him to the palace and handed him over to the princess, who adopted him as her son. He was named Moses (in Hebrew, Moshe), derived either from a Hebrew word meaning 'to draw out (from the water),' or from an Egyptian word for child. As a member of the royal household, the boy was reared in luxury, imbued with the intellectual traditions of an ancient culture, and exposed to affairs of state in an imperial court.

However, Moses remained aware of his true identity, and identified with his oppressed people. When he was already a grown man, he went out one day to watch the Hebrews at work and saw one of them being flogged by an Egyptian overseer. In a rage, Moses attacked and killed the Egyptian, and buried his body in the sand. Nobody else witnessed the deed, but the man saved by Moses must have told others about the incident. The next day Moses intervened between two Israelites fighting with each other. One of them turned on him and said, 'Who made you a prince and a judge over us? Do you mean to kill me as you killed the Egyptian?' (Ex. 2:14). Moses realized that his act had become known. He fled eastward into the Sinai desert before Pharaoh could seize him.

*With the Midianites* Resting at a well, Moses assisted some young women to water their flocks, and protected them from interference by other shepherds. They told their father Jethro (also called Reuel) about the stranger that had helped them. Jethro invited Moses to share their meal. Moses found his host was a wise priest of a clan of nomads from Midian, the desert region south of the Dead Sea. As was their custom, these bedouin had wandered westward in search of grazing and water. Moses remained with them, married Zipporah, one of Jethro's seven daughters, and settled down to the life of a shepherd.

For Moses, this was an abrupt transition to a different world. He now became inured to the harsh life of the desert, and the simple, slow-moving ways of the nomad. He learnt to endure patiently the scorching heat of noon, the cold at night, the dust storms before which he and his flock huddled in the shelter of rocky outcrops. He acquired the exacting skills of the shepherd: finding his way through the bleak and pathless terrain; locating water holes, and the scant vegetation for the sheep and goats at the bottom of wadis; beating off predatory animals; and evading marauders. At night, around the cooking fires, he listened to the talk of his father-in-law Jethro and the other men, and came to understand their customs and their stern code of conduct. The years with the Midianites were Moses' apprenticeship as a future desert chieftain.

They were also no doubt years of deep reflection, of religious and legal concepts slowly evolving in a profound and searching mind. In the solitude and space of the desert far from the teeming Nile valley, God could be felt as a single, invisible, omnipotent and brooding presence, before whom man seemed puny. Moses must have given much thought to the traditions about the covenant between his patriarchal ancestors

Moses and the Burning Bush. A woodcut by the German artist Jochem Pechau.

and their God – a relationship quite different in spirit from all the pagan religions of the Middle East, including the pantheon of Egyptian gods.

*The Burning Bush* The first revelation of his special destiny came to Moses at the mountain of Horeb (Mount Sinai), where he was tending his father-in-law's flocks. One day he saw a strange sight: a desert bush that was in flames without being burnt. The voice of the Lord called his name from the bush and said, 'Do not come near; put off your shoes from your feet, for the place on which you are standing is holy ground' (Ex. 3:5). The Lord then revealed to Moses that he had been chosen to deliver the Children of Israel from their oppression, and lead them to the goodly land that had been promised to the descendants of Abraham, Isaac and Jacob.

Moses shrank from this task: 'Who am I that I should go to Pharaoh, and bring the sons of Israel out of Egypt?' (Ex. 3:11). The Lord assured him of divine support in his mission, and revealed to him the sacred name of Yahweh (Jehovah). He was also given certain magic signs with which to convince Pharaoh and the Israelites: turning his staff into a snake, making his hand white with leprosy, and turning water into blood. Moses still demurred, claiming that he was unfit for such an undertaking as 'I am slow of speech and of tongue' (Ex. 4:10). But the Lord impatiently brushed aside this excuse, saying that Moses' brother Aaron could serve as his spokesman.

Moses obtained the permission and blessing of his father-in-law Jethro for the journey back to Egypt. He set out with his wife Zipporah on a donkey, holding their elder son Gershom and the newly-born Eliezer. At a wayside halt Moses became very ill. Zipporah feared that his life would be forfeited to the Lord because their infant son had not been circumcised. She therefore performed the rite herself with a sharp flint stone.

In the brief account of this episode, Zipporah touched Moses' 'feet' (probably a euphemism for genitals) with the severed foreskin, calling him her 'bridegroom of blood'. The meaning of this action is obscure; it may relate to a primitive custom among the Midianites, Zipporah's people, of circumcision before marriage.

Aaron, the elder brother of Moses, came out to meet him and was told what the Lord had commanded. Their first task was to arouse the Israelites themselves from their apathy. They had to be given enough hope and faith to make them uproot themselves and follow Moses across the desert to an unknown future.

A meeting was arranged with the elders, the hereditary leaders of the Israelite clans and tribal groups. Here Aaron's role was decisive. He was a respected priest of the tribe of Levi, while Moses had been remote from his own people, first as a young aristocrat at the court and then as a shepherd with the Midianites. The elders were persuaded by Aaron's eloquent exposition of God's design for their deliverance, and by the magic signs he produced as corroboration. With their backing, the general community accepted the message as authentic and 'they bowed their heads and worshipped' (Ex. 4:31).

## Let My People Go

THE BROTHERS GAINED AN AUDIENCE WITH THE Pharaoh, the successor to the one from whom Moses had fled many years before. They did not dare disclose their real objective; instead, they asked for permission for the Israelites to hold a religious festival and offer sacrifices at a place in the desert three days away. Even this limited request aroused the ruler's ire. As a punishment for the presumption of the Israelites in wanting to take time off from their work, he decreed that they would be made to work even harder. Their *Pharaoh's* main job was to make bricks of clay mixed with *Reaction* straw and baked in the sun. From now on, they would have to find their own straw instead of having it issued to them and they would be flogged if their work fell short of the required quota of bricks. (Contrary to popular belief, nothing was said about making bricks without straw.) A deputation of Israelite foremen came to plead with Pharaoh, who berated them for the idleness of their people. The Israelites complained bitterly to Moses and Aaron that their intervention had only made matters worse, 'because you have made us offensive in the sight of Pharaoh and his servants, and have put a sword in their hand to kill us' (Ex. 5:21). Moses, too was despondent at this setback, and he in turn reproached the Lord that 'thou hast not delivered thy people at all' (Ex. 5:23). The Lord replied that he had hardened Pharaoh's heart so that the Egyptians should understand the power of God when he finally took the Children of Israel away from them.

*The Ten Plagues*  Egypt now experienced a succession of plagues. After each one Pharaoh promised to relent, but changed his mind when the affliction passed.

First, the water of the Nile was turned to blood and became foul, so that it was undrinkable and all the fish in it died. Then, frogs swarmed out of the river and spread everywhere, even into beds and cooking utensils. There followed plagues of lice, flies, cattle disease, boils, hail, locusts, and three days of darkness.

Since the cumulative effect of these disasters had failed to secure freedom for the Hebrews, the tenth and last plague was the most crushing of all – the deaths of Egyptian first-born sons. The Lord instructed Moses and Aaron that on the fourteenth day of that month, each Israelite family should slaughter a lamb or a kid and roast its flesh for a sacrificial meal; at the same time, everything was to be prepared for an immediate move. 'In this manner you shall eat it; your loins girded, your sandals on your feet, and your staff in your hand; and you shall eat it in haste. It is the Lord's passover' (Ex. 12:11). Blood from the slaughtered animals was to be daubed on the doorposts of Israelite homes so that the Lord could pass them over in smiting the Egyptians. There was grief and panic throughout the country as the first-born died in every Egyptian family, and even among their domestic animals. That same night Pharaoh hurriedly sent for Moses and Aaron and demanded that they lead their people away at once.

In the spring of each year Jews commemorate this event in the seven-day festival of Passover (in Hebrew, Pesach). They eat matzah or unleavened bread, for their ancestors had departed in such haste they could not wait for the leaven to rise in the dough. At the ceremonial *seder* meal bitter herbs are tasted as the symbol of the bondage to Egypt, and a roasted shank bone represents the lamb consumed on that fateful night thirty-three centuries ago.

*The Exodus*  The shortest route from Egypt to Canaan followed the Mediterranean coast across Sinai. It was known as the 'Way of the Philistines', and would normally take a week for merchant caravans or marching troops. Moses decided this was too risky a road for his horde of runaway slaves; they would certainly be driven back at Gaza, on the Canaan border, if they ever got as far. He therefore chose to make a longer and more arduous detour through the open desert, 'Lest the people repent when they see war, and return to Egypt' (Ex. 13:17). They headed southeast, moving in frantic haste for fear that Pharaoh would come after them. 'And the Lord went before them by day in a pillar of cloud to lead them along the way, and by night in a pillar of fire to give them light, that they might travel by day and by night' (Ex. 13:21).

Their first camp was at Succoth, thirty-two miles south of Raamses; their second at Etham at the edge of the desert, with the Reed Sea before them. (The Hebrew term *yam suf*, has been incorrectly translated as the Red Sea.) Here Pharaoh caught up with them, with a powerful mobile force that included six hundred war chariots. The terrified Israelites felt themselves trapped, and cried out to Moses, 'Is it because there are no graves in Egypt that you have taken us away to die in the wilderness?' (Ex. 14:11). They were saved by a miracle. When Moses stretched out his hand the water was pushed aside by a strong east wind, and the Israelites were able to cross to the other side. Pharaoh's chariots were bogged down in the soft surface and men and horses were drowned in the rush of the returning water. The Israelites sang a hymn of praise to the Lord for their deliverance, while Moses' sister Miriam, playing on a tambourine, led the women in a dance of gratitude.

There is no consensus among Bible scholars about the route of the Exodus and the location of Mount Sinai. Several theories have been put forward which might fit both the scriptural account and the geographical terrain.

By the version that has become traditional, the Israelites crossed the Sea of Reeds where the Suez Canal now runs in the vicinity of the Bitter Lakes. They then turned southward along the eastern side of the Gulf of Suez, following the route to the Egyptian turquoise and copper mines in southern Sinai. That brought them to a granite mountain range, with gaunt peaks rising up to 8,000 feet above sea-level. One of these peaks, which the Arabs call Jebel Musa (Mountain of Moses), was identified as the biblical Mount Sinai by Christian hermits who penetrated into this wild, deserted area in the second and third centuries AD. Near the foot of the mountain, at the reputed site of the burning bush, a chapel was built for the hermits in the fourth century by Constantine, the first Roman emperor to embrace

Christianity, or possibly by his devout mother, Helena. Two centuries later, the emperor Justinian expanded the isolated chapel into a large monastery complex, enclosed by a strong wall to protect the monks from brigands. Subsequently, the monastery became identified with Saint Catherine of Alexandria, an early christian martyr, who was tortured to death on a wheel in fourth-century Alexandria, and became the patron saint of wheelwrights. The monastery has been in continuous occupation for fifteen hundred years. From Mount Sinai the Israelites would have headed northward to the top of the Gulf of Akaba and continued to the oasis of Kadesh Barnea.

Another school of thought favours a shorter northern route for the Exodus. The crossing of the Reed Sea would be Lake Bardawil, a large, shallow lagoon on the Sinai coast east of Port Said. It is separated from the open sea by a narrow strip of land along which runs the coastal highway. By this theory, Pharaoh's chariots would have been caught by the sea-water surging across the strip in a storm after the Israelites had crossed. The Israelites would then have headed across the line of sand-dunes into the open desert, in the direction of the Kadesh Barnea oasis. The most likely location along this route for Mount Sinai would be the peak of Jebel Halal, a short distance to the south of Kadesh Barnea.

A third theory suggests a still shorter but more difficult central route, eastward across the wilderness of Shur and the Wilderness of Paran to Kadesh Barnea. Along this route there are two peaks either of which might possibly be identified with Mount Sinai.

*Rigours of the Desert* Wherever the crossing of the Reed Sea took place, the relief of the Israelites at their narrow escape and the intoxication of their new-found freedom soon evaporated, as the rigours of the desert closed in on them. They trekked for three days through the Wilderness of Shur, a wasteland of sand and gravel intersected with dry water-courses, where their sheep, goats and cattle cropped hungrily at the thin scrub. Already they were up against the key problem of desert travel – water. At Marah (which means bitter in Hebrew), there was a pool too brackish to drink. Here 'the people murmured against Moses' (Ex. 15:24). Using his desert lore, he reduced the salinity by throwing in a certain type of bush. A day's march further on, they were able to camp at the oasis of Elim, 'where there were twelve springs of water and seventy palm trees' (Ex. 15:27).

The next crisis arose when they ran out of food, as they moved through the barren Wilderness of Sin. They hurled at Moses and Aaron all the pent-up resentment they felt over a 'liberation' which had brought them nothing but misery: 'Would that we had died by the hand of the Lord in the land of Egypt, when we sat by the fleshpots and ate bread to the full; for you have brought us out into this wilderness to kill this whole assembly with hunger' (Ex. 16:3).

Moses promised them that the Lord would provide meat and bread. In the evening flocks of quails covered the ground around their encampment and were easily caught. Next morning when the dew cleared the ground was strewn with manna, 'like coriander seed, white, and the taste of it was like wafers made of honey' (Ex. 16:31). The people were told to gather and prepare each morning just enough manna for the day, as the rest would decay in the heat. A double portion could be gathered on the sixth day to tide them over the Sabbath.

To this day, huge flocks of quail migrating from Europe come down to rest among the desert bushes, and are snared for food by the bedouin tribes. The practice has been forbidden in the State of Israel. In seeking a natural explanation for the manna, scholars suggest it may have been a resin that is exuded by the tamarisk trees in Sinai and falls to the ground in white particles as it dries.

When the Children of Israel again suffered from thirst, at a place called Rephidim, their complaints were so vehement that Moses cried out to the Lord 'What shall I do with this people? They are almost ready to stone me' (Ex. 17:4). Once more the situation was saved by a miracle. Moses was told to assemble the elders and in their presence to strike a certain rock with the rod used to work wonders in Egypt. He did so, and fresh water gushed out. Moses called the place Massah and Meribah (proof and contention) because the Israelites had found fault with God and put him to the test.

Before they moved from this encampment, a human adversary was added to the hostility of nature. They were threatened by a band of Amalekite desert marauders. Until then, no arrangements had been made for self-defence. Moses at once selected as commander a stalwart

The Flight of the Israelites out
of Egypt. A painting by the
nineteenth-century English artist
Richard Dadd.

young man who had impressed him – Joshua the son of Nun, an Ephraimite. Joshua was told to improvise a fighting force of selected young men. When the attack came, Moses took up his position on top of a hill, holding his rod in his right hand. He was accompanied by Aaron and by Hur (traditionally regarded as his brother-in-law, married to Miriam). As long as Moses was able to stretch out his arms with the rod extended, the Israelites held their own in the battle. When he tired, Aaron and Hur seated him on a rock and supported his arms 'so his hands were steady until the going down of the sun' (Ex. 17:12). At nightfall the surviving Amalekites fled.

## Mount Sinai

IN THE THIRD MONTH AFTER LEAVING EGYPT, the Israelites reached a rugged mountain terrain in the heart of Sinai. They camped facing the peak of Mount Sinai (or Mount Horeb). It was here that Moses had heard the voice of the Lord coming out of the burning bush. His father-in-law Jethro came to see him, bringing Zipporah and her two sons, who had apparently been on a visit to her family. When Jethro heard all that had happened, he exclaimed 'Now I know that the Lord is greater than all gods' (Ex. 18:11), and himself offered a sacrifice to the Hebrew deity. The Israelite elders were invited to a feast in honour of the Midianite leader.

Next day Jethro was present while Moses dealt with a throng of persons bringing disputes and complaints to be settled. In the tent that evening the sagacious old man remonstrated with Moses for trying to carry the whole burden by himself. He recommended that the Israelites be divided into groups and sub-groups of uniform size, each in charge of a competent person. These subordinates should have authority to deal with day-to-day matters and disputes, leaving Moses free for more important cases and for questions of general policy. Moses accepted the proposed system and appointed 'rulers of thousands, of hundreds, of fifties, and of tens. And they judged the people at all times; hard cases they brought to Moses' (Ex. 18:25–26). For the discharge of their functions, Moses gave his deputies brief guidelines which could serve for any magistrate in any age. They were charged to 'judge righteously between a man and his brother or the alien that is with him. You shall not be partial in judgment;

you shall hear the small and the great alike; you shall not be afraid of the face of man, for the judgment is God's' (Deut. 1:16–17).

Moses must for some time have felt the need to organize his people more effectively. He had led out of Egypt a dispirited rabble, loosely grouped under traditional tribal elders. The battle with the Midianite raiders at Rephidim had shown how ill-equipped for military encounters was this amorphous mass. To gain cohesion, and even to survive, they needed a firm hierarchy of leadership and responsibility. It would take Moses another forty patient and painful years before the Israelites would be able to enter the Promised Land and establish themselves on its soil.

The decisive moment in the nation-building process came almost at its beginning: the handing down of the Law on Mount Sinai.

*The Sinai Covenant*

Moses climbed alone to the top of the mountain, and was instructed by the Lord to say to the people encamped below 'if you will obey my voice and keep my covenant, you shall be my own possession among all peoples' (Ex. 19:5). When Moses repeated this to them the Israelites replied in unison: 'All that the Lord has spoken we will do' (Ex. 19:8), thereby expressing their acceptance of the covenant.

The idea of a divine covenant was not new in Hebrew history. God had made one in turn with each of the three Patriarchs – Abraham, Isaac and Jacob. At Sinai the concept was given a fresh and lofty dimension. The human party to the agreement was not an individual but a whole people; while its content marked a revolution in the moral history of mankind.

The Sinaitic form of the covenant has a superficial resemblance to the treaties made by the rulers of the ancient Hittite empire with their vassals. In such a pact, it was agreed that the subject people would be protected by the conqueror as long as it remained loyal to him and paid the agreed tribute. At Sinai, God promised to protect the Israelite nation and secure its future, and it undertook in turn to observe God's moral code. This unique concept of a covenant relationship between God and man has remained the cornerstone of the Jewish faith.

*The Ten Commandments*

For two days after their acceptance of the covenant, the Israelites washed and purified themselves. On the third day the mountain was covered with a thick cloud, and out of it came thunder and lightning. A loud trumpet blast was

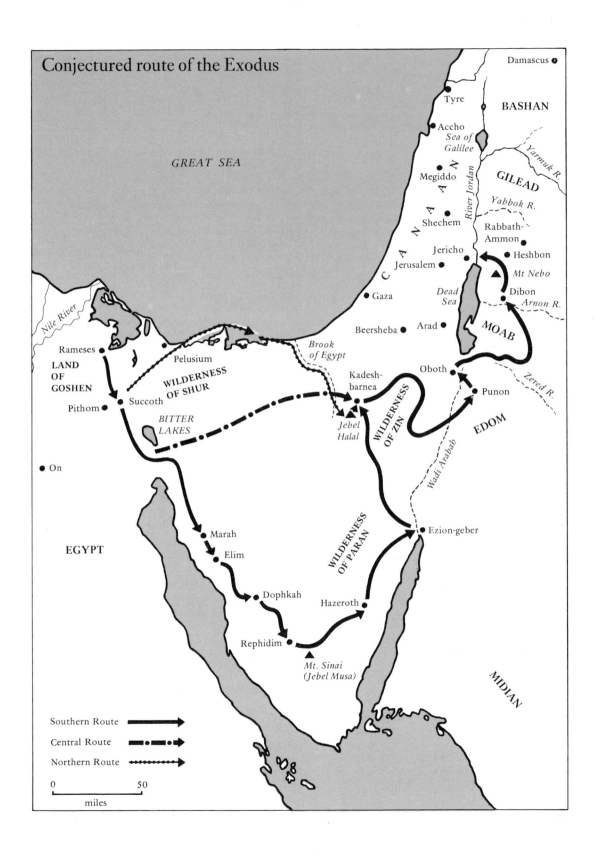

Conjectured route of the Exodus

Damascus

BASHAN

GREAT SEA

Tyre

Accho
Sea of
Galilee

Yarmuk R.

GILEAD

Megiddo

Yabbok R.

C A N A A N

Shechem

Rabbath-
Ammon

River Jordan

Jericho

Heshbon

Jerusalem

Mt Nebo

Dibon

Dead
Sea

Arnon R.

Gaza

MOAB

Nile River

Beersheba

Arad

Zered R.

Rameses

Brook
of Egypt

Kadesh-
barnea

Oboth

LAND
OF
GOSHEN

Pelusium

Punon

Pithom

Succoth

WILDERNESS
OF SHUR

WILDERNESS
OF ZIN

EDOM

BITTER
LAKES

Jebel
Halal

Wadi Arabah

On

Marah

WILDERNESS
OF PARAN

Elim

EGYPT

Ezion-geber

Dophkah

Hazeroth

Rephidim

Mt. Sinai
(Jebel Musa)

MIDIAN

Southern Route

Central Route

Northern Route

0        50

miles

the signal for the crowd to draw closer. The peak burst into flames as the Lord descended on to it and 'the whole mountain quaked greatly' (Ex. 19:18). The voice of the Lord was then heard, pronouncing the Ten Commandments:

I am the Lord your God, who brought you out of the land of Egypt, out of the house of bondage.
You shall have no other gods before me.
You shall not make for yourself a graven image . . .
You shall not take the name of the Lord your God in vain;
Remember the sabbath day, to keep it holy. Six days you shall labour, and do all your work; but the seventh day is a sabbath to the Lord your God;
Honour your father and your mother;
You shall not kill.
You shall not commit adultery.
You shall not steal.
You shall not bear false witness against your neighbour.
You shall not covet your neighbour's house; or anything that is your neighbour's.

(Ex. 20:2–17)

The first three commandments call for a total adherence to monotheism and the rejection of pagan cults. The fourth commandment consecrates the sabbath day. The remaining six concern dealings between man and man.

*The Covenant Code*
To mark the solemn occasion, Moses built a stone altar at the foot of the mountain, with twelve pillars representing the tribes of Israel. Oxen were sacrificed on the altar and blood from the sacrifices was sprinkled on the people as a sign of the covenant. Moses then read out to them a set of detailed legal precepts contained in a 'book of the covenant' (Ex. 24:7). This Covenant Code, as it has come to be called, is set out in Chapters 20–23 of the Book of Exodus. It was expanded and edited in a later age, as is shown by some passages that reflect a settled agricultural life in the Land of Israel. But there is no reason to doubt that the essence of the Code came from Moses as the great lawgiver.

The Code deals with a wide range of subjects: religious observance, criminal law, relations between master and slave or creditor and debtor. The progressive and humane spirit of the Mosaic Code can be illustrated by this ordinance concerning the needy:

If you lend money to any of my people with you who is poor, you shall not be to him as a creditor, and you shall not exact interest from him. If ever you take your neighbour's garment in pledge, you shall restore it to him before the sun goes down; for that is his only covering, it is his mantle for his body; in what else shall he sleep? And if he cries to me, I will hear, for I am compassionate. (Ex. 22:25–27).

It is also laid down that, 'You shall not wrong a stranger or oppress him, for you were strangers in the land of Egypt' (Ex. 22:21). Fields and vineyards were to lie fallow every seventh year, and in that year those in want could garner whatever grew in them.

*The Golden Calf*
The Lord said to Moses: 'Come up to me on the mountain, and wait there; and I will give you the tablets of stone, with the law and the commandment, which I have written for their instruction' (Ex. 24:12). Moses climbed up again, leaving Aaron and Hur in charge of the camp. His trusted lieutenant Joshua accompanied him for part of the ascent and waited for his return.

Meanwhile, as the inexplicable absence of their leader dragged on, the Israelites feared that he had deserted them. Their brittle faith in Moses and in the divine Covenant started to crumble. They came to Aaron and said, 'Up, make us gods, who shall go before us; as for this Moses, the man who brought us up out of the land of Egypt, we do not know what has become of him' (Ex. 32:1). Aaron gave way before their anger and despair. He asked for all the gold earings worn by both men and women, melted them down, and moulded a golden calf. The people made sacrifices to the effigy, and they sang, feasted and danced around it. (This lapse into pagan rites may have echoed the worship by the Egyptians of the bull-god Apis.)

Forty days after he had left, Moses came down again carrying two tables or tablets of stone engraved with the Ten Commandments, 'written with the finger of God' (Ex. 31:18). When Moses and Joshua arrived at the camp, they were met by the shattering spectacle of the revels around the golden calf. In a rage at this betrayal, Moses hurled the tablets to the ground and smashed them – an act signifying that the Covenant embodied in them had been broken. He burnt the image of the calf, ground the remains into powder, mixed it with water and forced the worshippers to drink it. He then ordered the Levites to arm themselves with swords and slay the ringleaders. The shamefaced Aaron managed to excuse his own part in the affair, and escaped serious punishment. Having carried out the drastic purge, Moses relented and prayed to the Lord to forgive his 'stiff-necked people', as they had now returned to the fold in penitent mood.

To symbolize the renewal of the Covenant, Moses hewed two more slabs of stone and went up the mountain with them. After another forty days he came down with the new engraved tablets. Because of his communion with the Lord, the skin of his face shone with such radiance that Aaron and the others were at first afraid to approach him. (The famous statue of Moses by Michelangelo, which stands in the Church of San Pietro di Vincoli in Rome, has an incongruous pair of small horns jutting from the forehead. The reason is that the Hebrew word for rays of light was mistaken by the translators of the Vulgate (Latin Bible) for a similar word meaning horns.)

*The Ark and the Tabernacle* On God's instructions, Moses had two sacred objects made: the Ark of the Covenant (or Ark of the Law) and the Tabernacle. The Ark was a box made of acacia wood covered with gold, and served as a receptacle for the Tablets of the Law. On top of the Ark were two small figures of cherubim, winged creatures somewhat like the Egyptian sphinx. The *shechinah* or Divine Presence, was supposed to rest between them. During periods of travel, the Ark was carried on poles threaded through rings in its sides.

The Tabernacle was a portable sanctuary, constructed of decorated linen hung on frames of acacia wood covered in gold. It was enclosed within a huge tent made from goat's hair with an outer covering of the skins of rams and goats. The Ark was kept in a holy of holies at one end, screened off with a fine linen curtain. Moses' directions also covered the altar and other sacred equipment, the rich priestly vestments, and recipes for incense and anointing oil.

When the Israelites were on the move, the Tabernacle was dismantled for ease of transport. In an encampment it was erected in the centre, with the tents of the Levites around it, and all the other tribes forming an outer square.

Biblical scholars have been puzzled by the costly and elaborate nature of this portable desert shrine, and by the close resemblance of its layout and fittings to Solomon's Temple, built three centuries later. It is surmised that the description in Exodus was drawn up by biblical compilers in a later age after the destruction of Solomon's Temple, and under the influence of its memory. In Exodus there is mention also of a much simpler tent with which God's presence was associated. 'Now Moses used to take the tent and pitch it outside the camp ... And every one who sought the Lord would go out to the tent of the meeting' (Ex. 33:7). Watched by the Israelites from afar, Moses would go alone to this tent, and there 'the Lord used to speak to Moses face to face, as a man speaks to his friend' (Ex. 33:11). This modest sanctuary appears to represent an earlier tradition, closer to the actual way of life in the desert wandering.

*The Priesthood* With the substance of religious life laid down in the Mosaic code, attention was given to organizing its cult, that is, its ceremonial and ritual system. For the first time, a professional priesthood was instituted. Aaron was formally ordained as the high priest and his four sons as priests. Their duties were defined and included a regular daily schedule of sacrifices. The rigid standard required of the priests in performing their functions was brought home by the fate of Aaron's two elder sons, Nadab and Abihu. For burning incense on the altar in a forbidden manner, they were struck dead on the spot, and Aaron and his family were not permitted to carry out the mourning rites for them.

## On to Kadesh

WHEN THE ISRAELITES HAD BEEN AT MOUNT Sinai for nearly a year, the time came for them to move forward towards the Promised Land. In *The Order of the March* preparation for the resumed journey, Moses took steps to organize his people into a more disciplined community, capable of effective self-defence at all times.

To start with, a census was taken of all men from the age of twenty upwards, capable of bearing arms. The census was carried out by Moses and Aaron, assisted by a team of twelve, one from each tribe. The tally did not include the Levites, who were responsible for the Tabernacle and for religious duties generally, and were exempt from military service. In the text the

A miniature from a thirteenth-century English Psalter (above) showing Moses in the Tabernacle. It shows him with horns because in some early English translations of the Hebrew Bible the word *karnaim*, which in this context means 'rays of light', was incorrectly translated as 'horns', another meaning of the word. The head of Moses (left), from the altar in Schleswig Cathedral, Germany, shows him correctly with rays of light shining from his head.

number is given for each tribe, and the total comes to 603,550. Adding women and children, young people below twenty, the elderly and the sick, and the Levites, the tally would represent an Israelite community of over two million souls. Such a number could hardly have been sustained in the desert. Bible critics have sought a rational explanation for these obviously unreal figures. One theory suggested by the eminent Bible scholar Professor W. F. Albright is that these numbers really relate to the census ordered by king David in the United Monarchy about two-and-a-half centuries later, and have somehow become misplaced in the text. Another theory concerns the Hebrew word for a thousand, *elef*. In an earlier sense, it could mean a household group or a subsection of a tribe. By this hypothesis, the number given for the Tribe of Reuben, for instance, would not read 'forty-six thousand five hundred' but 'forty-six households, five hundred (men)'. By this reading, the total number of men in the census would not be 603,550 but 5,550 which would bring the size of the community to the more realistic figure of some twenty thousand.

In the marching order, every tribe and sub-tribe had a fixed position, with the men of Judah in the lead and the men of Dan bringing up the rear. A system of trumpet blasts gave the signals to advance or to halt. When encamped, the column quickly arranged itself into a square formation, with three tribes in front, three at the back and three on each flank.

Slowly they moved northward. Their guide through the rough, uncharted terrain was Moses' Midianite brother-in-law Hobab, a man born and bred in the desert.

*Sagging Morale* It was an empty expanse without human foe. But in this second year of their desert odyssey, the morale of the Israelites had sunk low, and discontent had become endemic. They complained endlessly about the meagre diet of manna and moaned to Moses: 'O that we had meat to eat! We remember the fish we ate in Egypt for nothing, the cucumbers, the melons, the leeks, the onions, and the garlic' (Num. 11:4–5). Moses too was becoming weary of his thankless task. He said to the Lord: 'I am not able to carry all this people alone, the burden is too heavy for me' (Num. 11:14). However, he rose above this moment of weakness. Seventy leading elders were called together in council, and infused again

with some of Moses' renewed spirit and determination. The hunger for meat was met once more by the seasonal flocks of migrating quail blown inland from the sea and settling in exhaustion around the camp. For two days the Israelites gorged themselves on the birds. As a result many of them became sick and some died.

To the great distress of Moses, the next attack on him came from the two people closest to him, his sister Miriam and his brother Aaron. Their criticism fastened on his marriage to a Cushite woman – a term that usually means Ethiopian, though it may here refer to Zipporah, the Midianite wife of Moses. But that was only a pretext. Their real grievance sprang from jealousy of their brother, because of his special relationship with God and his towering authority with the people. They said: 'Has the Lord indeed spoken only through Moses? Has he not spoken through us also?' (Num. 12:2). Miriam seems to have been the main source of this resentment. She was punished by the Lord by being smitten with leprosy, and was driven out of the camp, as was the custom. When Moses pleaded for her with the Lord, she recovered in seven days and returned.

They had now reached the wilderness of Paran, and were able to base themselves on the remarkable oasis of Kadesh-Barnea. It is situated about fifty miles south-west of Beersheba and possesses springs of fresh water and lush green vegetation.

*The Twelve Spies* The long trek from Egypt had brought them close to the southern border of the Promised Land. They knew very little about it, and Moses prudently decided to send forward a small reconnaissance party of twelve picked men, one from each of the tribes. Joshua represented his own tribe of Ephraim. Moses briefed them on their intelligence mission:

Go up into the Negeb yonder, and go up into the hill country, and see what the land is, and whether the people who dwell in it are strong or weak, whether they are few or many, and whether the land that they dwell in is good or bad, and whether the cities that they dwell in are camps or strongholds, and whether the land is rich or poor, and whether there is wood in it or not. Be of good courage, and bring some of the fruit of the land. (Num. 13:17–20).

The spies returned safely some six weeks later,

ABOVE Joseph's brothers throwing him into the well. A scene from the twelfth-century enamelled Verdun Altarpiece in Klosterneuburg in Austria.

RIGHT Joseph is visited by the Archangel Gabriel. An illustration from the epic poem on Joseph by the eleventh-century Persian poet Firdausi. The theme was popular in Islamic literature, based on the Joseph story in the twelfth Sura (chapter) of the Koran, that broadly follows the Old Testament account.

جبرئیل ایندی الهی اجازت ویرکه می کندو می اکا یعقوب صورتنده
کوستره م که غایبنده مشتاق در یوسف اول

دمیشن پداراولوب اول لشکر مجبندن هشیار
اولدی قده جبریسی یعقوب حانوسب فریاده کلدی که ایتاه کورو که ل خوانا

bringing with them pomegranates, figs, and a bunch of grapes so large that it was slung on a pole carried on the shoulders of two men. (It had been cut in the Valley of Eshkol, a vineyard area near Hebron.) Moses called together a general assembly to hear their report. They had found, they said, a fertile country that 'flows with milk and honey' (Num. 13:27), and produced the fruit as evidence. But, they warned, the population was strong and the cities were large and well fortified. Some of the men they saw were of gigantic stature, descendants of Anak, the Hebrew word for a giant. The Amalekites occupied the Negev in the south; the Hittites, Jebusites and the Amorites the hill country; and the Canaanites the coastal plain and the Jordan valley.

The boldest spirit among the twelve was Caleb from the tribe of Issachar. He proposed that the Israelites should advance at once into Canaan and occupy it, 'for we are well able to overcome it' (Num. 13:3). With the exception of Joshua, the others flatly contradicted him and gave a much more pessimistic opinion. It was, they maintained 'a land that devours its inhabitants' (Num. 13:32); and the men in it were so formidable in size that the Israelites seemed like grasshoppers by comparison.

The assembly broke into an uproar at hearing this. They railed against Moses and Aaron, and a demand was heard for some other leader to take them back to Egypt. In vain did Caleb and Joshua plead for faith in the Lord's promises. Passions ran so high that the leaders were in danger of being stoned. The Lord declared to Moses that because of the general lack of trust shown in him, none of the adults then living would see the Promised Land, except for Joshua and Caleb.

Some of the more militant Israelites organized an expedition that tried to penetrate to the hill country through the northern Negev. Moses was against this attempt, but his objections were brushed aside. The thrust was repulsed with heavy losses by the king of Arad, a Canaanite town on the plateau west of the Dead Sea.

*The Korah Revolt* The simmering disaffection now broke into open revolt. The trouble came from two different quarters. By tradition, the tribe of Levi carried out general religious duties among the Israelites. A number of them, led by a certain Korah, refused to accept the newly-created priestly office and the authority Aaron had been given. These Levites said to Moses and Aaron, 'You have gone too far! For all the congregation are holy, every one of them, and the Lord is among them; why then do you exalt yourselves above the assembly of the Lord?' (Num. 16:3). Another rebellious group headed by three men from the tribe of Reuben, Dathan, Abiram and On, gave vent to the general feeling of hopelessness that followed the spies' report and the defeat at Arad.

These two factions made common cause, and mustered the support of two hundred and fifty 'well-known men'. The dangerous challenge to Moses' leadership and God's authority was suppressed by swift and dire means. Moses made everybody else move away from the tents of the three ringleaders. The earth split open and they were swallowed up in it, together with their families and possessions. Their 250 supporters were brought together before the tent of meeting and died in a fire that broke out. When the people protested at this punishment, a plague broke out among them; it was halted only when Aaron walked among them swinging a censer of incense.

Some miraculous act was needed to remove doubt about Aaron's status and to establish him as the leader of the Levites. Moses demanded that a rod from each tribe be deposited overnight in the sanctuary. The tribe of Levi was represented by Aaron's own rod. In the morning his rod had blossomed and produced ripe almonds.

As the years rolled by, the Israelites settled down to a semi-nomadic tribal way of life, with the focal point of their territory at the Kadesh oasis. The men and women led out of Egyptian bondage gradually died off. Moses' sister Miriam was one of them and was buried at Kadesh. Beside this passing 'generation of the wilderness' there grew up a hardy, free new generation that had been born in the desert and knew no other existence. (From it would come the fighting men who would erupt into Canaan under Joshua.) Moses had long shed any illusion that a short interval of time would suffice between the Exodus from Egypt and the settlement in the Promised Land. He now grasped that the transition involved not the physical crossing of the desert but the remoulding of a people. Over decades, under his patient and consistent guidance, the Children of Israel absorbed the religious and legal code handed down at Sinai, and gained a national cohesion that transcended their tribal divisions.

## Before the Promised Land

*The Detour* FORTY YEARS AFTER THE EXODUS MOSES, BY now an aged man, decided that the time had come to resume the long-suspended journey. Since the direct route into Canaan from the south seemed blocked, the alternative was to skirt round the Dead Sea and come into the country from the east across the Jordan river.

The area to be traversed contained a number of small kingdoms inhabited by Semitic peoples who had recently migrated down from the north, as Abraham had done centuries earlier. Round the southern end of the Dead Sea lay the rugged desert terrain of Edom. On the tableland east of the Dead Sea, and three thousand feet above it, was Moab. North of Moab the Amorite kingdom of Heshbon stretched down to the Jordan river fords. To its east was Ammon. Further to the north (on what is now known as the Golan Heights) was Bashan. Through these Trans-jordan kingdoms ran the ancient caravan route from Arabia to Damascus, known as the King's Highway. According to biblical tradition, the Moabites and the Ammonites were descended from Abraham's nephew Lot, while Jacob's twin brother Esau was the ancestor of the Edomites.

From Kadesh, Moses sent messengers to the king of Edom, asking permission for the Israelites to cross. Moses undertook that 'We will not pass through field or vineyard, neither will we drink water from a well; we will go along the King's Highway, we will not turn aside to the right hand or to the left, until we have passed through your territory' (Num. 20:17). The king refused, and placed a fighting force on his border to prevent transit. The Israelites were obliged to make a long detour to the south.

*The Death of* Soon after they had moved off from Kadesh, *Aaron* they reached a height called Mount Hor. As Aaron was nearing his end, Moses took him up the mountain together with his son Eleazar, who was robed in Aaron's vestments and became high priest in his stead. Aaron died, was buried on the mountain, and was mourned by the people for thirty days.

Aaron had from the beginning shared the historic task God had thrust upon his younger brother Moses. Together they had appeared before Pharaoh, and carried the burden of leadership in the wilderness. With all the closeness of this association, Aaron did not measure up to the vision and moral stature of Moses. He is important in the Bible story chiefly as the founder of the Hebrew priesthood. In the centuries that followed, all the high priests claimed descent from him.

The Israelites proceeded in a southerly *The* direction through the Negev desert to Ezion *Conquests in* Geber (near Eilat) at the head of the Gulf of *Trans-jordan* Akaba. One desolate spot along the way was infested with venomous snakes that bit many of the people. Moses set up a bronze serpent on a pole, and the sight of it acted as a magic cure.

From Ezion Geber they swung northward again, bypassed Edom and Moab round their eastern flank, and reached the deep canyon of the Arnon river that flows into the Dead Sea half-way along its shore. The Moabite territory north of the Arnon had recently been occupied by Amorite tribesmen under King Sihon, with his capital at Heshbon. He not only refused to allow the Israelites to cross over to the Jordan fords but marched out to push them back into the desert. In the battle that followed, Sihon's forces were routed. The Israelites took Heshbon and occupied the Amorite region between the rivers Arnon and Jabbok. They then continued their advance northwards through Gilead, and defeated King Og of Bashan. The whole belt of territory along the east bank of the Jordan, from the Dead Sea to the Sea of Galilee, was now in Israelite hands.

After the defeats inflicted on Sihon and Og, the *Balaam the* Israelites encamped in the plains of Moab near *Soothsayer* the river fords opposite Jericho. King Balak of Moab was filled with alarm at the Israelite advent on his border. But he shrank from a direct military confrontation with these tough desert warriors, and sought first to weaken them by occult means. Balak sent messengers laden with gifts to engage the services of Balaam, a noted Aramean soothsayer and diviner who lived at Bethor on the northern Euphrates. He was offered a lavish reward if he would come and lay a curse on the Israelites. In a dream, the Lord told Balaam he could go on condition that he pronounced only the words the Lord put in his mouth.

Riding on his ass along a country road to meet his royal client, Balaam had a strange experience. The ass balked, and was beaten by his angry master. When this happened twice more, the animal said to him reproachfully, 'What have I

'Israel in Egypt', a painting by the nineteenth-century English artist Sir Edward Poynter, RA.
The realistic detail illustrates the vogue which Egyptian archaeology enjoyed in Victorian England.

done to you, that you have struck me these three times? ... Am I not your ass, upon which you have ridden all your life long to this day? Was I ever accustomed to do so to you?' (Num. 22:28,30). The astonished Balaam looked up and for the first time saw what had bothered his ass. An angel of the Lord with drawn sword in his hand blocked their path. Balaam threw himself prostrate in the dust, and once more swore that he would say nothing to the Moabites except what the Lord told him to say.

King Balak and his retinue came out to meet the diviner, and escorted him to the heights of Baal from where they could look down on the distant Israelite encampment. At Balaam's request seven altars were erected, and on each altar a bull and a ram were sacrificed. To the king's consternation, Balaam refused to pronounce curses. Instead he praised the special status of the Israelites as 'a people dwelling alone, and not reckoning itself among the nations!' (Num. 23:9). The ceremonial acts were repeated at two more high places, with similar results. The angry Moabite king did not dare touch the diviner, who returned to his own country without the promised reward. The poetic oracles attributed to Balaam are preserved in the Bible. In them, he blesses the Israelites in the name of the Lord, exclaiming:

> how fair are your tents, O Jacob,
>     your encampments, O Israel!
> Like valleys that stretch afar,
>     like gardens beside a river,
> like aloes that the Lord has planted,
>     like cedar trees beside the waters.
>                         (Num. 24:5,6)

Balaam prophesies that the Israelite nation will subdue Moab, and he foresees the emergence of the Davidic monarchy:

> a star shall come forth out of Jacob,
>     and a sceptre shall rise out of Israel;
> it shall crush the forehead of Moab,
>                         (Num. 24:17)

In a later chapter of the Book of Numbers, Balaam appears again – this time in a different and more sinister light. It seems that life in the desert had not prepared the Israelites for the temptations that arose from close contact with alien peoples. In the plains of Moab, Israelite men started cohabiting with local Moabite and Midianite women. Through these women they were seduced into practising the erotic fertility rites that were an integral part of Canaanite cults. For reasons left unexplained, the influence of Balaam was blamed for this insidious corruption of the Mosaic faith. A plague that broke out in the Israelite camp was attributed to the wrath of the Lord.

The problem was highlighted by a dramatic incident. While there was weeping in the camp for the plague victims, an Israelite man brazenly brought a Midianite woman to his tent. Phinehas, a grandson of Aaron, seized a spear and plunged it through the bodies of the couple during intercourse.

Moses took drastic steps to preserve the physical and moral health of the community. He ordered a military attack on a Midianite tribe in the area from which had come most of the pagan women involved with the Israelites. A thousand men were enrolled from each Israelite tribe for this punitive expedition. The Midianite camp was practically wiped out, and Balaam himself was killed in the battle. The captured livestock was divided into two parts, one for the fighting men and the other for the rest of the community, with a special share set aside for the priests.

It is difficult to explain the sharp contrast in behaviour between Balaam who refuses to curse the Israelites from the mountain top above, and Balaam who undermines their morals in the plain below. The generally accepted view today is that two separate traditions of quite different origins have come together in the text.

Under the direction of Joshua and the high priest Eleazar, another census was taken of all the men of military age, tribe by tribe. Of those *Preparing for the Settlement* numbered in the first census, taken in the desert thirty-eight years earlier, only three men were left alive: Moses, Joshua and Caleb. The new census was also to serve as a basis for allocation of tribal settlement areas in the Promised Land. Moses was told by the Lord what would be the overall borders of the Land of Israel.

The tribe of Levi, that performed purely religious functions, would not have a separate territory. Each of the other tribes would give the Levites land for their towns, with a strip of pasturage around each town for their animals. Six of these Levitical towns would be designated as 'cities of refuge', where a man who had killed another could find asylum from the kinsmen of

D az ez niemant sider vant
V nd ez nie menschen wart erchant
D urch daz wann in den zieten
V ie Israheliten
S o liehte warn gmvt
D az gein im solde sin behvt

D az si den gots erwelten man
f vr got iht solden letten an
W ann si ze sruden weren balt
S wentzich vnd hvndert iar alt
W as moyses do er verdarp
S o daz er an dem liebe starp

God the Father burying Moses, whose grave is unknown to man. A miniature
from a fourteenth-century Chronicle of World History in German.

El figura de aquellos reyes com̃o los mato Josue apuntura de espada:

ij vn rey de ebron:
iij vn rey de iarmuth:
iiij vn rey de lachis:
v vn rey de eglon:
vj vn rey de gezer:
vij vn rey de debir:
viij vn rey de geder:
ix vn rey de horma:
x vn rey de arad:
xj vn rey de libna:
xij vn rey de adullam:
xiij vn rey de maqueda:
xiiij vn rey de betel:
xv vn rey de tappua:
xvj vn rey de hefer:
xvij vn rey de afech:
xviij vn rey de lasaron:
xix vn rey de madon:
xx vn rey de açor:
xxj vn rey de simron meroon:
xxij vn rey de achsaf:
xxiij vn rey de thanach:
xxiiij vn rey de magedo:
xxv vn rey de cedes:
xxvj vn rey de yochnaan del carmel:
xxvij vn rey de dor con napha dor:
xxviij vn rey de goym saçal gilgal:
xxix vn rey de tirça:

Asi el numero de estos reyes son treynta
j vn reyes:

xiij platiria que gano

S erca de Josue biejo entrado en
dias dixole el señor tu eres
vn biejo entrado en dias i
abn queda por ganar mucho
dela tra: Esta tra q̃ aqui por
panar queda ca es esta q̃ se sigue todas las
prouincias delos filisteos i todo el yesuri:
G desde el rio que va faza egypto fasta el ter
mino de echron faza aquilon todo esto

LEFT The Canaanite Kings who were defeated by Joshua. A page from the Duke of Alba's Bible produced in fifteenth-century Spain.

ABOVE Slaying of the first-born; the tenth plague in Egypt. From a nineteenth-century Ethiopian manuscript.

the deceased until he could have a proper public trial. (There was no room for lynch law in the Mosaic code.)

The tribes of Reuben and Gad wanted to remain permanently in the areas that had already been occupied by the Israelites east of the Jordan river. They were cattlemen and found suitable grazing on these Trans-jordan uplands. Moreover, they could take over the towns abandoned by the defeated Amorite subjects of King Sihon. The Machir clan of the tribe of Manasseh also elected to stay in Trans-jordan. The settlement area they requested was the Land of Gilead that had been wrested from King Og of Bashan. At first Moses frowned on the proposal. These tribes, he held, would be shirking their duty if they opted out of the coming push into Canaan. Eventually it was agreed that their fighting men would cross the river with the other tribes, and later return. Meanwhile, their families and livestock would be left in fortified towns where they could be protected.

Moses handed down an important judgment at this time concerning the inheritance of land. Zelophehad, a man of the Machir clan of Manasseh, died without leaving sons. His five unmarried daughters appeared before Moses and the assembly of elders at the tent of meeting, and claimed that they should be recongized as their father's heirs. The claim was accepted, with the proviso that daughters inheriting land would have to marry only men of their own tribe, so as to keep intact the territory of that tribe.

*The Death of Moses* Moses was now nearing the end of his task. The Book of Deuteronomy, compiled six centuries later, contains three lengthy farewell discourses attributed to the great leader. In them he surveyed the events of the forty years since the Exodus, and painted an encouraging picture of the country they were about to enter:

> For the Lord your God is bringing you into a good land, a land of brooks of water, of fountains and springs, flowing forth in valleys and hills, a land of wheat and barley, of vines and fig trees and pomegranates, a land of olive trees and honey, a land in which you will eat bread without scarcity, in which you will lack nothing, a land whose stones are iron, and out of whose hills you can dig copper.
>
> (Deut. 8:7–9).

The religious and legal code is expanded and interpreted in these Deuteronomic discourses. The central theme is the renewal of the Sinai Covenant. Moses says to the people: 'Hear, O Israel: The Lord our God is one Lord; and you shall love the Lord your God with all your heart, and with all your soul, and with all your might' (Deut. 6:4–5). (These are the opening sentences of the familiar prayer *Shemah Yisrael* – Hear, O Israel – that pious Jews repeat twice daily.) In concluding his addresses, Moses blesses each of the tribes in turn.

Joshua the son of Nun was appointed to succeed Moses as leader. In the Tabernacle, in the presence of the whole assembly, Moses solemnly placed his hands on Joshua and said: 'Be strong and of good courage; for you shall go with this people into the land which the Lord has sworn to their fathers to give them; and you shall put them in possession of it (Deut. 31:7).

Before he died at the age of one hundred and twenty, Moses was taken up 'to Mount Nebo, to the top of Pisgah,' (Deut. 34:1) and from there was given by the Lord a panoramic view of the Promised Land he was not to enter. In this vision, his gaze travelled across the Dead Sea glittering thousands of feet below, beyond the khaki-coloured rampart of the Judean desert on the other side, as far as the Mediterranean to the west, the Negev to the south, and the Galilee to the north. This was the land that had been his unswerving destination from the moment that God's voice had come to him out of the burning bush, as he humbly tended the sheep of his Midianite father-in-law. With that one sweeping glimpse, Moses died upon the solitary mountain-top. He was buried by the Lord somewhere in the Moabite landscape, 'but no man knows the place of his burial to this day' (Deut. 34:6). For thirty days the Children of Israel wept and mourned for the departed leader and lawgiver whose unruly and often reluctant followers they had been for so long.

Moses is the pivotal character in the Old Testament story, and looms majestically through the mists of later legend. Many centuries later, the compilers of the Old Testament would attribute its first five Books to him, and would declare that there has not arisen a prophet since in Israel like Moses, whom the Lord knew face to face.

# 4
# THE CONQUEST AND
# THE SETTLEMENT

## *Joshua*

T HE LORD SAID TO JOSHUA, 'MOSES my servant is dead; now therefore arise, go over this Jordan, you and all this people,´ into the land which I am giving to them, to the people of Israel' (Josh. 1:2).

The political conditions were propitious. Canaan was not a unified country under a central regime. Over its hills and plains were scattered a number of little city-states, each under its own independent king. They were apt to carry on feuds with each other, and at best would form temporary local coalitions against a common enemy. For centuries, Canaan had been within the imperial orbit of their powerful southern *The Invasion* neighbour, Egypt, which had exercised control *Problem* through high commissioners, and through mobile garrisons stationed in key strategic towns. But before the Israelite advent the sway of Egypt had declined, and it could no longer give effective protection to its Canaanite vassals.

Yet in plain military terms, Joshua's mission seemed almost impossible. As he and his fellow-spies had reported to Moses a generation earlier, the cities were large, and fortified with massive walls. Joshua was a brilliant and resourceful commander. He could rely on the fitness, bravery and religious zeal of his desert fighting men. But he lacked the equipment and skills to overcome a fortified stronghold – such as battering rams, scaling ladders, catapults and tunnelling techniques. Except for the miraculous and puzzling fall of Jericho, those cities that fell into Israelite hands did so because their defenders had been defeated in open battle outside the walls, or had surrendered without resistance. A number of important Canaanite cities were not taken at all at that time, including Jerusalem, Gezer, Megiddo, Beth-shan and Gaza. On the whole, the Israelites would keep to the sparsely populated hill-terrain and not gain control of the more densely inhabited coastal plain and broad inland valleys, where they would have been at the mercy of chariot forces.

The first obstacle was Jericho, five miles west of *The Fall of* the Jordan fords. Joshua sent ahead two spies. *Jericho* They slipped unnoticed into the town and found lodgings for the night with Rahab, a prostitute who occupied one of the dwellings built into the city walls. Word reached the authorities that she

Arach leide sijn heer optie Scolaſt hiſt
ſtat azor en yabin quam wt wut euen
groeten heer hem te gemoet en barach cloechē
doot alco yoſephus ſeyt Text Capittel · v·

The Canaanite general Sisera is slain by Jael
after his defeat by Barak and Deborah. From
a fifteenth-century Dutch illuminated manuscript.

was harbouring two suspicious strangers and a squad of men were sent to find them. Rahab hid them under bundles of flax drying on the roof and pretended they had departed before the city gate was closed at sunset. During the night she lowered the two Israelites down the wall with a rope. They were able to escape into the hills and hide for three days until the search parties had given up. They then returned to base and reported to Joshua that the city was full of fear at the prospect of being attacked by the invaders who had already overrun the Trans-jordan kingdoms of King Sihon and King Og.

The Israelites were led across the river, its flow temporarily halted in an echo of the miraculous Reed Sea crossing. A new encampment was established in the plain beyond, at a place called Gilgal, between the river Jordan and Jericho. Here, as a memorial of their entry into the Promised Land, Joshua set up a circle of twelve boulders carried from the river-bed. At Gilgal the Israelite males were circumcized, a custom that had been neglected during the desert wandering. The Passover feast was celebrated, recalling the deliverance from bondage in Egypt. They were now living from locally grown produce, the manna and quail of the desert having been left behind.

The capture of Jericho was preceded by a remarkable display of psychological warfare. Once a day for six days the Israelites marched round the walls in a procession, led by priests carrying the Ark of the Covenant and blowing rams' horns. On the seventh day this perform-ance was repeated seven times. The priests then gave a final loud blast, amplified by a shout from all the Israelite soldiers. The city walls came tumbling down, and Joshua's men rushed in. All the inhabitants were put to the sword, except Rahab and her family who had been promised protection by the two spies she had sheltered. The city was then burnt down.

*The Capture of Ai* Joshua now faced the Judean escarpment, four thousand feet above the level of the Jordan valley. The direct route up the mountain was blocked by the strong Jebusite city of Jerusalem. A track a little further to the right led up a defile to the town of Ai. A reconnaissance patrol reported back that the place was poorly defended, and could be taken by a relatively small force. This intelligence assessment was inaccurate. The contingent sent by Joshua was repulsed by the

defenders of Ai and chased down the mountain-side, losing thirty-six men.

Joshua was dismayed at this ignominious setback, and feared the heartening impact it would have on Canaanite morale: 'O Lord, what can I say, when Israel has turned their backs before their enemies!' (Josh. 7:8). He was told that this defeat was a punishment because one of the Israelites had broken the ban against carrying off loot from Jericho; the Lord's help would be withheld until the misdeed had been expiated. The drawing of lots indicated that the culprit was Achan of Judah, who had hidden his spoils in the floor of his tent. He and his family were stoned to death.

Joshua now mobilized all his forces against Ai. They were deployed so as to take the town by stratagem. Part of the Israelite forces concealed themselves near the town, under cover of darkness. Next morning other units pretended to flee when attacked, and lured the defenders out of the walls in pursuit. The hidden Israelites promptly occupied the undefended town. They then closed in on the men of Ai from the rear, catching them in a pincer movement and wiping them out. Ai was reduced to rubble and its king hanged from a tree.

Seven miles west of Ai, and six miles from *The Battle* Jerusalem, lay the hill-town of Gibeon, now *for Gibeon* directly in the path of the advancing Israelites. The Gibeonite leaders shrank from a military encounter with the recent victors of Jericho and Ai, and preferred coming to terms with them. Fearing that Joshua would fight rather than parley, they used devious means to secure a pact. A delegation of Gibeonites arrived at the camp at Gilgal. They claimed they had travelled from a distant land to offer peace, since they had heard the Lord would make the Israelites masters of the country. To lend this story colour, their clothes, sandals and wineskins and the sacks on their asses' backs were worn and patched, and their food was dry and mouldy. Their story was believed, and oaths of mutual friendship were exchanged. The Israelite elders were angry when they found they had been duped, but felt their commitment remained binding. However, Joshua declared that in future the Gibeonites would carry out the menial tasks for the Israelite sanctuary, as 'hewers of wood and drawers of water for all the congregation' (Josh. 9:21).

The defection of Gibeon left the towns in

southern Canaan more exposed to the Israelite threat, and produced a hurried defence alliance among some of the local rulers. The king of Jerusalem took the initiative. He joined forces with the kings of Hebron and three towns in the foothills and coastal plain: Lachish, Eglon and Jarmuth. When they laid siege to Gibeon, the men of that city, relying on their friendship treaty, sent urgent messages calling for help from its Israelite allies. After a forced night march from Gilgal, Joshua attacked and routed the forces of the five kings and pursued them down the pass at Bethhoron into the broad valley of Aijalon. On the way the hapless Canaanites were battered by a fierce hail storm that killed many of them. To gain time for mopping-up operations before nightfall, Joshua prayed: 'Sun, stand thou still at Gibeon, and thou Moon in the valley of Aijalon' (Josh. 10:12). (Today the Latrun road to Jerusalem runs through this valley.) Having been granted suspension of the natural order, the Israelites were able to press home their victory. The defeated kings were discovered hiding in a cave. They were put to death and their bodies strung up on trees.

*The Southern Campaign* Joshua's forces were now able to sweep southward through the foothill region taking one town after another with little resistance. The most important of them was Lachish, to the west of Hebron. The king of Gezer, the powerful Canaanite city on the coastal plain, marched to the help of Lachish, but was beaten back. With all the approaches from the lowlands to the southern hill-country now in their hands, the Israelites swung east up to Hebron and captured it. The taking of Debir, in the foothills south-west of Hebron, completed the southern phase of the campaign. 'So Joshua defeated the whole land, the hill country and the Negeb and the lowland and the slopes, and all their kings' (Josh. 10:40).

*The Assembly at Shechem* Joshua, the victorious general, now took up the moral legacy of Moses. He gathered all the tribes in a convocation at Shechem, that lay in a valley between Mount Ebal and Mount Gerizim, twenty miles north of Jerusalem. Joshua erected an altar on Mount Ebal and offered sacrifices, while the people were drawn up on the slopes with the Ark of the Covenant in the middle. Joshua read out to them all the laws that had been handed down by Moses.

There is no suggestion that the Israelites fought with the local inhabitants of Shechem and the surrounding countryside. This gives credence to the assumption by some Bible scholars either that not all the Hebrew tribes had migrated to Egypt, or that some of them had returned at an earlier period. If so, the incoming Israelites would have linked up with groups of kinsmen in the Shechem area. Such 'sojourners who lived among them' (Josh. 8:35) would not have shared in the historic experience of the Exodus, the Sinai Covenant and the desert wandering; for them, Joshua's exposition of the Mosaic Law would have come as fresh gospel.

*The Northern Campaign* The scene of action now shifted to the northern part of the country. The most important city in that region was Hazor, in the Huleh valley through which the Jordan river flows before it enters the Sea of Galilee. Hazor commanded a section of the Via Maris, the 'Way of the Sea', from Egypt to Damascus, before it crossed the Jordan river at the Bridge of the Daughters of Jacob. Its king, Jabin, rallied the neighbouring cities in a united front against the advancing Israelites. Their joint forces, strengthened with chariot troops, were defeated by Joshua in a decisive battle 'by the waters of Merom' in the Galilee hills overlooking the lake. Joshua immediately marched on Hazor and burnt down the city.

*The Archeological Evidence for Joshua's Campaigns* The excavations at Hazor have provided striking confirmation of the biblical record. They show that an extensive and well-developed Canaanite city was destroyed by fire about 1230 BC. This discovery clarified the date of the Conquest, which one group of scholars had tended to place about one century earlier. Lachish and Debir, that figure in the account of the southern campaign, have also been shown by archaeological evidence to have been destroyed about that time.

Regarding Jericho and Ai, however, there are serious problems in reconciling the account in the Book of Joshua with the results of excavations on the sites.

The first city walls of Jericho were constructed nine thousand years ago, making it the oldest fortified town found anywhere in the world. The remains of its last fortifications are dated several centuries before Joshua; and other structures in the city appear to have been demolished in the fourteenth century BC – that is, a century before Joshua. The evidence on the site does not support the story that the walls were demolished at the

The walls of Jericho tumble down at the blast of the Israelite trumpets.
An illustration from an eighteenth-century German Bible.

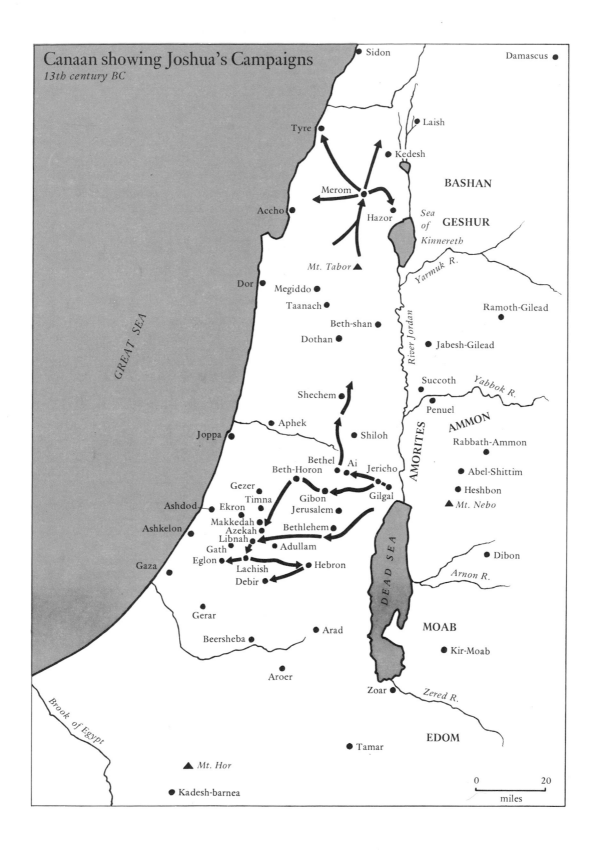

# Canaan showing Joshua's Campaigns
### 13th century BC

Sidon

Damascus

Tyre

Laish

Kedesh

BASHAN

Merom

Accho

Hazor

GESHUR

Sea of Kinnereth

Mt. Tabor ▲

Dor

Yarmuk R.

Megiddo

Taanach

Ramoth-Gilead

Beth-shan

Dothan

River Jordan

Jabesh-Gilead

Succoth

Yabbok R.

Shechem

Penuel

AMMON

Aphek

Joppa

Shiloh

Rabbath-Ammon

Bethel   Ai

Jericho

Beth-Horon

Gilgal

Abel-Shittim

Gezer

Gibon

AMORITES

Heshbon

Timna

Jerusalem

▲ Mt. Nebo

Ashdod   Ekron

Makkedah

Bethlehem

Azekah

Libnah

Adullam

Gath

Ashkelon

Eglon

Lachish

Hebron

Dibon

Gaza

Debir

DEAD SEA

Arnon R.

Gerar

Arad

MOAB

Beersheba

Kir-Moab

Aroer

Zoar

Zered R.

Tamar

EDOM

▲ Mt. Hor

GREAT SEA

Brook of Egypt

Kadesh-barnea

0      20
miles

time of the Israelite conquest in the late thirteenth century BC. Various theories have been suggested to explain the discrepancy in dates. On the problem of the fortifications, the noted Israel archaeologist, Professor Yigael Yadin, has suggested that the massive stone foundations of an earlier wall, found in the Jericho excavations, carried an upper wall of mud bricks that existed in Joshua's time and has since disappeared.

It is hard anyway to find a natural explanation for the biblical story that the city wall 'fell down flat' when the Israelites blew their trumpets and shouted. Here all is pure conjecture. Either the walls were overthrown by a providential earth tremor; or it was really the morale of the defenders that collapsed; or the account must be regarded as a legend attributing the fall of the city to divine magic.

At Ai, the excavations indicate that the town was destroyed a thousand years before Joshua, and the site only re-occupied well after his time. On the other hand Bethel, less than two miles from Ai, was partly demolished about the time of the Israelite conquest. It is surmised that the two places became confused with each other in oral traditions that were collected in written form centuries later.

*The Tribal Settlement Areas* After the successful military campaigns in the south and the north, the time had come to allocate separate settlement areas to the tribes and to lay down the borders between them.

The men of Reuben, Gad and the Machir clan of Manasseh were now allowed to return to the territories east of the Jordan originally allotted to them, and rejoin their families there. The two Joseph tribes – Ephraim and the rest of Manasseh – remained in the central hill-country around Shechem. The tribe of Judah obtained the Hebron hills south of Jerusalem, with Hebron itself given to Caleb and his clan as a reward for his faith in the Lord when he was one of the twelve men sent to spy out the land. That left seven tribes for whom territory had to be found. Joshua sent out a survey team made up of three men from each tribe, and instructed them to 'describe the land in seven divisions and bring the description here to me' (Josh. 18:6). On the basis of their report, lots were drawn by the seven tribes for these remaining areas. The ceremony took place at a gathering at Shiloh, about halfway between Jerusalem and Shechem. The Ark of the Covenant and the tent of meeting had been placed at Shiloh, that became the central sanctuary of the Israelite tribes in the period of the Judges. By the drawing of lots, Benjamin's portion was a narrow strip running across the hills just north of Jerusalem. Dan was assigned an area in the foothills to the west of Benjamin. Simeon stayed in the Negev round Beer-sheba. Four tribes were assigned to the northern part of the country: Asher in western Galilee; Naphtali in central and western Galilee; Zebulun in the Carmel range; and Issachar in the eastern Jezreel and Beth-shan valleys, sloping down to the Jordan river.

The tribe of Levi was not allotted an area of its own, but received a number of towns in the other tribal areas. They carried out religious duties for all the tribes, and 'the Lord God of Israel is their inheritance' (Josh. 13:33). Six Levite towns were designed as 'cities of refuge', three on each side of the Jordan.

At the age of one hundred and ten, Joshua felt *The Death of* his end was near. He summoned the people to *Joshua* another assembly at Shechem. In a moving farewell address, he reaffirmed the Sinai Covenant, exhorted them to walk in God's ways and begged them to resist the inroads of paganism. Joshua died and 'they buried him in his own inheritance at Timnath-serah, which is in the hill country of Ephraim' (Josh. 24:30).

## The Period of the Judges

THE BOOK OF JOSHUA LEAVES THE IMPRESSION that the Promised Land was conquered in a swift and decisive campaign under a single leader, and that the Israelite tribes then settled down peacefully in it: 'So Joshua took the whole land, according to all that the Lord had spoken to Moses; and Joshua gave it for an inheritance to Israel according to their tribal allotments. And the land had rest from war.' (Josh. 11:23).

The account in the Book of Judges is more *Settlement* blurred. The Book covers two centuries, from the *Struggles* entry of the Israelites into the country, about 1220 BC, to the beginning of the monarchy, about 1020 BC. Here it is indicated that even after the conquest, the process of settlement was slow and difficult, with individual tribal areas harassed from time to time by hostile neighbours. Some portions of the territory allocated to the tribes in Joshua's time did not come under Israelite control at that time, especially in the plains.

At least, they did not have to contend with external Big Powers. Egypt, in the south, had lost control of the country. The expansion of the Hittite empire was halted further to the north. Canaan lay in a colonial no man's land during that period, and the Israelite struggle for possession was played out on a local stage.

West of the Jordan river, the Israelites managed to settle mainly in the sparsely populated hill areas, where the limited resources of land and water made subsistence difficult. They were not strong enough to subdue the Canaanite cities in the fertile coastal plain or the broad valley of Jezreel-Bethshan. It ran from west to east, cutting off the Israelite tribes in the Galilee highlands from their brethren further south.

The elders of Manasseh and Ephraim complained to Joshua that, 'The hill country is not enough for us; yet all the Canaanites who dwell in the plain have chariots of iron' (Josh. 17:16). Joshua bluntly told them to make more room for themselves by clearing the wooded hillsides. Similarly, in the Hebron hills, Judah 'took possession of the hill country, but he could not drive out the inhabitants of the plain, because they had chariots of iron' (Judg. 1:19). The tribe of Asher failed to occupy the coastal strip allotted to it, from Acre to Tyre. In the Shephelah (Judean foothills), the position of Dan became precarious under Philistine pressure, and the tribe later migrated to the extreme north-east corner of the country. The Jebusite city of Jerusalem remained an unconquered enclave in the Judean hills until the time of King David.

Archaeological remains bear out that in the territory settled by the Israelites the population gradually increased, and more land was cleared and cultivated. New towns and villages sprang up, sometimes on the sites of destroyed Canaanite cities. Israelite towns were as yet unfortified, and the standard of building was still relatively primitive, showing the transition from a semi-nomad to a settled society. Development of the hill areas was made easier by two technological advances. Rainwater was collected in rock-hewn cisterns lined with plaster, reducing the traditional dependence on natural wells and springs. Iron work-tools came into use, obtained from more advanced neighbours.

In the Old Testament, all events are related to one overriding theme: the relation of the people of Israel to the Lord, and their observance of his commandments. Wars with neighbouring peoples or incursions by bands of desert raiders were regarded as retribution for the constant backsliding into pagan ways:

> And the people of Israel did what was evil in the sight of the Lord and served the Baals; ... they went after other gods, from among the gods of the peoples who were round about them, and bowed down to them; ... So the anger of the Lord was kindled against Israel, and he gave them over to plunderers, who plundered them; and he sold them into the power of their enemies round about, ... and they were in sore straits' (Judge. 2:11–15).

The most skilled and sophisticated of the Canaanite peoples were the Phoenicians, who inhabited the coastal plain today included in Lebanon. From their port-cities of Tyre and Sidon, the Phoenician merchant galleys plied along the whole length of the Mediterranean, setting up colonies and trading depots as far afield as Spain.

In the southern coastal plain, between Gaza and Joppa (Jaffa), a new people appeared in the twelfth century BC, during the period of the Judges. They were the Philistines, one of the 'sea peoples' who came from the Aegean area and harassed the eastern Mediterranean. These invaders were repulsed with difficulty by the Egyptians, but penetrated the Hittite empire from the coast and hastened its demise. In southern Canaan the Philistines established five city-states: Gaza, Ashdod, Ashkelon, Ekron and Gath. Each was ruled by its own king, but they were linked in a military league. They constituted the most serious of the threats to the Israelite settlers in the period of the Judges.

An important advantage held by the Philistines was their knowledge of smelting and working iron, a much harder and more effective metal in peace or war than copper or bronze (an amalgam of copper and tin). For a long time they maintained a local monopoly of the craft:

> Now there was no smith to be found throughout all the land of Israel; for the Philistines said, 'Lest the Hebrews make themselves swords or spears'; but every one of the Israelites went down to the Philistines to sharpen his plowshare, his mattock, his axe, or his sickle' (1 Sam. 13:19–20).

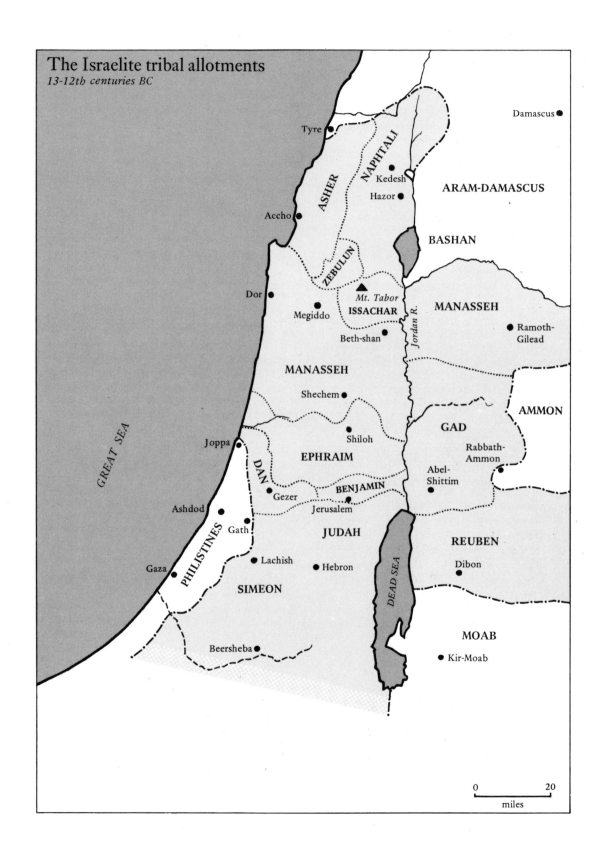

The Israelite tribal allotments
*13-12th centuries BC*

Damascus

Tyre

ASHER

NAPHTALI

Kedesh

Hazor

ARAM-DAMASCUS

Accho

BASHAN

ZEBULUN

Dor

Mt. Tabor

ISSACHAR

MANASSEH

Megiddo

Beth-shan

Jordan R.

Ramoth-Gilead

MANASSEH

Shechem

GAD

AMMON

Shiloh

Rabbath-Ammon

Joppa

DAN

EPHRAIM

Abel-Shittim

Gezer

BENJAMIN

Jerusalem

Ashdod

Gath

JUDAH

REUBEN

GREAT SEA

Gaza

PHILISTINES

Lachish

Hebron

Dibon

DEAD SEA

SIMEON

MOAB

Beersheba

Kir-Moab

0    20
miles

The dispersal of the tribes, each in its own defined territory, gave greater tribal autonomy. The enforced cohesion of the desert odyssey slackened in the Land of Israel. Moses and Joshua were the last leaders to exercise supreme authority until the beginning of the kingship two hundred years later. The tribes were held together by ethnic ties, by shared traditions about their origin and early history, by their unique faith, and by the pressures of external enemies that sometimes compelled a number of tribes to come together briefly for mutual defence. But they had no central institutions – no common ruler, capital city, administration or army.

However, it was an overstatement to say that, 'In those days there was no king in Israel; every man did what was right in his own eyes' (Judg. 21:25). In fact, the patriarchal order of the nomadic desert life remained intact, though weakened by the change to farming and town life. The basic social unit was the *bet-av* (father's house) in which the head of the extended family had undisputed authority over his wives and concubines, his children and grandchildren, and the family property and retainers. A group of such households, descended from a common ancestor some generations back, formed a clan or sub-tribe. The heads of the clans, or the more important figures among them, were the hereditary 'elders' that formed a kind of tribal council, responsible for keeping order and settling disputes.

This loose system of authority gave each tribe sufficient internal cohesion for normal purposes. It was not one that provided effective military leadership in an emergency, and even less so when more than one tribe was involved. In times of trouble the elders would turn to some individual to rally and lead the fighting men of the tribe. The tribesmen would have to leave their daily work at the call to arms, since there were no professional soldiers.

It was accepted that the 'spirit of the Lord' inspired and guided such an ad hoc leader: 'Then the Lord raised up judges, who saved them out of the power of those who plundered them' (Judg. 2:16).

The word 'judges' is misleading. The word in the original Hebrew, *shoftim*, is used in a sense that has little to do with the judicial function. Seven of the Judges were persons who were made leaders in a crisis and were involved in military operations. They were 'charismatic' in the sense of a mortal on whom the gods had bestowed a special grace. In each case, after the emergency was over, the person concerned is stated to have 'judged Israel' for a number of years. That probably meant that such a deliverer afterwards enjoyed a unique prestige and moral authority in the affairs of the tribe, and would be called upon to help settle disputes. The Judges who fit into this general description are the following seven: Othniel of Judah; Ehud of Benjamin; Shamgar (tribe unknown); Deborah of Issachar; Gideon of Manasseh; Jephthah of Gilead, inhabited by Gad and Reuben; and Samson of Dan. The prophet Samuel, of the tribe of Ephraim, may be regarded as the last and greatest of the Judges and the transitional figure between the period of the Judges and the period of the monarchy.

The Book of Judges also refers to five 'minor Judges' who belong to a different category. In these cases, there is no mention of deliverance from an external enemy or of any military role at all. There is only a brief paragraph devoted to each, with a few details hinting at his wealth and importance. These were no doubt leading men in their respective tribes, but it is hard to understand their inclusion among the Judges, unless later biblical compilers wanted to bring the number up to twelve, corresponding to the number of tribes. These were the minor Judges:

Tola lived at Shamir in the hill country of Ephraim and judged Israel twenty-three years.

Jair of Gilead judged Israel twenty-two years. 'And he had thirty sons who rode on thirty asses' (Judg. 10:4).

Ibzan of Bethlehem in Judah judged Israel for seven years. 'He had thirty sons; and thirty daughters he gave in marriage outside his clan, and thirty daughters he brought in from outside for his sons' (Judg. 12:9).

Elon of Zebulun judged Israel ten years.

Abdon of Pirathon in Ephraim judged Israel eight years. 'He had forty sons and thirty grandsons, who rode on seventy asses' (Judg. 12:14).

Othniel was the son of Kenaz, the younger *Othniel* brother of Caleb. He is given credit for the capture of Debir (also known as Kiriath-sepher), one of the Canaanite cities in the Shephelah that were destroyed by the Israelites at the end of the thirteenth century BC. In the Book of Judges, the conquest of the Hebron hill region and the adjacent foothills is attributed only to the tribe of Judah, and not to the main Israelite body under Joshua. Caleb, who took and retained Hebron, offered his daughter Achsah in marriage to whomever would overcome Debir. She therefore became Othnicl's wife, and persuaded her father to give her as a dowry certain vital springs of water in the area. Othniel later delivered his people after eight years of subjection by 'Cushan-rishathaim king of Mesopotamia' (Judg. 3:8). This brief claim remains completely obscure. There is no other record of a ruler bearing that name; nor did any Mesopotamian power penetrate into the country at that time.

*Ehud* For some centuries after the Conquest there were uneasy relations, and at times open warfare, between the Israelites and the three Trans-jordan kingdoms of Ammon, Moab and Edom. The background to the Ehud story is the dominant position achieved by Moab under its king Eglon in the twelfth century BC. It reoccupied the tableland east of the Dead Sea and north of the Jabbok river, pushed down into the Jordan valley and took Jericho. The Israelite tribes in the area tried to resist this advance, but were defeated by Eglon with the help of Ammonite auxiliaries and bands of Amalekites (desert nomads). For the next eighteen years Moab exacted tribute from the tribe of Benjamin, whose territory stretched across the Judean hills and down towards the Jordan river. The Moabite hold was broken by Ehud the son of Gera, a member of a leading Benjaminite family.

Ehud headed the delegation carrying the annual tribute to the obese Moabite king, who was at his winter palace at Jericho. After performing its obsequious duty, the delegation withdrew to nearby Gilgal, a little north-east of Jericho. From here Ehud returned on his own and once more appeared before the king, who was taking his ease in the cool roof-chamber. On being told that Ehud had a secret message to deliver to him, the king dismissed his attendants and was left alone with his Israelite visitor. Ehud declared that his message was from God, at which the king rose to his feet. With his left hand Ehud snatched a short two-edged sword that had been strapped to his right thigh under his garments, and plunged it into the flabby royal belly 'and the hilt also went in after the blade, and the fat closed over the blade, for he did not draw the sword out of his belly; and the dirt came out' (Judg. 3:22).

Ehud locked the doors of the chamber and escaped through the vestibule. The servants did not try to enter for some while, thinking that their master 'is only relieving himself in the closet' (Judg. 3:24). When they became worried enough to unlock the doors, they found the king's body lying on the floor in a pool of blood.

The delay made it easier for Ehud to get away into the hills. He blew the trumpet of revolt and returned into the Jordan valley with a force raised from the men of Ephraim and Benjamin. They cut the line of retreat of the Moabites by seizing the Jordan river fords and then attacked and wiped out all of them who were trapped on the western side. 'So Moab was subdued that day. . . . And the land had rest for eighty years' (Judg. 3:30).

Of the exploits of Shamgar, all that is *Shamgar* preserved in the Old Testament is a one-sentence fragment. It reads: 'After him (Ehud) was Shamgar the son of Anath, who killed six hundred of the Philistines with an oxgoad; and he too delivered Israel' (Judg. 3:31). There is no way of determining when or where this event took place, nor what was Shamgar's tribal identity. One surmise is that he was a non-Israelite hero whose blow at the common Philistine enemy is gratefully remembered. His action probably took place in the northern area. He is mentioned in the victory song of Deborah, and his father's name may derive from the Galilee village of Bet-Anath.

Deborah the wife of Lappidoth, prophetess and Judge, gained a prestige and authority unmatched by that of any other woman in the Old Testament. In the late twelfth century BC she led a successful uprising that broke the twenty-year hold the Canaanites had on the northern part of the country.

Two parallel accounts are given of the decisive battle, one a prose narrative (Chapter 4 of the Book of Judges) and the other an ancient victory poem, The Song of Deborah (Chapter 5). These two versions are at variance with each other in certain respects.

Deborah regularly took her seat under a tree *Deborah* between Bethel and Ramah in the hill country of Ephraim, where 'the people of Israel came up to her for judgment' (Judg. 4:5). She came from the tribe of Issachar in the eastern Jezreel valley and was acutely aware that the valley was controlled by the Canaanite strongholds of Megiddo, Taanach and Beth-shan. Her tribe was thus dominated by the Canaanites, as was the tribe of Asher, near the western Galilee coast. The two tribes further north in the Galilee highlands, Zebulun and Naphtali, retained more independence, but were isolated from the Israelite areas of settlement to the south.

Deborah sent for Barak, a well-known fighting commander from the town of Kedesh in the territory of Naphtali. She instructed him to muster ten thousand men from Naphtali and Zebulun and to concentrate them on Mount Tabor, a cone-shaped hill overlooking the whole valley. At Barak's insistence, Deborah agreed to accompany him in this daring venture.

The Canaanite force that massed against them was commanded by Sisera, a great general, and possessed a large number of chariots as its main striking force (the figure of nine hundred given in the text was probably inflated). It was clear that the poorly equipped Israelite militia, operating on foot, would be mowed down by the chariots if they were caught on flat ground. Fortunately it was the winter rainy season. A rainstorm turned the valley floor into a sea of mud in which the chariots were bogged down. The Israelite highlanders rushed down the hillside in a fierce charge and overwhelmed the floundering Canaanites. Sisera's remaining forces retreated towards their fortified bases at Megiddo and Taanach, along the southern rim of the valley, but were blocked by the small Kishon river, swollen by the rains. Here the pursuing Israelites turned the retreat into a rout, and inflicted heavy casualties.

The enemy general Sisera escaped on foot. Exhausted and thirsty, he reached the nomad encampment of a Kenite clan that had moved up from the Negev in the south. Yael, wife of the clan leader Heber, invited him into her tent, gave him milk to drink and covered him with a robe when he lay down. As soon as he fell asleep, she grabbed a sharp tent peg and with one blow of a mallet drove it through his head. When Barak came in pursuit of Sisera, Yael produced his body.

The Song of Deborah exults:

> The kings came, they fought;
> > then fought the kings of Canaan,
> at Taanach, by the waters of
> > Megiddo;
> they got no spoils of silver.

> From heaven fought the stars,
> > from their courses they fought
> > against Sisera.
> The torrent Kishon swept them away,
> the onrushing torrent, the torrent Kishon.
> March on, my soul, with might!
> > (Judg. 5:19–21)

The song gives a pathetic picture of Sisera's mother peering through the lattice of her window for his return after the battle, and listening in vain for the hoof-beats of his chariot horses.

One problem raised by the prose account is its reference to 'Jabin king of Canaan, who reigned in Hazor' as the main Canaanite ruler at the time. This encounter took place several generations after Joshua had defeated Jabin and his allies at the battle of the Waters of Merom, and had then razed Hazor to the ground – a fact confirmed by modern excavations on the site. The editor of the prose narrative centuries later may well have added this reference in an attempt to correlate the Books of Joshua and Judges. The Song of Deborah, an older written document than the prose account, does not mention either Jabin or Hazor.

The main difference between the prose and poetry versions concerns the extent to which different Israelite tribes were involved in the fight. The prose account refers only to the tribes of Naphtali and Zebulun. The Song of Deborah suggests that she issued a general call to arms; Naphtali and Zebulun bore the brunt of the battle, but help came also from Issachar, and from three tribes in the central hill-region: Ephraim, Benjamin and the Machir clan of Manasseh. Deborah chides the tribes that did not respond at all: Asher, Dan, Reuben and Gad – the latter two in Trans-jordan. Those who did rally behind Deborah and Barak constituted the widest inter-tribal alignment forged at any time during the period of the Judges. It is interesting to note that nowhere is there any mention of the two most southerly tribes, Judah and Simeon. It shows that a gulf already existed between the northern and southern tribes. Some two centuries later, they would part company with each other into two separate and rival kingdoms.

After the victory of Deborah and Barak, the tribes in the Galilee and those in the central hill country were no longer separated by a Canaanite wedge. 'And the land had rest for forty years.'

Mount Tabor at the edge of the Jezreel Valley, where the forces of Deborah
and Barak were assembled for the battle against Sisera.

*Gideon*    The story of Gideon was one episode in the perennial struggle with the desert nomads who erupted from time to time into the settled countries around Arabia: Mesopotamia, Syria, Canaan and Egypt. Sometimes these were migrants who stayed; they were either absorbed into the local population or they preserved their own identity, like the Hebrews. At other times, the nomads were raiders who swept through the countryside pillaging farms and villages, carrying off cattle, sheep and grain, filling up their waterskins and vanishing back into the empty spaces that were their home.

Of the latter kind were 'the Midianites and the Amalekites and the people of the East' (Judg. 6:3). They had harried the country for seven years, like periodic locust swarms, before Gideon emerged as an Israelite Judge towards the end of the twelfth century BC. It was a period when the country was weak and divided, and its borders vulnerable to outside intruders. With the decline of Egyptian protection, the Amalekites in the south were able to penetrate as far as Gaza. In the north-east, Deborah's victory had destroyed Canaanite power and with it the chain of strongholds that protected the Jezreel and Beth-shan valleys. These fertile fields now lay exposed to the Midianite bands that crossed the Jordan fords from the east, and cut a swathe of destruction before retiring. The recent domestication of the camel, 'the ship of the desert', had given the nomads a capacity to cover great distances with little water.

Gideon the son of Joash belonged to the clan of Abiezer, in the tribe of Manasseh, that inhabited the central hill country up to the Jezreel valley. Like the other farmers in the area, Gideon's family would take refuge in hill-caves when the Midianites appeared. One of the precautions forced on them was threshing their grain harvest inside the wine-press instead of on an open hill-top, where the breeze would separate the wheat from the chaff. Gideon was busy with this task when he suddenly saw a man sitting under a nearby oak tree. It was an angel in disguise, who told Gideon that he had been chosen as a deliverer, and brushed aside his hesitations.

The perplexed Gideon went into the house and prepared for his strange visitor a meal of stewed kid, soup and unleavened bread. The angel asked him to put the food on a rock and touched it with the end of his staff. It was consumed by fire. This sign impressed Gideon but did not entirely convince him. He put the Lord to further tests before he was satisfied about his mandate. On two successive nights a sheep's fleece was left outside. The first night it was wet with dew, but the ground around it was dry. The next night the fleece remained dry while the ground was wet.

Gideon was a godfearing man. He assumed that the Israelite misfortunes were due to the pagan customs and religious practices they had picked up from their neighbours. For his mission to succeed he felt impelled to carry out a forceful purification, at least in his own village of Ophrah. Taking ten servants with him, Gideon went out at night, smashed the local altar of Baal, cut down the sacred grove of the goddess Asherah (Astarte) and used the wood to sacrifice a bullock to the Lord. Next morning a group of enraged villagers came to Joash and demanded that his son be put to death. Joash replied sarcastically 'Will you contend for Baal? . . . If he is a god, let him contend for himself' (Judg. 6:31). That day Gideon acquired the second name of Jerubbaal, that is to say, 'Let Baal contend against him, . . .' (Judg. 6:32).

The Midianites had amassed a large force under two of their tribal kings, Zebah and Zalmunnah. They encamped in the eastern Jezreel valley near the hill of Moreh, between Mount Gilboa and Mount Tabor. Gideon first rallied the men of Manasseh, then gained reinforcements from the three Galilee tribes of Naphtali, Zebulun and Asher, to whom he had sent messengers. He was dismayed by the unwieldy and unreliable mass of thirty-two thousand men that mustered on the lower slopes of Mount Gilboa, above the spring of Harod. When he declared that those who were afraid of battle could return to their homes, all but ten thousand promptly left. Those who remained were put through a peculiar aptitude test. They were sent down to drink from the pool of water formed from the spring. The great majority knelt, put their faces down to the water and lapped it up with their tongues, 'as a dog laps' (Judg. 7:5). They were held back, and the assault force limited to three hundred men who had scooped up water in their hands a little at a time. This behaviour presumably revealed that they had self-restraint and a high state of alertness, and showed care not to make any unnecessary noise near the enemy lines.

The biblical text gives a theological reason for the small size of the attacking unit – that the credit for victory should be due to God's favour and not to human skill. Gideon had his own military reason. He had decided on novel tactics in the form of a surprise commando raid at night, with a spectacular use of psychological weapons to induce panic. For such an operation his three hundred picked men were adequate.

Gideon needed to know the precise layout of the Midianite camp, so he stole into it at night with his servant Pureh. He overheard a Midianite tell his comrade about a bad dream, in which a loaf of barley bread rolled into the camp and knocked over a tent. The two of them gloomily interpreted the dream as a portent of Israelite victory over them. This defeatist spirit bore out the psychological calculations that underlay Gideon's battle plan.

That night, under cover of darkness, three companies of a hundred men each crept towards the Midianite camp, and took up their positions on different sides of the perimeter. The hour was carefully chosen – about midnight just after the camp sentries had been changed for the middle watch. In addition to his weapons, each Israelite carried a trumpet and a flaming torch concealed in a jar. Gideon himself led the first company. At a signal from him, all three hundred let out a deafening blast on their trumpets, shouted at the top of their voices, smashed the jars and rushed into the camp waving their torches, that were then used to set the tents alight.

As Gideon had planned, the sleeping Midianites were taken totally by surprise and fled in disorder, leaving behind their dead and all their herds and possessions. They made their way eastward to the Jordan and then south along the river valley. Gideon invoked the help of the Ephraimites, in the central hill terrain, who rushed down and seized the river fords. The Midianites had to fight their way across, losing a number of men, including their two battle commanders Oreb and Zeeb (names that in Hebrew mean 'crow' and 'wolf'). The Ephraimites cut off the heads of the commanders and brought them to Gideon. They were indignant that they had been called in at such a late stage, after the main battle was over. Gideon soothed them down by saying that theirs had been the vital role: 'What have I done now in comparison with you? Is not the gleaning of the grapes of Ephraim better than the vintage of Abiezer?' (Judg. 8:2).

With his original three hundred, Gideon stubbornly kept up the pursuit across the Jordan and eastward along the gorge of the Jabbok river. The first Israelite town he reached was Succoth, where he asked for food for his weary and famished men. The elders of the town fobbed him off, for fear that the Midianites would come back and take revenge on them. Referring to the two Midianite kings, they asked pointedly, 'Are Zebah and Zalmunnah already in your hand, that we should give bread to your army?' (Judg. 8:6). Gideon lost his temper and promised that when the kings had been taken he would return and flog the elders with thorn-bushes. The next town, Penuel, also rebuffed Gideon and he swore he would destroy its tower on his way back.

Gideon picked up the ancient caravan route and followed it for over a hundred miles to the desert town of Karkur situated in a deep canyon. Again his attack on the Midianite camp was totally unexpected. He not only inflicted another defeat but took the two kings captive. On the return journey, he made good his threat to punish the towns of Penuel and Succoth.

The kings were interrogated by Gideon and admitted that at Mount Tabor they had killed his brothers who, they said, resembled Gideon in princely bearing. Gideon declared that by the accepted tradition of the blood feud he was obliged to put them to death. He called on his eldest son to do so, but the young man shrank from the execution. With dignity the desert chieftains asserted that their honour required death only at the hands of Gideon: 'Rise yourself, and fall upon us; for as the man is, so is his strength' (Judg. 8:21). Then Gideon slew them 'and he took the crescents that were on the necks of their camels' (Judg. 8:21), the glittering emblems of their rank and wealth.

Leading men of the tribes that had been involved in the war now came to Gideon and said: 'Rule over us, you and your son and your grandson also; for you have delivered us out of the hand of Midian' (Judg. 8:22). Hereditary kingship was the form of political rule among all the surrounding peoples. It was, however, completely alien to Israelite history and belief, as summed up in Gideon's terse reply: 'I will not rule over you, and my son will not rule over you; the Lord will rule over you' (Judg. 8:23).

Gideon devised a tribute to the Lord that would remain a permanent memorial of the deliverance. The booty taken by the Israelites included a quantity of the golden earings worn by the Midianites. Gideon collected them, made an ephod, and set it up in his village of Ophrah. The idea backfired, since the ephod itself became an object of cultworship by Israelites who were corrupted by paganism.

The nature of the ephod in this passage is uncertain. In the later Jerusalem Temple an ephod was one of the high priest's vestments, woven of fine wool and linen and ornamented with gold. Attached to it was a golden breastplate, with twelve precious stones set in it to represent the twelve tribes. The ephod and breastplate had ritual functions of a mystic nature.

After the campaign, Gideon returned to his village and remained there until his death. The young farmer who had once reluctantly obeyed the angel messenger became a rich and famous man, with a number of wives and concubines and seventy sons. He had rejected a throne for himself and his offspring. But one tough and ambitious son, Abimelech, nursed his own dream of royal estate. It was significant that his name in Hebrew means 'my father is king'.

*Abimelech*    Abimelech was only half-Israelite. His mother was a Canaanite woman from Shechem whom Gideon had taken as a concubine. After his father's death. Abimelech saw his mother's people as a stepping-stone to power. Shechem was still a largely Canaanite city, though an enclave in the territory of Manasseh, Gideon's tribe. Abimelech came to his mother's relatives, and with their help persuaded the citizens of the town that they should accept his undivided authority over them: 'Which is better for you, that all seventy of the sons of Jerubbaal rule over you, or that one rule over you? Remember also that I am your bone and your flesh' (Judg. 9:2). The elders agreed to support him, and financed his venture with seventy pieces of silver from the temple treasury of their local god Baal-berith. Abimelech used the money to hire a band of cutthroats from the local riff-raff, 'worthless and reckless fellows'. With these mercenaries at his heels, he proceeded to the family home at Ophrah and had his brothers and half-brothers put to death. Only the youngest, Jotham, managed to hide himself and escaped the wholesale fratricide. On his return to Shechem, Abimelech was

crowned king. The ceremony took place, ironically enough, at the same sacred oak where Joshua had renewed the Israelite covenant with the Lord, more than a century earlier.

The one disturbing note was the sudden appearance on nearby Mount Gerizim of Abimelech's younger brother Jotham. He cried out to the assembly, 'Listen to me, you men of Shechem, that God may listen to you' (Judg. 9:7). He then told them the caustic parable of the trees that wanted a king of their own. In turn the olive tree, the fig tree and the grapevine declined the honour, since they had useful things to do: producing olive oil, sweet figs and 'wine which cheers gods and men,' (Judg. 9:13). The choice then fell on the sterile and thorny bramble, likely to catch fire when dry and burn down the tallest trees in the forest. Jotham, applying the parable, denounced the citizens of Shechem who had so shabbily repaid Gideon for saving them from the marauding Midianites, and had connived in the murder of Gideon's other sons. Like the bramble in the forest, the Shechemites and their new king would destroy each other. After that grim prediction, Jotham got away before he could be caught.

It soon became evident that Abimelech was not content to be just the ruler of Shechem. He appointed Zebul as governor of the city, and set up his own headquarters at the Israelite village of Arumah, five miles south of Shechem in the territory of Ephraim. From here he tried to expand his kingdom by gaining the allegiance of the Israelite population.

At first, the notables of Shechem had believed that Abimelech had identified himself with his mother's Canaanite community, and would restore the sway of their city over that part of the country. When they realized that he was using them for his own ends, they turned against him. They saw to it that robberies and ambushes made the hill roads in the vicinity unsafe. Then a boastful bandit leader called Gaal moved into the town with his followers and incited the citizens to open defiance against their absent ruler. He gained wide support. The revolt was launched with a feast in the local sanctuary, where they 'ate and drank and reviled Abimelech' (Judg. 9:27). Zebul, the governor, sent a message to Abimelech at Arumah, urging him to march up at once and restore control. At daybreak, when some of Abimelech's advancing forces were observed from the city gate, Zebul provoked Gaal to risk an encounter in the open. 'Are not these the men whom you despised? Go out now and fight with them' (Judg. 9:38). Gaal ventured out with his followers, who were attacked and fled back through the gate, leaving behind many dead. The discredited Gaal was expelled from the city by the governor.

Abimelech appeared again with a larger army, forced his way into Shechem, and 'razed the city and sowed it with salt' (Judg. 9:45). About a thousand men and women held out in the 'Tower of Shechem', and perished in the flames when Abimelech set the stronghold alight with the aid of dry brushwood laid around the wall.

(Excavations at the site of biblical Shechem confirm that the city was destroyed in the twelfth century BC, and that in it had stood a temple-citadel on raised ground, the 'Tower of Shechem' in the biblical account.)

Abimelech next besieged and took the nearby Canaanite town of Thebez, that had presumably joined in the revolt against him. Here too, a number of the citizens held out in the fortified citadel, which Abimelech and his men tried to set alight. When he drew close to the doorway, a woman on the roof dropped a millstone that split his skull. The dying Abimelech said to his young armourbearer: 'Draw your sword and kill me, lest men say of me, "A woman killed him"' (Judg. 9:54).

That abruptly ended Abimelech's three-year attempt to establish dynastic rule. It was only much later, with the election of Saul towards the end of the eleventh century BC, that kingship would become an accepted Israelite institution.

*Jephthah*  Jephthah was a man of Gilead, the central Trans-jordan area north and south of the Jabbok river, a tributary of the Jordan. It was an area of wooded hills, ravines and pasture lands. The territory to the south of the Jabbok, towards the Dead Sea, had been settled by the tribes of Reuben and Gad. Northern Gilead, stretching up towards the Sea of Galilee, was allocated to the Machir clan from the tribe of Manasseh. During the period of the Judges, the Israelite inhabitants of Gilead were involved in periodic strife either with their southern neighbour, the kingdom of Moab or their eastern neighbour, the kingdom of Ammon with its capital at Rabbath-ammon (today Amman, the capital of the Hashemite Kingdom of Jordan).

After Ehud had assassinated the king of Moab and defeated his forces, that kingdom declined, while the Ammonites grew stronger and more militant. In Jephthah's time, possibly the beginning of the eleventh century BC, they were encroaching into Gilead, and even raiding across the Jordan river into the territories of Judah, Benjamin and Ephraim. The situation became grave when the Ammonites assembled an army that threatened to overrun Gilead. The Israelites mustered at the town of Mizpah, a little south of the Jabbok river, and prepared to resist invasion. In desperation, the Israelite elders in Gilead turned to a man they regarded as an outcast.

Jephthah, the son of a prostitute, had been thrown out by the legitimate sons of his father, to prevent him from sharing with them in the future inheritance. He gathered around him a group of other outlaws, and became renowned as a bold and resourceful bandit chief in 'the land of Tob' – probably on the fringes of the desert east of the Sea of Galilee. A delegation of elders from Gilead sought Jephthah out and proposed that he take command of the Israelite forces against Ammon. His reply was scornful: 'Did you not hate me, and drive me out of my father's house? Why have you come to me now when you are in trouble?' (Judg. 11:7). The elders then offered him a more far-reaching inducement – to be not only the military commander but also the ruler over Gilead. The agreement was sealed in a public religious ceremony at Mizpah.

Jephthah sent messengers to the king of Ammon, in an effort to settle the conflict by negotiation. The king maintained that he was resorting to arms in order to regain the Trans-jordan territory between the Arnon river (half-way along the eastern shore of the Dead Sea) and the Jabbok river. That land, he claimed, had been Ammonite land when the Israelites seized and occupied it on their way to the Promised Land. Jephthah's reply refuted this claim. He recalled that the disputed area had been gained by the Israelites in a war with the Amorite king Sihon. Since then it had been in Israelite occupation for centuries, without their rights being challenged. 'I therefore have not sinned against you, and you do me wrong by making war on me' (Judg. 11:27). Since the Ammonite ruler remained unmoved by this historical reasoning, the parley broke down and hostilities became inevitable.

To improve his prospects in the coming battle

Jephthah made a dramatic but rash vow to the Lord: 'If thou wilt give the Ammonites into my hand, then whoever comes forth from the doors of my house to meet me, when I return victorious from the Ammonites, shall be the Lord's, and I will offer him up for a burnt offering' (Judg. 11:30, 31).

Having augmented his force with fresh levies from Gilead and Manasseh, Jephthah advanced and inflicted a defeat on the Ammonites. He demolished a defensive line of border forts to the west and south of Rabbath-ammon, but did not reach the city itself, nor did he penetrate deep into Ammonite territory. While the victory was not decisive, it relieved the Israelite area in Trans-jordan from Ammonite pressure for generations to come.

When Jephthah returned to Mizpah, he was met by a procession of women, celebrating the victory with song and dance in the traditional manner. To Jephthah's horror, the women were led by his young daughter, his only child. Stricken with grief, he told her about the vow he had made before the battle. She accepted that her father was compelled to abide by the vow. Her only request was for two months' grace, which she wanted to spend with her companions wandering in the hills, mourning the fact that she would die a virgin without a chance to become a wife and mother. It later became a custom among the Israelites for young women to mourn Jephthah's daughter for four days each year.

The story is difficult to explain. Human sacrifice had very ancient and primitive roots in the Near East, as in other parts of the world. It was a ritual sacrament, renewing the mystic blood ties between the tribe and its deity. But the Hebrew faith rejected and fought the practice as a pagan abomination. With Abraham's call to sacrifice Isaac centuries earlier, the substitution of a ram for the boy symbolized the sacrifice of animals instead of human beings. The vow to which Jephthah's daughter fell victim could not have conformed with Israelite beliefs and customs at that time, and may well be an echo of a more archaic tradition.

Later rabbinical literature passes a harsh judgment on Jephthah. The Talmudic sages asserted that he could have been absolved from his immoral vow by the high priest, and could have made a donation to the sanctuary as a ransom for his daughter's life.

The story has an interesting parallel in the later Homeric legend of Iphigenia, the beautiful virgin daughter of the Greek prince and commander-in-chief Agamemnon. On their way to the Trojan war, the Greek forces were becalmed at Aulis. Pressure was brought on Agamemnon to agree that Iphigenia should be offered up in sacrifice to appease the anger of the goddess Artemis. The girl was lured to Aulis on a pretext and the sacrifice prepared, but at the last moment the goddess relented, spirited Iphigenia away from the altar and substituted a hind. This legend was the theme of Euripedes' great tragedy, 'Iphigenia at Aulis'.

Jephthah's successful campaign against the *The War* Ammonites had an unhappy sequel in an Israelite *with Ephraim* inter-tribal clash. Ephraim regarded itself as the leading Israelite tribe in the central and northern region of the country. The Ephraimites had resented having been left out of Gideon's victory over the Midianites, and had been pacified with an important role in the pursuit stage – plus, no doubt, a share in the booty. After Jephthah's defeat of the Ammonites, the men of Ephraim again protested that they had not been drawn into the campaign. Jephthah angrily retorted that they had ignored his initial call for help and that he had risked his life in battle while they had stood aside. The Ephraimites crossed the Jordan river in force and entered Gilead. Jephthah launched a crushing attack on them and routed them. His men seized the river fords to cut off the fugitives. Any person trying to cross was made to say *shibboleth*, the Hebrew word for an ear of corn. If he pronounced it *sibboleth*, it disclosed that he spoke the dialect of Ephraim, and he was killed on the spot.

Jephthah remained the leader of Gilead until his death six years later.

Samson the Danite does not fit at all into the *Samson* pattern of the charismatic leaders known as the Judges. The biblical text makes the standard statement that he 'judged Israel in the days of the Philistines twenty years' (Judg. 15:20). But there is nothing in the actual narrative to suggest that he filled any position of tribal authority – as a military commander, a judicial arbiter of disputes or a religious figure. On the contrary, Samson was a boisterous folk-hero of a type that down the ages has captivated the popular mind with feats of superhuman strength, from Hercules in ancient Greece to Superman in modern cartoons.

In the Israelite settlement of Canaan, the small tribe of Dan was allotted a strip of territory in the region of undulating Judean foothills. This Israelite salient in the lowlands came under pressure from the confederation of five Philistine city-states established in the southern coastal plain from the twelfth century BC. For a while, the two peoples co-existed as neighbours, with an ill-defined border running through the Shephelah. However, Philistine power started pushing towards the hill-country of Judah. The tribe of Dan struggled for survival in the Shephelah, but most of the Danite families eventually migrated to the north-eastern corner of the Galilee.

That was the historical background for the singlehanded exploits of Samson. Their main physical setting was the vicinity of the Sorek valley, between the Danite villages of Zorah and Eshtaol on the high ground, and the Philistine town of Timnah in the valley five miles to the west.

Samson's parents, Manoah and his wife, were a childless couple living in Zorah. An angel of the Lord appeared to them and told them that they would have a son. He would be from birth a Nazirite, a person consecrated to the service of the Lord. During her pregnancy his mother had to refrain from drinking wine or eating any food that was not ritually pure. When the boy was born, he was given the name of Samson (in Hebrew, Shimshon, probably derived from *shemesh*, the word for sun).

When Samson grew up, he fell in love with a Philistine girl in the town of Timnah. His parents could not persuade him to find a bride among his own people, so they reluctantly went with him to Timnah to arrange the marriage. There Samson was threatened by a young lion in the vineyards. He grappled with the beast and with a burst of strength he killed it with his bare hands by tearing the jaws apart. He returned to the scene later and found that a swarm of bees had settled in the lion's body. He scooped up some of the honey and went his way eating it. Samson did not tell his mother nor anyone else about his encounter with the lion.

As was the custom, Samson gave a feast in his bride's home, to which thirty young men of her town were invited. During the week of eating and drinking, the time was taken up with the telling of tales and the asking of riddles. Samson made a

wager with the thirty Philistine guests, whereby each of them would receive a piece of fine linen and a set of good clothes if they could solve the riddle he would put to them. If not, they would each give him the same. His riddle was:

> Out of the eater came something to eat.
> Out of the strong came something sweet.
> (Judg. 14:14)

The Philistines puzzled over their conundrum for three days, then came to Samson's wife and threatened to burn down her father's house unless she found out the answer for them. After nights of coaxing and wheedling, Samson gave in and told her. On the last day the Philistines produced the answer:

> What is sweeter than honey?
> What is stronger than a lion?
> (Judg. 14:18)

In a rage Samson shouted that they could not have found out 'If you had not ploughed with my heifer' (Judg. 14:18). To meet the terms of the wager, he went off to the Philistine city of Ashkelon, killed thirty men, took their clothes and flung them at the wedding guests. He then stalked out, left his deceitful wife and returned to his parents' home.

Her family handed the abandoned girl to someone else. To their acute embarrassment, Samson turned up again to be with her, bringing a young goat as a gift. The father explained tactfully why Samson could no longer be given access to her, and proposed that he take her younger sister instead. Samson refused, and sought an ingenious and malicious revenge on his wife's people. He caught three hundred foxes, tied them together in pairs by the tails, fixed a torch to each pair of tails, set the torches alight and turned the foxes loose in the Philistine wheatfields and olive orchards. They were destroyed by fire. The Philistines reacted by punishing the family into which he had married. They burnt down the house and Samson's wife and father-in-law perished in the flames.

Samson killed a number of Philistines involved in the deed. He then escaped into the Judean hills and took refuge in a rock-cave at Etam, just south of Bethlehem. A Philistine force marched into the hills to capture him, to the dismay of the men of Judah, whose territory had been invaded through no fault of their own. They came to Samson and demanded that he let them hand him over to his pursuers. 'Do you not know that the Philistines are rulers over us? What then is this that you have done to us? (Judg. 15:11). Samson consented to have his arms bound with new ropes, and was brought to the Philistines. When they ran towards him, shouting with glee at their prize, he exerted his enormous strength 'and the ropes which were on his arms became as flax that has caught fire, and his bonds melted off his hands' (Judg. 15:14). He snatched up the jawbone of an ass and laid about him with such vigour that he killed a thousand Philistines before the rest fled. His burning thirst after these exertions was miraculously quenched by a spring of water that suddenly bubbled out of a cleft rock.

Some time later, Samson audaciously ventured again into the heart of Philistine territory, to spend the night with a prostitute in the city of Gaza. When word of his presence reached them, the Philistines prepared to ambush him when the city gates were opened at daybreak. Samson did not wait for them. He got up at midnight, pulled up the gateposts, walked off with the gates on his back and carried them forty miles until he dumped them on a hilltop outside Hebron.

Samson became involved with a third Philistine woman, who was to prove his undoing. The seductive Delilah lived in the valley of Sorek, not far from Samson's home village. When it became known that he was visiting her regularly, she was approached by a group of the Philistine leaders. They offered each to pay her eleven hundred pieces of silver if she would worm out of Samson the secret of his fabulous strength, so that they could find some way to tie him up. To satisfy her questions, Samson told her that he could be subdued if he were bound with seven new bowstrings that had not dried out. The Philistines supplied her with the bowstrings. When Samson was sleeping in her room that night, she used them to tie him. Before that, she had hidden a number of men in another room. When she shouted out 'The Philistines are upon you, Samson!' (Judg. 16:9), he jumped up and snapped the bowstrings as if they were threads.

Delilah made two more abortive attempts to have Samson captured, based on what he told her. Once she bound him with new ropes but he snapped them with ease. The next time seven locks of his hair were woven into a web and pegged to a loom. But he pulled his hair free

without any trouble. Delilah complained bitterly that he had made a fool of her, and nagged him day after day, until he gave in and told her the truth: 'A razor has never come upon my head; for I have been a Nazirite to God from my mother's womb. If I be shaved, then my strength will leave me, and I shall become weak, and be like any other man' (Judg. 16:17). One of the restrictions imposed by the vows of a Nazirite was that his hair should remain uncut.

Delilah informed the Philistine leaders that at last she had succeeded in learning the secret. They arrived at her house with the money they had promised her. That night, when Samson was asleep with his head in her lap, she had a man shave off his hair. This time he was helpless when he was seized and bound. His eyes were gouged out; he was taken to Gaza, put in chains, and set to work turning the prison millstone to grind the corn. The legendary hero had become a pitiable hulk of a man, groping in darkness and performing the task of a beast of burden. In the words of John Milton's epic poem *Samson Agonistes*:

Ask for this great deliverer now, and find him
Eyeless in Gaza at the mill with slaves,

But God's grace and strength built up in him again as his hair began to grow.

All the leading citizens of Gaza gathered at a great feast in the temple of the god Dagon, to celebrate the capture of their enemy. (Dagon was a Canaanite corn-god absorbed into the Philistine cult after they settled in the country.) With a boy leading him by the hand, Samson was brought into the temple so that he could be an object of sport and derision for the merrymakers. The temple was full, and three thousand more people had gathered on the roof to join in the fun.

Samson asked the lad to place him between the two pillars that stood in the middle of the temple and supported the roof. He prayed to the Lord to restore his power for the last time. As his strength came surging back, he pressed his two hands against the pillars and said: 'Let me die with the Philistines' (Judg. 17:30). Then he pushed with all his might. The columns collapsed and the roof came crashing down, killing the whole crowd together with Samson himself. His family recovered his body and buried it in the family tomb between Zorah and Eshtaol.

In the manner of his death, the roistering fighter and lover became a noble and tragic figure.

The Blinding of Samson by his Philistine captors. An engraving
by the Viennese artist Alfred Hrdlicka.

Life in the Shephelah lowlands became precarious for the small tribe of Dan. It sent out a party of five men to look for another territory that did not already belong to one of the other Israelite tribes. They reported that in the north-east of the country they had seen the Canaanite city of Laish in a fertile and well-watered area. Its inhabitants seemed a 'quiet and unsuspecting' people, poorly defended, and too far removed from the Phoenicians on the coast for help to reach them from that quarter.

Six hundred armed Danites, with their wives and possessions, set out on the long trek to conquer a new home in the north. On their way through the hills of Ephraim, they reached the homestead of a farmer called Micah, where the exploration party of five had previously spent the night. Micah had made a shrine for himself, installed in it a silver idol made out of money provided by his mother, and engaged a young Levite from Bethlehem as his family priest. The Danites confiscated the idol and persuaded the priest to come with them. Micah and his neighbours tried to retrieve both, but were frightened off.

On arrival at Laish, the men of Dan attacked and wiped out the city and its inhabitants. The town they built on the site was named Dan. The graven image that belonged to Micah was set up in its sanctuary. A certain Jonathan was appointed as the priest, an office handed down to his descendants.

In its final form, the biblical account of this migration may have been coloured by the antipathy of the Jerusalem priesthood towards the northern kingdom of Israel, after it had split away from Judah and set up its own sanctuaries at Dan and Bethel. The temple at Dan, in particular, was charged with being the seat of idolatrous practices.

The last episode in the Book of Judges concerns the war of the other Israelite tribes against the tribe of Benjamin, sparked by a gruesome sex crime.

A Levite living in the hills of Ephraim acquired a concubine (what today would be called a common law wife) from Bethlehem in Judah. After four months she left him and returned to her family. With a servant and two donkeys he went to fetch her, to the evident satisfaction of her father, who made him welcome. On the journey back, they came at nightfall to the town of Gibeah, in the territory of Benjamin. None of the local inhabitants was prepared to give them shelter for the night until an old man, who also hailed from the tribe of Ephraim, took them into his home.

The unusual lack of hospitality shown to a passing traveller indicates that there was already friction between the neighbouring tribes of Ephraim and Benjamin. Ephraim claimed a pre-eminent position among the tribes. The Benjaminites, though small, were not subservient to any other tribe. They were renowned as fighting men, skilled with the bow and the sling. Not for nothing had Jacob's blessing of his sons declared that:

> Benjamin is a ravenous wolf,
> in the morning devouring the
> prey, and at even dividing the spoil.
> (Gen. 49:27)

Trouble broke out that night over the Levite and his concubine. A gang of young toughs beat at the door and demanded that the Levite be handed to them for sexual purposes. The old man's protests had no effect. In the end they got hold of the concubine and 'knew her, and abused her all night until the morning' (Judg. 19:25). When the Levite ventured out at daybreak, he found the woman lying there dead with her hands outstretched to the door. He placed her body on the donkey, took it back to his home in Ephraim, hacked it into twelve pieces and sent them to the leaders of the twelve tribes – an ancient ritual for a call to war.

Representatives of the tribes assembled at Mizpah, where the Levite appeared before them and told his story. A large combined force was mustered, each tribe contributing one-tenth of its fighting strength, with provisions for its own contingent. An ultimatum was sent to the elders of Benjamin, demanding the surrender of the men in Gibeah who had perpetrated the outrage. The demand was refused and the tribe of Benjamin mobilized for war. Its army included a crack unit of slingsmen, 'seven hundred picked men who were left-handed; every one could sling a stone at a hair, and not miss' (Judg. 20:16).

On two successive days, the allied army advanced on Gibeah, but was repulsed with heavy losses. On the third day, they resorted to the precise tactics Joshua had used in the capture of Ai. Part of the attacking force concealed itself at night behind the town. Another part feigned flight, to lure the defenders away from the city. The men waiting in ambush then entered it and set it alight. When the smoke rose into the air the units that appeared to be running away turned round and attacked. Caught in the middle, the army of Benjamin was practically wiped out, only six hundred men escaping to Rimmon, a stronghold on the escarpment east of Bethel. The territory of Benjamin was then devastated, its towns and villages destroyed and their inhabitants annihilated.

The leaders of the other tribes belatedly realized that they might bring about the total extinction of one of the twelve Israelite tribes. The way to preserve Benjamin was to find wives for its six hundred surviving warriors. The one Israelite town that had refused to join in the combined attack was Jabesh-gilead in Trans-jordan, a place that seems to have had special ties with the tribe of Benjamin. A punitive expedition launched against that town destroyed it, leaving alive only four hundred young women, who were delivered to the Benjaminites as wives. For the two hundred brides still required, the men were encouraged to seize girls dancing in the fields at the sanctuary of Shiloh, in celebration of the annual vintage festival.

It is difficult to know what factual basis there was for the biblical account of this inter-tribal war, that is not corroborated from any other source. If a group of other tribes did indeed have an armed encounter with Benjamin, it would probably have taken place at an early stage of the settlement, and would have been far less devastating in its consequences than is depicted in this account. At the end of the period of the Judges, Benjamin was a strong and well-established tribe that provided the people of Israel with its first king, Saul. Gibeah was his home town and capital. The Trans-jordan town of Jabesh-gilead was certainly intact at that time. Saul first came to public notice when he led an expedition to relieve the town when it was under siege by the Ammonites.

## Samuel

SHILOH WAS SITUATED IN THE HILLS OF Ephraim thirty miles north of Jerusalem and a little east of the road to Shechem. In the period of the Judges the town was the central place of worship for the Israelite tribes. The Ark of the Covenant, the most sacred cult-object of the Hebrew faith, was kept in the Tabernacle at the sanctuary. On major feast days families would come on pilgrimage from the surrounding region and offer up their sacrifice to the Lord.

One day the venerable high priest Eli was sitting on a bench at the entrance to the sanctuary. He observed an agitated woman sobbing, and mumbling incoherently. Thinking she was drunk he rebuked her, until she explained that she had been 'pouring out my soul before the Lord' (1 Sam. 1:15). The woman was Hannah, one of the two wives of Elkanah, a man from the Ephraimite town of Ramah further to the south. The other wife, Pninah, had a number of children and would deride the barren Hannah. She turned to the Lord for help in her affliction – as other Old Testament women, including Sarah, Rebekah, Rachel and the mother of Samson, had done for the same reason. The kindly priest gave her his blessing, and promised that the Lord would give heed to her prayers. *Hannah's Prayer*

Hannah conceived and bore a son whom she called Samuel, meaning 'the name of God'. She now fulfilled the vow she had taken when praying at Shiloh for a child: 'I will give him to the Lord all the days of his life, and no razor shall touch his head' (1 Sam. 1:11). When the infant was weaned she handed him over to Eli to be brought up in the sanctuary, saying 'I have lent him to the Lord' (1 Sam. 1:28). He remained in the personal care of the aged high priest and 'continued to grow both in stature and in favour with the Lord and with men' (1 Sam. 2:26). Each year, when the family came on the annual pilgrimage, Hannah visited her son and brought a new robe she had made for him. *Samuel the Novice*

The assistant priests were Eli's two sons, Hophni and Phinehas. They were 'worthless men' who abused their office by appropriating for themselves the choicest portions of the sacrifices, and by seducing the women who worked at the sanctuary. Their distressed father tried in vain to reform them, saying, 'If a man sins against a man, God will mediate for him; but if a man sins against the Lord, who can intercede for him?' (1 Sam. 2:25).

The misdeeds of Eli's sons brought about a direct revelation of the Lord's presence to Samuel – an event that 'was rare in those days; there was no frequent vision' (1 Sam. 3:1). The young neophyte slept inside the sanctuary near the Ark. One night he awoke to hear his name being called and ran into Eli's room, thinking the priest had summoned him. When this happened three times, Eli understood that Samuel must have heard the voice of God himself, and told him to answer next time, 'Speak, Lord, for thy servant hears' (1 Sam. 3:9). The Lord then told Samuel he was about to take an action that would make 'the two ears of every one that hears it tingle' (1 Sam. 3:11). Eli's two corrupt sons would be killed and his line wiped out. Next morning Samuel was reluctant to repeat this grim message, but did so when Eli insisted. The old man said resignedly, 'It is the Lord; let him do what seems good to him' (1 Sam. 3:18). According to Jewish tradition, Samuel was twelve years old when this happened. The revelation marked him out for a special destiny.

*The Defeat at Aphek* At that time (about the middle of the eleventh century BC), the growing power and superior military technology of the Philistines in the southern coastal plain had become a major threat to the Israelite tribes in the hills. Philistine forces concentrated at Aphek at the edge of the coastal plain north-east of Joppa (Jaffa). The Israelites mustered in the nearby hills at Ebenezer. Battle was joined and on the first day went badly for the Israelites, four thousand of whom fell. The commanders sent an urgent message to Shiloh requesting that the Ark of the Covenant be sent forward to them, in the belief that its presence would turn the tide of battle in their favour. A great shout of excitement went up from the Israelite camp when the two priests Hophni and Phinehas arrived with this powerful secret weapon. At first the Philistines were afraid that supernatural forces were being arrayed against them. But they rallied and attacked. The Israelite army was routed, and the Ark captured by the enemy. Eli's two sons were killed in the fighting.

Eli, ninety-eight years old and blind, sat anxiously waiting for news of the battle. When a runner arrived and told him about the disaster, he fell over backwards with the shock and died of a broken neck. Eli's daughter-in-law, the wife of Phinehas, was expecting a child. The dreadful tidings brought on the premature birth of an infant son. The dying mother named him Ichabod (in Hebrew, 'no glory') because, she cried out, 'The glory has departed from Israel' (1 Sam. 4:22).

After the victory the Philistines advanced into the hills, and established their hold over the tribal territory of Ephraim and Benjamin. Excavations at the site of biblical Shiloh indicate that it was destroyed about this time.

The Ark of the Covenant proved to be a very troublesome trophy for its Philistine captors. It was brought from Ebenezer to the Philistine city of Ashdod and triumphantly placed in the temple of Dagon, before the great statue of the god. During the night the statue toppled over. It was heaved back onto its pedestal but the next night it fell down again, and this time the head and arms were smashed off. What was worse, there was an outbreak of tumours (apparently bubonic plague) in the city and the surrounding countryside, and many died of the disease. The people of Ashdod hurriedly passed the Ark on to Gath and from there it continued to Ekron (both Philistine cities), with the plague following it. *The Journey of the Ark*

By this time the Philistines had had possession of the Ark for seven months, and were more than anxious to see the last of it. On the advice of their priests and diviners, they placed it on a new cart drawn by two milch cows and sent it on its way in the direction of the nearest Israelite town, Beth-shemesh in the foothills. With the Ark they put on the cart a box containing five golden tumours and five golden mice (probably rats) to serve both as a 'guilt-offering' to the Israelites and as a symbolic way of moving the plague out of their territory.

The cows ambled straight across the border and reached the fields outside Beth-shemesh where the men were reaping the wheat harvest. A great boulder was set up; the Levites reverently placed the Ark upon it together with the box of golden images; and the cows were sacrificed as a burnt offering to the Lord, in gratitude. The inhabitants of Beth-shemesh felt less grateful when seventy of them died for the sacrilegious act of peering into the Ark. They persuaded the men of Kiriath-jearim to come and remove it to their own town up in the Judean hills, near the border between Judah and Benjamin (the present Arab village of Abu Ghosh is close to the site). Here the Ark remained for twenty years in the custody of one of the villagers, Eleazar, and his son.

After their victory at Aphek, the Philistines did not establish direct rule over the Israelite tribes as that would have meant keeping a large occupation army in the hills. It was rough terrain, with poor communications, and unsuitable for the deployment of the chariot troops that were the mainstay of the Philistine army. They exacted tribute and stationed garrisons in strategic towns commanding the main roads. For the rest, they left the Israelites to carry on with their own way of life, provided they did not revive their fighting capacity.

*Samuel becomes Leader*  Samuel emerged during this period as the dominant Israelite figure. As priest, prophet and judge, his moral authority was unquestioned, and he became accepted as the mouthpiece through whom God's will was made known. 'And all Israel from Dan to Beersheba knew that Samuel was established as a prophet of the Lord' (1 Sam. 3:20). With the Shiloh sanctuary wiped out, he returned to his birthplace at Ramah, where he married and had two sons, Joel and Abijah.

Samuel was convinced that only a spiritual revival could bring about an end to Israelite subjection. He summoned a meeting of the tribes at Mizpah, just north of Ramah. Here he made them fast all day and pour libations of water to the Lord while he exhorted them to set aside pagan ways and adhere strictly to the Mosaic code. The Philistines interpreted the rally as the beginning of a resistance movement against them, and marched up a force to disperse it. A violent thunderstorm sent them scurrying back. The Israelites pursued them into the coastal plain, regaining some lost territory. This local success raised morale, though it did not break the Philistine occupation. It also established Samuel more firmly in his leadership. He dispensed justice at Ramah, and once a year went on circuit to three other Israelite towns that had become local centres of worship; Bethel, on the border between Benjamin and Ephraim; Gilgal, down in the Jordan valley near Jericho; and Mizpeh. He appointed his two sons as judges in Beersheba, but to his grief they 'turned aside after gain; they took bribes and perverted justice' (1 Sam. 8:3).

# 5

# THE UNITED MONARCHY

### *The Reign of Saul* [*1020–1000* BC]

THE TRIBAL ELDERS AGREED AMONG themselves that they would never be able to stand up to the well-organized Philistine enemy unless a single ruler led them in battle. In some trepidation a deputation of the elders came to put the proposal before Samuel: 'Behold, you are old and your sons do not walk in your ways; now appoint for us a king to govern us like all the nations' (1 Sam. 8:5).

As they had feared, Samuel reacted badly. In a classic anti-monarchical passage he warned them that a king would oppress them and exploit them. He would take their sons to be his chariot drivers and horsemen. They would have to plough his ground, reap his harvest and make the implements of war for him. Their daughters would serve the palace as perfumers, cooks and bakers. The best of their fields, vineyards and orchards would be appropriated for the royal use. Their servants and animals would be put to work for the king, and a tenth part of their crops and flocks would be levied as taxes. 'And in that day you will cry out because of your king, but the Lord will not answer you in that day' (1 Sam. 8:18).

His visitors listened with respect to the formidable old man of God, but stuck stubbornly to their request, and insisted that they had to have a king who would 'go out before us and fight our battles' (1 Sam. 8:20). To Samuel this was blasphemy, for God himself was their ruler. But the Lord told him to meet their request. *The Elders insist on a King*

The choice fell on Saul the son of Kish, a man of the tribe of Benjamin who lived in Gibeah, just north of Jerusalem. Saul is described as 'a handsome young man, from his shoulders upward he was taller than any of the people' (1 Sam. 9:2). On the manner of his election the biblical text is confusing, as two different versions are woven together.

According to one version, after yielding to the demand of the elders Samuel called an assembly of the tribes at Mizpah. Once again making clear his own disapproval, he upbraided them for rejecting the Lord by demanding an earthly king. The election then proceeded by a process of elimination through the drawing of lots. The field was narrowed first to the tribe of Benjamin, then to the family clan of the Matrites in that tribe, and finally to Saul in that clan. He was found hanging *Saul's Election: The Later Version* back among the supplies, brought forward and presented by Samuel to the crowd that shouted, 'Long live the king!' (1 Sam. 10:24). Samuel explained the rights and duties of the kingship, and wrote them down.

In a final speech at the ceremony, he warned the Israelites to remember that with or without a king the power resided in the Lord, while he, Samuel, would remain the intermediary between God and the people. 'Only fear the Lord, and serve him faithfully with all your heart; but if you still do wickedly, you shall be swept away, both you and your king' (1 Sam. 12:24,25). To stress the point that the Lord's authority was behind his words Samuel caused a rainstorm to come down on their heads, though it was the harvest season in late summer, when the country is rainless. The drenched assembly then dispersed and Saul returned to his home in Gibeah.

*Saul's Election: The Earlier Version*

Into the narrative there intrudes a version from an earlier source. Saul was sent by his father with a servant to look for some she-donkeys that had strayed. After days of combing through the hills of Ephraim and Benjamin, Saul was about to abandon the quest and return lest his father become anxious at their long absence. His servant suggested that they consult the famous seer Samuel in the nearby town (probably Ramah, where the prophet lived). When Saul protested that they had used up their provisions and had nothing left to offer as a gift to the seer, the servant produced a silver quarter-shekel. As they went up the hill to the town they met a group of young women coming down to draw water at the well. The young women told them that if they wanted to see Samuel they would have to hurry, as he was about to make a sacrifice to the Lord on the altar at the 'high place', and would then preside over the ceremonial meal.

The previous day the Lord had revealed to Samuel that a young man from Benjamin would come to him, who should be anointed as ruler over Israel, and would save the people from the Philistines. When Saul approached, Samuel told him not to worry about his donkeys as they had already been found. The prophet heaped attentions on the astonished Saul, giving him the seat of honour and the choicest morsels at the table, and inviting him to sleep that night on the flat roof of the house. At daybreak Samuel accompanied Saul through the streets to see him on his way. When they came out of the town Samuel

sent the servant ahead. He then took out a vial, poured a little sacred oil on Saul's head, and told him of the destiny the Lord had bestowed on him.

On Saul's way home certain things happened exactly as Samuel had foretold. First, he met two men near Rachel's tomb who confirmed that the donkeys had been returned. Three other men going to offer a sacrifice at the sanctuary of Bethel supplied him with provisions. At Gibeathelohim (the Hill of God), where there was a Philistine garrison, Saul encountered 'prophets' coming down from the 'high place' and playing on their musical instruments. They were some of the religious ecstatics who went about in bands and lived off the alms given to them by the pious. Saul was suddenly filled with the 'spirit of God' and joined in the fervent dancing and chanting of the group. This spiritual experience left its mark on him and provoked a well-known saying: 'Is Saul also among the prophets?' (1 Sam. 10:12). On his return home, the first person he saw was his uncle, who wanted to know where he had been. Saul told him that the prophet Samuel had helped him recover the donkeys, but kept silent about the strange anointing. (It may be noted that in this earlier version the Hebrew Bible does not use the word *melech*, king, but the word *nagid*, prince or governor.)

Saul soon had an opportunity to prove his ability as a leader in battle. Nahash, the king of Ammon, laid siege to the Israelite town of Jabesh-gilead in Trans-jordan. When the town elders were willing to discuss surrender terms, Nahash stipulated that the right eyes of all the townsmen would have to be gouged out. The town stalled for time and sent out urgent messages for help. Saul was coming from the field behind his oxen when he heard the news. Inspired by the Lord, he killed the oxen and sent pieces of the meat with messengers to the other tribes – the ritual call to arms. He mustered a large body of men, made a forced night march, and at dawn launched a three-pronged attack on the Ammonite camp. By midday, the enemy had been defeated and routed and the siege lifted. After this victory, Samuel convened an assembly at Gilgal in the Jordan valley and publicly proclaimed Saul as king, 'and all the men of Israel rejoiced greatly' (1 Sam. 11:15).

Here the election of Saul is presented as the expression of God's will, and appears to have the unqualified support of Samuel. This earlier version is free of the negative view of kingship that strongly colours the other account of Saul's election. How can these two conflicting attitudes mingle in the same chapters? The Old Testament, in its final form, was evolved over many centuries, and drew on earlier documents and oral traditions that reflected different periods in Hebrew history. In the Book of Samuel, the earlier tradition was probably recorded in the reign of King Solomon, when it was accepted that the monarchy was the divine instrument for the salvation and guidance of God's chosen people. The later source may have been written down two or more centuries later when the institution of Hebrew kingship was no longer held in great esteem. At the time the Hebrew prophets were thundering that not kings and armies but only a return to the ways of God could save the nation from its doom. The final text of the Book of Samuel is an amalgam of both attitudes: the pro-royalist and the anti-royalist.

Saul may have reigned for about twenty years – the exact period is uncertain as the Hebrew text is mutilated at this point. His rule fulfilled the limited purpose for which it had been established. He provided the Israelite tribes with an overall command and a focus of solidarity against their enemies. At the same time, the tribal system remained intact. The centralized political, religious and administrative institutions of the monarchy would only be developed under Saul's successors David and Solomon. Saul continued to live at Gibeah a modest life-style, with hardly any of the royal state that would later mark the palace in Jerusalem. Excavations at Tel el-Ful, the modern Arabic name for Gibeah, have revealed the foundations of a simple rectangular citadel built of rough stone blocks. It is thought to have served as Saul's fortress-residence. Today the hill is surmounted by an unfinished building, the summer palace that King Hussein of Jordan started to construct during the Jordanian occupation of East Jerusalem between 1948 and 1967.

*Revolt against the Philistines*
Soon after his election, Saul raised the standard of revolt against Philistine domination. He had selected and trained a force of three thousand men. The first objective he chose was the Philistine garrison at the town of Geba, a few miles north of Gibeah. An assault force of one thousand men, led by Saul's son Jonathan, attacked from Gibeah. Saul deployed the remainder of his troops at Michmash north of Geba, and in the hills towards Bethel in the northeast, cutting off the enemy line of retreat. Jonathan's force overwhelmed the Philistine garrison, and its commander was killed in the engagement.

This success was only the opening round in a war that would sway back and forth for decades to come. But it boosted the morale of the Israelite tribes and stiffened their will to resist. Saul immediately issued a general call to mobilize, with Gilgal in the Jordan valley as a secure mustering area and base of operations.

The Philistines responded strongly to the challenge. With an army of foot soldiers, cavalry and chariot troops they advanced into the hills, encamped at Michmash and restored their occupation of the area. The intimidated local Israelite inhabitants hid themselves in caves and cisterns, or streamed as refugees down the escarpment and across the Jordan fords.

At Gilgal, Saul tried to stem the panic. He planned a counter-attack, and waited for Samuel to come and make the sacrifices required before the battle. When the prophet failed to arrive within seven days, as he had promised, Saul felt he could delay no longer as his hurriedly recruited army was disintegrating. He himself therefore made the burnt offerings on the altar. Samuel appeared immediately after, bitterly upbraided the king, and declared that God would reject him. The old man's fury was not hard to understand. The king he had reluctantly appointed was acquiring an independent authority, and had even presumed to encroach on Samuel's religious domain. The open rift between king and prophet would not be closed again.

*The Battle of Michmash*
With the hard core of six hundred men left to him, Saul moved up the mountainside and faced the Philistine camp at Michmash across a deep ravine. He was in no position to seek an open military encounter with his formidable enemy. His force was heavily outnumbered and poorly equipped. Since the Philistines still had a monopoly of iron smelting, the Israelites could not make their own weapons, and only the king and Prince Jonathan carried swords. Saul was forced to remain passive while the Philistines sent out three companies in different directions from their main base, to consolidate their hold on the surrounding countryside.

The situation was saved by Jonathan in a daring single-handed exploit. Without his father's knowledge, he and a young armour-bearer crossed the ravine, scaled the cliffs on the other side and leapt on the Philistine guard, killing twenty of them. Panic spread in the camp after this attack from a totally unexpected quarter. Saul's sentries reported to him that the Philistine soldiers were rushing about in disorder. A roll call of his men showed that Jonathan and his armour-bearer were missing. Realizing what had happened, Saul gave the order to advance and attack. The Philistines started fleeing. Israelites from all over the area rushed to join in the pursuit, which continued down to the valley of Aijalon in the lowlands.

Saul had gone to great lengths to ensure the Lord's approval for the battle. Before leaving his camp, he had asked his priest Ahijah to bring out the sacred ephod. He had also ordered his men to fast all day. The night after the battle Saul wanted to press home the advantage by carrying the pursuit into Philistine territory. But the priest sensed that something had happened to provoke divine displeasure. The Urim and Thummim, the divining device associated with the ephod, indicated that Jonathan was the guilty party. It appeared that he had not known about the fasting order and had tasted some honey from a hive of wild bees. Saul ruled that Jonathan had incurred the death penalty, but spared him in response to the pleas of the soldiers for whom Jonathan was the hero of the day.

Saul ran into another religious problem at the end of the day. His famished soldiers started killing and cooking livestock captured from the Philistines, without first draining the blood as prescribed by the dietary laws. Saul made the soldiers bring the cattle to the altar he erected, and had them ritually slaughtered for food.

*The Amalekite Campaign*

The victory at Michmash relieved the Philistine pressure for a number of years. Saul could turn his attention to other hostile neighbours. There is mention of campaigns against the Trans-jordan kingdoms of Edom, Moab, Ammon and Zobah, but no details are given. More stress is laid on an expedition Saul led against the Amalekites, the marauding nomad tribesmen in the southern desert.

Samuel had grudgingly yielded to pressure regarding the election of a king. In playing the role of king-maker, he had assumed that the step was required only by military necessity; that the king would be subservient to him; and that his own moral authority as God's spokesman would remain supreme. As Saul became accepted in his own right as the national liberator and leader, the old prophet was increasingly filled with bitter rancour towards him. The campaign against the Amalekites led to a final rupture in the relations between the two.

Samuel called for a holy war, in which the Amalekites were to be wiped out without taking prisoners or booty. Saul defeated them, but allowed his men to keep the best of their herds and flocks as spoils of war. He himself brought back the Amalekite leader, Agag, as his personal prisoner. When Samuel heard this, he descended in a rage on Saul at the Gilgal base, and accused him of flouting the Lord's injunction. Since none of the Amalekite livestock was to be spared, Samuel asked sarcastically, what was all the bleating and lowing he heard. Saul tried to placate the prophet. His men, he explained, had brought back the pick of the animals in order to sacrifice them to the Lord. Samuel poured scorn on this excuse:

> Has the Lord as great delight in
>   burnt offerings and sacrifices,
>   as in obeying the voice of the
>   Lord?
> Because you have rejected the word
>   of the Lord,
>   he has also rejected you from being king.
>
> (1 Sam. 15:22,23)

The chastened Saul asked to be forgiven, and begged the prophet to appear at his side when he gave formal thanks to the Lord in the presence of the elders. At first Samuel refused; when Saul clutched at the edge of his robe and it tore, Samuel promptly declared this to be a sign that the Lord had torn the kingdom of Israel from Saul. Samuel then changed his mind and appeared with Saul. He demanded, however, that the captive Amalekite king be brought before him. Agag walked forward confidently, thinking that the risk of death had receded. Just as Agag's sword had made other women childless, Samuel shouted, so should his mother be, 'And Samuel hewed Agag in pieces before the Lord in Gilgal' (1 Sam. 15:33). After this grim demonstration Samuel retired to his home in Ramah. He did not see Saul again in his lifetime.

Claiming the Lord's guidance, Samuel now anointed a gifted but unknown boy as the future successor to Saul. The prophet made an unexpected visit to the small Judean town of Bethlehem, causing a flurry of trepidation among its citizens. The elders of the town came out to meet the great man, anxiously enquiring whether he had come in peace. He reassured them that he had come only to make a sacrifice to the Lord. They were required to sanctify themselves and attend the ceremony.

*The Boy David*   One of these citizens was Jesse, a respected sheep farmer. Seven of his fine-looking sons were presented to the prophet in turn. To Samuel's enquiry whether he had any more sons, Jesse explained that the youngest one, David, was out tending the sheep. Samuel insisted on seeing him too. An attractive lad was brought in, with a ruddy complexion and beautiful eyes. Without explaining his unusual action, Samuel anointed the head of the young David with oil. The prophet returned to Ramah, David went back to his sheep and Bethlehem resumed its quiet ways.

From the biblical portrait of David, and the landscape around his birthplace, it is not hard to reconstruct his boyhood. Bethlehem is spread over a hilltop looking down into terraced valleys of olive groves, fig trees, vineyards and vegetable patches. The ridges beyond the valley are covered with boulders and scrub. From their tops the young shepherd could gaze over the rolling expanse of the Judean hills, and eastward down to the Dead Sea, beyond which rise up the purple ramparts of Moab. Here he found grass and shelter for the sheep and protected them from wild animals with stones from his sling. The boy grew agile and strong. He composed lyrics and sang them to the sweet notes of his *kinor* (lyre). Among these solitary hills, under the vast sky, he developed a strong religious streak; God was a father-figure who would punish him when he sinned but would bring him to greatness and sustain him against his enemies. That feeling of close communion with the Lord was to remain with him through all the trials and triumphs of his life.

King Saul began to suffer from fits of melancholy, tinged with violence. Feelings of guilt, and of rejection by the Lord, preyed on his mind after he had been spurned by his spiritual mentor Samuel. 'Now the Spirit of the Lord departed from Saul, and an evil spirit from the Lord tormented him' (1 Sam. 16:14). One of his retainers had heard of the handsome youth in Bethlehem who was skilled with the lyre, and brought him to the palace in the hope that the music might soothe his disturbed master. Saul was charmed by the young David, and made him his personal armour-bearer. When his black moods came on him, David played to him 'so Saul was refreshed, and was well, and the evil spirit departed from him' (1 Sam. 16:23).

*David and Goliath*   The Bible also tells another, probably later, story of how David first came to Saul's attention. In the valley of Elah, in the Judean foothills, Saul's army faced the Philistine forces across a narrow ravine. Neither side wanted to launch an attack, as its soldiers would be exposed to clouds of arrows while crossing the boulder-strewn stream bed and climbing up the opposing slope. In this military stalemate, the Philistines resorted to the time-honoured custom of single combat between two champions. They produced a massive soldier from the city of Gath, wearing a helmet and armour of bronze and equipped with a javelin, a great sword and a spear. His name was Goliath. Every morning he would parade up and down between the two armies, preceded by his shield-bearer, and shout, 'I defy the ranks of Israel this day; give me a man, that we may fight together' (1 Sam. 17:10). No Israelite soldier was prepared to take on the jeering giant. Day by day Saul watched helplessly as the morale of his humiliated army sank lower.

The Israelite tribesmen enlisted for a campaign depended on the food supplies sent by their families. Jesse's three eldest sons were serving with Saul. David was sent with provisions for them loaded onto a small cart, and told to bring back a report on his brothers' welfare. Jesse prudently included ten cheeses as a gift for the officers of his sons.

From Bethlehem to the valley of Elah was a distance of some twelve miles down a mountain ravine. David set out at dawn and arrived in the camp in time to witness the daily spectacle of Goliath's challenge. David went around speaking indignantly to the soldiers about the need to kill 'this uncircumcised Philistine'. He was told that whoever did so would gain riches and the hand of the king's daughter in marriage. His exasperated eldest brother rebuked him for impudence and said he should be home minding the sheep. Saul heard about the unusual young man in the camp

David playing to the disturbed Saul. A lithograph
by the modern German artist Otto Dix.

and sent for him. When David volunteered to go and fight Goliath, the king did not take it seriously. Unabashed, David declared that the Lord who had helped him to slay lions and bears when they attacked his flocks would enable him to stand up to Goliath as well. Impressed by the youth's utter conviction, Saul agreed to let him try. The king's own armour was put on David and a sword girded at his side. Thus equipped, David 'tried in vain to go, for he was not used to them' (1 Sam. 17:39). He shed the accoutrements and went out towards Goliath armed with nothing but a staff in one hand, his sling in the other and five smooth stones from the stream in his shepherd's bag. The astounded Goliath gazed with disdain at this puny foe. 'Am I a dog,' he roared, 'that you come to me with sticks? ... I will give your flesh to the birds of the air and to the beasts of the field' (1 Sam. 17:43,44). David called back that he needed no sword or spear because he came in the name of the Lord.

As Goliath lumbered forward, David put a stone in his sling and let fly. The stone embedded itself in the forehead of the giant who was killed on the spot, falling forward on his face. David leapt forward, seized Goliath's sword and lopped off his head. With their champion so dramatically eliminated, the Philistines turned and fled, with the Israelites in hot pursuit.

Once more David was brought before the king, this time carrying the bloody trophy of Goliath's head. Saul took him into his service on the spot. Jonathan, the king's son, was so captivated by David that he bestowed on him his own robe, armour and weapons. The two young men were to remain devoted friends.

*Saul's Resentment* As the king's favourite, David rose rapidly at court. He also distinguished himself as a battle commander when Saul sent him to lead forays. Handsome and brave, he became a hero with the public. When they returned from the Philistine campaign, the women came out to greet them, singing 'Saul has slain his thousands, and David his ten thousands' (1 Sam. 18:7). The royal favourite changed in Saul's eyes to a royal rival, and his love for David turned to hatred. In one of his fits of depression, Saul twice hurled his javelin at David without hitting him. Since a seasoned warrior like Saul could hardly have missed a man at close quarters, it would seem that he shrank from shedding David's blood with his own hand. Instead, David was sent on dangerous missions,

but each time he came back successful, and a more popular figure than before.

As an added inducement to fight 'the Lord's battles' at the risk of his life, David was promised the king's elder daughter Merab as his wife. However, while he was away in the field, she was married to someone else. Learning that David and his younger daughter Michal were in love with each other, Saul pretended to approve the match. When David demurred that he came from a poor family and would not be able to afford a marriage price suitable for a royal princess, Saul said that the only gift he required from the prospective bridegroom was to slay a hundred Philistine soldiers and bring back their foreskins as proof. (The Philistines, comparative newcomers from the Aegean Sea, were the only people in the Canaanite area who did not practise circumcision.) Saul assumed that David would not come back alive from the impossible task he had been set. David amply proved the contrary by returning with no less than two hundred Philistine foreskins. Saul was compelled to carry out his commitment, and David was married to Michal. He had become the son-in-law of a ruler whose mind was bent on his destruction.

Caught between his father and his friend, *David's* Jonathan tried in vain to persuade Saul that there *Flight* was no reason to doubt the loyalty of David. In one of the king's evil moods, David had to flee for his life. That night Saul sent men to ambush and assassinate David when he came out of his house next morning. Michal saved him by lowering him through the window. To gain time for his escape she put a dummy under his bedclothes, with goats' hair at the head, and pretended that her husband was ill.

David found asylum with the prophet Samuel at Ramah. The men Saul sent to capture him were deflected by the frenzied leaping and singing of the band of prophets maintained by Samuel. From Ramah, David made his way back by stealth to the vicinity of Gibeah and arranged a secret meeting with Jonathan in an empty field. Jonathan undertook to find out how his father now felt about David, and to let his friend know by a prearranged signal. When Saul enquired why David had failed to appear for the ceremonial meal at the new moon, Jonathan replied that David had gone off to Bethlehem to attend his family sacrifices. Saul flew into a rage, abused Jonathan for his devotion to David, and even

David slays Goliath. Engraving from Julius Schnorr von Carolsfeld's *De Bibel in Bilden*, published in Germany (1851) and in English translation (1860).

threatened to kill his son. In deep distress, Jonathan went to the field where David was hiding behind a pile of boulders. Pretending to practise his archery, Jonathan shot three arrows beyond the boulders. By this sign, David knew the worst. The youth attending Jonathan was told to pick up the arrows and go ahead towards the city. David then came out of his hiding place. The two friends embraced and took tearful leave of each other. They would not meet again.

As a destitute and unarmed fugitive, David reached the sanctuary at Nob, just outside Jerusalem, where the survivors of the Shiloh priesthood had settled. David pretended to Ahimelech, the high priest, that he was on urgent business for the king, and that his men were waiting nearby. He asked for food and arms. After assuring the priest that his men had not had sexual intercourse recently and were in a state of ritual purity, David was given some of the holy bread from the altar, since no ordinary bread was available. He was also handed the sword of Goliath, that had been preserved in the sanctuary. David then went on his way.

The priests were to pay a dreadful price for their help. By chance, David's visit was observed by the king's chief herdsman, Doeg the Edomite, who went and told his master about it. Saul sent for the priests, had them brought before him, and charged them with conspiring with David against the king. Ahimelech denied the charge. How, he asked, could they be blamed for assisting the king's distinguished son-in-law, the commander of his palace guard? Beside himself with fury, Saul remained deaf to the plea. He ordered his men to kill all the eighty-five priests lined up before him, but none of the Israelites present was prepared to commit so sacrilegious an act. The order was carried out by the non-Israelite, Doeg. He then went to Nob and killed everyone left there – except for Abiathar the son of Ahimelech, who escaped carrying with him the sacred ephod.

*The Hunted Outlaw*  Realising that he could not be safe anywhere in Saul's realm, David crossed into Philistine territory and slipped into the city of Gath, ruled by king Achish. One of the palace retainers thought he recognized the stranger as the famous Israelite commander, and hauled him before the king. The quick-witted David feigned madness, scratching at the door with his nails and drooling down his beard. Achish reprimanded the servant for bothering him with an obvious lunatic and ordered him to turn David loose.

Making for the familiar hills of his boyhood, David went into hiding in a large cave at Adullam, a little southwest of Bethlehem. Here he was joined by his brothers, together with a motley collection of fugitives, outcasts and rebels. He turned them into a band of four hundred tough guerrilla fighters, ready to follow him anywhere. Fearing that Saul might take reprisals against his parents, David brought them across the Dead Sea and persuaded the king of Moab to give them asylum. The shepherd lad who had made such a dazzling rise to fame and high command now suddenly found himself a hunted brigand chief.

David heard that the town of Keilah, in southern Judah, was being threatened by Philistine raiders. He led his men to the town's rescue and drove back the Philistines. The grateful inhabitants feted them and invited them to stay. When Saul received a report about this, his soldier's mind promptly saw a chance to trap David and his elusive hillmen inside the walls. David forestalled this move. Feeling insecure inside the town, he turned for advice to Abiathar, the surviving priest from Nob, who had joined him. Using the divining powers of the ephod, the priest warned David that the citizens of Keilah would hand him over if Saul's troops descended on them.

David immediately forsook the amenities of the town and withdrew into the rocky ridges of Ziph, looking down the great escarpment of the Judean desert towards the Dead Sea gleaming far below. The men of Ziph betrayed the presence of these bandits to Saul. David moved further south, where he was cut off in the hills by an expedition led by Saul. Luckily for his cornered quarry, Saul had to turn back to meet a new Philistine attack.

David took his men down to the Dead Sea where they went to earth in the cave-riddled cliffs above En-gedi (the Spring of the Wild Goat). Saul resumed his obsessive pursuit. With a force of three thousand men he tried to flush David and his followers out of their bleak refuge.

Saul entered an opening in the rock to relieve himself, unaware that David and a handful of his men were hiding in the dark recesses of the cave. David's excited followers whispered to him that this was a heaven-sent chance to kill his enemy.

David refused to lay a hand on 'the Lord's anointed'. Instead, he crept stealthily forward and cut a piece of cloth from the hem of Saul's robe. Emerging from the cave behind Saul, David called out to him. When Saul spun round, David threw himself to the ground and swore that he had never done anything to merit Saul's anger. He held up the piece of cloth to show that he had spared Saul's life when the king had been at his mercy. Overcome with emotion, Saul called back, 'You are more righteous than I; for you have repaid me good, whereas I have repaid you evil' (1 Sam. 24:17). Saul then abandoned the expedition and withdrew his troops.

According to another version of this incident from an earlier source, David stole at night into Saul's camp, accompanied only by his nephew Abishai. They reached the place where Saul lay sleeping on the ground next to his cousin and army commander, Abner the son of Ner. David was urged by Abishai to kill the king, but he refused. Instead, he took Saul's spear and water jar, and they made their way out of the camp without rousing anyone. The next morning David shouted across the ravine, brandished the sword and jar and taunted Abner for not keeping better watch over his royal master. When Saul recognized his voice, David protested that he was guiltless and Saul had no reason to seek his life, 'like one who hunts a partridge in the mountains' (1 Sam. 26:20). Saul admitted that he had erred, and withdrew his troops. David moved back into the southern hill country to the district of Maon, on the edge of the Judean desert.

It was now that the prophet Samuel died, and was mourned by all the Israelites. He was buried in his hometown of Ramah.

*Abigail*    In the village of Carmel, just north of Maon, there lived a wealthy but surly sheep farmer called Nabal, a member of the Caleb clan. David sent a group of his young men to Nabal at the time of the customary feast given after the sheep-shearing. They courteously asked Nabal for some provisions, pointing out that David's band had throughout the winter protected Nabal's flocks grazing in the hills. (A prudent guerilla leader, David was careful to maintain good relations with the local farmers, on whom he depended for his supplies.) Nabal roughly rebuffed David's men. He said he had never heard of David; the countryside was full of runaway slaves and he had no food to spare for them. When David's men

came back with this insolent answer, he swore he would get even. Leaving part of his men behind, he led a raiding party along the mountain trail towards Nabal's homestead, threatening to wipe out the farmer with all his retainers.

Nabal's wife Abigail was a comely and intelligent woman. When she heard from the servants what had happened, she acted on her own to ward off David's reprisals. Without saying anything to her disagreeable husband, she had a large quantity of provisions loaded onto donkeys: bread, wine, carcasses of sheep, grain, raisins and dried figs. Setting out towards David's base, she met him coming the other way. She threw herself on the ground in front of him, begged him to ignore her husband's meanness and offered him the gifts she had brought. She was sure, Abigail declared, that David was destined to greatness; he would not want to look back and recall that he had shed blood just to revenge an insult from an unworthy man. David's anger died down at the plea of this attractive farmer's wife. He accepted the provisions and turned back.

On her return home, Abigail found her husband in drunken good spirits at the feast. She did not tell him about her meeting with David until he had sobered up next morning. Nabal was so enraged that he suffered a paralytic stroke and died ten days later.

When the news reached David, he sent Abigail a proposal of marriage. She promptly accepted it and went to join David, accompanied by five maids. This union served a useful political purpose as it gave David a tie with the sub-tribe of Caleb, the dominant group in Hebron and the surrounding hill area. Some time after, David took another wife, Ahinoam, from the village of Jezreel, also in the Hebron hills. Meanwhile, Saul had married off his daughter Michal, David's first wife, to someone else, a certain Palti the son of Laish.

Despite the incidents in which David had *David Serves* spared Saul's life, the breach between the two *Achish* men remained unhealed. All David and his followers could hope for was to continue their precarious existence on the fringes of society. The life of outlaws had become even more difficult for them now that they had acquired wives and children. David decided to lead his followers out of Israelite territory and to seek service with King Achish of Gath. For David's men, who now numbered six hundred, this meant a respite from Saul's relentless pressure and easier conditions for their families. Achish, for his part, no doubt saw in this unexpected Israelite defection a chance to undermine the allegiance to Saul of southern Judah. Moreover, a large contingent of such seasoned fighting men strengthened his own forces.

At David's request, Achish sent him and his men southward to operate in the region where the border between Philistia and Judah merged into the open desert. David was given command over the town of Ziklag, between Beersheba and Gaza. From this base, he carried out forays against the troublesome nomad tribes in the northern Negev, wiping out their encampments and capturing their livestock as booty. These activities enhanced David's reputation among the Israelite inhabitants in the border areas of southern Judah, who had been suffering from the nomad raids. However, in reporting to his master Achish, David pretended that he was operating against his own countrymen, or against tribes allied with the Israelites like the Kenites. As a result, Achish came to believe that David had thrown in his lot with the Philistines for good.

The chronic conflict between the Israelites and the Philistines moved towards a climax. Still smarting from the blows Saul had dealt them in the early part of his reign, the five Philistine kings gathered their forces for a decisive battle. Their marshalling area was at Aphek at the edge of the central coastal plain, where half a century earlier they had defeated the Israelites and captured the sacred Ark. From Aphek a powerful Philistine army marched northward along the plain of Sharon and then swung eastward into the valley of Jezreel, where they already held the strategic fortified cities of Megiddo and Beth-shan. They pitched camp on the hill of Moreh at Shunem. Saul mobilized the Israelite forces and deployed them on the slopes of Mount Gilboa, across the valley from the Philistines and out of reach of their dreaded battle chariots.

The launching of the Philistine campaign placed David in an agonizing predicament. Achish insisted that David and his men join in the advance and march in the rear of the Philistine forces. David had no intention of going into battle against his own people. But he did not know how to extricate his men and himself from the expedition. Fortunately the other Philistine kings did not share Achish's trust in his Hebrew

henchmen. What, they maintained, was to stop David's men going over to the other side in the heat of the battle? Achish had to yield to the pressure of his colleagues. Rather apologetically he told David to take his men back to Ziklag. Barely concealing his relief, David promptly complied.

On the eve of the fateful battle Saul was in an *The Witch of* agitated frame of mind. He had tried to obtain *Endor* some reassuring sign from the Lord through all the usual means – prophets, dreams, and the casting of the sacred lots – but there had been no response. He was haunted by the memory of the old prophet Samuel who had made him king and then fiercely rejected him in the name of God. Only Samuel could help him now; Samuel was dead, so had to be sought out beyond the grave. Saul asked his servants to find out discreetly whether there was in the vicinity a medium whom he could consult. They reported that there was an old woman at the village of Endor, in the Jezreel valley near Mount Tabor, who was reputed to possess occult powers.

That night Saul put on simple garments to conceal his identity and, with two men accompanying him, found his way on foot to the old crone's cottage. When asked whether she would summon up a spirit, she answered tartly that the king had banished all fortune-tellers and mediums on pain of death, and she was not going to fall into any trap. Saul assured her that no harm would come to her and asked her to 'Bring up Samuel for me' (1 Sam. 28:11). Recognizing her royal visitor, she agreed to comply.

In a little while the wraith of an old man in a cloak rose from the ground, and demanded to know why he had been disturbed. Saul bowed down to the ground and voiced his distress: the Philistines were about to attack; God had deserted him; what was he to do? Samuel was as grim and unforgiving in death as he had been with Saul when alive. Saul, he insisted, had been rejected by God. On the following day, the Israelites would be defeated. Saul and his sons would be killed!

At these words of doom Saul fell down, overcome with fear and grief. He was also faint with hunger, as he had fasted all day while trying to communicate with the Lord. The old woman and the two men lifted him onto her bed, and she prepared food for him. When he had recovered, he returned to the camp.

The next day the Philistine troops stormed up the slopes of Mount Gilboa and broke through the Israelite lines, overcoming the defence in savage hand-to-hand fighting. Jonathan and two of his brothers were killed. Saul was badly wounded by an arrow and begged his armour-bearer to despatch him, rather than allow him to be captured alive. The man could not bring himself to kill the king, who then fell upon his own sword.

*The Death of Saul*

When the Philistines found Saul's body among the slain they cut off his head, stripped off his armour for display in the temple of their goddess Ashtaroth, and hung his body on the wall of Beth-shan together with the bodies of his three sons. When the men of Jabesh-gilead across the Jordan river heard the dreadful news, they recalled how Saul had rescued the town from the Ammonites many years before. A group of them went to Beth-shan under cover of darkness, retrieved the bodies and had them cremated and buried under a tamarisk tree outside their town. They mourned the dead king for seven days.

Sent back by Achish, David and his men reached Ziklag on the third day, after forced marches. They were met by a desolate scene. During their absence, an Amalekite raiding party had seized and looted the town and carried off the women and children. David's tired men broke down and wept, then bitterly blamed him for having left their families unprotected. David set aside his grief for his own two wives and rallied his men to set out in pursuit. At the Besor wadi south of Gaza, two hundred men who were too exhausted to go further were left behind with most of the baggage, while the rest pushed forward. In the desert they found a youth in a state of collapse. He was an Egyptian slave who had been taken ill and had been abandoned without food and water by his Amalekite master. He guided them to the encampment where the nomads were celebrating their successful raid. David's men made a surprise attack on them at dusk and wiped out those who did not get away on the camels. The Israelite women and children were recovered unharmed, and the livestock and possessions of the Amalekites were taken as spoil. David ordered that the two hundred men left behind with the equipment should get their full share of the booty. Part of it was handed back to the Israelite towns and villages in the area.

A few days after their return to Ziklag, a young man staggered into the town with his clothes torn and earth upon his head – the traditional signs of mourning. He said he was an Amalekite living among the Israelites. On Mount Gilboa he had seen the Israelites defeated, and at the request of the badly wounded king Saul he had killed the king with a sword. As proof of his story he produced Saul's crown and bracelet. He added that the king's son Jonathan was among the slain. David and all his fellow-Israelites in the town were plunged into grief. The man who had brought the tidings was put to death on David's order, because on his own admission he had slain the Lord's anointed.

Out of David's bereavement and shock came his immortal lament for Saul and Jonathan:

Thy glory, O Israel, is slain upon thy high
    places!
  How are the mighty fallen!
Tell it not in Gath,
    publish it not in the streets of Ashkelon;
lest the daughters of the Philistines rejoice,
    lest the daughters of the uncircumcised exult.

Ye mountains of Gilboa,
    let there be no dew or rain upon you,
    nor upsurging of the deep!
For there the shield of the mighty was
    defiled,
    the shield of Saul, not anointed with oil. . . .

Saul and Jonathan, beloved and lovely!
  In life and in death they were not divided;
they were swifter than eagles,
  they were stronger than lions. . . .

I am distressed for you, my brother Jonathan;
    very pleasant have you been to me;
    your love to me was wonderful, passing the
    love of women.
                              (2 Sam. 1:19–21,23,26)

## The Reign of David ( 1000–961 BC )

THE SHATTERING ISRAELITE DEFEAT ON MOUNT Gilboa again opened the northern and central hill regions to Philistine control. Saul's kinsman and general, Abner, gathered the remnants of his forces and retreated across the river Jordan to Mahanaim, the main Israelite town in the land of Gilead. With him went Saul's youngest son. His name was Ish-baal (Man of God) but later biblical writers contemptuously dubbed him Ish-bosheth (man of shame). The text mentions that he was forty years old, but that may be a corruption, since it is unlikely that he was an adult at that time. In Mahanaim, Abner had him crowned king of all Israel, in order to maintain Saul's line intact and make his heir a focus of resistance.

*David King in Hebron*  With Saul gone, David was free to lead his men back to Israelite territory. He established himself in Hebron, where he was elected king of Judah. The largest and most important of the tribes, Judah had always tended to be somewhat apart from the others. It was free of Philistine domination and felt no allegiance to Saul's son in Mahanaim, so the way was clear for David to head an independent Judahite state. One of his first acts was to make a gesture to the land of Gilead where Ish-bosheth had been proclaimed. David sent a message to the inhabitants of the town of Jabesh-gilead, commending them for recovering and interring the bodies of Saul and his sons.

*Encounter at the Pool of Gibeon*  There followed a period of a confused power-struggle between the two Israelite thrones – that of David in Hebron and that of Ish-bosheth in Mahanaim. A contingent of soldiers led by Abner crossed over from Trans-jordan and reached Gibeon, a town in the territory of Benjamin, north-west of Jerusalem. Here they were intercepted by a detachment from Judah led by Joab, David's nephew and commander. The two forces faced each other across 'the pool of Gibeon', a huge round cistern connected by a tunnel to springs outside the town wall. After a parley, it was agreed that the battle should be decided by a contest between twelve men picked from each side. They faced each other in pairs, 'And each caught his opponent by the head, and thrust his sword in his opponent's side; so they fell down together' (2 Sam. 2:16). With the issue left undecided, general fighting broke out. Abner retreated with his surviving men, pursued by those of Joab. Joab's younger brother Asahel was as fast as a gazelle. He caught up with Abner and attacked him. Abner tried in vain to head him off and was forced to kill him with his spear.

For the time being, a truce was arranged and the pursuit called off. Abner and his men marched all night to get across the Jordan, and returned to Mahanaim. Joab and his brother Abishai, sons of David's eldest sister Zeruiah, brought their men back to Hebron. The body of the third brother, Asahel, was buried in the family tomb at Bethlehem. From then on, Joab nursed an implacable blood-feud against Abner.

*Civil War*  The intermittent civil war between the two Israelite monarchies dragged on for another two years, with David's prestige and influence steadily rising. Abner, a fine soldier and an honourable man, had acted out of loyalty to Saul's memory. But he became disillusioned with Ish-bosheth, the weak and petty puppet king he had put on the throne. The final break came when Ish-bosheth accused Abner of having intercourse with Saul's concubine Rizpah, an act which could be construed as a symbolic claim to the succession.

The outraged Abner made up his mind that the time had come to unite the kingdom under David. He secretly sent a message to David offering to bring about this union. David made one stipulation: his former wife Michal must be restored to him. Abner insisted that Ish-bosheth have his sister brought back to David. Her distraught second husband ran weeping behind the chariot until Abner ordered him to go back home. Whatever feeling David may still have had for Michal after their years of separation, her return was a shrewd political move. With his marriage to Saul's daughter revived, David had a straight claim to Saul's throne.

Abner conferred with the elders of the other tribes and persuaded them to transfer their allegiance to David. It was of great importance that he managed to win over Benjamin, his own tribe and that of Saul. Benjamin was also in a key geographical position, since its narrow strip of territory was a border-land between Judah and the other tribes in the centre and north.

With the ground prepared, Abner went to visit David at Hebron, with a bodyguard of twenty men. David gave a feast in his honour. Abner then left to arrange a formal covenant between David and the northern tribes, as a basis for his election as their king. Just after his departure, Joab returned from a foray and was furious to learn what had happened. Behind David's back, he sent a runner to catch up with Abner and invite him to return. Joab waited for Abner at the city gate, drew him away from his men on the pretext of wanting to speak to him privately, and suddenly stabbed him to death. By this ruthless assassination, Joab avenged the killing of his younger brother Asahel at the hands of Abner.

David's Empire
Early 10th century BC

Euphrates R.

Tiphsah

CYPRUS

Hamath

HAMATH

Arvad

Tadmor

GREAT SEA

Gebal
(Byblos)

SIDONIANS

ZOBAH
ARAM

Lebo-Hamath

BETH — REHOB

Sidon

ARAM DAMASCUS

Izon

Damascus

Tyre

Dan

Kedesh

MAACHAH

Accho

ISRAEL

Dor

Meggido

Beth-shan

Ramoth-Gilead

Shechem

Mahanaim

Joppa

Rabbath-
Ammon — AMMON

Bethel

Ashdod

Jerusalem

Karkor

PHILISTINES

Gath

Gaza

Dead Sea

Aroer

Hebron

MOAB

Beersheba

Kir-Moab

JUDAH

Zoar

Kadesh-barnea

EDOM

EGYPT

Teman

Judah and Israel

Conquered Kingdom

Sphere of Influence

Ezion-geber

Interior Border    Border of David's Empire    0          50

miles

There may also have been another hidden motive: the accession to David of Saul's redoubtable and experienced general would certainly have endangered Joab's position as commander-in-chief.

Abner's murder came as more than a personal shock to David. It also imperilled the election by the northern tribes that Abner had negotiated for him. They would find it hard to believe that Joab, David's kinsman and trusted commander, had acted entirely without David's knowledge. In a rolling curse the angry David wished on the male members of Joab's household the afflictions of gonorrhea, effeminacy, starvation and death in battle. As for Joab and his brother Abishai, David declared feelingly that 'these men the sons of Zeruiah are too hard for me' (2 Sam. 3:39). At the same time he refrained from punishing or even dismissing them. His two nephews were tough and dangerous men; they had been at his side through thick and thin in the lean outlaw years; and he would need them in the struggles to come.

In public, David put the best face he could on the ugly affair. Abner was buried with full honours, with the king himself leading the mourners. At the graveside David recited a poem of lament for Abner. A general fast and period of mourning were decreed. 'So all the people and all Israel understood that day that it had not been the king's will to slay Abner the son of Ner' (2 Sam. 3:37).

Abner's death knocked out the main prop of Ish-bosheth's shaky kingship, and he slumped into a mood of pessimism. Soon after, he too was murdered. Two brothers serving as officers in his army came to his home while he was having a siesta in the heat of the day. The woman at the door had dozed off while sifting wheat. They stole past her into the house, stabbed Ish-bosheth, cut off his head, and brought the grisly trophy to David in Hebron, expecting a rich reward. He had them executed on the spot for slaying 'a righteous man in his own house upon his bed' (2 Sam. 4:11). The head of Ish-Bosheth was decently interred in Abner's tomb at Hebron.

There was now no obstacle left to David's assuming rule over a united Hebrew nation. The leaders of the northern and central tribes came together at Hebron, entered into a covenant with David, and anointed him as their king. (That was the last occasion when a Hebrew king came to power by election through the representatives of the people in the way that the charismatic judges had received their mandate in an earlier period.)

Hebron had been an adequate capital for David as long as he held jurisdiction only over the territory of Judah. With his rule extended over all the Israelite tribes, he needed a national capital more centrally located and less identified with his own tribe. The city of Jerusalem would ideally meet these two requirements. It lay twenty miles north of Hebron in the territory of Benjamin, between the two leading Israelite tribes, Judah and Ephraim. At the same time, it had remained an enclave in possession of the Jebusites, a Canaanite people, and therefore did not belong to any Israelite tribe. The problem was that the capture of the city by armed assault was a daunting task. *The Taking of Jerusalem*

The Jebusite city was small and narrow, perched along the spur of Ophel. On three sides the spur was bounded by steep valleys – Kidron to the east, the Tyropean valley (as it was later called) to the west, and the vale of Hinnom at the southern end. The actual taking of the city is described in the Bible in a few brief and puzzling verses. The defenders declared to David, 'You will not come in here, but the blind and the lame will ward you off' (2 Sam. 5:6). David told his men: 'Whoever would smite the Jebusites, let him get up the water shaft to attack the lame and the blind' (2 Sam. 5:8). The Book of Chronicles adds that Joab was the first to break through, and the city fell.

The Jebusites had apparently lined up these afflicted persons along the ramparts – but why? The usual explanation is that they felt secure behind their walls and natural defences, and were showing their contempt for the Israelite attackers. That is improbable, however, since they were facing the renowned David with all the strength of a united Israelite nation at his disposal. Another theory, pointing in the opposite direction, was that the Jebusites felt isolated and afraid, and resorted to a psychological barrier instead of relying just on their physical fortifications. It was a common superstition that whoever harmed an afflicted person would himself be afflicted. If so, it took the tough and intrepid Joab to lead the attack in disregard of supernatural fears.

The biblical account raises a second scholastic question, concerning the Hebrew word *tsinnor*, rendered in the above-quoted passage as 'water shaft'. The accepted interpretation has been that the attackers gained their initial access to the city by creeping through the conduit that brought water from the spring of Gihon outside the wall. For historical and technical reasons that is not a credible surmise. Some Bible experts have suggested that the Hebrew word *tsinnor* does not in this context have its ordinary meaning of a water pipe or conduit, but stands either for a weapon shaped like a trident, or a grappling iron with several points used for scaling walls.

*The Battle of Rephaim* While David sat in Hebron as king only of Judah, he had not been under any Philistine pressure. The nearest Philistine city-state on the coastal plain was Gath; its king, Achish, had been David's overlord and seems to have remained well-disposed towards him. In any event, the Philistine leaders had observed an internal power-struggle going on that had kept their Israelite neighbours weak and divided. They now woke up to the fact that all the Israelite tribes had united under David, who had by the capture of Jerusalem eliminated the last Canaanite stronghold in Israelite territory. The Philistines promptly reacted to this display of strength and independence from the people they still regarded as their vassals. An army was sent to take Jerusalem away from David. It probably marched up the pass of Sorek (through which the railway now runs) and reached the open vale of Rephaim to the southwest of the city. Here David's men attacked and repulsed them, capturing and destroying the idols they carried with them.

The Philistines advanced a second time and again took up a position in the vale of Rephaim. David attacked them from the rear at dusk. The signal for the assault was the rustling of the evening breeze in a balsam grove, like the sound of an army on the march. The Philistines retreated in disorder down the pass of Horon to the northwest of Jerusalem, and were pursued by the Israelites as far as the edge of Philistine territory.

*The Bringing of the Ark* As Jerusalem had not previously been in Israelite possession, it became known as David's City in honour of its conqueror. He left the Jebusite town intact within its walls but extended it northward to meet the needs of a capital. An area along the ridge above the city was filled in to provide a site for an unpretentious palace of stone and cedarwood, with additional buildings for the royal retinue and the palace guard. A tomb was also constructed for the royal family, the only persons who by tradition could be buried within a walled city.

With Jerusalem securely established as the political capital of the kingdom, David decided to make it the religious centre as well. The Ark of the Covenant, the most sacred object of the Hebrew faith, had for twenty years been lying in obscurity in the village of Kiriath-jearim, eleven miles west of Jerusalem. At the head of a great procession, David went to fetch the Ark. It was carried on a newly-made cart drawn by oxen, to the jubilant sound of singing and music. The cart was guided by two sons of Abinadab, the man who had taken care of the Ark from the time it had been recovered from its Philistine captivity. One son, Uzzah, walked alongside the cart, and the other Ahio, led the oxen. Along the way the animals stumbled and Uzzah grabbed the Ark to steady it. He was struck dead on the spot. Fearful of this sign of divine displeasure, David suspended the project. A house nearby belonged to Obed-edom, a native of the Philistine city of Gath who had settled in the Judean hills. David arranged for him to take custody of the Ark, presumably because an Israelite would have dreaded doing so.

During the next three months, nothing untoward happened to Obed-edom. On the contrary, he and his household prospered. David felt that it was safe to resume the interrupted journey of the Ark. It was brought in triumph into Jerusalem and deposited in a tabernacle he had prepared. A great crowd of worshippers gathered and David led the ritual dancing, dressed in a short ephod, the priestly apron. His wife Michal watched the spectacle from a window of the palace. When David returned home that evening, she greeted him with scorn. The king, she said, had been leaping about and exposing his person like a vulgar fellow in front of all the common serving maids. David retorted angrily that the Lord had chosen him to reign in place of her father's house: 'I will be abased in your eyes; but by the maids of whom you have spoken, by them I shall be held in honour' (2 Sam. 6:22).

Michal's outburst must have given vent to years of bitterness and wounded pride. As a king's daughter, she had fallen in love with and married the young and dazzling David. Life had been cruel to her since then. Her father and brothers had been slain. She herself had been forced to leave her second husband, and had become one of many women in David's harem. What was worse, she had remained barren, in a household teeming with the offspring of David's wives and concubines. Now the festive day of the Ark's arrival had been ruined for David by the ugly quarrel she had forced on him. On this note their relationship came to an end. The last reference to her in the Bible is the terse statement that she had no child to the day of her death.

David's family had grown steadily. During the seven to eight years he reigned in Hebron, the number of his wives had increased to six, each of whom had a son at that time. Three of these sons were to play an important part in later events: Amnon the first-born, whose mother was Ahinoam of Jezreel; Absalom the son of Maacah, daughter of Talmai king of Geshur; and Adonijah, the son of Haggith. During the Jerusalem years, David took a number of additional wives and concubines, thereby gaining a large harem befitting the status and prestige of a monarch. He also had eleven more sons and an unknown number of daughters. Only one of the daughters is mentioned by name, Tamar.

*Saul's Offspring*  A three-year drought and famine in the kingdom was interpreted as a punishment for the wrong Saul was alleged to have committed against the Gibeonites. They were a small Canaanite community northwest of Jerusalem that had, by a subterfuge, obtained from Joshua a guarantee of their safety at the time of the Conquest. They now claimed that in his zeal to clear the hill-country of Canaanite elements, Saul had attacked them and killed a number of them. When David was informed that the disastrous drought was linked to this charge, he offered the Gibeonites any compensation they might want in order to expiate the blood-guilt. They insisted that the only way was to hand Saul's male descendants over to them for execution. David was reluctantly persuaded to yield to this grim accounting. Two sons Saul had had by his concubine Rizpah, and five sons of his elder daughter Merab were delivered to the Gibeonites. They hanged them on the top of a hill next to their town, and left the bodies exposed on a flat rock.

The bereaved Rizpah made herself a shelter of sackcloth and kept a lonely vigil next to the rock. From the beginning of the barley harvest in early summer to the first rains in autumn she protected the bodies against carrion crows by day and animal scavengers by night. When the drought had broken David tried to make amends for the tragedy. He sent to Jabesh-gilead in Transjordan for the bones of Saul and Jonathan and had them reinterred in the tomb of Saul's father Kish together with the bones of Saul's seven hanged offspring.

David was able to help one, at any rate, of Saul's descendants. The love David had felt for Jonathan prompted him to make enquiries whether any member of his dead friend's family was still alive. A man called Ziba, who had been one of Saul's chief retainers, was brought to the king. He disclosed that Jonathan's son Mephibosheth was in Gilead across the Jordan. He had been a child of five when his father and grandfather were slain in the battle of Mount Gilboa. During the hurried flight across the Jordan river after the battle his nurse had dropped him, and he was so badly injured that he remained a cripple in both legs. He was now living in the house of Machir, in the village of Lodebar. David immediately had the young man brought to Jerusalem and kept him in the royal household as if he were one of David's own sons. All the lands that had belonged to Saul were given to Mephibosheth, and their care and cultivation entrusted to Ziba as steward. In this way David carried out the oath of mutual loyalty, and of concern for each other's descendants, that he had sworn with Jonathan when they parted.

*The Expansion of the Kingdom*  In David's time, the Israelite territory and the surrounding area lay in a power-vacuum, free from domination by the great imperial centres of Egypt to the south-west and Mesopotamia to the north-east. A brilliant political and military leader, David exploited this situation and extended the sway of his kingdom until it became the strongest state in the region.

His first task was to break the power of the Philistine league of city-states, that for the best part of a century had been the most formidable foe of the Israelites. The Philistine defeat in the vale of Rephaim had blocked their bid to reassert control of the hill terrain. David now launched a counter-offensive against the Philistine territory in the coastal plain. He captured Gath where he had once served its king Achish. The remaining Philistine cities – Gaza, Ashkelon, Ashdod and Ekron – appear to have come to terms with

David, as there is no mention of an attack on them. A shrunken Philistine area remained subject to Israelite mastery. In due course the Philistines lost their separate identity and became assimilated into the surrounding population.

The Canaanite enclaves that had survived since the Conquest along the maritime plain and the valley of Jezreel were absorbed into the Israelite kingdom. Their lands became royal estates administered by David's stewards. The only Canaanite people west of the Jordan that retained their autonomy were the Phoenicians along what is now the Lebanese coast, with their two great port-cities of Tyre and Sidon. Their kings were careful to maintain ties of friendship and economic co-operation with David and his successor Solomon, and with the northern kingdom of Israel after the monarchy split.

A series of campaigns was carried out east of the Jordan against the kingdoms of Edom, Moab and Ammon. The first two were subdued, and the resistance of their people broken by ruthless punitive measures. In Moab the captive soldiers were made to lie on the ground in three rows, only one of which was spared. Moab probably remained a tribute-paying vassal; while Edom, south of the Dead Sea, was placed under direct Israelite administration, supported by military garrisons.

*The Ammonite War*  The war against Ammon was tougher and more prolonged, and drew in the Aramean (Syrian) kingdoms further to the north – Maacah, Aram-Damascus, Zobah, and the unidentified district of Tob on the Hauran plateau east of the Sea of Galilee. David tried to avoid a military confrontation with Ammon. He had been on friendly terms with its king Nahash. When Nahash died and was succeeded by his son Hanun, David sent a delegation to Rabath-ammon, the capital, to convey his good wishes. The new king's counsellors persuaded him that David meant to annex his country, and that the real object of the delegation was to spy out the land. Hanun therefore treated the goodwill ambassadors in the most insulting fashion. He humiliated them by shaving off half their beards and cutting away their garments from the waist down. To spare their shame and save his own face David sent them instructions that, on their way home, they should remain in Jericho until their beards grew again.

The provocation made war inevitable. Joab led

an expeditionary force against the enemy capital, and found the Ammonite army drawn up in battle array in front of the city. In the rear of the Israelites appeared an army of Aramean mercenaries enlisted on Hanun's behalf from Zobah, Maacah and Tob. Joab found himself caught in a pincer movement and forced to fight on two fronts. Part of the Israelite force commanded by Joab's brother Abishai held the Ammonites in check, while Joab led an assault on the enemy to the rear. The Arameans broke and fled, and the Ammonites retreated within the city walls. Joab disengaged his forces and marched them back across the Jordan.

Although this first campaign against Ammon was inconclusive, the rout of the auxiliary force stunned the Aramean leaders into mounting a more serious challenge to the growing strength of David's kingdom. Hadadezer king of Zobah took the lead in organizing a joint army from the small Aramean kingdoms west of the Euphrates river. Under the command of Hadadezer's general Shobach, the army marched southward. David's strategy was to intercept and fight the Arameans before they could join forces with their Ammonite allies. Led by David in person, the Israelites advanced through Gilead, east of the Jordan river, and defeated the Aramean army at the battle of Helam, in what is now northern Jordan. Their commanding general was fatally wounded, and their chariots and horses were captured. Enough of the war-horses were kept for a hundred chariots to be absorbed into the Israelite army, and the remaining animals were hamstrung.

After the victory at Helam, the kingdoms of Zobah, Aram-Damascus and Maacah were reduced to the status of vassals. An Israelite garrison was installed in the city of Damascus. As part of the tribute exacted from the Arameans, some gold shields were handed over by Hadadezer and carried as trophies to Jerusalem.

To the north of Zobah on the Orontes river lay the kingdom of Hamath. Its ruler, Toi, now thought it politic to send a deputation to David with gifts and assurances of friendship.

The following spring, 'the time when kings go forth to battle' (2 Sam. 11:1), the campaign against Ammon was renewed – this time with Aramean intervention effectively neutralized. Joab was again in command, and laid siege to the strongly fortified Rabbath-ammon. The capture of the positions protecting the city's water supply made its fall inevitable. At Joab's suggestion, David came from Jerusalem to take personal charge of the final assault. When the city surrendered, Hanun was deposed and his crown placed on David's head, thereby making the Ammonites his subjects. They were afterwards made to serve as a reservoir of forced labour for building projects.

*David and*     The Ammonite war formed the background *Bathsheba* for David's affair with Bathsheba – the most romantic and at the same time the least worthy episode in his career.

Late one afternoon, after his siesta, the king was strolling on the flat roof of the palace. Looking down, he was captivated by the sight of a beautiful woman bathing herself in the courtyard of a house below. He sent a servant to make discreet enquiries and learnt she was Bathsheba the wife of Uriah, a Hittite officer serving with the army in the siege of Rabbath-ammon. David's messengers brought her secretly to the palace, where he made love to her. To David's dismay, he later received a message from her to tell him that she was pregnant. Since she had been carrying out the prescribed ritual washing after her menstrual period when he first saw her, only he could have been the father of the unborn child. To avert a scandal, it was imperative that Uriah should have access to his wife without delay. David sent a hurried dispatch to the army commander, Joab, requesting that Uriah be sent back with a campaign report. When he arrived, David questioned him about the progress of the war and the welfare of the troops, then sent him off with a gift to relax at his home.

To David's chagrin, Uriah spent the night in the servants' quarter of the palace. When David asked him next morning why he had not returned to his own home, the officer replied primly that while he was on active service he felt obliged to conduct himself like his fellow soldiers in the field, and do without domestic comforts. David plied him with food and drink but that did not alter his attitude; he remained in the palace compound that night as well.

When Uriah returned to the front next day, he carried with him a sealed letter from David to Joab. It read, 'Set Uriah in the forefront of the hardest fighting, and then draw back from him, that he may be struck down, and die' (2 Sam. 11:15). Joab included him in a dangerous sortie

against a sector of the city wall, and he was among those who fell in the action. After the required period of mourning David married Bathsheba, and in due course she gave birth to an infant son.

Inspired by the Lord, Nathan the court prophet had the moral courage to tackle the king about his conduct. Nathan broached the delicate subject in an indirect way. He related to David a parable about a rich man with many flocks and herds, and a poor man who owned only a single ewe lamb that had been raised in his home with his children: 'it used to eat of his morsel, and drink from his cup, and lie in his bosom, and it was like a daughter to him' (2 Sam. 12:3). When he had to extend hospitality to a visitor, the rich man took the poor man's lamb for the meal. Incensed at such heartless behaviour, David exclaimed that the rich man in the story deserved to be punished with death. The prophet dramatically pointed at the king and cried out: 'You are the man' (2 Sam. 12:7). The Lord, he said, would punish David for the evil he had done; and the child born of the illicit union would die.

When Bathsheba's child took ill, David fasted and prayed to the Lord to spare the baby. It died on the seventh day of his vigil. David rose, changed his clothes, and sat down to a meal. His perplexed retainers asked him why he had fasted and wept when the child was alive, but had returned to normal living when it died. David replied sadly, 'But now he is dead; why should I fast? Can I bring him back again? I shall go to him, but he will not return to me' (2 Sam. 12:23). After some while Bathsheba bore David another son, who was named Solomon.

David's empire now extended from the tip of *Organization* the Negev desert in the south to northern Syria. *of the Regime* Its heartland was the territory settled by the Israelite tribes on both sides of the Jordan river, between the Mediterranean coast and the desert. To the southeast, east and northeast, were the conquered neighbouring kingdoms of Edom, Moab, Ammon, Maacah, Aram-Damascus and Zobah. Within the Israelite sphere of influence also lay the kingdom of Hamath, north of Zobah, the Phoenicians (or Sidonians) along the Lebanese coast, and the Philistines in the southern maritime plain.

The campaigns had produced a sweeping reorganization of the military establishment. The hard core of the professional army came from the six hundred veterans who had been with David in

ABOVE A scribe in his workshop, copying a sacred text. An illustration from a medieval French manuscript.

RIGHT Page from the illuminated French ninth–century Alcuin Bible produced on the order of Charlemagne.

his guerilla years. They included Benjaminite archers and slingmen who could use their weapons with either hand; and Gadite spearsmen who are described as fierce-looking as lions and as swift-footed as gazelles. David's nephews Joab and Abishai were respectively the commander-in-chief and his deputy.

A special status was held by a group of 'mighty men' who had distinguished themselves by acts of valour. The roster of these famous soldiers is divided into two orders: the 'Three' and the 'Thirty'. (Actually, thirty-six names are listed.) The citations of the three outstanding heroes all describe their exploits against the Philistines. One killed eight hundred of the enemy with his spear. A second held his ground when the Israelites retreated, and fought until his hand was so stiff that he could not let go of his sword. A third made a lone stand in a field of peas till the tide of battle turned.

The leader of the Thirty was Abishai, who was credited with having personally slain three hundred of the enemy. But more space is given to another member of the group, Benaiah, who was appointed captain of David's bodyguard and later became commander-in-chief under Solomon. Several of Benaiah's great deeds are cited: he slew two powerful Moabite warriors; he killed a lion in a pit on a snowy day; and armed only with a club, he overcame a huge Egyptian spearman in single combat. Ironically, one name listed in the Thirty is Uriah the Hittite, the husband of Bathsheba.

The regular soldiers included groups of Philistine mercenaries under the command of Benaiah. It may be that the royal bodyguard was drawn from these non-Israelite soldiers because they would be immune to palace intrigues. Among them were the Cherethites, probably immigrants from the island of Crete settled in the area of the Philistines, a kindred sea-people; and Gittites, men from the Philistine city of Gath who may have joined David when he was serving their king Achish.

In the period of the Judges the fighting men had been tribal levies mobilized in an emergency and disbanded when it was over. David organized this part-time militia into a regular system of civilian reserves. Twelve formations were set up, each consisting of twenty-four thousand men commanded by one of David's senior officers. These formations were each called up for a month a year, in rotation, though in wartime there would be a more general mobilization. This balance between full-time soldiers and reserve units is the pattern followed by the modern army of the State of Israel.

Although the tribal system remained nominally in existence, the autonomy of the tribes was steadily superseded by the central powers of the kingdom, and the traditional authority of the elders by that of the king. However, some tension remained under the surface between the tribe of Judah, from which the royal dynasty was drawn, and the northern tribes grouped together under the name of Israel. A generation after David, the kingdom would break into two along these lines.

The supreme political and religious power concentrated in the hands of the king was exercised through a small royal cabinet. The person closest to David was his nephew Joab, in charge of the armed forces. The sophisticated Ahithophel, from the small town of Gilo, became the king's chief political counsellor. Jehoshaphat the *mazkir* (recorder) was the keeper of the court records and the official chronicler; Suriah the *sopher* (scribe) was the official responsible for drafting royal decrees and supervising their implementation. The two high priests, appointed by David and subordinate to him, were Zadok and Abiathar, the latter having been with David in the early outlaw days. Nathan and Gad were resident prophets at the court. Adoniram had the unpopular task of levying the corvée, the forced labour for building projects.

The tribute paid by vassal kingdoms and the income from the royal estates were the main sources of revenue for the palace exchequer.

David decided to carry out a census of the whole nation, from Dan to Beersheba. It may have served taxation purposes as well, but its primary objective was to provide the data for organizing the militia, as is shown by the appointment of Joab to carry out the census, and the tally it produced of all the 'valiant men who drew the sword'. Joab tried to talk David out of the project since by popular belief the numbering of people, or even of livestock, was an unholy act that might offend God. David was adamant and Joab carried out his orders, assisted by a team of senior army officers. *The Site for the Temple*

The census party started at Aroer, on the Arnon river east of the Dead Sea. From there they worked their way northward through Transjordan, crossed over past Dan to Tyre on the

Lebanese coast, and proceeded southward to Beersheba. The task lasted nine months and twenty days. The number of men of military age is given as five hundred thousand for Judah and eight hundred thousand for the northern tribes.

If Joab had feared retribution from the Lord, he appeared to be justified by the epidemic that broke out. A legend sprang up that it was directed by an angel of the Lord who had been seen on Mount Moriah, the top of the ridge upon which stood Jerusalem. On the advice of the prophet Gad, David and his retinue went up the hill to see Araunah the Jebusite who owned the threshing-floor where the angel was said to have appeared. Araunah offered the king the threshing floor to build an altar, together with his oxen for the sacrifice and the yokes and threshing sledges as wood for the fire. David replied, 'No, but I will buy it of you for a price; I will not offer burnt offerings to the Lord my God which cost me nothing' (2 Sam. 24:24). Araunah accepted fifty shekels of silver. The burnt offering was made on the altar and the act of expiation brought the epidemic to a halt. Araunah's threshing floor was destined to become the site of Solomon's Temple.

It seems strange that David did not himself build the Temple. An impressive permanent sanctuary would have adorned the capital he had chosen, and provided a fitting home for the Ark he had brought to it. That David had in mind to build a temple was revealed by his remark to the prophet Nathan: 'See now, I dwell in a house of cedar, but the Ark of God dwells in a tent' (2 Sam. 7:2). Nathan's spontaneous reaction was a positive one. But after communing with God that night, Nathan discouraged the king next morning. Since the Exodus, the Lord had said to Nathan, his dwelling had been a tent; why should he now want a house of cedar? It was the Lord who would give David a 'house', that is, a royal dynasty. (This is the only example in the Bible of a pun attributed to the Almighty.)

The Book of Chronicles supplies an explanation why the Temple should have been built not by David but by his son Solomon. In a farewell address to the people David claimed that God had said to him: 'You may not build a house for my name, for you are a warrior and have shed blood' (1 Chron. 28:3). The Chronicler does, however, give David a share in the credit for the Temple, by recording that he handed over to

Solomon a detailed plan for the structure together with the gold, precious stones and materials to be used for it.

With his kingdom united and peaceful and his external enemies subdued, David was at the height of his prestige. Suddenly he faced an agonizing and perilous crisis that erupted from within his own family. As so often happens in history, great political events sprang from the infatuation of a man for a woman.

Amnon, whose mother was Ahinoam, was David's eldest son and the presumptive heir to the throne. The second son was Chileab, born to Abigail in Hebron; he may have died as a child, as he disappears from the record. The next son was Absalom, born to Maacah, the daughter of the ruler of Geshur, a tiny kingdom east of the Sea of Galilee.

Absalom had a beautiful young sister called Tamar. Her half-brother Amnon fell in love with her. Tormented because there seemed to be no way he could be alone with her (since young virgins were kept in seclusion), Amnon resorted to a devious stratagem suggested by a shrewd cousin in whom he confided. He feigned illness and took to his bed. When David came to see his ailing first-born son, Amnon asked with an innocent air whether Tamar could not come and bake him some of his favourite cakes. As a solicitous father, David arranged that this be done. When she brought the cakes to his bedside, he seized hold of her and urged her to come into the bed with him. She resisted his advances, protesting that such an act would shame her and disgrace him. If he wanted to marry her, why did he not discuss the matter with their father?

By now Amnon was completely carried away by passion. He pulled her onto the bed and raped her. Then his feelings of guilt turned to hatred of his victim. He had his manservant throw her out of his house, and locked the door behind her. The distraught girl tore her long robe, put ashes on her head as a sign of grief and wandered away sobbing. Absalom took her into his house and persuaded her to keep quiet about the rape. She remained in her brother's home, a sad and lonely figure. Absalom said nothing to Amnon, but nursed thoughts of revenge. David was angry with Amnon but did nothing which might publicly discredit his crown prince.

Two years later, Absalom arranged a feast after the sheep-shearing at his estate in the hills of

*The Rape of Tamar*

Ephraim. David declined an invitation to attend, but at Absalom's insistence he gave his permission for the other princes to go, including Amnon. At the feast Amnon was made drunk, and at a prearranged signal from Absalom he was set upon and killed by the retainers. David's other sons left on their mules and rushed back to Jerusalem. Absalom fled and took refuge with his grandfather the king of Geshur. David declared him exiled from the kingdom, but longed constantly for his attractive and impulsive son.

*The Return of Absalom* When three years had gone by, Joab took steps to bring his uncle David and his cousin Absalom together again. However rough and fearless Joab was, he shrank from taking up such a sensitive matter directly with his master. Instead, he approached a clever woman he knew in the village of Tekoa, near David's home town of Bethlehem. Instructed by Joab, she dressed herself in mourning and obtained an audience with the king. According to the story she told, she had been left a widow with two sons. One day they quarrelled in the fields and one killed the other. Her family were now demanding that she hand over the other son, who would be put to death for his crime. She appealed to David for help, lest she be bereft of both sons and there would be nobody left to carry on the family name. David told her not to worry; he would take care of the matter and see to it that neither she nor her son would be harmed. At this point the woman asked leave to say just one more thing. In the light of what the king had ruled in her case, why did he not let his own son return from exile. 'We must all die, we are like water spilt on the ground, which cannot be gathered up again; but God will not take away the life of him who devises means not to keep his banished one an outcast' (2 Sam. 14:14). The startled David guessed that Joab must be behind the woman's approach. She admitted the truth when the king taxed her with it. Deeply moved, David sent for Joab and agreed to let him bring Absalom back to Jerusalem.

Yet after Absalom's return David refused to see him. 'Let him dwell apart in his own house; he is not to come into my presence' (2 Sam. 14:24). Absalom appeared to settle down in Jerusalem with a large household of his own. His wives bore him four children: three sons and a daughter, whom he named Tamar after his ravished sister. But he brooded incessantly about his rejection by his father. After two years had

gone by, he sent for Joab. To his chagrin, Joab ignored the summons, no doubt out of loyalty to David. When this happened once more, Absalom had his servants set fire to Joab's field of barley. This brought the old soldier to Absalom in a rage. When he calmed down, he listened to Absalom's plea, 'Now therefore let me go into the presence of the king; and if there is guilt in me, let him kill me' (2 Sam. 14:32). At the meeting arranged by Joab, David received Absalom and kissed him in forgiveness.

The reconciliation had been delayed too long, for Absalom's rancour was already turning to thoughts of rebellion. His charm and good looks made him a popular figure 'Now in all Israel there was no one so much to be praised for his beauty as Absalom, from the sole of his foot to the crown of his head there was no blemish in him' (2 Sam. 14:25). His most striking physical attribute was a great shining mane of hair; once a year some five pounds weight of hair was trimmed from his head.

Slowly and persistently, Absalom prepared the ground for revolt. He did everything he could to build up his own prestige and undermine the king's authority. 'Absalom stole the hearts of the men of Israel' (2 Sam. 15:6). He rode around the streets of Jerusalem in a chariot with an escort of fifty mounted men, as if he were already the monarch. He would station himself at the city gate and intercept people coming in from the surrounding area to seek the king's justice. Absalom would treat them cordially, explain that under David there was really nobody to listen to their complaints and stress that the situation would be different if he were the ruler. In this way Absalom exploited a weakness in David's regime: no proper judicial system had been built up for the expanded kingdom, and the king still dealt personally with the disputes of his subjects, in the paternalistic tribal tradition of a simpler age.

After four years of subversion, Absalom was *The Revolt* ready to make his bid for power. It is true he was now the eldest surviving son, and therefore might have hoped to succeed in the natural course when David died. On the other hand, the monarchy was a new institution for the Israelites, and there was as yet no firm tradition of primogeniture, that is, succession by the first-born. It was at the king's discretion to nominate his heir. In spite of David's apparent forgiveness, Absalom could feel no assurance that his father really intended to overlook the murder of Amnon. An immediate bold seizure of the throne appealed more strongly to Absalom's temperament than dubious prospects in the distant future.

Absalom obtained permission from David to go and make a sacrifice at Hebron, claiming that this was a promise to the Lord that he had made while still in exile at Geshur. He came to Hebron with an escort of two hundred picked men and proclaimed himself king. Hebron was a shrewdly chosen launching-pad for the revolt. Not only had Absalom been born there, but the town had declined since David had moved his capital to Jerusalem.

Adherents flocked to Absalom from other parts of the country where his agents had been active. He had suddenly become the catalyst for all the multiple discontents in the realm. The most important of his supporters was Ahithophel, David's sagacious and influential counsellor. No reason is given in the Bible why he should have turned against David in this way. He may well have been convinced that Absalom would succeed, as he so nearly did. It might also be inferred from the text that Bathsheba was his granddaughter; if so, he may have nursed resentment over David's relations with her.

At the head of a large force, Absalom marched on Jerusalem. David was caught completely off guard. He had not taken Absalom's mischief-making seriously, and had underrated the smouldering disaffection in his kingdom. Certainly Ahithophel, and maybe others at the palace, had sensed that trouble was brewing; but it is not the habit of courtiers to tell their masters unpleasant truths. Now that he was directly threatened, all David's earlier instincts for survival came to the surface. The immediate danger was that he might be trapped in the city. He therefore took a swift and painful decision – to abandon his capital to the rebels and flee eastward with his family and his most trusted followers. Across the river in Trans-jordan there were reliable garrisons and loyal vassals. If he could reach there, he could gain precious time to prepare for a comeback.

*David Flees from Jerusalem* David stood at the side of the road where it left the city and dipped down into the Kidron valley, while those who were following him came marching by. He halted Ittai the Gittite who led out the Philistine palace guard. As foreign mercenaries, David said, they had no obligation to go into exile with him, let them return and serve the new king. Ittai refused and declared that he and his men would stay with David until death. Deeply moved, David motioned him to pass on.

The two high priests Zadok and Abiathar came next, the group of Levites with them carrying the sacred Ark taken from the tabernacle. Beneath the emotional stress of the moment, David's cool wits were already at work. He told the priests to go back, resume their duties, and act as his eyes and ears in the capital. When he reached the river ford, he would wait for their sons to bring him a confidential report.

David crossed the valley and followed the road up the Mount of Olives, 'weeping as he went, barefoot and with his head covered' (2 Sam. 15:30). All the people who were with him were also in tears. At the top of the rise he met his devoted adviser Hushai the Archite, a member of a Canaanite clan north of Jerusalem that had been absorbed into the people of Israel. Distressed at the turn of events, Hushai was hurrying to offer him help. David gave him a delicate and risky assignment. He was to attach himself to Absalom, gain the prince's trust and counteract the guidance of Ahithophel, the man David feared most in the rebellion. Hushai could secretly communicate with David through the high priests.

On his way down the Judean escarpment towards Jericho and the river, David's heaviness of heart was increased by two disturbing encounters. Saul's old retainer Ziba, now in the service of Jonathan's crippled son Mephibosheth, brought David a gift of two riding asses loaded with bread, fruit and wine. When David asked after the young man he had befriended, Ziba answered that his master had remained behind in the hope that the upheaval would bring him to the throne of his grandfather Saul. Hurt at this ingratitude, David promised to transfer to Ziba all Saul's property given to Mephibosheth.

Further down there suddenly appeared on the ridge above them an old Benjaminite called Shimei, a distant kinsman of Saul. In a frenzy of malicious glee, the old man flung stones at the men below and heaped curses on David: 'Begone, begone, you man of blood, you worthless fellow! The Lord has avenged upon you all the blood of the house of Saul, in whose place you have reigned' (2 Sam. 16:7,8). David had to restrain his nephew Abishai who drew his sword and wanted to rush at the old man. 'Behold,' David said, 'my own son seeks my life; how much more now may this Benjaminite! Let him alone, and let him curse; for the Lord has bidden him' (2 Sam. 16:11). The accounting with Shimei was left open for the future.

As Absalom entered Jerusalem, he was surprised to see Hushai among those waiting to greet him at the city gate. Oddly enough, Absalom upbraided him for deserting his friend David. Hushai declared that just as he had loyally served David when he was king, he would now serve the son who had been chosen by the Lord and the people to reign in David's stead. The gratified Absalom took him at his word.

On Ahithophel's advice, Absalom pitched a tent on the flat roof of the palace and had intercourse in turn with each of the ten royal concubines David had left behind to take care of the palace. The significance of this act of possession was clear to the populace. By enjoying the women that had belonged to the deposed monarch, the new ruler demonstrated the takeover in a most conspicuous manner.

What now concerned Ahithophel most of all was that David was still at large. He understood full well that his former master was a resourceful and dangerous foe, even as a fugitive on the run. He pressed Absalom to let him take a force of twelve thousand men and set out at once in pursuit, so that David could be caught and eliminated before he had a chance to rally support: 'I will strike down the king only, and I will bring all the people back to you as a bride comes home to her husband' (2 Sam. 17:2,3). Absalom agreed at first, but wanted to hear Hushai's opinion as well. Hushai skilfully argued against the plan. It did not take into account, he pointed out to Absalom, that 'your father and his men are mighty men, and that they are enraged, like a bear robbed of her cubs in the field' (2 Sam. 17:8). They were capable of inflicting heavy casualties, and the morale of the attackers would suffer. Besides, David was too wily an old fighter to be caught in his camp, but would have concealed himself and would escape. Would it not be more sensible, Hushai asked, to mobilize the tribal levies, raise a large army, and make sure of victory?

In the minds of Absalom and the others present at the discussion, Hushai's words invoked their fear of David's legendary name and the prowess of his grizzled veterans. They became doubtful about Ahithophel's proposal, and the discussion became bogged down in the rival merits of the two courses of action that had been put forward. Uncertain what would be decided, Hushai sent an urgent message through the high priests to David, urging him to get across the Jordan with his followers without delay. The two runners sent from Jerusalem with the message were Zadok's son Ahimaaz and Abiathar's son Jonathan. They were spotted moving off and chased by Absalom's soldiers. A kindly housewife in the village of Bahurim just east of Jerusalem hid them in her well until the coast was clear. They reached David that night. Before dawn next morning the whole party had crossed over the ford.

Back in Jerusalem, Absalom and his counsellors decided in favour of Hushai's line of action. The farsighted Ahithophel concluded that Absalom had missed his chance, and that his own gamble in joining the revolt had failed. Without any fuss, Ahithophel saddled his ass and rode back to his home in Gilo, where 'he set his house in order, and hanged himself' (2 Sam. 17:23).

In Trans-jordan David reached the land of Gilead, where the local population had remained loyal to him, and established his base in the town of Mahanaim on the Jabbok river. After their hurried flight his people arrived weary, hungry and without any basic equipment. Three local leaders – Shobi, Machir and Barzillai – supplied their immediate needs: 'beds, basin, and earthen vessels, wheat, barley, meal, parched grain, beans and lentils, honey and curds and sheep and cheese from the herd' (2 Sam. 17:28,29). (Shobi was actually a brother of Hanun, the defeated Ammonite king. He had probably been installed by David as governor in the Ammonite capital of Rabbath-ammon after it had fallen to the Israelites.)

David concentrated on organizing for the decisive battle. His forces were divided into three formations, commanded by Joab, Abishai and Ittai the Gittite. David announced that he would personally take the field with his troops, but was dissuaded by his commanders. They argued that Absalom's target was David himself. If they were defeated, and David was not with them, the other

*Absalom's Defeat and Death*

side would not press the pursuit very hard. David agreed to remain behind in Mahanaim, with one stipulation: 'Deal gently for my sake with the young man Absalom' (2 Sam. 18:5).

Absalom advanced across the river with a large army under the command of Amasa, another of David's nephews, through his sister Abigail. But this force was hastily assembled, inexperienced and poorly trained. In the rough terrain of Gilead it was heavily defeated by David's veteran commanders and men, and turned into a rabble fleeing through the woods. Dashing along a path on his mule, Absalom was caught by the head in the fork of an overhanging branch of an oak tree. His mule went on and left him hanging in mid-air. One of Joab's soldiers found him but was afraid to harm him because of David's order to his commanders. The soldier went to fetch Joab, who without any hesitation plunged three javelins into the helpless Absalom's chest. Joab's men closed in on Absalom, finished him off, and buried his body in the wood, under a pile of stones. Joab then ordered his trumpeter to sound the signal for the troops to break off the pursuit and return to their base.

Joab had to send a runner to Mahanaim to bring David a report on the outcome of the battle. Ahimaaz the son of the high priest Abiathar volunteered to go, but Joab wished to spare him the unhappy task of bearing the news of David's personal tragedy. With unexpected kindness Joab said: 'you may carry tidings another day, but today you shall carry no tidings, because the king's son is dead' (2 Sam. 18:20). Instead, an Ethiopian slave was despatched to Mahanaim. Ahimaaz persisted, and was allowed to follow. He took the longer but more level route through the Jordan valley and was the first to arrive and tell the king about the victory. Asked about Absalom, Ahimaaz did not have the heart to tell David the truth; he mumbled that in the noise and confusion of the battle he had been unable to see what was going on. Soon after, the Ethiopian runner arrived. To David's question, he replied simply that Absalom had suffered the fate that should overtake all the king's enemies. David was crushed with grief. He went up to the roof chamber and wept, crying out 'O my son Absalom, my son, my son Absalom! Would I had died instead of you, O Absalom, my son, my son!' (2 Sam. 18:33).

Joab came back to find that a general air of mourning pervaded the town and the king was secluded in his own quarters. Joab burst into David's room and lashed out at him. Why, he demanded to know, did David behave as if he loved his enemies and not his friends. Did the devoted officers and men who had won him victory mean nothing to him? 'If Absalom were alive and all of us were dead today, then you would be pleased' (2 Sam. 19:6). He demanded that the king show himself to his soldiers and commend them for their deeds. Joab's blunt words jolted David out of his private sorrow and reminded him of his public duty. He pulled himself together and went to review the army returning from the battle.

With the rebellion quashed, the leaders of the *David* northern tribes discussed sending a deputation to *Resumes the* David calling on him to resume his throne. David *Throne* forestalled their demand, thinking it was more important that the initiative should come from his own tribe of Judah, especially as Absalom's revolt had sprung from that tribe. At his request, the two high priests arranged for an appeal to come to David from Jerusalem. The Judahite notables went in a body down to Gilgal in the Jordan valley in order to welcome David and escort him back to the capital.

There were others who came to Gilgal. One was Shimei, the old man of Benjamin who had reviled David on his flight from Jerusalem. He now craved pardon and David spared his life. It was no time to reopen old wounds with Saul's tribe of Benjamin.

Mephibosheth, Jonathan's son, also appeared and declared he had grieved for David throughout the crisis. During all that time he had not washed his feet, cut his beard or changed his clothes. David asked him sharply why he had stayed behind. Being a cripple, Mephibosheth explained, he had asked Ziba to saddle up his ass so that he could accompany David. However Ziba had left him behind and then told lies about him to the king. Uncertain where the truth lay, David ordered that Ziba and Mephibosheth should have equal shares in the property left by Saul.

Barzillai of Gilead, who had helped David and his men after their flight, accompanied the king as far as the Jordan ford. David invited him to live in Jerusalem at the palace. Barzillai courteously declined; he was eighty years old and would only be an added burden to the king, so asked for leave to return and die in his ancestral home. He proposed that Chimham (probably his son) should remain in the king's service in his stead, and David agreed.

At Gilgal, latent antagonism flared up between the notables of Judah and a crowd of men who had gathered there from Benjamin and the northern tribes. The latter resented the fact that only Judah had been informed of David's return and arranged to receive him back officially. The king did not only belong to Judah, they protested; the northern tribes had no lesser stake in him, and indeed they had been the first to propose bringing him back. In the heat of the quarrel one of the men of Benjamin, Sheba son of Bichri, blew a trumpet and shouted out:

> We have no portion in David,
> and we have no inheritance in the
> son of Jesse;
> every man to his tents, O Israel.
>
> (2 Sam. 20:1)

All the Benjaminites and the northerners then departed with Sheba, leaving only the Judahites to escort David up to Jerusalem.

Installed back in his palace, David acted quickly to nip the Sheba revolt in the bud. He had appointed his nephew Amasa, who had been Absalom's general, to replace Joab as commander-in-chief – no doubt to punish Joab for slaying Absalom. Amasa was ordered to organize a task force and suppress the revolt before it could spread. On the way, Amasa was treacherously murdered by Joab. His body was left lying in a field with a blanket over it. The palace guard was sent out under the command of Abishai when Amasa failed to report back. Joab promptly took charge of the sortie. They pursued Sheba and his clansmen northward to the walled town of 'Abel of Beth-maacah', in the north-east part of the country near Dan. Joab's men laid siege to the town. They started to build ramps against the wall and to dig a tunnel beneath it. A 'wise woman' stood on the wall and demanded to talk to Joab. She asked him why he should want to destroy one of the most peaceful and loyal cities in the kingdom. He replied that he had nothing against the city, but only wanted Sheba who had taken shelter in it. The woman persuaded the citizens of the town to kill Sheba and toss his severed head over the wall. Joab raised the siege and marched back to Jerusalem, where David reluctantly reinstated him as commander-in-chief.

At the start David had taken the revolt very much to heart, saying 'Now Sheba the son of Bichri will do us more harm than Absalom' (2 Sam. 20:6)' He must have been relieved when it ended so quickly. In the long run his fears were well founded. The Sheba episode was a reminder that the union within the kingdom of north and south remained brittle.

One sensitive matter David had to settle concerned the ten concubines violated by Absalom. As they could not be taken back into the royal harem, David provided for their keep and arranged for them to live in seclusion as if they were widows.

In David's declining years his bodily vigour *The Struggle* dimmed and he constantly shivered with cold. *for the* His worried servants brought to the palace *Succession* Abishag, a beautiful girl from the town of Shunem in the Jezreel valley. They said to David, 'let her wait upon the king, and be his nurse; let her lie in your bosom, that my lord the king may be warm' (1 Kings 1:2). A touching friendship sprang up between the ailing monarch and the young woman who attended him.

David gradually retired from the active conduct of public affairs. The faith in God that had sustained him all his life was expressed in a lengthy hymn of praise, tinged with nostalgia for the pastoral scenes of his boyhood:

> When one rules justly over men,
>    ruling in the fear of God,
> he dawns on them like the morning light,
>    like the sun shining forth upon a
>       cloudless morning,
>    like rain that makes grass to
>       sprout from the earth.
>
> (2 Sam. 23:3,4)

With the king old, unwell and withdrawn, the question of the succession came to the fore. After the violent deaths of Amnon and Absalom, the senior surviving prince was the dashing Adonijah, generally regarded as the heir. Yet the ambitious Bathsheba still had great influence over the king, and aspired to gain the throne for her son Solomon.

Adonijah set about establishing his claim. Of the key figures at the court, Joab the commander-in-chief and the high priest Abiathar encouraged him to go ahead and pledged their support. The

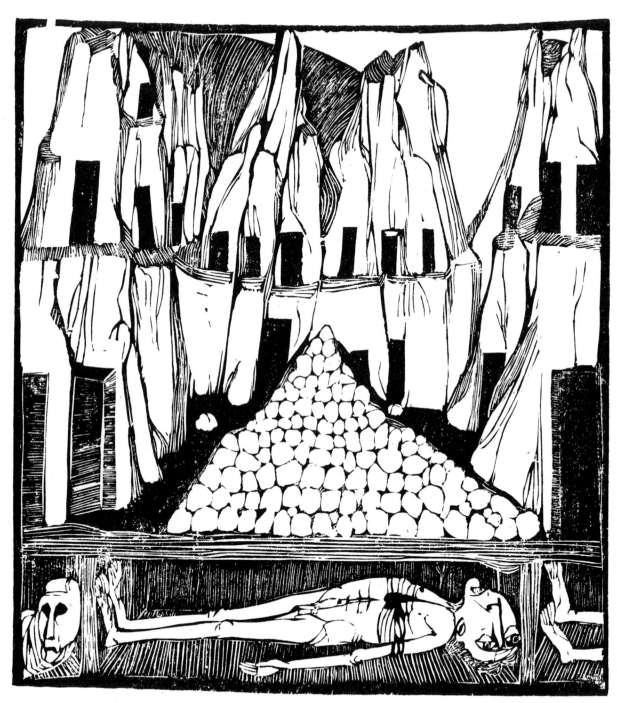

'Absalom's Grave.' His body was flung into a pit in the Gilead Woods and a pile of stones heaped over it. Woodcut by the contemporary German artist Franz Rumpf.

other high priest Zadok, Benaiah the commander of the palace guard and Nathan the prophet all hung back. Presumably they had already been drawn into the design to enthrone Solomon, a much younger but much abler prince.

Adonijah forced the issue. He invited the other princes (except Solomon) and his supporters to a gathering at the spring of En-rogel, in the valley of Kidron outside the city. Here he sacrificed sheep and oxen on a sacred rock known as the Serpent's Stone. Then they all sat down to a feast in his honour, and hailed him as king.

Prompted by the prophet Nathan, Bathsheba entered the king's bedroom, where Abishag was attending to him, and bowed to the ground. When he asked her what she wanted, she reminded him that he had promised her to make their son Solomon his successor. Why then, she asked, had Adonijah proclaimed himself king? Nathan came in next, confirmed her story, and urged the king to make his wishes known. David agreed to renounce the throne there and then in favour of Solomon. He instructed Nathan, Zadok and Benaiah to take Solomon on the king's own mule to the spring of Gihon, escorted by the palace guard. There they were formally to anoint him as the new ruler with the holy oil from the tent of the Ark. They immediately performed the ceremony. A trumpet was blown and everyone present shouted 'Long live King Solomon!'

The group feasting with Adonijah heard the trumpet and the shouting. Jonathan, the son of the priest Abiathar, then arrived with the news of what had happened. Adonijah's guests dispersed in a panic. Fearing for his life, Adonijah rushed to the altar and grasped the horns that protruded from its corners, the traditional way of claiming sanctuary. Solomon had him brought to the palace, where he bowed down before his junior half-brother. Solomon told Adonijah that he would be spared as long as he remained loyal; he was then summarily dismissed and sent back home. The youthful Solomon was already acting with regal authority.

*The Death of David* On his deathbed David said to Solomon: 'Be strong, and show yourself a man, and keep the charge of the Lord your God' (1 Kings 2:2). He requested his successor to settle accounts with Joab and with Shimei the old man of Benjamin, and to show kindness to the sons of Barzillai the Gileadite. 'Then David slept with his fathers, and was buried in the city of David' (1 Kings 2:10).

Scholars consider that the biblical account of David's life from his infatuation for Bathsheba to his death was written by a single unknown author with an intimate firsthand knowledge of the facts. The main theme is the question of the succession involving four of David's sons – Amnon, Absalom, Adonijah and Solomon. The writer of these eighteen chapters may possibly have been the high priest Abiathar or Zadok's son Ahimaaz. They form the finest narrative writing in the entire Bible, with a dramatic flow of action, vivid personal details and a superb and concise style. Above all, the story is remarkable for its candour. This is no conventional eulogy of a departed monarch, but the portrait of a brilliant and complex man that reveals his greatness together with his human weakness. David's character is full of contradictions. He is steadfast and humble in his faith, yet capable of sordid opportunism. He has a shrewd grasp of power, yet is indulgent and naive in his relations with his own children. He is the man of action, a warrior and an empire builder; and with it a dreamer, a poet and a lover of beauty. His faults are the shadows that throw his genius into relief. The greatest of the Hebrew kings, David is also the most fascinating personality in the Old Testament.

## The Reign of Solomon (961–922 BC)

IN THE LONG ARRAY OF HEBREW MONARCHS David and his son Solomon were the two outstanding figures. Their careers were markedly different. David rose from humble beginnings and carved out an empire. Solomon, born into royal estate, consolidated the realm and gave it forty years of peace and prosperity. Solomon's story lacks the drama and intense human interest that marks that of David. Solomon is remembered for his sagacity and intellectual gifts, for the Temple, and for the sumptuous style of his court, notably its huge harem.

On reaching the throne Solomon secured his *Securing the* hold on it by rapidly getting rid of his older rival *Throne* and half-brother Adonijah and the latter's chief sponsors, Joab and Abiathar. Adonijah exposed himself to attack by his desire to wed Abishag the Shunammite, the beautiful girl who had tended David at the end of his life. Adonijah persuaded the queen-mother Bathsheba to ask for Solomon's approval for the union. The young king reacted sharply: 'Ask for him the kingdom also; for he is my elder brother' (1 Kings 2:22). These ominous words implied that Adonijah's claim to a woman who had belonged to David could be interpreted as a claim to David's throne. Benaiah the captain of the guard was sent at once to execute Adonijah.

Solomon said sternly to Abiathar that he deserved death for his support of Adonijah's attempt to usurp the throne. He would be spared because he had been the priest and constant companion of David. However, he was banished from Jerusalem to the village of Anathoth, where he owned a piece of property. With Abiathar's removal Zadok remained the sole high priest.

When he heard what had happened to Adonijah and Abiathar, Joab realized that he was in mortal danger. He fled to the tent of the Ark and held onto the horns of the altar. Sent after him, Benaiah shrank from violating the sanctuary. But on Solomon's firm order, he went in and struck Joab down. Solomon justified the deed as retribution for Joab's murders of Saul's general Abner and of Joab's own cousin Amasa. Benaiah was given the post of commander-in-chief that Joab had held.

In this manner Solomon acted decisively to eliminate the men who had opposed his election and might have remained a threat to his regime. 'So the kingdom was established in the hand of Solomon' (1 Kings 2:46).

There remained the accounting with Shimei that the dying David had handed on to Solomon. Shimei was ordered not to leave Jerusalem on penalty of death. Three years later the old man went off to Gath to look for two runaway slaves. When he got back he was killed by Benaiah at the king's command.

*The Wisdom of Solomon* Since the Temple did not yet exist, the king made a practice of worshipping and offering sacrifices at different 'high places' or local shrines. He came for this purpose to Gibeon, to the north-west of Jerusalem. The Lord appeared to him in a dream that night and asked him what he desired. Solomon answered with great humility that though the Lord had seen fit to put him on the throne after his father David, he was 'but a little child'. What he wanted most was 'an understanding mind to govern thy people, that I may discern between good and evil' (1 Kings 3:9). Pleased that Solomon had not asked for long life, wealth or triumph over his enemies, the Lord

bestowed on him 'a wise and discerning mind,' together with a promise of riches, honour and longevity.

Solomon's wisdom was soon tested in a dispute that produced the most celebrated judgment in the Bible. Two harlots appeared in audience before the king. They lived in the same house, where each had given birth to a male child. One infant had died, and both mothers claimed the other. Solomon sent for a sword and ordered the child cut in two, with a half going to each of the women. One of them accepted the verdict. The other cried out that she would rather give up her claim than have the child killed. Solomon ruled that she was the rightful mother, and the baby was handed to her.

This Solomonic judgment helped to spread Solomon's fame. His wisdom became legendary throughout the area, and was said to surpass 'the wisdom of all the people of the east, and all the wisdom of Egypt' (1 Kings 4:30). It was further claimed that he composed three thousand proverbs and a thousand and five songs; and that he could discourse learnedly about all trees, plants, animals, birds, reptiles and fish.

*Solomon's Policies* The period of military expansion had been concluded in David's reign. Solomon's policies were pacific; they concentrated on ties of friendship with neighbouring states, external trade and reorganizing the kingdom from within. Continuity with the preceding reign was ensured by retaining in the chief offices of state men, or their sons, who had served David.

Solomon used marriage as a means to cement political alliances with vassal states and with other independent rulers in the region. His extensive harem included foreign princesses who were Moabite, Ammonite, Edomite, Sidonian (Phoenician) and Hittite. However, the biblical figure of a thousand women – seven hundred wives and three hundred concubines – may be regarded as oriental hyperbole rather than a genuine statistic. Solomon's most important nuptial prize was the daughter of the Egyptian pharaoh, who may have been Siamun, the second-last Pharaoh in the twenty-first dynasty. Her dowry was the Canaanite city of Gezer, presumably under Egyptian control at the time. The Egyptian princess and her servants were given special quarters in the royal compound in Jerusalem.

The foreign princesses at the Israelite court

were allowed to set up their own pagan shrines, where they worshipped according to their own cults. This tolerance is criticized by the scriptural editors as spiritual corruption. The Bible complained that when Solomon was older 'his wives turned away his heart after other gods; and his heart was not wholly true to the Lord his God, as was the heart of David his father' (1 Kings 11:4). The difficulties Solomon encountered in the later years of his reign, and the ultimate split in the kingdom after his death, are attributed to the Lord's displeasure over his easygoing attitude in religious matters.

Solomon reorganized the kingdom into twelve districts administered by commissioners appointed by the king and directly responsible to him. Only the tribal area of Judah remained outside this framework and was administered directly from Jerusalem. The reorganization made for more efficient government under central direction. On the other hand, it provoked a backlash of resentment. The residual authority of the tribal leaders was still further impaired by it, while the district lines did not everywhere correspond to the old tribal boundaries.

The division into districts was made the basis for 'taxation in kind' to feed the palace. Each district commissioner had to raise the required supplies for one month in the year. The daily quota was five thousand litres of fine flour, ten thousand litres of meal, ten stall-fed cattle, twenty pasture-fed cattle and a hundred sheep, besides deer and poultry. It has been calculated that this quantity of food was enough to maintain an establishment of five to six thousand persons. In addition, the districts had to provide fodder for all the king's horses throughout the country. Here too, the king's own tribe of Judah was in a privileged position. It was exempt from the food tax – a fact that added to the sense of grievance among the other tribes.

Commerce developed in several directions. The kingdom lay astride the main caravan routes between Asia Minor and Mesopotamia to the north and north-east, and Arabia and Egypt to the south and south-west. One such route was the Via Maris, the Way of the Sea, through the coastal plain. Another was the desert route east of the Jordan known as the King's Highway. The needs of the passing caravans provided a market for local produce, while the tolls they paid filled the royal treasury. In

addition, the king's agents acted as middlemen in lucrative trading activities between north and south. One striking example is given in the Bible. Chariots were imported from Egypt and horses from Cilicia (now southern Turkey); both were then resold at a profit in Syria, after the requirements of Solomon's army had been met.

With his father's friend Hiram, king of Tyre, Solomon maintained business relations that were advantageous to both sides. The Phoenician kingdom supplied timber, minerals, skilled artisans and know-how for Solomon's building projects. In return, the Israelite kingdom disposed of its surplus grain and olive oil to Hiram. As a joint venture, Solomon and Hiram opened a trade route from the southern Israelite port of Ezion-geber (near modern Eilat) through the Gulf of Akaba to the Red Sea. The expert Phoenician shipwrights helped to construct the vessels, that were then manned by mixed crews of Phoenician and Israelite sailors. These flat-bottomed boats with their banks of oars and square sails plied as far as the coasts of southern Arabia and east Africa. Somewhere in that region was situated the fabulous gold-producing land of Ophir. The round-trip trading voyage took three years, and the vessels brought back rich cargoes of 'gold, silver, ivory, apes, and peacocks' (1 Kings 10:22). These commodities were in part re-exported by the Phoenicians to their customers around the Mediterranean.

In the Red Sea region reached by the Israelite merchants, there was a small country called Sheba, located either at the corner of Arabia adjacent to the southern entrance to the Red Sea, or on the Ethiopean side of the sea. Living at a crossroads of land and sea routes, the inhabitants of Sheba were a trading people. They dealt mainly in Arabian spices and incense, besides gold and precious stones. The Queen of Sheba was intrigued by the reports that reached her of Solomon's wealth and wisdom. No doubt, there were also practical interests to be served in co-operating with Israel along the trade routes. She decided to make a royal visit to the court in Jerusalem, and set out on an arduous fifteen-hundred-mile journey over desert and mountains.

The queen's advent at Solomon's court was impressive. She came with a large retinue and a string of camels laden with costly gifts, which included a large quantity of spices. She was also

*The Queen of Sheba*

armed with a collection of 'cunning riddles' to challenge Solomon's reputation for wisdom. He resolved them without much difficulty. She was dazzled by Solomon's sumptuous life-style:

> And when the queen of Sheba had seen all the wisdom of Solomon, the house that he had built, the food of his table, the seating of his officials, and the attendance of his servants, their clothing, his cupbearers, and his burnt offerings which he offered at the house of the Lord, there was no more spirit in her (1 Kings 10:4,5).

The queen accepted Solomon's reciprocal gifts and started out again for her own country.

The visit seems to have been a cordial social occasion, with common trade interests no doubt figuring in the talks. There is no suggestion in the Bible that the relations between the two rulers were any more intimate than that. Nevertheless the folk history of Ethiopia has it that the Queen of Sheba bore Solomon a son, Menelik, who founded the Ethiopian dynasty. For that reason the Emperors of Ethiopia, including the late Haile Selassie, numbered 'Lion of Judah' among their official titles.

*The Royal Builder*  The peaceful conditions in Solomon's reign and the flow of revenues into his treasury enabled him to launch extensive building projects. The main beneficiary was Jerusalem. The city expanded to the top of Mount Moriah, doubling the area within the walls. The summit of the hill, where Araunah had had his threshing floor, was levelled and filled as a site for the Temple and its compound – a seven-year construction project. Below that, on a lower terrace, the palace complex was built during the next thirteen years. It contained the quarters for the royal household and a number of auxiliary buildings. Notable among these buildings were the House of the Forest of Lebanon, so-called because of the rows of massive cedar columns that supported its roof, and the Judgment Hall which held the great gold and ivory throne. The blocks of stone for the Jerusalem buildings were quarried in the nearby hills. The timber, mainly cedarwood, was supplied by Hiram of Tyre. The logs were brought to the Lebanese coast, floated on rafts to the port of Jaffa, and hauled from there up the mountain to Jerusalem. Hiram also provided masons and carpenters, and some of the gold that was lavishly used in the Temple and palace.

In spite of the grain and olive oil Hiram received in exchange, the trade gap caused an Israelite debt that mounted from year to year. To cover it, Solomon ceded to Hiram a strip of territory in the Acre plain adjacent to the Phoenician border, together with the twenty villages it contained.

The labour force was a perennial problem. It was said to number eighty thousand men working on the buildings, in the stone quarries and on haulage; while thirty thousand more were sent to Phoenicia, in shifts of ten thousand a month, to fell the trees and transport them to the coast. Solomon had to introduce the unpopular measure of forced labour.

*The Temple*  The building of the Temple started in the fourth year of Solomon's reign and was completed in the eleventh year. A great crowd attended the consecration ceremony, including notables from all over the country. In solemn procession the priests carried the Ark of the Covenant to the new sanctuary, and deposited it in the Holy of Holies. In the courtyard outside, the king blessed the congregation, then knelt at the altar and uttered a prayer to the Lord. The prayer stressed the point that the royal dynasty was an instrument of God's will. Sacrifices followed, and the inaugural feast lasted seven days.

Not a single stone of the First Temple has been found. It can be roughly visualized from certain biblical passages, taken together with the ground plans of other ancient Canaanite and Israelite temples of which the remains have been excavated. Among these parallel structures are two small temples in the Canaanite city of Hazor, destroyed by Joshua in the thirteenth century BC, a Syro-Hittite temple at Tel Tinet in northern Syria, dating from the eighth or ninth century BC; and the little Israelite shrine at Arad above the Dead Sea. The relevant Old Testament passages occur in the Books of Kings, Chronicles and Ezekiel. A general outline of Solomon's Temple emerges from these varied sources.

The ground plan had three chambers of equal width, one behind the other: the *Ulam* (vestibule), the *Hechal* (main hall) and the *Davir* (Holy of Holies), where the Ark was kept. Round the back and sides of the building was a double tier of smaller rooms, used for robing, storage and so forth. The overall dimensions were about fifty metres (165 feet) long, twenty-five metres (82 feet) wide and fifteen metres (49 feet) high.

The Temple was therefore smaller and simpler in design than its fame would lead one to expect. It must be borne in mind that the worshippers remained in the courtyard outside, and did not gather inside the building as with the later church, synagogue or mosque. The structure itself served primarily as a dwelling for the Ark of the Law and for the *Shechina* (Divine Presence), that was thought to be poised over the Ark.

The inside of the stone building was panelled in cedar wood, richly carved and overlaid with gold. The motifs in the carving and the sumptuous curtains were cherubim, together with palm trees, pomegranates and flower designs. The cherubim were winged images probably resembling the Egyptian sphinx, with a human head and a lion's body. Two huge cherubim, each sixteen feet high, made of olive wood covered with gold, flanked the Ark in the Holy of Holies.

In the courtyard before the Temple stood a group of monumental bronze works, designed and executed by a master craftsman from Tyre, also called Hiram like the king. His mother was an Israelite woman from the tribe of Naphtali. The most conspicuous of these bronze objects were two great columns, one on each side of the main entrance. They were nearly forty feet high and six feet in diameter. The origin of their names, Jachin and Boaz, remains obscure. The main altar for sacrifices, plated with bronze and rising in steps, stood in the courtyard facing the entrance. Its base was a square with three-foot sides. The 'molten sea' was a large bronze bowl of water over sixteen feet in diameter. It stood on the backs of twelve sculptured oxen, three in each corner. It is estimated that the bowl together with its base weighed thirty tons. Near it were ten smaller lavers mounted on wheels and used by the priests for their ceremonial ablutions.

The beauty of the Temple, its superb craftsmanship and its costly decorations made it one of the wonders of the ancient Near East, and added to the lustre of Solomon's reign. For the Israelites, its importance went far beyond its physical details. It stood for a new covenant between the Lord and the Davidic dynasty, and made Jerusalem a Holy City for all time. Long after the final destruction of the Temple its memory would remain for the dispersed Jewish people a symbol of their future return.

Outside Jerusalem, Solomon's building programme concentrated on defence needs. He constructed a network of forts and supply points, carefully designed to control strategic routes and passes and to subdue restless subject peoples. The key military centres were the three 'chariot cities'. Hazor, near the river Jordan in eastern Galilee, controlled the highway to Damascus. Megiddo controlled the pass from the coastal plain through the Carmel range, and was located where the pass opened into the Jezreel valley. Gezer commanded the central coastal plain and the approaches to the pass leading up to Jerusalem. In each of these cities Solomon's engineers erected identical fortifications. They consisted of external walls of the casemate type – that is, double walls with rooms between them – and a gateway of striking design, flanked by twin towers at the entrance to a vestibule which had three guardrooms on each side. This may also have been the design for the gateway to the Temple compound in Jerusalem, judging by the description in a vision of the prophet Ezekiel. Both at Megiddo and at Hazor modern excavations have disclosed elaborate water systems with underground tunnels leading to springs, in order to withstand siege.

*The Defence of the Realm*

In an earlier period the Israelite hillmen had been at a disadvantage in open country against their enemies' horsedrawn chariots, the battletank of ancient times. That was the weapon Deborah and Barak had to counter in their battle against the Philistines; and also the reason why Saul tried to draw the Philistine armies into the hill terrain. David acquired the first Israelite chariots and horses as spoils of war in his victory over the Aramean kingdom. By Solomon's time, the Hebrew kingdom had the resources and skills to build up substantial chariot and cavalry forces. Part of these forces were kept in Jerusalem, and the rest divided among the three chariot cities.

Towards the end of his reign Solomon could feel satisfied about the state of the nation. The kingdom was united and peaceful and he had kept it free of foreign wars and entanglements. The Israelite population had greatly increased, its material standards had risen, and new towns had developed. An urban middle-class grew up of officials, merchants, artisans and army officers. Excavations show that four-roomed stone houses were the standard family unit at that time, and imported goods were in common use. Solomon's

*Cracks in the Edifice*

court was renowned in the region for its wealth and culture. The Bible describes a golden age in which the Israelites 'ate and drank and were happy' and where they 'dwelt in safety, from Dan even to Beersheba, every man under his vine and under his fig tree, all the days of Solomon' (1 Kings 4:20,25).

Yet under this idyllic surface cracks were appearing in the edifice of the kingdom. The revenues were eaten up by the extravagance of the royal establishment and by the ambitious building programme. Heavy taxation and forced labour caused discontent. The northern tribes resented the favoured position of Judah. Their latent disaffection accounted for an incident that was ominous for the future. During the building operations in Jerusalem, Solomon had appointed an able young man called Jeroboam as overseer of the labourers from his tribal area of Ephraim. He started plotting against the king, and was encouraged by a prophet called Ahijah who came from the former sanctuary town of Shiloh. Ahijah may also have been influenced by the repugnance felt in orthodox religious circles for the pagan ways that were introduced into the cosmopolitan court by Solomon's foreign wives. Meeting Jeroboam along the road one day, the prophet tore his cloak into twelve pieces and handed ten of

them to Jeroboam – a symbolic act denoting that he would be the future leader of ten of the Israelite tribes. Jeroboam's planned revolt was foiled by Solomon's officers and he himself escaped the death penalty by fleeing to Egypt, where the pharaoh Shishak gave him political asylum.

As Solomon grew older the royal authority over the vassal kingdoms became eroded. When Edom was annexed in David's time its young prince Hadad, then still a child, was taken to Egypt by faithful retainers. He was brought up at the Egyptian court, where he married the queen's sister. He now returned to his own country and 'made mischief' for Solomon's regime. It is not clear whether Edom broke away at this time, but clearly the Israelite hold on it was weakened. In the north, the Aramean subject kingdom of Aram-Damascus regained its independence under Rezon, who proclaimed himself king.

Thus, even before Solomon's death, the empire built up by David was beginning to disintegrate. Solomon's great prestige and sagacity kept the united monarchy intact in spite of growing internal strains. When he died, it split into two. The Trans-jordan kingdoms of Ammon and Moab then also broke away from Israelite rule.

# 6

# THE TWO KINGDOMS

## The Split

SOLOMON WAS SUCCEEDED BY HIS SON Rehoboam (922–915 BC) whose mother was Naamah, an Ammonite princess. He was forty-one years old at the time. His succession was taken for granted in his own tribe of Judah. For the northern tribes, the question was more uncertain. Rehoboam went specially to Shechem to accept their allegiance. The assembly of notables gathered there was joined by Jeroboam, who hurried back from Egypt when the news of Solomon's death reached him.

*The Secession of the North* The northern leaders were in no mood for docile acceptance of the new king. They presented him with a list of grievances and demanded relief from the tax burdens Solomon had imposed on them. Taken aback, Rehoboam promised to give them a reply within three days, and dispersed the gathering. Meanwhile he sought the advice of his counsellors. The older ones among them, who had served his father, urged him to meet the demands and thereby retain their loyalty. Rehoboam's own contemporaries pressed for a tough, no-nonsense line. Unfortunately the king was swayed by them.

When the assembly met again, he addressed it in harsh language. He would, he declared, make their yoke heavier than before: 'My father chastised you with whips, but I will chastise you with scorpions' (1 Kings 12:11). The 'scorpion' was a cruel type of scourge, so-called because of its stinging tips.

The backlash to this attempted browbeating was instant revolt. Adoniram, the official in charge of the forced levies, was stoned to death. The king himself escaped the fury of the crowd by leaping into his chariot and galloping back to Jerusalem. The northern tribes declared their secession, set up the separate kingdom of Israel and elected Jeroboam as their first king (922–901 BC).

Rehoboam was left as ruler of the rump kingdom of Judah. He started to raise an army in order to recover the northern area by force. But he was dissuaded by Shemaiah the prophet, who conveyed a message from the Lord: 'You shall not go up or fight against your kinsmen the people of Israel. Return every man to his home, for this thing is from me' (1 Kings 12:24). A long and costly civil war had been narrowly averted.

It had taken Saul, David and Solomon a century to construct a united kingdom out of the twelve autonomous Israelite tribes, and to make of it the leading power in the area. Overnight, it was reduced to two bickering successor states, each exposed to external enemies. They would co-exist for the next two centuries until Israel, the northern kingdom, would come to an end in 722 BC. Judah would survive for another one hundred and thirty-five years until 587 BC.

Of the two kingdoms, Judah was smaller in size and poorer in resources. Although in addition to the original tribal area of Judah, it had absorbed the tribe of Simeon in the Beersheba district. The split also left most of the territory of Benjamin with Judah. Its great advantage was its internal stability. Throughout its separate existence it was ruled by the dynasty David had founded, while Jerusalem remained its political centre and the Temple the unique focus of its religious life.

Israel comprised the remaining tribes, spread over the central hill country, the Galilee, the coastal area and Trans-jordan. It had a greater area and population than Judah, and more fertile land. Moreover, it had a substantial share in regional trade because of the caravan routes, the sea coast, and the friendly ties with its enterprising Phoenician neighbour. On the other hand, it never acquired a durable ruling dynasty, and suffered from chronic political instability. Nor did it develop a central sanctuary comparable in appeal to the Temple. Its proximity to Phoenicia was a mixed blessing, since the pagan cults and customs of that sophisticated people were insidious infiltrators into the northern kingdom. To the north-east, the growing strength of Aram-Damascus posed a constant military threat to Israel.

The southern kingdom had a total of twenty rulers (including one queen) and the northern kingdom nineteen. In the biblical account, the parallel histories of the two states are woven together in a manner which is often confusing.

*The Campaign of Shishak* Five years after the division, both kingdoms were invaded and plundered by an expeditionary force led by the pharaoh Shishak, a vigorous Libyan colonel who had seized the Egyptian throne during Solomon's reign, He advanced along the coast through Gaza and marched on Jerusalem. Rehoboam headed off an assault on the city by handing over the treasures of the Temple and the palace as tribute. The ransom included the shields of gold that Solomon had hung on the palace walls; they were replaced by bronze substitutes.

The Bible attributes the invasion to religious backsliding under Rehoboam. It is stated that 'Asherot' – sacred trees or wooden poles that were symbols of the Canaanite fertility goddess Asherah – were set up on the hilltops, and that sacred male prostitutes were allowed. Rehoboam himself came to a more prosaic military conclusion – that Shishak's force had penetrated with ease through southern Judah because it was inadequately protected. Fifteen towns in that area were thereupon fortified, stocked with supplies of weapons and linked by internal roads into a defence network.

The biblical text is silent about the rest of Shishak's campaign, but it can be reconstructed from the place-names he had inscribed on a temple wall in Luxor, Upper Egypt. It appears that he swung through Trans-jordan, along the Jezreel valley and back down the coastal plain to Egypt. One detachment went south through the Negev to Ezion-geber. A portion of a stele (inscribed stone slab) left by Shishak has been found at Megiddo.

*Israel: The Reign of Jeroboam* The later biblical scribes remained loyal to the Davidic line and the Jerusalem Temple. Jeroboam figures as a political renegade and a religious heretic about whom nothing good is said. In fact, he must have been a man of unusual personality and stature to have been unanimously chosen as head of the breakaway northern kingdom. His main task was to develop its separate institutions. The name given to the kingdom, Israel, itself carried an air of legitimacy, since it had powerful associations with the past. It was the name acquired by Jacob, the common ancestor of all the Israelite tribes, after he had wrestled with the angel at the ford of Jabbok. His descendants became known as the Children of Israel, and the country God promised them was called the Land of Israel (in Hebrew, *Eretz Israel*).

Jeroboam's first capital was at Shechem, the main northern city, where he built a fortified citadel for its defence. After a brief interval at Penuel in the land of Gilead (where he also built a citadel, no doubt to secure the allegiance of the Trans-jordan tribes), he established a new capital at Tirzah, seven miles north-east of Shechem. It was a small town in beautiful surroundings,

The Prophet receiving God's Word. Woodcut by
the contemporary German artist Wilhelm Gross.

commanding both the north-south highway through the hills and the road down to the Jordan river ford at Adam (Damia).

Since religion played a vital part in the daily lives of the people, Jeroboam understood that their minds and hearts had to be turned away from the Temple in Jerusalem: 'If this people go up to offer sacrifices in the house of the Lord at Jerusalem, then the heart of this people will turn again to their lord, to Rehoboam king of Judah, and they will kill me' (1 Kings 12:27). As a counter-attraction, Jeroboam developed and gave royal status to two ancient sanctuaries: Bethel in the southern part of his kingdom and Dan at its extreme north-east corner. Both had a long Hebrew background – Bethel from the time of Abraham, and Dan from its conquest and settlement by the tribe of that name in the early period of the Judges. In each of these sanctuaries Jeroboam placed a golden image of a calf. The Bible describes this as a swing to outright idolatry. Jeroboam is quoted as saying: 'You have gone up to Jerusalem long enough. Behold your gods, O Israel, who brought you up out of the land of Egypt' (1 Kings 12:28). Yet scholars today do not find it credible that the northern kingdom should have turned its back on the Hebrew faith and the Mosaic code. The bulls may have been meant to serve as a footstool or throne for the Divine Presence, corresponding to the cherubim in the Holy of Holies of the Jerusalem Temple. Nevertheless, the choice of the calf symbol was easily misinterpreted, for it was associated with the worship of the Egyptian bull-god Apis, and with Canaanite fertility cults.

Jeroboam further antagonized orthodox religious circles by getting rid of the Levites. By tradition they carried out religious duties for all the Israelite tribes and provided the priesthood. Jeroboam doubtless considered that they were too closely identified with Jerusalem and the Temple. He emphasized the break by appointing priests at Bethel and Dan who were not drawn from the hereditary Levite families. He also fostered worship at the local shrines or 'high places'. The annual feast of Succoth was set in Israel for the ninth month of the Jewish calendar, instead of the eighth month as in Judah. All these changes were regarded by the religious establishment in Jerusalem as further evidence of the drift towards paganism in the northern kingdom.

The scriptural hostility to Jeroboam is reflected in two stories told at some length. The first concerns an unnamed 'man of God' from Judah who suddenly appeared in the Bethel temple when Jeroboam was standing by the altar about to burn incense. When the prophet cursed the altar it fell apart and the ashes were scattered, as a sign of the Lord's anger. As the king pointed at the old man and called for his arrest, the king's outstretched arm was paralysed in that position. It was healed only when he appealed to the prophet to pray for him. The chastened Jeroboam invited the visitor to come home with him for a meal and a reward, but the old man refused, saying that God had forbidden him to eat or drink in Bethel.

A local prophet hurried after the man from Judah and deceived him into accepting hospitality. On riding back home, the old man was attacked and killed by a lion for having disobeyed the Lord's injunction. Strangely, his donkey and the lion remained standing side by side next to the body. The Bethel prophet retrieved the body and buried it in his own family tomb.

In the second story, Jeroboam's infant son fell ill and was taken by his mother to Shiloh to consult the prophet Ahijah, now old and practically blind. Jeroboam knew that Ahijah, who had once promoted his kingship, had since turned against him (an echo of the strained relations between Samuel and Saul). He therefore told his wife to disguise herself and take a generous gift with her. Ahijah identified her at once and told her the child would die. He then denounced the king for doing evil and predicted a dire fate for his descendants. The Lord, the prophet cried, would 'utterly consume the house of Jeroboam, as a man burns up dung until it is all gone' (1 Kings 14:10).

Jeroboam died after twenty-two years on the northern throne, and was briefly succeeded by his son Nadab (901–900 BC). Fighting flared up on the border with Philistia, and Nadab laid siege to the town of Gibbethon on the coastal plain. It had been one of the Levitical cities in David's empire, and had been retaken by the Philistines. During the siege Nadab was murdered by a ruthless army officer called Baasha, from the tribe of Issachar. He usurped the throne in Tirzah and promptly had all Jeroboam's male descendants put to death. This was the first of a number of occasions that a change of regime in the northern kingdom was brought about by assassination and coup.

Baasha reigned for a total of twenty-four years (900–877 BC).

*Judah:*
*Abijah and*
*Asa*

Rehoboam was succeeded by his son Abijah (915–913 BC). The total size of Rehoboam's harem is given as eighteen wives and sixty concubines who between them bore him twenty-eight sons and sixty daughters. Abijah's mother was Maacah the daughter of Abishalom (also called Absalom). If the reference was to David's son, she would be a member of the royal family in her own right. Rehoboam prudently made provision for his other sons by appointing them governors of provincial towns outside the capital, 'and he gave them abundant provisions, and procured wives for them' (2 Chron. 11:23).

Abijah raised a substantial army to crush the northern kingdom that had seceded from his father, and to restore the united monarchy. He launched the offensive by proclaiming from a hilltop that there could be no legitimate dynasty other than the House of David, and that Jeroboam led his followers after pagan idols. The battle that followed swung in favour of Judah. Jeroboam retreated with heavy losses, but retained his kingdom. Judah gained some territory in the tribal area of Benjamin, and an adjacent strip of the hills of Ephraim. It included several towns and villages, the most important of them being the sanctuary town of Bethel. This was one episode in an inconclusive half-century of border warfare between the two kingdoms, with territory in the borderland of Benjamin passing from one side to the other.

Abijah is credited with fourteen wives, twenty-two sons and sixteen daughters. After his short reign of three years, he was succeeded by one of his sons, Asa, who reigned for forty-one years (913–873 BC). While the new king was still a minor, the dominant personality in the kingdom was his grandmother Maacah, the widow of Rehoboam. As queen-mother she became regent, and was in virtual control until Asa came of age.

Asa is one of the few Hebrew kings who is commended in the Bible for his piety. During his grandmother's regency religious observance had grown slack in the kingdom and pagan practices had become common. On assuming power Asa carried out a sweeping purge. He deposed his grandmother from her official position, and publicly burnt in the valley of Kidron an 'abominable image' she had·used in the cult of the Canaanite fertility goddess Asherah. Throughout the kingdom idols were smashed and sacred prostitution banned. However, local shrines or 'high places' were left in use. In Jerusalem Asa repaired the great altar in front of the Temple and replenished with gold and silver the depleted Temple treasury. In the fifteenth year of his reign, Asa convened in Jerusalem a religious assembly with representatives from all over Judah, as well as pious people who had moved into Judah from the northern kingdom. A solemn oath of obedience to God was taken in an atmosphere of great fervour, 'with shouting, and with trumpets, and with horns' (2 Chron. 15:14). In his religious reforms Asa had the spiritual guidance of a prophet called Azariah the son of Oded.

During Asa's reign the intermittent border tension between the two kingdoms flared up again into open warfare. King Baasha of Israel marched south and re-occupied Bethel. He then captured and started to fortify Ramah. On the high ground only five miles north of Jerusalem, Ramah commanded the north-south highway through the hills. Alarmed at this threat but without the military strength needed to drive the northerners back, Asa sought outside help. He hurriedly sent messengers to Ben-hadad I, king of Damascus, carrying with them a quantity of gold and silver from the palace and Temple treasuries. Not reluctant to exploit the conflict between the two Hebrew kingdoms, Ben-hadad invaded and occupied north-eastern Galilee as far as Lake Kinnereth (the Sea of Galilee). This second front opened in his rear compelled Baasha to withdraw and rush back. The piles of timber and cut stone abandoned at Ramah were used by Asa to fortify two other nearby hill towns, Geba and Mizpah. The northern approach to Jerusalem was thereby safeguarded, and the border between Israel and Judah permanently settled.

Asa had to cope with another military thrust against his kingdom, this time from the south. An Egyptian force led by Zerah the Cushite (Ethiopian) advanced from the Sinai desert through Philistine territory and reached the Israelite town of Mareshah in the Judean lowlands. It was defeated by Asa's army and pursued as far as the Philistine city of Gerar. That city and the surrounding countryside were sacked and plundered, with large herds of cattle, sheep and camels captured as booty. The identity of Zerah is obscure. One theory is that he was the pharaoh Osorkon I, son and successor of the pharaoh Shishak who founded the 'Libyan' dynasty in Egypt. The Book of Chronicles refers to the invading force as made up of Ethiopians and Libyans.

In spite of his record of religious zeal, Asa was criticized by the orthodox because he did not put his faith entirely in the Lord in time of trouble. He should not, it was said, have appealed to the king of Damascus to relieve the pressure from Baasha. This complaint was voiced directly to the king by a prophet named Hanani, who was put in the stocks for his temerity. Another criticism was that, instead of just praying to God, Asa called in a physician for a disease that afflicted both his legs in the last two years of his life. When he died the disease (probably dropsy) must have caused rapid decomposition. The Bible mentions that his body was laid on 'a bier which had been filled with various kinds of spices prepared by the perfumer's art' (2 Chron. 16:14).

*Judah: The Reign of Jehoshaphat*

At the age of thirty-five Jehoshaphat succeeded his father Asa and reigned for twenty-five years (873–849 BC). For Judah it was a period of peaceful consolidation. The king was not only God-fearing like his father, but also energetic and practical.

In Judah's relations with the northern kingdom of Israel conflict gave way to co-operation. As was customary political understanding was sealed by a dynastic marriage: Jehoshaphat's crown prince Jehoram was married to Athaliah, a princess from the household of Ahab the reigning king of Israel. (It is unclear whether she was Ahab's sister or a daughter by his Phoenician queen Jezebel.)

Judah and Israel joined forces in two military campaigns during Jehoshaphat's reign. One was the battle of Ramoth-gilead in Trans-jordan against the army of the king of Damascus. The Israelites were defeated and King Ahab killed. Jehoshaphat withdrew his troops and returned to Jerusalem.

The earlier expedition had been against Moab, which had come under the domination of Israel. Since Moab subsisted mainly on pasturage, the annual tribute was fixed in sheep, goats and wool. Towards the end of Ahab's reign Mesha the king of Moab successfully rebelled against his Hebrew overlord. (Mesha's account of this event was inscribed on a stele (monumental slab) of black basalt discovered in 1868 by a Prussian missionary at the site of Dibon, the ancient Moabite capital.)

Ahab's younger son, also called Jehoram, made an alliance with King Jehoshaphat in an attempt to subjugate Moab once more. (He had succeeded his older brother Ahaziah who had reigned for about two years.) Their plan of campaign was to march round the southern end of the Dead Sea through the territory of Edom, and to attack Moab from the south. They were joined by the king of Edom, a vassal of Judah at the time. After a seven-day trek through broken desert terrain their supply of water ran out. In desperate plight, they called on the help of the prophet Elisha, who agreed to consult the Lord for the sake of the respected Jehoshaphat. Going into a trance under the influence of music, the seer predicted that a dry watercourse nearby would miraculously fill with water, though there would be no rain. By next morning a flash flood came tearing down the stream-bed, providing water for the men, cattle and pack animals. To the Moabite soldiers some distance away, the red light of a desert dawn reflected in the water made it look like blood. They rashly jumped to the conclusion that the followers of the three kings had turned upon and slaughtered each other. As the Moabites rushed forward to loot the camp, they were attacked and driven back across their own border, suffering heavy casualties.

The invading force devastated the Moabite countryside, cutting down fruit-trees, blocking up wells and springs, and heaping stones on fertile fields. King Mesha and the remnants of his army were besieged in his capital city of Kirharaseth. In desperation Mesha invoked the help of the national Moabite god, Chemosh, by sacrificing his eldest son on the city wall. Filled with superstitious dread by this spectacle the Israelites withdrew and returned the way they had come.

Prophetic circles in Judah were unhappy about Jehoshaphat's collaboration with the northern kingdom. On his return from the battle of Ramoth-gilead, these reservations were publicly uttered by a prophet called Jehu. The dissent was, however, muted because of the vigour with which Jehoshaphat stamped out the lingering paganism in his kingdom, particularly such practices as fertility images and cult prostitution.

The king did not content himself with repressive measures in the field of religion. He launched a public campaign of education in the laws and traditions of the ancestral faith. The programme was carried out by a high-level mission composed of five of the royal princes, two priests and nine Levites. They travelled from place to place in the country, giving instruction in 'the book of the Law of the Lord' – probably an early version of the Book of Deuteronomy. The king also made personal visits to different parts of the realm, and spread piety and religious observance among his subjects.

In a spirit of realism Jehoshaphat accepted the split in the nation as a permanent fact. On that basis he reorganized the military, judicial and administrative framework of Judah in order to give it greater internal cohesion. The country was divided into five military districts, each under a regional commander. Three of them were in Judah and two in Benjamin. Additional fortifications were constructed in key towns and the armed forces and supply depots were dispersed among them. These security dispositions, and Judah's improved relations with the sister kingdom of Israel, made an impression on other neighbouring peoples. The Philistines resumed the payment of tribute that had lapsed for some time. There were propitiatory gifts of livestock from 'the Arabs' – that is, the nomad tribes in the southern desert.

Jehoshaphat developed a regular judicial system for Judah. Professional judges were appointed in the main provincial centres, with royal terms of reference that were not only devout but remarkably enlightened at that time – and indeed remain so today! 'Consider what you do, for you judge not for man but for the Lord . . . for there is no perversion of justice with the Lord our God, or partiality, or taking bribes' (2 Chron. 19:6,7). In Jerusalem the king set up an upper tribunal composed of both clerical and lay members. The high priest Amariah presided over the court 'in all matters of the Lord' and the chief minister Zebadiah in all the king's matters. Jehoshaphat urged the tribunal: 'Deal courageously, and may the Lord be with the upright!' (2 Chron. 19:11).

It is likely that Jehoshaphat also organized Judah into districts for administrative and tax purposes, along the lines his ancestor King Solomon had done for the whole of the united kingdom. Under this system the palace in Jerusalem would exercise authority through district governors, who were royal appointees. In the Book of Joshua there is a list of Judean towns grouped into ten districts; it has been suggested by scholars that the list actually represents a division by King Jehoshaphat who reigned three centuries later.

Jehoshaphat established firm and direct control over the conquered kingdom of Edom in the south. One result was to secure access through the Negev desert to the small port of Ezion-geber (near modern Eilat) at the head of the Gulf of Akaba. The king thereupon attempted to revive the lucrative southern sea-route to the Red Sea area, that had lapsed after Solomon's death and the split in the kingdom. Jehoshaphat had some 'ships of Tarshish' constructed on the Phoenician model. Unfortunately they foundered in stormy weather as soon as they set sail. Perhaps the vessels were not seaworthy; there is no mention of his using skilled Phoenician shipwrights, as Solomon had done through his partner, Hiram king of Tyre. The Book of Chronicles offers a theological reason for the debacle of Jehoshaphat's maritime enterprise. It states that King Ahaziah of Israel (the son of Ahab) joined in the venture, that came to grief because the Lord disapproved of Jehoshaphat's choice of a business associate. This comment reflects the strong bias of the Chronicler against the northern kingdom. On the other hand, the Book of Kings says that Ahaziah wanted to join but his offer to do so was rejected.

Towards the end of Jehoshaphat's reign, there is mention of a raid across the Dead Sea into southern Judah by elements from Ammon, Moab and the rugged Mount Seir region of Edom. (Remains of Israelite forts on the escarpment overlooking the Dead Sea from the west would indicate that such incursions by bands of marauders from Trans-jordan constituted a chronic problem.) In the Book of Chronicles there occurs an obviously legendary account of this raid. It serves as a didactic parable to illustrate that prayer to the Lord is a reliable weapon in an emergency. According to this story, the invaders were a 'great multitude'. They reached En-gedi on the Dead Sea shore and from there climbed up the Judean escarpment by the ascent of Ziz, to penetrate into the Tekoah area of the Hebron hills. Jerusalem was panic-stricken.

A great assembly of worshippers came together in the courtyard of the Temple, offered sacrifices and prayed for salvation. Inspired by one of the Levites, the congregation set out towards the enemy with the Temple choir singing in the lead. The Lord provoked the enemy to quarrel among themselves and slay each other. When the Israelites arrived on the scene they found a pile of corpses and so much booty that it took three days to collect. Jehoshaphat's faith in the Lord had gained him a victory without the use of weapons.

In the twenty-fifth year of his reign Jehoshaphat died and was succeeded by his son Jehoram (849–842 BC).

## Israel Under Omri and Ahab

IN THE NORTHERN KINGDOM OF ISRAEL, BAASHA was succeeded by his son Elah (877–876 BC). Within two years, he was assassinated by Zimri, a senior commander of chariot troops. The wretched Elah met his end while getting drunk in the quarters of the official in charge of the royal household. *Omri gains the Throne* Zimri declared himself king and promptly put to death all the male members of the house of Baasha, together with the leading supporters of that house. These bloody measures to secure the throne proved futile, since his 'reign' lasted just one week. At the time of Zimri's coup, the Israel army general Omri was conducting a renewed siege of the rebellious Philistine town of Gibbethon in the coastal plain. Omri was proclaimed king by his troops, marched on Tirzah the capital and gained control of it. Trapped in the citadel, Zimri set it on fire and perished in the flames. For the next year, Omri was challenged by another would-be usurper, an officer called Tibni. With that bid for power also crushed and Tibni killed, Omri emerged as the undisputed master of the northern kingdom.

In his firm seven-year rule (876–869 BC), Omri imposed much-needed internal stability and gained his kingdom a fresh regional strength and importance. His son King Ahab further developed the prosperity and prestige of Israel to a level it would not achieve again. A century later, Assyrian documents still referred to the northern kingdom as Bit-Humri – the House of Omri. Nevertheless the Bible condemns Omri (and later Ahab) for his permissive attitude to the inroads of paganism. It is bluntly stated that he 'did more evil than all who were before him' (1 Kings 16:25).

The overlapping reigns of Omri in Israel and Asa in Judah ended the struggle between the two kingdoms, and ushered in a period of peaceful co-existence. A little later, in Ahab's reign, the two Hebrew royal houses would be linked by marriage. *Israel and its Neighbours*

Omri also strengthened the traditional ties of friendship with the trading and seafaring people of Phoenicia, on the Mediterranean coast to the north and west of the kingdom of Israel. This alliance was sealed by the marriage of Ahab to Jezebel, daughter of Ethbaal, king of the Phoenician port city of Sidon. The co-operation was of economic benefit to both sides. Israel acquired from Phoenicia lumber, minerals and the products of its developed arts and crafts, and supplied in return grain and olive oil. They also had a common interest in the general commerce of the region. The Phoenician trading vessels plied between the islands and shores of the Mediterranean, while the kingdom of Israel was astride the two main caravan routes from the south: the Via Maris from Egypt to Mesopotamia, and the King's Highway from Arabia through Trans-jordan.

The kingdom of Moab was brought under subjection by Omri. The inscribed stele of Mesha king of Moab confirms that fact. 'As for Omri, king of Israel, he humbled Moab many years for Chemosh was angry with his land.'

With his other borders secure, Omri was free to cope with the growing aggressiveness of his neighbour to the north-east, the Syrian kingdom of Aram-Damascus. In the reign of Baasha, the Syrians had taken advantage of a brief war between Israel and Judah to move into eastern Galilee and advance southward to the Sea of Galilee. They had partially withdrawn again but the Israelite town of Ramoth-gilead remained in their hands. It was an important strategic point, as it commanded the King's Highway before it crossed the gorge of the Yarmuk river. Since then Syria had continued to pose a threat to the Galilee and to Israelite territory in Trans-jordan. Omri was able to contain Syrian expansion, though not to roll it back. The struggle with Syria in what is now northern Jordan was to continue in the reign of his son Ahab. The Bible mentions the curious fact that Syrian merchants had their own bazaar quarter in the capital of Israel. That would indicate a measure of economic penetration.

Omri had taken over as his capital the small hill-town of Tirzah. He determined to replace it with a spendid new national centre for the northern kingdom, that would compete with the lustre of Jerusalem. For two talents of silver he purchased a conspicuous hill eight miles north of Shechem. It rose out of a level, fertile valley and could easily be defended, as three of the sides were very steep. Two important roads passed nearby: the main north-south route through the hills, and an east-west one from the Jordan valley to the coastal plain. From the top, the Mediterranean could be seen as a blue, shining strip over twenty miles away to the west.

The summit of the hill was cleared to the bedrock. On it, Omri constructed a rectangular citadel enclosed by massive walls of stone blocks. The lower courses can still be seen today, nearly three thousand years later. Within this compound stood the complex of palace buildings, together with storerooms, a water reservoir lined with plaster, and a royal tomb. Hundreds of clay fragments inscribed in ancient Hebrew have been found at the place where the records room must have stood. The lower town was built below the citadel, on the easier southern slope of the hill. It was enclosed by another wall in Ahab's time.

*Samaria the Capital*    Omri named the new capital Samaria, *Shomron* in Hebrew. The name may have been derived either from Shemer, the original owner of the hill, or from the Hebrew word for a watchtower. In the course of time the whole surrounding hill-region became known as Samaria, and its inhabitants as Samaritans.

On Omri's death he was buried in the royal tomb at Samaria. He was succeeded on the throne by his son Ahab (869–850 BC).

*Queen Jezebel*    In the scriptural account of Ahab's reign attention is focused neither on his constructive achievements nor on his military struggles, but on the issue of paganism. The two main protagonists in this drama were Jezebel, Ahab's haughty and strong-willed Phoenician queen, and the gaunt and terrifying figure of the prophet Elijah. At times the king himself seemed helplessly caught between the two.

Jezebel came from an affluent and cosmopolitan culture, with standards of architecture, craftsmanship and material comfort that were among the most advanced in the region. In the court circles and prosperous upper class of Samaria, Phoenician manners, dress and decoration became fashionable. This pervasive social influence was not as serious as the religious penetration that went with it. Jezebel made no attempt to embrace her husband's faith. On the contrary, she tried to replace it with her own in her adopted land. With great vigour she promoted the cults of Melkart, the Phoenician Baal or chief god, and of Asherah the fertility goddess. She brought in four hundred and fifty 'prophets' or priests of Baal and four hundred of Asherah, and maintained them in Samaria as part of her extensive household. A temple to Baal was built in the courtyard of the palace, with smaller shrines in the surrounding hills. The Israelite priests who resisted this intrusion of an alien faith were liquidated or hounded into exile.

In the biblical indictment against Ahab, he is charged with actually taking part in the worship of his wife's gods. It does seem that he gave her a remarkably free hand to undermine the ancestral faith of his people. The reasons may have been his own religious indifference, his absorption in the political and military affairs of the state, or simply that he was weak in his relations with his imperious consort.

*The Prophet Elijah*    About the middle of Ahab's reign, there suddenly appeared before him a wild and unkempt figure wearing the rough robe of a religious ascetic. From first to last Elijah carried an aura of mystery. Nothing is known of his background before this abrupt eruption into the story, except that he came from Tishbe, an unidentified place in the land of Gilead east of the Jordan. Glaring at the astonished king, Elijah cried out a dire prediction of drought: 'As the Lord the God of Israel lives, before whom I stand, there shall be neither dew nor rain these years, except by my word' (1 Kings 17:1). His words implied a challenge to the potency of the Phoenician Baal regarded by his followers as the controller of the life-giving rain. (The challenge would later be dramatized on Mount Carmel.)

Before an order could be given for his arrest, the prophet had gone. He escaped across the Jordan and hid himself in a desolate spot next to a stream called Cherith. Here he lived as a hermit, fed by ravens. When the stream dried up in the drought that had settled over the land, Elijah sought refuge across the Phoenician border. Outside the gate of Zarephath, a town near the port city of Sidon, he met a widow gathering sticks for firewood. Elijah asked her for a drink of water and a piece of bread. She replied sadly that she had no bread; all the food left in her home was a handful of meal in a bowl and a little oil in a jar. When she had cooked this for her son and herself, there would be nothing more to stop them from starving to death. Elijah told her not to worry: 'The jar of meal shall not be spent, and the cruse of oil shall not fail, until the day that the Lord sends rain upon the earth' (1 Kings 17:14). The woman offered Elijah lodging in the upper room of her house. The remnant of her food replenished itself, so that there was enough for the three of them for many days to come.

Some time later the widow's child fell ill and died. In her grief she blamed Elijah for having brought misfortune on her by reminding God of her sins. He took the boy from her arms, carried him upstairs to the upper room and stretched him out on the bed. Three times the prophet covered the dead child with his own body and prayed fervently to the Lord. The boy started to breathe again and revived. Elijah brought him down again to the overjoyed mother, who cried out: 'Now I know that you are a man of God, and that the word of the Lord in your mouth is truth' (1 Kings 17:24).

These two miracles – food replenishing itself, and the dead brought to life – were forerunners of those that would be attributed more than eight centuries later to Jesus of Nazareth.

*Confrontation on the Carmel*
In the third year of the drought the Lord instructed Elijah to go and see King Ahab once again. In Samaria the king was faced with the need to slaughter all the royal horses and mules, since there was no feed for them. Before that drastic step was taken, Obadiah, the official in charge of the palace, was sent out to scour the countryside for pasturage that might be left near riverbeds or springs. Obadiah was a devout man who had at great personal risk hidden a hundred Israelite prophets in caves to save them from Jezebel's persecution, and had secretly provided them with food and water. On his way to search for grazing he met Elijah striding towards the capital, and bowed down before the prophet. Elijah asked him to return and inform his royal master that he wanted to see him.

Ahab came out to meet Elijah and said sternly to him, 'Is it you, you troubler of Israel?' (1 Kings 18:17). The undaunted prophet flung back at the king: 'I have not troubled Israel; but you have, and your father's house, because you have forsaken the commandments of the Lord and followed the Baals' (1 Kings 18:18). The prophet then demanded that the king summon an assembly on Mount Carmel, and have it attended by the pagan priests kept by Jezebel, for a trial of strength. Strangely enough, Ahab acceded to this extravagant request. He was probably awed by the moral force with which Elijah spoke; and he also hoped that the prophet would intercede with God to end the drought that was crippling the kingdom.

On Mount Carmel there then took place one of the most memorable scenes in the Bible, marking a climactic point in the age-long conflict between monotheism and paganism. In the clear light of early morning the crowd stood hushed and expectant in the presence of the king. Elijah took up his position before them. To one side were ranged the four hundred and fifty prophets of Baal. Below them to the west stretched the gleaming blue expanse of the Mediterranean. To the east, across the Jezreel valley, wave after wave of the Galilee hills spread out to the tip of Mount Hermon on the distant skyline. The whole vast landscape was bathed in the radiance of the mounting sun. Elijah drew closer to the people, and his voice rang out: 'How long will you go limping with two different opinions? If the Lord is God, follow him; but if Baal, then follow him' (1 Kings 18:21). The crowd remained silent. This, Elijah continued, was how the issue would be tested. Let the prophets of Baal prepare a bullock and lay the pieces on an unlit altar. He would do the same. Let it then be seen whose god would send down fire to consume the sacrifice. The pagan priests should try first; after all, they were many in number, while here he was, God's only prophet.

All morning long the prophets of Baal leapt and swirled around their altar in a ritual dance, shouting out to Baal. There was no response. At noonday, Elijah's voice rose above the din in stinging ridicule. 'Cry aloud, for he is a god.' Maybe their Baal was musing, or was relieving himself, or had gone on a journey? Perhaps he was asleep and needed to be woken up? Goaded into a frenzy by these taunts, the pagan prophets started slashing themselves with knives until the blood ran down their bodies. There was still no response.

In the middle of the afternoon Elijah turned to

his part of the test. He constructed an altar of twelve rough stones, one for each of the Israelite tribes. Around it he dug a trench. The sacrificial bullock was prepared and cut up, and the pieces laid on the altar. Three times Elijah had jars of water poured over the meat, the firewood and the altar, until the water filled the trench. He then prayed to the Lord to answer him 'that this people may know that thou, O Lord, art God' (1 Kings 18:37). Fire came down from heaven, consumed the burnt offering and licked up the water in the trench. The assembly shouted 'The Lord, he is God; the Lord, he is God' and threw themselves onto the ground in awe. At Elijah's command the pagan priests were seized by the people, hauled down the mountainside to the Kishon brook in the valley below, and there put to death.

During the day everyone had fasted because of the solemn religious nature of the occasion. With complete confidence Elijah now told King Ahab to eat and drink, for he would soon hear the rushing sound of the rain. The prophet climbed to the highest point of the Carmel where he crouched down on the ground. He sent his servant time after time to gaze out over the water. The seventh time the man reported that he had seen that 'a little cloud like a man's hand is rising out of the sea' (1 Kings 18:44). The servant was sent to tell Ahab the drought would soon be over and that he should prepare to leave in his chariot at once if he did not want to get bogged down in the mud. Soon the whole sky was covered with dark clouds. The wind howled and torrents of rain poured down. The king drove through the storm to his winter palace at Jezreel, seventeen miles away. The exultant prophet, filled with 'the spirit of the Lord', tied his clothes around his waist and loped ahead of the chariot to the entrance of the Jezreel valley.

*Elijah at Mount Sinai*   When Ahab told Jezebel what had happened she flew into a rage, and dispatched a message to Elijah that by the following day he would suffer the fate he had meted out to her prophets. Seeing that the queen retained the power to carry out her threat, Elijah fled southwards into the kingdom of Judah.

With his faithful servant the prophet reached Beersheba, one hundred and thirty miles from Samaria. Leaving the servant there, he walked all day into the barren desert. At nightfall, he sank down exhausted beneath a bush. Sick at heart, he

begged the Lord to let him die. In a vision during the night, he felt an angel touch him on the shoulder and awoke to find bread and a jar of water on the ground beside him. Once again, as at the stream of Cherith, food had miraculously been provided to keep him alive. When this happened a second time, Elijah felt strong enough to set out on a gruelling trek across the rugged and barren terrain into the heart of the Sinai peninsula. His journey's end was Mount Sinai (also called Mount Horeb) where Moses had received the Law from God. Elijah had been driven by a compulsion to renew his faith at its source.

At the mountain, Elijah took shelter in a cave. The coming of the Lord was heralded by convulsions of nature. A gale, an earthquake and a fire swept over the landscape. Then the word of the Lord came to Elijah as 'a still small voice', asking him why he had come there. Elijah replied that in the kingdom of Israel the people had forsaken the Lord and turned to idolatry. For clinging to the true faith he had had to run for his life. The Lord told Elijah to go back and resume his mission. The Baal-worshippers would be destroyed by a new regime in Israel, by the attacks on Aram-Damascus, and by the efforts of a successor prophet, Elisha, who would continue Elijah's work.

On his way northward through the Jordan valley, Elijah passed a field where Elisha was ploughing with a team of his father's oxen. Elijah took off his cloak and flung it over the young man, who promptly accepted the call to service. He took leave of his parents and attached himself to the great prophet as his life-long disciple.

King Ahab had set his heart on acquiring a *Naboth's* vineyard in Jezreel belonging to a local citizen *Vineyard* called Naboth. The vineyard adjoined the grounds of the winter palace, and the king wanted it for a vegetable garden. He offered the owner either a better vineyard elsewhere in exchange, or a fair purchase price. Naboth declined to part with it, on the ground that it was a family inheritance.

Ahab was so angry and upset that he refused to eat, and lay on his bed with his face to the wall. Jezebel demanded to know what was the matter. When she heard about the vineyard, she scornfully asked Ahab whether he was the king or not. She told him to relax and to let her deal with the matter. She wrote letters to the town officials in

RIGHT Title page of The Bishops' Bible of 1568, with a portrait of Queen Elizabeth I.

# The.holie.Bible.

Non me pudet Euangelij Christi.
Virtus enim Dei est ad salutem
Omni credenti Rom. 1.

the name of the king and with his seal attached to them. The instructions in the letters were to call a town assembly, with Naboth in the seat of honour. By arrangement, two scoundrels were to appear and denounce him for uttering blasphemy against God and treason against the king. The hapless Naboth was then to be condemned, taken outside the wall and stoned to death. When Jezebel received confirmation that the plan had been carried out, she told the king he could take immediate possession of the vineyard. (By law, the property of a man condemned for treason was forfeited to the crown.)

Ahab went to the vineyard and found himself confronted by Elijah. Taken aback, the king exclaimed, 'Have you found me, O my enemy?' (1 Kings 21:20). 'Have you killed, and also taken possession?' (1 Kings 21:19). the prophet demanded. In the Lord's name he pronounced a doom on Ahab and all his house, that would be wiped out like those of Jeroboam and Baasha before him. As for the queen: 'The dogs shall eat Jezebel within the bounds of Jezreel' (1 Kings 21:23).

The king was overcome with guilt and remorse on hearing Elijah's fierce denunciation. He tore his clothes, put sackcloth next to his skin, fasted and 'went about dejectedly'. There is no reason to believe that he was a party to Jezebel's plot. Ahab, it should be noted, had not tried to seize the vineyard when his subject Naboth refused to part with it. A Hebrew king was not above the law. However, as a foreign princess accustomed to a ruler's despotic powers, Jezebel clearly had no understanding or respect for the curbs on her husband's royal prerogatives.

Ahab's penitence earned him a reprieve; Elijah was told by the Lord that the doom pronounced on the house of Ahab would take effect only in the next reign. The scene in the vineyard was the last encounter the king had with his old adversary.

*The War with Syria* In Ahab's reign, as in that of his father Omri, the Syrian kingdom of Aram-Damascus was the major threat to the kingdom of Israel. Its king Ben-hadad 1 gained control of all the smaller Aramean kingdoms and principalities in the area, and made their rulers his vassals. He mobilized a large army, including thirty-two vassals and their contingents, and marched against Samaria. Encamped near the city, Ben-hadad sent messengers to Ahab with humiliating demands. The gold and silver in the palace treasury were to be handed over to him, and also a number of royal wives and children – presumably to be held as hostages. Ahab sent a deferential but evasive reply: 'As you say, my lord, O king, I am yours, and all that I have' (1 Kings 20:4). When nothing happened, a second and more arrogant message arrived from Ben-hadad. It stated that he was sending a party of men the following day to search the palace and the residences of the chief courtiers, and to carry away everything of value.

Ahab called a council of his advisers and the city notables and explained the position to them. The consensus was that the Syrian pressure should be resisted. Ahab sent a reply rejecting the demands. This defiance reached Ben-hadad as he and his vassals lolled at their ease, tippling in their pavilions. This time the Israelite king received a blustering threat: the Syrian troops would flatten the city and carry away the rubble in their hands. Ahab's sarcastic retort was: 'Let not him that girds on his armour boast himself as he that puts it off' (1 Kings 20:11) – in other words, a real soldier does his boasting after the battle, not before.

A military showdown was now inevitable, and Ahab prepared to strike first. He was encouraged by a prophet to believe that the Lord would give him victory. A picked unit of two hundred and thirty-two young men was sent ahead as an armed reconnaissance party, followed by the main force of seven thousand men led by the king in person. When the Syrian outposts reported that they had sighted the advance guard, Ben-hadad still did not take it seriously. He ordered that the approaching enemy soldiers be captured and brought in alive, whether they came to fight or to parley. Contrary to accepted military practice, the main Israelite attack came in the heat of the day and caught the enemy camp unprepared. The Syrian army broke up and fled in disorder with the men of Israel in hot pursuit. On their return the same unnamed prophet warned the king that he should prepare for a renewed Syrian offensive the following spring.

In planning the next campaign, Ben-hadad's generals analysed their defeat at Samaria and drew lessons from it. The most important one concerned the choice of battleground. The Israelites were hill men and fought best among their native ridges and valleys. They should be drawn out into the open where the advantages of the terrain would not be on their side. 'Their gods are gods of the hills, and so they were stronger than we; but let us fight against them in the plain, and surely we shall be stronger than they' (1 Kings 20:23). The second point they made was a more sensitive one. As soldiers, they must have suffered from the presence in the field of a group of vassals, each giving orders to his own men. Like all army men down the ages, the Syrian generals insisted that war was a matter for professionals, not amateurs. They demanded: 'Remove the kings, each from his post, and put commanders in their places' (1 Kings 20:24).

Ben-hadad rebuilt his defeated army 'horse for horse, and chariot for chariot'. In the spring he moved forward along an axis that would have taken him past the southern end of the Sea of Galilee and westward along the valley of Jezreel, keeping out of the hill country. But Ahab had anticipated this Syrian thrust and blocked it on the Golan Heights, just north of the Yarmuk river ravine. In the battle that followed, the Israelite army was again victorious. The remnants of the Syrian forces, including Ben-hadad and his staff, escaped into the walled town of Aphek, near the eastern shore of the Sea of Galilee. When the town was about to fall, Ben-hadad sent a group of senior officers to Ahab to seek surrender terms. They wore sackcloth and ropes around their necks as signs of submission. To their relief the Israelite monarch was a magnanimous victor. He referred to Ben-hadad as his brother, sent for him and invited him to ride in the royal chariot.

In exchange for his freedom, Ben-hadad offered two concessions which were accepted. One was to restore Israelite towns and territory in northern Trans-jordan that had been occupied by the Syrians in the previous reign. The second was to grant the merchants of Israel a bazaar quarter in Damascus like the one the Syrians had enjoyed in Samaria.

The leniency Ahab had shown towards the defeated Syrian enemy upset the more extreme religious elements in his country. On his way back from Aphek Ahab was accosted by a member of a band of prophets who predicted that the king would be slain and his army routed, because his release of Ben-hadad and his soldiers had displeased the Lord. But Ahab probably had a farsighted and statesmanlike reason for wanting to end the chronic strife with Israel's north-eastern neighbour. A formidable common enemy was beginning to loom on the horizon. For the next three years there would be a truce between Samaria and Damascus, while they joined forces against the dreaded Assyrian war-machine rolling towards them from Mesopotamia.

Since the time of Joshua's conquest, nearly four centuries earlier, the Syrian–Israelite region had not known domination by an external imperial power. Egypt to the south had been in decline. The Mesopotamian area was engaged in local struggles for hegemony. The Hittite empire, stretching down from Asia Minor as far as Syria, had crumbled by the thirteenth century BC. In the intervening period the peoples of Syria and Canaan – Arameans, Israelites, Phoenicians, Philistines and others – had been concerned only with each other. They had set up kingdoms and city-states, fought wars, forged alliances, and developed trade. The lengthy interlude of imperial power-vacuum was about to end. Assyria, a kingdom astride the upper Tigris valley, had become the paramount state in the Mesopotamian basin, and its might was spreading across the Near East in every direction. The long shadow of its capital, Nineveh, was moving towards the Israelite kingdoms and their neighbours.

*The Shadow of Nineveh*

In excavating the ruins of Nineveh and other Assyrian cities, archaeologists have revealed a wealth of written and visual material about this ancient people, whose history and civilization overlapped those of the Babylonians further south on the Mesopotamian plain. Whatever their impressive achievements were in architecture, sculpture, astronomy and other arts of peace, the national obsession of the Assyrians was with war and conquest. They raised the military art to a technical level new in human history. The superbly detailed palace bas-reliefs and other treasures, now seen in leading western museums, depict the arrogant faces of Assyrian kings adorned with great curled beards, while the representatives of subject peoples kneel down before them offering tribute. Boastful inscriptions of victories are illustrated by scenes of battle and carnage: the chariots, cavalry, archers and spearmen advancing in serried ranks; city fortifications being overcome with battering rams, scaling ladders and tunnels; piles of dismembered corpses; and the dejected lines of captives being led away.

In 853 BC the smaller countries of the eastern Mediterranean were drawn together by a common fear as the Assyrian monarch Shalmanezer III marched westward at the head of a powerful army. Ahab of Israel and Ben-hadad of Aram-Damascus were among the leading members of a coalition of kings that combined their forces to halt the Assyrians. The battle took place at Karkar, on the Orontes river in northern Syria. In a palace inscription that has survived, Shalmanezer claimed that he had won a decisive victory, and that so many of the enemy slain were thrown into the river that he and his men were able to cross it on a bridge of corpses. Actually, the battle must have been less than conclusive, for Shalmanezer withdrew his army and did not resume the westward thrust for another five years. The inscription lists the eleven (possibly twelve) kings in the coalition, with the contingents contributed by each to the combined force. Ahab the Israelite is credited with providing ten thousand foot soldiers and two thousand chariots, about half the total force – a measure of the relative military importance of the kingdom of Israel at that time.

*Ahab's Building Programme*

Ahab was one of the most notable builders among the Hebrew kings. He further developed Samaria, the capital city founded by his father Omri. Among his additions were a defence wall surrounding the lower town, sturdy enough to withstand battering rams. The palace buildings in his time must have been adorned and furnished with considerable luxury, judging by the thousands of fragments of ivory found in the ruins, some of them decorated with gold and lapis lazuli. They were used as inlays in thrones, beds and other pieces of furniture, as well as on wall panels. Although some of these fragments bear the ancient Hebrew script, their design and motifs show the strong cultural influence of Phoenicia and to a lesser extent that of Egypt and Damascus. The Bible refers to an 'ivory house' built by Ahab, while the prophet Amos speaks of ivory houses and beds of ivory as marking the sumptuous life style which he attacked. Ivory was a rare and costly commodity, rated in value with gold, gems and spices.

Ahab's ambitious building programme was concerned with strengthening the defences of the realm. That was understandable, given the chronic struggle with Aram-Damascus, and the alarm over Assyrian expansion in the latter part of Ahab's reign. While the Bible refers generally to 'all the cities that he built' (1 Kings 22:39),

archaeological interest focuses on two places of the highest strategic priority, Megiddo and Hazor. These were two of the three 'chariot cities' on which Solomon had concentrated. The third, Gezer, lay in the territory of the kingdom of Judah in the coastal plain.

Megiddo controlled the vital pass of Wadi Ara that led from the coastal plain and cut through behind the Carmel range into the Jezreel valley. The Via Maris, the main route from Egypt to Mesopotamia, came through this pass. Five years after Solomon's death its fortifications had been partly demolished by the expeditionary force of the pharaoh Shishak. Ahab reconstructed the public buildings, including quarters for the regional governor. The massive city wall was rebuilt of blocks of stone, with salients and recesses to provide crossfire. These were solid walls of stone blocks, not the casemate type (double walls enclosing small rooms) that had been used by Solomon. This important change in military engineering came about in response to the battering rams employed in Assyrian tactics.

A distinctive feature of the Megiddo ruins is the extensive row of stalls equipped with stone tethering posts and limestone mangers. The stables could accommodate four hundred and ninety-two horses. Until recently they were known as 'Solomon's stables' as they were thought to have been constructed by that monarch for his chariot horses. It is now accepted that they date from the time of Ahab, nearly a century after Solomon.

Also attributed to Ahab's engineers is the elaborate water system at Megiddo. A vertical shaft with a stairway goes down for twenty-four metres (seventy-eight feet). At the bottom, a tunnel leads off through the sheer rock for sixty-eight metres (two hundred and twenty-one feet) to natural springs outside the city walls. This underground system provided a constant and protected supply of fresh water, essential to withstand a long siege in a hot country that is rainless for the greater part of the year.

Hazor in the Huleh valley near the upper Jordan river was of special importance, as it was the key citadel facing the northern sector of the frontier with hostile Aram-Damascus. The Via Maris passed close by, went over the Jordan at the ford that became known as B'not Ya'acov (the daughters of Jacob), and then crossed the Golan Heights to Damascus. Ahab reconstructed

Solomon's citadel, doubling its area and enclosing it in a thick solid wall. Here too, the complex water system dates from Ahab's time. A stairway spirals round the sides of a huge shaft. Forty metres (one hundred and thirty feet) down, a wide flight of steps leads through a gallery to a pool of water fed by a spring.

*Ahab's Last Campaign* After the battle of Karkar the Assyrian threat receded, and the ad hoc common front against Shalmanezer broke up again. King Ahab chafed at the fact that the Syrians had not carried out their promise to withdraw from Israelite territory in Trans-jordan, including the town of Ramoth-gilead. King Jehoshaphat of Judah came at this time on a royal visit to Samaria, the northern capital. It was the first time such a visit had been made since the united monarchy had split, and it marked the reconciliation between the two Hebrew kingdoms. Ahab took advantage of the cordial atmosphere to propose that Jehoshaphat should be his ally in a military expedition to regain Ramoth-gilead. Jehoshaphat was willing to do so but, being a devout ruler, asked that God's will should first be sought.

For this purpose the whole prophetic community, some four hundred in number, was assembled at the threshing floor outside the city gate of Samaria. The two monarchs sat side by side on thrones in their royal robes. Ahab put the formal question: 'Shall I go to battle against Ramoth-gilead, or shall I forbear?' (1 Kings 22:6). The reply was unanimous: The Lord would give him victory. The leader of the prophets, Zedekiah, produced a pair of horns made of iron as a symbol that the Syrian army would be pushed back and destroyed.

The king of Judah was not entirely convinced by this chorus of yes-men. He enquired whether there were any prophets who had not been included in the group. Yes, Ahab replied, there was one called Micaiah 'but I hate him, for he never prophesies good concerning me, but evil' (1 Kings 22:8). To satisfy the scruples of his royal visitor, Ahab sent an official to fetch Micaiah. The messenger advised the independent-minded prophet that for his own good he had better conform with the affirmative opinion already given. When Micaiah meekly echoed the other prophets, it was so out of character that Ahab refused to believe him and ordered him to say what he really thought. This time the prophet did not mince his words. He grimly predicted that the expedition would end in failure and that Ahab would be slain; the Lord was leading him to his fate by putting 'a lying spirit' into the mouth of the other prophets. Zedekiah, the spokesman for the others, was so indignant that he struck Micaiah in the face. The outspoken man of God was arrested on the spot and Ahab ordered that he be kept in prison on bread and water until the king returned safely from the war.

Apparently, Ahab was unable to put Micaiah's prediction out of his mind. When battle was joined at Ramoth-gilead he concealed his identity and refrained from putting on his royal robes over his armour, as his ally King Jehoshaphat did. The Syrian ruler, Ben-hadad, had instructed his thirty-two chariot commanders to concentrate their attack on the king of Israel. They converged on the conspicuous figure of the king of Judah until they heard his battle cry and realized their mistake. Ahab's disguise might have saved him, but one of the Syrian archers 'drew his bow at a venture, and struck the king of Israel between the scale armour and the breastplate' (1 Kings 22:34).

The wounded king behaved with great gallantry. He had himself driven to the edge of the swirling battle and propped himself up in his chariot facing the enemy, to maintain the morale of his troops. He died at sunset with a pool of blood on the floor of the chariot. The cry of retreat went through the army of Israel. The soldiers broke away and escaped under cover of darkness. Jehoshaphat withdrew to Jerusalem. Ahab's body was brought back to Samaria for burial, 'And they washed the chariot by the pool of Samaria, and the dogs licked up his blood, and the harlots washed themselves in it' (1 Kings 22:38).

## Decline and Resurgence

AFTER THE DEATHS OF AHAB KING OF ISRAEL and Jehoshaphat king of Judah, in the middle of the ninth century BC, the fortunes of both kingdoms were at a low ebb for more than sixty years. They would revive only in the eighth century BC during the long and successful reigns of Jeroboam II in Israel and Uzziah in Judah.

Ahab was succeeded by his eldest son Ahaziah (850–849 BC). The new king of Israel was badly injured by falling through the lattice of an upper-storey room in the palace and was confined to his *The End of Elijah* bed. He sent messengers to the temple of the Philistine god Baal-zebub in Ekron, to enquire whether he would recover. On the way the king's messengers were intercepted by Elijah, who told them to go back and ask their master, 'Is it because there is no God in Israel that you are going to inquire of Baal-zebub?' (2 Kings 1:3). Ahaziah, the prophet added, would die of his injuries.

The story now moves into the mist of folk-legend that so often envelops the figure of Elijah. The angry king sent an officer and fifty men to capture him. They saw him sitting on top of a hill, and called out: 'O man of God, the king says, "Come down"' (2 Kings 1:9). To that Elijah replied that if he was indeed a man of God, fire would come down from heaven and consume the soldiers. That is what happened. The same fate befell the next platoon. The commander of the third one begged Elijah to spare him and his men. The prophet went back with him to the recumbent king and repeated his dire message in person.

The name of the god of Ekron in this account, Baal-zebub, means 'Lord of the fly'. It is a derisive scriptural pun on the name of Baal-zebul, that means 'Lord of the lofty abode', and was one of the titles of the chief Canaanite deity Baal. By the time of the New Testament the name had become Beelzebub or Beelzebul, and was used in the Gospels as a synonym for Satan.

The injured Ahaziah died less than two years after he had mounted the throne. Since he had no male heir he was succeeded by his younger brother Jehoram (or Joram; 849–842 BC) – not to be confused with his contemporary and brother-in-law Jehoram of Judah who was married to Athaliah, a princess of the house of Omri.

Elijah felt that his work on earth was drawing to a close. With Elisha he walked from Gilgal, on the plain of Jericho, up the Judean escarpment to Bethel and then down again to Jericho. At each place he tried to persuade Elisha to stay behind and let him go on alone, but his faithful disciple refused to leave him. The local prophetic communes somehow became aware that the departure of the revered Elijah was near. In Bethel, and again in Jericho, they asked Elisha whether he knew that the Lord would take away his master that day. With the curtness of grief Elisha answered them: 'Yes, I know it; hold your peace' (2 Kings 2:3).

From Jericho, Elijah and Elisha, deep in talk, walked slowly to the bank of the river Jordan, about four miles away. A band of fifty of the local prophets followed at a respectful distance. Elijah took off his mantle, rolled it up and struck the surface of the river with it. The water parted and the two of them crossed over to the other side. Elijah asked what he could do for Elisha before they parted. Elisha asked for 'a double share of your spirit' (2 Kings 2:9).

Suddenly a fiery chariot drawn by fiery horses appeared next to them. Elijah stepped into it and it flew upwards with him in a great whirlwind until it vanished from sight. Elisha picked up the mantle his master had left lying on the ground and used it to recross the Jordan dry-shod. The group of prophets came up to him in great excitement. They were convinced that the whirlwind had deposited Elijah somewhere. For the next three days they searched for him among the hills and valleys in the area.

Jewish tradition has indeed clung to the belief that Elijah has not died, but will return one day with the Messiah. In the popular mind he has remained a mystic figure who might appear on festive occasions. It is customary to provide a special place for him at the Passover feast, and at a circumcision ceremony.

Elijah's mantle was the visible symbol of Elisha's succession. Although each devoted himself to the great crusade against pagan gods, there were marked differences in personality between the two holy men. Where Elijah was stern and solitary, Elisha was a gentler spirit, often associating with the groups of ascetics that followed the prophetic vocation. While Elisha appears in the Bible mainly as a worker of miracles, he played an important part in the political events leading to Jehu's seizure of power in the kingdom of Israel.

The city fathers of Jericho appealed to Elisha to purify their spring. The water was so saline that it made the fields barren and caused the women to have miscarriages. Elisha sprinkled some salt from a new bowl into the spring and its freshness was restored. Today, good water still wells up at Jericho from a spring that accounts for the remarkable oasis in a desert plain. The spring is by tradition named after Elisha.

From Jericho Elisha set off up the mountain to Bethel. Along the way a group of mischievous small boys from the town jeered at his bald head.

*Elisha the Wonder-Worker*

When Elisha lost his temper and cursed them, forty-two of them were mauled by two she-bears that appeared on the scene. (This incident is puzzling, as it seems out of character for so mild a prophet.)

Elisha spent a long time living in the Gilgal area as a member of the desert commune of holy men, 'sons of the prophets'. He performed a number of wonders to help his needy brethren.

One of the group died leaving his family in debt. The widow came to seek Elisha's aid because she owned nothing but a single jar of oil. The creditors were about to seize her two sons as bondsmen. Elisha told the family to borrow a large number of empty jars. They were all miraculously filled from the widow's one, and were sold to pay the debt and support the family.

During a famine the members of the commune kept themselves alive by gathering edible wild plants and cooking them. One day Elisha was teaching a group of disciples and requested that a pot of food be prepared for them. One of them sliced up into the pot yellow gourds he had picked off a vine without knowing what they were. The plant was poisonous and those who ate cried out: 'O man of God, there is death in the pot!' (2 Kings 4:40). Elisha sprinkled a little meal in the food, which promptly became wholesome.

A local farmer brought Elisha some loaves of barley bread and ears of grain as a gift of first-fruits from his field. Elisha told his servant to feed the hundred brethren in the commune from this gift. To the servant's astonishment there was enough for all, with some to spare.

Elisha went with some of the brethren to chop down trees at the river's edge, in order to build a hut. They used a borrowed axe, since they were too poor to own one. To their great distress, the axe fell into the water and sank from sight. When Elisha threw a twig into the water, the axe floated up to the surface and was retrieved.

These minor episodes illustrate the simple and austere existence of these groups of holy men living in the wilderness, and sustained by little more than their religious zeal.

Elisha and his servant Gehazi moved to Mount Carmel. From here the prophet went to and fro on devotional journeys, doing the Lord's work. From time to time he would pass through the village of Shunem twenty miles down the Jezreel valley. Here he would stop at the home of a well-to-do and devout woman who would give him

and his servant a meal. She persuaded her husband that the holy man should have a place to rest, so they built him a small room on their flat roof and furnished it with a bed, chair, table and lamp. Once, when Elisha was resting there, he asked his servant how the kindness of the mistress of the house could best be repaid. Gehazi pointed out that they were a childless couple and her husband was already an elderly man. Elisha sent for her and promised that she would bear a son. When the prediction came true, her joy was unbounded.

One hot day at harvest time the child went to the fields with his father, and was brought home with a blinding headache (possibly sunstroke). The same day he died in his mother's arms. She laid him on the bed in Elisha's room, hurried on her donkey to find the prophet on Mount Carmel and implored his help. He sent Gehazai ahead with his miraculous rod and followed more slowly with the woman. When the use of the rod by the servant did not help, Elisha closed himself in the room 'lay upon the child, putting his mouth upon his mouth, his eyes upon his eyes, and his hands upon his hands' (2 Kings 4:34). When he had done this a second time, the boy stirred, opened his eyes and sneezed seven times. Elisha called in the mother who was overcome with gratitude.

Since Elisha feared there would be a famine, the woman of Shunem moved away with her family to an unnamed place in Philistine territory. On returning seven years later, she petitioned the king for the return of her house and lands in Shunem. She obtained an audience at the palace just as the king was hearing an account from Elisha's servant Gehazi of the wonders performed by the prophet. The story of the woman's child restored to life made a deep impression on the king. At that moment the petitioner was brought in and identified by Elisha's servant. The king immediately instructed an official to restore her property to her, together with the value of the produce gathered during her absence.

The story of Elisha resuscitating the young son of the woman of Shunem is very similar to the story of Elijah and the young son of the widow with whom he lodged at Zarephath. It was believed that a prophet might be endowed by the Lord with a special life-force that in certain cases would enable him to revive the dead. In the New Testament, the raising of Lazarus is an example nine centuries after Elijah and Elisha.

OVERLEAF Samson being bound by the Philistines while Delilah jeers at him. A painting by the nineteenth-century British artist Solomon J. Solomon.

The Prophet Elisha makes the axe-head miraculously float on the water.
Drawing by Rembrandt van Ryn.

Elisha moved to Samaria and became a well-known religious figure in the capital. At that time the commander-in-chief of the armed forces of Aram-Damascus was called Naaman. He was the man responsible for his country's military *Naaman's* prowess and was highly regarded by his king. *Leprosy* Naaman contracted the dread disease of leprosy. His wife's maid was a young Israelite girl carried away in one of the Syrian incursions into the kingdom of Israel. She asked her mistress why her master did not seek a cure from the renowned prophet who lived in Samaria. Naaman obtained permission to do so from the king of Damascus, who gave him a letter of introduction to Jehoram, the king of Israel. It read: 'When this letter reaches you, know that I have sent to you Naaman my servant, that you may cure him of his leprosy' (2 Kings 5:6). The Syrian general set out for Samaria with a large party. They travelled in a convoy of chariots, taking with them a splendid gift of 'ten talents of silver, six thousand shekels of gold, and ten festal garments' (2 Kings 5:5). When King Jehoram read the letter he tore his clothes in dismay. How, he asked, could the king of Damascus possibly expect him to cure leprosy? This could only be a devious way of provoking a quarrel. (Israel and Aram-Damascus were not at war at the time.)

Elisha got word of the visit, and sent a message to the palace proposing that the Syrian be sent round to his house. When Naaman arrived, the prophet neither invited him in nor came out to greet him. Instead he sent a servant to tell Naaman that he would get rid of his disease by bathing seven times in the river Jordan. Naaman was surprised and offended at this treatment: 'I thought that he would surely come out to me, and stand, and call on the name of the Lord his God, and wave his hand over the place, and cure the leper' (2 Kings 5:11). Besides, he asked, were not the rivers back in Damascus better than any in Israel? His servants soothed him down and persuaded him to try the prophet's suggested cure. He went down to the Jordan and immersed himself seven times. To his delight, his flesh became as firm and healthy as that of a child.

Naaman rushed back to the prophet in Samaria and declared that he had been converted to a belief in the Hebrew God. He offered Elisha all the wealth he had brought with him, but the man of God declined to accept any reward. Naaman asked for two mule-loads of earth to take back

with him to Damascus so that he could pray to the Lord on Israel soil. He hoped the Lord would forgive him if his official position required him from time to time to accompany his ruler to worship at the temple of the god Rimmon in Damascus.

The money Elisha had declined aroused the greed of his servant Gehazi. He ran after the Syrian party. When Naaman stopped and asked him what was the matter, he came out with a concocted story. Two destitute young prophets, he said, had arrived at his master's home, and Elisha would like to be able to give them a talent of silver and a change of clothing. Naaman promptly pressed on the servant two bags of silver instead of one, and two changes of fine raiment. The servant hid these gains for himself. Unfortunately for him, the prophet divined what he had done. As a punishment, Gehazi was inflicted with the leprosy that Naaman had shed and turned 'as white as snow'.

Some time later the king of Damascus, Ben- *Samaria* hadad, resumed the war against the kingdom of *under Siege* Israel. In the first phase of the operations, armed detachments penetrated across the border into Israel territory. Each time they found the Israel defenders waiting for them and were repulsed. It was clear that the Israelites somehow knew in advance where and when the Syrians would strike. Ben-hadad called together his senior officers and charged that one of them was a traitor. This they all denied. One officer asserted that the security leaks were due to the uncanny powers of the prophet Elisha who could tell the Israel king even 'the words that you speak in your bedchamber' (2 Kings 6:12).

Learning that the prophet was then in Dothan, a town ten miles north of Samaria, Ben-hadad sent a mobile column of chariots and horsemen to capture him. They surrounded the town at night. Next morning Elisha found himself trapped and prayed to the Lord for help. The Syrian soldiers were struck with temporary blindness. Pretending to be someone else, Elisha came up to them and undertook to guide them to the man they were seeking. He led them straight into Samaria and handed them over to the royal guards before their sight was restored. King Jehoram asked whether the captives should be slain but the prophet advised that they should be given food and sent back unharmed across the border. After this act of clemency, the raids stopped for a short time.

ABOVE King Solomon and the Queen of Sheba. A painting by the Scottish artist Duncan Grant (1912).

RIGHT Solomon's Temple, with some of the kings, priests and prophets in the early Divided Monarchy period. A German woodcut from the Nuremberg Chronicle (1493).

Templum Salomonis

## Linea der Bischoff
### Sadoch der sun Achitob

Sadoch ein höhster brie=
ster in der zal der bischoff
der achtend fieng an zesitzē
im anfang des reich Sa=
lomonis.

### Achimas ein sun Sadoch

Difer Achimas d newnd
höhst briefter der hebrey,
fcheit was berümbt vnnd
in großer erwirdigkeit bey
den iuden gehalten.

## Achias der prophet

A Chias filonites der
prophet weyffaget
dē roboā dz er regnē wurd
über zehen geflecht ifrahel
Anfang des reichs ifrahel
Ieroboam empfieng.x.
Treißung des mantels
vō achia dē prophetē vñ
fluhe in egiptē. do falomō
ftarb do wardt er vō den
x.geflechten zu könig erwelt.vnd leget guldine gegoß
ne kelber i Dañ vñ neptali. vñ wardt der ergft abgöt
tereyer.vñ vrfacht dz volck ifrahel zu fünde vñ abgöt
terey. darauß volget zerftörũg des gätz vocks ifrahel

### Semeias

S emeias der prophet ge=
fwayget Roboā do er
ftrit wid hieroboam vnd be=
fchribe ire d könig gefchihte.
vñ er weiffaget do Sefac der
egyptifch könig in dē lād iuda
vil übels thet nemlich im.v.
iar Roboam.

N adab des königs iheroboās fun d and könig if=
rahel hat in dē andern iar Aza des königs iude
ze regirn angefange.vnnd als fein vater vil übels ge=
than.aber Baafa hat ine geflage vñ für ine geregiert.
nach der weyffagung Achie des propheten.

B aafa vō de geflecht ifachar d drit ifrahelifch kö=
nig hat auch übel vor dē herrñ getan vñ in alle
fünde ieroboās gewadert.vñ de prophetē hieu d zu
ime gefedet wardt nit wolle höñ fund getödtet.aber
er wardtauch vō Chreone vmbracht.

### Abdo

A bdo d prophet weiffaget
wid die guldine kelber vñ
die häd ieroboās dorrct.vñ do
er gein iherufale wid keret ward
er vō eine leoben ertödtet.

H Ela des königs baafe fun
der vierd könig ifrahel.

## Linea der könig ifrahel
### Ieroboam

### Nadab

### Baafa

### Hela

ward vō feinē knecht zambri mit allem haws fems vaters bis auff den pūtzenden
an die wand ertödtet nach der weyffagung hieu des propheten.

Ben-hadad then mounted an invasion of Israel with a large Syrian army and laid siege to Samaria. After some months the food reserves gave out and the city was starving. In the market-place, a donkey's head (although it was forbidden meat) sold for eighty shekels of silver, and a bowl of pigeon dung for five shekels of silver. Walking along the city wall one day, the king came upon two squabbling women, one of whom asked for his intervention. She claimed the two of them had made a pact to cook and eat each other's infant in turn. Hers had been consumed but the other woman had broken faith and concealed her own child. The horrifying story threw King Jehoram into despair. He blamed Elisha for bringing them to these straits by his misplaced faith in the Lord, and swore that the prophet's head would be lopped from his shoulders before the day was over.

Bursting into the house of Elisha, where some of the town elders had gathered, the king cried bitterly that it was no use waiting for the Lord to help them since it was the Lord who had brought this trouble upon them. Elisha solemnly assured him that by the following day there would be abundant food for everyone. One of the king's officers remarked that even if the Lord were to open the windows of heaven and let the rain come right away, what the prophet had said was not possible. Elisha snapped back at him that it would indeed happen, but the officer would no longer be around to eat the food.

As it was getting dark that evening, the Lord caused the Syrians to hear the noises of a great army approaching, with the beat of horses' hooves and the rumble of chariot wheels. Convinced that allied forces were marching up in strength to raise the siege, and fearful that their line of retreat was being cut, the Syrian soldiers abandoned their camp as it stood and disappeared into the darkness to try to get back across the river.

The same night, four lepers were sitting in the place of quarantine set aside for them outside the city gate. They decided that instead of dying of hunger they would risk being killed by going to the Syrian camp to scavenge for scraps of food. To their astonishment they found the camp totally deserted, with all the tents, equipment, supplies and personal belongings left intact, and the horses and donkeys still tethered in their places. The lepers went through some of the tents, ate and drank their fill and collected money and other valuables which they hid. They then realized that they might be in trouble if they delayed until the next day in reporting what they had seen. They approached the city gate and shouted their news to the guards. The information was relayed to the palace, where the king was awakened.

Together with his military advisers, he was suspicious that the Syrians had set a trap for them. The deserted camp full of food would lure out the starving defenders. They would then be captured and the city taken. With this suspicion in mind, the reaction was cautious. Two men were sent out to reconnoitre, mounted on a pair of the remaining horses. They went as far as the Jordan ford, easily following the escape route of the Syrians by the items of baggage and clothing shed along the way. When they got back, they confirmed that the invaders had gone and the siege was over.

The inhabitants of the city rushed out in a wild mob to loot the Syrian camp and carry away the food. The officer whose scepticism had annoyed Elisha the previous day happened to be on duty at the gate. He was trampled to death by the mob.

A period of truce must have followed between the kingdoms of Israel and Aram-Damascus, *Elisha in* since Elisha is next heard of in the city of *Damascus* Damascus. King Ben-hadad, who was seriously ill, heard that the renowned Israelite prophet who had cured his general Naaman was in the city. He sent a senior army officer called Hazael with forty camel-loads of gifts, to enquire of the prophet whether he would recover. Elisha's strange reply was that the king would recover from his ailment, but would soon die. Elisha stared fixedly into Hazael's face until the latter grew uncomfortable. Then tears ran down the prophet's cheeks. Hazael would himself become king, he predicted, and would do terrible things to Israel: 'set on fire their fortresses, and . . . slay their young men with the sword, and dash in pieces their little ones, and rip up their women with child' (2 Kings 8:12).

Hazael returned to the palace and told the king simply that Elisha had promised him recovery. The next day Hazael assassinated Ben-hadad by smothering him with a soaked blanket, and had himself proclaimed the new ruler.

With the militant Hazael on the throne in Damascus, the war between Syria and Israel flared up again. Once more, the struggle focused on possession of the strategic town of Ramoth-gilead in Trans-jordan. Wounded there in battle, King Jehoram returned to his winter palace at Jezreel to recuperate, after handing over command in the field to his general Jehu. Ahaziah, who had recently become king in Judah, had joined in the Syrian war on Israel's side. He now came to Jezreel to visit his wounded ally.

*The Revolt of Jehu*

The prophet Elisha believed that the time had come to end the Omri dynasty, and with it the influence of the hated queen-mother Jezebel. In his plan Jehu would serve as the Lord's instrument. Elisha sent a young prophet to the Israelite headquarters at Ramoth-gilead, carefully instructing him what to do. When the prophet arrived there, he found that Jehu was in a staff conference. The general rose and went into a nearby room with the odd visitor, to see what message he had brought. The young man solemnly produced the vial of oil Elisha had given him, and anointed Jehu with it. He declared that the Lord had chosen Jehu to be king and to wipe out the house of Ahab. With his mission accomplished, the prophet fled.

Jehu rejoined his brother officers, who asked out of curiosity what that 'mad fellow' had wanted of them. He was evasive at first, but when they pressed him, told them what had happened. They leapt to their feet, flung their cloaks across the staircase for him to walk on, and proclaimed him king to the sound of trumpets. Their spontaneous reception swept away any doubts Jehu may have felt about the role thrust upon him. He instructed the commanders to make sure that nobody slipped away from the camp in Ramoth-gilead to warn King Jehoram in Jezreel. He then leapt into his chariot and sped off on the fifty-mile journey to the king's winter palace, with a troop of horsemen galloping behind him.

A sentry in the watch-tower at Jezreel reported that he could see a party in the distance approaching in a cloud of dust. A horseman was sent out to see who they were. He rode up to Jehu and asked him in the king's name whether they came in peace. Jehu shouted at him: 'What have you to do with peace? Turn round and ride behind me' (2 Kings 9:18). The same thing happened with a second messenger. The sentry in the watch-tower observed that 'the driving is like the driving of Jehu, the son of Nimshi; for he drives furiously' (2 Kings 9:20).

Eager to find out what tidings the commander

was bringing in such haste, the two kings rode out to meet him, each in his own chariot. As they drew close Jehoram called out 'Is it peace, Jehu?' (2 Kings 9:22). The insolent reply was: 'What peace can there be, so long as the harlotries and the sorceries of your mother Jezebel are so many?' (2 Kings 9:22). Shouting 'treachery', Jehoram spun his chariot round and tried to escape, as did Ahaziah. Jehu snatched up his bow and loosed an arrow that hit Jehoram in the back and pierced his heart, killing him instantly. King Ahaziah was chased and wounded. He managed to reach Megiddo before he died. His staff carried his body to Jerusalem for burial. On Jehu's orders, Jehoram's body was flung into Naboth's vineyard, which lay close to where the king had been killed. Turning to his aide, Jehu recalled that both of them had been in King Ahab's escort on the occasion when the prophet Elijah had at this very spot foretold the doom of Ahab's dynasty.

The queen-mother Jezebel met her own end with all the pride and spirit of her royal lineage. When told of the grim events she went up to her room, where she carefully groomed her hair and applied her make-up. She then took her stand at the open window. As Jehu drove through the gate in the courtyard, she cried out to him in scorn: 'Is it peace, you Zimri, murderer of your master?' (2 Kings 9:31). (Zimri had also usurped the throne through assassination, forty years earlier.) Jehu halted, and shouted up to two or three palace eunuchs who were peering out. He ordered them to fling Jezebel through the window, which they did. She fell to her death in the courtyard below. Her blood spattered against the wall and splashed on the legs of Jehu's horses as he drove his chariot over her body. Without a backward glance, Jehu strode into the palace and sat down to a meal. Only then did he say to his servants: 'See now to this cursed woman, and bury her; for she is a king's daughter' (2 Kings 9:34). All they found left in the courtyard was her skull and the bones of her feet and hands. The dogs had eaten her, as Elijah had prophesied.

The gruesome account of Jezebel's death betrays the revulsion the biblical writers felt for her. More than any other character, she is presented as the embodiment of evil.

Jehu had seized Jezreel, but it was only a minor provincial town where the king's winter palace was located. The capital and main city of the kingdom was Samaria. That was where the ruling

ABOVE Queen Jezebel flung to her death on the orders of King Jehu seated in his chariot. The sixteenth-century Jezebel Tapestry now in Bath, England.

RIGHT King Hezekiah, a painting by the contemporary American artist Jack Levine.

classes were concentrated and where seventy of Ahab's descendants lived. Jehu's claim to the throne was worth little until he was accepted in Samaria. He threw out a bold challenge to the leadership there either to fight him or to submit. In a letter addressed to the top officials, and to the guardians of Ahab's descendants, Jehu proposed that they choose a suitable member of the royal family as a successor to King Jehoram, and then prepare to defend him. Intimidated by the stories reaching them of Jehu's ruthless methods, they sent a reply pledging allegiance to him and offering to carry out whatever orders he gave.

*The Bloody Purge*

Jehu sent them a second letter. It was ambiguous in its terms, but craftily devised to make them dispose of all the potential legitimate heirs to the throne. The letter read: 'If you are on my side, and if you are ready to obey me, take the heads of your master's sons, and come to me at Jezreel tomorrow at this time' (2 Kings 10:6). The word 'heads' could be read as leaders, but the frightened recipients of the letter took it literally. They killed all the seventy princes who were Ahab's sons and grandsons, put their severed heads in baskets and had them taken to Jehu in Jezreel. He ordered them to be heaped in two piles at the city gate. When a crowd had collected there, he came and addressed them. He had conspired against and killed the king, Jehu said to them; but who, he asked, was responsible for killing the princes? Surely their deaths carried out God's will, as expressed in Elijah's prophecy about the doom of the house of Ahab.

Continuing the blood-bath, Jehu rounded up and put to death all those in Jezreel who had been associated with the royal family, whether as relatives, officials or priests. Jehu then set out for Samaria. On the way, he met a group of forty-two people from the kingdom of Judah. They told him that they were kinsmen of the late King Ahaziah of Judah, and were going to Jezreel on a visit of condolence to the children and family of Queen Jezebel. It was a fatal admission; Jehu had them seized and killed, and their bodies flung into a pit.

Further along, Jehu came upon Jehonadab, the leader of the Rechabites. They were an ascetic sect that refused to touch wine, shunned houses and cultivation, and lived in tents. Jehu invited Jehonadab to ride in his own chariot, and to witness how devoted he was to the Lord.

In Samaria, Jehu had all the surviving relatives of Ahab put to death. He next turned his attention to the adherents of the Baal cult introduced by Jezebel. Pretending that he was one of them, he proclaimed that on an appointed day he would offer sacrifices in the temple of Baal. The priests and worshippers of that cult in the kingdom were to attend the ceremony, on penalty of death. With all of them assembled in the temple, Jehu entered with Jehonadab the Rechabite at his side, and made the ritual sacrifice on the altar. At a given signal, eighty of his soldiers burst into the temple with drawn swords and slew the congregation. The sacred pillar of Baal was dragged out of the inner sanctum and burnt. The temple was razed to the ground and a latrine built on the site.

By this act Jehu completed the purge called for by Elijah and Elisha. The dynasty of Omri and Ahab had been liquidated. The pagan deviation had been dealt a shattering blow. It was a victory that exacted a heavy price in bloodshed, and ushered in a period of misrule and national decline.

After his dramatic coup, Jehu occupied the throne of Israel for twenty-eight years (842–815 BC). The dynasty he founded was to last nearly a century – longer than any other in the history of the northern kingdom.

*The Reign of Jehu*

In 841 BC, a year after Jehu seized power, the region was invaded by an Assyrian army under Shalmanezer III. He defeated the kingdom of Aram-Damascus, moved through Israel and reached Mount Carmel, where he received tribute from the rulers of Israel and Phoenicia. A black stone obelisk from Assyria shows Jehu kneeling at the feet of Shalmanezer. Carrying their spoils with them, the Assyrians returned to their own country.

For the kingdom of Israel, the relief was short-lived. The upheaval of the Jehu coup left it internally disorganized and externally isolated. The bonds Omri and Ahab had so carefully nurtured with Phoenicia to the north-west and Judah to the south were destroyed by Jehu's murders of Queen Jezebel and of King Ahaziah.

Hazael, the army officer who had usurped the throne in Damascus, took advantage of the vulnerable condition of Israel. With little serious resistance his troops occupied all the Israelite territory in Trans-jordan, as well as parts of eastern Galilee. One of the Syrian columns cut right through Israel, reached Gath on the coastal plain and exacted tribute from Judah before turning back.

By the time Jehu died, and was succeeded by his son Jehoahaz (815–801 BC), the kingdom of Israel had shrunk in size and was virtually a vassal of Damascus. Its military impotence is indicated by the figures given in the Bible for its total armed forces at that time: 'fifty horsemen and ten chariots and ten thousand footmen' (2 Kings 13:7).

The Syrian domination of Israel was abruptly ended by outside intervention, nearly a decade after Jehu's death. In 806 BC another Assyrian force swept through the area under king Adad-nirari III. Syria was crushed and Damascus taken. According to the Assyrian records, heavy tribute was also collected from Israel, Edom and Philistia. To the people of the northern Hebrew kingdom that mattered less than the crippling of their traditional enemy Aram-Damascus. They felt gratitude for the lifting of the Syrian pressure: 'Therefore the Lord gave Israel a saviour, so that they escaped from the hand of the Syrians; and the people of Israel dwelt in their homes as formerly' (2 Kings 13:5).

It could not be foreseen that a half century later this same 'saviour' – Assyria – would finally extinguish the kingdom of Israel.

*Athaliah Queen of Judah*

Under Jehoshaphat's successors the kingdom of Judah also declined sharply. Its moral fibre started slackening in the reign of Jehoshaphat's son Jehoram (849–842 BC). He seems to have been dominated by his queen Athaliah, a princess of the Omri dynasty in the northern kingdom. A determined and ambitious woman, she was responsible for pagan infiltration into Judah, under the influence of Jezebel in Israel.

The hold of Judah over subject peoples also grew weaker at this time. Edom in the south revolted and regained its independence. An expedition led by Jehoram to subdue it was cut off in the rugged Mount Seir area, south-east of the Dead Sea. When Jehoram and his aides escaped at night, his force disintegrated and his soldiers scattered to their homes. The Philistines were also restive, while Libnah, a Canaanite town in the territory of Judah on the coastal plain, successfully broke away.

At the age of forty King Jehoram died of a painful intestinal ailment. The Book of Chronicles asserts that his suffering was a punishment for his religious laxity. It adds that 'he departed with no one's regret', and was denied burial in the royal tomb. He was succeeded by his son Ahaziah (842 BC). Within a year Ahaziah was caught up in the Jehu uprising in the northern kingdom and killed. The queen-mother Athaliah had acted as regent in his absence. On her son's untimely death, she had herself proclaimed as the new ruler. Athaliah was the only woman to occupy a Hebrew throne, and the only monarch in the history of the kingdom of Judah who was not a direct descendant of David.

Athaliah ruthlessly eliminated other potential heirs to the throne by having all the male members of her husband's family executed. Only one escaped – Joash (also called Jehoash), the infant son of Ahaziah and therefore Athaliah's grandson. His aunt, Ahaziah's half-sister, was married to Jehoiada the high priest at the Temple. She spirited the child away and hid him with his nurse in the Temple compound, where she took care of him.

When Athaliah had reigned for six years (842–837 BC), the high priest conspired with the commanders of the palace guard to put the boy Joash on the throne. The ceremony was set for a Sabbath. Before then, the officers visited other towns in Judah and quietly arranged for their leading citizens and Levites to come to Jerusalem on the Sabbath to attend the Temple service. The commanders also ensured that the guard coming off duty on that day did not return to its quarters, but took up positions in the Temple courtyard with drawn swords for the security of the prince. Jehoiada presented the seven-year-old boy to the Temple crowd, anointed him and placed the crown on his head. The whole assembly shouted 'Long live the king!' with much clapping of hands and sounding of trumpets.

Hearing the din from the palace, the queen came over to the adjoining Temple compound to find out the cause. Her startled gaze fell on the spectacle of the boy standing at the place next to a pillar that was reserved for the monarch, with members of her own bodyguard drawn up round him. Shouting 'Treason! Treason!', she turned to flee but was seized by the soldiers. On Jehoiada's orders, she was dragged away from the Temple precincts to one of the palace gates and there put to death. The whole assembly then streamed over to the palace, where the boy-king was placed on the throne. The temple that Athaliah had built to

OVERLEAF The wrath of King Ahasuerus against Haman, with Queen Esther in the foreground. An undated painting by the seventeenth-century Dutch artist Jan Steen.

Baal in the palace grounds was wrecked; the images in it were broken up and the pagan priest, Mattan, was killed at his altar.

*Joash's Reforms*    Joash reigned in Judah for thirty-eight years (837–800 BC). As long as the high priest Jehoiada was alive, the young king was guided by him in religious matters. When he grew up, he ordered extensive renovations to be carried out on the neglected Temple. The funds were raised from two sources: donations from the worshippers, and a special tax collected throughout the kingdom. The control of this revenue was taken out of the hands of the priests. The funds were deposited in a large chest with a slit in the lid, placed next to the altar. The contents of the chest were regularly counted and recorded by representatives of the king and the high priest. The money was then handed over directly to the contractors for the payment of wages, the buying of materials and other expenses. The balance left over was used to replace the Temple vessels and utensils that had been defiled through the Baal-worship in the time of Queen Athaliah.

After the death of the high priest Jehoiada, the clerical establishment lost its influence on the king. The atmosphere at the court became more secular, and Joash sought the advice of leading notables rather than that of the priests. Friction developed between church and state. Religious circles criticized the king for deviating from his earlier piety, even accusing him of permissiveness about renewed Baal worship. The spokesman for the resentment was the priest Zechariah, the son of Jehoiada. Zechariah's outspoken public attack on the king cost him his life. At the instigation of the palace he was stoned to death. Joash's image was further impaired by this act of ingratitude to the memory of the man who had protected him as a child, put him on the throne and acted as his spiritual mentor.

The weakness of both Hebrew kingdoms during this period was exploited by Hazael, king of Aram-Damascus. A Syrian military expedition crossed the kingdom of Israel, reached the city of Gath on the coastal plain and threatened to invade Judah. Joash bought it off with a crippling ransom that took nearly all the gold and silver in the treasuries of the palace and the Temple. The humiliating submission, coming on top of the Zechariah affair, led to the assassination of Joash by two of his officials. He was succeeded by his son, twenty-five-year-old Amaziah (800–783 BC).

The new king's first act was to execute the assassins of his father. The biblical passage stresses the fact that their children were not harmed, on the Mosaic principle that: 'The fathers shall not be put to death for the children, or the children be put to death for the fathers; but every man shall die for his own sin' (2 Kings 14:6). This precept, unique to the Hebrew faith in the ancient Near East, stressed the responsibility of the individual for his actions, as against the traditional blood-feuds between families and clans.

*Amaziah invades Edom*    Amaziah sought to reassert the sway of Judah over Edom in the south, and to restore access through the Negev desert to the port of Ezion-geber at the head of the Gulf of Akaba. He first had to reorganize the fighting capacity of the nation that had sunk to a low ebb under his predecessors. Each clan had to provide a quota of men. They were formed into units of thousands and sub-units of hundreds, commanded by officers appointed by the king.

The expeditionary force inflicted a decisive defeat on the Edomites in the Valley of Salt (Wadi Araba), running southwards from the Dead Sea. They advanced from there into the heart of Edom and captured the city of Sela. The location of this place has not been established. Its name means 'rock', and some scholars identify it with Petra (Greek for rock), the extraordinary cliff-city in southern Trans-jordan that later became the capital of the Nabatean desert civilization.

The Book of Chronicles, faithful to its own religious angle on events, states that the campaign brought about a lapse in the faith of Amaziah, who until then had been accounted a God-fearing ruler. He became tainted with the Edomite cult and brought back pagan images to Jerusalem. A prophet who remonstrated with him provoked an angry threat: 'Have we made you a royal counsellor? Stop!' (2 Chron. 25:16) Undaunted, the prophet predicted the calamities that would befall Amaziah for straying from the fold.

*The Mercenaries from the North*    In preparation for the Edomite campaign Amaziah had augmented his levies by recruiting auxiliary units from the northern kingdom of Israel. He handed over a substantial amount of silver to the mercenary troops as advance payment for their services. A prophet came to the king and urged him to dispense with military support from the infidel north; otherwise, the

Lord would be displeased and the reinforcements would bring not victory but defeat. When Amaziah referred to the money he had already paid, the prophet assured him that 'The Lord is able to give you much more than this' (2 Chron. 25:9). Amaziah then sent the hired soldiers back to their homes. Deprived of the loot they had anticipated from the campaign in Edom, the returning mercenaries pillaged towns and villages in Judah on their way back. When he returned, angry at the havoc caused, and over-confident after his Edomite success, Amaziah provoked a quarrel with Israel that had disastrous consequences for him. He failed to grasp that the kingdom of Israel had recovered from the weakness of the Jehu period and was now a formidable adversary.

*The Death of Elisha*
The upward swing in the fortunes of the northern kingdom started in the reign of Jehu's grandson Jehoash (Joash), (801–786 BC). His major achievement was to regain practically all the Israelite territory that had been lost to Aram-Damascus during his father's time. The king of Damascus, Ben-hadad II, was unable to hold on to these occupied lands because his country was still suffering from the Assyrian invasion five years before the accession of Jehoash.

Success against Syria had been predicted by the aged and dying Elisha, when the new king came to pay his respects to the prophet and seek his blessing. At the request of the bedridden old man, Jehoash opened a window facing east and shot an arrow in the direction of Syria. The king, Elisha declared, would be the arrow of the Lord to drive back the Syrian foe. Elisha told the king to take the rest of the arrows from his quiver and strike the floor with them. Jehoash did so three times and then stopped. The prophet was upset that he had not done so five or six times; that would have been a portent that Israel would finally subdue Aram-Damascus, instead of just winning three battles against it.

Elisha's fame as a wonder-worker was so great that legend attributed miraculous powers to him even after death. One day the mourners at a funeral took fright at an approaching band of Moabite marauders. They threw the corpse they were carrying into the nearby tomb of Elisha and fled. On contact with the prophet's bones the man came to life and walked out of the tomb.

With the Syrians repulsed and lost territory regained, the kingdom of Israel built up a military strength much greater than that of Judah. The challenge thrown down by King Amaziah of Judah after his Edomite campaign was therefore a rash one. The reply from King Jehoash of Israel was contemptuous: 'You have indeed smitten Edom, and your heart has lifted you up. Be content with your glory, and stay at home; for why should you provoke trouble so that you fall, you and Judah with you?' (2 Kings 14:10). He reminded Amaziah of the parable about the lowly thistle on Mount Lebanon which asked for the daughter of the noble cedar as a wife for his son. The thistle was trampled down by a wild animal for its temerity.

*The War between the Kingdoms*

Amaziah brushed caution aside and threw himself into a war that brought quick and inglorious results for Judah. Its forces were defeated by the army of Israel and King Amaziah was captured in a battle at Beth-shemesh in the Judean foothills. Jehoash then advanced on Jerusalem, partly demolished its northern defence wall, and returned to Samaria with the Temple treasures and a number of hostages. Amaziah was evidently released.

Jehoash died soon after, and was succeeded on the throne of Israel by his son Jeroboam II (786–746 BC). Amaziah reigned in Judah for another three years, when a revolt broke out against him. He fled to Lachish on the coastal plain, where he was pursued and killed by the conspirators. His body was slung across a horse and brought back to Jerusalem for burial. His sixteen-year-old son Uzziah (also called Azariah; 783–742 BC) was put on the throne of Judah.

In the long parallel reigns of Jeroboam II in Israel and Uzziah in Judah (each lasting over forty years), the Hebrew nation enjoyed a strength and material well-being it had not known since the golden age of David and Solomon a century and a half earlier. Jeroboam and Uzziah were able and statesmanlike monarchs. They put behind them the brief and futile war their fathers had fought and lived in peace with each other. Both kingdoms expanded.

*A Period of Revival*

Israel consolidated its hold over Trans-jordan, where estates were granted to leading families loyal to the king. The balance of power was reversed, with Aram-Damascus now under the suzerainty of Israel. The growth in the security and affluence of the northern kingdom under Jeroboam produced a fresh surge of building activity. The archaeological excavations at the

sites of Samaria and Hazor reveal a number of
fine buildings dating from Jeroboam's time.
Nevertheless, the prophets Amos and Hosea
railed against the luxury and selfishness of the
ruling classes, and predicted disaster:

> Woe to those who are at ease in Zion,
>     and to those who feel secure on the
>     mountain of Samaria,
>
>                                   (Amos 6:1)

The doom was to come upon the kingdom of
Israel only a generation later.

As Jeroboam extended his sway to the east and
north of Israel, so did Uzziah to the south and
west of Judah. Edom and Philistia were brought
under the firm rule of Jerusalem. The general
conditions in the region made it possible for the
Hebrew kingdoms to regain a dominant status.
Assyrian power was fully engaged in
Mesopotamia for the time being. Egypt remained
withdrawn and dormant. The main local adversary, Aram-Damascus, had not recovered from
the devastating blow it had suffered earlier from
an Assyrian army. By the middle of the eighth
century BC Israel and Judah controlled between
them an area roughly corresponding to David's
empire at its zenith. This interlude of Hebrew
prestige and power would not outlast the two
outstanding kings who presided over it.

*Judah under*   Uzziah reasserted the status of Judah as a local
*Uzziah*   military power. He waged a successful campaign
to subdue Philistia and dismantled the fortifications of the Philistine cities of Gath, Ashdod
and Javneh. He established fortified places in this
part of the coastal plain to protect the access of
Judah to the Mediterranean. At the same time
the port of Ezion-geber was restored at the top of
the Gulf of Akaba, reopening the trade route to
the Red Sea. Judah also became the overlord of
Ammon, the desert kingdom east of the Jordan.

To secure his expanded kingdom, Uzziah gave
special attention to defence measures. The army
was increased and equipped with helmets, coats
of mail, shields, spears, bows and slings. The city
walls of Jerusalem were strengthened, especially
the vulnerable northern sector where there was
no steep ravine to serve as a natural defence, as on
the other three sides. Uzziah added three towers
and 'he made engines, invented by skilful men, to
be on the towers and the corners, to shoot arrows
and great stones' (2 Chron. 26:15). The 'engines'
in this puzzling sentence have been construed as

shielded platforms constructed in the walls for
the defenders.

Uzziah also built 'towers in the wilderness' –
that is, desert forts to safeguard trade routes,
borders, and grazing areas. The remains of some
of these forts have been excavated. The best
preserved of them is at the oasis of Kadesh-
barnea in north-eastern Sinai. It is rectangular in
shape, and has casemate walls with eight towers.

Uzziah did much to improve agriculture in his
realm. He 'hewed out many cisterns, for he had
large herds, both in the Shephelah and in the
plain, and he had farmers and vinedressers in the
hills and in the fertile lands, for he loved the soil'
(2 Chron. 26:10).

Some time in the latter part of Uzziah's reign
he contracted leprosy. From then until his death
he lived isolated in quarantine in a separate
house, and withdrew from public duties. As the
disease made him ritually unclean, he could no
longer go to the Temple. The conduct of affairs
of state was taken over by his son and eventual
successor Jotham, acting as regent. The Book of
Chronicles attributes Uzziah's affliction to
punishment for an act of sacrilege by him. It is
alleged that he arrogantly came into the Temple
and attempted to burn incense on the altar, a
function reserved to the priesthood. Eighty of the
priests intervened, headed by the high priest
Azariah, who courageously protested and asked
the king to leave. Standing next to the altar with
the incense burner in his hand, Uzziah flew into a
rage. To the horror of the priests, the white marks
of leprosy appeared on his forehead, and he
rushed away.

When Uzziah died he was buried in the
grounds outside the royal tomb. His body was
later reinterred outside the city walls – probably
in the time of Herod the Great, seven centuries
later. The tombstone placed over the new grave
was found on the Mount of Olives and is now
preserved in the Israel Museum. The Aramaic
inscription on it reads: 'Hither were brought the
bones of Uzziah, king of Judah. Do not open.'

On his father's death Jotham became king in
his own right, and reigned for another eight years
(742–735 BC). He continued the policies pursued
in Uzziah's reign, including the development
of strong defences. In Jerusalem he extended
the city wall and constructed a north gate to
the Temple compound. To Uzziah's chain of
outlying forts he added further strongpoints in

The biblical city of Lachish, in the Judean foothills thirty miles south-west of Jerusalem. The excavated summit of the Tell, in the centre of this aerial photograph, is eighteen acres in size.

the hill areas. From the Ammonites he exacted for three years a heavy annual tribute of silver, wheat and barley.

Jotham is commended in the Bible for his devotion to the Lord. In contrast, his son and successor Ahaz (735–715 BC) is branded as one of the wickedest of the kings of Judah. 'He even burned his son as an offering, according to the abominable practices of the nations whom the Lord drove out before the people of Israel' (2 Kings 16:3).

For the biblical writers it followed that he was unsuccessful because he was so impious a ruler. The kingdom declined, and the gains made under the king's illustrious grandfather Uzziah were lost again. The Edomites in the south threw off the yoke of Judah and took back the port of Ezion-geber. Philistia successfully rebelled as well. A weak and shrunken Judah was then sucked into momentous events that shook the whole region. The dreaded might of Assyria had reappeared upon the scene – this time to stay.

In 745 BC the vigorous Tiglath-pileser III (also called Pul in the Bible) came to the throne in Nineveh, and launched Assyria into the period of the greatest imperial expansion. He was not satisfied to send armies just on looting expeditions, like his predecessors. Tiglath-pileser was an empire-builder. His policy was to annex conquered countries as provinces, deport their ruling classes and bring in settlers from other parts of the realm. Within less than a decade the Assyrian empire reached as far as northern Syria.

## The Fall of Samaria

AFTER THE REIGN OF THE GREAT JEROBOAM II the northern kingdom of Israel entered a period of decline and internal instability. Jeroboam's son and successor Zechariah (746–745 BC) was murdered within a year, bringing to an end the Jehu dynasty that had ruled for almost a century. *Disintegration in Israel* His assassin Shallum usurped the throne but a month later was himself killed and replaced by Menahem (745–738 BC), who may have been the governor of Tirzah, the former capital. Menahem brutally repressed opposition to his seizure of power, and sacked the town of Tappuah when it refused to accept him as king.

Weakened by this series of revolts, Israel did not even attempt to resist the southward expansion of Assyria. Instead, Menahem bought

off attack by paying a huge tribute to Tiglath-pileser. The money was raised by a levy of fifty shekels of silver from every man of property in the kingdom. Menahem's son and successor Pekahiah (738–737 BC) remained subservient to Assyria. After two years he fell victim to another coup. The throne was seized by an army officer called Pekah (737–732 BC) with the help of fifty Gileadite troopers.

Three years later the army of Tiglath-pileser swept down the coastal plain as far as Gaza. King Pekah of Israel and King Rezin of Aram-Damascus were frightened into forming an anti-Assyrian alliance. When King Ahaz of Judah prudently refused to join it, the forces of Pekah and Rezin invaded the southern kingdom to force its submission, or at least to neutralize it in the coming confrontation with Assyria. The invaders planned to depose Ahaz and instal in his place a certain Tabeel, from a well-known family in northern Trans-jordan.

With his back to the wall, Ahaz appealed for help to Tiglath-pileser. He sent messengers saying: 'I am your servant and your son. Come up, and rescue me' (2 Kings 16:7). The messengers carried as a gift all the gold and silver Ahaz could scrape together from the treasuries of the palace and the Temple. The great prophet Isaiah, held in deep respect at the Jerusalem court, had tried to talk the king out of seeking so dangerous an ally. He urged Ahaz not to lose courage because of Pekah and Rezin: 'these two smoldering stumps of firebrands' (Isa. 7:4). But the king could not be dissuaded.

The Assyrian monarch needed little encouragement to respond to the call for help from Judah. He attacked and took Damascus, killing King Rezin and carrying off many captives. His army then swept into the kingdom of Israel and occupied the land of Gilead in Trans-jordan, the Galilee, the valley of Jezreel and the Sharon plain. Modern excavations show evidence of the destruction wrought at the two strategic cities of Hazor and Megiddo. At one blow the northern Hebrew kingdom had been reduced to its capital Samaria and the hill district around it. The occupied parts of the kingdom were turned into three Assyrian provinces and a number of their inhabitants were taken away as captives. In Samaria, King Pekah was assassinated by Hoshea (732–724 BC) who was allowed by the Assyrians to be a puppet ruler paying tribute to the new masters. He was to be the last ruler of the kingdom of Israel.

King Ahaz of Judah travelled to Damascus to pay homage to Tiglath-pileser. He was so impressed by the altar he saw in the temple at Damascus that he sent a scale model of it to Uriah the high priest in Jerusalem with an order that a copy be made and installed in the courtyard of the Temple. To make room for it the existing bronze altar was moved to one side and reserved for the king's use only. The twelve bronze oxen that supported the huge bowl known as 'the sea' were removed and replaced with stone supports, while the bronze trolleys for the lavers were replaced with wooden ones. The bronze was no doubt used by Ahaz to help pay the crushing tribute to the Assyrians.

*The Fall of Samaria*

In 727 BC Tiglath-pileser died and his son, Shalmazar, V, mounted the Assyrian throne. Encouraged by Egypt, King Hoshea of Israel foolishly revolted and withheld the tribute payment due from him. Shalmanezer invaded what was left of the kingdom of Israel, and laid siege to Samaria in 724 BC. Hoshea was taken captive and disappeared, but the siege of Samaria continued until 722 BC, when Shalmanezer died and the city fell to his successor Sargon II. The territory was annexed to the Assyrian empire. The northern Hebrew kingdom had ceased to exist.

According to an inscription left by Sargon, he rounded up and deported 27,290 of the inhabitants, including all the important citizens. They were transferred to locations in Assyria west of the Tigris river, and also to Media east of the river, that had been conquered a short while before. These deportees were the origin of the 'lost ten tribes of Israel', the descendants of whom have by popular belief been 'discovered' in various countries. In accordance with the general practice, Sargon brought into the annexed territory fresh settlers from Babylonia and the Hamath area of northern Syria, and a few years later also from Arabia. These immigrant communities merged with the local Israelite population. From the mixture there evolved the people known as the Samaritans, (i.e. the people of Samaria).

## Judah: The Age of Hezekiah

SOON AFTER THE FALL OF SAMARIA AND THE end of the northern kingdom, Ahaz of Judah was succeeded by his son Hezekiah (715–687 BC), one of the outstanding Hebrew kings. His major concern was the survival of Judah, a small state precariously clinging to life on the southern fringe of the Assyrian empire. In this struggle Hezekiah was supported by the greatest of the Hebrew prophets, Isaiah the son of Amoz. Isaiah served in Jerusalem as political adviser to three successive kings – Jotham, Ahaz and Hezekiah. He was not a comfortable counsellor for any ruler. Of independent mind and powerful moral authority, Isaiah had faith only in salvation from God, not in the alliances of expediency which rulers under pressure tend to seek. For him, the nation was in danger because it sinned, and could redeem itself only by drawing fresh strength from the wellspring of the Mosaic faith. In this respect the king and the prophet were of like mind. Hezekiah devoted himself to building up the spiritual defences of his people. However since his religious conviction was balanced by political realism, he also devoted himself to building up the military defences of the kingdom. While concentrating on this dual task Hezekiah was careful for a decade not to provoke the Assyrian power that had swallowed up the sister Hebrew kingdom of Israel.

*The King and the Prophet Isaiah*

Hezekiah carried out a thorough rehabilitation of the Temple. He called together the priests and Levites and instructed them to carry out the work. The doors and lamps were repaired. The building and everything in it were ritually purified. Any objects defiled by improper use were taken away and thrown into the valley of Kidron. The regular sacrifices were restored, with the king providing the animals from his own flocks and herds. Rules were laid down for the maintenance of the Temple staff from public offerings and gifts. The street shrines permitted in Jerusalem in the lax reign of Ahaz were removed. The local hilltop shrines or 'high places' in the rural areas, that had become tainted with pagan practices, were closed down.

*Hezekiah's Religious Reforms*

Hezekiah then invited the notables from all parts of the country to take part in a special Passover celebration in Jerusalem. The invitation was also sent by messenger to the remnants of the Hebrew population in what had been the northern kingdom of Israel, now under direct Assyrian rule. The letters carried by the couriers urged the northerners to come to the sanctuary in Jerusalem and to renew the devotion to God from which their fathers had strayed: 'For if you return to the Lord, your brethren and your children will find compassion with their captors, and return to this land. For the Lord your God is gracious and merciful' (2 Chron. 30:9). Hezekiah's couriers were rebuffed. Two centuries after the secession of the northern tribes, no sense of allegiance to the Davidic dynasty and the Jerusalem Temple could be revived. In any case, the northerners may have feared the disapproval of the Assyrian authorities who were now their masters. A small number of the more devout among them did make the pilgrimage to the Passover feast. A problem arose because they had not carried out the ritual purification required for entry to the Temple area; but they were admitted after the king had offered up a prayer on their behalf.

The festival lasted a week and was extended for another week. It was marked by lavish sacrifices and the singing of psalms accompanied by Levite musicians on their harps, cymbals and trumpets. 'So there was great joy in Jerusalem, for since the time of Solomon ... there had been nothing like this in Jerusalem' (2 Chron. 30:26).

*The Defences of Jerusalem* The army was revitalized and re-equipped, and commanders appointed for the tribal levies that acted as reserves in time of war. Hezekiah addressed a parade of these officers in front of the city gates. He told them to be strong and courageous, and not to fear the Assyrian power, 'for there is one greater with us than with him'.

The defence wall of Jerusalem was strengthened, with new towers constructed upon it. Hezekiah's most important single project concerned the city's water supply in time of siege. His engineers carved out a tunnel nearly eighteen hundred feet long through solid rock. It went underneath the city wall and connected the spring of Gihon outside with a reservoir constructed inside, known as the pool of Siloam. The mouth of the cave in which the spring arose was then blocked up to protect the water source and deny it to an enemy. The tunnel was accidentally discovered in 1880. Halfway along it, part of an inscription on the rock wall described in biblical Hebrew how the work was done. The inscription was damaged and the upper part was missing. The six lines that were left indicated that two groups of miners had started at opposite ends and had met in the middle. The translation of the portion that survives is as follows:

... And this was the way in which it was cut through: while ... [were] still ... axe[s], each man toward his fellow, and while there were still three cubits to be cut through [there was heard] the voice of a man calling to his fellow, for there was an overlap in the rock on the right [and on the left]. And when the tunnel was driven through, the quarrymen hewed [the rock], each man toward his fellow, axe against axe; and the water flowed from the spring toward the reservoir for 1,200 cubits, and the height of the rock above the head[s] of the quarrymen was 100 cubits.

*The Invasion of Sennacherib* In 705 BC Hezekiah joined in a revolt against Assyrian domination. The background was the death of the mighty Assyrian monarch Sargon II who had crushed the kingdom of Israel, and the succession of his less forceful son Sennacherib. Babylonia flared up in rebellion, and it looked as if the Assyrian empire might break up. For some of the small vassal kingdoms along the Mediterranean seaboard in the west, the time seemed right to assert their own independence. They were encouraged and promised support both by the king of Babylon and by the Egyptian pharaoh, who shared a common desire to loosen the grasp of Nineveh.

About this time Hezekiah contracted an infection and nearly died of it. He was cured by the learned Isaiah, who prescribed poultices made of figs. As a sign from the Lord that the king's life would be spared, Isaiah caused the shadow on the sundial to move ten steps backward instead of forward.

A Babylonian delegation arrived in Jerusalem, ostensibly to bring the good wishes of their own ruler on Hezekiah's recovery. It was obvious that the real purpose was to draw Judah into the anti-Assyrian front. Hezekiah welcomed the envoys and personally conducted them round the palace and the royal treasure houses. Isaiah was alarmed at the show of cordiality. He predicted that involvement with Babylonia would have disastrous consequences in the future. The king did not openly argue with the prophet but remarked to himself: 'Why not, if there will be peace and security in my days?' (2 Kings 20:19).

In an act of defiance, Hezekiah stopped payment of the annual tribute to the Assyrian overlord. A coalition started to take shape with some of the neighbouring city-states, including

Phoenician Tyre and the two Philistine cities of Ashkelon and Ekron. The king of Ekron, Padi, who refused to co-operate, was deposed and sent in chains to Hezekiah in Jerusalem, where he was kept captive. The three kingdoms east of the Jordan, Ammon, Moab and Edom, may also have been implicated in the resistance movement, though they kept well in the background.

Hezekiah sent ambassadors to Egypt to discuss the support offered by that power. Again, Isaiah raised a dissenting voice. He railed against the 'rebellious children' who put their faith in the chariots and horsemen of Egypt rather than in the Lord.

> The Egyptians are men, and not
>  God;
> and their horses are flesh, and
>  not spirit.
>
> (Isa. 31:3)

At first the bid for freedom seemed to succeed. It took several years before Sennacherib subdued Babylonia. Only then could he set out from Mesopotamia to regain control of the western part of the Assyrian empire. In 701 BC he led his army southward along the Mediterranean littoral into Phoenicia, deposed the king of Tyre and appointed another in his place. Most of the rulers in the area hastened to swear allegiance to him, bringing their tribute. Advancing along the coastal plain he met and defeated an Egyptian force that had come northward to give battle. The two rebellious Philistine cities of Ashkelon and Ekron were taken. Judah was left isolated. The Assyrian army swung inland and started devastating the Shephelah, the foothill region of Judah. In his inscriptions Sennacherib claimed the sacking of forty-two towns and a great number of villages in Judah, and the deportation of most of the inhabitants.

The main Assyrian attack was on the strongly fortified lowland city of Lachish. It was besieged for some time, then captured in a fierce battle. The archaeological excavation of the site shows that the massive fortifications were partially destroyed. The remains of some fifteen hundred bodies were found in a large pit. In the British Museum there is a series of wall reliefs from Sennacherib's palace at Nineveh, depicting scenes from the storming of Lachish. In precise detail they show the battering rams and scaling parties moving up ramps at the city gate, supported by units of heavy archers, auxiliary archers, slingmen, spearmen and shieldbearers; the savage hand-to-hand fighting; and the Hebrew captives impaled or led with their women and children in a pathetic line past the king, seated on a throne in front of the royal pavilion.

Sennacherib records about Hezekiah: 'I imprisoned him in Jerusalem his residence, like a bird in a cage.' Hezekiah's position did indeed appear hopeless. He sent a humble message of subjection to Sennacherib at Lachish: 'I have done wrong; withdraw from me; whatever you impose on me I will bear' (2 Kings 18:14). To meet the tribute demanded of him, Hezekiah had to empty the royal coffers and the Temple treasury of gold and silver and strip the gold from the Temple doors and posts. Even that did not satisfy the Assyrian ruler. He sent three top Assyrian officials with a force to demand the voluntary surrender of Jerusalem. The titles of these three officials are given in the Bible as the Tartan (commander-in-chief), the Rabsaris (Master of the Harem) and the Rabshakeh (Head of the Royal Staff). The last-named was the spokesman. He was obviously a highly educated and articulate man with a command of languages, including Hebrew. The envoys took up a position on the road before the city gate at the place where the clothmakers worked, using water from the upper reservoir. Three of Hezekiah's officials were sent out to parley: Eliakim, the head of the royal household, Shebnah, the palace secretary, and Joah, the king's recorder.

Speaking in Hebrew, the Rabshakeh took a tough line with the local officials. To start with he dismissed the capacity of Hezekiah to offer resistance. 'Do you think,' he asked, 'that mere words are strategy and power for war?' (2 Kings 18:20) Hezekiah's reliance on Egypt was like a man leaning on a 'broken reed of a staff' that would pierce his hand. Nor would help come from the Lord, for it was the Lord himself who had sent the Assyrian army to destroy Judah. The Rabshakeh mocked at Hezekiah's military strength; the Assyrian monarch would provide him with two thousand horses, he offered, if Hezekiah could find that number of horsemen to ride them.

The city wall above them was crowded with soldiers and citizens listening to the taunts of the Assyrians. The officials of Judah begged the

*Jerusalem Saved*

Jerusalem from the Pool of Hezekiah (Shiloah), with the Mount of Olives in the background.
Engraving from *Jerusalem, Bethany and Bethlehem*, by the Reverend J. L. Porter (1887).

Rabshakeh to switch to Aramaic. (At that time Aramaic was used for regional diplomacy and commerce, but it would not be understood by the people on the wall.) The Rabshakeh adroitly seized the psychological opening he had been handed. He turned to the crowd on the wall and with raised voice addressed them directly in Hebrew. Let their king not deceive them, he cried out, by pretending that their God would save them. Other peoples conquered by Assyria had appealed in vain to their own deities. If Jerusalem surrendered they would be left in peace until such time as they were taken away to another country, where a good life awaited them. The people kept silent, as King Hezekiah had previously cautioned.

The Judahite officials returned in dismay to the palace and reported to the king. While he went to the Temple to pray, the officials were sent off to ask Isaiah what he thought should be done on this 'day of distress, of rebuke, and of disgrace'; (2 Kings 19:3). The prophet's advice was to stand firm, for the Lord would make the Assyrians withdraw.

The Assyrian envoys saw that they had failed to talk King Hezekiah into capitulation. They returned to Sennacherib to seek fresh instructions. After the fall of Lachish, the Assyrian forces had moved a few miles further north to attack the town of Libnah. Sennacherib sent Hezekiah a blunt message, threatening to destroy Jerusalem. Again Isaiah gave the king courage: 'By the way that he came, by the same he shall return, and he shall not come into this city, says the Lord' (2 Kings 19:33). That night, according to the biblical account, an angel of the Lord slew a great number of the Assyrian troops; as a result, the rest of the invading army was withdrawn and returned to Nineveh.

There may have been more mundane reasons for Sennacherib to break off the campaign in Judah, without actually laying siege to Jerusalem. Domestic problems in his own country may have compelled his return; or the 'angel of the Lord' in this case may have been an epidemic, possibly bubonic plague, that swept through his camp. Moreover, the main object of the offensive had been achieved, for his campaign had suppressed the spirit of revolt for some time to come. Whatever the cause of the Assyrian departure, Hebrew tradition held to the belief that Jerusalem was saved at that time by divine intervention.

This episode marked the last appearance of Isaiah in the biblical narrative.

Hezekiah's son Manasseh was twelve years old *Manasseh the* when he succeeded to the throne and reigned for *Impious* forty-five years (687–642 BC). He remained a docile vassal of Assyria, which reached the zenith of its power at that time with the conquest of Egypt. Manasseh was mentioned by the Assyrian emperor Asshurbanipal as one of the vassals who assisted in the Egyptian campaign.

The biblical account of Manasseh's reign is chiefly concerned with the abandonment of his father's religious reforms and his relapse into the impious ways of his grandfather Ahaz. Canaanite pagan 'abominations' crept in again, with fertility images and altars springing up in the very precincts of the Temple. It was even said that the practice of child sacrifice reappeared in the valley of Hinnom, and that the king offered up one of his own sons. The practice of Mesopotamian astrology and witchcraft intruded under the influence of the Assyrians. It is said that the king 'worshipped all the host of heaven ... and practised soothsaying and augury, and dealt with mediums and with wizards' (2 Kings 21:3,6). The prophets cried out that these evils would bring about the destruction of the kingdom, and predicted that the Lord would 'wipe Jerusalem as one wipes a dish, wiping it and turning it upside down' (2 Kings 21:13).

The Book of Chronicles relates that Manasseh eventually offended his Assyrian masters. They stuck hooks in him, put him in chains and took him away into captivity. When he repented of his evil ways he was allowed to return, and restored the purity of the faith. This story is dubious, as the religious reform movement was revived only in the time of Manasseh's grandson Josiah. The moral laxity continued in the short reign of Manasseh's son Amon (642–640 BC). He was murdered by palace officials who were themselves then caught and executed. The assassination brought to the throne Amon's eight-year-old son Josiah (640–609 BC).

## Judah: The Last Phase

JOSIAH WAS DEEMED THE MOST RIGHTEOUS OF all the Hebrew kings. His reign marked the last chapter of independence in the history of the *The Good* kingdom of Judah before its final decline and fall. *King Josiah*

At the age of eighteen the young king ordered

that the Temple be repaired and purified. The work was to be paid for with the donations collected from the public by the Levite door-keepers and handed over to the supervisors for wages, stone and timber. The king sent Shaphan the court secretary to convey his instructions to the high priest Hilkiah. The priest showed Shaphan a 'book of the law' that had come to light in a Temple storeroom in the course of the reconstruction. It was probably an early version of the Book of Deuteronomy. The court secretary took the scroll to his master and read it aloud to him. Josiah wept with emotion to hear the sacred precepts, and to realize how far his people had strayed from them. He sent a delegation of officials headed by Hilkiah to consult the Lord through Hulda the prophetess. She was married to Shallum, the keeper of the Temple robes and lived in the New Quarter of the city. According to Hulda's oracle, the Lord would destroy Jerusalem for the wickedness committed in it, but that would not be in Josiah's lifetime.

In conformity with what he had learnt from the Book of the Law, Josiah carried out comprehensive measures to wipe out all traces of paganism and restore the purity of the Mosaic creed. All objects in the Temple compound that had been associated with pagan deities, Canaanite or Mesopotamian, were burnt in the valley of Kidron – including the statues of horses and chariots his father had set up in the Temple courtyard in honour of the Assyrian sun-god. The shrine in the valley of Hinnom connected with child sacrifices was destroyed. All over the country images were broken up, errant priests dismissed, and altars that had been used for pagan sacrifices were defiled by burning human bones on them. The measures were extended beyond the borders of Judah into the northern areas that had comprised the kingdom of Israel. When the great purge had been completed, Josiah organized a Passover feast in Jerusalem for the whole country, as his great-grandfather Hezekiah had done. The assembly summoned to prayer in the Temple courtyard solemnly reaffirmed the ancient covenant between the Lord and his chosen people.

*The Collapse of Assyria* The freedom with which Josiah acted was in sharp contrast with the subservience to the Assyrian colossus shown by his grandfather Manasseh. With the death of the emperor Asshurbanipal in 627 BC (half way through

Josiah's reign), the vast, sprawling empire started to disintegrate. Both Egypt and Babylonia threw off the Assyrian yoke. The Medes to the east of Assyria went over to the offensive. In 612 BC Nineveh fell and was sacked in a combined onslaught by the Babylonians and the Medes. The imperial power that had been master of the whole Near East had crumbled in less than two decades. The fear and hatred it had inspired among subject peoples, and the general rejoicing at its downfall, were vividly expressed by the contemporary Hebrew prophet Nahum in his Oracle Concerning Nineveh:

Woe to the bloody city,
all full of lies and booty –
no end to the plunder!
The crack of whip, and rumble of wheel,
galloping horse and bounding chariot!
Horsemen charging,
flashing sword and glittering spear,
hosts of slain,
heaps of corpses,
dead bodies without end – ...
All who hear the news of you
clap their hands over you.
For upon whom has not come
your unceasing evil?

(Nahum 3:1–3,19)

For the kingdom of Judah, 'the clapping of hands' would not last long. Its survival was soon threatened again, from another quarter.

The collapse of Assyrian might left a power-vacuum in the area. Egypt sought to reassert *Egypt and* the hold it had lost centuries earlier. Its rival *Babylonia* was a resurgent Babylonia. To contain the Babylonians, an Egyptian army under pharaoh Neco marched northwards along the Via Maris in 609 BC, ostensibly to support Assyrian garrisons still holding out in the Haram area of northern Syria. King Josiah was alarmed at the prospect that Judah had become free of the Assyrian orbit only to land in that of Egypt. He mustered his forces and tried to block the Egyptian advance at the Megiddo pass. His army was defeated and the king himself fatally wounded by an arrow. His body was brought back to Jerusalem for burial.

The defeat at Megiddo marked the virtual end of Judean independence, though the kingdom continued to exist for another twenty-two years. For a while it remained under Egyptian domi-nation, as Josiah had feared would happen. He was succeeded by his son Jehoahaz but three months later the new Egyptian overlords took Jehoahaz off to captivity and placed on the throne his young brother Jehoiakim (609–598 BC). The first measure the new ruler had to take was to tax his subjects in order to raise the heavy tribute demanded by Egypt.

Four years later there was another dramatic tilt in the Near Eastern power balance. The new Babylonian ruler Nebuchadnezzar defeated an Egyptian army at the battle of Carchemish on the Upper Euphrates river in northern Syria. Now an irresistible force, Nebuchadnezzar's troops swept southward along the coastal plain as far as Gaza. The Babylonians, so recently the liberators from the Assyrian yoke, had now in their turn become the oppressors.

In Jerusalem there were differences of opinion on how to react. The king and his immediate advisers tended to advise resistance in order to regain the freedom from external control that Judah had enjoyed under King Josiah. Others thought it more prudent to submit without a fight. Among the latter was Jeremiah, as notable a Hebrew prophet as Isaiah had been.

*The Prophet Jeremiah* For many years Jeremiah had seriously attacked the moral laxity and social abuses he saw around him. With the advent of Nebuchadnezzar, Jeremiah's warnings took on a desperate note:

My heart is beating wildly;
I cannot keep silent;
for I hear the sound of the trumpet,
the alarm of war.

(Jer. 4:19)

It was futile, he cried, to resist by force of arms. The Babylonians were the instruments of God's anger against his people. If they did not mend their ways they would be destroyed. In a dramatic gesture the prophet smashed a pottery jar in front of a crowd listening to him. Thus, he shouted, the Lord would 'break this people and this city'.

Jeremiah's attacks on the establishment stirred up resentment against him. After he had delivered a scathing sermon to the worshippers in the Temple courtyard, the high priest Pashhur had him seized, beaten and clapped into the stocks. On his release next day, the unrepentant prophet told the priest that he would be among the captives carried off to Babylon when Jerusalem met its fate, and would die in exile.

Jeremiah's sermons and oracles were collected by his faithful disciple and scribe Baruch, and recorded on a scroll. The document came into the hands of palace officials who brought it to King Jehoiakim. It was read aloud to him while he warmed himself before a fire in his chamber. The infuriated king hacked off pieces as they were read, and threw them into the flames. Jeremiah's friends at the palace warned him to keep out of sight. He dictated the whole book over again to Baruch, who was sent to read it aloud in front of the Temple.

*Jerusalem Occupied* King Jehoiakim remained outwardly submissive to the Babylonians, but kept in touch with Egypt and bided his time. In 601 BC Nebuchadnezzar fought an inconclusive battle against Egypt, then returned to Mesopotamia where Babylon faced other problems. Jehoiakim chose what seemed an opportune moment to rebel. Again Jeremiah's dissenting voice was drowned out by patriotic elation.

For more than two years, Judah had had to defend itself against harassing tactics from the neighbouring states of Moab, Ammon and Syria (all of them still subject to Babylon) and from Babylonian garrisons stationed elsewhere in the area. But by 598 Nebuchadnezzar was free to march against Judah in force. At this moment Jehoiakim died. His eighteen-year-old son Jehoiachin (598 BC) came to the throne, and was left to face the Babylonian juggernaut his father had rashly set in motion. The promised support from Egypt failed to materialize.

Within three months resistance was over. The young king surrendered and was taken off to Babylon as a captive, together with his mother and family, his officials and 'all the mighty men of valour, ten thousand captives, and all the craftsmen and the smiths; none remained, except the poorest people of the land' (2 Kings 24:14). The palace and the Temple were stripped of everything valuable. The king's uncle Zedekiah was installed by Nebuchadnezzar as a puppet ruler. He was to reign for eleven years (598–587 BC) and was destined to be the last king of Judah.

According to the Bible, the exiled Jehoiachin remained alive in Babylon; thirty-seven years later he was released from prison and treated with kindness by the new Babylonian king who had succeeded Nebuchadnezzar. The records found in the basement of Nebuchadnezzar's excavated palace mention that among the captives issued

Jeremiah's prophecy: the Fall of Jerusalem and the Jews driven into
Babylonian exile. Etching by the contemporary Jewish artist Marc Chagall.

with rations from the royal stores were the 'king of Judah', his five sons and a number of his countrymen.

*Zedekiah's Revolt*

A few years after Zedekiah had been put on the throne there was unrest in Babylon. Hopes of liberation sprang up among the conquered peoples, including the shrunken Judah. Envoys came to Jerusalem from the neighbouring vassal kings of Tyre and Sidon in Phoenicia, and Moab and Edom in Trans-jordan, to plan a combined revolt. The Egyptian pharaoh promised his backing.

Jeremiah campaigned with all his fervour and eloquence against this hazardous course. Carrying a wooden yoke on his neck as a symbol, he preached God's message of submission as the price of survival: 'Bring your necks under the yoke of the king of Babylon, and serve him and his people, and live. Why will you and your people die by the sword' (Jer. 27:12–13). Jeremiah was incensed by the optimism spread by other religious leaders in Jerusalem. He had a public confrontation at the Temple with one of them, the prophet Hananiah, who predicted that within two years the exiled king and the other captives would be safely back and the looted Temple utensils recovered. To emphasize his point, Hananiah snatched the yoke from Jeremiah's neck and broke it in two. Jeremiah flung back that Hananiah was feeding lies to the people; he would not live the year out. (He died seven months later.)

King Zedekiah's confidence may have been sapped by Jeremiah's grim warnings. For whatever reason, the preparations for revolt were shelved at that time. Nebuchadnezzar restored his control, and Zedekiah thought it prudent to send a delegation to Babylon reaffirming his loyalty. Jeremiah knew two members of the delegation, who carried a letter from him to the exiles from Judah. In it he predicted that the captivity would last seventy years, and warned them not to be misled by those who were talking of an imminent return home. They should settle down, adjust themselves to the new conditions and try to build up normal, productive lives. What the Lord required of them was: 'Build houses and live in them; plant gardens and eat their produce. Take wives and have sons and daughters; ... multiply there, and do not decrease ... and I will bring you back to the place from which I sent you into exile' (Jer. 29:5,6,14).

The longing for independence simmered below the surface in Judah for another five years. In 589 BC Zedekiah went into open revolt, in league with Egypt and Tyre. Once more Nebuchadnezzar invaded Judah at the head of a powerful army. This time the campaign was more prolonged and bitter than had been the case nine years earlier. The account in the Book of Kings moves straight to the siege of Jerusalem. Babylonian records and archaeological evidence indicate, however, that Nebuchadnezzar adopted a broader invasion strategy like the one that the Assyrian ruler Sennacherib had used against King Hezekiah more than a century earlier. He advanced from the coastal plain and one by one took the towns in the foothill region of the Shephelah and in southern Judah.

The archaeological excavations show the destruction caused at Beth-shemesh, Lachish and Debir in the Shephelah, and at Ramat Rachel and Beth-zur on the southern edge of Jerusalem. The town of Arad in the northern Negev was apparently demolished at this time by the Edomites from the region round the Dead Sea. They had taken advantage of the situation to raid the territory of Judah from the south. With Jerusalem outflanked and isolated, and potential Egyptian help blocked, Nebuchadnezzar moved on the city.

The Book of Jeremiah mentions that the last two places to hold out outside the capital were the fortified city of Lachish and the town of Azekah, a few miles to the north-east of Lachish. This is strikingly borne out by the *ostraca* (inscribed pottery fragments) that are known as the Lachish Letters as they were found in the ruins of that city. Eighteen of them were written by an army officer called Hoshaiah, stationed in an outlying fort, to his superior officer Yaosh, commander of Lachish and the surrounding military district. One of these letters ends: 'We are watching for the fire signals of Lachish, according to all the signs my lord gave, because we do not see Azekah.' At the time that was written, Azekah had probably just been overrun by the Babylonian troops.

In another of the Lachish Letters the writer reveals how disturbed he is at reports describing the atmosphere of pessimism and ebbing morale among the ruling circles in Jerusalem. Shortly after, the siege of the capital was raised and the Babylonian troops were withdrawn. Apparently

Nebuchadnezzar had redeployed his forces to meet a threatened Egyptian thrust in the south. In Jerusalem the mood changed to one of rejoicing in the mistaken belief that the danger had passed.

Jeremiah had bought a piece of property from a cousin in his birthplace of Anathoth. He set out to inspect it, but was arrested at the city gate and imprisoned in the palace courtyard, on suspicion of deserting to the enemy. Uncertain about what lay ahead, Zedekiah secretly sent for the prophet. He was taken out of confinement and brought before the king, who asked for his honest opinion. Jeremiah replied that the Babylonians would come back; the only way to save the city was to surrender. He was thrown back into the dungeon.

*The End of the Kingdom* The Babylonians returned and the siege of Jerusalem was resumed. The defenders of the city held on heroically for more than a year. In the summer of 587 BC they were finally overcome by the famine that gripped the city from within, and by the Babylonian siege engines that battered a breach in the walls from without. The attackers poured in, killing and plundering from house to house. In the darkness and confusion King Zedekiah, his family and some of his officials and soldiers fled across the palace gardens, through the eastern gate and along the road down to the Jordan valley. They were pursued and caught on the Jericho plain. The whole party was taken to the town of Riblah in northern Syria, where Nebuchadnezzar had his temporary headquarters. The Babylonian monarch showed no mercy to his rebel vassal. Zedekiah's sons were slain in front of him, then his eyes were put out and he was taken off to Babylon in chains.

A month later the Babylonian general Nebuzaradan arrived in Jerusalem with orders to destroy the city: 'And he burned the house of the Lord, and the king's house and all the houses of Jerusalem' (2 Kings 25:9). The defence walls and fortifications were broken down. All the Temple equipment was collected and carried away, including the gold and silver utensils, the two great bronze pillars, and the 'bronze sea' and lavers in the courtyard. The high priest, the military commander of the city, five members of the king's council and other notables were arrested and also taken to Riblah, where Nebuchadnezzar had them summarily executed. A much larger number of representative citizens were rounded up with their families and deported to Babylonia. Those who were left were mainly 'some of the poorest of the land to be vinedressers and ploughmen' (2 Kings 25:12). Jeremiah explains that these were landless peasants who were given the deserted fields and vineyards in order to maintain food production.

*After the Fall* With the fall of Jerusalem the kingdom of Judah had come to an end, and Hebrew independence had been wiped out in blood and rubble. A Jewish state would not arise again for five centuries. The grief of the survivors was sharpened by the bitter feeling that God had turned against them. Gone was the Temple that had housed the Divine Presence. Gone was the throne that had been promised to David's dynasty for all time.

> The Lord has become like an enemy,
>    he has destroyed Israel . . .
> and in his fierce indignation has spurned
>    king and priest.
> The Lord has scorned his altar,
>    disowned his sanctuary;
> he has delivered into the hand of the enemy
> the walls of her palaces;
>
>           (Lam. 2:5–7)

What was left of Judah was annexed and turned into a minor Babylonian province. Gedaliah, a former palace official, was appointed as the local governor. His father Ahikam had been a respected adviser of Josiah and had later befriended Jeremiah. Gedaliah established himself at Mizpeh, just north of Jerusalem, and tried to restore some order. He gathered together and cared for the uprooted and the destitute, and was joined by remnants of the disbanded army. On all of these he urged acceptance of their lot: 'Dwell in the land, and serve the king of Babylon, and it shall be well with you' (Jer. 40:9). He put them to work harvesting and making wine and olive oil.

Jeremiah was among a group of captives who were about to be taken away in chains to exile. By order of the Babylonian commander he was released and brought to headquarters. The general treated with deference this holy man who had so vehemently opposed resistance to Babylonian rule. Jeremiah was asked whether he wished to come to Babylon, where he would be free and well-treated, or preferred to remain in the care of Gedaliah. He chose to remain, and was allowed to depart with food and a gift.

One member of the royal family, Ishmael, had

escaped across the Jordan river with a group of soldiers. They were given asylum by the king of Ammon, and from there planned to start a resistance movement. To them, Gedaliah was a quisling collaborating with the enemy. Johanan, one of the former officers who had joined Gedaliah, warned him that Ishmael was plotting to take his life. The governor refused to believe the story. When Ishmael came with ten men to visit him, they were well received. As the visitors were being entertained to a meal, they suddenly leapt to their feet and drew their swords. They slew Gedaliah and his entourage, and some soldiers from the Babylonian garrison whom they took unawares. A group of pilgrims arriving from the north were also wiped out, except for a few who were spared when they handed over the food supplies of the party. The bodies were thrown into a disused cistern. Ishmael then left, taking with him as hostages a number of the refugees who had gathered at Mizpah. Johanan and his men pursued them and caught up with them at the pool of Gibeon, north-west of Jerusalem. In the melee that followed Ishmael

escaped but the captives he had taken were freed.

Johanan and other members of the little community at Mizpah were fearful of the reprisals the Babylonian authorities might take for Gedaliah's murder. They wished to move to Egypt for safety, but first sought the advice of Jeremiah. He replied that the Lord forbade them to leave Judah; the remnant that was left had to maintain their presence there. They ignored this counsel and left, taking with them the protesting prophet and his scribe Baruch. They found refuge at Tahpanhes, a fortified border town on the eastern edge of the Delta. Here the aged Jeremiah remained true to his vocation. Towards the end of the Book of Jeremiah, there is recorded a stiff sermon he gave the Jewish diaspora community in Egypt, taking it to task (especially the women) for burning incense to the 'queen of heaven', the fertility goddess of the ancient world. (She appeared as Ishtar in Mesopotamia, Astarte in Canaan, Aphrodite in Greece and Venus in Rome.) The sermon, and the altercation that followed it, were no doubt recorded by Baruch. It is not known when Jeremiah died.

7

# EXILE AND RETURN

## *By the Waters of Babylon*

**A**FTER THE ASSASSINATION OF Gedaliah, Judah ceased to exist as a separate territory. Most of it was incorporated into the province of Samaria. The Hebron hill country to the south of Jerusalem was gradually occupied by Edomites from the adjacent desert areas, and later became known as Idumea. The cities of Judah had been destroyed. The population had been drained by war, starvation, executions, deportations and the exodus of refugees, such as the flight that carried Jeremiah into Egypt. Only a remnant was left, subsisting from the soil. Unlike the Assyrians after the destruction of the kingdom of Israel a century and a half earlier, the Babylonians did not bring into Judah new settlers from other parts of their empire.

*The* *Uprooted* The actual deportations to Babylonia were not as sweeping and general as is often suggested. They were deliberately and shrewdly selective, with the object of removing all the elements of the population that possessed official, religious, intellectual and property status. That left behind an amorphous and leaderless mass, incapable of organizing resistance. At the end of the Book of

Jeremiah the following statistics are given: 3023 in the first deportation of 598 BC, with the young king Jehoiachin; 832 in 587 BC, after the destruction of Jerusalem; and another 745 five years later after what may have been a last spasm of unrest – making a total of 4,600. It is likely that these figures refer only to heads of families. Adding all the members of their households, the total number may have been roughly 20,000. The quality of the deportees, rather than their numbers, made it easier for them to remain a cohesive and distinctive group after they were transplanted. Moreover, they seemed to have been settled in one area. Allusions in the Books of Jeremiah and Ezra indicate that this area was a group of towns or villages along the Chebar canal near the city of Nippur, a little south east of Babylon.

The initial anguish of the uprooting, and the longing to return home, found immortal expression in Psalm 137:

> By the waters of Babylon,
> there we sat down and wept,
> when we remembered Zion.

On the willows there
we hung up our lyres.
For there our captors
required of us songs,
and our tormentors, mirth, saying,
'Sing us one of the songs of Zion!'
How shall we sing the Lord's song
in a foreign land?
If I forget you, O Jerusalem,
let my right hand wither!
Let my tongue cleave to the roof of
my mouth,
if I do not remember you,
if I do not set Jerusalem
above my highest joy!
(Psalm 137:1–6)

But gradually they settled down to new lives, in the spirit of the letter Jeremiah had addressed to the first wave of exiles.

*Prophecies of Return*

In the preceding centuries, the prophets who had predicted the downfall of the two Hebrew kingdoms had at the same time held out the promise of a future restoration. The Book of Amos ends on this hopeful note:

'I will restore the fortunes of my
people Israel,
and they shall rebuild the ruined
cities and inhabit them;
I will plant them upon their land,
and they shall never again be plucked up
out of the land which I have given them,'
says the Lord your God.
(Amos 9:14,15)

Isaiah paints a glowing vision of a return to Zion in a Messianic kingdom. Jeremiah, in his remarkable letter to the first group of deportees to Babylonia, assures them that in seventy years' time, the Lord will 'gather you from all the nations and all the places where I have driven you ... and I will bring you back to the place from which I sent you into exile' (Jer. 29:14).

This confidence in the future acquired a greater meaning for the community of exiles in Babylonia after the end of the kingdom of Judah. It helped to maintain their morale and their national identity. The promise of return was powerfully reinforced by the two great prophets of the exile: Ezekiel and the unidentified preacher who has become known as the Second Isaiah.

Ezekiel's life and work straddled the last years of the kingdom and the Babylonian exile. He sought to comfort his fellow-exiles by describing the future restoration to their lost homeland. There they would live at peace in a kingdom ruled by a descendant of David, with the Temple rebuilt and the holy covenant restored between God and his people. The prophet's visions illustrated this prospect – such as the parable of the valley filled with dry bones that came to life; and the imaginary tour of the reconstructed Temple, described in minute detail.

The utterances of the unknown sixth-century prophet known as Second Isaiah are contained in the Book of Isaiah from Chapter 40 onward. They open with a message of consolation:

Comfort, comfort my people,
says your God.
Speak tenderly to Jerusalem,
and cry to her
that her warfare is ended,
that her iniquity is pardoned,
that she has received from the Lord's hand
double for all her sins.
(Isa. 40:1)

*The Edict of Cyrus*

Cyrus, king of Persia, is presented by Second Isaiah as God's instrument for the restoration. The reference was related to developments that completely altered the political map of the Near East. In the middle of the sixth century BC Cyrus successfully revolted against his overlords, the neighbouring kingdom of Medes, which lay between the Persian Gulf and the Black Sea. In 550 BC Cyrus captured the Medean capital of Ecbatana and brought Medea under his control. A series of brilliant campaigns extended the sway of Persia over one Near Eastern country after another. In 539 BC Babylon fell to Cyrus. When his son and successor Cambyses II conquered Egypt, Persia ruled over the greatest empire the world had seen until then, spreading from Asia Minor to the borders of India. This far-flung domain was divided into a number of satrapies (provinces), each under a governor. Judah became the district of Yahud in the Fifth Satrapy, known as Beyond the River – that is, west of the Euphrates.

Cyrus was an exceptionally enlightened ruler. Where the preceding empires of Assyria and Babylonia had repressed and partially displaced conquered peoples, Cyrus encouraged them to foster their own cultures and creeds. When he

TOP The Euphrates and the Plains of Babylon, where the Jews were taken into exile from Judah.
BOTTOM The fords of the Kishon River, whose flooding swept away the army of Sisera
in the battle against Deborah and Barak.

Two engravings from *The Rivers and Lakes of Scripture*, by the Reverend W. K. Tweedie (1857).

conquered Babylonia he behaved as the liberator of its people from their oppressive rulers. His troops were ordered to ensure that no harm should come to the Babylonian cities and their religion. Cyrus even made the gesture of attending worship in the temple of the chief Babylonian deity Marduk. His policy was to win the allegiance of his new subjects by benevolence towards them. In that broad context, the community of Jewish exiles in Babylonia was given the chance to return to Jerusalem and rebuild their sacred Temple. The story of that Return is told in the Books of Ezra and Nehemiah.

In 538 BC, a year after the Persian conquest of Babylonia, Cyrus issued the historic edict or royal proclamation that led to the Return. The text, as given in the Book of Ezra, reads:

> Thus says Cyrus king of Persia: The Lord, the God of heaven, has given me all the kingdoms of the earth, and he has charged me to build him a house at Jerusalem, which is in Judah. Whoever is among you of all his people, may his God be with him, and let him go up to Jerusalem, which is in Judah, and rebuild the house of the Lord, the God of Israel – he is the God who is in Jerusalem; and let each survivor, in whatever place he sojourns, be assisted by the men of his place with silver and gold, with goods and with beasts, besides freewill offerings for the house of God which is in Jerusalem. (Ezra 1:2–4)

*The Beginning of the Return*  Only a minority of the exiles responded to the call. In the half century since the fall of Jerusalem many of the community had taken root in the Babylonian diaspora, and some of them were already prosperous traders. The tolerance of the new Persian regime made them even less inclined to move again. As suggested in the edict, those who did not join the Return provided some financial support for those who did, in the form of money, supplies and pack animals. Sheshbazzar, a prince of the exiled royal house of Judah, was appointed leader of the returning group. Cyrus ordered the royal treasurer to hand over to him the collection of gold and silver Temple vessels that the Babylonian army had carried away from Jerusalem. The inventory of the vessels contained the following items:

| | |
|---|---|
| gold bowls for offerings | 1000 |
| silver bowls for offerings | 1000 |
| censers | 29 |
| small gold bowls | 30 |
| small silver bowls | 2410 |
| other utensils | 1000 |
| Total | 5469 |

When preparations had been completed, the caravan set out on the hazardous six-hundred-mile journey across the desert.

The first period after their arrival was spent on the practical arrangements for life in difficult circumstances. The returnees were organized according to their family clans, some of them going back to the towns and localities from which they had come originally. The Temple site on Mount Moriah was cleared, an altar constructed and regular prayers and sacrifices started. Authority at this stage was exercised by two men: Zerubbabel as the lay leader and Jeshua the high priest. Zerubbabel was also a member of the royal family of Judah. Since there is no further mention of Sheshbazzar, it is possible that this may have been another name for Zerubbabel.

## The Second Temple

IN THE SEVENTH MONTH, ALL THE ABLEBODIED men were called together to start work on the Temple site, including those who had set up their homes in places other than Jerusalem. They commenced with the foundations. As David and Solomon had done more than five centuries earlier, Zerubbabel obtained cedar logs from Tyre and Sidon in Phoenicia, in exchange for olive oil and other agricultural products. Skilled stonemasons and carpenters were also hired from Phoenicia, and money to pay their wages was collected from the settler community. Levites were appointed to supervise the construction. When the foundations were laid there was a moving service of thanksgiving to the Lord:

> For he is good,
> for his steadfast love endures for
> ever toward Israel.
>
> (Ezra 3:11)

Everyone shouted for joy, except for a few old men who wept with emotion as they remembered the First Temple.

The Samaritans inhabited the hill region that had been part of the former northern kingdom of

Israel. They were descended from the Hebrew survivors of the destroyed kingdom, mixed with settlers brought in from elsewhere by the Assyrian conquerors. The Samaritans practised a simple form of the Mosaic faith. When the news reached them that the foundations had been laid for a second Temple in Jerusalem, a group of their leaders came to demand a share in the work. They said: 'Let us build with you; for we worship your God as you do' (Ezra 4:2). Zerubbabel and Jeshua bluntly refused: 'You have nothing to do with us in building a house to our God' (Ezra 4:3). Antagonized at this rebuff, the Samaritans turned hostile and tried to block the project. They harassed the builders on the spot, and bribed Persian officials to create difficulties. As a result of these obstructive tactics the work on the Temple was suspended.

*Trouble with the Samaritans*

In the years that followed the initial impetus faded. The energies of the small community were absorbed in the daily struggle for existence. Two prophets in Jerusalem, Haggai and Zechariah, laboured ceaselessly for the work on the Temple to be resumed. It was not for them an end in itself, but part of a wider vision. They preached the revival of national independence, with Zerubbabel, a direct descendant of David, as king. The key to that dream was that the Divine Presence should once more reside in the house of the Lord.

*The Support of Darius the Great*

Such aspirations sprang from political upheaval in the Persian empire that affected even a quiet backwater like Jerusalem. In 530 BC Cyrus died and was succeeded by his son Cambyses. Eight years later Cambyses was returning from the conquest of Egypt when he heard that his brother had revolted and seized the western part of the empire. He was so disturbed by this report that he committed suicide. Cambyses' kinsman and general, Darius, proclaimed himself king. A period of civil war ensued before Darius I (the Great) was able to consolidate his power.

One of the matters that came to the attention of Darius in the second year of his reign was a despatch from Tattenai, the regional governor in Damascus, concerning the problem of Jerusalem. Under the moral pressure of the two prophets, Zerubbabel and Jeshua, work had started again on the Temple, thereby arousing fresh disputes. On a visit to Jerusalem, Tattenai enquired who had authorized the structure. To his surprise, he was told that King Cyrus himself had given

permission, and had ordered the gold and silver vessels looted by the Babylonians to be restored. The governor wrote to King Darius requesting that a check be made of the royal archives to verify the story of such a decree by Cyrus. Darius had the records searched. In the summer palace at Ecbatana a scroll was found containing the following note by the royal scribe:

> In the first year of Cyrus the king, Cyrus the king issued a decree: Concerning the house of God at Jerusalem, let the house be rebuilt, the place where sacrifices are offered and burnt offerings are brought; its height shall be sixty cubits and its breadth sixty cubits, with three courses of great stones and one course of timber; let the cost be paid from the royal treasury. And also let the gold and silver vessels of the house of God, which Nebuchadnezzar took out of the temple that is in Jerusalem and brought to Babylon, be restored and brought back to the temple which is in Jerusalem, each to its place; you shall put them in the house of God. (Ezra 6:3–5)

The king sent a copy of this document to Tattenai the governor, with instructions to let the building of the Temple proceed. The cost was to be borne out of the provincial revenues, and the priesthood was to be provided with daily needs: animals for the sacrifices, wheat, salt, wine and oil. Anyone who tried to interfere with the work should be put to death by impalement and his house demolished. The Temple services should include a prayer to the Hebrew God for the welfare of the king and his sons.

The governor and his staff diligently carried out these orders. The Second Temple was completed within five years, by 515 BC. The dedication took place in the spring, the sacrifices including twelve he-goats for the twelve tribes of Israel.

*The Second Temple Completed*

By the standards of Solomon's splendid Temple, the new building and its equipment were modest and simple, though the ground plan was the same. It no longer served as the central sanctuary of a kingdom, but as the house of worship for a small and struggling minority in an unimportant corner of the vast Persian empire. But the historical and emotional significance of the Second Temple far surpassed the physical aspect of the building or the size of its congregation. The scattered Jewish people had

RIGHT Jeremiah's prophecy: an Angel heralds the return of the Jewish exiles to a restored Jerusalem. Etching by Marc Chagall.

once more been provided with a focus for its faith and identity, in its holy city and its ancestral homeland. The bonds were strengthened between the homeland and the growing diaspora communities in Babylonia, Egypt and Asia Minor.

The next seventy years are a blank page in the biblical narrative. The population of Judah grew slowly by the absorption of those elements that had remained in the area after the destruction of Jerusalem, and maybe by the arrival of more small groups of returnees from Babylonia. It is conjectured that a century after the edict of Cyrus there may have been about forty thousand inhabitants in Judah. They would have remained inconspicuous, and would probably have disappeared in the course of time, but for the impact on their lives of two outstanding Babylonian Jews: Nehemiah and Ezra. One organized the administration and defences of Jerusalem; the other gave a fresh shape and dynamism to the Jewish faith.

## Nehemiah the Governor

NEHEMIAH HAD BEEN THE CUPBEARER TO THE Persian monarch Artaxerxes I – an honourable, ceremonious position that required him to serve the wine to his royal master, tasting it first himself in case it had been poisoned. After his term as governor in Jerusalem, he wrote a first-hand account that is preserved in the biblical book named after him. The memoir starts with Nehemiah at the winter palace in Susa with the royal entourage. His kinsman Hanani from Jerusalem came to visit him with a group of fellow-Judahites. Nehemiah, a devout Jew, was deeply upset by their report of the conditions in the holy city, where the people were 'in great trouble and shame; the wall of Jerusalem is broken down, and its gates are destroyed by fire' (Neh. 1:3).

Some while before, an attempt had been made to repair the city's defence walls. A letter of protest drawn up by the officials in the province was forwarded to the king by the provincial governor, Rehum. The letter complained that Jerusalem had in the past been 'a rebellious and wicked city'. If allowed to restore its defences, it would again become seditious. It would stop paying taxes and tolls to the royal revenues, and the control of the whole province would be undermined. On the strength of that negative report, Artaxerxes had authorized Rehum the governor to stop the construction work on the Jerusalem walls.

Nehemiah was apparently unaware of the *The Mission* earlier attempt and its suppression. The description of the defenceless city he heard from his Jerusalem relative filled him with a desire to go there himself and remedy the situation. He waited for a suitable moment to broach the subject with his master. Some four months later, he was serving wine to the king and queen at dinner. The king asked him why he was looking so sad; since he was not ill there must be something else troubling him. Startled at this show of concern, Nehemiah blurted out that he was unhappy because the city where his ancestors were buried was in ruins. The emperor asked him in a kindly tone what it was that he wanted. Nehemiah sent up a hurried prayer to the Lord, and plucked up the courage to make a bold request. Would the king allow him to travel to Jerusalem and organize the repairs in the city? The king graciously granted the request, only asking how long he would be away, 'and I set him a time' (Neh. 2:6). The king also agreed to provide Nehemiah with a letter of safe conduct addressed to the authorities in the 'Beyond the River' province. The chief royal forester was instructed to supply him with all the timber he might require for the work.

Nehemiah set out from Susa with an official *The Work* escort of armed horsemen on a journey of over a *Commences* thousand miles, across mountains and deserts. On arrival in Jerusalem, he rested quietly for three days without presenting himself to the city authorities. Then he rose at midnight and, riding on a donkey, he made an inspection by moonlight of the broken city walls and gates, accompanied by a few of his men. He records that in places the donkey could not pick its way through the piles of rubble, so he rode along the floor of the Kidron valley looking at the ruined battlements above him.

The following day Nehemiah called together a meeting of leading men from the city and the surrounding towns: priests, officials, notables, and heads of artisan guilds. He called on them to co-operate in rebuilding the walls, a project that was God's work and had the support of the king. They responded with enthusiasm: 'Let us rise up and build' (Neh. 2:18).

Nehemiah organized his voluntary labour

force in a methodical fashion. Each gate and each section of the wall was allocated to a separate group: the priesthood, the levitical orders, merchants, guilds such as the goldsmiths and perfume-makers, and contingents from Jericho, Tekoa, Gibeon, Mizpah, Beth-zur and other towns in Judah. Some of the well-to-do merchants were made responsible for the sections adjoining their homes. A district official called Shallum is on record as having drafted his daughters to work with him on his section. Nehemiah's detailed work schedule lists ten gates that had to be reconstructed: The Sheep, Fish, Old, Valley, Dung, Fountain, Water, Horse, East, and Watch Gates.

*Nehemiah's Opponents*

In the districts adjacent to Judah, there were men in official positions who were opposed to restoring the fortifications of Jerusalem. They resented the arrival of Nehemiah and did their best to frustrate his plans. Nehemiah's memoir identifies them as Sanballat the Horonite, Tobiah the Ammonite and Geshem the Arab. Non-biblical sources throw some light on their backgrounds and motives.

Sanballat was a Samaritan from the town of Beth-horon to the north-west of Jerusalem, on the strategic pass leading down to the vale of Aijalon. He had been appointed governor of the province of Samaria. As such, his authority had extended over Judah and was curtailed by Nehemiah's royal warrant as governor in Jerusalem. In any case the Samaritans had been hostile to the Return ever since the time when Zerubbabel had refused to let them share in rebuilding the Temple.

Tobiah was the head of an Israelite land-owning clan in Gilead, east of the Jordan, with important family connections in Jerusalem. Apparently he had been appointed to the office of governor of a sub-province that included Gilead and the former Trans-jordan kingdom of Ammon.

Geshem was a desert chieftain in the south. The Persian authorities had put him in charge of a wide area that extended into the Hebron hills to the south of Jerusalem, occupied by Edomites. Nehemiah also refers to trouble from the district of Ashdod in the coastal plain, without specifying an individual leader.

The project Nehemiah had launched thus faced a formidable alliance of adversaries all round Judah. They resorted to a succession of manoeuvres to stop him. Fortunately, he was a strong-willed and tenacious man, confident in the sense of both Divine and royal protection.

Before the work commenced, Sanballat, Tobiah and Geshem appeared together in Jerusalem and derided the whole undertaking, asking in jest whether Nehemiah was making preparations to rebel against the emperor. Nehemiah dismissed them curtly, pointing out that they had no standing in the city and did not share in its traditions: 'you have no portion or right or memorial in Jerusalem' (Neh. 2:20). Come what may, he told them, the people would 'arise and build'. With the construction in progress, Sanballat and his associates became angry. They attempted to undermine the morale of the builders. Bringing up Samaritan troops, Sanballat scornfully asked in their hearing what 'these feeble Jews' were doing. Did they think that by offering sacrifices they could get the work done quickly? Could they make building stones out of heaps of burnt rubble? Tobiah added that even a fox would be able to knock down the stone wall they were erecting.

When the walls were half-way up the opponents moved from psychological pressure to more direct action. They secretly plotted to organize surprise attacks by bands of armed raiders from their territories. Nehemiah received advance warnings of these plans from Jews residing in the adjoining provinces. He organized a home guard with each clan assigned defence duties in its own sector, and equipped them with swords, spears and bows. These measures deterred the planned attacks. From then on, the work proceeded under strict security arrangements. On each shift half the men worked and the other half stood guard. Even the workers were armed: 'And each of the builders had his sword girded at his side while he built' (Neh. 4:18). Nehemiah kept a trumpeter with him at all times, in case of sudden attack. His instructions to the work teams scattered round the city were that, at the blast of the trumpet, they were to gather where he was. The job was kept going at such a feverish pace that neither Nehemiah nor his staff and bodyguard took their clothes off at night. A number of the volunteer workers from places outside Jerusalem used to return to their homes after the day's labour. Nehemiah asked them to remain over in the city so that they could share in the nightly guard duties.

Sanballat, Tobiah and Geshem gave up the idea of armed attack. But they continued to conspire against Nehemiah. When the city walls were completed but the gates not yet placed in position, they sent a message to Nehemiah asking him to meet them in one of the villages on the coastal plain near Lydda, in order to talk things over. Nehemiah surmised that they wanted to lure him away from Jerusalem and do him harm. He replied simply that he was too busy to leave the work. The invitation was conveyed four more times and each time he sent the same reply.

His opponents now tried to frighten him in a devious way. He received from Sanballat a letter that was unsealed, with the obvious intention that its contents should become known to others. Sanballat wrote as if he was a friend. He had heard from Geshem about damaging rumours circulating among neighbouring peoples. It was alleged that Nehemiah and the Jewish people intended to rebel against Persia, once the walls of Jerusalem were completed; Nehemiah would be proclaimed king of Judah by the local prophets. Since this story was bound to come to the attention of the emperor, Sanballat suggested that he and Nehemiah should meet to discuss what could be done about it. Nehemiah wrote back that the contents of the letter were completely untrue, and that 'you are inventing them out of your own mind' (Neh. 6:8).

Soon after, Nehemiah called on a Jerusalem prophet called Shemaiah, who was ill at home. The prophet warned him that an attempt would be made to kill him and urged him to hide in the Temple behind locked doors. Nehemiah retorted that he was not the kind of man to run away, or to save himself by hiding in the Temple. Nehemiah concluded that Shemaiah had been bribed by Tobiah and Sanballat to put him in a position that would be both sacrilegious and humiliating.

*The Dedication of the Walls* When the reconstruction of the city fortifications and gates had been completed, Nehemiah arranged a public celebration to which the inhabitants of all the outlying Judean towns were also invited. First the priests and the Levites performed the purification rites. Then the leading citizens were assembled on the southern part of the wall, near the Dung Gate, and divided into two groups. Each group led half the assembled crowd in procession along the wall, accompanied by the singing and music of the Levite choirs. Going in opposite directions, the two companies met at the entrance to the Temple. Sacrifices were offered, 'And the joy of Jerusalem was heard afar off' (Neh. 12:43).

With the primary task that had brought him to Jerusalem – the rebuilding of the city walls – behind him, Nehemiah devoted himself to organizing the city and the surrounding area.

*Nehemiah's Reforms*

Trustworthy men were made responsible for the security of Jerusalem: Nehemiah's relative Hanani, and Hananiah, the commander of the fortress. On Nehemiah's instructions, they had the gates closed at sunset each evening and not reopened until well after sunrise each morning. Guards were appointed from among the local residents, some to serve as sentries in fixed posts, others to patrol the areas near their own homes.

Nehemiah placed on a regular basis the collection of tithes and the first fruits of the fields for the maintenance of the Temple and its staff – the priests, Levites, guards and musicians.

Nehemiah also carried out much-needed social and economic reforms. Judah was going through hard times. Many poor families complained that they did not have enough to eat. Others had to mortgage their homes and fields to keep alive, or borrow money to pay taxes. In a number of cases, they were dispossessed and evicted for failure to pay debts or their children became bondsmen. When these complaints were brought to Nehemiah, he was very angry with the officials and more affluent citizens, whom he accused of oppressing their brothers. At a meeting called to discuss the problem, he publicly rebuked those responsible. He ordered that all outstanding debts be cancelled and all property seized for default be returned. He made the officials and leading citizens take an oath before the priests that they would carry out these orders. To emphasize the point, Nehemiah took off the sash he was wearing round his waist and shook it out, saying: 'So may God shake out every man from his house and from his labour who does not perform this promise' (Neh. 5:13). (Money and valuables were usually carried in the sash.)

In recording these measures to help the poor, Nehemiah noted that he had never accepted the allowances and perquisites to which he was entitled as governor, since that would have added to the burdens of the people. He went on to say that he and all his servants had taken part in the voluntary work, and that some one hundred and fifty of the other workers had been fed at his expense. For this purpose he had provided an ox, six choice sheep and many chickens daily, and a fresh supply of wine every ten days. Nehemiah contrasts his unselfish conduct with that of other governors who had enriched themselves from the public purse.

*The Population of Jerusalem*

Nehemiah was concerned that Jerusalem was still to a large extent ruined and underpopulated. 'The city was wide and large, but the people within it were few' (Neh. 7:4). As a basis for redistribution he had the inhabitants registered and compared the results with the original lists of returnees from Babylon. The leading men of Judah were encouraged to make their homes in Jerusalem. In addition, each of the other towns was asked to arrange for one-tenth of its citizens, drawn by lot, to settle in the capital. The list of localities involved in this population shift included towns in the Beersheba area, the Judean foothills and the territory of Benjamin north of Jerusalem. It is probable that these areas of Judah fell outside the Jerusalem district at the beginning of the Return, but were integrated with it in Nehemiah's time.

*Nehemiah's Second Term*

In 433 BC, after serving twelve years in Jerusalem, Nehemiah returned to Persia and rejoined the service of the emperor Artaxerxes. Some time later (the date is unknown), Nehemiah persuaded his master to send him back to Jerusalem for a second term as governor. He found that during his absence religious observance had grown slacker, the rate of intermarriage with non-Jewish peoples in the area had increased, and abuses had appeared in high places. Nehemiah took firm hold of affairs and carried out sweeping changes.

At the outset, he came into collision with Eliashib, the high priest. The priest had for a long time been friendly with Tobiah of Gilead, Nehemiah's old opponent. Nehemiah was shocked to find that Tobiah had been given a room in the Temple precincts for his personal use while in Jerusalem. It had been a storeroom for Temple equipment, and for offerings of grain and incense. Nehemiah promptly had Tobiah's belongings flung out, the room ritually purified and the items previously stored there returned to it.

Eliashib was connected with another old adversary, for his grandson was married to the daughter of Sanballat. This was regarded as a mixed marriage, since the Samaritans were not accepted by orthodox Jews as true followers of

the Mosaic faith. Nehemiah had the offender exiled from Jerusalem for having degraded the priesthood.

The context of this action was Nehemiah's general campaign against marrying foreign wives, on the ground that they undermined the religious and cultural identity of the Jewish community. Many of these women were Philistines, Moabites or Ammonites; at least half their children knew no Hebrew, but spoke only the language of the mothers. Nehemiah called together the husbands concerned and lectured them on the dangers of intermarriage. Even the wise king Solomon, he pointed out, had come under the pernicious influence of the pagan princesses in his harem. Nehemiah made the men solemnly undertake that their sons and daughters would not be permitted to make mixed marriages.

Nehemiah was dismayed to find that the Temple had been neglected and its revenues from tithes and first-fruits had largely ceased. As a result, most of the Levites and other Temple attendants were unable to subsist and had gone back to their villages, to work on the land. Nehemiah put the matter in order. The regular offerings of corn, wine and olive oil were resumed in full, and the Levites were brought back to their duties in the sanctuary.

Nehemiah next clamped down on the laxity in Sabbath observance. He noted that the farmers were pressing their grapes on the holy day, or coming into Jerusalem with donkeys laden with produce for sale. There were also Phoenician merchants from the coast, bringing fish and other wares. Nehemiah ordered that the gates of the city should be shut before the Sabbath started and remain shut until it was over. Levites were posted at all the gates to ensure that the orders were observed. To get round the ban, merchants traded outside the walls, until Nehemiah threatened to use force against them.

Nehemiah was anxious to gain merit in the eyes of the Lord for all he had done to strengthen the purity of the faith in Judah. His memoir ends with the pious prayer, 'Remember me, O my God, for good' (Neh. 13:30).

## Ezra the Scribe

EZRA BELONGED TO THE COMMUNITY IN BABYlonia descended from the Judahite exiles. He came from a distinguished priestly family, and was a gifted scholar and preacher, well versed in the Mosaic laws and Jewish traditions. He is always known as Ezra the Scribe (Hebrew *sofer*). The term had been used under the monarchy for the palace secretary, but by Ezra's time had come to mean any man learned in religious law.

*Ezra's Mission*
It has been surmised that Ezra was attached to the Persian court as a commissioner or adviser on the affairs of the Jewish minority. He certainly seems to have had no difficulty in obtaining royal support for the mission he had set himself. That mission was to go to Jerusalem in order to reform and organize the religious life of the Jews who had returned from Babylonia.

The date when Ezra launched this enterprise remains one of the unresolved problems of biblical study. The Book of Ezra simply states that it was 'in the seventh year of Artaxerxes the king' (Ezra 7:7). If the reference was to Artaxerxes I, who was Nehemiah's royal master, Ezra would have gone to Jerusalem in 458 BC, five years before Nehemiah did. That view has generally been rejected by modern authorities, who maintain that Ezra came after Nehemiah. If the monarch concerned was Artaxerxes II, the date of Ezra's mission would be sixty years later, in 398 BC. A third supposition is that the 'seventh year' in the text is a textual error, and should read 'thirty-seventh year'. That would make the date 428 BC, maybe a decade or two after Nehemiah's period as governor.

The royal warrant authorizing Ezra's mission is quoted in its original Aramaic language in the Hebrew Bible. The first part of it reads:

> I make a decree that any one of the people of Israel or their priests or Levites in my kingdom, who freely offers to go to Jerusalem, may go with you.
>
> For you are sent by the king and his seven counsellors to make inquiries about Judah and Jerusalem according to the law of your God, which is in your hand, (Ezra 7:13,14).

The documents contain instructions on a number of other points.

Ezra was to take with him, for the Temple in Jerusalem, the gold and silver granted to him by the king and his counsellors, or donated by his fellow-Jews in the province of Babylonia. The money was to be used for the purchase of animals to be offered as sacrifices on behalf of the royal house. What was left over could be devoted to other religious purposes at Ezra's discretion.

The authorities in the 'Beyond the River' province were ordered to provide Ezra with certain amounts of silver, wheat, wine and oil and with an unlimited quantity of salt, for use in the Temple services. The provincial treasurers were advised that the priests and other members of the Temple staff would be exempt from paying taxes.

Ezra was given extensive powers over the Jews residing in the Beyond the River province, including the right to appoint judges and officials for them. Those who did not obey the Mosaic laws as well as those of the king would be liable to drastic penalties of death, banishment, confiscation of property or imprisonment. Where his fellow-Jews were not acquainted with the Mosaic Laws, Ezra was to teach them.

*The Journey to Jerusalem*
Assured of official sponsorship and practical support, Ezra persuaded a number of clan and family heads to join his party, with their households. When the time for departure came they all gathered at a place on the Ahava canal. There were fifteen hundred families, or about five thousand people in all, divided into twelve clans. Ezra found that though there were a few priests there were no Levites. He sent a deputation to Iddo, probably the chief priest at the Jewish shrine in the city of Casiphia. Iddo recruited several family groups of Levites for Ezra, together with a number of men from families that traditionally provided workmen for the Temple. For safe custody on the journey, Ezra divided the gold, the silver and the additional vessels for the Temple among twelve priests, prudently drawing up an inventory before doing so.

In his diary (Chapters 7 to 9 of the Book of Ezra), Ezra notes with refreshing candour that 'I was ashamed to ask the king for a band of soldiers and horsemen to protect us against the enemy on our way' (Ezra 8:22). He had already explained to the king that the Lord protected those who put their trust in him. To make up for the lack of a military escort, Ezra concentrated on spiritual armament. He proclaimed a fast and led the assembly in prayer. The appeal was effective, Ezra records, for the Lord delivered them from enemies and ambushes along the way. On arrival in Jerusalem the money and valuables were delivered at the Temple, and the powers vested in Ezra by his royal warrant were made known to the provincial authorities.

It filled Ezra with grief that in the restored homeland the Jewish religion and identity should be eroded by inter-marriage and assimilation. The chief offenders were to be found among the priests and leading citizens. In his prayers, Ezra confessed to the Lord that the remnant returned *The Mixed* to the holy land had strayed from God's *Marriages* commandments: 'our iniquities have risen higher *Problem* than our heads, and our guilt has mounted up to the heavens' (Ezra 9:6). Disturbed by the situation, a group came to Ezra and urged him to have all the foreign women and children sent away: 'Arise, for it is your task, and we are with you; be strong and do it' (Ezra 10:4).

Using the powers conferred on him by the king, Ezra issued a proclamation summoning the men of Jerusalem and the surrounding towns and villages to attend a public meeting in the capital. Failure to attend would be punished by confiscation of property and expulsion from the community. The assembly took place in the open Temple square on a wet winter day. Everyone's spirits were further dampened by Ezra's strictures and the drastic demands he made on them.

The people agreed in principle that men with non-Jewish wives should divorce them. But, they pointed our forlornly, this could not be done immediately, and certainly not while they were standing huddled in the pouring rain. They made the sensible proposal that officials be appointed to handle the matter in each town. The persons who were to get divorces would appear before these registrars at appointed times. Ezra agreed, and the gathering dispersed.

*The Reading* Ezra appointed a tribunal of leading heads of *of the Law* clans that investigated each case separately, over a period of two months. The foreign wives retained the custody of their children. The Book of Ezra gives a list of one hundred and eleven husbands involved in these proceedings, seventeen of them priests. 'All these had married foreign women, and they put them away with their children' (Ezra 10:44).

The time had come for Ezra to bring the Law to the people. On the first day of Tishri, the seventh month in the Hebrew calendar (September-October), the whole community gathered in the square at the Water Gate. Children were included who were old enough to follow the proceedings. Ezra stood on a high wooden platform, flanked by a group of leaders.

The most precious object Ezra had brought with him from Babylonia was a copy of 'the book of the law of Moses'. Though it is unclear what this book contained, it may well have been an early version of the Torah or Pentateuch (the Five Books of Moses) collated during the Babylonian exile. As Ezra opened the sacred work, the congregation rose to its feet. He recited a blessing, to which they shouted 'Amen, Amen,' bowing down with their faces to the ground. They seated themselves and fixed their eyes intently on Ezra's face as he started to read from the Hebrew text. With the help of his Levite assistants, each passage was translated and explained in Aramaic, the daily language of the people. The reading lasted from sunrise to noon. The audience was so moved that many of them wept. Ezra told them that it was a day for rejoicing, not grief, 'for this day is holy to our Lord; and do not be grieved, for the joy of the Lord is your strength' (Neh. 8:10). They returned to their homes to feast and celebrate.

Through the study of the Law, the community *The Feast of* was aware that the Feast of Succoth described in *Succoth* the Book of Leviticus should be celebrated at that time of the year. During the monarchy it had been one of the three traditional festivals of pilgrimage to the Temple in Jerusalem, but apparently it had not been observed for a long time. They now carried out the biblical injunction: 'Go out to the hills and bring branches of olive, wild olive, myrtle, palm, and other leafy trees to make booths' (Neh. 8:15). From these branches, family booths were made on the flat rooftops and large communal booths in the courtyard of the Temple and in the public squares. For seven days the people lived in the booths, in memory of the sojourn of the Children of Israel in the desert at the time of the Exodus from Egypt. Each day, under Ezra's guidance, the study of the Law continued.

On the eighth day there was a general assembly for worship. In a long prayer, Ezra recalled the wondrous things the Lord had done for his people: the covenant with Abraham, the Exodus, the giving of the Law on Mount Sinai, and salvation from the enemies they had brought upon themselves by disobeying the Lord's commandments. Ezra ended by calling on the priests and the leaders to sign a written covenant on behalf of the whole community. Its provisions committed them to obey the Mosaic code, to refrain from mixed marriages, to observe the

Sabbath, to leave their land fallow and release their debtors each seventh year, and to bring their first-fruits and tithes for the upkeep of the Temple and its personnel.

*Ezra's Achievement*　　Ezra's concept of religious observance was shaped in the Babylonian exile. The Hebrew state had been swept away; the national sanctuary, the Temple, destroyed; and a good part of the people uprooted. To survive this shattering experience, the exiled community groped for ways of maintaining their faith and their group cohesion as minorities in alien lands. What held them together was no longer the institutions of statehood, or the Temple cult with its priestly hierarchy, but the Mosaic code enshrined in their sacred Book. Ezra's great achievement was to make the Bible, with its system of laws and precepts, the framework for a group way of life that could function in any land and under any political regime. His work was a pilot project that would be of profound importance in the centuries of dispersion that lay in the future. Next to Moses, Ezra is regarded as the pivotal figure in the early history of Judaism.

# 8

# FOUR STORIES FROM THE OLD TESTAMENT

## *Ruth and Naomi*

ONCE UPON A TIME, IN THE DAYS of the Judges, there lived in Bethlehem a man called Elimelech, of the clan of Ephrath in the tribe of Judah. Driven by famine, he moved with his wife Naomi and his two sons Mahlon and Chilion to the mountain plateau of Moab beyond the Dead Sea. There Elimelech died. The sons married Moabite girls, Ruth and Orpah. About ten years later the sons died childless, leaving only the three widows in the family.

Some time after, Naomi heard that there had been a good harvest in Judah, and decided to return home. She set out with her daughters-in-law, but on the way she said to them: 'Go, return each of you to her mother's house. May the Lord deal kindly with you, as you have dealt with the dead and with me. The Lord grant that you may find a home, each of you in the house of her husband!' (Ruth 1:8,9).

Naomi kissed them fondly, and all three broke down and wept. When the young women insisted on staying with her, Naomi wryly pointed out that she was unlikely to marry again and have more sons. Even if she did, the two of them would

hardly wait for two sons to grow up and marry them. (By Hebrew law, a man was obliged to marry his deceased brother's widow so that the dead man's family line could be continued.) After some emotional discussion, Orpah reluctantly consented to return to her own family. Ruth refused. She clung to her mother-in-law and said: 'Entreat me not to leave you ... for where you go I will go, and where you lodge I will lodge; your people shall be my people, and your God my God; where you die I will die, and there will I be buried' (Ruth 1:16,17).

The two women arrived on foot in Bethlehem, a sleepy country town four miles south of Jerusalem. Their arrival caused a flurry of interest in the town. When Naomi's old friends welcomed her, she said sadly to them: 'Do not call me Naomi, call me Mara, for the Almighty has dealt very bitterly with me' (Ruth 1:20). (In Hebrew, Naomi means pleasure and Mara means bitter.)

It was the time of the barley harvest. Since they were without means, Ruth volunteered to go and join the women gathering the corn in the fields behind the reapers. By chance, the field she

'Ruth and Boaz.' A drawing by the nineteenth-century English artist
Sir Edward Burne-Jones, published in 1881.

chose belonged to Boaz, a wealthy and important man in Bethlehem who was related to Elimelech, Naomi's late husband. Boaz arrived at the field and greeted the reapers. Noticing the comely young woman among the gleaners, he asked the foreman who she was. The answer was that she was the foreign girl who had come back with Naomi from Moab, and had been gleaning since early morning. Boaz came up to Ruth and urged her to remain working in his field. His men would take care of her. If she was thirsty, she could drink from their water jars.

Bowing down in gratitude, Ruth humbly asked why he should concern himself with a foreigner like her. Boaz told her that he had heard all about her selfless devotion to her mother-in-law. At the midday meal he had her join the workers and share his food. She ate her fill and saved what was left over to bring to Naomi. When she went back to her gleaning, Boaz instructed his labourers to leave for her some of the stalks from the sheaves. By evening, when she beat out the grains from the stalks she had gathered, she was able to carry home twenty kilos of barley, to Naomi's great surprise.

Naomi heard an account of the day's happenings. She told Ruth that Boaz was a close relative and therefore responsible for taking care of them. It would be best for Ruth to go on working in his fields.

At the end of the harvest, Naomi said to Ruth that it was time for her to get married again and have a home of her own. As a kinsman, Boaz could be a suitable husband. To promote the match, Naomi entered into a gentle plot with her daughter-in-law. Boaz would be supervising the work at the threshing floor, and would sleep there that night. Ruth was to bathe, put on perfume, and dress in her best robe. She was to go to the threshing floor but remain concealed until Boaz had finished eating and lay down on the barley to sleep. She was then to lie down at his feet under the cover.

Ruth did what she was told. Boaz woke up in the night and was startled to discover a woman lying at his feet. He called out, 'Who are you?' Ruth identified herself. Following Naomi's instructions, she plucked up her courage to claim that Boaz was responsible for her and should marry her. Boaz was obviously pleased with the suggestion, and flattered that Ruth should prefer him to a younger man. At the same time, he

explained to her, there was a legal problem. Another citizen of the town was a closer relative than he was. If the other were willing to do so, it would be his right and duty to marry her. Boaz promised to clarify the matter the next day. Before dawn, he filled Ruth's cloak with threshed barley, helped her to sling it on her back, and sent her home.

The following morning Boaz took up his position at the entrance to the town and waited for the other relative to appear. Boaz had arranged for ten of the town elders to be there as witnesses. In their presence, Boaz told his kinsman that Naomi wanted to sell a field that had belonged to her husband Elimelech. If the other relative did not exercise his option to buy it he, Boaz, intended to do so. The kinsman promptly said he wanted to buy the field. But he changed his mind when Boaz explained that he would also have to make himself responsible for Ruth, the widow of Elimelech's eldest son. The other waived all his rights in favour of Boaz, and handed his sandal to Boaz in the presence of the elders, to seal the transaction. Boaz solemnly declared that he had that day bought from Naomi everything that had belonged to her husband and sons, and that he was taking Ruth as his wife in order to continue the dead man's name and to keep the property in the family. The way was now clear for the marriage of Boaz and Ruth.

In due course Ruth had a son, who was given the name of Obed. The delighted Naomi took care of the infant, and was congratulated by her women friends. They exclaimed that her daughter-in-law Ruth, who loved her and had done more for her than seven sons, had now given her a grandson who would bring her new life and give her security in her old age.

When Obed grew up, he married and became the father of Jesse, one of whose sons was David. Ruth the Moabite was thus the great-grandmother of the most illustrious of Hebrew kings.

In the Hebrew Bible the Book of Ruth is in- *Comments on* cluded among the Writings, the third and last *the Book of* division of the Old Testament. In the Christian *Ruth* Bible, it has been moved forward to appear immediately after Judges.

Textual analysis indicates that the Book of Ruth in its present form may have been written about 400 BC, though the story on which it is based may well have come down from a much earlier time. The setting for the story is the latter half of the period of the Judges, about the eleventh century BC. Historically, that was a period of struggle for the Israelite tribes settling down in the Promised Land. None of that turbulence is reflected in the book, which depicts an idyllic rural life in the Judean hills.

The story concerns intermarriage between an Israelite and a non-Israelite, and the adoption of a Moabite girl into the Hebrew community and faith. If it was written down at the end of the fifth century BC (as scholars are inclined to believe), its theme would be completely at variance with the ban on foreign marriages introduced about that time by Nehemiah and Ezra, in order to preserve the purity of the Mosaic faith.

## Jonah and the Whale

ONE DAY THE LORD SPOKE TO THE PROPHET Jonah the son of Amittai, and told him to go to the city of Nineveh. He was to speak out against it because the people were wicked. (Nineveh, on the upper Euphrates river in Mesopotamia, was the capital of the Assyrian empire.)

Jonah did not want to go. Instead, he ran away in the opposite direction. He arrived at the port of Joppa (now Jaffa), found a ship about to sail for Tarshish in Spain and bought a passage on it.

The Lord caused such a violent storm at sea that the ship was in danger of foundering. The terrified crew started to pray for help, each to his own god. They also threw the cargo overboard to lighten the ship but the storm did not abate. Jonah had gone below and fallen asleep in the ship's hold. The captain shook him awake and said: 'What do you mean, you sleeper? Arise, call upon your god! Perhaps the god will give a thought to us, that we do not perish' (Jon. 1:6).

When the sailors drew lots to find out who might be to blame, Jonah's name was drawn. They wanted to know who he was, where he came from and what he had done to bring this peril on them. Jonah replied that he was a Hebrew; he worshipped the Lord of Heaven who had made the land and the sea. He admitted that he was now running away from the Lord, and told them that the only way to calm the water was to throw him into the sea. The sailors shrank from doing so. They manned the oars of the galley and pulled with all their strength for the shore. But they were unable to make progress.

The storm got worse. The desperate sailors prayed to Jonah's God not to punish them with death if they were compelled to take his life. They pointed out that it was the Lord who was responsible for their plight. They then took Jonah and threw him overboard. The sea calmed down at once. Overawed, the ship's crew immediately converted to Jonah's faith and offered up a sacrifice to the Lord.

God ordered a great fish to swallow up Jonah. He remained in its belly for three days and nights. From inside the fish, Jonah sent up a prayer of gratitude to the Lord who had saved him from drowning. 'And the Lord spoke to the fish, and it vomited out Jonah upon the dry land' (Jon. 2:10).

Once again the Lord told Jonah to go to Nineveh and proclaim to its inhabitants 'the message that I tell you'. This time Jonah obeyed. He found Nineveh so large that it took three days to walk across it. Jonah walked for a day into the city. He then proclaimed that in forty days it would be destroyed.

Believing the message, the citizens were thrown into a panic. The king of Nineveh got up from his throne, removed his robe, covered himself with sackcloth and sat in ashes. He issued a proclamation that all the inhabitants, and even their domestic animals, should stop eating and drinking, and should wear sackcloth. They were all to put aside their wicked ways and pray to the Lord, in the hope that he would change his mind and let them live. On seeing this display of penitence the Lord decided to spare the city.

This cancellation of the fate he had been sent to prophesy 'displeased Jonah exceedingly, and he was angry' (Jon. 4:1). (He considered that the wicked should have been punished.) The reason he had not wanted to carry out the mission, he complained, was that he knew God would be merciful. In the event, it was better for him to die than to live.

Jonah left the city towards the east. He made a shelter and sat down under it, to wait and see what would actually happen to Nineveh. The Lord made a castor-oil plant spring up overnight to give Jonah more shade from the heat. Jonah was very pleased with the plant. But at dawn the following day, the Lord made a worm attack the plant and it withered. Later that morning, Jonah felt faint from the sun that beat down on him, and from the hot east wind the Lord sent to add to his discomfort. Once more Jonah wished he were dead. God asked him what right he had to be angry about the destruction of the plant. Jonah replied that he was entitled to be angry – in fact, angry enough to want death. The Lord pointed out that Jonah was being sorry for a plant that had sprung up one night and disappeared the next, without Jonah's having done anything to make it grow. How much more should the Lord have pity on the great city of Nineveh, that contained a hundred and twenty thousand innocent people and a great number of animals.

*Comments on the Book of Jonah* The Book of Jonah is included among the twelve Minor Prophets, but has little in common with the other eleven. It is not a compilation of prophetic utterances but a brief prose narrative, relating the prophet's experiences. However simple, even droll, the story may seem, everything about it is debatable – from its date of origin to its spiritual message.

Some authorities hold that the story has an historical connection with an eighth-century BC prophet of the same name; he is mentioned in the Book of Kings as advising king Jeroboam II of Israel. Others place the Book as late as the fourth or third century BC; in God's concern with Nineveh they see an expression of the broader universalist strand in Judaism as opposed to the exclusive and inward-looking trend developed by Ezra and Nehemiah at that time.

The book has been described in certain Jewish circles as a mystic parable of a period in the national history. In this interpretation, Jonah is Israel; the sailors, the surrounding nations; Nineveh, paganism; the ocean, the Near Eastern political scene; and the storm that churns it up, the rising might of Babylonia. In synagogue liturgy the Book of Jonah holds an honoured place, being the Haftarah (passage from the Prophetic Books) read during the afternoon service on the Day of Atonement.

Christian theologians, for their part, tend to regard Jonah as a precursor of Jesus. The three days spent in the belly of the fish are regarded as symbolic of the three days Jesus was in the tomb before the Resurrection.

Clearly, there are attributes of God in the story that commend themselves to Jews and Christians alike. God is merciful and forgiving to repentant sinners – even if Jonah thinks they deserve to be punished. God also appears as the deity of all living creatures, and in control of nature.

Jonah figured in the nineteenth-century battles between scientific rationalism and religious fundamentalism. The sceptics gleefully pointed out that the anatomy of a whale's throat made it impossible for it to swallow a man. Unfortunately for them, this point was derived from an error in translation. There never have been whales in the Mediterranean, and the ancient Israelites knew nothing of such animals. The Book of Jonah speaks only of a *dag gadol*, a big fish.

Whatever the problems of interpretation, what the average man recalls about Jonah is that he was swallowed by a whale and got away – surely the greatest fish story of all time!

## Queen Esther

SEATED ON HIS IMPERIAL THRONE IN THE Persian capital of Susa, King Ahasuerus ruled over one hundred and twenty provinces, all the way from India to Ethiopia.

In the third year of his reign he gave a banquet for his top officials, to which he invited the army heads, and the governors and nobles of the provinces. For six months he displayed to them 'the riches of his royal glory and the splendour and pomp of his majesty' (Est. 1:4). After that the king proffered a feast to all the male citizens of Susa, which lasted a whole week in the palace gardens. The courtyard was decorated with blue and white cotton curtains, tied by cords of fine purple linen to silver rings on marble columns. Couches made of gold and silver were set out on the mosaic pavement of white and red marble inlaid with mother-of-pearl and turquoise. The royal wine flowed freely, served in golden goblets of different designs. At the same time, Queen Vashti entertained the ladies inside the palace.

On the seventh day, 'the heart of the king was merry with wine' (Est. 1:10), and he sent the seven eunuchs who were his personal attendants to bring out his beautiful Queen, wearing her royal crown. The king wanted to show her off to his male guests. To his rage, she refused to humiliate herself by complying with his order.

The king made a major issue out of the queen's disobedience. He consulted his seven leading counsellors on the legal position. Their spokesman, Memucan, declared that the queen had done wrong not just to the king but to the whole empire. Her example would lead other wives to treat their husbands with contempt. The advisers proposed that a royal decree be published deposing Vashti. When that had been done, the king's entourage suggested how Vashti could be replaced. The officials in all the provinces should be instructed to send 'all the beautiful young virgins to the women's quarters of the palace in Susa' (Est. 2:3), where the chief eunuch would take charge of them. The one who pleased Ahasuerus most would become the new queen. The king accepted the proposal.

There lived in Susa a Jew called Mordecai. He was a member of a Benjaminite family descended from Kish, the father of King Saul. His cousin Esther, whose Hebrew name was Hadassah, had lost her parents as a child. Mordecai had adopted her and brought her up as his own daughter. She was a beautiful and charming young woman, and was among those selected to be brought to the palace. The chief eunuch took a liking to her. He gave her the best quarters in the harem, with seven maids to attend on her, and arranged for her to start her beauty treatment right away. On Mordecai's advice, she did not disclose that she was Jewish. Each day Mordecai would walk up and down in front of the women's quarters, to keep in touch with Esther and find out how she was getting on.

The girls were given a special diet and beauty treatment for a year, including massage for six months with oil of myrrh and six months with other spices and unguents. At the end of the year, each girl was taken to the king's quarters and spent the night with him. She then remained in the harem of the concubines, and did not see the king again unless he sent for her by name.

When Esther's turn came, her friend the chief eunuch advised her what to wear and how to behave. Her looks and personality captivated the king, who placed the royal crown on her head and made her his queen. The king arranged a great wedding feast in her honour. To mark the occasion, he granted a remission of taxes to the provinces, and 'gave gifts with royal liberality' (Est. 2:18).

Mordecai, who had gained a position on the palace staff, overheard two of the royal eunuchs plotting to assassinate the king. He asked Esther to warn the king. The report was investigated and found to be true. The two eunuchs were hanged for treason. On the king's orders, the incident was recorded in the royal archives.

Some time later King Ahasuerus appointed as his chief minister a man called Haman. He was descended from the eleventh century BC King Agag of the Amalekites, traditional enemies of the Hebrews. All the palace officials were ordered to show their respect for Haman by kneeling and bowing to him. As a proud Jew, Mordecai refused to comply. Haman's wrath was directed not only against Mordecai but against all the Jews under Persian rule. He decided to organize a pogrom against the Jews.

In order to pick the most propitious time, he had lots, called *purim*, cast before him day after day. The date finally determined by this means was the thirteenth day of the twelfth month, Adar (some time in March).

Haman then went to the king and said:

There is a certain people scattered abroad and dispersed among the peoples in all the provinces of your kingdom; their laws are different from those of every other people, and they do not keep the king's laws, so that it is not for the king's profit to tolerate them. If it please the king, let it be decreed that they be destroyed (Est. 3:8,9)

To make the proposal more tempting, Haman claimed he would be able to bring in a huge sum of money to the royal treasury. The king replied that the people and their money were at the disposal of Haman and he could do with them as he saw fit. The king drew off his finger the signet ring with which royal edicts were sealed and handed it to Haman.

Haman dictated to the palace secretaries edicts in the king's name and sealed with the king's ring, addressed to the authorities throughout the vast empire, 'to every province in its own script and every people in its own language' (Est. 3:12). The edicts were sent out by couriers. They contained instructions to slaughter all Jews – young and old, men, women and children – on a single day, the thirteenth day of Adar, and to seize all their property. The edict was published in Susa as well, and threw the city into confusion.

The Jewish communities everywhere were plunged into mourning when the dreadful news reached them. Mordecai put on sackcloth and ashes, the traditional sign of grief, and wept before the palace gate. He was not admitted because of his appearance. Queen Esther sent one of the eunuchs to ask Mordecai what the matter was. He told the servant what had happened, and gave him a copy of the edict to show Esther, with a plea that she should intervene with the king. She sent a message back pointing out that the penalty was death for anybody who came into the royal presence without being summoned. (This rule was doubtless a precaution against assassination – the fate that did eventually befall king Ahasuerus.) Esther added that she had not seen the king for a month.

Mordecai refused to be satisfied. He replied with a stern warning: 'Think not that in the king's palace you will escape any more than all the other Jews' (Est. 4:13). Maybe, he suggested, it was for just such an emergency that Esther had become queen. Deeply moved, she requested that all the Jews of Susa should fast for three days. She and her maids would do the same. After that she would go to the king 'and if I perish, I perish' (Est. 4:16).

Three days later Esther, dressed in her royal robes, took her stand in the inner courtyard facing the throne room. Sitting on his throne the king caught sight of her and pointed towards her with the golden sceptre in his hand – a sign that he pardoned her intrusion and was willing to see her. She came up to him and touched the tip of the sceptre. He asked her what she wanted. She could have anything she desired, he said kindly, even half his kingdom. Esther's only request was that the king and his chief minister Haman would honour her by dining with her in her quarters that night. It was promptly granted.

During the meal the king again asked her if there was anything she wanted from him. She would tell him the following evening, she replied, if he and Haman would do her the honour of dining with her again.

Haman left Esther's quarters feeling very pleased with himself. But when he saw Mordecai at the palace entrance, he was again furious that the Jew did not kneel to him. He restrained himself and continued on his way. In his home, Haman boasted to his wife and friends about the wealth and importance he had gained. The king, he claimed, held him in greater honour than anyone else: 'Even Queen Esther let no one come with the king to the banquet she prepared but myself. And tomorrow also I am invited by her together with the king' (Est. 5:12). Yet all this, he added, did him no good as long as he had to see Mordecai the Jew sitting at the king's gate.

His wife and guests proposed that Haman have a gallows erected twenty-two metres high. He should persuade the king to have Mordecai hanged on it next morning, 'then go merrily with the king to the dinner' (Est. 5:14). Haman thought this was an excellent idea and had the work carried out at once.

Unable to sleep that night, the king occupied himself by having the official records read to him. He came across the entry about Mordecai's exposure of the two eunuchs who had conspired to kill him. Ahasuerus asked his officials what had been done to reward the man who had saved his life. They admitted that the answer was nothing. At that moment Haman came into the palace. He was summoned by Ahasuerus who asked him what could be done for a man the king wished to honour. Believing that he himself was the man, Haman advised that such a person should be dressed in royal robes and mounted on the king's horse with a crown on its head. He should be led through the public square by a nobleman who would call out as they went: 'Thus shall it be done to the man whom the king delights to honour' (Est. 6:9).

To Haman's dismay, he was ordered by the king to have Mordecai honoured in exactly the manner he had described, with Haman himself leading the horse. After this ordeal Haman hurried home, covering his face in shame, and told his wife and friends of his humiliating experience. His wife commented coldly that he was losing his power to Mordecai the Jew and there was nothing he could do about it.

At this point, the king's eunuchs arrived to escort Haman to the second dinner Queen Esther had prepared. During the dinner she boldly pleaded that her people be spared. She would have held her peace, she said emotionally, if they were just being sold into slavery; but in fact they had been sold for slaughter.

King Ahasuerus was aghast at this story. He demanded to know who it was that presumed to carry out such a deed. Pointing at her other guest, Esther cried out: 'A foe and enemy! This wicked Haman!' (Est. 7:6). The king was so wrought up over the dramatic disclosure that he rushed out of the room and paced in the garden. The terrified Haman flung himself onto the couch where the queen was sitting and pleaded for his life. That was the sight that met the king's eyes when he came back into the room. He shouted out: 'Will he even assault the queen in my presence, in my own house?' (Est. 7:8).

The attendants flung a cloth over Haman's face, as was customary with a doomed man. One of them revealed that Haman had prepared a gallows for Mordecai. The king barked out an order that Haman should be hanged upon it himself. That was promptly done. 'Then the anger of the king abated' (Est. 7:10).

Haman's property was given to Queen Esther. The king sent for Mordecai and handed him the royal signet ring as a sign that he was appointed to replace Haman as chief minister. Esther put all Haman's property in Mordecai's hands to administer for her.

Though Haman had met his end, the evil design he had set in motion against the Jews remained in force. Esther flung herself weeping at the king's feet and begged him to repeal Haman's decree. Ahasuerus explained that a proclamation issued in the name of the king and stamped with his ring could not be revoked. However, Mordecai was given permission to write letters to all the Jewish communities and instruct them on royal authority what they should do. The letters dictated by Mordecai went out with imperial couriers mounted on fast horses. They authorized the Jewish communities to arm themselves in self-defence. If they were attacked they would be entitled to fight back and destroy their assailants.

Having made these arrangements to thwart Haman's anti-Semitic decree Mordecai left the palace, splendidly dressed in royal robes of blue and white and a cloak of fine purple linen, with a great golden crown on his head. As he went through the streets the Jews of the capital 'had light and gladness and joy and honour' (Est. 8:16). Wherever the king's couriers arrived in the provinces with Mordecai's despatch, the local Jewish communities declared a holiday and held a feast. Many other people converted to Judaism out of a new respect for the Jews.

The thirteenth day of Adar arrived, the day that had been appointed for the slaughter. But the Jewish communities everywhere were organized and armed, and ready to repulse attacks. The provincial officials gave them support for fear of Mordecai, since it was known that he had become powerful at the imperial court. In the clashes that took place on the thirteenth of Adar, five hundred enemies of the Jews were killed in Susa and seventy-five thousand elsewhere in the empire. Three hundred more were killed in Susa the following day. The dead included the ten sons of Haman, whose bodies were hung on the gallows their father had erected for Mordecai. Nowhere did the Jews loot the property of their slain enemies.

The day after these outbreaks had ceased (the fourteenth of Adar in the provinces and the fifteenth in Susa the capital) was celebrated by the Jews as a feast of thanksgiving for their deliverance. The feast was kept on those dates every year afterwards, in accordance with a letter of instruction sent by Mordecai to all the Jews in the empire, together with a confirming letter from Queen Esther.

The festival is celebrated to this day and is known as Purim, after the lots Haman had cast to fix a date for the pogrom.

**Comments on the Book of Esther**

The Scroll of Esther (*Megillet Esther* in Hebrew) is by tradition read out in every synagogue on Purim, the early spring festival that takes place during March. Unlike the three festivals of Passover (*Pesach*), the Feast of Weeks (*Shavuoth*) and the Feast of Booths (*Succoth*), Purim is not mentioned in the Pentateuch. It was introduced much later into the calendar of Jewish feasts, probably by immigrants to the Land of Israel from the Jewish community in Persia.

The possible Mesopotamian origin of the story is suggested by the names of some of its chief characters. Biblical scholars regard the name of Mordecai as derived from Marduk the chief Babylonian god; and Esther from Ishtar, the Babylonian goddess of love and fertility. In Babylonian mythology Marduk and Ishtar were cousins like Mordecai and Esther. Vashti was the name of the goddess of Elam, the homeland of the Persians to the east of Babylonia.

The Book of Esther accounts for the origin of the Purim festival by relating events that are supposed to have taken place at the court of the Persian monarch Xerxes I (in Hebrew, Ahasuerus) who ruled from 486 to 465 BC. Shushan (or Susa in Greek) was the winter capital of the Persian empire at the time. The unknown author of the Book shows surprising familiarity with Persian court customs. He embellishes his account with touches of oriental hyperbole – such as a feast that lasts for six months, or a gallows twenty-two metres high constructed in a single night. Whether the events actually took place is

'The Triumph of Mordecai.' An engraving from the Doré Bible (1865).

doubtful. There is nothing in Persian records to corroborate the story.

It is a matter of speculation when the book was actually written. One theory places it in the context of the Maccabean revolt against the Seleucid ruler Antiochus IV, in the second century BC. An alternative suggestion dates the work a little later, in the time of John Hyrcanus I, the Hasmonean high priest and ethnarch at the end of the second century BC.

One of the subtle literary devices used by the author of the book is to make Mordecai a descendant of Saul's father Kish, and Haman a descendant of the Amalekite chief Agag. The Amalekites were a fierce nomad tribe in the Negev desert, to the south of the Israelite area of settlement. The two peoples lived in constant strife. Saul carried out a successful campaign against the Amalekites and captured Agag, who was slain by the prophet Samuel. Against that background, the readers of the Book of Esther would readily conclude that Mordecai and Haman were destined to be mortal enemies.

A conspicuous feature of the book is its secular spirit. It is out of step with the Old Testament generally, in that the Lord is not mentioned even once. There is no appeal to God in time of trouble, nor gratitude to him for deliverance. It is hardly surprising that there were rabbinical reservations about the inclusion of this work, when the canon of the Hebrew Old Testament was finally settled in the first century AD. The Septuagint, the early Greek translation of the Old Testament, included additional material that aimed at injecting a religious element into the book. These additions were retained in the Catholic Bible but the Protestant Bible relegated them to the Apocrypha.

In spite of its lack of a religious dimension, the story of Esther has always had a profound emotional impact on Jews. It is the earliest account of the forces of anti-Semitism that have stained the pages of Diaspora Jewish history with so much bloodshed and suffering. Haman is the prototype of a long line of anti-Semitic persecutors, of whom Hitler was the most devastating.

In the ancient Persia of the story, the important thing about the planned pogrom is that it did not happen. Haman was foiled; the lovely Queen Esther and the sagacious Mordecai triumphed and saved their people. That turn of events was certainly a matter for celebration.

Purim is the gayest occasion in the Jewish year. In Israel it is carnival time, marked by masquerades, folk-dancing in the streets, and the consumption of vast quantities of three-cornered buns stuffed with poppy seeds, called 'Haman's ears'. Above all, it is the children's festival, though their fancy-dress costumes today include as many Walt Disney characters as Queen Esthers.

The Book of Esther is one of five Scrolls (*Megillot*) that are the shortest works among the Writings in the Old Testament. Each is read out in synagogue on a different religious day. The other four are: The Song of Songs (Passover); Ruth (the Feast of Weeks); Lamentations (the ninth day of Av, the fast commemorating the destruction of the Temple); and Ecclesiastes (the Feast of Succoth).

## Daniel in the Lions' Den

NEBUCHADNEZZAR, THE SIXTH-CENTURY BC king of Babylonia, captured Jerusalem and carried into captivity the king of Judah and a number of the leading families. He also took the Temple treasures and stored them in the temple of his gods in Babylon.

Nebuchadnezzar ordered Ashpenaz, his chief minister, to select some young men of good family among the Hebrew captives, and to train them for service in the palace. They had to be handsome, intelligent, quick to learn and free of any physical defect. Ashpenaz was to give them a three-year course that included reading and writing the Babylonian language. *The Four Young Judeans*

Among those chosen were Daniel, Hananiah, Mishael and Azariah, all from the tribe of Judah. The chief minister gave them Babylonian names: Daniel was called Belteshazzar and the other three Shadrach, Meshach and Abednego.

By the king's orders the young men received the same food as the rest of the palace staff. Daniel went to Ashpenaz and appealed to him for help, as this food was not in accordance with the Jewish dietary laws. If he and his friends ate it, they would become ritually unclean. The official was sympathetic. But he was afraid his life might be in danger if these four Jews did not eat what the king had stipulated, and were seen to be in poorer condition than the others. Daniel persuaded a palace servant to let them live on vegetables and water for a trial period of ten days.

At the end of that time they were healthier than the others who were eating the rich food from the royal table, so the arrangement was continued indefinitely.

Daniel and his companions proved themselves outstanding students. They became proficient not only in the Babylonian language, but also in literature and philosophy. In addition, Daniel had a special gift from the Lord: the ability to interpret visions and dreams. At the end of three years, the pupils on the training course were presented to the king who talked with each of them. The four young men from Judah impressed the monarch more than the others and he appointed them to the staff of the court. 'And in every matter of wisdom and understanding concerning which the king inquired of them, he found them ten times better than all the magicians and enchanters that were in all his kingdom' (Dan. 1:20).

*Nebuchadnez-zar's Dream*     One night the king had a most disturbing dream. Next day he sent for his wise men, magicians, sorcerers and wizards and asked them to interpret his dream. They replied, very reasonably, that if the king would tell them what he had dreamt they would tell him what it meant. No, said the king, they had first to tell him what his dream had been, otherwise 'you shall be torn limb from limb, and your houses shall be laid in ruins' (Dan. 2:5). The wise men were dumbfounded. They protested that there was no man on earth who could meet such a demand. What he required could be done only by the gods. The king became furious with them and ordered that all his wise men and magicians be executed without exception. The task was given to Arioch, the captain of the palace guard.

Since they were employed as 'wise men' the decree applied to Daniel and his friends. Daniel cautiously sounded out Arioch to find out how the harsh order had come about. He received an audience with the king and obtained a short suspension of the order so that he could have a little more time to come up with the explanation of the dream. He rushed home to consult his friends. They prayed to the Lord for help. That same night the mystery was revealed to Daniel in a vision, and he offered a prayer of thanks to God:

> for thou hast made known to us
> the king's matter.
>
> (Dan. 2:23)

First thing next morning Daniel rushed to the captain of the guard and told him not to kill the wise men, as he could now interpret the dream. Arioch hastily brought Daniel in to the king.

Daniel opened with the remark that while no wise man could give him the answer he sought, there was a God in heaven who revealed mysteries, and would do so in this case. In his dream, the king had seen an enormous bright statue of terrifying appearance. Its head was made of fine gold; its chest and arms were of silver; the waist and hips of bronze; its legs of iron; and its feet partly of iron and partly of clay. A great stone broke loose of its own accord, struck the feet of the image and shattered them. The whole statue then disintegrated and became like the chaff on a threshing floor in summer. The wind carried away the dust of the gold, silver, bronze, iron and clay, leaving not a trace behind. The stone that had destroyed the image grew into a mountain that covered the earth.

Having told the dream, Daniel proceeded to give its meaning. The golden head of the statue was Nebuchadnezzar himself, to whom God had 'given the kingdom, the power, and the might, and the glory' (Dan. 2:37), and who ruled over all living things. After him would come inferior empires, represented by the silver and then the bronze parts of the statue. The lower limbs of the statue denoted a fourth empire that would arise. It would be as strong as iron, and shatter the others. But its feet would be partly clay, showing that it would be divided and have weaknesses that would lead to its downfall. Finally, the stone that grew into a mountain was the kingdom that God would establish. It would completely wipe out all the earlier empires, and would itself be everlasting. In the dream, Daniel concluded, God was telling the king what would happen in the future.

King Nebuchadnezzar was overwhelmed by the revelation he had heard from Daniel, who had accurately described his dream. He bowed down to the ground in front of Daniel, and gave orders for sacrifices and offerings to be made in his honour. 'Truly,' he said, 'your God is God of gods and Lord of kings, and a revealer of mysteries' (Dan. 2:47). Daniel was presented with lavish gifts, appointed as governor over the province of Babylon, and made the chief royal adviser. At Daniel's request, his three friends were put in charge of the Babylon province instead of him, while he remained as an adviser.

Three sixteenth-century tiles from the Tilehous, Otterloo, Netherlands.

ABOVE LEFT The Angel announces the coming birth of Samson to Manoah and his wife, who offer a sacrifice.

LEFT 'The wicked draw their swords . . .' (Psalm 37:14).

ABOVE RIGHT Tobias, the Angel Raphael and the Fish.

*The Fiery Furnace*

King Nebuchadnezzar had a gold statue made that was twenty-seven metres high and nearly three metres wide. It was set up in the plain of Dura, in the province of Babylon. All the royal officials were ordered to assemble for the dedication of the statue. When they heard the sound of the trumpet and other musical instruments they were to bow down and worship the image. The penalty for failing to do so would be to be thrown into a fiery furnace.

The ceremony was duly carried out. But some officials jealous of the high positions given to Shadrach, Meshach and Abednego, Daniel's three friends, reported to the king that they had not bowed down to the statue as had been ordered. The angry king sent for them and offered them another chance to comply; if they did not they would be cast into the furnace. Let their own God then save them if he could. The three Jews replied with dignity and courage. They would not compromise their faith by worshipping the statue, whether the Lord rescued them from the furnace or not.

The king lost his temper at this defiance. He had the furnace heated up to the maximum. Soldiers were ordered to tie up the three Jews fully dressed, and cast them into the fire. The heat was so intense that the men who carried the victims to the furnace themselves succumbed to the flames.

Gazing through the door of the furnace from a safe distance, the king was astonished to see not three but four men walking about inside it, apparently unharmed. He came closer and shouted for Shadrach, Meshach and Abednego to come out. The crowd of officials who had gathered to watch the proceedings then witnessed an incredible sight. The three Jews emerged from the furnace untouched: 'the hair of their heads was not singed, their mantles were not harmed, and no smell of fire had come upon them' (Dan. 3:27). Nebuchadnezzar realized that God had sent an angel (the fourth man in the furnace) to effect the miracle. The king proclaimed that if anyone in the realm henceforth spoke with disrespect of the Hebrew God he would be severely punished, 'for there is no other god who is able to deliver in this way' (Dan. 3:29). The rescued men were promoted to even higher positions.

King Nebuchadnezzar was filled with dread after another ominous dream. He saw a beautiful tree, so tall that it reached the sky. The fruit it bore was enough for the whole world to eat. The wild animals rested in its shade and the birds built their nests in its branches. An angel came down from heaven and had the tree cut down, leaving only the stump in the ground, with an iron and bronze band around it. The angel predicted that a man would live with the animals for seven years and his mind would be like that of an animal.

*Nebuchadnezzar's Second Dream*

Once more the king's leading magicians were unable to explain his dream. He sent for Daniel, who was reluctant to do so, until his royal master insisted. The tree, Daniel declared, was Nebuchadnezzar himself, whose greatness covered the world. But the Lord, who had supreme power over human rulers, would reduce him to the level of the animals. For seven years 'you shall be driven from among men, and your dwelling shall be with the beasts of the field; you shall be made to eat grass like an ox, and you shall be wet with the dew of heaven, and seven times shall pass over you, till you know that the Most High rules the kingdom of men' (Dan. 4:25). Leaving the stump of the tree in the ground meant that he would eventually get his kingdom back. Daniel begged the king to repent and change his ways while there was yet time.

A year later, Nebuchadnezzar was strolling on his palace roof. He gazed round him at the great city of Babylon, and boasted that it displayed his might and majesty. Suddenly a voice came out of heaven and proclaimed that his royal power had been taken away from him. For the next seven years he lived like an animal in the field, as Daniel had foretold, till his hair grew as long as eagles' feathers and his nails as long as birds' claws. He then regained his sanity, and his throne and former power were restored to him. He praised the Hebrew God, 'for all his works are right and his ways are just; and those who walk in pride he is able to abase' (Dan. 4:37).

*Belshazzar's Feast*

The next story concerns King Belshazzar, who is described (inaccurately) as Nebuchadnezzar's son and successor. One night he gave a splendid banquet to which a thousand of his noblemen were invited. While they were drinking, the king ordered his servants to bring in the gold and silver vessels his father had looted from the Temple in Jerusalem, so that they could use them to toast their pagan gods 'of gold and silver, bronze, iron, wood, and stone' (Dan. 5:4).

Suddenly a man's hand appeared and started writing on a patch of wall lit by the lamps. When the king caught sight of it he turned pale, and his knees knocked together with fright. He shouted for his magicians and wise men, promising that whoever deciphered the writing on the wall would be dressed in purple robes, have a chain of gold about his neck and rank third in the realm. None of the royal advisers could make anything of the four words the hand had written: *MENE, MENE, TEKEL, PARSIN.*

The queen heard the commotion and entered the banqueting hall. When she found what was troubling the king she told him that there was a man in the kingdom who had the spirit of the holy gods in him. Her husband Nebuchadnezzar had made him chief of the wise men because of his extraordinary ability in interpreting dreams and explaining riddles. His name was Daniel, and he had been given the Babylonian name of Belteshazzar.

Daniel was at once brought before the monarch, but declined the proffered reward. He recalled what had happened to the king's father, who had been deposed from his throne and made to live like an animal until he accepted that the Lord was supreme and could set anyone he chose over the kingdom of men. Belshazzar in turn had 'lifted up yourself against the Lord of heaven' (Dan. 5:23), and had desecrated the sacred Temple vessels in honour of heathen deities.

Daniel then proceeded to interpret the writing on the wall. *MENE* (number): God had numbered the days of Belshazzar's kingdom and brought it to an end; *TEKEL* (weight): the king had been weighed in the scales and found wanting; *PARSIN* (divisions): the kingdom would be divided up and given to the Medes and Persians. In spite of this grim interpretation, the king bestowed the promised reward on Daniel.

That very night Belshazzar was assassinated, and the throne seized by 'Darius the Mede', then sixty-two years old.

*Daniel in the Lions' Den*   King Darius made Daniel one of the most powerful men in the kingdom. The empire was divided into one hundred and twenty satrapies or provinces, each under its own governor. Daniel was one of the three top officials appointed to supervise the governors and to protect the king's interests. He was so outstanding that the king planned to make him the chief minister in charge of the affairs of the whole empire.

Naturally, Daniel's power and influence provoked jealousy and resentment among other senior officials. It was impossible to find fault with his loyalty or religion, so they sought some other way to bring him down. They persuaded Darius to issue a decree that for thirty days nobody was permitted to petition for anything from any god or man, other than the king. Whoever violated the order would be thrown into the den of lions.

Daniel was accustomed to say his prayers three times a day, in front of an open window that faced in the direction of Jerusalem. His enemies went to the king and laid a charge that Daniel had violated the royal decree by invoking his God. In great distress, the monarch spent the day trying to find some loophole that could save Daniel. That evening his other advisers returned and reminded him that, according to the law of the Medes and Persians, a royal decree once issued could never be revoked or altered.

Against his will Darius was obliged to order that Daniel be arrested and thrown into the lions' den. He said to Daniel, 'May your God, whom you serve continually, deliver you!' (Dan. 6:16). The sentence was then carried out. The opening to the pit was blocked by a boulder, and the royal seal fixed to ropes across it.

The king returned to his palace and spent a sleepless night, fasting and refusing to be diverted from his remorse and grief. At dawn he hurried back to the pit and cried out in a tone of anguish, hoping that Daniel's God had kept him alive. To the king's astonishment and relief, Daniel's voice was heard calling back: 'My God sent his angel and shut the lions' mouths, and they have not hurt me, because I was found blameless before him; and also before you, O king, I have done no wrong' (Dan. 6:22). The king ordered that Daniel be taken out of the den. His accusers were thrown in instead, with their families. The lions instantly tore them to pieces.

King Darius issued a proclamation throughout his empire that all men should fear and respect Daniel's God, who performed wonders and miracles in heaven and on earth. Daniel prospered during the reign of Darius and the subsequent reign of 'Cyrus the Persian'.

*Comments on the Book of Daniel*   The first six chapters of the book contain the series of stories about the difficulties and triumphs of Daniel and his three companions at the Babylonian court. Daniel's rise to power is in

**Der Form schneider.**

RIGHT A blockmaker carving wooden blocks for printing bibles on parchment or paper. A woodcut by Jost Amman, the sixteenth-century printmaker and book illustrator.

ABOVE Page from the *Biblia Pauperum (The Bible of the Poor)*, a fifteenth-century block-book in which parallel incidents from the Old and New Testaments are placed side by side in order to illustrate spiritual truths. Here the Entombment is flanked by Joseph being dropped into the well and Jonah being thrown to the whale. All three are good men being dropped into the jaws of death, from which all three will rise again.

the same tradition as the story of Joseph at Pharaoh's court, and Mordecai at the Persian court. Like Joseph, Daniel launches his career through his extraordinary gift for intepreting dreams. The moral in this part of the Book is that faith in the Lord enables Daniel and his friends to survive the trials that come upon them.

From internal evidence, the main part of these chapters appears to have been written about 304 BC, with additions about the middle of the third century BC. The author's knowledge of earlier Mesopotamian history is poor, for he has muddled up the rulers that appear in the stories. Belshazzar was not the son of Nebuchadnezzar but his great-great-grandson; nor did he become king, but only acted as regent in the absence of his father Nabonidus. There was no 'Darius the Mede' among the Babylonian rulers before Cyrus. Darius I (the Great) was the third ruler of the Persian empire after Cyrus.

In the stories of both Esther and Daniel it is a feature of the plot that 'the laws of the Medes and Persians' cannot be revoked. In the ancient Near East, the Medes were a people of Indo-European stock who established their kingdom in the mountainous areas to the north and east of the Mesopotamian plain. Towards the end of the Assyrian empire, they pressed southward into the plain, and joined forces with the Babylonians in the taking of Nineveh in 612 BC. That event marked the end of the Assyrian empire.

In the first half of the sixth century BC, when Nebuchadnezzar was on the Babylonian throne, the Medes were still a rival power to the Babylonians. At that time Persia was a tribute-paying vassal-state of the Medes. In 550 BC the Persian ruler Cyrus revolted against his Medean overlords. In a successful campaign he took over Medea, deposed its king and merged it with Persia, which thus became the dual nation of the Medes and Persians, under a single ruler. The Medean law that a royal decree could not be revoked at the will of the king, without the consent of his counsellors, apparently remained in force in the Persian empire.

The whole of the Book of Daniel was written in Aramaic, in general use at the time as the colloquial language of the region. The version that survived was partly in Aramaic (from chapter 2:4 to the end of chapter 7) and the rest in Hebrew.

The Second half of the Book of Daniel (Chapters 7 to 12) was written more than a century after the first half, in the reign of Antiochus IV Epiphanes, the Seleucid ruler whose anti-Jewish decrees touched off the Maccabean Revolt. These chapters contain apocalyptic visions that are dealt with more fully in the section on the Hebrew Prophets. The prediction that the Seleucid tyrant would be destroyed and a messianic kingdom established served to instil hope in the oppressed Jews.

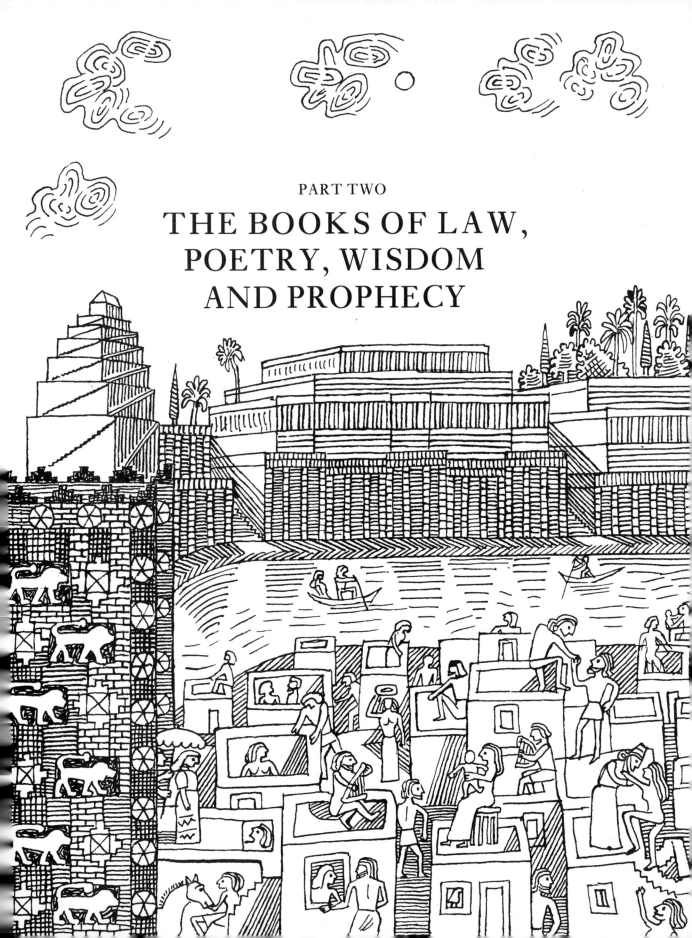

PART TWO

# THE BOOKS OF LAW, POETRY, WISDOM AND PROPHECY

## I

# THE MOSAIC CODE

THE ANCIENT HEBREWS DREW NO
clear distinction between legal, moral
and religious precepts. All laws were
God's commandments, whether they
governed personal conduct, family
life, property or worship. Even kings were not
above the rule of law; they were rebuked by
prophets when they flouted it.

The climactic moment of the Old Testament
story is the handing down of the Law to Moses on
Mount Sinai. The cornerstone of the Hebrew
legal system was the Ten Commandments,
engraved on two stone tablets by the finger of
God, and kept in the Holy of Holies of the
Temple as the most sacred object of the Israelite
faith. By the Sinai Covenant, God undertook to
give his protection and favour to his chosen
people provided it lived by the Mosaic Code:

And because you hearken to these ordinances,
and keep and do them, the LORD your God will
keep with you the covenant and the steadfast
love which he swore to your fathers to keep; he
will love you, bless you, and multiply you; he
will also bless the fruit of your body and the

fruit of your ground, your grain and your wine
and your oil, the increase of your cattle and the
young of your flock, in the land which he swore
to your fathers to give you (Deut. 7:12–13).

### The Books of the Law

THE FIRST FIVE BOOKS OF THE OLD TESTAMENT
are grouped together in the Hebrew Bible as the
Law (*Torah*). The strictly legal provisions are
spread over four of these books: Exodus,
Leviticus, Numbers and Deuteronomy.

Since the laws were expressions of God's will,
they were in theory immutable. In practice, they
were constantly being revised and adapted, as the
conditions of life and the outlook of the Israelite
people changed. In the Old Testament period,
this process of evolution went on for some seven
centuries or more from the time of Moses. Many
priests and prophets, sages and scribes shared in
the moulding of the Mosaic Code in its final
biblical form.

It is accepted that the oldest set of laws in the *Exodus*
Old Testament is that in Exodus – the Ten
Commandments, and the Covenant Code that

follow them in Chapters 20 and 23. The Code contains miscellaneous provisions dealing with the protection of human rights, property, social relations, the regulation of worship, and a calendar of feast days. Although the scriptural setting of the Covenant Code is the Sinai revelation, much of it reflects a later period of settled agricultural life in the Land of Israel. The substance of the Code was eventually woven into the Book of Deuteronomy.

*Leviticus*     The Book of Leviticus gets its name in the Christian Bible from the Levites, the tribe that carried out religious duties. The priesthood was by tradition drawn from certain specific Levite families. The book is primarily the major part of a priestly manual that begins in the latter part of Exodus and extends through Leviticus to the first chapters of Numbers. These portions of the three books focus on the cultic aspects of religion – that is, on its organization, rituals and Temple equipment. The topics covered include the construction of the Ark of the Covenant, the Tabernacle, the altar and other furnishings; the ordination and vestments of priests; types of sacrifices; the rules for ritual cleanliness; sacred vows, and the observance of the Sabbath and the Day of Atonement.

At the heart of the Book of Leviticus is a Holiness Code (Chapters 17 to 25). Its scope is much wider than ritual. It is based on the far-reaching concept that the Children of Israel are a holy people and must behave accordingly. Side by side with provisions concerning the holiness of priests and offerings, the Holiness Code also deals with moral and social issues: sexual mores, justice, fair business practice and the protection of the disadvantaged – debtors, slaves, hired labourers, and the disabled.

The Book of Leviticus in its present form was compiled about the middle of the fifth century BC. At that time the bulk of the Jewish people formed an ethnic and religious minority group in the Persian empire, subject to Persian laws and with no state of their own. The priestly editors of Leviticus set out to codify and strengthen formal religious observance as a means of preserving Jewish identity and holding scattered communities together.

*Numbers*     The Book of Numbers tells the story of the Israelites in their desert wandering for nearly forty years, from the time they left Mount Sinai in the second month of the second year until they reached the border of the Promised Land. Scattered through the earlier chapters of the book there are various laws and regulations that form a supplement to Leviticus. They mostly deal with the consecration and duties of the Levites.

Deuteronomy is the last of the five Books of *Deuteronomy* Moses. Its name is a Greek word meaning 'the second law'. The book was probably written late in the seventh century BC, when Israelite fortunes were at a low ebb. The northern kingdom of Israel had been destroyed by the Assyrians. The southern kingdom of Judah was clinging to survival, shrunken and insecure, and with its traditional faith permeated by the pagan environment. The unknown author of Deuteronomy, an erudite and devout preacher or priest, sought to revive the spirit of the original Sinai Covenant, and to adjust the Covenant Code to contemporary thought. Deuteronomy, or an early version of it, was probably the 'book of the law' that came to light in the Temple of Jerusalem in 621 BC, and inspired the sweeping religious reforms of King Josiah.

The book is in the form of three farewell addresses by Moses to the Children of Israel, while they were encamped east of the Jordan before entering the Promised Land. Moses recounts all that the Lord has done for them in the wilderness, warns them not to yield to idolatrous temptations in the Promised Land, and pleads with them to accept love of God and obedience to his laws as the basis of their existence there. In this framework, the Deuteronomist reinterprets the Mosaic Code, blending it with the ethical and humane ideals of the great prophets who had preached before him: Amos, Hosea, Isaiah and Micah. While Deuteronomy stresses the centrality of the Jerusalem Temple, it lays less stress than Leviticus on ritual, and more on the social content of legislation: protection for the underprivileged, equal justice for all, restraints on royal power, and even exemptions from military service on compassionate grounds. The ideals and the style of Deuteronomy were to have a profound influence on the subsequent development of Jewish jurisprudence.

## Facets of the Mosaic Code

THE RITUALS OF THE OLD TESTAMENT, LIKE THAT of all cults in the ancient Near-East, focused on animal sacrifices. They were offered up on altars that always stood under the open sky – whether in the courtyard of the Jerusalem Temple or on the 'high places' of rural shrines. This universal custom, long since obsolete, was derived originally from the belief that offering food and drink to the gods was needed to ensure the fertility of the flocks and fields on which the life of the community depended. This origin is implied in the scriptural injunction to bring to the Temple the first-fruits of the harvest and the firstling males of the flocks and herds; and in the statement that there arose from the altar fires 'a pleasing odour to the Lord'. Later Hebrew theology linked sacrifices with the concept of expiation for sins.

*Rituals*    The first seven chapters of Leviticus provide a detailed code of regulations for sacrifices. The animals used were cattle, goats, sheep and pigeons, all without blemish. Working beasts or wild animals were not acceptable. The sacrifices were made for a variety of different purposes, and were classified as burnt, sin, guilt, fellowship, peace, votive, free-will and ordination offerings. Burnt offerings meant that the whole carcass was consumed in the altar fire. In other cases only parts of the entrails or fatty tissues were burnt, and the meat served as food for the Temple priests and attendants.

As a rule, the animal offerings were accompanied by libation offerings of wine, and grain offerings of flour mixed with olive oil. Token amounts of these were burnt away, and the rest was eaten by the Temple staff.

The blood of the animals was always drained away and sprinkled on the sides of the altar, in accordance with the mystic concept that 'the life of the flesh is in the blood,' and it was, therefore, forbidden to eat blood.

One sacrificial rite with primitive roots was that of the scapegoat, which on the Day of Atonement carried the collective sins of the community into the Judean desert.

The classical Hebrew prophets objected to sacrifices that were just empty rituals, not accompanied by genuine piety and a special conscience.

Animal sacrifices ceased in Jewish religious observance with the destruction of Jerusalem and the Temple by the Romans, in 70 AD.

Incense played an important part in the Temple ritual. It was burnt twice daily on a small altar made of cedarwood and gold. It stood inside the main chamber of the sanctuary, in front of the curtain that screened off the Holy of Holies. Once a year, on the Day of Atonement, the high priest would enter the Holy of Holies carrying a censer of incense.

The Book of Leviticus gives the original formula for making the incense: stacte, onycha, gelbanum and frankincense. It contained equal parts of four ingredients. Stacte were drops of gum from a certain desert bush that grew plentifully in the land of Gilead in Trans-jordan, hence the expression 'balm of gilead'. Onycha was made from the shell of a mollusc found in the Red Sea area. Gelbanum was a gum resin obtained from the Syrian fennel plant. Frankincense was also a gum resin, from a type of terebinth tree that grew in south-western Arabia. In the course of time other spices were added to the incense, since the Land of Israel lay on the caravan route of the lucrative spice trade from Arabia. The exact recipe for the incense became a closely guarded secret handed down in the priestly family of Avtinas and it was prepared only in the home of that family. The recipe was later given in the Talmud and is included in the daily prayers.

The Book of Exodus sets out the formula for making the holy oil, consisting of pure olive oil blended with a number of spices. It was used to consecrate the Temple and its equipment and utensils, and to anoint kings and priests when they took office. The term 'messiah' is a Hebrew word meaning 'the anointed one'. The word Christ is from the Greek for messiah.

The Pentateuch lays stress on the observance    *Festivals* of the three pilgrimage festivals that were the main religious events of the year, with the Jerusalem Temple as their centre. Their origin lay in the agricultural cycle of the year, but each acquired an historical meaning related to the great national saga of the Exodus.

Passover (in Hebrew, *Pesach*) occurred in March-April. It marked the end of the winter rains and the beginning of the spring planting season; at the same time, it commemorated the events that attended the departure of the Israelites from Egypt.

The Feast of Weeks (in Hebrew, *Shavuoth*), in early summer, was the feast of the first-fruits; it also celebrated the giving of the Law at Mount Sinai.

'Noah's Sacrifice', a painting by Joseph Anton Koch, showing the ritual of sacrifice.

An aerial photograph of Mount Sinai (Jebel Musa), in the rugged mountain region of the southern Sinai Peninsula.

Moses writing the Tables of The Law, from a modern
Dutch Bible illustrated by the Dutch artist Kees de Kort (1972).

The Feast of Booths (in Hebrew, *Succoth*) was the autumn harvest festival; the booth made of branches symbolized the nomadic life of the Children of Israel in the wilderness.

On these festivals pilgrims crowded into Jerusalem from all parts of the kingdom, with their families and their offerings. They went to the Temple area in joyful procession, singing psalms of thanksgiving accompanied by musical instruments.

Since the sacred Temple area could not be defiled, the Pentateuch (especially in the Book of Leviticus) gives precise instructions about persons who are deemed ritually unclean, and the rites for their purification. These instructions applied to women during their monthly periods or after childbirth; to persons who had had contact with the dead or with unclean animals; to certain types of chronic skin diseases; to specific bodily discharges; and to mildew in clothes and homes.

*Dietary Laws* The Books of Leviticus and Deuteronomy make a distinction between living creatures that are fit or unfit for food. These rules still form the basis for the kashrut laws observed by orthodox Jews. (The terms 'kashruth' and 'kosher', from a Hebrew root meaning 'fit' or 'proper', came into use for food in the post-biblical period.)

Animals must satisfy two requirements: they must have cloven hooves and chew the cud. These criteria cover such domestic animals as cattle and sheep, but exclude pigs (they do not chew the cud) or camels and rabbits (they do not have cloven hooves). Fish must have both fins and scales; shellfish and eels are therefore among the sea-food excluded. No general rule is given for birds, but twenty-four species of them are listed as unclean, including birds of prey like eagles and hawks, or scavengers like vultures and crows.

The provision concerning insects was relevant to the life of desert nomads. Winged insects can be eaten if they hop on the ground – for instance, locusts.

An animal of a clean species cannot be eaten if it has died a natural death or from injuries – where, for example, it has been lacerated by a wild beast.

All species of fruit and vegetables can be eaten.

Preparing an animal for food takes into account the prohibition in Leviticus against consuming blood, which is held to contain the life-force.

Methods of ritual slaughter are designed to drain the blood from the carcass.

It is twice stated in Exodus, and repeated in Deuteronomy, that 'thou shalt not boil a kid in its mother's milk'. From that scriptural point of departure, an elaborate set of rules was later evolved to separate meat from milk in preparing or eating food. Certain types of food, including fish, eggs, fruit and vegetables are 'parva' – that is, they can be eaten with either meat or milk. Modern commentators tend to explain this separation, as well as the rules of kashrut generally, in terms of health and hygiene factors in the biblical Near-East (but see p. 364 for another possible explanation).

The Deuteronomic directive to judges is: 'You *Administration* shall not take a bribe, for a bribe blinds the eyes of *of Justice* the wise and subverts the cause of the righteous' (Deut. 16:19). Where a local judge found the application of the law too difficult in a particular case, it could be referred to the Temple priesthood.

The Book of Numbers lays down that a conviction for murder requires the evidence of at least two eye-witnesses. Deuteronomy extends the requirement to all charges: 'A single witness shall not prevail against a man for any crime or for any wrong in connection with any offense that he has committed; only on the evidence of two witnesses, or of three witnesses, shall a charge be sustained' (Deut. 19:15). Deuteronomy adds that if one person brings a false or malicious charge against another, the accuser will incur the same penalty as would have been inflicted on the accused if the charge had been proved. Trials were as a rule held in public 'in the city gate' – that is, in the open square at the entrance to the city.

A unique biblical provision was the establishment of six 'cities of refuge' under the control of the Levites. A man who had unintentionally killed someone else could gain asylum in a city of refuge from the vengeance of the dead man's kinsmen, until he could be properly brought to trial. This provision was of special legal interest because it distinguished between murder and manslaughter, and excluded for the latter the ancient tradition of the blood-feud.

Deuteronomy makes plain that even the king is expected to know the law, abide by it and apply it to his subjects '. . . that his heart may not be lifted up above his brethren' (Deut. 17:20).

The Book of Deuteronomy contains re-

*Protection of the Under-privileged*

markably progressive social legislation, clearly influenced by the Hebrew prophets. The concept of the Covenant between God and his chosen people implied that all Israelites were equal in God's eyes, and that the human dignity and welfare of each had to be safeguarded.

Slavery was a universal institution, unquestioned until the nineteenth century AD. It existed in Hebrew society as well, but in a relatively benign fashion. The general attitude was expressed in the maxim, 'You shall remember that you were a slave in the land of Egypt, and the Lord your God redeemed you' (Deut. 15:15).

In Hebrew the word for a slave, *eved*, was a variant of the word for any worker, *oved*. Slaves were in effect unpaid labourers, legally protected against ill-treatment just as hired labourers were. Only a foreigner (a non-Israelite) could be bought and permanently owned as a slave. An Israelite unable to pay his debts to a fellow-Israelite could 'sell' himself as a bondsman to his creditor. However, he would have to be automatically released, and his debt cancelled, at the next 'sabbatical year' – the seventh year when all the fields had to be left fallow. The released slave could choose to remain in the service of his master, in which case the lobe of his ear would be pierced as a visible mark of his status.

It was an offence under the law to treat a slave with cruelty, or to overtax his strength. A master who killed a slave was liable to a murder charge. It was a crime punishable by death for one Israelite to kidnap another in order to use or sell him as a slave. Where an Israelite for any reason became a slave to foreigners, his relatives were obliged to redeem him. A runaway slave who sought refuge had to be assisted, and was not to be handed back to his owner against his will. (It was no doubt presumed that he had run away because he had been badly treated.)

Generally, the slave and his family were part of the household, under the control of the family head. A slave was allowed to possess property of his own, and could inherit his master's estate where there were no blood heirs.

One form of servitude was the right of a father to sell his daughter into domestic service with another family, in the expectation that it would lead to marriage. If no son of that family accepted her as his bride, she was entitled to be released.

The Deuteronomic law was protective about any poor people who got into debt: 'For the poor will never cease out of the land; therefore I command you, You shall open wide your hand to your brother, to the needy and to the poor, in the land' (Deut. 15:11). A loan to a fellow-Israelite was free of interest. A poor man's millstone could not be taken as a pledge, for it was needed for the family bread. If his cloak was pledged, it had to be returned to him at night to keep him warm. Out of regard for a debtor's feelings, a creditor who went to collect a pledge had to wait for it outside and was not entitled to enter the debtor's home. A hired labourer had to be given his wages before sunset each day.

Special provision was made for the support of three classes of person if they were destitute: widows, orphans and foreigners living in Israelite territory (what today would be called resident aliens). Chapter 27 of Deuteronomy lists twelve solemn curses for the Levites to read out to the community. One of the curses is placed on anyone who deprives widows, orphans and foreigners of their rights. When fields, olive groves and vineyards are harvested, what is left in them is reserved for gleaning by needy widows, orphans and foreigners. Every third year, the tithes of the produce can be used for the support of widows, orphans and indigent foreigners as well as Levites serving in areas outside Jerusalem. A widow's garment cannot be taken as a pledge.

When a man dies without leaving a child, his brother or male next-of-kin is obliged to marry the widow. The object of this 'levirate marriage' was to enable the widow to bear a child who would be regarded as continuing the family line of the deceased. If the brother refused to carry out this duty, the widow had to lay her complaint before the court. They would summon the brother, and if he still refused, she was required in the presence of the elders to remove one of his sandals, to spit in front of him, and to declare that that was what happened to a man who refused to give his brother a descendant. His family would then be known as the 'house of him who had his sandal pulled off'. The most interesting case of levirate marriage in the Old Testament is that of Tamar, the daughter-in-law of Judah in the Book of Genesis. Another example is in the Book of Ruth: before Boaz could marry Ruth, a nearer kinsman of her late husband had to waive his right to do so. A widow could legally remarry anyone except a priest.

OVERLEAF 'The Feast of Tabernacles' – this painting by Marc Chagall depicts the traditional tabernacle or booth (in Hebrew, *Succah*) in a small Jewish community in Eastern Europe.

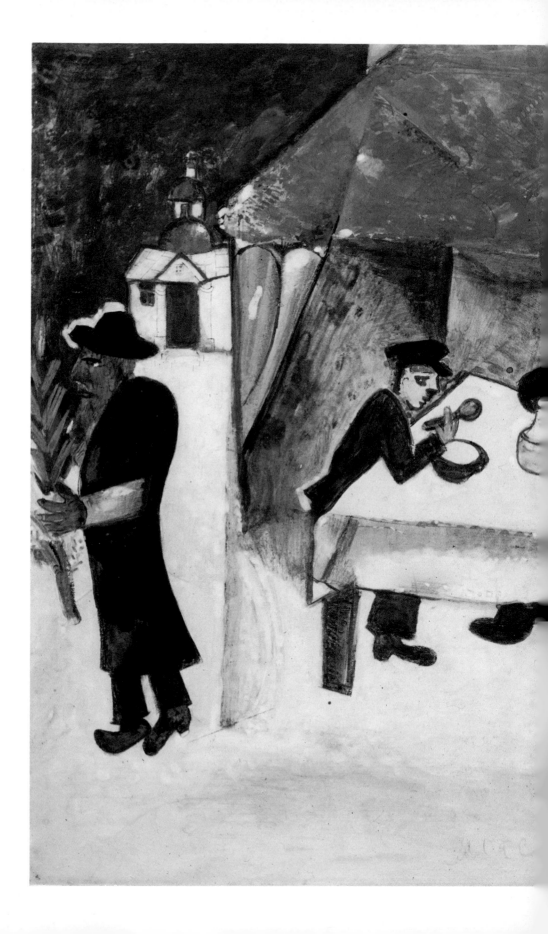

The marriage tie was so hallowed that adultery brought the death penalty on both parties. The rape of a girl betrothed to someone else was also punishable by death. However, if the girl was not betrothed, the man was compelled by law to marry her and to pay the bride-price to her father. In such a case, the husband was not allowed to divorce his wife.

A newly married man was given exemption from compulsory military service: 'he shall be free at home one year, to be happy with his wife whom he has taken' (Deut. 24:5). There were also other grounds for exemption. Going into battle was a holy venture that required the approval of the Lord, and therefore the wholehearted dedication of the fighting troops. Each officer was required to find out which of his men had built a house but not yet dedicated it, had planted a vineyard but not yet harvested the first crop, or had recently become engaged to be married. All these were allowed to return home if they chose. (The same rule applied to those who had lost their nerve and were likely to undermine the morale of their comrades.)

A humane attitude extended to animals, who were also accepted as the creatures of God. The ox treading out the grain on the threshing floor must not be muzzled while he is working. Someone who sees a donkey that has fallen down is ordered to help it to its feet. Animals that have strayed must be returned to their owner, and looked after until that can be done.

## The Torah and the Talmud

THE PROCESS OF DISCUSSING, APPLYING, REVISING and developing the laws of the Old Testament was carried on continuously by the Jewish rabbis and sages in the post-biblical period. At the end of the first century BC the two leading scholars in Jerusalem, Hillel and Shammai, headed rival schools where the Oral Law, commentaries on the Scriptures, were expounded.

After the destruction of Jerusalem in 70 AD marking the end of the Second Temple period and the beginning of Diaspora life, the Law became central to the Jewish faith. Judah the Prince, the patriarch of the Jewish community surviving in Palestine under Roman rule, initiated the systematic codification of rabbinical rulings and opinions. As a result a single compilation, the Mishnah, appeared about 220 AD. It formed the core of the Jerusalem Talmud, which appeared in the fourth century AD, and the even vaster Babylonian Talmud completed in the sixth century AD. In these works Jewish law and tradition had been elaborated into a culture that embraced every detail of daily life. The Talmud has continued to be the subject of intense and uninterrupted study and adjustment up to the present. When an observant Jew seeks a ruling on *halacha*, Jewish law, he is invoking a comprehensive system of jurisprudence that has evolved over more than three thousand years from the time of Moses.

## 2

# THE PSALMS

### Nature and Authorship

THE BOOK OF PSALMS IS AN ANTHOLOGY of ancient Hebrew hymns and sacred lyrics, most of them composed to be sung to music during worship in the Temple. The depth of feeling in the Psalms, and the beauty of their language and imagery, makes them the most superb collection of religious poetry ever produced. They have had a profound spiritual and literary impact on the Jewish and Christian worlds.

*The Name of the Book*

In the Hebrew Bible the work is called *Tehillim* (Songs of Praise), and is the first and longest book in the Writings, the third section of the Old Testament. The name Psalms comes from a Greek word that means a poem sung to the harp. It was probably meant to be a translation of the obscure Hebrew term *mizmor* that appears in the heading to a number of the Psalms and may refer to the accompaniment by the Temple musicians. A Psalm-book is also commonly called a Psalter. That term originates from a Greek word for a stringed instrument. It was first used as the name for this Book in the Septuagint, the Greek translation from the Hebrew Bible which was produced in ancient Alexandria.

The book contains 150 psalms, divided into five books in imitation of the Pentateuch. It is actually a 'collection of collections', assembled from smaller groups of psalms dating from different periods. The whole work evolved over a span of about a thousand years, going back to the eleventh to tenth centuries BC, the period of King David. Some of the earliest of the songs may have been handed down orally among the Israelite tribes before the beginning of the monarchy. The book was compiled, edited and given its present shape during the Second Temple period, between 400 BC and 100 BC.

*The Dating of the Psalms*

Most of the psalms have a few words as a heading. With 101 out of the 150 psalms, the headings indicate to whom the authorship is ascribed, as follows: 73, David; 1, Moses; 2, Solomon; 12, Asaph; 11, The Sons of Korah; 1, Ethan; 1, Heman. Asaph, Ethan and Heman were heads of levitical guilds of Temple singers and musicians; 'The Sons of Korah' was the name of one such guild.

*The Attribution to David*

Although nearly half the psalms are marked in the headings as 'of David', his authorship of them was improbable in many of these cases – for

225

instance, where these are references to the Temple that did not yet exist in his reign. It was natural, however, that popular belief came to regard David as the father of the Psalms, just as Solomon was regarded as the father of the Proverbs. David was reputed to be a skilled musician and a lover of poetry, as well as a devout man in intimate communion with God. The Bible calls him 'the sweet psalmist of Israel' (2 Sam. 23:1). The Book of Chronicles, written some six centuries after David, actually claims him as the founder of Hebrew liturgical music and the organizer of the Temple choir guilds. True, the Chronicler was more concerned with an idealized image of David than with a factual biography; yet this assertion on his behalf does indicate how strong the legend had grown of David the psalmist.

Yet a few Psalms, written in the first person, give an overwhelming impression that they have come from David. For instance, Psalm 18 is a song of thanksgiving that, according to its heading, was addressed to the Lord by David when he was saved from his enemies, especially 'from the hand of Saul':

> In my distress I called upon the Lord;
>     to my God I cried for help.
> From his temple he heard my voice,
>     and my cry to him reached his ears.
>
> He reached from on high, he took me,
>     he drew me out of many waters.
> He delivered me from my strong enemy.
>     and from those who hated me;
>     for they were too mighty for me.
> They came upon me in the day of my
>         calamity;
>     but the Lord was my stay.
> He brought me forth into a broad place;
>     he delivered me, because he delighted
>     in me.
>
> Great triumphs he gives to his King,
>     and shows steadfast love to his anointed,
> to David and his descendants for ever.

Psalm 89, on the other hand, is filled with a sense of betrayal and abandonment because the Lord seems to have broken his promise to David:

> I have found David, my servant;
>     with my holy oil I have anointed him;

> so that my hand shall ever abide with him,
>     my arm also shall strengthen him.
> But now thou hast cast off the rejected
>     thou art full of wrath against thy anointed.
> Thou hast renounced the covenant
>         with thy servant;
>     thou hast defiled his crown in the dust.
> Lord, where is thy steadfast love of old,
>     which by thy faithfulness thou
>     didst swear to David?

## The Themes

THE PSALMS ARE NOT EASY TO CLASSIFY, SINCE they represent a variety of theme and mood. They fall into a few broad types. The largest group is that of the hymns, songs of praise for the greatness and goodness of the Lord. The second largest group, about one-third of the total number, is that of laments bewailing the misfortunes and suffering of the nation or the individual and pleading for divine help. There are also songs of trust, thanksgiving and penitence; royal psalms stressing the role of the king as God's anointed; widsom psalms, meditating on the nature of life; and execration psalms against the nation's enemies.

All mankind is called upon to praise the Lord: *Hymns of Praise*

> Kings of the earth and all peoples,
>     princes and all rulers of the earth!
> Young men and maidens together,
>     old men and children!
> Let them praise the name of the Lord,
>     for his name alone is exalted;
>         his glory is above earth and heaven.
>             (Ps. 148:11–13)

But special praise is due from his chosen people:

> Let Israel be glad in his Maker,
>     let the sons of Zion rejoice in their King!
> Let them praise his name with dancing,
>     making melody to him with tim-
>         brel and lyre!
> For the Lord takes pleasure in his people;
>             (Ps. 149:2–4)

God's majesty has enobled unworthy man:

> When I look at thy heavens, the work
>     of thy fingers,
>     the moon and the stars which thou
>         hast established;

What is man that thou art mindful of him,
   and the son of man that thou dost
      care for him?
Yet thou hast made him little less
      than God,
   and dost crown him with glory and
      honour.

                 (Ps. 8:3–5)

The fertility of the earth is the gift of God:

Thou visitest the earth and waterest it,
   thou greatly enrichest it;
the river of God is full of water;
   thou providest their grain,
   for so thou hast prepared it.
Thou waterest its furrows abundantly,
   settling its ridges,
softening it with showers,
   and blessing its growth.
Thou crownest the year with thy bounty;
   the tracks of thy chariot drip with fatness.
The pastures of the wilderness drip,
   the hills gird themselves with joy,
   the meadows clothe themselves with
      flocks,
   the valleys deck themselves with grain,
   they shout and sing together for joy.

               (Ps. 65:9–13)

God is filled with goodness and compassion:

The Lord is gracious and merciful,
   slow to anger and abounding in
      steadfast love.
The Lord is good to all,
   and his compassion is over all that
      he has made.

               (Ps. 145:8–9)

Some of the hymns of praise are called Enthronement Hymns, as they stress that God is 'a great king over all the earth' (Ps. 47:2):

Say among the nations, 'The Lord reigns!
Yea, the world is established, it
      shall never be moved;
he will judge the peoples with equity.'

               (Ps. 96:10)

Another group of hymns are known as Songs of Zion, for they praise Jerusalem as the Holy City of God:

Great is the Lord and greatly to be praised
   in the city of our God!

His holy mountain, beautiful in elevation,
   is the joy of all the earth,
Mount Zion, in the far north,
   the city of the great King.
Within her citadels God
   has shown himself a sure defence.

               (Ps. 48:1–3)

For the Lord has chosen Zion;
   he has desired it for his habitation:
'This is my resting place for ever;
   here I will dwell, for I have desired it . . .'

               (Ps. 132:13–14).

The Lord is praised as the Creator of the whole natural order. Passages such as the following indicate that the ancient Hebrews were mainly an agricultural people, living close to the sights and sounds of nature:

Thou dost cause the grass to grow for
      the cattle,
   and plants for man to cultivate,
that he may bring forth food from the
      earth,
   and wine to gladden the heart of man,
oil to make his face shine,
   and bread to strengthen man's heart.
The trees of the Lord are watered
      abundantly,
   the cedars of Lebanon which he planted.
In them the birds build their nests;
   the stork has her home in the fir trees.
The high mountains are for the wild goats;
   the rocks are a refuge for the badgers.
Thou hast made the moon to mark
      the seasons;
   the sun knows its time for setting.
Thou makest darkness, and it is night,
   when all the beasts of the forest
      creep forth.
The young lions roar for their prey,
   seeking their food from God.
When the sun rises, they get them away
   and lie down in their dens.
Man goes forth to his work
   and to his labour until the evening.

               (Ps. 104:14–23)

Some of the royal Psalms may have been composed to celebrate a coronation or a royal wedding. They generally relate to David, the greatest of the Hebrew monarchs. They stress that a Hebrew king is the anointed of God, derives his authority and success from God's blessing, and is required to fear the Lord and rule justly.

> Now therefore, O kings, be wise;
>     be warned, O rulers of the earth.
> Serve the Lord with fear,
>     with trembling kiss his feet,
> lest he be angry, and you perish in the way;
>     for his wrath is quickly kindled.
> Blessed are all who take refuge in
>     him.
>
> (Ps. 2:10–11)

> Give the king thy justice, O God,
>     and thy righteousness to the royal son!
> May he judge thy people with
>     righteousness,
>     and thy poor with justice!
>
> (Ps. 72:1–2)

*Psalms of Lament*  About forty of the Psalms deal with personal suffering and anguish.

In some of them it is asserted that the suffering is unmerited, or God is reproached for being tardy in responding to the plea for help.

> Be gracious to me, O Lord, for I am
>     languishing;
> O Lord, heal me, for my bones are
>     troubled.
> My soul also is sorely troubled.
>     But thou, O Lord – how long?
>
> (Ps. 6:2–3)

> How long, O Lord? Wilt thou
>     forget me for ever?
> How long wilt thou hide thy face from me?
> How long must I bear pain in my soul,
>     and have sorrow in my heart all the day?
> How long shall my enemy be exalted
>     over me?
>
> (Ps. 13:1–2)

> I wait for the Lord, my soul waits,
>     and in his word I hope;
> my soul waits for the Lord
>     more than watchmen for the morning,
> more than watchmen for the morning.
>
> (Ps. 130:5–6)

In other cases, the psalms stress guilt and punishment:

> For I know my transgressions,
>     and my sin is ever before me.
>
> (Ps. 51:3)

> Make them bear their guilt, O God;
>     let them fall by their own counsels;
>     because of their many transgressions,
>         cast them out,
>     for they have rebelled against thee.
>
> (Ps. 5:10)

Some of the laments do not concern the individual but the misfortunes that have befallen the Hebrew nation, and turn to the Lord to save it from its enemies:

> O God, the heathen have come
>     into thy inheritance;
>     they have defiled thy holy temple;
>     they have laid Jerusalem in ruins.
> They have given the bodies of thy servants
>     to the birds of the air for food,
>     the flesh of thy saints to the beasts
>         of the earth.
> Help us, O God of our salvation,
>     for the glory of thy name;
>     deliver us, and forgive our sins,
>         for thy name's sake!
>
> (Ps. 79:1–2, 9)

> O God, do not keep silence;
>     do not hold thy peace or be still, O God!
> For lo, thy enemies are in tumult;
>     those who hate thee have raised
>         their heads.
> They say, 'Come, let us wipe them
>     out as a nation;
> let the name of Israel be remembered
>     no more!'
>
> (Ps. 83:1–2, 4)

There are desperate passages in these psalms that blame God for having failed to avert disaster:

> Thou hast made us like sheep for
>     slaughter,
>     and has scattered us among the nations.
> Thou hast sold thy people for a trifle,
>     demanding no high price for them.
> Rouse thyself! Why sleepest thou,
>     O Lord?
> Awake! Do not cast us off for ever!
> Why dost thou hide thy face?
>     Why dost thou forget our affliction
>         and oppression?
>
> (Ps. 44:11–12, 23–24)

Like certain of the oracles in the Books of the Prophets, the Psalms call down fierce curses on

ABOVE LEFT The first page of the Book of Joshua from the first complete printed Hebrew Bible produced in 1488 by the famous Soncino family of Jewish printers.

ABOVE RIGHT The Great Bible (1539). The title page is said to have been designed by Holbein and shows King Henry VIII, Archbishop Cranmer and Thomas Cromwell distributing bibles to the people.

RIGHT A woodcut showing printers at work. A block by Jost Amman which appeared in H. Scropperus's *Book of Trades* (1574).

the nation's enemies, and ask God to destroy them. These Imprecation Psalms are disturbing to those who seek in the Scriptures only a spirit of *Psalms of* love and forgiveness. Yet the Psalms are the *Imprecation* authentic and uninhibited voice of a small nation battling to survive against powerful foes, suffering at times the bitter experience of bloodshed, destruction, occupation and exile.

> O God, break the teeth in their mouths;
>    tear out the fangs of the young
>       lions, O Lord!
> Let them vanish like water that runs away;
>    like grass let them be trodden down
>       and wither.
> Let them be like the snail which dissolves
>       into slime,
>    like the untimely birth that never
>          sees the sun.
>
> (Ps. 58:6–8)

> Remember, O Lord, against the
>       Edomites
>    the day of Jerusalem,
>    how they said, 'Rase it, rase it!
>       Down to its foundations!'
> O daughter of Babylon, you devastator!
> Happy shall he be who requites you
> with what you have done to us!
> Happy shall he be who takes your
>       little ones
> and dashes them against the rock!
>
> (Ps. 137:7–9)

*Psalms of* There are Psalms that are infused with a serene *Trust* confidence in divine goodwill and protection:

> I lift up my eyes to the hills.
>       From whence does my help come?
> My help comes from the Lord,
>    who made heaven and earth.
>
> (Ps. 121:1–2)

The balance between human frailty and human faith has never been more movingly expressed than in Psalm 23, the best known of all the one hundred and fifty Psalms in the Book:

> The Lord is my shepherd, I shall not want;
> he makes me lie down in green pastures.
> He leads me beside still waters;
>    he restores my soul.
> He leads me in paths of righteousness
>    for his name's sake.
> Even though I walk through the
>    valley of the shadow of death,
>       I fear no evil;
>    for thou art with me;
>       thy rod and thy staff,
>          they comfort me.
> Thou preparest a table before me
>    in the presence of my enemies;
>    thou anointest my head with oil,
>       my cup overflows.
> Surely goodness and mercy shall
>    follow me
>    all the days of my life;
> and I shall dwell in the house of the Lord
>    for ever.

The Book of Psalms is not just a chapel for quiet devotion. The emotions that rack the human heart, and the turbulence of the national saga, surge through the work with a sonorous power that cannot be fully rendered in translation from the Hebrew. Praise of the Lord has a fervour and intensity unmatched elsewhere. Calm and consolation coexist with agitation of spirit; hope and trust with doubt, despair and loneliness; joy with grief; love of God with fierce execration of human enemies; self-righteousness with a sense of sin and shame. What the Psalms do mirror in full is the unsparing candour of the Hebrew mind.

# 3
# LAMENTATIONS

THE BOOK OF LAMENTATIONS IS A series of five poetic dirges mourning over the sacking of Jerusalem in 587 BC, and the sufferings of its up-rooted inhabitants. The name in the Hebrew Bible is *Eichah* (How), taken from the opening word of the book. Lamentations is a translation of *kinnot*, the name frequently used in the Talmud.

In form the first four chapters (poems) are acrostics of twenty-two stanzas, corresponding to the number of letters in the Hebrew alphabet, with each stanza starting with the succeeding letter of the alphabet. The fifth and last chapter also has twenty-two stanzas, but without their initial letters in alphabetical order.

From the earliest Christian times the work was ascribed to the authorship of the prophet Jeremiah, and in Christian bibles it is printed immediately after the Book of Jeremiah. Textual analysis makes this attribution improbable. Nevertheless, it has produced the general word 'jeremiad' for a lengthy expression of lamentation, grief or complaint.

The Hebrew Bible does not associate Lamentations with Jeremiah. It is one of the five scrolls (*megillot*) included in the Writings, the last section of the Old Testament. In synagogue services the work is traditionally recited on the ninth day of Av, the fast-day that commemorates both the first destruction of Jerusalem and the Temple in 587 BC, and their second in 70 AD.

The first verses set the melancholy mood that pervades the book:

> How lonely sits the city
> that was full of people! . . .
> She weeps bitterly in the night,
>     tears on her cheeks;
> among all her lovers
>     she has none to comfort her;
> all her friends have dealt
>     treacherously with her,
>     they have become her enemies.
> Judah has gone into exile because of
>     affliction
>     and hard servitude;
> she dwells now among the nations,
>     but finds no resting place;
>                     (Lam. 1:1,2,3)

The anguish is sharpened by a feeling of abandonment by God:

> The Lord has become like an enemy,
>    he has destroyed Israel; . . .
> Why dost thou forget us for ever,
>    why dost thou so long forsake us?
>
> (Lam. 2:5; 5:20)

Despite this note of reproach, Lamentations develops the theme that the calamity and the Exile are the Lord's punishment for the nation's sins. The suffering must be borne without complaint, and redeemed by penitence, before the Lord will relent and restore his people.

> Who has commanded and it came to
>    pass,
>    unless the Lord has ordained it?
> Is it not from the mouth of the Most High
>    that good and evil come?
> Let us test and examine our ways,
>    and return to the Lord!
> Let us lift up our hearts and hands
>    to God in heaven:
> 'We have transgressed and rebelled,
>    and thou hast not forgiven.'
> Restore us to thyself, O Lord, that we
>    may be restored!
> Renew our days as of old!
>
> (Lam. 3:37–38; 40–42; 5:21)

# 4

# THE SONG OF SONGS

## Origin

O that you would kiss me with the
kisses of your mouth!
For your love is better than wine
(S. of S. 1:2)

THE SONG OF SONGS, ALSO CALLED the Song of Solomon, is a startling work to find in the Bible. From its opening lines quoted above, to its concluding words that compare the maiden's beloved to 'a young stag upon the mountains of spices', (8:14) the work is a celebration of human love, with no gesture to religion and no mention of the Lord. It found its way into the final canon of the Old Testament for two reasons: the fiction that it was composed by King Solomon, and the rabbinical willingness to read the poem as an allegory for the relationship between God and his chosen people. Christian theologians were later to take over the allegorical approach and to interpret the work as applying to the relationship between Jesus and the Church. The full title is 'The Song of Songs, which is Solomon's'. In the Hebrew original the heading is ambiguous: *le-Shlomo* could mean either 'by Solomon' or 'about Solomon'. One passage in the book actually suggests that the marriage of Solomon is being celebrated:

Go forth, O daughters of Zion,
and behold King Solomon,

with the crown with which his mother
crowned him
on the day of his wedding,
on the day of the gladness of his heart.
(S. of S. 3:11)

The attribution of the authorship to the illustrious monarch was tempting. Solomon had become legendary not only for his wisdom but also as a lover of many women and as a writer of many songs. However, it is generally accepted today that the book was compiled about the third century BC, some seven hundred years after Solomon, and was woven together from a number of love lyrics, some of them very ancient.

## Contents

THE SONG OF SONGS HAS NO UNIFIED STRUC-ture, nor does it tell a coherent story. In form it is a series of some twenty-five poems or fragments of poems, spoken either by the man or the woman lover, or on occasion by an unidentified chorus. On the assumption that the book was meant to be recited or sung at weddings, the man and the

233

woman who speak the lines would be filling the parts of the bride and bridegroom, engaged in a somewhat disconnected dialogue.

At the beginning, the woman is diffident about her dark beauty:

> I am very dark, but comely,
>   O daughters of Jerusalem,
>   like the tents of Kedar,
>   like the curtains of Solomon.
> Do not gaze at me because I am swarthy,
> because the sun has scorched me.
>               (S. of S. 1:5,6)

Her lover does not find her colouring a drawback. He lists her charms in a rush of rapturous images:

> You are all fair, my love;
>   there is no flaw in you.
>               (S. of S. 4:7)
> How graceful are your feet in sandals,
>   O queenly maiden!
> Your rounded thighs are like jewels,
>   the work of a master hand.
> Your navel is a rounded bowl
>   that never lacks mixed wine.
> Your belly is a heap of wheat,
>   encircled with lilies.
> Your two breasts are like two fawns,
>   twins of a gazelle.
>               (S. of S. 7:1–3)

She is equally lyrical about his appearance:

> My beloved is all radiant and ruddy,
>   distinguished among ten thousand.
> His head is the finest gold;

> his locks are wavy,
>   black as a raven.
> His speech is most sweet,
>   and he is altogether desirable.
> This is my beloved and this is my
>   friend,
>   O daughters of Jerusalem.
>               (S. of S. 5:10–11,16)

The sensuous delight the lovers take in each other is blended with the sights and sounds of the Israel countryside in the freshness of early spring:

> for lo, the winter is past,
>   the rain is over and gone.
> The flowers appear on the earth,
>   the time of singing has come,
> and the voice of the turtledove
>   is heard in our land.
> The fig tree puts forth its figs,
>   and the vines are in blossom;
>   they give forth fragrance.
> Arise, my love, my fair one,
>   and come away.
> Catch us the foxes,
>   the little foxes,
>   that spoil the vineyards,
> for our vineyards are in blossom.
>               (S. of S. 2:11–13,15)

Whatever subtle interpretation may have included the Song of Songs in the Old Testament, later generations could only be grateful for the handing down of a poem so rich in language and simile, so filled with the frank joy of love.

# 5
# PROVERBS

## The Nature of the Book

THE BOOK OF PROVERBS DERIVES from the wisdom literature that was prevalent in the ancient Near-East and was expressed in a love for fables, parables, proverbs, riddles and acrostic poems. In the Old Testament there are three works usually classified as Wisdom Books – Job, Proverbs and Ecclesiastes – although they are very dissimilar. Two more works in this genre, The Wisdom of Solomon and The Wisdom of Jesus the son of Sirach (or Ecclesiasticus), are among the Apocrypha.

*Solomon and the Wisdom Books* Of the Old Testament Wisdom Books, Proverbs and Ecclesiastes were by tradition attributed to King Solomon, who is described in the Bible as the wisest of men: 'so that Solomon's wisdom surpassed the wisdom of all the people of the east, and all the wisdom of Egypt... He also uttered three thousand proverbs; and his songs were a thousand and five' (1 Kings 4:30,32).

*The Scope of the Work* Proverbs is an anthology of brief moral maxims and discourses of the Hebrew wise men in ancient times. It is meant mainly for the instruction of young men starting out in life. The book is not a uniform work from a single source, but was compiled from different collections of sayings dating from different periods.

While fear of the Lord and obedience to his commandments are stressed, Proverbs does not have the emotional fervour of the Psalms, nor the spiritual power and soaring eloquence of the great prophets. The prophets were concerned with the fate of the nation and its special covenant with God; the priests with the formal and ritual aspects of religious observance; and the wise men (in Hebrew, *hahamim*) with practical morality in the daily concerns of the life of the individual. Proverbs therefore deals with family and social relations, business ethics, and personal behaviour. It extols the virtues of piety, hard work, patience, humility, charity to the poor, willingness to accept good advice, truthfulness and avoiding self-indulgence in women and drink. A young man who follows these injunctions may hope for a long and happy life and a successful career.

*The Form of the Proverbs* Most of the book is taken up with the proverbs in the standard form, each a self-contained saying of one sentence. In the Hebrew (a very condensed language) the typical proverb consists of a sentence of six, seven or eight words, divided into two halves balancing each other in content and printed one on each side of the page. This tight form becomes blurred in translation. Here is a familiar proverb that has thirteen words in English translation:

> A soft answer turns away wrath,
> but a harsh word stirs up anger.
>
> (Prov. 15:1)

The Hebrew has eight words, and looks as follows:

מַעֲנֶה רַךְ יָשִׁיב חֵמָה וּדְבַר עֶצֶב יַעֲלֶה אָף

Certain sections of the book depart from the one-sentence standard type of proverb, and contain longer dissertations on specific themes.

*The Structure of the Work*

The general title of the book is 'The proverbs of Solomon, son of David, king of Israel'. That is followed by a brief introductory note inserted by the compiler, stressing that a study of the proverbs will help the reader to lead a life of honour, give understanding to simple people, knowledge to the young and increased learning to the wise. In the body of the book there are four main groups of sayings.

The first section of nine chapters contains a series of didactic discourses in praise of wisdom, or advising young men to follow a righteous path. They are particularly cautioned to keep away from loose women, especially married women who might try to seduce them. This section is of comparatively late date, and may have been composed by the anonymous scholar or teacher who assembled the whole work about the fourth century BC.

The second section is headed 'The proverbs of Solomon', and is the longest in the book. It extends from Chapter 10 to Chapter 22 and contains 375 proverbs.

The third section (Chapters 22 to 24) comprises two groups of precepts called 'Sayings of the Wise'. These sayings were clearly influenced by an Egyptian book of wisdom entitled, 'The Instruction of Amenemope', which predates the time of Solomon.

The fourth section (Chapters 25 to 29) has another collection called 'proverbs of Solomon which the men of Hezekiah king of Judah copied'. There are 128 proverbs in this group, similar in type to those in the second section.

In addition to these groups the last two chapters of the book (30 and 31) contain four passages unrelated to each other in style and theme. They are:

a) 'The words of Agur son of Jakeh of Massa'. This is a fragment of dialogue between a sceptical man who insists with irony that he is incapable of grasping the ways of the Almighty, and a believer who affirms that God's promises are true. The brief exchange echoes the Book of Job.

b) A collection of folk-sayings, based on the mystical numbers three and four.

c) Advice to an unidentified young king named Lemuel, from his mother. She urges him to avoid sexual and alcoholic excess and to protect the poor and needy among his subjects.

d) An acrostic poem in praise of the qualities of a good wife.

## The Themes

IN THE FIRST PART OF THE BOOK THE TEACHER impresses on his pupil that true wealth is not measured in material things, but in the long life, respect and peace of mind which are the fruits of wisdom.

> Happy is the man who finds wisdom,
>     and the man who gets understanding,
> for the gain from it is better than
>     gain from silver
>         and its profit better than gold.
> She is more precious than jewels,
>     and nothing you desire can com-
>     pare with her.
> Long life is in her right hand;
>     in her left hand are riches and honour.
> Her ways are ways of pleasantness,
>     and all her paths are peace.
> She is a tree of life to those who lay
>     hold of her;
>         those who hold her fast are called happy.
>
> (Prov. 3:13–18)

*Wisdom personified*

In the poetical passages that occur in this introductory section, Wisdom speaks in the first person. In one such passage, she is a prophetess exhorting the simple, the scoffers and the fools to give heed to her counsel before it is too late for them to redeem themselves:

> Wisdom cries aloud in the street;
>     in the markets she raises her voice;
> on the top of the walls she cries out;
>     at the entrance of the city gates she speaks:

'How long, O simple ones, will you
   love being simple?
How long will scoffers delight in
   their scoffing
   and fools hate knowledge?
Give heed to my reproof;
behold, I will pour out my thoughts
   to you;
   I will make my words known to you.'
'For the simple are killed by their
   turning away,
   and the complacence of fools
      destroy them;
but he who listens to me will dwell secure
   and will be at ease, without dread of evil.'
                    (Prov. 1:20–23, 32–33)

In another passage, Wisdom makes the more fundamental claim that she was involved in God's original act of creation:

The Lord created me at the beginning
   of his work,
the first of his acts of old. . .
   when he assigned to the sea its limit,
   so that the waters might not trans-
      gress his command,
   when he marked out the foundations
      of the earth,
   then I was beside him, like a master
      workman;
   and I was daily his delight,
      rejoicing before him always,
   rejoicing in his inhabited world
      and delighting in the sons of men.
                    (Prov. 8:22, 29–31)

*The Wise and*   The attitude to religion in the Book of Proverbs
*the Pious*   is on two distinct levels: the secular and the pious. The two main collections of Solomonic proverbs, which are of ancient origin (Chapters 10–22 and 25–29), have relatively little concern with the religious basis for the practical affairs of life. On the other hand, in the first section of the book, of relatively late date, a reverent attitude to God is regarded as inseparable from true enlightenment:

The fear of the Lord is the beginning
   of wisdom,
and the knowledge of the Holy One
   is insight.

                    (Prov. 9:10)

The first section generally exhorts young men to piety. It stresses that the moral order in human affairs comes from the Lord, and that wisdom is an aspect of Divine grace:

Trust in the Lord with all your heart,
   and do not rely on your own insight.
In all your ways acknowledge him,
   and he will make straight your paths.
                    (Prov. 3:5–6)

However the general tone of the Solomonic proverbs is secular and pragmatic. They are acute and sometimes caustic social comments, based on direct observation of human nature. No theology is visible in such statements as:

Many seek the favour of a generous
   man,
   and everyone is a friend to a man
      who gives gifts.
                    (Prov. 19:6)

Like a dog that returns to his vomit
   is a fool that repeats his folly.
                    (Prov. 26:11)

He who meddles in a quarrel not his own
   is like one who takes a passing dog
      by the ears.
                    (Prov. 26:17)

The Book of Proverbs reflects a picture of
family relations that would have been completely   *All in the*
acceptable in the Victorian era, but less so in the   *Family*
permissive society of today. The household is monogamous and patriarchal; the husband is its undisputed master; the wife's place is the home; the children are strictly reared; and old people are treated with respect.

Concerning education, nobody would query the general aim:

Train up a child in the way he should go,
   and when he is old he will not
      depart from it.
                    (Prov. 22:6)

The pedagogic *method* is another matter. Modern educators and psychologists no longer accept the validity of such repeated maxims as:

He who spares the rod hates his son,
   but he who loves him is diligent to
      discipline him.
                    (Prov. 13:24)

The rod and reproof give wisdom,
  but a child left to himself brings
    shame to his mother.
                    (Prov. 29:15)

Children are expected to have a proper deference for their elders:

The eye that mocks a father
  and scorns to obey a mother
will be picked out by the ravens
  of the valley
and eaten by the vultures.
                    (Prov. 30:17)

The aged must not be despised or cast aside:

A hoary head is a crown of glory;
  it is gained in a righteous life.
                    (Prov. 16:31)

The Book of Proverbs assigns a worthy and respected role to the wife:

House and wealth are inherited from
    fathers,
but a prudent wife is from the Lord.
                    (Prov. 19:14)

The last passage in the book is an acrostic poem with the verses in Hebrew starting with the successive letters of the alphabet. It depicts the ideal wife and mother:

A good wife who can find?
  She is far more precious than jewels.
The heart of her husband trusts in her,
  and he will have no lack of gain.
She does him good, and not harm,
  all the days of her life.
                    (Prov. 31:10–12)

The good wife weaves and spins and makes the clothes for the family. She rises before dawn to prepare the meals and organize the work of the maids. She is generous to the poor and needy. Her reward is the love she gains from her family:

Her children rise up and call her blessed;
  her husband also, and he praises her:
'Many women have done excellently,
  but you surpass them all.'
                    (Prov. 31:28–29)

A less happy view of the marital state is conveyed in a proverb that compares a nagging woman to 'A continual dripping on a rainy day' (Prov. 27:15)

or the one that declares:

Like a gold ring in a swine's snout
  is a beautiful woman without discretion.
                    (Prov. 11:22)

It is of interest to note that the ideal Hebrew wife in the alphabetical poem does not remain secluded in the home, as women of upper-class families generally were in oriental lands. She goes out to buy food, and carries out business transactions, such as selling to merchants linen garments she has made, or buying a field.

At the same time, an independent career for a *Loose Women* woman was unthinkable beyond the concerns of the home and family. The women a man might encounter outside the circle of his own kinfolk were likely to be those who would corrupt him and lead him astray. The Book of Proverbs, especially in its introductory chapters, sternly warns young men to beware of such loose women. Nothing they can offer can compare with a happy marriage:

Let your fountain be blessed,
  and rejoice in the wife of your youth,
  a lovely hind, a graceful doe.
Let her affection fill you at all times
  with delight,
    be infatuated always with her love.
Why should you be infatuated,
  my son, with a loose woman
  and embrace the bosom of an adventuress?
                    (Prov. 5:18–20)

In Chapter 9, folly is personified as a loud-mouthed, ignorant and shameless woman, who sits before the door of her house or in a public place and tempts passers-by to come and visit her, saying to them:

Stolen water is sweet,
  and bread eaten in secret is pleasant.
                    (Prov. 9:17)

Chapter 7 gives a vivid description of the *Warning* faithless wife who lures foolish young men to her *against* house: *adultery*

I have decked my couch with coverings,
  coloured spreads of Egyptian linen;
I have perfumed my bed with myrrh,
  aloes, and cinnamon.
Come, let us take our fill of love till
  morning;

let us delight ourselves with love.
For my husband is not at home;
he has gone on a long journey;
(Prov. 7:16–19)

The teacher uttering this warning feels obliged to explain his knowledge of such behaviour. He states that he looked through his window and himself saw such a married woman picking up a young man in the street at night.

The Book of Proverbs clearly reflects a male-dominated society. The members of the female sex, whether virtuous or wanton, are depicted by men to other men. It was not thought necessary to set out what was required of the ideal husband, to paint an unsavoury picture of the adulterous husband, or to warn young women against amorous males.

Proverbs is ambivalent about wealth. On the one hand the book holds that there are attributes worth more than being rich: wisdom, righteousness, peace of mind, integrity, and a good reputation.

Better is a little with righteousness
than great revenues with injustice.
(Prov. 16:8)

A good name is to be chosen
rather than great riches,
and favour is better than silver or gold.
(Prov. 22:1)

Better is a poor man who walks in his
integrity
than a rich man who is perverse in his ways.
(Prov. 28:6)

Do not toil to acquire wealth;
be wise enough to desist.
When your eyes light upon it, it is gone;
for suddenly it takes to itself wings,
flying like an eagle toward heaven.
(Prov. 23:4–5)

Anyway, all men are equal in God's eyes:

The rich and the poor meet together;
The Lord is the maker of them all.
(Prov. 22:2)

*The Rich and the Poor* At the same time, the book is unabashed in admitting that it is better to be rich than poor:

The rich rules over the poor,
and the borrower is the slave of the lender.
(Prov. 22:7)

A rich man's wealth is his strong city,
and like a high wall protecting him.
(Prov. 18:11)

Wealth brings many new friends,
but a poor man is deserted by his friend.
(Prov. 19:4)

However, charity is required by the Lord, who will protect those in need:

He who is kind to the poor lends to
the Lord,
and he will repay him for his deed.
(Prov. 19:17)

Do not rob the poor, because he is poor,
or crush the afflicted at the gate;
for the Lord will plead their cause
and despoil of life those who spoil them.
(Prov. 22:22–23)

*Guard your Tongue* Proverbs is much concerned with the evil results of loose talk, lies and gossip. The wise man will strive for ways of speech which are prudent, truthful, pleasant and relevant:

Even a fool who keeps silent is considered wise;
when he closes his lips, he is
deemed intelligent.
(Prov. 17:28)

He who keeps his mouth and his tongue
keeps himself out of trouble.
(Prov. 21:23)

A perverse man spreads strife,
and a whisperer separates close friends.
(Prov. 16:28)

Put away from you crooked speech,
and put devious talk far from you.
(Prov. 4:24)

A lying tongue hates its victims,
and a flattering mouth works ruin.
(Prov. 26:28)

Pleasant words are like a honeycomb,
sweetness to the soul and health to
the body.
(Prov. 16:24)

To make an apt answer is a joy to a man,
and a word in season, how good it is!
(Prov. 15:23)

Proverbs wastes no sympathy on the slothful, and does not believe they will get anywhere in life:

*The Diligent and the Lazy*

> How long will you lie there, O sluggard?
> When will you arise from your sleep?
> A little sleep, a little slumber,
>     a little folding of the hands to rest,
> and poverty will come upon you like
>     a vagabond,
> and want like an armed man.
>
> (Prov. 6:9–11)

> In all toil there is profit,
>     but mere talk tends only to want.
>
> (Prov. 14:23)

The working man who has mastered his trade has his own dignity and self-respect:

> Do you see a man skilled in his work?
>     he will stand before kings;
>     he will not stand before obscure men.
>
> (Prov. 22:29)

The model for organized labour can be found in the nearest ant-heap:

> Go to the ant, O sluggard;
>     consider her ways, and be wise.
> Without having any chief, office or ruler,
> she prepares her food in summer,
>     and gathers her sustenance in harvest.
>
> (Prov. 6:6–8)

*The Danger of Drink*

Proverbs has a very commonsense approach to alcohol. There is no call to total abstinence. Wine in moderation can be pleasant, and in special cases a drink may be helpful:

> Give strong drink to him who is perishing,
>     and wine to those in bitter distress;
> let them drink and forget their poverty,
>     and remember their misery no more.
>
> (Prov. 31:6–7)

But excessive drinking must be shunned:

> Wine is a mocker, strong drink a brawler;
> and whoever is led astray by it is not wise.
>
> (Prov. 20:1)

In the advice the queen-mother gives to her son, she explains that drink may cause him to rule unjustly:

> It is not for kings, O Lemuel,
>     it is not for kings to drink wine,

> or for rulers to desire strong drink;
> lest they drink and forget what has
>     been decreed,
>     and pervert the rights of all the afflicted.
>
> (Prov. 31:4–5)

The section on 'Sayings of the Wise' gives a classic description of the effects of drinking and the inevitable hangover:

> Who has woe? Who has sorrow?
>     Who has strife? Who has complaining?
> Who has wounds without cause?
>     Who has redness of eyes?
> Those who tarry long over wine,
>     Those who go to try mixed wine.
> Do not look at wine when it is red,
>     when it sparkles in the cup
>     and goes down smoothly.
> At the last it bites like a serpent,
>     and stings like an adder.
> Your eyes will see strange things,
>     and your mind utter perverse things.
> You will be like one who lies down in
>     the midst of the sea,
>     like one who lies on the top of a mast.
> 'They struck me,' you will say,
>     'but I was not hurt;
>     they beat me, but I did not feel it.
> When shall I awake?
>     I will seek another drink.'
>
> (Prov. 23:29–35)

*The Power of Rulers*

To exercise their power properly, rulers should be wise:

> When the righteous are in authority,
>     the people rejoice;
> but when the wicked rule, the
>     people groan.
>
> (Prov. 29:2)

But in reality kings are likely to be capricious and arbitrary, and prudent subjects will be careful not to offend them:

> A king's wrath is like the growling of
>     a lion,
> but his favour is like dew upon the grass.
>
> (Prov. 19:12)

For the ordinary man, danger may lurk in any authority – divine or human:

> My son, fear the Lord and the king,
>     and do not disobey either of them;

for disaster from them will rise suddenly,
and who knows the ruin that will
come from them both?
(Prov. 24:21–22)

A king must remind himself that he is no greater
than the nation over whom he rules:

In a multitude of people is the glory
of a king,
but without people a prince is ruined.
(Prov. 14:28)

*Friends and Enemies*  One of life's greatest boons is a friend or relative on whom one can rely in need:

A friend loves at all times,
and a brother is born for adversity.
(Prov. 17:17)

But access to a friendly neighbour should not be abused:

Let your foot be seldom in your
neighbour's house,
lest he become weary of you and hate you.
(Prov. 25:17)

Good intentions are not an excuse for inconsiderate actions:

He who blesses his neighbour with a
loud voice,
rising early in the morning,
will be counted as cursing.
(Prov. 27:14)

A wise man is magnanimous to his enemies, instead of trying to repay them in kind:

Do not rejoice when your enemy falls,
and let not your heart be glad
when he stumbles;
(Prov. 24:17)

If your enemy is hungry, give him
bread to eat;
and if he is thirsty, give him water
to drink;
for you will heap coals of fire on his head,
and the Lord will reward you.
(Prov. 25:21–22)

*Beware of Fools*  Fools tend to be self-opinionated, credulous and aggressive:

A fool takes no pleasure in understanding,
but only in expressing his opinion.
(Prov. 18:2)

The simple believes everything,
but the prudent looks where he is
going.
(Prov. 14:15)

It is an honour for a man to keep aloof
from strife;
but every fool will be quarrelling.
(Prov. 20:3)

Let a man meet a she-bear robbed of
her cubs,
rather than a fool in his folly
(Prov. 17:12)

A silly question from a fool puts a wise man in a quandary: Should he give an equally silly answer or should he not?

Answer not a fool according to his folly,
lest you be like him yourself.
Answer a fool according to his folly,
lest he be wise in his own eyes.
(Prov. 26:4–5)

*Attributes of the Wise*  The attributes already mentioned do not exhaust the manual of conduct that leads to a life of wisdom. There are a number of additional virtues that Proverbs commends to the wise men:

A cheerful heart is a good medicine,
but a downcast spirit dries up the bones.
(Prov. 17:22)

Better is a dinner of herbs where love is
than a fatted ox and hatred with it.
(Prov. 15:17)

A tranquil mind gives life to the flesh,
but passion makes the bones rot.
(Prov. 14:30)

Better is a dry morsel with quiet
than a house full of feasting with strife.
(Prov. 17:1)

Pride goes before destruction,
and a haughty spirit before a fall.
(Prov. 16:18)

Let another praise you, and not your
own mouth;
a stranger, and not your own lips.
(Prov. 27:2)

Bread gained by deceit is sweet to a man,
but afterwards his mouth will be full of gravel.
(Prov. 20:17)

Diverse weights are an abomination
   to the Lord,
and false scales are not good.
(Prov. 20:23)

A rebuke goes deeper into a man of
   understanding
than a hundred blows into a fool.
(Prov. 17:10)

A hot-tempered man stirs up strife,
   but he who is slow to anger quiets
   contention.
(Prov. 15:18)

If you have found honey, eat only
   enough for you,
   lest you be sated with it and vomit it.
(Prov. 25:16)

A man without self-control
   is like a city broken into and left
   without walls.
(Prov. 25:28)

*Folk proverbs: Things that Come in Fours*

Chapter 30 contains a special form of numerical folk-proverb. Each example lists four objects that have a common factor. The first group concerns insatiable things; the second, things that have wondrous ways; the third, situations that are hard to tolerate; the fourth, tiny creatures from which man can learn; and the fifth,

examples of arrogance. Examples of these groups are as follows:

Three things are too wonderful for me;
   four I do not understand:
the way of an eagle in the sky,
   the way of a serpent on a rock,
the way of a ship on the high seas,
   and the way of a man with a maiden.
(Prov. 30:18–19)

Four things on earth are small,
   but they are exceedingly wise:
the ants are a people not strong,
   yet they provide their food in the
     summer;
the badgers are a people not mighty,
   yet they make their homes in the rocks;
the locusts have no king,
   yet all of them march in rank;
the lizard you can take in your hands,
   yet it is in kings' palaces.
(Prov. 30:24–28)

Three things are stately in their tread;
   four are stately in their stride:
the lion, which is mightiest among beasts
   and does not turn back before any;
the strutting cock, the he-goat,
   and a king striding before his people.
(Prov. 30:29–31)

# 6

# JOB

SOME TIME IN THE SIXTH OR FIFTH century BC an unknown genius took a familiar folk-tale and used it as a vehicle for a profound and powerful masterpiece. The Book of Job is unique in the Bible both for its verse-drama form and for its theme – a debate on human suffering and divine justice. Job stands as a lonely peak in Hebrew Wisdom writings and has no close parallel in human literature, ancient or modern.

*The Composition of the Book*

The brief folk-tale is set in an early patriarchal society. It appears with a prologue and an epilogue framing the main body of the work, which is in a different and much loftier poetic style. The character of Job also changes dramatically. The Job of the folk-tale is a simple man of unshakable faith and patience. The Job of the poem is complex, impatient with the conventional morality of his friends, and challenging God to justify his actions. The proverbial expression 'the patience of Job' is anything but appropriate to the work as a whole.

The main work is divided into a number of parts. First comes a monologue by Job, cursing his fate. There follow three sets of dialogues between him and his three friends Eliphaz, Bildad and Zophar. A separate poem in praise of wisdom is here inserted in the text. Job's final summation leads to the Lord's answer. But between the summation and the answer there appear three speeches by another friend, Elihu, probably written at a later date by a different and less gifted author.

## *The Prologue*

THERE WAS A MAN NAMED JOB WHO LIVED 'IN the land of Uz' (possibly Edom, south of the Dead Sea). He was upright, God-fearing and prosperous, and the leading figure in the region. Job had seven sons and three daughters, and many servants. He owned seven thousand sheep, three thousand camels, a thousand head of cattle and five hundred donkeys. Each of the sons would give a feast in turn, to which all the others were invited. Each time, Job would rise early in the morning and offer sacrifices for all his children, in case one of them had inadvertently offended the Lord.

On the day that all the heavenly beings

assembled before the Lord, God asked Satan where he had been. He replied that he had been roaming round the earth. God enquired whether he had noticed Job, that good and faithful man. Satan remarked with sarcasm that it was easy for Job to worship the Lord as long as he and his family were protected from all harm and he was blessed with great wealth. But if Job lost what he had he would curse the Lord to his face. Confident in Job's rectitude, the Lord gave Satan permission to put Job to the test, provided his person was not harmed.

The next day a succession of disasters struck Job. His donkeys, camels and cattle were carried off by marauders and his sheep were killed in a hailstorm. His eldest son's house collapsed in a storm when all Job's children were gathered in it. They all died. Job flung himself into mourning, but his faith remained intact. He said: 'Naked I came from my mother's womb, and naked shall I return; the Lord gave, and the Lord has taken away; blessed be the name of the Lord' (Job 1:21).

At the next meeting of the heavenly council, the Lord pointed out to Satan that calamity had not changed Job. Satan maintained that Job's faith would not withstand physical affliction. Again, permission was given for a test, provided Job's life was spared. Job's body broke out in dreadful sores from head to foot. He sat all day next to the rubbish heap and scraped at his skin with broken pieces of pottery. His wife said to him bitterly, 'Do you still hold fast your integrity? Curse God, and die' (Job 2:9). Job rebuked her as a foolish woman; if one accepted good things from God, why not bad things as well?

Word of Job's misfortunes reached three of his friends: Eliphaz of Teman, Bildad of Shua and Zophar of Naamar. When they hurried to comfort him, they found it difficult to recognize him. They wept and tore their clothes in grief and sat with him on the ground for seven days, to keep him company in his suffering. At this point the prologue breaks off and the main work begins.

## The Debates between Job and his Friends

### JOB'S FIRST STATEMENT OPENS WITH DESPAIR:

Let the day perish wherein I was born,
and the night which said,
'A man-child is conceived.'
(Job 3:3)

His life has become intolerable, and he longs for the peace of the grave:

There the wicked cease from troubling,
and there the weary are at rest.
(Job 3:17)

Why should anyone want to continue an existence of misery and bitterness of soul?

Presumably the senior among the three friends, Eliphaz, is the first to respond to Job's outburst. He starts on a courteous note. Job has helped others in trouble, but is too stunned to face up to his own. Eliphaz hints that maybe Job is not as blameless as he might think. God does not punish the righteous, only the wicked. How can puny man, a creature of clay and dust, be wholly pure in the eyes of the Lord? When a man finds himself in difficulties, he must have brought it on himself:

For affliction does not come from the dust,
nor does trouble sprout from the ground;
but man is born to trouble
as the sparks fly upward.
(Job 5:6–7)

Let Job have confidence and hope. Let him present his case to God, who is merciful. Suffering must be accepted as God's chastening of a man for his own good. Where God wounds, he heals again. In Job's case, everything will be restored to him and he will still enjoy long life, peace, security and abundance.

Why, Job asks, should his wild words come as a surprise after what God has done to him? Is he made of stone or bronze?

My flesh is clothed with worms and dirt;
my skin hardens, then breaks out afresh.
My days are swifter than a weaver's shuttle,
and come to their end without hope.
(Job 7:5–6)

All he wants from God is to kill him off. The consolation his friends are offering him is worthless, like a stream dried up in summer when its water is most needed. If they can show him in what way he has erred, he is willing to be silent. He requires their proof, not their reproof.

Job bitterly accuses God of being a jailer who must watch and test his prisoner all the time. Supposing he has sinned, what harm has that done God, and why should it matter to God? His life is like a cloud that disappears; he will be gone, forgotten, and even God will not be able to find him.

> I loathe my life; I would not live for ever.
> Let me alone, for my days are a breath.
>
> (Job 7:16)

Stung by Job's attack, the second of his friends uses harsher language. Since God is always just, Job's children must have been sinful or they would not have been killed. God does not abandon the faithful, nor does he help the wicked. Quoting ancient proverbs, Bildad describes the wicked as reeds that wither when the water dries up, weeds that get pulled up or a spider's web that is easily brushed aside. If Job thinks himself innocent, let him appeal to God and all will be well again.

Out of the depths of Job's anguish there is now wrenched a terrifying indictment of the Lord himself. What is the use, he cries out to his friends, of telling him to argue his case with God? What chance does he have of winning the argument? God is all-wise and all-powerful. He can move mountains and make the sun stand still; and he can crush Job whenever he wishes. Who is there to be the impartial judge between them? If he took God to court, who would make God come? Can he use force against God? Even if he is innocent, with God as his accuser he can do nothing but beg for mercy. Let God not condemn him but tell him what the charge is against him. The same God that shaped him out of dust, and gave him life and love, is now hunting him down.

> Let me alone, that I may find a
> little comfort
> before I go whence I shall not return.
>
> (Job 10:20–21)

By this time Job's would-be comforters are appalled and angry at his blasphemy, and have no sympathy left for him. The third of his friends, Zophar, upbraids him:

> Should your babble silence men,
> and when you mock, shall no one
> shame you?
>
> (Job 11:3)

Job, asserts Zophar, is incapable of grasping the limitless power and wisdom of God, who alone knows which men are worthless. For the first time Zophar directly accuses Job, and suggests that his punishment is maybe even less than he deserves.

Let him repent and stretch out his hands to God and 'you will forget your misery' (11:16).

Zophar's words provoke Job to sarcasm. No doubt, he retorts, Zophar is the voice of the people, and wisdom will die with him. However, Job's dispute is not with him but with God and God does not need Zophar to defend him. Job is ready to risk his life rather than keep silent, because he knows he is in the right. He accepts that God has complete power over all living things, and that men are weak and helpless:

> Man that is born of woman is
> of few days, and full of trouble.
>
> (Job 14:1)

Why then should God bother to pursue him for his sins and imperfections? God has ordained in advance how long each person will live. That cannot be changed. When he is dead he will never rise again. Therefore let God look away from him, and let him enjoy his day on earth if he can.

As the discussion continues, the three friends tell Job that his anger against God will only hurt himself. Wicked men may be successful for a while, but what they gain is insecure. Sooner or later, their punishment catches up with them. Job must have abused his wealth and position, and wronged the weak and needy. Let him cleanse himself of sin and pray to the Lord, to gain release from his sufferings:

> Agree with God, and be at peace;
> thereby good will come to you.
>
> (Job 22:21)

Job feels that his companions are 'miserable comforters' who have failed him, and that he is left isolated:

> All my intimate friends abhor me,
> and those whom I loved have
> turned against me.
>
> (Job 19:19)

Why, he asks, should he not be impatient when everybody who sees him is shocked? It is not the wicked who are punished – they prosper, live to a ripe old age and die in peace. His friends are trying to comfort him with lies and 'empty nothings'.

Chapter 28 of the Book of Job is a beautiful *A Poem on* poem on wisdom, probably by some other author, *Wisdom* that breaks into the flow of the argument. It describes how men mine in remote places for gold, silver, iron, copper and sapphires. The miners dig tunnels through rocks and mountains, working in lonely darkness while they cling to ropes. But where can wisdom be sought?

> Man does not know the way to it,
>     and it is not found in the land of
>     the living.
>
> (Job 28:13)

It cannot be valued in gold or precious stones. Only the Lord knows the source of wisdom. God has said to men that to be wise they must worship the Lord, and to understand, they must turn away from evil.

*Job's Summation* In a last and deeply moving plea, Job contrasts his former happy state with his pitiable present plight. If only he could return to the time 'when the friendship of God was upon my tent'. Then he was surrounded by his children, his affairs prospered, and he helped all who were in distress:

> I was eyes to the blind,
>     and feet to the lame.
> I was a father to the poor,
>     and I searched out the cause of
>     him whom I did not know.
>
> (Job 29:15–16)

At the time he was held in honour among his peers, who listened to his counsel with deference.

But all that is gone now. He is mocked by younger men whose fathers he would not have employed as shepherds. The rabble laugh at him, and outcasts spit in his face. He is racked by ceaseless pain:

> My skin turns black and falls from me,
>     and my bones burn with heat.
>
> (Job 30:30)

Yet his spirit has remained unbroken, and he insists on his innocence. God is persecuting him but does not tell him why:

> I cry to thee and thou dost not answer me;
>     I stand, and thou dost not heed me.
>
> (Job 30:20)

Job emphatically denies that there is any reason for him to feel guilty or ashamed. If only his adversary would write down the charges against him, he would be glad to refute them:

> I would give him an account of all my steps;
>     like a prince I would approach him.
>
> (Job 31:37)

*The Speech of Elihu* The six chapters of the book that follow Job's summation are taken up by a lengthy and moralistic speech by a fourth friend, Elihu, 'the son of Barachel the Buzite, of the family of Ram,' (Job 32:2). At the outset he states that he is a younger man who has kept silent while his three elders argued with Job. Now that they have failed to bring him to reason, Elihu feels compelled to express his own opinion.

Elihu's intervention was clearly added by a later author. This is apparent from its awkward position between Job's final challenge and God's answer, from the difference in style, and from the fact that only the three other friends are mentioned in the prologue and the epilogue. Like the others, Elihu rebukes Job for presuming to doubt God's justice. He offers a number of examples to prove God's concern with human beings and all living creatures. In order to spare men God communicates warnings to them through visions, dreams and illnesses. It is God that gives breath to men, and could make them perish at any time if he withdrew his breath from them. God endows men with the capacity to tell right from wrong. God sends down the rain to water the earth and provide food.

Elihu's main ideological contribution to the debate is the thesis that suffering is an expression of God's grace, for its purpose is to chasten and discipline men.

*God's Discourse* Speaking out of a whirlwind God asks:

> Who is this that darkens counsel by
>     words without knowledge?
>
> (Job 38:2)

In the form of rhetorical questions to Job the Lord discourses on the sweep and splendour of Creation:

> Where were you when I laid the
>     foundations of the earth?
> when the morning stars sang together,
>     and all the sons of God shouted for
>     joy?
>
> (Job 38:4,7)

Who has shut in the proud ocean, brings the dawn, guides the stars, alternates light and darkness, and discharges rain upon the empty desert? Can Job feed the young lion and the raven, or turn the wild ass loose to roam, or tame the wild ox? Who has given its power to the war-horse, pawing and snorting before the battle?

Is it by your wisdom that the hawk soars,
and spreads its wings toward the south?
Is it at your command that the eagle
    mounts up
and makes his nest on high?

(Job 39:26–27)

As for Job's complaints,

Shall a faultfinder contend
    with the Almighty?...
    Will you condemn me that you
    may be justified?

(Job 40:2,8)

A second discourse by God gives vivid portraits of two powerful creatures. One is the Behemoth, the hippotamus, whose belly is plated with muscles and whose bones and limbs are like bronze and iron. The other is the Leviathan, the legendary sea-monster of whom all are afraid. These also are under God's control for 'Whatever is under the whole heaven is mine' (Job 41:11).

Overwhelmed, Job at long last repents of his doubts and confesses his limitations:

Therefore I have uttered what I did
    not understand,
    things too wonderful for me,
    which I did not know.

(Job 42:3)

*The Meaning of Suffering* Down the ages, thoughtful minds have been perplexed by the 'why' of human tragedy and pain, and have shrunk from the conclusion that they are without meaning, the product of blind chance. It is more comforting to believe, like Job's friends, that the good are rewarded and the wicked punished; where the facts seem otherwise, that must be because only God can know the whole truth.

Various religions have propounded various answers to the problem: a balancing of accounts will not be made in this life but in the heaven and hell of the hereafter; suffering is sent to test and redeem us; trouble is inflicted on mortals to satisfy the egoes of offended deities; merit and demerit will be weighed in the endless cycle of reincarnation.

But in Job's case, no answer at all is offered to his insistent question. Instead, he is given a spiritual experience that transcends the question – a direct communion with God, and a glimpse of the majestic cosmos that the Lord has created and directs. After that revelation, Job contritely renounces his right to query God's conduct.

*The Epilogue* In the epilogue, the Book of Job abruptly returns to the simple prose style of the folk-tale with which it started. It provides a conventional happy ending. The three friends are rebuked by the Lord, but Job intercedes with prayer on their behalf. He is restored to his former position and attains double the wealth he had lost. All his friends and kinsmen come to greet him with respect, bearing gifts. Once more he produces seven sons and three daughters – the latter exceptionally beautiful girls who bear the romantic names of Jemimah (dove), Keziah (cassia or cinnamon) and Keren-happuch (a small box for eye make-up). In their father's estate, the daughters get equal shares with their brothers. Job lives for another one hundred and forty years, long enough to see four generations of his descendants.

# 7

# ECCLESIASTES

*The Inclusion
of the Work*

KOHELETH, THE HEBREW NAME FOR this biblical book, means a person who speaks before a *Kahal* or assembly. The word was translated into Greek as Ecclesiastes, and into English as the Preacher. But Koheleth was no preacher, in the normal sense of one who exhorts to religious faith. An anonymous Jewish intellectual in the Judea of the third century BC, he had a brilliant but cynical mind that questioned the accepted tenets of the Jewish religion. Under the influence of rational Greek philosophers like Epicurus, Koheleth evolved an outlook on life difficult to reconcile with that pervading the rest of the Old Testament. Where the Hebrew creed is marked by optimistic belief, Koheleth is filled with pessimistic disbelief. His is a doctrine of futility.

The strangest aspect of this strange treatise is that it was accepted into the Old Testament at all. When the rabbinical council sat at Javneh in the first century AD to finalize the canon of the Hebrew Bible, reservations must have been felt about a writing so far removed from orthodoxy. Its inclusion may be attributed to several factors.

The first of these was the identification of the Preacher with King Solomon, who personified traditional Hebrew wisdom. Solomon is not actually mentioned by name. The full title of the Book is 'The words of the Preacher, the son of David, king in Jerusalem'; and later in the first chapter, Koheleth states that 'I the Preacher, have been king over Israel in Jerusalem.' (Ec. 1:12). To a modern scholar, both the language and the ideas in the book establish beyond doubt that it was written in the Hellenistic period, about six centuries after Solomon. The implied references to the royal sage were a literary device but they served as an entry to the Scriptures.

Koheleth was also made more acceptable by a brief epilogue appended by a later editor, in an effort to give the book a positive slant. The epilogue awards the author a testimonial as a wise and honest teacher. The disturbing nature of the work is explained away by the observation that the sayings of wise men are like the goads used to drive sheep, and that they come from God, the one Shepherd of us all. The last words of the epilogue end the work on a suitably pious note:

The end of the matter; all has been heard. Fear

God, and keep his commandments; for this is the whole duty of man. For God will bring every deed into judgment, with every secret thing, whether good or evil. (Ec. 12:13–14)

Another factor that made the acceptance of Koheleth theologically possible for the rabbis was that the target of his scepticism was not God but man. Koheleth is not an atheist. He does not question the existence and authority of God, nor that the world functions by a divinely ordained design. What Koheleth regards as a delusion is the belief that human beings can grasp God's design, much less change it. He insists that man's life is both fleeting and unpredictable, therefore it is futile to try and control one's destiny.

The inclusion in the Hebrew Bible of so bleak and negative a philosophy demonstrates that Judaism never rested on absolute dogma. From early times, the Hebrew genius invoked a critical and questing spirit. Koheleth became one of the three Wisdom Books in the Old Testament. The other two are Job, also full of unanswered questions about man and God; and Proverbs, which sidesteps philosophic doubt altogether in order to dispense practical advice for daily life.

*The Pattern of Life* The underlying thesis of Koheleth, and its sparkling literary style, are both evident in the famous opening passage:

> Vanity of vanities, says the Preacher,
>   vanity of vanities! All is vanity.
> What does man gain by all the toil
>   at which he toils under the sun?
> A generation goes, and a generation comes,
>   but the earth remains for ever.
> The sun rises and the sun goes down,
>   and hastens to the place where it rises.
> The wind blows to the south,
>   and goes round to the north;
> round and round goes the wind,
>   and on its circuits the wind returns.
> All the streams run to the sea,
>   but the sea is not full;
> to the place where the streams flow,
>   there they flow again.
> All things are full of weariness;
>   a man cannot utter it;
> the eye is not satisfied with seeing,
>   nor the ear filled with hearing.
> What has been is what will be,
>   and what has been done is what
>     will be done;

> and there is nothing new under the sun.
> Is there a thing of which it is said,
>   'See, this is new'?
> It has been already,
>   in the ages before us.
>
> (Ec. 1:2–10)

The concept that life and nature are like a roundabout ever revolving on itself at the same place was inherent in the beliefs of ancient Babylon, Egypt and Greece. But it was a concept alien to the more hopeful Hebrew mind, that saw God propelling history forward to a future messianic world.

As an integral part of Koheleth's fatalistic outlook, he held that the whole pattern of man's life was predetermined. Everything happened at the time appointed for it, and there was nothing one could do to change the course of events:

> a time to be born, and a time to die;
> a time to plant, and a time to pluck
>   up what is planted;
> a time to kill, and a time to heal;
> a time to break down, and a time to
>   build up;
> a time to weep, and a time to laugh;
> a time to mourn, and a time to dance;
> a time to cast away stones, and a time
>   to gather stones together;
> a time to embrace, and a time to re-
>   frain from embracing;
> a time to seek, and a time to lose;
> a time to keep, and a time to cast away;
> a time to rend, and a time to sew;
> a time to keep silence, and a time to speak;
> a time to love, and a time to hate;
> a time for war, and a time for peace.
> What gain has the worker from his toil?
>
> (Ec. 3:2–9)

*The Search for Goals* The Preacher relates how he sought different ends in life – wisdom and knowledge, pleasure, acquisition of wealth, the fruits of toil, social justice – but always arrived back at futility.

This is what he has to say about wisdom and knowledge:

And I applied my mind to know wisdom and to know madness and folly. I perceived that this also is but a striving after wind.

For in much wisdom is much vexation, and he who increases knowledge increases sorrow. (Ec. 1:17–18)

Then I said to myself, 'What befalls the fool will befall me also; why then have I been so very wise?' And I said to myself that this also is vanity.

For of the wise man as of the fool there is no enduring remembrance, seeing that in the days to come all will have been long forgotten. How the wise man dies just like the fool! (Ec. 2:15–16)

And about pleasure:

I said to myself, 'Come now, I will make a test of pleasure; enjoy yourself.' But behold, this also was vanity. I said of laughter, 'It is mad,' and of pleasure, 'What use is it?' (Ec. 2:1,2)

The Preacher imagines himself to have acquired all King Solomon's fabulous wealth.

I made great works; I built houses and planted vineyards for myself; I made myself gardens and parks, and planted in them all kinds of fruit trees. I made myself pools from which to water the forest of growing trees.

I bought male and female slaves, and had slaves who were born in my house; I had also great possessions of herds and flocks, more than any who had been before me in Jerusalem. I also gathered for myself silver and gold and the treasure of kings and provinces; I got singers, both men and women, and many concubines, man's delight.

Then I considered all that my hands had done and the toil I had spent in doing it, and behold, all was vanity and a striving after wind, and there was nothing to be gained under the sun (Ec. 2:4–8,11).

He has this to say about the fruits of hard work:

I hated all my toil in which I had toiled under the sun, seeing that I must leave it to the man who will come after me; and who knows whether he will be a wise man or a fool? Yet he will be master of all for which I toiled and used my wisdom under the sun. This also is vanity. So I turned about and gave my heart up to despair over all the toil of my labours under the sun, because sometimes a man who has toiled with wisdom and knowledge and skill must leave all to be enjoyed by a man who did not toil for it. This also is vanity and a great evil. What has a man from all the toil and strain with which he toils beneath the sun? For all his days

are full of pain, and his work is a vexation; even in the night his mind does not rest. This also is vanity (Ec. 2:18–23).

He has no hope for social justice:

Moreover I saw under the sun that in the place of justice, even there was wickedness, and in the place of righteousness, even there was wickedness (Ec. 3:16).

Again I saw all the oppressions that are practised under the sun. And behold, the tears of the oppressed, and they had no one to comfort them! On the side of their oppressors there was power, and there was no one to comfort them (Ec. 4:1).

With all his pessimism, Koheleth wryly urges that life be accepted as it is. What happens, happens. In spite of the uncertain outcome, men must go on living and working. *Making the Best of Things*

Cast your bread upon the waters, for you will find it after many days . . . In the morning sow your seed, and at evening withhold not your hand; for you do not know which will prosper, this or that, or whether both alike will be good (Ec. 11:1,6).

Moreover, there are compensations in work and in the enjoyment of material things:

So I saw that there is nothing better than that a man should enjoy his work, for that is his lot; who can bring him to see what will be after him? (Ec. 3:22)

Whatever your hand finds to do, do it with your might; for there is no work or thought or knowledge or wisdom in Sheol, to which you are going (Ec. 9:10).

Bread is made for laughter, and wine gladdens life, and money answers everything. (Ec. 10:19)

In the last resort, it is better to be alive than dead:

But he who is joined with all the living has hope, for a living dog is better than a dead lion. For the living know that they will die, but the dead know nothing, and they have no more reward; but the memory of them is lost. Their love and their hate and their envy have already perished, and they have no more for ever any share in all that is done under the sun. (Ec. 9:4–6)

8

# THE HEBREW PROPHETS

## *Who the Prophets were*

THOUSANDS OF YEARS AGO THERE appeared in the small Hebrew nation a succession of remarkable spiritual leaders: the Prophets. Their message had such moral force and was clothed in such inspired language that it has remained unsurpassed in the annals of religious literature. Through the three monotheistic faiths of Judaism, Christianity and Islam, their teachings have profoundly influenced half the world.

The call to prophesy came to persons of different temperaments and occupations. Among them were Moses, brought up in the sophisticated palace of an Egyptian pharaoh; Samuel, the young novice in the sanctuary at Shiloh; Elijah, the fierce desert hermit; Amos tending his sheep; Elisha ploughing with his father's oxen; court chaplains like Nathan and Gad; Isaiah, the cultivated statesman and adviser of kings; Hulda, the Jerusalem housewife; Jeremiah and Ezekiel with a priestly background. All of them had one thing in common: they received and transmitted revelations of the divine will.

The Hebrew prophetic movement started in the thirteenth century BC with the towering figure of Moses, and lasted for nearly a thousand years until the end of the Old Testament period. It was based on the belief that God communicated with his people through individuals selected by him for this purpose. Prophecy was, therefore, a much wider concept than the prediction of future events. The Hebrew word for a prophet, *navi*, denotes a spokesman. This meaning is brought out clearly in a passage in Exodus. When Moses was told to go and speak to Pharaoh, he demurred, pleading that the talking would be hard for him. The Lord said to him 'See, I make you as God to Pharaoh; and Aaron your brother shall be your prophet. You shall speak all that I command you; and Aaron your brother shall tell Pharaoh to let the people of Israel go out of his land' (Ex. 7:1–2). Here it is Aaron who is called the prophet (*navi*), for he is delegated to be the spokesman for Moses, as Moses is for God.

In the Septuagint, the earliest Greek translation of the Old Testament, the Hebrew word *navi* was rendered as *prophétés*, which means a person who speaks on behalf of another. The English word 'prophet' is derived from this Greek term.

*The Prophetic Movement*

251

*The Former Prophets*

The Hebrew Bible is divided into three sections: the Law (Pentateuch), the Prophets and the Writings. In the section called the Prophets, there are two groups of Books, usually distinguished as the Former and Latter Prophets. The Former Prophets are the Books of Joshua, Judges, 1 and 2 Samuel, and 1 and 2 Kings. These are historical narratives, covering the period from Joshua's Conquest to the destruction of Jerusalem in 587 BC, a period of over six centuries. It is puzzling that they should be included in the prophetic works. But the Old Testament writers did not see the annals of their people as secular history. They believed that the national saga was written by God, and reflected his will. The prophetic strain runs through the course of events recorded in the historical books. It produced exponents in every generation of that period, from notable personalities like Samuel and Elijah to the humble and anonymous members of the bands of ascetics who were called 'Sons of the Prophets'.

*'Sons of the Prophets'*

The first appearance of such a prophetic group in the Bible is in the First Book of Samuel. The young Saul was on his way home after a strange encounter with the prophet Samuel, who had privately anointed him as the first Hebrew king. At Gibeah Saul met a band of prophets, and was swept up into their ecstatic dancing and singing to the sound of music.

Such groups or guilds of holy men were a common phenomenon throughout the Near-East. In the Old Testament, they occur only in the books of the Former Prophets. Samuel apparently had a band of this kind permanently attached to him in his home town of Ramah. It is mentioned in connection with Saul's pursuit of David, who had taken refuge with Samuel.

A graphic description of pagan group frenzy occurs in Elijah's confrontation on Mount Carmel with the false prophets of Baal. For hours they circled round their altar in a kind of limping ritual dance, ranting and raving, and gashing themselves with knives until the blood flowed.

The Elisha story provides interesting glimpses of life in a commune of ascetic 'sons of the prophets' in the desert near Jericho. He lived with them for a while after the ascent of Elijah.

The Books known as The Latter Prophets comprise the oracles and teachings of the great classical prophets who lived from the eighth to the fourth centuries BC. Their messages were written down by themselves or by their disciples and scribes, hence they are also known as the Literary Prophets.

*The Latter Prophets*

Three of them, Isaiah, Jeremiah and Ezekiel, are called 'major' prophets. Theirs are the longest of the prophetic books. Biblical scholars have shown that the latter part of the Book of Isaiah reflects the words of an unknown prophet of the Babylonian Exile, more than a century after Isaiah. For want of a better name, he is referred to simply as Deutero-Isaiah or the Second Isaiah, and is certainly one of the loftiest figures of the prophetic movement.

Another twelve 'minor' prophets are grouped together in the Hebrew Bible as The Book of the Twelve. Christian bibles print them as separate books, though in the same order.

The Book of Daniel is placed in the Hebrew Bible not in the Prophets but in the Writings, the last section of the Old Testament to be received into the canon; in the Christian Bible, Daniel appears immediately after the three major prophets.

Counting the Second Isaiah and Daniel, there are thus seventeen works of Literary Prophets in the Old Testament.

The utterances of these prophets must be seen in their historical context. They are therefore treated here in chronological order, which differs somewhat from the arrangement in the Bible. The dating of some of the shorter Books is uncertain, but the following order would be generally accepted as approximate:

*The Kingdom of Israel* (Eighth century BC): Amos; Hosea.

*The Kingdom of Judah* (Eighth – Sixth century BC): Isaiah, Micah, Zephaniah, Nahum, Habakkuk, Jeremiah.

*The Exilic Period* (Sixth century BC): Obadiah, Ezekiel, Second Isaiah.

*The Post-Exilic Period* (Sixth – Fourth century BC): Haggai, Zechariah, Malachi, Joel, Jonah. (Second century BC): Daniel (Second half of the Book).

## The Classical Prophets

*Amos*

AMOS WAS THE PIONEER FIGURE IN THE CLASsical trend of Hebrew prophecy. He emerged in the eighth century BC, during the parallel reigns of two outstanding Hebrew monarchs: Uzziah of

Judah and Jeroboam II of Israel. The Hebrew nation was enjoying a period of peace, material wellbeing and regional prestige it had not known since the golden age of David and Solomon. The aim of Amos' missionary zeal was to shatter the prevailing mood of complacency, and to revive the true values inherent in the Mosaic covenant with God.

Amos was a shepherd and also tended sycamore trees (a kind of fig) in the village of Tekoah in the Hebron hills, about ten miles south of Jerusalem. God called him to prophesy not in his own kingdom, Judah, but in the northern kingdom, Israel. He first appeared in the sanctuary town of Bethel, and preached against the selfishness, luxurious life-style and lack of social conscience he perceived among the privileged classes. He uttered grim warnings of the fate that awaited the nation if it did not mend its ways.

About thirty years later the northern kingdom would be crushed by the imperial might of Assyria, but in the time of Amos such a possibility was remote from men's minds. Amaziah, the head priest of the Bethel sanctuary, was incensed by Amos' campaign and laid a charge of sedition against him with the palace authorities in the capital, Samaria: 'For thus Amos has said, "Jeroboam shall die by the sword, and Israel must go into exile away from his land."' (Amos 7:11).

Officialdom apparently had other things to worry about than the utterances of an obscure agitator from the south. No notice was taken of the complaint. When the priest pressed Amos to go back to Judah, the prophet repeated his warnings in even fiercer terms, adding a curse on Amaziah and his family.

The Book of Amos is relatively short, nine chapters in all. In the first two chapters he assails the surrounding nations for their violence and militarism. Here Amos takes a leap forward in the evolving theology of the Old Testament. The Lord is not just the Israelite God but the deity of other peoples as well, though the Hebrew nation is in a special covenant relationship with him and must, therefore, make sterner moral demands on itself.

The succeeding chapters focus on the religious and social corruption the prophet sees in the kingdom of Israel. God's pending judgment of his people is prophesied in five visions, each built round a tangible metaphor: a swarm of locusts, a consuming fire, a builder's plumbline, a basket of fruit, and a devastated sanctuary.

In spite of Amos' humble village background, his Book is marked by a keen grasp of political and social issues and great literary skill.

The prophet Hosea, the son of Beeri, appeared *Hosea* in the northern kingdom soon after Amos, with a message bearing similar themes. The kingdom was entering the last quarter-century of its existence, a period marked by political unrest and moral erosion. Like Amos, Hosea identified himself with the poor and oppressed. He also vigorously attacked the pagan influence that was prevalent in Israel.

Nothing is known of Hosea's origin and background, though the Book shows a countryman's familiarity with nature and farming scenes. The one aspect of his personal life that is painfully revealed is his disastrous marriage to Gomer the daughter of Diblaim. She had been a prostitute, and continued her loose ways after marriage. The three children she bore were given disturbing symbolic names: a boy called Jezreel (the place where the ruling Jehu dynasty made its bloody start); a girl called No-pity; and a second boy called Not-my-people. Hosea discarded Gomer, but remained emotionally tied to her. He later rescued her from her degrading life and took her back into his household. Hosea asserts that the marriage was carried out at the Lord's command, and he draws a close parallel between it and God's relations with the sinful people of Israel. God would drive them into exile, but continue to love them and eventually redeem them. It is a matter of disputed interpretation whether Hosea's account of his marriage was factual or an imaginary parable to convey his message.

The rest of the fourteen-chapter Book of Hosea develops the prophet's indictment against the depravity and decay he saw in the kingdom. He warns his countrymen of the doom that awaits them from God unless they repent and reform themselves in time: 'For they sow the wind, and they shall reap the whirlwind' (Hos. 8:7). Hosea proclaims, however, that God is not only a stern father but a loving and merciful one, and that not everything will be lost in the impending calamity.

After the fall of the northern kingdom in 722 BC, the southern kingdom of Judah lasted for another century and a half. The unique prophetic strain that Amos and Hosea had started in the north was carried forward in Judah by Isaiah, the greatest of the classical Hebrew prophets.

*Isaiah*    Isaiah states that God's call to prophesy came to him at the age of twenty-five, the year that King Uzziah died – that is, about 742 BC. For the next fifty years he occupied a position of great eminence in Jerusalem, and served as a royal consultant to three successive kings, Jotham, Ahaz and Hezekiah. In his time Judah was struggling to survive the Assyrian might that had overwhelmed its sister kingdom. The part played in these turbulent events by Isaiah the statesman is told in the Book of Kings. That portion of the prose narrative in Kings was also inserted by a later compiler into the Book of Isaiah, where it forms chapters 36 to 39.

The authentic voice of the great prophet rings through the first thirty-five of the sixty-six chapters in the Book of Isaiah. They contain the most sublime religious writing in the Old Testament. These chapters include Isaiah's personal reflections, oracles against Judah's enemies, castigation of the religious, ethical and social short-comings of his people, and apocalyptic visions of future divine judgment and redemption.

*Micah*    Where Isaiah was a sophisticated urbanite in the capital, his younger contemporary Micah was a son of the common people from the village of Moresheth in the Judean foothills. In the unique sixth-century AD mosaic floor-map of the Holy Land discovered at Madeba in southern Jordan, the place is expressly marked as 'Moresheth, from which came Micah, the prophet'. The prophet's rural background is echoed in his frequent allusions to ploughed fields, vineyards, flocks of sheep, the howling of jackals at night and the idyllic picture of a future when:

> . . . they shall sit every man under his
>     vine and under his fig tree,
>   and none shall make them afraid
>
> (Micah 4:4)

Some of a countryman's dislike and distrust of urban ways comes through in Micah's fierce attacks on the two capital cities of Jerusalem and Samaria. He sees them as hotbeds of corruption and deceit, where elaborate Temple rituals and sacrifices are a substitute for the true faith of the heart. Micah foretells the destruction of the northern capital that would take place in his time:

> Therefore I will make Samaria a
>     heap in the open country,
>   a place for planting vineyards;
> and I will pour down her stones into
>     the valley,
>   and uncover her foundations.
>
> (Micah 1:6)

Jerusalem too, he predicts, will become 'a heap of ruins' for its wickedness – but that would happen only much later.

The seven chapters in the Book of Micah include substantial portions that were added much later in the exilic period, and do not emulate the prophet's forceful and picturesque style.

*Zephaniah*    A little more than a century after Micah, in the era of Jeremiah, three more minor prophets appeared in Judah – Zephaniah, Nahum and Habakkuk. From the contents of the brief Book of Zephaniah, it can be deduced that the prophet was a young Jerusalem aristocrat of royal blood. The superscription claims that he was a great-grandson of King Hezekiah, and that he lived in the reign of King Josiah. Zephaniah's prophecies probably occur between 620 BC and Josiah's sweeping religious reforms in 612 BC.

Zephaniah is concerned less with social protest than with the religious abuses in the upper class to which he belonged. He rails against the infiltration of Assyrian star-worship and local Canaanite cults, and warns that at the time of judgment:

> 'I will utterly sweep away everything
>     from the face of the earth,' says the Lord.
>
> (Zeph. 1:2)

Zephaniah's uncompromising moral fervour leads him to denounce the whole Jerusalem establishment: the court circles decked out in foppish foreign attire, the greedy merchants, the corrupt judges, and the false prophets and priests. On the day of the wrath of the Lord,

> their blood shall be poured out like
>     dust,
>   and their flesh like dung.
>
> (Zeph. 1:17)

Only the humble and godfearing remnant will be spared in Judah.

At the same time, Zephaniah lashes out at the traditional foreign enemies of the nation, whom

RIGHT    The Vision of Isaiah when receiving his call to prophesy. Illustration from a German Isaiah manuscript *c*. AD 1000.

God will humiliate and destroy. Moab and Ammon, for instance, will be left,

> a land possessed by nettles and salt pits,
> and a waste for ever.
>
> (Zeph. 2:9)

*Nahum*    The personal background of the prophet Nahum is unknown. The superscription to the Book states that he came from Elkosh, but that place has not been identified. The main feature of the work is a powerful and graphic poem describing the impending siege, capture and destruction of Nineveh, the Assyrian capital on the upper Euphrates river. At the time when Nahum wrote (approximately 614 BC), the Assyrian empire was in its death-throes, plunging into collapse under the blows of two resurgent neighbours, the Medes and the Babylonians. Nineveh fell to their armies in 612 BC – the event Nahum had anticipated with such confidence. The Assyrian era was ended for all time.

The first of the three chapters of the Book is a prologue to the main theme. The Lord is 'avenging and wrathful' and proclaims to the Assyrians that 'I will make your grave, for you are vile' (Nah. 1:14).

The second chapter launches straight into the preparations for the defence of Nineveh: 'Man the ramparts; watch the road; gird your loins; collect all your strength' (Nah. 2:1).

The Assyrian forces are drawn up in their full force and splendour:

> The shield of his mighty men is red,
> his soldiers are clothed in scarlet.
> The chariots flash like flame
> when mustered in array;
> the chargers prance.
>
> (Nah. 2:3)

But the defences crumble, and panic grips the city as desolation and ruin sweep through it. The assault troops pour into it, putting the inhabitants to the sword. The survivors are carried off into captivity, with the leaders in chains.

The fierce exultation that will sweep throughout the Near-East at the crushing of Assyria is voiced in the concluding lines of the Book:

> All who hear news of you
> clap their hands over you.
> For upon whom has not come
> your unceasing evil?
>
> (Nah. 3:19)

Among the Dead Sea Scrolls is a fragmentary commentary on the Book of Nahum which has helped to clarify certain passages in it.

While the identity of the minor prophet    *Habakkuk* Habakkuk is obscure, the historical context of his book is fairly clear.

In 605 BC the Babylonian ruler Nebuchadnezzar defeated an Egyptian army at the battle of Carchemish on the Upper Euphrates river. The Babylonians had become the new masters of the Near-East in place of the defunct Assyrian empire. Eight years later, in 598 BC, they invaded Judah and occupied Jerusalem.

Habakkuk's ministry fell between these two events, at a time when Judah was already threatened by the emergent power of Babylon. The prophet was evidently a thoughtful and sensitive man, deeply troubled by God's apparent acquiescence in evil and oppression. In the form of a dialogue with God, he raises perplexing questions about the violence and injustice he sees:

> O Lord, how long shall I cry for help,
> and thou wilt not hear?
> For the wicked surround the righteous,
> so justice goes forth perverted.
>
> (Hab. 1:2,4)

The Lord replies that the Babylonians, 'that bitter and hasty nation', are the chosen instrument to do his work. The Lord describes their irresistible advance, '... swifter than leopards, more fierce than the evening wolves' (Hab. 1:8). The conquerors make sport of kings, overrun fortresses and scoop up captives like sand.

The prophet cannot accept that the Lord would impose an unjust fate on his people. Are the Babylonians to go on mercilessly slaying nations for ever? The Lord does not deal directly with Habakkuk's questions, but urges him to believe that ultimately justice will be done:

> Write the vision;
> make it plain upon tablets,
> so he may run who reads it.
> For still the vision awaits its time;
> it hastens to the end – it will not lie.
> If it seem slow, wait for it;
> it will surely come, it will not delay.
> Behold, he whose soul is not upright
> in him shall fail,
> but the righteous shall live by his faith.
>
> (Hab. 2:2–4)

The dialogue with the Lord is followed by five curses directed at the Babylonians, each starting with 'Woe to him who . . .' They predict that the idolatrous nation that has raped and plundered other peoples will meet the same fate.

The Book ends with a prayer or psalm, reaffirming the prophet's faith despite every adversity:

> God, the Lord, is my strength;
>    he makes my feet like hinds' feet,
>    he makes me tread upon my high places.
>
>                             (Hab. 3:19)

*Jeremiah*   About a century after Isaiah came the other giant of classical Hebrew prophecy, Jeremiah. He was born in the village of Anathoth, two miles north-east of Jerusalem. Jeremiah's father Hilkiah was a priest in the village, and the boy was no doubt brought up in a simple and devout home. At the age of eighteen the word of the Lord came to him, revealing his destiny:

> Before I formed you in the womb
>    I knew you,
> and before you were born I conse-
>    crated you;
> I appointed you a prophet to the nations.
>
>                             (Jer. 1:5)

From that moment of revelation, Jeremiah bore the painful burden of his prophetic vocation. Living in the capital, he was deeply involved in the turbulent and tragic events that marked the forty years from the death of King Josiah (609 BC) to the end of the kingdom of Judah.

In the reign of Josiah's son Jehoiakim (609–598 BC) the prophet was in constant trouble with the authorities for his outspoken diatribes against religious and moral corruption. When the king decided to defy Babylonia, relying on Egyptian support, Jeremiah protested against such a policy:

> You shall be put to shame by Egypt
>    as you were put to shame by Assyria.
> From it too you will come away
>    with your hands upon your head,
> for the Lord has rejected those in
>    whom you trust,
>    and you will not prosper by them.
>
>                        (Jer. 2:36–37)

His views were ignored with disastrous results.

In 587 BC a Babylonian expedition invaded Judah, Jehoiakim died and was succeeded by his eighteen-year-old son Jehoiachin. Within three months Jerusalem had surrendered and the young king was taken off into captivity, together with the leading citizens. The king's uncle, Zedekiah, was installed as a puppet ruler. Some years later he too conspired with neighbouring vassals to throw off the Babylonian yoke. Jeremiah campaigned vehemently against this rash action and in favour of submission. He was regarded as a defeatist and imprisoned.

Some time after the sack of Jerusalem in 587 BC, the aged prophet was taken by a group of refugees to Egypt, where he died in exile.

The Book of Jeremiah has fifty-two chapters. The first half contains sermons against the shortcomings of the prophet's own people, with a group of harsh 'oracles against the nations' – chiefly Babylon, but also other hostile neighbouring peoples:

> The clamour will resound to the ends
>    of the earth,
> for the Lord has an indictment
>    against the nations;
> he is entering into judgment with all
>    flesh,
> and the wicked he will put to the
>    sword,
>             says the Lord.
>
>                        (Jer. 25:31)

The second part of the work gives more personal glimpses of the prophet's inner conflicts, with episodes from his struggles with the authorities. They were presumably recorded by his faithful scribe and disciple Baruch.

The Book of Obadiah is the shortest in the Old *Obadiah* Testament, consisting of one chapter with twenty-one verses. Nothing is known of the prophet's identity or date. The main theme of the book is the role played by the Edomites after the destruction of Jerusalem. They were a desert people whose kingdom lay round the southern end of the Dead Sea, extending from southern Jordan to the Negev. By biblical tradition, their legendary ancestor was Esau, Jacob's twin brother. After the end of the kingdom of Judah in 587 BC the Edomites occupied the depopulated Hebron hills south of Jerusalem. Centuries later, when they were known as Idumeans, they were absorbed into the Judean population.

OVERLEAF A messenger bringing Job tidings of his misfortunes. A painting by William Blake, the mystical English artist and poet.

Obadiah fiercely denounces the Edomites for collaborating with the Babylonian conquerors:

> For the violence done to your
>         brother Jacob,
>     shame shall cover you,
>     and you shall be cut off for ever.
>                                   (Obad. 10)

The prophet accuses them of gloating over Judah's disaster, looting its property, cutting off the fugitives and delivering the survivors to the enemy:

> you should not have rejoiced over the
>         people of Judah
>     in the day of their ruin;
> you should not have boasted
>     in the day of distress.
> You should not have entered the gate
>     of my people
>     in the day of his calamity;
>                                 (Obad. 12–13)

On the Lord's coming day of judgment Edom will suffer what it has done to others. On that day the Hebrew nation will be restored to independence and will regain all its former territories, including dominion over Edom.

*Ezekiel*    Ezekiel ranks with Isaiah and Jeremiah as one of the three major figures of the classical prophetic movement. He served as a priest at the Temple in Jerusalem, and was carried away into exile when the city was first occupied by the Babylonians in 598 BC. The call to prophecy came to him five years later in the refugee community of Tel-Abib, on the large irrigation canal of Chebar north of Babylon.

The Book of Ezekiel has forty-eight chapters covering four main visions. The first one relates to the period before the destruction of Jerusalem. Ezekiel transmutes the impending doom into a series of vivid symbolic actions. For example, he draws a map of Jerusalem on a clay tablet, places it on the floor, and acts out before it the siege and famine that will be suffered by the city.

After the wiping out of the kingdom of Judah, Ezekiel preached to his own people a message of hope for a future Return. A series of hard-hitting oracles are directed against neighbouring nations that have rejoiced in the Hebrew downfall, or taken advantage of it: Ammon, Moab and Edom; the Philistines; the two great Phoenician port-cities of Sidon and Tyre; and Egypt. (He is

perforce silent about Babylonia, the power that had crushed Judah and now held Ezekiel and his fellow-exiles in captivity.)

The long invective against Tyre graphically describes its seemingly impregnable position on a rocky offshore island, and the seafarers and merchants who are the source of its wealth and power. But Ezekiel predicts that the Babylonians 'shall destroy the walls of Tyre, and break down her towers; and I [the Lord] will scrape her soil from her, and make her a bare rock' (Ezek. 26:4).

In the last part of the Book, Ezekiel details plans for the future messianic kingdom and the rebuilt Temple. In a vision he is given a guided tour over the Temple by a celestial architect carrying a measuring rod. A notable feature of the building is the elaborate gateway. It corresponds in design to the Solomonic gateways revealed by the archaeological excavations at Hazor, Megiddo and Gezer, presumed to have been modelled on that of Solomon's Temple with which Ezekiel would have been familiar as a young priest. Ezekiel's architectural blueprint is supplemented by a manual for the duties of Temple priests and Levites.

The second-last chapter of the Book contains another burst of fantasy. A sacred river starts below the threshold of the Temple and flows eastward down the arid declivity of the Judean desert into the Dead Sea. Along its course fruit trees spring up in the desolate landscape, while the waters of the Dead Sea turn fresh and teem with fish. In this way Ezekiel dramatized for his congregation of exiles the prospect that their lost homeland would again come to life.

Ezekiel is the most complex and baffling of the Hebrew prophets. His bizarre, surrealist visions are set out in a wealth of precise, almost pedantic detail, and sometimes in a matter-of-fact style. He was a religious mystic and at the same time an ordained priest immersed in the details of Temple rites.

Ezekiel's disturbing visions had a profound influence on later apocalyptic works such as the Book of Daniel, and the Revelation of John in the New Testament. They were to be echoed in the paintings of mystical European artists like Hieronymus Bosch in fifteenth-century Flanders and William Blake in nineteenth-century England.

The noble and gentle utterances of the unknown exilic prophet Second Isaiah may be

LEFT Ezekiel and the Boiling Pot representing Jerusalem. Wood engraving by Sir Edward Burne-Jones.

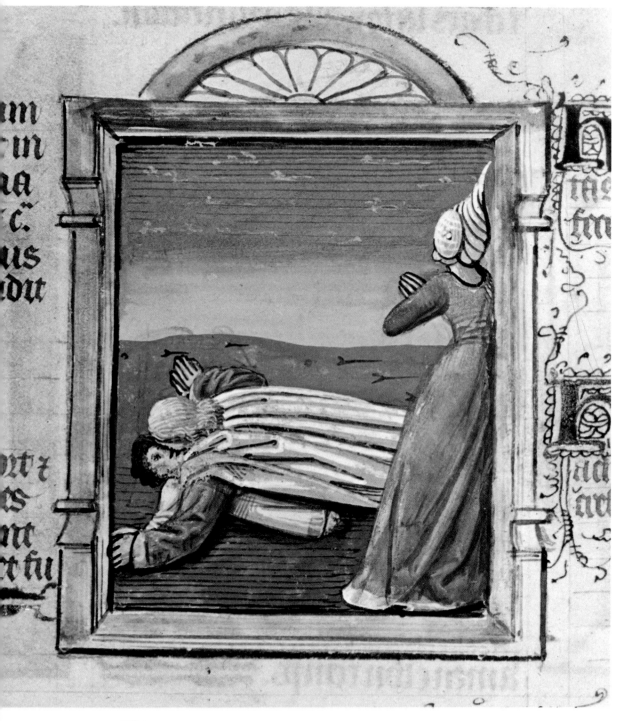

ABOVE Elijah restoring life to the widow's son. From a fifteenth-century French manuscript.

RIGHT Jesus, the son of Sirach, author of second-century Apocryphal work Ecclesiasticus, addresses a female figure of Wisdom. From a tenth-century Byzantine manuscript.

ϹΟΛΟΜΩΝ

dated about half-a-century after the destruction of Jerusalem. Cyrus, king of Persia, captured *Second* Babylon in 539 BC and became the new master of *Isaiah* the Near-East. Second Isaiah hails him as God's appointed liberator of the exiled Jewish people: 'He is my shepherd, and he shall fulfil all my purpose' (Isa. 44:28); 'he shall build my city and set my exiles free' (Isa. 44:13). (In this passage Cyrus is referred to as the Lord's 'anointed', the only case in the Old Testament where a non-Jew is so described.)

The last eleven chapters of the Book of Isaiah (56–66) appear to have been written by anonymous followers of Second Isaiah during the first generation of the Return – maybe between 530 BC and 510 BC. In these chapters (sometimes called Third Isaiah) the glowing vision of the restored kingdom has faded somewhat, and the stress is on religious rather than on national revival. It is surmised that this part of the Book was influenced by the hard post-exilic realities of life for the settlers in Judah, after the Return.

*Haggai* The Book of Haggai consists of two prose chapters, written in Jerusalem in the year 520 BC. Eighteen years had passed since the beginning of the Return under the Edict of Cyrus. Haggai indicates that the small community was living in difficult conditions, with poor harvests, insufficient food and clothing, and low pay for the labourer who 'earns wages to put them into a bag with holes' (Hag. 1:6).

Haggai, together with his fellow-prophet Zechariah, preached that these privations were due to the failure to rebuild the ruined Temple. In the Lord's name he called upon the two leaders of the community, Zerubbabel the governor and Joshua the high priest, to resume the project that had been abandoned after the foundations were laid: 'Go up to the hills and bring wood and build the house, that I may take pleasure in it and that I may appear in my glory, says the Lord' (Hag. 1:8). If that were done, the prophet predicted, the Lord's blessing would bring renewed independence and prosperity under Zerubbabel as king. It was an over-confident promise, for the kingdom was not to arise again for centuries. But under the moral pressure of the two prophets the work was in fact put in hand, and the Second Temple completed within five years.

Zechariah, the son of Berechiah, prophesied in Jerusalem in 520–519 BC – that is, some two decades after the beginning of the Return, and early in the reign of King Darius of Persia. Zechariah and his contemporary prophet Haggai *Zechariah* pressed Zerubbabel the governor and Joshua the high priest to proceed with the rebuilding of the destroyed Temple. At the same time, he called for the community to set its religious and moral house in order.

It was a time of political upheaval in the Persian empire. Zechariah shared with Haggai the expectation that Judah would regain its independence. He visualizes a messianic kingdom with the coronation of a leader 'who shall build the temple of the Lord, and shall bear royal honour, and shall sit and rule upon his throne' (Zech. 6:13).

In the manner of Ezekiel a generation or two earlier, Zechariah receives the word of the Lord in a series of strange mystical visions: angels mounted on horses patrol the earth; four horns representing hostile powers are destroyed by the Lord's smiths; an angel with a measuring rod comes to measure Jerusalem and proclaims, 'For I will be to her a wall of fire round about, says the Lord, and I will be the glory within her' (Zech. 2:5). The high priest Joshua appears before a heavenly court, and the filthy robes he is wearing are replacd by shining new raiment, as a sign that his people has shed its guilt; a golden lampstand is flanked by two olive trees representing Zerubbabel and Joshua; an immense flying scroll symbolizes God's word; a woman named Wickedness, sitting inside a container, is transported to Babylon by angels; four chariots drawn respectively by red, black, white and piebald horses set out in different directions, presumably to carry the messianic message to the nations.

Zechariah depicts the Jews living in peace under God's protection in their restored kingdom: 'I will return to Zion, and will dwell in the midst of Jerusalem, and Jerusalem shall be called the faithful city, and the mountain of the Lord of hosts, the holy mountain' (Zech. 8:3).

Of the fourteen chapters in the Book of Zechariah, only the first eight can be attributed to the prophet himself. The remaining six are anonymous oracles written two to three centuries afterwards, in the period of Greek rule over Judah. A compiler appended them to the Book of Zechariah because they developed the messianic themes of that prophet. Certain passages in these chapters are regarded by some Christians as presaging the advent of Jesus two centuries later. Passages that find their echo in the Gospels include the description of the future messianic king coming into Jerusalem 'humble and riding on an ass', (Zech. 9:9); the thirty shekels of silver paid as the Lord's wages; and the parable of the good shepherd rejected by his flock.

*Malachi*    Malachi appeared in Jerusalem in the first half of the fifth century BC, roughly half-a-century after the completion of the Second Temple, but before the missions of Ezra and Nehemiah. Nothing is known about his personal life. Even his name, which means 'my messenger', may have been taken from chapter 3, verse 1: 'Behold, I send my messenger to prepare the way before me'.

The fortunes of the Judean community, as described by Malachi, are at a low ebb. The crops have been poor, due to drought and locust swarms. Religious observance has become slack; the priests accept blemished animals for sacrifice; and the Temple tithes and offerings are not paid in full. A number of the men have divorced their Jewish wives and married pagan women, thereby producing 'ungodly' children.

Malachi demands a genuine revival of the faith. The Lord says to his people, 'Return to me, and I will return to you' (Mal. 3:7). The priesthood must live up to its sacred task: 'For the lips of a priest should guard knowledge, and men should seek instruction from his mouth, for he is the messenger of the Lord of hosts' (Mal. 2:7).

When the day of judgment comes only the observant will be spared. Before then, the Lord will send the prophet Elijah to reform the people while there is yet time: 'And he will turn the hearts of fathers to their children and the hearts of children to their fathers, lest I come and smite the land with a curse' (Mal. 4:6).

The short Book of Malachi has two unusual features. One is the post-exilic emphasis on strict Temple worship, an attitude far removed from that of the great classical prophets of the previous centuries. The other is the distinctive question-and-answer method of making a point; it later became characteristic of the talmudic mode of argument.

*Joel*    The prophet Joel, the son of Pethuel, lived in Judah under Persian rule, about 400 BC, or a little later.

The most notable feature of his short book is a superb description of a plague of locusts that lays the country waste. Anyone who has witnessed a gigantic swarm of these insects descend from their desert breeding-grounds, forming a dense, whirring cloud that can cover scores of square miles and blot out the sun, will recognize the power and precision of Joel's documentary account:

> Their appearance is like the appear-
>     ance of horses,
>     and like war horses they run . . .
> Before them people are in anguish,
>     all faces grow pale.
> Like warriors they charge,
>     like soldiers they scale the wall . . .
> They do not jostle one another,
>     each marches in his path;
> they burst through the weapons
>     and are not halted.
> They leap upon the city,
>     they run upon the walls;
> they climb up into the houses,
>     they enter through the windows
>         like a thief.
>                                    (Joel 2:4–9)

The destruction is sweeping:

> What the cutting locust left,
>     the swarming locust has eaten.
> What the swarming locust left,
>     the hopping locust has eaten,
> and what the hopping locust left,
>     the destroying locust has eaten.
>                                    (Joel 1:4)

Joel presents the scourge as a portent of divine judgment, the coming 'day of the Lord'. He calls upon the people to repent and return to God, to 'rend your hearts and not your garments' (2:13). Then the Lord will bring rains and renewed fertility, so that:

> The threshing floors shall be full of grain,
>     the vats shall overflow with wine and oil.
>                                    (Joel 2:24)

In the new era that will dawn after the 'day of the Lord', and the restoration of Judah:

> . . . I will pour out my spirit on all
>     flesh;
> your sons and your daughters shall
>     prophesy,

your old men shall dream dreams,
and your young men shall see visions.

(Joel 2:28)

*Jonah*  The story of Jonah, and the meanings that have been attributed to it, are dealt with in the chapter entitled 'Four Stories from the Old Testament'.

The first half of the Book of Daniel contains stories of Daniel and his companions at the *Daniel* Babylonian court. These episodes are related in the chapter entitled 'Four Stories from the Old Testament'.

The second half of the book was written by several different authors in the Hellenist period, between 167 and 165 BC, just before the Maccabean Revolt. Judea was under the Seleucid throne of Antiochus IV, who sought to suppress the Hebrew faith and impose Greek ways and pagan worship on his Jewish subjects. In a series of weird visions attributed to Daniel, the history of the region after its conquest by Alexander the Great (332 BC) is traced with the help of vivid symbols and veiled allusions. The visions project the contemporary scene into the future, in a manner that has become known as apocalyptic – that is, mystical revelations of a general calamity to come ('the end of days') followed by the redemption of the righteous. In the two centuries after the Book of Daniel, a number of other works of this kind appeared in Judea, culminating in the Revelation of St. John in the New Testament.

The four visions of Daniel are told in the first person. The 'historical' setting is taken from the stories in the earlier part of the book – that is, the Babylonian court in the reigns of Belshazzar, 'Darius the Mede' and Cyrus, king of Persia.

In the first vision, four huge beasts arise in turn out of a stormy sea: a winged lion, a bear, a four-headed winged leopard, and a fourth beast, 'terrible and dreadful and exceedingly strong; and it had great iron teeth; it devoured and broke in pieces, and stamped the residue with its feet' (Dan. 7:7). As Daniel watches, the fourth beast is slain and its body thrown into the fire. In the dream an angel explains to him what he has seen. The four beasts stand for four successive empires. They will be succeeded by a fifth kingdom, given to 'the saints of the Most High' and lasting forever.

In his second vision Daniel finds himself standing on the bank of a river in the Persian city of Susa. He sees a ram with two horns that dominates everything else, until a goat with a single long horn rushes at the ram and overcomes it. The single horn is replaced by four horns, each pointing in a different direction. Out of one of these horns comes a smaller one, with a power that extends over the Promised Land. It defies the Lord, represses the true religion, desecrates the Temple and stops the sacrifices.

The angel Gabriel interprets this vision to Daniel. The ram with two horns represents the united kingdoms of Medea and Persia. The goat that overthrows the ram is Greece, and the great horn between its eyes is its king (Alexander the Great). The four horns that come up are the four successor kingdoms after Alexander's death. Towards the end of their rule, a cunning and deceitful king will arise (a guarded reference to Antiochus IV) and will cause great destruction until he is broken by the Lord. Gabriel adds, however, that this deliverance will not come for a long time; until then Daniel must keep his vision secret.

Daniel prays to God, confessing that the people of Israel had sinned but pleading for an end to its suffering and the restoration of the Temple. The Angel Gabriel comes to him again in a vision, to say that God loves him and will answer his prayer in due course. But before that, Jerusalem and the Temple will be destroyed by the invading army of a powerful ruler, who will make pagan sacrifices in the Temple.

In the fourth and longest of his visions, Daniel sees a shining angel on the bank of the river Tigris. The angel soothes the trembling Daniel, and in enigmatic language outlines the history of the region from the advent of Alexander the Great to the reign of the 'contemptible person' who will profane the Temple (again Antiochus IV). The resistance to that regime will receive 'a little help from people who will stand firm in their faith' (a reference to the Maccabean Revolt, which began in 165 BC). The angel then predicts that the age will end with a period of trouble greater than any that has gone before. At that time, all those of the Jewish nation whose names have been written in God's book will be saved. Many of the dead will then rise again, some to enjoy eternal life and others to suffer eternal disgrace. Daniel, too, will then stand in his allotted place. Daniel is told to 'shut up the words, and seal the book, until the time of the end' (Dan. 12:4).

## The Meanings of the Classical Prophets' Names

| | |
|---|---|
| Amos | Burden |
| Hosea | Deliverance |
| Isaiah | God is Salvation |
| Micah | Who is like God |
| Zephaniah | God has protected |
| Nahum | Comforted |
| Habakkuk | Basil plant (in Assyrian) |
| Jeremiah | God will elevate |
| Obadiah | Servant of God |
| Ezekiel | God's Strength |
| Haggai | Festive |
| Zechariah | God has remembered |
| Malachi | My Messenger |
| Joel | The Lord is God |
| Jonah | Dove |
| Daniel | God is my judge |

## The Prophetic Vocation

AS THE MORAL CONSCIENCE OF THE COMMUNITY, the prophet had a task that was tough, unpopular and at times hazardous. Some of the greatest of the prophets shrank from accepting God's call, and felt inadequate to carry it out.

When the voice of the Lord came to Moses out of the burning bush, he raised every possible argument against accepting the assignment. He first pleaded that nobody would believe him, then stressed that he stammered. The Lord brushed aside these suggestions.

*The Burden of Prophecy* Isaiah protested that 'I am a man of unclean lips' (Isa. 6:5). Jeremiah argued that, 'I do not know how to speak, for I am only a youth' (Jer. 1:6). Ezekiel had to be braced by the Lord to meet the hostility he would encounter from his fellow-exiles: 'And you, son of man, be not afraid of them, nor be afraid of their words, though briers and thorns are with you and you sit upon scorpions; be not afraid of their words, nor be dismayed at their looks, for they are a rebellious house' (Ezek. 2:6). As for Jonah, when the word of the Lord came to him to go and prophesy in Nineveh, he simply ran away to sea.

Once the prophets were launched on their vocation, they were fearless and independent in carrying it out. They were God's chosen servants, and there was no evading his demands:

> Surely the Lord God does nothing,
> without revealing his secret

> to his servants the prophets...
> The Lord God has spoken;
> who can but prophesy?
> (Amos 3:7,8)

They did not hesitate to attack the powerful, the privileged and the rich, nor to fight the battles of the underdog. It was inevitable that their opinions should arouse against them the anger of rulers, priests and the common people. They had to be prepared for punishment, derision, indifference and loneliness.

Elijah was hounded by Queen Jezebel and had to flee for his life. When King Ahab of Israel consulted the prophets before the campaign against Ramoth-gilead, Micaiah the lone dissenter was flung into prison and kept on bread and water. Jeremiah was clapped into the stocks, then locked up, for his vigorous criticism of the official war policy. But physical penalties in these and other cases were of less importance than the emotional stress the prophets underwent when their preaching fell on deaf ears, and when they felt helpless to avert the calamities they saw coming. There is a great frustration and weariness of spirit in the cry of Isaiah:

> Therefore the word of the Lord will
> be to them
> precept upon precept, precept
> upon precept,
> line upon line, line upon line,
> here a little, there a little;
> that they may go, and fall backward,
> and be broken, and snared, and taken.
> (Isa. 28:13)

Hosea sadly sums up the popular attitude towards his calling:

> The prophet is a fool,
> the man of the spirit is mad.
> (Hos. 9:7)

Micah has no illusions about the kind of spiritual mentor the community would prefer:

> If a man should go about and utter
> wind and lies,
> saying, 'I will preach to you of
> wine and strong drink,'
> he would be the preacher for this people!
> (Micah 2:11)

Ezekiel is given a caustic warning by the Lord

that his task would be easier if he were sent to 'a people of foreign speech and a hard language'. His own people would probably reject him, yet he was to bring them the Lord's message 'whether they hear or refuse to hear' (Ezek. 2:7).

It was hard for the prophets to be messengers of doom, for they were filled with anguish at the thought that their own grim warnings would come true. Isaiah, for instance, found it intolerable that his beloved city of Jerusalem might be destroyed, even if that was the Lord's will:

> Look away from me,
>  let me weep bitter tears;
> do not labour to comfort me
>  for the destruction of the daughter
>   of my people.
>
> (Isa. 22:4)

The Book of Jeremiah reveals the prophet's intense personal conflict and suffering. Behind the abrasive manner was a lonely and sensitive man, tormented by self-doubt. Because of the disasters he witnessed and foresaw he did not marry and have children, and felt unable to share in the ordinary joys of life. He was deeply hurt by the enmity and rejection he encountered: 'Woe is me, my mother, that you bore me, a man of strife and contention to the whole land! I have not lent, nor have I borrowed, yet all of them curse me' (Jer. 15:10). At times he was oppressed by a sense of futility over his mission:

> O Lord, do not thy eyes look for truth?
> Thou hast smitten them,
>  but they felt no anguish;
>  thou hast consumed them,
>  but they refused to take correction.
> They have made their faces harder
>  than rock;
>  they have refused to repent.
>
> (Jer. 5:3)

He went through a crisis of faith, and reproached God for having failed his own people:

> Why shouldst thou be like a man
>  confused,
>  like a mighty man who cannot save?
> Yet thou, O Lord, art in the midst of us,
>  and we are called by thy name;
>  leave us not.
>
> (Jer. 14:9)

At the same time, Jeremiah could not shake off the compulsion of his prophetic task, which was like 'a burning fire shut up in my bones'.

The prophets did not confine themselves to the one-way role of being God's mouthpiece. They also appeared as defence counsel for their human clients, pleading with God to withhold retribution however deserved.

*Interceding with God*

Abraham, a precursor of the prophets, interceded with the Lord whenever he could. The most conspicuous example concerned the fate of Sodom and Gomorrah, the sinful Canaanite cities near the southern end of the Dead Sea. The kindly Abraham pleaded that they be spared because some of the inhabitants might be innocent. 'Wilt thou indeed destroy the righteous with the wicked?' (Gen. 18:23).

When the Children of Israel in the desert worshipped the golden calf, the Lord decided that they were hopelessly corrupt and had to be destroyed. Moses had been so angry and disillusioned when he came down from Mount Sinai that he had smashed the stone tablets of the Law he was carrying. Yet he turned to God and stubbornly argued for clemency. The Egyptians, he said, would note with glee that the Lord had brought the Israelites out of Egypt 'with great power and a mighty hand' only to slay them himself. Moreover, what about the Lord's promises to Abraham, Isaac and Jacob, that he would multiply their descendants and give them the Land of Israel forever? 'And the Lord repented of the evil which he thought to do to his people' (Ex. 32:14).

In times of emergency, the prophet Samuel was invariably asked by the elders to use his influence with God. When it looked as if the Israelite tribes would be overrun by the Philistines from the coastal area, the prophet gathered the people together at Mizpah, offered sacrifices, 'and Samuel cried to the Lord for Israel, and the Lord answered him' (1 Sam. 7:9). By divine intervention the enemy was thrown into confusion and routed.

Amos cried out:

> O Lord God, forgive, I beseech thee!
> How can Jacob stand?
> He is so small!
>
> (Amos 7:2)

Jeremiah was rebuked by God for trying to deflect judgment: 'As for you, do not pray for this people, or lift up cry or prayer for them, and do not intercede with me, for I do not hear you' (Jer. 7:16). The hunger and death caused by a great drought drove the prophet to wail bitterly:

Hast thou utterly rejected Judah?
  Does thy soul loathe Zion?
Why hast thou smitten us
  so that there is no healing for us?
We looked for peace, but no good came;
for a time of healing, but behold, terror.
(Jer. 14:19)

Ezekiel was already in exile in Babylonia when Jerusalem was finally destroyed in 587 BC. In a vision he sees six 'executioners of the city' sent by the Lord to put the inhabitants to the sword for their iniquity. This is more than Ezekiel can bear: 'And while they were smiting, and I was left alone, I fell upon my face, and cried, "Ah Lord God! wilt thou destroy all that remains of Israel in the outpouring of thy wrath upon Jerusalem?"' (Ezek. 9:8).

*Involvement in Public Events* The Hebrew prophets were not religious recluses turning their backs upon the world. They were men of their time, deeply involved in public affairs and at times influencing them. For them no dividing line existed between the spiritual and the secular. The God they served was in control of history, and everything that happened to their people came from him.

No person in the Old Testament story played a more decisive political role than Moses. He was the liberator, the leader and the lawgiver of the small Hebrew nation emerging from a rabble of runaway slaves. For forty years he guided them in the wilderness and moulded them as an entity. By the time he handed over his trust to Joshua, at the gateway to the Promised Land, the Israelites were an organized people.

At the end of the period of the Judges, the dominant Israelite figure was Samuel, who combined the vocations of priest, prophet and judge. He was an unofficial national leader, who had the moral authority to rally the tribesmen in times of danger. However reluctantly, Samuel played a key political role as king-maker. He selected and anointed first Saul, then the young David.

During the monarchy some of the prophets had an important impact on political affairs, either as advisers to kings or as instigators of revolt against them.

Nathan, the prophet at King David's court, was instrumental in blocking the succession of David's eldest surviving son Adonijah and gaining the throne for a younger brother, Solomon. For this purpose, Nathan conspired with Solomon's mother Bathsheba.

Ahijah, a prophet attached to the sanctuary at Shiloh, had a hand in the events that led to the split in the monarchy after Solomon's death.

The prophet Elisha took steps to overthrow the hated Ahab dynasty in the northern kingdom of Israel. He incited the army general Jehu to lead a revolt that succeeded in bloodthirsty fashion.

The highly respected Isaiah was a royal counsellor to three successive kings of Judah, and there were times when his advice was decisive. One such occasion is related in graphic detail. In 701 BC the Assyrian monarch Sennacherib swept through Judah and sent his emissaries to demand that King Hezekiah surrender Jerusalem. Isaiah firmly insisted that the demand be rejected. Hezekiah was thus emboldened to hold out, and the Assyrians withdrew.

A century later Jerusalem was again threatened, this time by a Babylonian force. In vain Jeremiah pleaded the folly of resistance, and tried to dissuade first King Jehoiakim and later King Zedekiah from revolt. His advice was spurned. In 587 BC Jerusalem was taken and sacked and the kingdom of Judah came to a tragic end.

To their own people, the prophets presented *The Prophets as Patriots* external foes as God's instrument of punishment. The enemy outside the gate had been sent on account of the moral decay within. At the same time, they were vehement patriots and nationalists in addressing other nations. A great part of the prophetic Books is taken up with oracles against hostile countries, and calls for their destruction. Some of these oracles are among the finest passages of invective in world literature.

Up to the eighth century, the enemy nations were small neighbouring peoples: Edom, Moab and Ammon east of the Jordan river and the Dead Sea; Aram-Damascus to the north-east; the Canaanites and the Philistines in the coastal plain; and the Amalekites, marauding nomad tribes in the southern desert. But the classical age of prophecy, from the eighth century BC onwards, had as its background the clash of mighty empires: Assyria, Babylonia and Egypt. The two small Hebrew states were caught up in the power struggle between these forces, and in the end crushed by them. It is these enemies who are

'The Valley of Dry Bones – Vision
of Ezekiel', by the English artist
David Bomberg (1912).

most fiercely assailed by Isaiah and his successors.

Isaiah threw his full weight against alliances of expediency. He denounced as futile and dangerous the tendency in Jerusalem to seek safety in balance-of-power politics, and to play off one external force against another. That was so when King Ahaz appealed for help to the king of Assyria. The immediate pressure on Judah was relieved, but she had placed herself in the Assyrian orbit. Thirty years later, Isaiah criticized King Hezekiah for seeking support from the Egyptians against the Assyrians.

Isaiah and the other prophets asserted that neither armed strength nor allies were of any avail if the Lord did not extend his protection. A foreign foe was the stick God used to discipline his erring people:

> Ah, Assyria, the rod of my anger,
>     the staff of my fury!
> Against a godless nation I send him,
>     and against the people of my wrath
>     I command him,
>
> (Isa. 10:5,6)

The only way for the nation to be secure was for the ruler and the ruled to purge themselves of wrong and to live in the spirit of the Covenant.

*Prophets and Seers*    The prophets did at times foretell what was going to happen. But that was incidental to their main function, which was to be the channel for conveying God's will. There is a revealing remark inserted into the First Book of Samuel by a later biblical editor. When the young Saul was out searching in the hills for his father's lost donkeys, his servant proposed that they should consult the man of God, Samuel. At this point the following observation appears in the text in brackets: '(Formerly in Israel, when a man went to inquire of God, he said, "Come, let us go to the seer"; for he who is now called a prophet was formerly called a seer.)' (1 Sam. 9:9).

Throughout the ancient world, divining the future – being a 'seer' – was a highly respected science, relying on the stars, the spirits of the dead, the drawing of lots, the entrails of animals, and the flight of birds. At an early stage, the Old Testament frowned on most of these practices as reeking of paganism and inappropriate for learning the will of the Lord. Leviticus forbids recourse to augurs, mediums or wizards and lays down that they should be stoned to death. In Deuteronomy, Moses in his farewell address declares that:

> There shall not be found among you any one . . . who practises divination, a soothsayer, or an augur, or a sorcerer, or a charmer, or a medium, or a wizard, or a necromancer. For whoever does these things is an abomination to the Lord . . . The Lord your God will raise up for you a prophet like me from among you, from your brethren – him you shall heed' (Deut. 18:10–12,15).

Before his final battle at Mount Gilboa, King Saul was deeply disturbed because he had failed to get a response from the Lord by the accepted means: dreams, Urim and Thummim, or prophets. In desperation he asked his retainers to find him a medium through whom he could consult the spirit of his dead mentor, the prophet Samuel. He was directed to a woman who lived in the village of Endor, and visited her in disguise at night. The moment he told her what he wanted of her, she replied: 'Surely you know what Saul has done, how he has cut off the mediums and the wizards from the land. Why then are you laying a snare for my life to bring about my death?' (1 Sam. 28:9). It was only when she recognized him as the king and he promised her immunity from the law that she agreed to the seance.

In the early Old Testament period, the casting of lots was used for taking important decisions with divine approval. This method was used, for instance, to divide the Promised Land among the twelve Israelite tribes after Joshua's Conquest. A special and sacred device for casting lots was the Urim and Thummim, the exact nature of which has remained a mystery. Apparently they were small objects kept in a pouch that was attached to the gem-studded breast-plate worn by the high priest on ceremonial occasions: 'And in the breastpiece of judgment you shall put the Urim and the Thummim, and they shall be upon Aaron's heart, when he goes in before the Lord' (Ex. 28:30). When Moses appointed Joshua to be his successor as leader, Joshua had to stand before the high priest 'who shall inquire for him by the judgment of the Urim before the Lord' (Num. 27:21). During the battle of Michmash against the Philistines, King Saul ordered his men to fast all day. His son Jonathan was unaware of the order and ate some wild honey. Sensing that someone had done wrong, the priest advised the king to consult the Lord before pursuing the enemy. The Urim and Thummim were used to disclose the culprit. Saul prayed to the Lord and said, 'If this guilt is in me or in Jonathan my son, O Lord, God of Israel, give Urim; but if this guilt is in thy people Israel, give Thummim.' And Jonathan and Saul were taken, but the people escaped. Then Saul said, "Cast the lot between me and my son Jonathan." And Jonathan was taken' (1 Sam. 14:41–42).

On another occasion, the Urim and Thummim were used by David in his outlaw period. They had been carried away from the sanctuary at Nob by the priest Abiathar, who escaped when the unbalanced Saul had all the other priests killed for giving aid to David.

From the reign of David onward there is no further mention in the Old Testament of casting lots as a means of predicting the future or finding out God's will.

*Dreams and Visions*   Three thousand years before Sigmund Freud, it was universally accepted that a dream was a communication from the gods. If the message was not understood by the dreamer, it could be interpreted by someone else, as Joseph did for the Egyptian Pharaoh and Daniel for the Babylonian king. The Book of Job refers to the way God communicates with men:

> In a dream, in a vision of the night,
>   when deep sleep falls upon men,
>   while they slumber on their beds,
> then he opens the ears of men,
>   and terrifies them with warnings,
>
> (Job 33:15)

Divinely inspired dreams are a feature of the Old Testament story from the period of the Patriarchs onward.

Abimelech, king of Gerar, took as his wife the beautiful Sarah, whom Abraham had passed off as his sister for his own protection. That same night, the Lord appeared in a dream to Abimelech and warned him that Sarah had to be returned at once as she was really Abraham's wife.

At Bethel Jacob had a celebrated dream about the ladder reaching up to heaven, with angels passing up and down it. In the dream, the Lord stood beside Jacob and renewed the promise that the land of Israel would belong to his descendants.

Soon after the youthful Solomon became king,

he went to the sanctuary at Gibeon to offer sacrifices. There the Lord came to him in a dream and asked him what he wanted as a gift. Solomon asked for wisdom to rule justly, and to know the difference between good and evil.

Dreams and visions were closely associated with prophecy as revelations of God's will. Moses was the only person of whom it was said that God spoke directly to him: 'If there is a prophet among you, I the Lord make myself known to him in a vision, I speak with him in a dream. Not so with my servant Moses; he is entrusted with all my house. With him I speak mouth to mouth, clearly, and not in dark speech; and he beholds the form of the Lord' (Num. 12:6–8). At the very end of the Book of Deuteronomy, after the death of Moses, his final epitaph is: 'And there has not arisen a prophet since in Israel like Moses, whom the Lord knew face to face' (Deut. 34:10).

Some of the classical prophets relate how God's call first came to them as an overpowering experience in a dream or vision. That is so with the three major prophets.

At the age of twenty-five, Isaiah had a sudden vision of the Lord sitting high upon his throne in the Temple. He was surrounded by seraphim; the sound of their voices shook the foundations of the Temple, which was filled with smoke. Isaiah cried out, 'Woe is me! For I am lost' (Isa. 6:5). One of the seraphim touched his lips with a burning coal from the altar. The voice of the Lord was heard saying, 'Whom shall I send, and who will go for us?' Then Isaiah said 'Here am I! Send me' (Isa. 6:8).

Jeremiah was a youth of eighteen when he was given the call to follow the vocation of a prophet. 'Then the Lord put forth his hand and touched my mouth; and the Lord said to me,

> "Behold, I have put my words in your
>   mouth.
> See, I have set you this day over nations
>   and over kingdoms,
> to pluck up and to break down,
> to destroy and to overthrow,
> to build and to plant."'
>
> (Jer. 1:9,10)

Ezekiel received his call in a manner typical of the detailed and disturbing visions to which this mystical prophet was given. He was one of the Jewish exiles in Babylonia, and was standing beside the river when 'the heavens were opened,

The young Jeremiah's lips being touched by the hand of God. Charcoal drawing
by the modern German artist Ludwig Meidner.

and I saw visions of God' (Ezek. 1:1). In the centre of a storm, the Lord was carried in the air by four bizarre winged creatures, each having four faces resembling those of a human being, a lion, a bull and an eagle respectively. The whole scene was bathed in flames and blinding light, and the whirring of the wings was like the noise of rushing water. A hand was stretched towards Ezekiel holding a scroll written on both sides with 'words of lamentation and mourning and woe'. The Lord ordered Ezekiel to eat the scroll, which he found had a taste of honey. Ezekiel was then told that he was being sent to minister to his own people. Ezekiel records that he returned to his fellow-exiles and 'sat there overwhelmed among them seven days' (Ezek. 3:15).

*Miracles and Symbols*
In all ancient faiths the magician played a prominent role. It was generally believed that he possessed the power to tap occult forces, perform miracles and influence people and events by supernatural means.

Miracles and wonders occur frequently in earlier Old Testament history as well. But, in contrast to the Egyptians, Babylonians and other Near-Eastern peoples, the Israelites never regarded magic as an occult science that a human being could master and use at his own will, for good or evil. In the Hebrew faith all miracles were signs from God, and their purpose was to reinforce God's message and make people believe.

The saga of the Exodus abounds in such miracles. When Moses heard the voice of God from the burning bush, he was told that before going to Pharaoh he had first to disclose God's liberation plan to the leaders of the Israelite community in Egypt. Moses replied: 'But behold, they will not believe me or listen to my voice, for they will say, "The Lord did not appear to you"' (Ex. 4:1). Three magical acts were then taught to him as a means of endorsing his credentials: his shepherd's stick was turned into a snake; his hand was struck white with leprosy and healed again; some Nile water was poured onto dry ground where it became blood. The miracles were later performed for the Israelite elders and they were convinced.

The demand to Pharaoh by Moses and Aaron to 'let my people go' was supported by a series of 'signs and wonders' that served to demonstrate the Lord's power. Pharaoh accepted the challenge and called on his best magicians to match the Hebrew miracles. The first test was turning a staff into a snake. The Egyptian magicians performed this too; though Aaron's snake showed its superiority by swallowing the Egyptian ones. Pharaoh did not relent. Pressure was then brought on him by the ten plagues. The Egyptian wise men were able to repeat the first two: turning the water of the Nile into blood and creating swarms of frogs. They failed however with the third test – the plague of gnats – and retired from the contest, admitting to their royal master that 'This is the finger of God'. It took seven more miraculous afflictions to persuade Pharaoh.

Once the Israelites had started out on their long and perilous trek, the miracles continued but their purpose had shifted. Unless Moses had obtained God's intervention at each moment of crisis, the whole venture would have collapsed in failure. Hence the waters were parted at the Reed Sea (wrongly translated as the Red Sea) so that the Israelites could cross, while Pharaoh's pursuing troops were engulfed. In the desert God sent manna to eat, and Moses struck water from a rock when his people were dying of thirst. They were navigated through the pathless wilderness by a pillar of cloud by day and a pillar of fire at night.

The eventual entry into the Promised Land, under Joshua's command, was also assisted by divine miracles – the secret weapon in the battles that had to be fought. The walls of Jericho that the Israelites were unable to breach tumbled down at the blasts of the trumpets. And when Joshua needed to stave off darkness in order to press home a victory against the Canaanites, God made the sun and moon stand still.

In the period of the monarchy, the two great miracle workers were the Former Prophets Elijah and his disciple and successor Elisha. The most dramatic moment in the Elijah story was the contrast between the true God and pagan deities on Mount Carmel. Fire came down from heaven to consume the sacrifice on Elijah's altar, after the priests of Baal had tried in vain all day to produce a similar wonder from their own deity.

Some of the miracles performed by Elijah and Elisha strikingly anticipated certain of those attributed to Jesus eight centuries later. Both these prophets raised the dead. Both also multiplied a small quantity of food – Elijah with the poor widow who gave him lodging when he was in hiding, and Elisha with the hungry band of prophets near Jericho to whom he had attached himself.

The line of wonder-working prophets in the Old Testament ended with Elijah and Elisha. The classical prophets from Amos onwards were preachers who expounded the word of God without miraculous aids. Their weapons were moral pressure, eloquence and zeal.

When these prophets wished to give their verbal message visual emphasis, they did so with symbolic objects and actions that were rhetorical devices without overtones of magic. In King Hezekiah's time, Isaiah strongly opposed seeking an alliance with Egypt against Assyria. To dramatize the pitiable plight the Egyptians would be in when defeated, the prophet himself went about naked and barefoot. Jeremiah had frequent recourse to dramatic gestures. At a public gathering he took an earthenware jar and smashed it on the ground, proclaiming in God's name: 'So will I break this people and this city, as one breaks a potter's vessel, so that it can never be mended' (Jer. 19:11). Urging submission to the Babylonians, Jeremiah walked about Jerusalem with a wooden yoke on his neck.

Ezekiel used elaborate mime, fraught with symbolism. For instance, as a warning sign that the inhabitants of Jerusalem would be driven into exile, Ezekiel emerged through a hole he had knocked in the wall of his house, hoisted a refugee pack on his shoulders, and moved off with his eyes covered to show that he did not know where he was heading.

*True and False Prophets*  In the Old Testament, the people of Israel was repeatedly warned against being led astray by false prophets. Yet there was no reliable criterion for distinguishing the true prophet from the false. When different prophets, each claiming to speak in the name of God, proffered conflicting opinions, which course was the audience to follow? As a rule, the prophet who said what people wanted to hear was the one likely to be believed.

The test proposed in Deuteronomy is whether the prediction turns out to be correct: 'when a prophet speaks in the name of the Lord, if the word does not come to pass or come true, that is a word which the Lord has not spoken; the prophet has spoken it presumptuously, you need not be afraid of him' (Deut. 18:22). But future events were not of much help in assessing the prophet's words at the time when they were spoken.

Some of the classical prophets suggested tests of character and conduct. Isaiah condemned priests and prophets who

> ...stagger with strong drink;
> they err in vision,
>     they stumble in giving judgment.
>
> (Isa. 28:7)

Jeremiah lashed out at the morally lax 'establishment' prophets:

> But in the prophets of Jerusalem
>    I have seen a horrible thing:
> they commit adultery and walk in lies;
> they strengthen the hands of evil-doers,
> so that no one turns from his wickedness;
>
> (Jer. 23:14)

Micah attacked those prophets who got paid for assuring people that all was well:

> ...its prophets divine for money;
> yet they lean upon the Lord and say,
>    'Is not the Lord in the midst of us?
>    No evil shall come upon us.'
>
> (Micah 3:11)

Looking back thousands of years later, it matters little whether the prophets were able to foresee accurately the events of their time. What have survived are the eternal truths they preached.

## The Teachings of the Prophets

THE PROPHETS STRESSED THE MORAL LAW rather than formal worship. They insisted that everyone had to behave justly towards his fellow-men. Kings were no exception: David was rebuked by Nathan over the Bathsheba affair, and Ahab by Elijah over the episode of Naboth's vineyard.

*Religion and Morality*  For the classical prophets, externals of religious practice were secondary to genuine faith, righteous conduct and social concern. They held that the practice of religion was worthless without its moral content. They valued human rights more than rites; devotion to God more than devotions.

Amos first raised the prophetic cry for a just society and a personal ethic:

> Therefore because you trample upon
>     the poor
> and take from him exactions of wheat,

you have built houses of hewn stone,
 but you shall not dwell in them;
you have planted pleasant vineyards,
 but you shall not drink their wine.
       (Amos 5:11)

He was echoed by his northern contemporary Hosea:

For I desire steadfast love and not sacrifice,
 the knowledge of God, rather than
  burnt offerings.
       (Hos. 6:6)

Micah of Judah summed up the ethical approach to religion in three moving lines:

and what does the Lord require of you
but to do justice, and to love kindness,
and to walk humbly with your God?
       (Micah 6:8)

Amos, Hosea and Micah were men of the people. But even the eminent Isaiah poured scorn on empty ritual:

What to me is the multitude of your
  sacrifices?
 says the Lord;
I have had enough of burnt offerings
  of rams
 and the fat of fed beasts;
I do not delight in the blood of bulls,
 or of lambs, or of he-goats.
       (Isa. 1:11)

Isaiah's feelings of repugnance for the arrogant and decadent life-style of upper-class Jerusalem in his time was epitomized in his attack on the ladies of fashion:

The Lord said:
Because the daughters of Zion are
  haughty
 and walk with outstretched necks,
 glancing wantonly with their eyes,
mincing along as they go,
 tinkling with their feet;
the Lord will smite with a scab
 the heads of the daughters of Zion,
 and the Lord will lay bare their
  secret parts ...
Instead of perfume there will be
 rottenness;
and instead of a girdle, a rope;
and instead of well-set hair, baldness;

and instead of a rich robe, a
 girding of sackcloth;
instead of beauty, shame.
     (Isa. 3:16–17,24)

Jeremiah fiercely rejected the notion that Temple attendance in itself cleansed the sinner in God's eyes:

Will you steal, murder, commit adultery, swear falsely, burn incense to Baal, and go after other gods that you have not known, and then come and stand before me in this house, which is called by my name, and say, 'We are delivered!' – only to go on doing all these abominations? (Jer. 7:9–10).

*The Prophet and the Priest*

The Mosaic Law had two main aspects. One concerned moral and social behaviour. The other concerned the regulation of religious life: the duties of the priests and Levites, offerings of animals and produce, ritual cleanliness, and the observance of festivals.

The priests were the guardians of formal worship, the cult. Their function was to represent the community before God, through time-honoured rituals and sacrifices. The prophets had a different function – to bring God's word directly to the community. The priests often resented the independent role of the prophets, particularly their sharp criticism of conventional worship. It was not surprising that the chief priest of the Bethel sanctuary should have complained to the king that Amos was subversive; or that the Jerusalem priests should have had Jeremiah arrested.

Yet this conflict need not be exaggerated. Both prophet and priest drew their authority from a single source – the Mosaic Code, sanctified by the covenant with God. In course of time the ethical and the cultic aspects of the Hebrew faith permeated each other. The religious reforms of King Josiah in 621 BC were derived from the early Book of Deuteronomy, which was strongly influenced by the teachings of the Prophets. On the other hand the Priestly Code, woven into the Pentateuch in the post-exilic period, stressed organized religion as the best means of holding together a dispersed and stateless people.

The prophets were religious reformers, not anti-religious revolutionaries. They were trying to purify and strengthen the faith, not to undermine it. While they worried that moral slackness would destroy the nation from within, they fought together with the priesthood against the idolatrous practices that crept in from surrounding pagan peoples.

Hosea pictures Israel as a harlot who will suffer public shame for the false gods she pursues:

> And I will punish her for the feast
>     days of the Baals
> when she burned incense to them
> and decked herself with her ring and
>     jewelry,
> and went after her lovers,
> and forgot me, says the Lord.
>
> (Hos. 2:13)

Zephaniah threatens in the name of the Lord:

> I will cut off from this place the
>     remnant of Baal ...
> those who bow down and swear to
>     the Lord
> and yet swear by Milcom;
>
> (Zeph. 1:4,5)

Jeremiah is scathing about his countrymen who turn to heathen deities:

> Do you not see what they are doing in the cities of Judah and in the streets of Jerusalem? The children gather wood, the fathers kindle fire, and the women knead dough, to make cakes for the queen of heaven; and they pour out drink offerings to other gods, to provoke me to anger. Is it I whom they provoke? says the Lord. Is it not themselves, to their own confusion? (Jer. 7:17–19)

Ezekiel castigates the 'vile abominations' of Hebrews who worship the sun, the stars and idols, and practise cult prostitution and child sacrifices.

*The Meaning of the Covenant*    The prophets warned against the comfortable belief that God would always protect his people. The divine covenant, they insisted, gave no automatic immunity. It set conditions. The choice of Israel carried not privilege but a heavier responsibility and sterner standards. Failure to live up to its covenant obligations would bring disaster on God's people:

> for they have rejected the law of the
>     Lord of hosts,
> and have despised the word of the
>     Holy One of Israel.

Therefore the anger of the Lord was
>     kindled against his people,
> and he stretched out his hand
>     against them and smote them,
>
> (Isa. 5:24,25)

Amos declares bluntly, in the Lord's name:

> You only have I known
>     of all the families of the earth;
> therefore I will punish you
>     for all your iniquities.
>
> (Amos 3:2)

Micah assails the erring leaders, priests and prophets in Jerusalem who complacently believe nothing will happen to them:

> Its heads give judgment for a bribe,
>     its priests teach for hire,
>     its prophets divine for money;
> yet they lean upon the Lord and say,
>     Is not the Lord in the midst of us?
>     No evil shall come upon us.
> Therefore because of you
>     Zion shall be ploughed as a field;
>     Jerusalem shall become a heap of ruins,
> and the mountain of the house a
>     wooded height.
>
> (Micah 3:11,12)

*The Call to Repent*    The prophets' harsh predictions were meant to shock their people into the repentance and reform that alone could avert disaster. God, they said, was merciful and would change his mind if the people changed their ways.

Joel gives a frightening picture of the coming 'Day of the Lord', but adds:

> Return to the Lord, your God,
>     for he is gracious and merciful,
> slow to anger, and abounding in
>     steadfast love,
> and repents of evil.
>
> (Joel 2:13)

Jeremiah is told by the Lord:

> If at any time I declare concerning a nation or a kingdom, that I will pluck up and break down and destroy it, and if that nation, concerning which I have spoken, turns from its evil, I will repent of the evil that I intended to do to it. (Jer. 18:7–8).

But the lack of response to their pleas and

warnings drove the prophets to despair. They were addressing themselves to a people that

> Hear and hear, but do not understand;
> see and see, but do not perceive.
>
> (Isa. 6:9)

Jeremiah saw the fate of Judah closing in and lapsed into utter pessimism:

> But this people has a stubborn and
> rebellious heart;
>   they have turned aside and gone away ...
> An appalling and horrible thing
>   has happened in the land:
> the prophets prophesy falsely,
>   and the priests rule at their direction;
> my people love to have it so,
> but what will you do when the end comes?
>
> (Jer. 5:23,30–31)

*The Messianic Vision* With all their pessimism and despair, the prophets held that it was not God's purpose to let his people disappear for good, however much it might stray.

In the eighth century BC, when both Hebrew kingdoms were still in existence, Amos warned about the coming destruction, but at the same time held out the hope of a future rebirth:

> I will restore the fortunes of my
>   people Israel,
>   and they shall rebuild the ruined
>     cities and inhabit them;
>   they shall plant vineyards and drink
>     their wine,
>   and they shall make gardens and
>     eat their fruit.
> I will plant them upon their land,
>   and they shall never again be
>     plucked up
>   out of the land which I have given them,
>     says the Lord your God.
>
> (Amos 9:14,15)

After the northern kingdom of Israel had been wiped out, and the southern kingdom was surviving precariously in the shadow of the Assyrian colossus, Isaiah proclaimed his immortal vision of the restored kingdom of peace and harmony, under a messianic king descended from David:

> The wolf shall dwell with the lamb,
>   and the leopard shall lie down with the kid,
>   and the calf and the lion and the

fatling together,
>   and a little child shall lead them.
> The cow and the bear shall feed;
>   their young shall lie down together;
>   and the lion shall eat straw like the ox.
> The suckling child shall play over the
>   hole of the asp,
>   and the weaned child shall put his
>     hand on the adder's den.
> They shall not hurt or destroy
>   in all my holy mountain;
>
> (Isa. 11:6–9)

In one of his visions Ezekiel was transported to a valley filled with dry bones, and was told by the Lord to prophesy to them. As he spoke,

> there was a noise, and behold, a rattling; and the bones came together, bone to its bone. And as I looked, there were sinews on them, and flesh had come upon them, and skin had covered them; but there was no breath in them. Then he said to me, 'Prophesy to the breath, prophesy, son of man, and say to the breath, Thus says the Lord God: Come from the four winds, O breath, and breathe upon these slain, that they may live.' So I prophesied as he commanded me, and the breath came into them, and they lived, and stood upon their feet, an exceedingly great host.
>
> (Ezek. 37:7–10)

The Lord then explained to Ezekiel that these bones were the house of Israel that would be raised from the grave, have the spirit of God infused into it, and be restored to its ancestral land.

The Return, the prophets believed, would usher in a new age not only for the Hebrew people but for all mankind. Nations would cease their strife and live in peace with each other, set aside their pagan creeds and accept the Lord as their God too, with Jerusalem as his holy city:

> and many peoples shall come, and say:
> 'Come, let us go up to the mountain
>   of the Lord,
> to the house of the God of Jacob;
> that he may teach us his ways
>   and that we may walk in his paths.'
> For out of Zion shall go forth the law,
>   and the word of the Lord from
>     Jerusalem.
> He shall judge between the nations,
>   and shall decide for many peoples;

and they shall beat their swords into
   ploughshares,
   and their spears into pruning hooks;
nation shall not lift up sword against
   nation,
   neither shall they learn war any more.

                              (Isa. 2:3–4)

(These verses are duplicated in the Book of Isaiah's contemporary, Micah. The 'swords into ploughshares' passage that foresees world disarmament is engraved on a stone wall facing the entrance to the United Nations building in New York.)

Isaiah had a wistful ecumenical dream of the two great imperial powers of his time co-existing in a community of faith with the small Hebrew nation that lay between them:

In that day there will be a highway from Egypt to Assyria, and the Assyrian will come into Egypt, and the Egyptian into Assyria, and the Egyptians will worship with the Assyrians.

   In that day Israel will be the third with Egypt and Assyria, a blessing in the midst of the earth, whom the Lord of hosts has blessed, saying, 'Blessed be Egypt my people, and Assyria the work of my hands, and Israel my heritage'. (Isa. 19:23–24)

(This passage was aptly quoted by the Israeli representative at the opening session of the historic Israel/Arab conference in Cairo in December 1977.)

Jeremiah shared the vision of a world faith:

At that time Jerusalem shall be called the throne of the Lord, and all nations shall gather to it, to the presence of the Lord in Jerusalem, and they shall no more stubbornly follow their own evil heart. (Jer. 3:17)

The Second Isaiah, preaching during the Babylonian exile, foretold a messianic age when 'the glory of the Lord shall be revealed, and all flesh shall see it together' (Isa. 40:5). At that time the Lord's word to mankind will be:

Turn to me and be saved,
   all the ends of the earth!
For I am God, and there is no other.

                            (Isa. 45:22)

Second Isaiah held that the Hebrew people, the 'suffering servant' of God, was destined to be a prophet-nation spreading a message universal in scope:

Behold my servant, whom I uphold,
   my chosen, in whom my soul delights;
I have put my Spirit upon him,
   he will bring forth justice to the nations.
He will not fail or be discouraged
   till he has established justice in the earth;
   and the coastlands wait for his law.
I have taken you by the hand and kept you;
I have given you as a covenant to the people,
a light to the nations.

                        (Isa. 42:1,4,6)

PART THREE

# THE APOCRYPHA

## I

# WHAT ARE THE APOCRYPHA?

THE GREEK WORD APOCHRYPHA MEANS THINGS that are hidden. It came to denote a specific group of fifteen works, or portions of works, that were included (except for 2 Esdras) in the Septuagint, the early Greek translation of the Old Testament, but were not part of the canon of the Hebrew Bible. These works were originally written in Hebrew, Aramaic or Greek, during the period from the third century BC to the first century AD.

The first version of the Septuagint was produced in the Alexandria of the third century BC, and expanded after that. It became the Old Testament in standard use by the early Christian Church. In the fourth century AD the great biblical scholar St. Jerome was commissioned by the Pope to produce a Latin translation of the Bible. Working in Bethlehem, Jerome translated the Old Testament directly from the Hebrew, and adhered to the Hebrew canon, though not in the same order of the books. The additional works that appeared in the Greek Bible he set aside as 'ecclesiastical' but lacking in scriptural authority. His Latin Bible became known as the Vulgate. Jerome's exclusion of the Apocrypha was not upheld by the Church. Under the influence of his illustrious contemporary St. Augustine, Church synods endorsed the wider Alexandrian canon contained in the Greek Bible.

The question was again examined by the Catholic Church in the sixteenth century AD, after the beginning of the Protestant Reformation. At the Council of Trent in 1546, the inclusion of all the Apocrypha was reaffirmed, except for three works: 1 and 2 Esdras, and the Prayer of Manasseh. These three were not entirely discarded, but printed as an appendix at the end of the New Testament.

The Septuagint used by the Greek Orthodox Church and (in translation) by other Eastern Churches, retains all the Apocrypha.

The leaders of the Protestant Reformation reverted to the position taken by St. Jerome. The Apocrypha were classified by them as human works, not divinely inspired. Nevertheless, reading these works was regarded as morally edifying, and they were generally printed as a separate unit sandwiched between the Old and New Testaments. That was the format adopted by Martin Luther in his German translation of the Bible, published in 1534; and also in the English translations up to and including the noble King James (or Authorised) Version of 1611. The Thirty-nine Articles of the Church of England, adopted in 1571, laid down that the Apocrypha were to be read 'for example of life and instruction of manners', but no doctrine could be derived from them. (Incidentally, the Articles marked the doctrinal break with Rome; in the following year Queen Elizabeth was excommunicated by the Pope.) Calvin's more puritanical ruling was to exclude the Apocrypha altogether from printed bibles, since they had no more standing for Protestants than any other non-scriptural religious works. In modern Protestant versions there is no fixed practice. The Apocrypha may be printed between the Old and New Testaments, after the New Testament, or in a separate volume.

The following is a list of the fifteen works that are traditionally included in the Apocrypha:

*The First Book of Esdras* (1 Esd.): see comments at the end of the story 'The Three Young Guardsmen'.

*The Second Book of Esdras* (2 Esd.): an apocalyptic work in the manner of the Book of Daniel, and the Revelations to John in the New Testament. The main part of the Book is a series of seven visions, in which the seer is under the guidance of the archangel Uriel. The unknown author denounces the wickedness of the Roman conquerors, disguised as 'Babylon'. Like Job, he also wrestles with the theological problem of reconciling divine justice and mercy with the evil in the world.

The origin of the work is obscure, and it survives only in translation. It may originally have been written in Hebrew or Aramaic in the first century AD, with additions in Greek by subsequent editors. Its late date may account for the fact that 2 Esdras is the only one of the Apocryphal works not included in the Septuagint, the early Greek Bible. In the Latin (Vulgate) Bible it appears in the appendix as 4 Esdras.

*Tobit* (Tob.): see comments at the end of the story 'The Blindness of Tobit'.

*Judith* (Jdt.): see comments at the end of the story 'Judith and Holofernes'.

*Additions to the Book of Esther* (Ad. Est.): in the Septuagint there were six additional passages written into the Book of Esther, in order to give it a more orthodox and less secular slant than the original Hebrew version.

*The Wisdom of Solomon* (Wis.): this work (simply called The Book of Wisdom in the Latin Bible) purports to be written by King Solomon. It extols Wisdom as the guide for a good and happy life, stresses faith in God and condemns the evils of pagan idolatry. It may have been composed by an Alexandrian Jew late in the first century BC. This work is another example of the Wisdom Literature that includes the biblical Books of Proverbs, Job and Ecclesiastes, and also another Apocryphal work, Ecclesiasticus.

*Ecclesiasticus, or The Wisdom of Jesus the son of Sirach* (Sir.): this important Jewish treatise on Wisdom was written in Hebrew in the Judea of the early second century BC, a decade or more before the Maccabean Revolt. The Hebrew form of the author's name would be Joshua ben Sira. The work is an anthology of short discourses and maxims, designed to reaffirm traditional Jewish values and counteract current trends of assimilation of Hellenist ideas. In 132 BC a Greek translation appeared, with a preface stating that the unnamed translator was the grandson of the author. The Book as a whole survived only in this Greek version. Portions of it in Hebrew have been known since mediaeval times, and their authenticity has been verified by comparison with tiny fragments found among the Dead Sea Scrolls near Qumran.

The Latin word Ecclesiasticus simply means 'The Church Book'. This name dates back to the third century AD, and indicates the importance the early Christian Fathers attached to the work. In the history of Judaism, it is a link between the kind of Wisdom expressed in the Book of Proverbs and the post-biblical thinking of the rabbis.

*Baruch* (Bar.): this prophetic work purports to have been written during the Babylonian exile in the sixth century BC, by Baruch, the faithful disciple and scribe of the prophet Jeremiah. In the Greek and Latin Bibles, it is placed immediately after the Books of Jeremiah and Lamentations. Although it has survived only in the Greek language, analysis of the text indicates that it was originally written in Hebrew, and compiled in the first century BC or the first century AD from several elements of different authorship.

*The Letter of Jeremiah* (Let. Jer.): this work claims to be a copy of a letter sent by the prophet Jeremiah to the Jewish captives taken into exile in Babylonia in 597 BC. This attribution is clearly untenable. In content and style, the Letter is a rhetorical sermon against the evils of idolatry and paganism. It is believed to have been written in the Hellenist period in the third or second century BC. A minute fragment in Greek was found among the Dead Sea Scrolls. In the Greek and Latin Bibles the Letter is printed as a sixth chapter of Baruch, though it is an independent work.

*The Prayer of Azariah and the Song of the Three Young Men* (S. of 3Y): these are among the Septuagint additions to the Book of Daniel, and in the Greek and Latin Bibles are inserted in Chapter 3 of that Book. The three young men were the companions of Daniel at the Babylonian court, who were thrown into the fiery furnace for refusing to worship a golden image. The Prayer was offered to God in the midst of the flames by one of the three, Azariah, whose Babylonian name was Abednego. The Song of the Three Young Men is a hymn of praise to the Lord for preserving them from the fire. These insertions were probably written in the second century BC.

*Susanna* (Sus.): see comments at the end of the story 'Susanna and the Elders'.

*Bel and the Dragon* (Bel): see comments at the end of the story 'Daniel in the Den of Lions'.

*The Prayer of Manasseh* (Man.): Manasseh was the wicked and idolatrous Hebrew king who reigned in Judah from 687 to 642 BC. The Book of Chronicles relates that he was carried off in chains to Babylon, repented of his sins and was restored to Jerusalem. This Apocryphal work is a beautiful, short prayer of penitence, attributed to the king. It probably dates from the second or first century BC. In the Latin Bible, it is excluded from the canon and placed in the appendix after the New Testament.

*The First Book of the Maccabees* (1 Macc.): *The Second Book of the Maccabees* (2 Macc.): see comments at the end of the story 'The Maccabean Revolt'.

## 2

# TALES FROM THE APOCRYPHA

*The Blindness of Tobit*

TOBIT THE SON OF TOBIEL BELONGED to the tribe of Naphtali in the eastern half of the Galilee highlands. It formed part of the northern kingdom of Israel that had seceded after the death of King Solomon in 922 BC and set up its own religious sanctuaries. Tobit claims that as a young man he refused to share in the apostasy of his tribe but remained loyal to the Temple in Jerusalem, in the southern kingdom of Judah. He often travelled to Jerusalem for the traditional festivals, bringing his first-fruits and tithes for the priests and Levites. He did so under the influence of his grandmother Deborah, for he had been left an orphan as a boy. When he grew up he married Anna, a relative. They had a son, Tobias.

*Tobit's Good Deeds* The kingdom of Israel was destroyed by Shalmanezer, king of the Assyrians, in the eighth century BC. Tobit and his family were among those who were carried away into captivity in Assyria. Living in Nineveh the capital, Tobit remained a devout Jew. Unlike his relatives and friends, he strictly maintained the dietary laws. His piety gained him God's favour. He prospered, and became a buyer of provisions for the king. Tobit was known in the community for acts of charity: 'I would give my bread to the hungry and my clothing to the naked; and if I saw one of my people dead and thrown out behind the wall of Nineveh, I would bury him' (Tob. 1:17).

Tobit's work for the king took him on journeys to Media, the kingdom to the east of Assyria. On one such journey, he left ten talents of silver (a very substantial sum) in trust with a kinsman called Gabael, in the Median city of Rages. When King Shalmanezer died and was succeeded by his son Sennacherib, the highways became unsafe and Tobit no longer went to Media.

Tobit's good deeds brought him into trouble with the new ruler. There were still Jews who had fled from their homeland and reached Assyria, only to be seized and put to death by the authorities. Their bodies were deliberately left lying unburied. This was more than the kindly Tobit could bear, so he secretly retrieved the corpses at night and buried them. Someone informed on him and he had to flee for his life, leaving behind his wife and son. All his property was confiscated.

Fifty days later, Sennacherib was assassinated

by two of his sons, who escaped to the mountains. Another son, Esarhaddon, gained the throne. Tobit's nephew Ahikar was appointed the chief official of the kingdom, serving as cupbearer, keeper of the signet, treasurer and head of administration. Tobit was able to return.

*The Afflictions of Tobit and Sarah*

It was the festival of Pentecost (the Feast of Weeks) when the joyful family reunion took place. Seated at the laden table, Tobit sent his son to find one of their poor brethren who could be invited to share the meal. Tobias came back to report that a Jew had been executed by strangling. His body had been thrown into the market place. Tobit rushed off and removed the body to a secure place where it could be kept until sunset. He came back to eat in sorrow. When darkness had fallen he went to bury the corpse. His neighbours derided him saying 'he once ran away, and here he is burying the dead again!' (Tob. 2:8). Returning home from this pious duty, Tobit did not enter his house, since he had been defiled by contact with the dead. Instead, he stretched himself out next to the wall of the courtyard, with his upturned face uncovered.

Fresh droppings from sparrows on the wall fell into Tobit's open eyes, causing a white film to form on them. Tobit's kind heart had brought blindness upon him. He consulted physicians but they were unable to help him. For two years he was maintained by his nephew Ahikar, who was then sent to another part of the empire. His wife Anna kept the household going by doing weaving at home for wages. Once, when she collected her money, her employers added a kid as a gift. Hearing the animal bleating, Tobit jumped to the conclusion she had stolen it and ordered her to take it back. When she denied the charge and chided him, Tobit broke down and wept with self-pity. He prayed to God, asking to die.

That was not the only cry of distress that arose to the Lord on the same day. In Ecbatana, the capital of Media, there lived another kinsman of Tobit whose name was Raguel. His beautiful and virtuous daughter Sarah had already been married seven times. On each occasion the demon Asmodeus, who loved Sarah, had slain the bridegroom before the marriage had been consummated. Sarah's maids taunted her:

Do you not know that you strangle your husbands? You already have had seven and have had no benefit from any of them. Why do you beat us? If they are dead, go with them! May we never see a son or daughter of yours! (Tob. 3:8,9).

The distraught girl thought of hanging herself. She held back because she was the only child of her parents and did not want to cause them pain and disgrace. She prayed to the Lord either to help her or to let her die.

The prayers of Tobit and Sarah reached God at the same time. The angel Raphael was promptly despatched to earth to deal with both problems. He was to restore Tobit's sight, to suppress the demon Asmodeus and to bring about the marriage of Tobias to Sarah.

*The Journey of Tobias*

Believing that he would soon die, Tobit sent for his son and instructed him in his filial duties. He was to give his father a decent burial, take good care of his mother and in due course bury her next to her husband. Tobias was enjoined to carry on the godfearing and charitable traditions of the family. He was to take a wife from among his own people, 'for we are the sons of the prophets' (Tob. 4:12). Tobit requested Tobias to fetch the ten talents of silver left many years before with Gabael in Media. The young man was handed the receipt and was sent to find a travelling companion who knew the way. Tobit undertook to pay the person's wages.

Tobias returned and reported to his father that he had found a fellow-Jew who claimed to know the route well, and had actually lodged with Gabael. When brought before Tobit for further questioning, the man said his name was Azarias (which means 'God helps'), and he was the son of Ananias. Tobit was delighted; Ananias was actually a relative who used to accompany him on his religious journeys to Jerusalem when they were still young men, before the captivity. Azarias was engaged on the spot for a drachma a day plus expenses, with the promise of an addition to his wages if they returned safe and sound. Neither father nor son could guess that they had just hired the angel Raphael.

At the thought of her son's imminent journey, Tobit's wife Anna burst into tears. 'Why have you sent our child away?... Do not add money to money, but consider it rubbish as compared to our child' (Tob. 5:17,18). Tobit soothed her down. Tobias and his companion-guide then set out on their way. The young man's dog trotted along behind them.

Tobit becomes blind. Woodcut from the Holbein Old Testament (1543).

At evening they came to the Tigris river and camped there for the night. Tobias went down to wash himself at the water's edge. A large fish leapt out of the water and attacked him. The angel shouted out to him to grab the fish and haul it up the bank. This he did. Raphael then told him to open the fish and remove its gall, heart and liver for medicinal use. They then cooked and ate the fish. Further along the road to Ecbatana, Tobias asked his companion to explain the uses of the fish's organs. The angel replied that the smoke made by burning the heart and the liver would drive away for good a demon afflicting a human being; while the gall could be used to cure blindness caused by a white film over the eyes.

*The Marriage* When they reached Ecbatana the angel said they would be lodging with Tobias' relative Raguel. He offered to arrange a marriage between Tobias and Raguel's only child Sarah, a beautiful and intelligent girl. He pointed out that, as the only eligible male relative, Tobias was entitled by the law of Moses to marry her, and in due course to receive her inheritance. Her father was an honourable man who would respect Tobias' claim. The angel suggested that he discuss the matter with Raguel right away, so that the wedding could take place when they returned from Rages.

Tobias objected that the demon Asmodeus would surely kill him, as he had done with Sarah's seven previous bridegrooms. But the angel told him not to worry. If he took some live ashes of incense into the bridal chamber, and put the heart and liver of the fish on them so as to make a smoke, the demon would flee and never return. Tobias and his bride should then pray to the Lord who would preserve them. At these words, Tobias' desire for Sarah was kindled and he agreed to all that the angel had proposed.

Raguel welcomed the two men with kindness and offered them hospitality. He politely enquired who they were and from where they had come. He sprang up in great delight when Tobias declared that he was the son of Raguel's relative Tobit. But Raguel, his wife Edna and his daughter were greatly distressed to hear about the blindness of Tobit, whom Raguel described as 'that good and noble man!' (Tob. 7:7).

Prodded by the eager Tobias, the angel broached the question of the marriage. Raguel answered: 'Eat, drink, and be merry: for it is your right to take my child. But let me explain the true situation to you' (Tob. 7:9,10). He then warned him about the demon. To Raguel's surprise, Tobias was quite undeterred by the untimely end of the seven previous bridegrooms. He insisted that the marriage contract be drawn up and signed there and then. That was solemnly done and Sarah given to Tobias with her father's blessing. Only then did they sit down to eat.

Edna prepared the guest room and left her daughter in it, after begging the weeping girl to be brave. When the meal was concluded Tobias was led in to his bride. He immediately made a smoke of the fish's heart and liver, as the angel had instructed him. The jealous demon was driven away by the smell and fled to Egypt (the traditional home of sorcery in the ancient world). Tobias asked Sarah to join him in a prayer of thanks to God, before consummating their marriage:

> Thou madest Adam and gavest
>    him Eve his wife
>       as a helper and support.
> From them the race of mankind
>    has sprung.
> Thou didst say, 'It is not good that
>    the man should be alone;
>       let us make a helper for him like himself.'
>                                      (Tob. 8:6)

During the night Raguel had got up and sadly dug a grave in the garden, so that he could bury his doomed son-in-law without the neighbours knowing about it. A maid sent to peer into the bridal chamber came rushing back to report that the young couple were both well and sleeping soundly. Raguel blessed God and ordered his servants to fill in the grave.

Next morning the joyful Raguel proclaimed a wedding feast that would last fourteen days instead of the customary seven. He took an oath whereby Tobias would remain with them for the fourteen days, and then return to his home with his bride. He was to be endowed immediately with half of Raguel's possessions; the other half would be bequeathed to him on the death of Sarah's parents.

Tobias was concerned lest his parents would start worrying at his long absence. To save time he asked his companion to take two camels and the receipt, and go alone to Rages to collect the money Tobit had left there. The angel reached Gabael in Rages, and was handed Tobit's money-

*The Home-coming*

bags with the seals still intact. Early next morning he set out again for Ecbatana. Gabael went with him to attend the wedding feast.

Back in Nineveh, the blind Tobit and his wife Anna had been counting the days since their son had set out on his journey. When Tobias had failed to return at the expected time, Tobit started fretting. Maybe, he thought, his relative Gabael had died and there was nobody else who could hand over the silver. Anna, however, feared that her son had been killed. She started to mourn for him, and Tobit was unable to console her. When he said to her, 'Be still and stop worrying; he is well,' she flung back at him, 'Be still and stop deceiving me; my child has perished' (Tob. 10:6,7). Torn between grief and hope, she could not eat or sleep, but went and stood every day at the side of the road that her son had taken.

Knowing that his parents would be anxious, Tobias wished to set out for home at the end of the wedding feast. Raguel offered to send a messenger to Tobit, if his daughter and son-in-law would remain a while longer, but Tobias was adamant. Raguel sent them away with his blessing and half his wealth in slaves, cattle and money. He instructed his daughter to honour her parents-in-law as if they were her own parents. To Tobias Edna said, 'See, I am entrusting my daughter to you; do nothing to grieve her' (Tob. 10:12). Their fondest hope now was that they would live to see their grandchildren.

When they reached Nineveh, Sarah stayed behind at the gateway while Tobias and Raphael went ahead, the little dog still trotting at their heels. Anna saw them coming, shouted the news to her husband and ran to meet them. She flung her arms round Tobias and said, 'I have seen you, my child, now I am ready to die' (Tob. 11:9). They both burst into tears.

The blind Tobit groped his way forward and stumbled. His son ran to catch him and immediately sprinkled some of the fish's gall on his father's eyes, as the angel had told him to do. When Tobit rubbed his smarting eyes, the white film came away from the corners and suddenly he could see his son. When the rejoicing had died down, Tobias reported all that had happened on his journey. His father came with him to welcome Sarah at the city gate. Another wedding feast now took place. Among the guests were Tobit's nephew Ahikar from the palace, and Ahikar's own nephew Nadab.

After the festivities were over, Tobit spoke to Tobias about the wages due to his companion and the extra reward he had been promised. Tobias listed all that Azarias had done for them and suggested that he should be given half of the wealth Tobias had brought back with him. Tobit readily agreed. When they informed the companion of this decision, he asked to see them privately. He then disclosed his identity: 'I am Raphael, one of the seven holy angels who present the prayers of the saints and enter into the presence of the glory of the Holy One' (Tob. 12:15). He explained that God had sent him to heal both Tobit and Sarah. Tobit and Tobias threw themselves down in alarm before the angel, who reassured them that they had nothing to fear. His work was done and he was ascending back to heaven. They should now give thanks to God and write down in a book everything that had happened. Tobit offered up a hymn of rejoicing.

Tobit was fifty-eight years old when he lost his sight, and regained it eight years later. He continued his pious and charitable way of life and lived to the ripe old age of one hundred and fifty-eight. Before he died, he told Tobias to leave Nineveh and settle in Media, since Nineveh would be destroyed, as foretold by the prophet Jonah. Tobit himself prophesied that Jerusalem would also be destroyed and its people scattered, but the Jews would one day be restored to their own country and the Temple rebuilt.

When his parents died, Tobias gave them splendid funerals. He then returned with his wife and sons to his parents-in-law at Ecbatana in Media, where he lived in honour and respect until the age of one hundred and twenty-seven. The news of the fall of Nineveh reached him before he died.

With superb narrative skill the unknown author of Tobit blended simple Jewish piety, romance, family sentiment and oriental folk-magic into a tale that has been popular over twenty centuries.

*Comments on the Book of Tobit*

The origin of the work is blurred. Scholarly conjecture ranges from the Persia of the fourth century BC to the Jerusalem or Alexandria of the second century BC. It is even uncertain whether it was originally written in Hebrew or Aramaic; fragments in both languages were found among the Dead Sea Scrolls.

The story is introduced with a biblical background that would be familiar to its Jewish readers. The tribe of Naphtali to which Tobit's family belonged was indeed settled in the eastern Galilee highlands. It was one of the northern tribes that broke away after the death of Solomon and set up the kingdom of Israel. As Tobit indicates, the northerners were accused of religious heresy by the scriptural writers in Jerusalem. The northern kingdom lasted just two centuries before it was destroyed by an Assyrian army. Many of its inhabitants were carried away into exile, some to Assyria, others to 'the cities of the Medes'. (The exiles disappeared from history, and many legends have since sprung up about the where-abouts of the 'Lost Ten Tribes'.) Media was the country to the east of Assyria. Its capital was Ecbatana, where Raguel lived in the story, and its other main city was Rages (or Ragai), the home of Tobit's other kinsman Gabael. This historical and geographical framework gives the story of Tobit a realistic atmosphere.

At the same time, there are factual in-accuracies. The chronology of the three Assyrian monarchs who are mentioned, is muddled. Shalmanezer V laid siege to Samaria, the capital of Israel, but died before it fell, and was succeeded by his son Sargon II. Shalmanezer could not, therefore, have been the king whom Tobit served while in captivity. Sennacherib was Shalmanezer's grandson, not his son; and he reigned not 'fifty days' but twenty-four years, before his son Esarhaddon succeeded him. Nineveh was not destroyed by Nebuchadnezzar and Ahasuerus, as stated at the end of the Book of Tobit. The angel Raphael could not have made an overnight journey on camel-back from Ecbatana to Rages and back; it took the soldiers of Alexander the Great eleven days of forced marches from one city to the other. But these discrepancies are of little consequence if one accepts the Book of Tobit as an imaginary story, not an historical work – any more than one need believe in the demon-lover Asmodeus or the magical properties of the fish organs.

Tobit is above all a morality tale. Its purpose is didactic, to show that goodness and belief in God are rewarded. That was an important message in the Jewish world at a time when it had no national independence and its ancestral faith was being eroded by Hellenist influence. The ethical teaching of the book is epitomized in Tobit's discourse to his son in Chapter 4. He underlines the virtues of piety, upright living, charity to the needy, industry, self-discipline and an attentive ear to the counsels of the wise. This practical morality has close affinities with the Book of Proverbs.

The most notable sentence in this passage is an early statement of what later came to be known as the Golden Rule: 'And what you hate, do not do to any one' (Tob. 4:15). The classical expression of this precept was that of the great Jewish sage Hillel, at the end of the first century BC. Asked by a heathen proselyte to teach him the entire Torah (the Law) while standing on one foot, Hillel replied: 'What is hateful to you, do not do unto your neighbour; this is the entire Torah, all the rest is commentary.' Hillel's words were echoed in the New Testament in the Gospel according to Matthew: 'So whatever you wish that men would do to you, do so to them; for this is the law and the prophets' (Mt. 7:12).

The Reformation in the sixteenth century AD revived esteem for the literary quality of the Book of Tobit. 'Is it history?' wrote Martin Luther, 'Then is it a holy history. Is it fiction? Then is it a truly beautiful, wholesome and profitable fiction, the performance of a gifted poet.'

The story stresses the legal right of Tobias to marry Sarah, a claim acknowledged by her father. Under the Mosaic Law, a childless widow had to be married to the nearest eligible male relative of her husband – an institution known as 'levirate marriage'. Examples in the Old Testament are Tamar and Judah, and Ruth and Boaz.

For an angel to appear in human form on an assignment from the Lord was not uncommon in the earlier Old Testament period. For instance, there were the three strangers who came to Abraham to announce that the barren Sarah would have a child; the two that went to Lot to warn him that Sodom would be destroyed; the angel that intervened when Abraham was about to sacrifice Isaac; the angel with the drawn sword that barred the passage of Balaam and was at first seen only by his ass; and the mysterious being with whom Jacob wrestled at the ford of Jabbok. The Hebrew word for an angel, *malach*, means a messenger.

During the classical period of prophecy – the period of the divided monarchy – God made his will known through the prophets, not through angels. But in post-biblical Judaism the concept of celestial beings surrounding and serving the

Lord was revived and developed, to a large extent under the influence of Babylonian, Persian and Hellenist pagan beliefs. As is mentioned in the Book of Tobit, there was a group of seven archangels who could 'enter into the presence of the glory of the Holy One'. They formed in the heavenly court a kind of inner cabinet that performed various functions, such as bringing the prayers of pious persons before the Almighty, or carrying out special missions for him. In addition to Raphael, the others were Uriel, Raguel, Michael, Sariel, Gabriel and Jeremiel. The 'el' at the end of each name means God.

The counterpart to belief in angels was belief in demons, also developed in post-biblical Judaism. Asmodeus (in Hebrew Ashmedai) was regarded as the king of the demons. His name means 'the destroyer'. In later Jewish folklore Asmodeus lost his lethal powers and turned into a rather droll and mischievous spirit, the butt or 'fall guy' of many a fireside tale.

The Book of Tobit refers in three places to Ahikar, a powerful court official who is presented in the story as Tobit's nephew, the son of his brother Anael and therefore one of the community in Nineveh formed by Jewish captives from Israel. Actually Ahikar the Wise was the hero of a work that may have been of Aramean origin, and had a wide circulation in the ancient Near East. Versions of it have survived in several of the languages in the region. A copy in Aramaic was found among the papyrus scrolls dating from the fifth century BC and belonging to the ancient Jewish community at Elephantine on the Upper Nile (near the present Aswan Dam). The original Ahikar was a court official who was not a Jew and had no specific association with Jews. He adopted and reared a youth called Nadab, who made trouble for his foster-father and landed up in jail. Ahikar admonished Nadab in a series of epigrammatic sayings typical of Near Eastern Wisdom Literature, and resembling passages in the Book of Proverbs. In speaking to his son Tobias before his own death, Tobit recalls the conflict between Ahikar and Nadab to show that in the end the righteous triumph and the wicked perish.

## The Three Young Guardsmen

THE FIRST BOOK OF ESDRAS RECOUNTS HOW King Darius of Persia gave a great banquet in his palace, attended by all the important men who served him throughout the empire, 'from India to Ethiopia'. When everyone had eaten and drunk their fill, the guests departed and the king retired to his bedchamber to sleep.

The three young soldiers of the royal bodyguard who were posted outside the chamber thought up a contest which they hoped would bring one of them fame and fortune. (The idea was no doubt born out of the boredom that afflicts all soldiers on peacetime guard duty.) Each was to give his own answer to the quiz question: what was the strongest thing in life? They reckoned that the one who, in the king's opinion, gave the wisest answer would be richly rewarded. They imagined the reward in glowing terms: 'He shall be clothed in purple, and drink from gold cups, and sleep on a gold bed, and have a chariot with gold bridles, and a turban of fine linen, and a necklace about his neck; and because of his wisdom he shall sit next to Darius and shall be called kinsman of Darius'. (1 Esd. 3:6–7)

Each wrote down and sealed his answer. They tiptoed into the chamber and slipped the answers under the pillow of the sleeping king. When he awoke, they told him what they had done. Darius was greatly entertained by the whole idea. He read the answers, then called together the entire court in the great council chamber, to hear each of the young guardsmen defend his opinion.

The first one had written that wine was strongest. He argued before the court that drink was the great leveller, without respect for anyone. 'It makes equal the mind of the king and the orphan, of the slave and the free, of the poor and the rich' (1 Esd. 3:19). Under the influence of wine men felt merry and rich and forgot their sorrows and their debts. It also made them quarrelsome, and ready to fight even their friends and brothers. When they were sober again, they could not remember what they had done while drunk. The guardsman ended with a rhetorical flourish: 'Gentlemen, is not wine the strongest, since it forces men to do these things?' (1 Esd. 3:24)

The second young bodyguard defended the proposition that the king was strongest. He was the lord and master of all his subjects, who had to obey him blindly. At his command they went out to make war, to kill and be killed. If they were victorious, all the spoils were brought to the king. Every farmer had to hand over to him a share of the harvest, and all had to pay him taxes. Whenever he reclined, ate, drank or slept, others had to attend on him and keep watch around him, instead of going about their own affairs. 'Gentlemen, why is not the king the strongest, since he is to be obeyed in this fashion? (1 Esd. 4:12)

The third youth, identified as Zerubbabel, had written down a double answer: 'Women are strongest, but truth is victor over all things' (1 Esd. 3:12). The king was great, he conceded, and wine was potent. But all men were borne and brought up by women – including kings, as well as the farmers who planted the vineyards from which came the wine. Men busied themselves gaining glory and wealth till they saw a beautiful woman. Then they would stare at her with open mouth and forget about their other desires. Why did a man cling to his wife rather than to his parents or his country? The answer was that women ruled over men. For the sake of a woman he loved a man would commit heroic deeds, face dangers, steal and sin. With great audacity, the young man pointed to the king as an example of man's abject servitude to a woman's charms. Here was a monarch feared in every land:

> Yet I have seen him with Apame, the king's concubine, the daughter of the illustrious Bartacus; she would sit at the king's right hand and take the crown from the king's head and put it on her own, and slap the king with her left hand. At this the king would gaze at her with mouth agape. If she smiles at him, he laughs; if she loses her temper with him, he flatters her, that she may be reconciled to him.
> (1 Esd. 4:29–31)

While the king and his courtiers looked at each other, embarrassed by such frankness, the young man deftly switched to the second part of his answer. He equated truth with righteousness and the will of God. Wine, the king, women – all these were unrighteous and would perish, but truth would endure forever. 'To her belongs the strength and the kingship and the power and the majesty of all the ages. Blessed be the God of truth!' (1 Esd. 4:40) Carried away, the audience shouted back, 'Great is truth, and strongest of all!' (1 Esd. 4:41)

The king rose and kissed the young man, commended him for his wisdom, and seated him next to the throne. When asked to state what he wished as a reward, Zerubbabel reminded Darius of the vow made by him to rebuild Jerusalem and the Temple, and to restore all the sacred vessels taken as loot by the Babylonians. Darius promptly wrote letters instructing his treasurers and provincial governors to give generous aid to the enterprise, and to honour the privileges he conferred on the returning Jews. There was general rejoicing when Zerubbabel went to Babylon with the royal letters and told his fellow-Jews there what had happened. He then recruited heads of clans and families to set out with him for Jerusalem.

*Comments on the Story* The First Book of Esdras was a rewritten Greek version of parts of the Books of Chronicles and Nehemiah and the whole of the Book of Ezra. Its probable date is the second century BC. In the Latin Bible, it is not included in the canon but relegated to the appendix with the title of The Third Book of Esdras.

The only well-known passage in 1 Esdras is the story of the three young guardsmen. It does not appear at all in the biblical books of Ezra and Nehemiah, but is based on a popular folk-tale. In its original form the story dealt only with the relative strength of kings, wine and women. The supreme power of truth, as the equivalent of righteousness, was a later insertion. The response of the audience in the Vulgate text of 1 Esdras became a famous Latin proverb: *Magna est veritas et prevalet* ('Great is truth, and it prevails').

The unknown author of 1 Esdras fitted the tale into the context of his work by giving the third young guardsman the identity of Zerubbabel, who became governor of the community of returnees in Jerusalem, near the end of the sixth century BC. In the story, the major credit for authorizing and encouraging the Return of the Jews from Babylonian exile is transferred from Cyrus the Great (559–529 BC) to Darius the Great (522–486 BC). Darius did indeed reconfirm the earlier decree by Cyrus, and ruled against those of his officials who objected to the rebuilding of the Temple. But the account in 1 Esdras of the support he gave Zerubbabel as a reward for winning a debating contest is clearly fictional.

## Judith and Holofernes

'YOU ARE THE EXALTATION OF JERUSALEM, YOU are the great glory of Israel, you are the great pride of our nation!' (Jdt. 15:9) This lavish praise was given to Judith, the lovely Jewish woman whose bold and singlehanded act saved her people from destruction by a mighty Assyrian army led by Holofernes the general.

*The Invasion*    Nebuchadnezzar, king of Assyria, waged an unsuccessful war against King Arphaxad of Media, Assyria's neighbour to the east. Other adjacent kingdoms sided with Media. Nebuchadnezzar sent envoys to the rulers in the western part of the Near East region, from Cilicia in Asia Minor through Syria and Judea to Egypt, demanding that they come to his assistance. None of them responded. They regarded Assyria as isolated and did not want to get involved in its struggle. The angry Nebuchadnezzar swore by his throne and his kingdom that he would take revenge on them for turning their backs on him when he needed them.

Five years later Nebuchadnezzar defeated Media, captured and sacked its capital city Ecbatana, and struck down King Arphaxad with a spear when he captured him in the mountains.

Nebuchadnezzar now ordered his commander-in-chief, Holofernes, to lead an army on a punitive expedition against the nations in the west. The king threatened to inflict a terrible fate on them:

> I am coming against them in my anger, and will cover the whole face of the earth with the feet of my armies, and will hand them over to be plundered by my troops, till their wounded shall fill their valleys, and every brook and river shall be filled with their dead, and overflow; and I will lead them away captive to the ends of the whole earth. (Jdt. 2:7–9)

The general's instructions were to slaughter and plunder any people that resisted him; those countries that capitulated were to be occupied, pending the king's decision about their disposal.

Holofernes assembled a huge army. It included 120,000 infantry, 12,000 mounted archers, divisions of chariot troops, herds of camels, asses and mules for transport, and innumerable oxen, goats and sheep for provisions. The camp followers were 'a mixed crowd like a swarm of locusts' (Jdt. 2:20).

Holofernes first marched to Cilicia, which he devastated. He then swung south, wiping out Arabian nomad tribes along the way. His troops overran the fertile plain of Damascus during the wheat harvest, burning and destroying towns,

fields and flocks. Panic spread through the area, and all the cities of the maritime plain rushed to pledge their allegiance to Nebuchadnezzar. Holofernes placed garrisons in them, and demanded that they demolish their own shrines and worship Nebuchadnezzar as their sole god.

The Assyrian army now reached the eastern end of the valley of Jezreel and pitched camp in the vicinity of Beth-shan, facing the hill terrain of Samaria. Here they rested for a month, and organized their lines of supply.

Not long before this invasion, the Jews had    *The Siege* returned to their homeland from exile in Babylonia and rebuilt the city of Jerusalem and the holy Temple. The nation was led by the high priest Joakim, assisted by the senate in Jerusalem. Terrified of destruction by the Assyrian army, Joakim sent out orders that the narrow passes from the valley of Jezreel into the hill country should be guarded, the mountain villages fortified, and food stored for a siege. Having decided to resist, the leaders in Jerusalem fasted and prayed at the Temple for several days, seeking the help of the Lord.

Holofernes was taken aback at reports that the small Jewish hill-nation was preparing to defend itself against the mighty force he commanded. Attached to his army were auxiliary contingents from other local peoples who had submitted to him, such as Moab and Ammon in Trans-jordan and the Phoenicians on the coast. He summoned their commanders and interrogated them about this puny Jewish adversary:

> Tell me, you Canaanites, what people is this that lives in the hill country? What cities do they inhabit? How large is their army, and in what does their power or strength consist? Who rules over them as king, leading their army? And why have they alone, of all who live in the west, refused to come out and meet me? (Jdt. 5:3–4)

The leader of the Ammonite auxiliaries, whose name was Achior, took it upon himself to reply. He gave a brief outline of the history of the Jewish people, from their origin in Mesopotamia to their migration to Canaan, the sojourn in Egypt, the Exodus and the Conquest, the destruction of their state and Temple, and their return from exile. Achior concluded that the Hebrews had suffered defeat and captivity only when they had sinned against their God; as long as they remained loyal to their faith, their God would protect them and an attack upon them would fail ignominiously.

The others present, both the Assyrian officers and the auxiliary commanders, were outraged at Achior's opinion and demanded that he be put to death. They insisted that there was no reason to be afraid of the Israelites, 'a people with no strength or power for making war' (Jdt. 5:23). Holofernes berated Achior as a hireling of the Jews. What other god, he asked, could measure up to Nebuchadnezzar? He would wipe out the Jews and their god would be powerless to help them. Their mountains would be drenched with blood and their fields filled with corpses. As for Achior, he would be taken to one of the Israelite towns blocking the passes, and would share its fate when the Assyrians took it. Until that day came Achior would not again see the face of Holofernes.

The key Israelite town in the area was Bethulia. (It has not been identified, and may be an indirect reference to Nablus.) Holofernes' slaves took Achior from the camp as far as the spring in the valley below the town. Its defenders saw them approaching and attacked them with slings, until they took shelter behind a ridge. They left Achior tied up on the ground and returned to their camp. The Ammonite was taken into the city and brought before its chief magistrate Uzziah, and his two colleagues Chabris and Charmis. A crowd of citizens collected. When he had related what had taken place at Holofernes' council, Achior was warmly welcomed. Uzziah took him to his home, and gave a banquet in his honour. All that night the leaders of the town prayed to God for help.

The Assyrian army moved forward into the hills and encamped in the valley below Bethulia. The next day Holofernes made a show of strength by parading his cavalry forces in full view of the city. He also inspected the nearby springs that supplied the city's water, and placed military guards over them.

Some of the auxiliary chiefs came to him with their own plan to reduce the city without fighting. They pointed out that with its water supply cut it would be driven by thirst to surrender. The auxiliary forces could be stationed in the hills round Bethulia to block escape routes. The general accepted this strategy and settled down to await results.

It was the hot, rainless summer season. After more than a month had gone by the cisterns in Bethulia were running dry and strict water rationing was in force. 'Their children lost heart, and the women and young men fainted from thirst and fell down in the streets of the city and in the passages through the gates; there was no strength left in them any longer' (Jdt. 7:22). A despairing crowd gathered before Uzziah and his fellow magistrates, and demanded that they surrender. It was better, they shouted, to live as captives than to die of thirst. Uzziah swore to them that if help did not come from God in the next five days, he would hand over the city to the enemy.

In Bethulia lived the widow Judith, the *Judith Goes* daughter of Merari. More than three years earlier *to Holofernes* her husband Manasseh had died of sunstroke, incurred while he was overseeing the workers binding the sheaves of barley in his fields. Judith carried on with the farming. Though young, attractive and well-to-do she did not marry again, but lived a life of rigorous piety. She wore only her widow's garments, occupied a shelter on the flat roof of the house, and frequently prayed and fasted.

Judith was greatly distressed when she heard about the undertaking given by Uzziah. She sent her maid to invite the three magistrates to come and see her. When they arrived, she took them to task for presuming to give God a deadline of five days to come to their rescue. How could God be put to the test in this fashion? God was putting *them* to the test, as he had done with their forefathers. Since the people had remained true to their faith, she was confident they had nothing to fear. Moreover, if Bethulia surrendered the whole of Judea would be lost, the Temple would be destroyed, and they would become a nation of despised slaves.

Uzziah replied sadly that everything she said was true and wise, but under the pressure of thirst and despair the people had compelled the town's leaders to take an oath they could not break. Everyone knew what a devout woman Judith was; he could only beg her to pray that rain would fall before the five days were up.

Judith declared that she had a plan of her own to save the city. She would not tell them what it was. All she required of them was to meet her at the city gate that night, and to let her go out with her maid.

When the magistrates had left her, Judith flung herself on the floor of her roof shelter and fervently prayed to God to give her strength for what she had to do. Since she was but a woman and a widow, she asked God to strike down the arrogant foe by means of 'the deceit of my lips'. She recalled the precedent of her ancestor Simeon the son of Jacob, who had misled the men of Shechem in order to take revenge on them for the rape of his sister Dinah.

Having invoked a divine blessing for her venture, Judith went down into the house from the rooftop. With the help of her maid she bathed and perfumed herself and put on the pretty clothes, the jewellery and the bright headdress that had been stored away since her husband's death. She took a skin of wine, a flask of oil, a closed bag filled with roasted grain, dried figs and fine bread, and her cooking and eating utensils. All these were given to her maid to carry, and they set out for the city gate. The three magistrates waiting for her were astonished at the dazzling beauty of the woman they had seen only that morning in her drab widow's sackcloth. They ordered the guards to open the gate, and watched anxiously while the two women walked down the valley towards the enemy camp until they disappeared into the darkness.

They were soon intercepted and questioned by an Assyrian patrol. Judith told them she was a Hebrew woman who had escaped from the doomed city. She had come to seek out their general Holofernes and show him a way to take all the hill country without losing a single man. The two were sent to the general's tent under armed escort. Soon the whole camp was buzzing with talk at the sudden advent of this beautiful and well-dressed woman. The admiring soldiers said to each other: 'Who can despise these people, who have women like this among them?' (Jdt. 10:19)

Holofernes was resting on his bed, under a splendid purple and gold canopy adorned with gems. (It may have served as protection against flies and mosquitoes.) He rose and came forward to greet his beguiling visitor, reassuring her that she would be safe and well treated. Would she explain to him, he asked, why she had come?

Judith heaped lavish praise on King Nebuchadnezzar, and on the wisdom and ability of his great general Holofernes. If he would accept her humble advice God's purpose would be served through him, as well as his own. What Achior the Ammonite had told him about the Hebrew nation was the truth. They could not be subdued by military force, unless they sinned against God. This they were now about to do, thereby arousing God's anger against them. Under the stress of hunger, the citizens of Bethulia had sent to the senate in Jerusalem for permission to eat the first-fruits and the tithes which under the Mosaic Law had to be preserved for the Temple priesthood. She, Judith, was a religious woman. God had sent her to ensure that through the Assyrians the people of the town would be punished when they transgressed the law. She would go outside the camp every evening to pray in the valley, and God would tell her when her people had sinned. She would then pass the word to Holofernes. From that moment he would be able to go in and destroy the city. After that she would lead him through the middle of Judea to Jerusalem, and set him upon the throne there, 'and not a dog will so much as open its mouth to growl at you' (Jdt. 11:19).

The general and his staff were delighted at her words. Holofernes commended her for her beauty and wisdom, and promised her a glowing future in the palace of his monarch. He ordered his slaves to serve her a meal from his own choice food and wine, and on his silver dishes. Judith declined, explaining that by her ritual laws she could eat only the provisions she had brought with her. She slept until midnight in a separate tent in Holofernes' quarters, then rose and was given permission to leave the camp with her maid in order to pray.

Judith was entrusted to the care of Bagoas, the eunuch in charge of the general's personal affairs. Each night she and her maid left the camp to pray in the valley and to wash themselves in the spring. The guards had been ordered not to hinder them, which was what Judith had intended.

*The Feast*

On the fourth evening after her arrival, Holofernes gave a feast in his tent for his personal staff. Bagoas was sent to bring Judith to the party. Holofernes remarked to Bagoas that it would be a disgrace to let such a woman go without first winning her favours. The eunuch advised Judith not to be bashful but to enjoy herself, and to behave like the Assyrian women did at Nebuchadnezzar's palace. Judith pretended to be enthusiastic at the invitation, and eager to please the general. She decked herself out in all her finery. Holofernes had been infatuated with Judith from the first moment he had seen her. Gazing at her stretched out before him on soft fleeces, he was carried away by desire for her and drank more wine than he had ever done before.

When it grew late, Bagoas sent all the servants to bed and closed the tent door from outside, leaving Judith alone with his master. By this time Holofernes was lying on the bed in a drunken stupor. She took down his sword that was hanging on the bedpost above his head, grabbed hold of his hair and cried out, 'Give me strength this day, O Lord God of Israel!' (Jdt. 13:7) At this, she struck his neck twice with all her force, cut off his head and rolled the body off the bed.

Judith had instructed her maid to wait outside the tent door with the food-bag. The head of Holofernes was quickly put in the bag, together with the canopy torn down from the bed; the two women walked out of the camp. None of the guards took any particular notice of them, since they appeared to be on their way to pray in the valley as usual. They continued up the hill to Bethulia. As they approached the gate, Judith called out to the sentries to open it and let them in.

An excited crowd quickly gathered in the square. The magistrates were fetched from their homes. By the light of a fire Judith displayed the head of Holofernes. In ringing tones she declared that her face had lured him to his destruction, but her honour had not been defiled. The astonished crowd bowed down and gave praise to God. On behalf of the whole city Uzziah expressed fervent thanks to the woman who had risked her life for her country.

At Judith's request, Achior the Ammonite was brought from Uzziah's house to confirm the identity of the severed head. He took one look at it and fainted. (Ironically, Holofernes had sworn that Achior would not see his face again until the city perished.) When he came round, Judith gave an account of all that had happened since she had left for the Assyrian camp. Overwhelmed by what God had enabled her to do, Achior announced that he wanted to adopt the Jewish faith and be circumcised. The head of Holofernes was stuck upon the parapet of the city wall.

*The Victory*  Judith advised the two leaders how her deed could be exploited to rout the Assyrian army. They accepted and carried out her proposal. At sunrise the armed defenders mustered in the open ground in front of the gate, with their commander at the head, as if they were about to advance against the Assyrian camp. The report from the Assyrian sentries on this hostile concentration was immediately conveyed to senior officers. They rushed to the tent of their general to inform him, and receive his orders. They said to Bagoas, 'Wake up our lord, for the slaves have been so bold as to come down against us to give battle' (Jdt. 14:13).

Bagoas discreetly called out at the door of the tent, believing that his master was in bed with Judith. When he could get no response, he went in and found the headless corpse of Holofernes lying on the floor. When he found Judith's tent empty, he rushed through the camp screaming that the Hebrew woman had tricked and disgraced them.

Soon the whole camp was in an uproar, and panic swept through it like wildfire. The soldiers fled across the hills by every path, pursued by the men of Bethulia. The Ammonite, Moabite and Edomite auxiliaries stationed on the high ground around the town also ran away. Uzziah sent messengers to other Israelite towns in the area and their men joined in the chase. As the Assyrians streamed eastward across the Jordan, they were harried from both flanks by the Israelites in Galilee to the north and in Gilead to the south. Great numbers of them were slaughtered, and a vast amount of booty collected. All those who had joined in the rout shared in the plunder of the abandoned Syrian camp.

As her personal reward, Judith was given the tent of Holofernes and all its contents, including its rich furniture and silver dishes. She had these possessions loaded onto mule-carts. The high priest Joakim and the members of the senate came from Jerusalem to visit the scene of the victory and to bring their greetings in person to Judith. She led the women in a dance of triumph, with garlands of olive leaves on their heads. Judith sang a hymn of thanksgiving to the Lord, in which the dramatic events were described as if by Judea personified:

> The Assyrian came down from the
>      mountains of the north;
>   he came with myriads of his
>      warriors;
>     their multitude blocked up the valleys,
>        their cavalry covered the hills.

He boasted that he would burn up my
territory,
and kill my young men with the sword,
and dash my infants to the ground
and seize my children as prey
and take my virgins as booty.
But the Lord Almighty has foiled them
by the hand of a woman.

(Jdt. 16:4–6)

The song ended in an exultant curse on all the
enemies of the Hebrew nation:

For every sacrifice as a fragrant offering is a small thing,
and all fat for burnt offerings to thee
is a very little thing,
but he who fears the Lord shall be
great for ever.
Woe to the nations that rise up against
my people!
The Lord Almighty will take vengeance
on them in the day of judgement;
fire and worms he will give to their flesh;
they shall weep in pain for ever.

(Jdt. 16:16,17)

Judith and her fellow-citizens went in procession from Bethulia to the Temple in
Jerusalem, to offer sacrifices and gifts. In the
Temple, Judith dedicated to God all Holofernes'
valuables she had been given, and also the
glittering canopy she had carried away with the
severed head. The celebrations in Jerusalem
lasted for three months.

Judith returned to her home in Bethulia as a
national heroine. She rejected many offers of
marriage, went back to the quiet life of a widow,
and continued to run the farm. The devoted
slave-maid who had shared her dangerous
mission was set free.

Judith lived to the ripe old age of one hundred
and five and was buried in the tomb of her
husband Manasseh. She was mourned by the
whole country for the traditional seven days.
During her lifetime, and for a long while after,
Judea was not again threatened by a foreign foe.

The historical background outlined in the
work is very confused, and attempts to relate it to
actual events have been unconvincing.

Nebuchadnezzar was not king of Assyria. His
father founded the neo-Babylonian kingdom and
with Media as an ally brought about the downfall

of the Assyrian empires with the capture of its
capital Nineveh, in 612 BC. Nebuchadnezzar
succeeded to the Babylonian throne in 605 BC,
and soon made himself the new master of the
Near East. His troops sacked Jerusalem in 587 BC,
bringing the kingdom of Judah to an end.

*Comments on the Book of Judith*

Holofernes, the main character in the story
next to Judith herself, seems to be a composite
figure. There was a Persian general of that name
who led a military expedition westward in the
reign of Artaxerxes III (358–338 BC). An account
of it is given in the works of the Roman historian
Diodorus Siculus, in the first century BC. Some
scholars have suggested that this fourth-century
BC campaign prompted the story of Judith. But
there is no record that the Persian Holofernes
marched southward to Judea, which was at that
time an obscure and docile province of the
Persian empire. In the middle of the second
century BC another Holofernes became king of
Cappadocia, a small country in Asia Minor that
had friendly contacts with Judea and did not
come into conflict with it.

There never was a high priest in Jerusalem
called Joakim. The name may have been derived
from the Jehoiachim who reigned in Jerusalem as
king of Judah from 609–598 BC. He rebelled
against his Babylonian overlord and died while
Nebuchadnezzar, at the head of an army, was on
his way to occupy Jerusalem.

Writing a work of fiction with a moral purpose,
the unknown author no doubt felt free to use the
names of historical personages in the imaginary
context of his story. This view is borne out by the
symbolic name given to the heroine. Judith
simply means a woman of Judah (in Latin,
Judea); in its wider sense, it could mean any
Jewess, not necessarily one in Judea.

It cannot be said with any certainty when the
work was written. The events in it are supposed
to have taken place some time after the return
from the Babylonian exile. The Judea of Judith's
time is described as governed from Jerusalem by
a high priest and a senate. This would fit in with
the Hasmonean period in the second half of the
second century BC, after the Maccabean Revolt.
Between 160 BC and 104 BC Jonathan and Simeon,
brothers of Judas Maccabeus, and Simeon's son
John Hyrcanus, each ruled Judea with the title of
high priest. They were assisted by a Great
Assembly, a body that could correspond to the
'senate' in the Judith story.

The Hasmonean period had a turbulent background. Judea was struggling to survive as an independent entity as the Seleucid empire disintegrated and Roman power pushed into the Near East. Assuming that the story of Judith was written in Judea during this period, its blend of religious and patriotic fervour would have been an appropriate message for the time.

The stirring story with its well-constructed plot, and the scene of high drama in Holofernes' tent, has been reflected in the arts more than any other work in the Apocryphal literature. From the Middle Ages to the present it has produced a notable list of paintings, plays, operas and oratorios.

## Susanna and the Elders

JOAKIM WAS A JEW WHO LIVED IN BABYLON during the Exile in the sixth century BC. He married Susanna the daughter of Hilkiah, a very beautiful and devout young woman, brought up in a religious household. Joakim was the wealthy and respected leader of the community, and his fellow-Jews used to gather in his spacious garden. Among them were two elders who had been appointed judges; at times legal disputes were brought to them at Joakim's house. Both these elderly men became madly infatuated with Susanna, so that 'they perverted their minds and turned away their eyes from looking to Heaven or remembering righteous judgments' (Sus. 1:9). Each was unaware of the other's desire. One day they went off from Joakim's house in different directions, pretending they were going home for lunch. When each sneaked back to the garden in the hope of spying on Susanna, they were embarrassed to meet face to face. They confessed their purpose to each other and decided they would together seek an opportune time to seduce her.

On a hot day, after all the visitors had left, Susanna decided to bathe in the garden. She sent her maids to bring her soap and oil from the house. The two elders had hidden themselves in the garden. As soon as the maids had left they came up to Susanna and said, 'Look, the garden doors are shut, no one sees us, and we are in love with you; so give your consent, and lie with us' (Sus. 1:20). They threatened that if she refused they would accuse her of having secretly met a young lover in the garden.

Poor Susanna wept in her distress. Whatever she did would expose her to the risk of a shameful death. She decided that rather than commit a sin she would expose the elders, even if that would afterwards leave her at their mercy. She shouted for help, with the elders trying to shout her down. One of them quickly opened the garden door to account for their entry. When the maid rushed back from the house, they were shocked at the story of the lover the elders told, since no breath of scandal had ever touched their mistress.

Next day all the leading members of the community came together at Joakim's house to hear the accusation formally presented against Susanna. She came in heavily veiled, surrounded by her children, her parents and her relatives. The two elders insisted that she remove the veil 'that they might feast upon her beauty' (Sus. 1:32). They solemnly placed their hands upon her head and repeated their story in public. They were walking alone in the garden, they said, when they saw Susanna come in with her two maids. She shut the garden doors and sent the maids away. A young man then emerged from hiding and made love to her. The two elders rushed up and seized the man, but he was too strong for them. He broke away and escaped from the garden. Susanna had refused to tell them who he was.

Nobody doubted the evidence of two such reputable elders and judges. The assembly condemned Susanna to death for adultery. She cried out to the Lord that she was innocent and that the two men had borne false witness against her. The Lord heard her appeal. As she was being led off to die, God inspired a young man called Daniel to raise his voice in protest. He called out that he would not stand by and have an innocent woman's blood on his head. Everybody turned round to him and asked what he meant. He declared that she had been condemned without a proper trial and a genuine effort to find out the truth; the evidence of her accusers was false and the case had to be reopened. The crowd hurriedly reassembled and the community leaders invited Daniel to join them and state his case.

Daniel requested that he be allowed to question each of the two accusers separately, out of earshot of the other. Confronting the first one, he immediately attacked his character and credibility. Daniel bluntly charged him with abusing his office by 'pronouncing unjust

Daniel in the Lions' Den, with the prophet Habakkuk, carried by an angel, bringing him food. Scene on a bronze Italian church door, dated 1076.

judgments, condemning the innocent and letting the guilty go free' (Sus. 1:53). Daniel then put a direct question to the shaken witness: under what kind of tree had Susanna sinned with the young man. Under a clove tree, said the elder. When the second elder was brought in, he was also given rough treatment by Daniel, who charged him with habitually intimidating and seducing young women until the virtuous Susanna had stood up to him. When the same direct question was flung at this witness, he affirmed that the tree had been a yew, thereby contradicting the first one. With a word play on the names of the trees, Daniel declared that the first elder would be cloven, and the second hewn, by the angel of the Lord.

By now it was clear to the assembly that the two elders had been lying. In accordance with the Mosaic Code, they were condemned to suffer the exact penalty their perjury would have brought down on Susanna, and they were put to death.

Susanna's husband and family gave praise to the Lord for having vindicated her honour. 'And from that day onward Daniel had a great reputation among the people' (Sus. 1:64).

*Comments on the Book of Susanna*

The story was probably written in the late second or early first century BC, and reflects the moralistic tone of Jewish writings at that time. Virtue and piety triumph and the wicked meet their deserts.

A special point is made of the right of an accused person to a proper trial. That was a matter stressed by the Pharisaic trend in the Judea of that period. To quote the German-Jewish historian Graetz, in his classical *History of the Jews*:

> Witnesses in the law courts were no longer to be questioned merely upon the place where, and the time when they had seen a crime committed, but they were expected to give the most detailed and minute evidence connected with it, so that the judge might be more certain of pronouncing a correct judgment and also more able to entrap the witnesses should they make contradictory statements (Vol. 2, page 50).

What is important about this brief tale is not its moral or legal merits but its literary and human quality. In quick strokes the unknown author sketches the two eminent elderly men catching each other out in lechery; the beautiful young matron surprised naked in her garden; the last-minute reprieve from execution; and the trial scene in which the concocted evidence is exposed through skilful cross-examination by a young defender of justice. Even the names fit into the theme: Susanna means a lily and Daniel, 'God is my judge'.

Susanna and the Elders is one of the masterpieces in world literature of the short story form.

## Daniel in the Lions' Den

*The Idol Bel and David*

THE BABYLONIANS HAD AN IDOL CALLED BEL whom the king went to worship every day. Daniel, the king's most trusted companion and friend, prayed to his own God. When the king asked him why he did not worship Bel, Daniel answered: 'Because I do not revere man-made idols, but the living God, who created heaven and earth and has dominion over all flesh' (Bel 5). The king insisted that Bel was a living god. As proof, he pointed to the amount of food and drink the god consumed every day – twelve bushels of fine flour, forty sheep and fifty gallons of wine. Daniel scoffed at this statement. He maintained that the idol was made of clay inside and brass outside, and could not eat or drink anything.

The king was offended by Daniel's scepticism. He declared that if the god consumed the provisions placed before him, Daniel would be put to death as a blasphemer; but if that was not proved, the priests who served at the temple of Bel would die. Daniel accepted the challenge. He and the king went to the temple, where the priests proposed a way of testing the matter. They would remain outside, while the king and Daniel personally set out the food and wine, then locked and sealed the door behind them. Without the knowledge of the priests, Daniel had his servants strew sifted ashes over the floor before he and the king left.

When they returned in the morning the king removed the royal seals, looked in through the door and saw that the food was gone. He shouted that Bel was great, and there was no deceit in him. But Daniel laughed. He stopped the king entering any further and asked him to look at the floor. The footprints of a number of men, women and children showed up clearly in the ashes.

The king promptly had the seventy priests arrested. They confessed that there was a secret entrance underneath the food-table that stood before the idol. Every night the priests entered through it, together with their wives and children, and consumed the food and drink. In a rage at this deception, the monarch had them and their families put to death. Daniel was given permission to destroy the idol, together with its temple.

*The Sacred Dragon* The Babylonians also worshipped a great dragon. The king pointed out to Daniel that this at least was a living god. Daniel answered that he would go on worshipping the Lord, the only living God. With the king's permission, he undertook to kill the sacred dragon without using a sword or club. The king agreed to let him try.

Daniel boiled a mixture of pitch, fat and hair, shaped it into cakes and fed them to the dragon until it burst. Daniel said sarcastically, 'See what you have been worshipping!' (Bel 27)

*The Lions' Den* Intense public resentment sprang up over the smashing of the idol Bel, the killing of the temple priests, and now the destruction of the sacred dragon. A rebellion threatened against the king, who was held responsible for these deeds and was accused of having become a Jew. The leaders of the revolt gave the king an ultimatum. Either he would hand over Daniel, or he and the royal household would be wiped out. The king yielded to the popular pressure. Daniel was handed over, and thrown into a den of lions. There were seven lions, who were accustomed to receive a daily ration of two human bodies and two sheep. Their food supply was suspended to make sure they would eat Daniel.

In Judea, the prophet Habakkuk was preparing food to take to the reapers in the field. He had boiled a thick soup and was breaking bread into the bowl. The angel of the Lord appeared and told him to take the food to Babylon for Daniel in the den of lions. The perplexed prophet answered that he had never been to Babylon and knew nothing about the den. The angel seized him by the hair and carried him through the air to Babylon, still clutching the food. All Habakkuk

heard on his airborne journey was the sound of the wind rushing past. Set down next to the den, he shouted out 'Daniel! Daniel! Take the dinner which God has sent you' (Bel 37). Daniel offered up thanks to the Lord, who had not forsaken him, then rose and ate the food. The angel brought Habakkuk back the way he had come.

On the seventh day after Daniel had been handed over, the king came to the den of lions to mourn for the friend he had lost. He looked into the pit, and to his utter astonishment there sat Daniel. The king cried out in praise of the Lord God worshipped by Daniel. He then had Daniel taken out of the den. The men who had tried to do away with him were thrown in instead. They were instantly torn to pieces and eaten before the king's eyes.

*Comments on Bel and the Dragon* These two interwoven tales are included in the Latin (Catholic) Bible as Chapter 14 of the canonical Book of Daniel. In Protestant bibles they appear among the Apocrypha under the single title of 'Bel and the Dragon'.

The work derides idolatry and stresses that there is only one true and living God. The setting is the Babylonian court in the time of 'Cyrus the Persian', who conquered Babylonia in 539 BC. Bel, short for Baal, is another name for the chief Babylonian god, Marduk or Merodach. The name Babylon means the Gateway of Bel. The dragon was probably a great snake. Worship of a serpent-deity was prevalent in Egypt and Babylonia.

The origin of the work is uncertain. The general belief is that it was written in Judea towards the end of the second century BC though it survived only in Greek, and no Hebrew or Aramaic original has been found.

One scholarly theory is that it reflects a period of anti-Jewish religious persecution in the reign of the Seleucid monarch Antiochus VII Sedetes (138–129 BC). The passage bringing in Habakkuk is probably a later addition to the story.

# 3

# THE MACCABEAN REVOLT

### Prologue: Encounter in Modi'in

THE SLEEPY HAMLET OF MODI'IN stood near the town of Lydda, where the coastal plain of Judea merged into the gently undulating foothills. Less than ten miles to the west glinted the Mediterranean sea. To the east rose the blue wall of the Judean hills, hazy in the midday heat. Cradled in those hills was Jerusalem, the capital. On the traditional festivals the villagers would dress in their Sabbath clothes and trudge up the pass of Beth-horon with their families, the donkeys laden with panniers of fruit, vegetables, wheat and olives as first-fruit offerings in the Temple.

The quiet rhythm of their life was about to be shattered. It was the beginning of summer, in the year 166 BC. Evil days had come upon the ancestral faith. Judea was a province of the sprawling Seleucid empire, ruled from its capital Antioch, in northern Syria. Hellenist (Greek) influence had eroded the traditional way of life of the small Hebrew nation. The current ruler, Antiochus IV Epiphanes (175–163 BC), was forcing his subjects to accept Hellenist ways in all spheres of life, including religion. In Judea, the Jewish faith was being brutally repressed and some of its adherents had been martyred. The holy Temple in Jerusalem had been profaned. Officers were being sent through the countryside to make the rural folk fall into line as well.

That was why the inhabitants of Modi'in had left their fields that day and lined up in the village square. In sullen silence they stared at the Seleucid officer facing them. The soldiers of his armed escort stood to attention behind him. In front of him, stones had been piled up into a rough altar, the burning wood on it sending up a plume of smoke into the clear air. A pig was tethered next to the altar. In careful Aramaic (the common language of the region) the officer explained to them what the edict of His Imperial Majesty required. They would sacrifice the pig to Zeus, the father of the Greek gods. Each of them would then eat a morsel of the flesh. Anyone who refused would be executed on the spot. As soon as the ceremony was over they could get back to their work.

A shudder of horror went through the crowd. The officer stared at the scene with distaste; he was a professional soldier, and resented the task of making defenceless peasants break their religious taboos. But orders were orders. His only concern was to get the job done quickly and without trouble, before he moved on to the next village.

In the centre of the front row stood the leader of the community, the priest Mattathias, flanked by his five stalwart sons – John, Simon, Judah, Eleazar and Jonathan. The officer understood that if the priest could be induced to co-operate the others would follow his lead. But there was nothing submissive about the erect stance of Mattathias, his strong, bearded face or his level gaze. Obviously this was no ordinary village headman who could be cowed by a barked command. The officer addressed him in tones of blandishment: 'You are a leader, honoured and great in this city, and supported by sons and brothers. Now be the first to come and do what the king commands, as all the Gentiles and the men of Judah and those that are left in Jerusalem have done. Then you and your sons will be numbered among the friends of the king, and you and your sons will be honoured with silver and gold and many gifts' (1 Macc. 2:17,18).

The priest's reply was firm and unhesitating: 'We will not obey the king's words by turning aside from our religion to the right hand or to the left' (1 Macc. 2:22).

At this open defiance, everyone present stood frozen in a tableau of tension. Suddenly one of the villagers panicked and shuffled towards the altar to comply with the command. Mattathias bounded forward, seized the sacrificial knife and plunged it into the offender. As the man fell screaming, the priest whipped round and stabbed the officer to death. With a push of his foot, he sent the makeshift altar tumbling to the ground. Before the startled soldiers could react, they were overwhelmed by a gang of young men who leaped on them, led by the sons of Mattathias.

Shortly after this abrupt and bloody end to the ceremony, the priest, his sons and their families left the village and made for the hills, together with those who were willing to follow them. The standard of revolt had been raised.

## The Struggle Against Hellenism

THE BACKGROUND TO THE REVOLT WAS A CENtury and a half of Hellenist rule. The word Hellenist is derived from Hellas, the inclusive Greek name for the motherland and all the Greek settlements elsewhere. The Hellenist period in Near Eastern history was launched by Alexander the Great of Macedonia (356–323 BC), one of the finest military geniuses of all time. Macedonia was the rugged kingdom just to the north of Greece. (It included what are today parts of Greece, Yugoslavia, Albania and Bulgaria.) Alexander's father, King Philip II, had conquered Greece and adopted the Greek language and culture in his realm. When Alexander came to the throne as a young man, he marched eastward and defeated the Persian monarch Darius III. By the age of twenty-three he had made himself master of the eastern Mediterranean and western Asia as far as the border of India. As the First Book of Maccabees succinctly puts it: 'He advanced to the ends of the earth, and plundered many nations' (1 Macc. 1:3).

*Alexander and his Successors*

Alexander died of illness in Babylon, in 323 BC. His top generals then fought each other over the disposal of the vast territory he had occupied. One of them, Seleucus, became the ruler of Persia, Babylonia, Syria and Asia Minor. Another, Ptolemy, established himself on the throne of Egypt. The Near East was thereby divided between these two rival Hellenist kingdoms. Judea lay on the borderland between them. For a century it came under the Ptolemaic dynasty of Egypt. In 198 BC the Seleucid ruler Antiochus III the Great (223–187 BC) routed an Egyptian army at Panias, at the foot of Mount Hermon near the sources of the Jordan river. As a result, Judea became part of the Seleucid empire.

Alexander had regarded himself as the heir and apostle of the dazzling Greek civilization. The city-states of ancient Greece, notably Athens in the golden age of Pericles, had attained new levels of achievement in philosophy, the natural sciences, political theory, architecture, drama, sculpture, and athletic pursuits (the Olympic Games). Alexander aspired to a universal empire based on a uniform Greek way of life. Under the two successor regimes in the Near East, the Ptolemaic and the Seleucid, Hellenist rule was accompanied by Hellenist culture. Groups of colonists from the mother country established new Greek cities and towns – some thirty of them in and around Judea alone. Greek was the accepted language of administration, of upperclass society, and of literature. Greek-style public buildings, schools, theatres and sports gymnasia

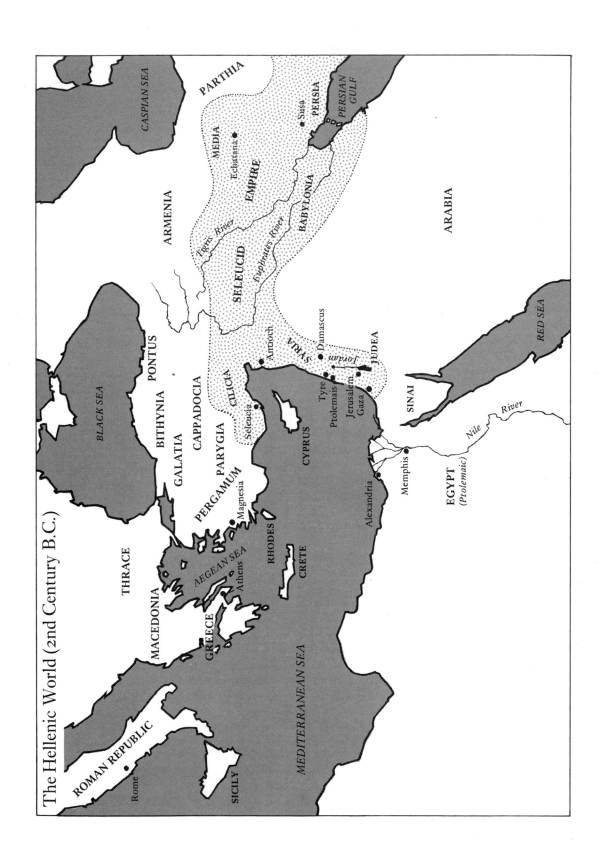

The Hellenic World (2nd Century B.C.)

sprang up everywhere. It became fashionable to take Greek names, wear Greek clothes, and adopt Greek manners.

Where local traditions were strong, as in Judea, the process was to some extent resisted. The Jewish diaspora communities that sprang up in the Hellenist world maintained their own identity, but were Greek-speaking. The largest and most important of these communities was in Alexandria. Founded by Alexander and named after him, it became the leading business and cultural centre in the eastern Mediterranean. In the third century BC, the sacred Hebrew scriptures were translated into Greek for the use of the Alexandrian community. That was the origin of the Greek Bible known as the Septuagint.

*Antiochus Epiphanes* Up to the reign of Antiochus IV, the absorption of Hellenist culture was spontaneous and unplanned. While Judea was under Egyptian rule, the Ptolemaic dynasty made no attempt to interfere with the religious practices or internal affairs of the Jews. When Antiochus III brought the country into the Seleucid orbit, with the help of the Jews of Jerusalem, he guaranteed them freedom of worship. These tolerant official attitudes changed under his son Antiochus IV. He made it a matter of state policy to force the Hellenist way of life upon the natives in the Seleucid realm.

Antiochus was a dynamic but unstable personality. His megalomania led him to adopt the grandiose title of Epiphanes ('god-manifest'), which his enemies suggested should have been Epimanes ('the madman'). Born and reared in Athens, he was an intense admirer of all things Greek. His overriding ambition was to conquer Egypt, become sole ruler of the whole Near East, and make it exclusively Hellenist in language, culture and creed. He was intolerant and suspicious of those peoples, like the Jews in Judea, who clung to their own traditions and ways. To him, these were manifestations of separatism that weakened his empire from within.

In Jerusalem Antiochus found a natural ally in an influential minority of Jewish Hellenists. They were a group of assimilated families with wealth and social position, who constantly sought favour with the regime. As against that, the traditional elements included most of the ordinary people in the cities, and practically all of the rural population.

The tension between the two camps focussed on control of the highest office in the nation, that of the high priest in Jerusalem. He was not only *The High Priest's Office* the top religious dignitary but also exercised considerable secular authority. When Antiochus came to the throne, the high priest was the aged Onias III, who was greatly respected for his orthodoxy and erudition. He fell victim to the intrigues of the Hellenist Jewish leaders, who persuaded the new ruler that Onias was disloyal to him and had retained contacts with the Ptolemaic throne in Egypt. The king deposed him, and his brother Jason (in Hebrew, Joshua) was appointed in his place. Onias was given sanctuary by the Jewish community of Antioch. Jason was much less observant than his brother, and more amenable to Hellenist influence. He served Antiochus as a docile vassal, regularly provided the required tribute, and was permissive about the growth of Greek institutions in the capital. One of these was a gymnasium or sports stadium which scandalized the Orthodox because young Jews wrestled naked in it and were inducted into pagan rites. It was said that some of them even tried to cover over their circumcision by having their prepuces stretched forward.

But worse was to come. Jason, after all, was a member of the family who had always held the office of high priest. During his tenure, there was no direct attempt to interfere with religious practices, and the Temple functioned normally. But after three years he too was ousted in favour of Menelaus, a lay leader of the Hellenists. He was probably a member of the wealthy Tobiad family who owned large feudal estates in Transjordan. Menelaus persuaded the king to appoint him, undertaking to provide greatly increased revenue from Judea for the royal treasury in Antioch, depleted by military campaigns in the East. Jason fled across the Jordan river, and Menelaus was installed under the protection of a Seleucid garrison stationed in Jerusalem.

In these years a number of observant Jews started to leave Jerusalem, seeking a less disturbed life in the rural areas. Among them was the priest Mattathias, who returned with his family to his native village of Modi'in.

In his second year as high priest, the hated Menelaus ran into serious trouble. Unable to pay the heavy tribute he had promised, he was summoned to Antioch to explain the default. He left his brother Lysimachus in charge and departed for the Seleucid capital, carrying with him some of the golden vessels from the Temple. Finding that the king was away, dealing with an uprising elsewhere, Menelaus handed the Temple vessels to the king's deputy in discharge of his debt. To observant Jews everywhere, the deposed Onias had remained the only legitimate high priest, since it was a hereditary office and not one dependent on royal appointment. Menelaus had him lured out of hiding in Antioch and killed him.

When it became known in Jerusalem that the Temple had been robbed by the high priest himself, and that the revered Onias had been murdered, there were angry demonstrations. In trying to quell them with the help of the Seleucid troops in the garrison, Lysimachus was killed in a clash. A deputation of reputable Jerusalem citizens was sent to King Antiochus to petition for the removal of Menelaus. But the king was easily persuaded that the high priest's detractors were subversives. The appointment was reconfirmed, and the process of Hellenization went on apace. As a mark of royal favour a new Greek quarter in the western part of Jerusalem was named Antiochia.

*Antiochus' Egyptian Campaign* In 169 BC Antiochus invaded Egypt, occupied most of the Delta region, had himself crowned in the ancient capital of Memphis, appointed a governor and returned to Syria. The following year he resumed the campaign and laid siege to Alexandria.

It is strange that Antiochus should have counted on non-intervention by the Roman republic. He had reason to know and fear that power. By 200 BC Rome had crippled its main rival, Carthage, and become mistress of the western Mediterranean. It then turned eastward, and immediately came into collision with two leading Hellenist states allied with each other: Macedonia and the Seleucid empire. Within less than a decade Macedonia had been subdued. The Seleucid monarch Antiochus III was defeated in the battle of Magnesia, in Asia Minor. By a humiliating peace treaty, Antiochus III was forced to surrender his domains in Asia Minor, pay a heavy annual tribute, and hand over a group of youths of noble birth to be kept in Rome as hostages for his good conduct. Among these hostages was the royal prince who would later come to the Seleucid throne as Antiochus IV.

By the time of Antiochus IV's Egyptian

venture, Rome was the dominant power in the Mediterranean world, and had taken under its protection the weak Ptolemaic dynasty in Egypt. Antiochus reckoned, however, that Rome was neutralized for the time being by its renewed struggle with Macedonia. That turned out to be a miscalculation. Rome could not tolerate the Seleucid bid to become master of the Near East, and the radical shift in the balance of power that would imply. The Senate despatched a high-level delegation bearing an ultimatum to Antiochus. It was headed by a tough legate named Caius Popilius Laenas. The delegation lingered on the way until it received the news that King Perseus of Macedonia had been decisively defeated. It then sailed at once for Egypt.

The showdown with Antiochus took place at his camp outside Alexandria, and is graphically described by the contemporary historian Polybius. At the outset, the envoy Popilius snubbed the Seleucid monarch by refusing to shake hands with him until the decree of the Senate had been read out. The document curtly called upon Antiochus to abandon the campaign and withdraw his troops from Egypt. When he asked for time to consider the message and consult with his advisers. Popilius drew a circle around the king's feet with a stick, and demanded that he remain in the circle until he had made up his mind. Unwilling to face a confrontation with Rome, the fuming Antiochus agreed to comply, and to leave Egypt within the stated time-limit. It was only then that there was hand-shaking all around and the diplomatic niceties were observed.

In a savage mood, Antiochus led his forces back along the coastal road. The news from Judea that reached him on the way threw him into an even greater rage. The story of his humiliation by the Romans had spread rapidly through the Near East, together with a false report that he had died in Egypt. Emboldened by these developments, the former high priest Jason mustered a force, crossed the river Jordan and advanced on Jerusalem. He was welcomed and supported by most of the populace, to whom even Jason seemed a deliverer compared to the incumbent high priest Menelaus. The latter took refuge with the garrison in Jerusalem and sent out urgent appeals for help.

Antiochus reacted swiftly. One of his top commanders, Apollonius, was diverted to

Jerusalem with a substantial body of troops to stamp out the incipient rebellion and restore order. The Seleucid force entered the city on the Sabbath, when religious Jews would not permit themselves to take up arms, even in self-defence. The soldiers slaughtered a number of the inhabitants, took others captive, and razed parts of the town. They broke into the Temple and carried off the contents of the treasury, together with the bulk of the holy vessels and furnishings. Menelaus was once more installed as high priest. A new citadel, called the Acra, was built on the high ground to the west of the Temple Mount, and occupied by a reinforced garrison. Its commanding officer, Philip, was appointed governor of the city.

*The Religious Persecution* Back in his capital, Antiochus grimly took stock of the situation. His dream of reviving Alexander's imperial glory had been frustrated. The regime was on the defensive. Unrest had spread through Persia, Media and Babylonia in the east, Cilicia in the north-west and Judea in the south. Beyond the eastern border the militant kingdoms of Parthia and Bactria were a growing threat. Rome would take advantage of any weakness and increase its pressure. Antiochus concluded that internal cohesion and control in his empire had to be tightened. Separatist tendencies could not be tolerated. The Hellenizing programme would be more rigidly enforced, even in the sensitive area of religion. Judea was a special target for these measures. It occupied a vital strategic position, as the southern outpost on the vulnerable border with Egypt. Experience had shown that the Jews were stubbornly committed to their own peculiar faith, worshipping a single invisible God, observing strict dietary laws, and rejecting Greek paganism with contempt. Their resistance had to be broken, by whatever means.

For the first time in its history, the Jewish people were subjected to an official policy of religious persecution. The experience would be repeated many times in the next twenty centuries. The First Book of Maccabees gives a bitter summary of Antiochus' decrees:

> Then the king wrote to his whole kingdom that all should be one people, and that each should give up his customs. All the Gentiles accepted the command of the king. Many even from Israel gladly adopted his religion; they

sacrificed to idols and profaned the Sabbath. And the king sent letters by messengers to Jerusalem and the cities of Judah; he directed them to follow customs strange to the land, to forbid burnt offerings and sacrifices and drink offerings in the sanctuary, to profane sabbaths and feasts, to defile the sanctuary and the priests, to build altars and sacred precincts and shrines for idols, to sacrifice swine and unclean animals, and to leave their sons uncircumcised. They were to make themselves abominable by everything unclean and profane, so that they should forget the law and change all the ordinances. 'And whoever does not obey the command of the king shall die.' (1 Macc. 1:41-50).

The Second Book of Maccabees records stories of Jewish martyrs who chose to be tortured to death rather than deny their faith. The accounts are amplified and embellished in a later work (not included in the Apocrypha) known as the Fourth Book of Maccabees. The gruesome fate meted out to these early martyrs no doubt frightened some Jews into submission. But among the devout they stiffened the mood of resistance as the following examples testified.

Two women were arrested for having circumcised their children. They were paraded through the streets with the infants hanging at their breasts, then hurled down to their deaths from the city wall.

A public conversion ceremony was arranged in the presence of the king and his retinue. Among the Jews herded together for the purpose, the outstanding figure was the venerable sage and teacher Eleazar, who was expected to set a lead in eating the flesh of a pig sacrificed to the Greek gods. (The Hellenic world knew little about the religion of the Jews, except that they were forbidden to eat pork; that is why breaking this dietary taboo became the symbolic act of apostasy.) The Fourth Book of Maccabees relates that the king at first addressed Eleazar in a courteous manner, and pleaded with him to obey:

> Before I commence inflicting torture upon you, graybeard, I would give you this counsel: eat of the swine's flesh and save yourself. I respect your age and your hoary head; but I cannot think you a philosopher when you have so long been an old man and still cling to the religion of the Jews. Why do you abominate

The Second Book of Maccabees: the sage Eleazar refuses to eat pork as
commanded by Antiochus IV. Illustration from *Histoire de Jerusalem*.

eating the excellent meat of this animal which nature has so freely bestowed upon us? (4 Macc. 5:5–8).

The reply attributed to Eleazar was dignified and eloquent. He declared that for observant Jews no constraint was more compelling than their own willing obedience to the Law. 'And do not regard the eating of unclean flesh a small offence; transgression is of equal weight in small matters as in large, for in either case the Law is equally despised ... so make ready your torturers' wheel, fan your fires to a fiercer heat ... unsullied shall my fathers welcome me' (4 Macc. 5:14,36). As the old man was being beaten and scourged, the blood spurting from his wounds, some of the king's courtiers came up to him and suggested a way to save his life. Meat that was permissible for him to eat would be brought to him, and he would pretend that it was the swineflesh of the sacrifice. In a voice already weak with suffering, the aged scholar refused. How could he mislead his young followers into believing that in his ninetieth year he had betrayed the faith of his ancestors? It was better for him to set an example 'of how to die happily and nobly on behalf of our revered and holy Law'. He was seized and bound to the rack, where he expired.

The next of these moving martyrdoms was the story of Hannah and her seven sons. The handsome youths and their mother were part of the group that had been brought into the king's presence and made to witness the killing of Eleazar. When they too were given a choice between conversion and a cruel death, the eldest brother replied for all of them. If their aged teacher Eleazar could triumph over torment and die for the faith, it was even more fitting that young men like themselves should be prepared to do so. He was seized, his tongue was cut out, his hands and feet were lopped off and he was burned in the fire. One by one, the other six brothers suffered the same end, after each had spurned the king's order. The mother then died with her sons.

The worst shock to the whole Jewish people was the desecration of the Temple in Jerusalem. The Temple was a unique focus of faith and sentiment, not only for the Judeans but also for the diaspora communities elsewhere. (More than two centuries later the greatest Jewish philo-sopher of his time, Philo of Alexandria, was to note: 'Countless multitudes from countless cities come to the Temple at every festival, some by land, others by sea, from east and west and north and south.' The Temple was pillaged by Antiochus' troops, who carried away everything of value. An altar was erected to Zeus and a statue of the god installed. Pigs were sacrificed on the altar to the Greek gods, and their blood sprinkled in the Holy of Holies. The sacred scrolls of the Law were torn up and burnt. Bacchanalian orgies took place in the Temple precincts: 'For the heathens ... took their pleasure with prostitutes and had intercourse with women in the sacred enclosures' (2 Macc. 6:4).

Orthodox Jews were plunged into mourning at the most dreadful blow their religion had suffered since the destruction of the First Temple by Nebuchadnezzar's Babylonian troops, more than four centuries earlier. In Modi'in, Mattathias and his sons clothed themselves in the traditional sackcloth. The priest cried out in anguish:

> Alas! Why was I born to see this,
>    the ruin of my people, the ruin of
>       the holy city,
> and to dwell there when it was given
>       over to the enemy,
>    the sanctuary given over to aliens?
> Her temple has become like a man
>       without honour;
>    her glorious vessels have been car-
>       ried into captivity.
> Her babes have been killed in her
>       streets,
>    her youths by the sword of the foe.
> What nation has not inherited her
>    palaces
> and has not seized her spoils?
> All her adornment has been taken
>       away;
>    no longer free, she has become a
>       slave.
> And behold, our holy place, our beauty,
>       and our glory have been laid waste;
>    the Gentiles have profaned it.
>       Why should we live any longer?
>                (1 Macc. 2:7-13)

Already, in the minds of Mattathias and his sons, the resolve was being formed to go down fighting, if the alternatives were to worship pagan gods or to be helplessly killed.

## Judah (166–161 BC)

AFTER THEY HAD STRUCK DOWN THE SELEUCID officer and his men in Modi'in, Mattathias and his handful of followers went up the Beth-horon pass under cover of darkness, and turned off into the Gophna hills, about half-way between Jerusalem and the town of Samaria, the seat of the Seleucid provincial governor. It was rough terrain – some twenty square miles of ridges and ravines, boulders, bush and caves. Here they set up a base of operations. At night men would go on foot along the stony paths to farms and villages in the hills and on the plain below. Their job was to obtain supplies and weapons for the small resistance movement, and to organize a network of contacts that would keep them informed of enemy dispositions. Those who wanted to join were carefully checked in case they were informers, and then led blindfold in the dark to the band's hideout.

*The Partisans*    The main reinforcements were a group of Hassidim, young religious zealots who had taken refuge from persecution in the caves of the Judean desert to the southeast of Jerusalem, overlooking the Dead Sea. A number of them had been killed by a Seleucid unit that had taken them by surprise on the Sabbath, when they would not fight back even in self-defence. This self-imposed religious restraint left the Jews at the mercy of their enemies, as had happened earlier when the Seleucid general Apollonius had turned his troops loose on the inhabitants of Jerusalem on the Sabbath. Mattathias listened to the story of the Hassidim who had reached him, and queried their extreme interpretation of the Law. He pointed out that if they did not take up arms for their survival, they would be wiped out. 'Let us fight against every man who comes to attack us on the Sabbath day; let us not all die as our brethren died in their hiding places' (1 Macc. 2:41). The Hassidim accepted his view. (It would be upheld by the rabbis in later centuries, who ruled that the Sabbath was not profaned by any action that was necessary to preserve life. They held that 'the Sabbath is given to man, not man to the Sabbath'.)

Other fugitives and malcontents found their way to the Hasmoneans, as Mattathias' family was later called, after his ancestor Hasmon. All the men were trained as fighters. Judah, the third son of Mattathias, emerged as a born com-mander, and developed the classical tactics of the guerilla. In open combat they would have been no match for the well-equipped regular units of the Seleucid army. They therefore confined themselves to small-scale raids, relying on speed, mobility and surprise, an intimate knowledge of the terrain, movement at night and the support of the local population. They never lost sight of the fact that they were fighting God's battle; their primary aim was to uphold the true faith and to disrupt the programme of enforced Hellenist conversion. Small groups would elude the Seleucid patrols and steal into the villages at night. They would knock down pagan altars, kill collaborators, have male infants circumcised, gather recruits and provisions and disappear before first light.

The First Book of Maccabees claims with pride that 'they rescued the law out of the hands of the Gentiles and kings, and they never let the sinner gain the upper hand' (1 Macc. 2:48).

The rigours of their new life proved too much for the aged Mattathias, who fell mortally ill. On his deathbed he gave his sons a last message of courage. He recalled their ancestors who had stood the test of faith: Abraham, Joseph, Joshua, Caleb, David, Elijah, Daniel's three companions in the fiery furnace, and Daniel himself in the lions' den: 'And so observe, from generation to generation, that none who put their trust in him [God] will lack strength' (1 Macc. 2:61). Two of the sons were singled out to bear special responsibilities. Simon, the second brother, said the old man, 'is wise in counsel; always listen to him; he shall be your father' (1 Macc. 2:65). The middle brother, Judah, had been 'a mighty warrior from his youth' and would be their commander in battle. (It is left unexplained why John, the eldest son, was passed over in silence. Apparently his father did not attribute to him the sagacity of Simon or the martial skill of Judah.) The priest then blessed his sons 'and was gathered to his fathers'. At night they carried his body down the mountain to the village of Modi'in – by then completely deserted – and buried it secretly in the family tomb.

History has no parallel to the five 'glorious brothers' now left to carry on the struggle for the religious liberty and ultimate independence of their people. They were an exceptionally able, brave and dedicated group. In the stormy period that lay ahead they would never waver in their

Daniel's Three Companions in the Fiery Furnace. Linocut by
the contemporary German artist Herbert Falken.

devotion to the cause and to each other. For the next third of a century, the burden of leadership would be borne successively by Judah, Jonathan and Simon. Not one of the five would die a natural death – they would all fall in battle or be murdered. The Hasmonean dynasty that sprang from Mattathias would last for 130 years from the beginning of the Revolt.

Judah acquired the second name of Maccabee, probably derived from a Hebrew word meaning a hammer. In due course, the whole family came to be called the Maccabees, and their successful struggle for freedom the Maccabean Revolt. In non-Hebrew writings the leader of the Revolt is remembered not as Judah the Maccabee but by the Greek form of his name, Judas Maccabeus. The reason is that the First Book of Maccabees has survived only in Greek translation, while the Second Book of Maccabees was written in Greek.

At first, the band of outlaws in the Gophna hills was regarded by the Seleucid authorities as a nuisance rather than a serious threat. No doubt there were the routine counter-measures that are usual in such colonial situations. Reprisals were taken against any village suspected of aiding the rebels. Efforts were made to get information through spies, informers, bribery or torture. These measures were counter-productive: they only deepened resentment against the regime and swelled the ranks of the Maccabean supporters. The resistance movement spread steadily. At its core in the Gophna hills there were some hundreds of full-time freedom fighters, with an armoury collected from ambushed Seleucid patrols and supply convoys. Far greater in number were the part-time partisans throughout the countryside. By day they were peaceful farmers; at night they would haul out weapons from places of concealment, disappear on a foray, and be back sleeping in their homesteads before dawn. The key to Judah's war of attrition was full and accurate intelligence about enemy movements. The men working in the fields, the women coming from market, labourers in the military camps, secret sympathizers in Jerusalem and the country towns, were his eyes and ears. A stream of intelligence reached him through a pre-arranged code system. Steadily, the rural areas became unsafe for the occupation forces. They were confined to Jerusalem, to military camps in the larger centres, and to movement only in well-protected convoys along main roads.

Disquietening reports came to General Apollonius, the regional governor in Samaria. They indicated that his subordinates in Jerusalem were no longer in control of the situation and that the Seleucid grip on the strategic Judean province was slipping. He decided on vigorous action to restore order. With a force of regular troops and mercenaries, Apollonius marched south from Samaria to Jerusalem, in order to take personal charge of operations.

Judah and his brothers anxiously debated what they should do. Prudence dictated that they should suspend their operations and lie low for a while, until the military pressure receded. A direct confrontation with Seleucid troops might invite a crushing defeat. At the very least, an open clash could exact a price in casualties that they could ill afford. But there were cogent arguments the other way. The strategy of insurgency obeyed its own inherent laws. Its momentum had to be maintained; if it were inactive, it would collapse. Furthermore, a first phase of harassment could not be kept up indefinitely; at the opportune moment, it needed to move into a second phase of military engagement. Apollonius' march from Samaria could be such an opportune moment. If the Seleucid force could be caught unawares on the move and defeated, such an action would arouse the country and give the struggle a new dimension. Aware of all its hazards, Judah took the bold decision to attack.

The hill road from Samaria to Jerusalem winds through valleys and over the tops of ridges. The spot that Judah chose to waylay the Seleucid force was probably the ascent of Libonah, three or four miles to the northeast of the Gophna district. Here the road passed through a broad dale and looped its way up the steep side through a defile. As the laden Seleucid soldiers marched sweating and panting up the pass, Judah's men suddenly emerged from their concealed positions on both sides of the defile and attacked them with swords, daggers and farm implements, after a bombardment of slingshots and rocks. The enemy forces were thrown into confusion. The forward units were driven back, while those in the rear kept on pressing forward, creating an inextricable tangle of men and animals. It was impossible for them to deploy in battle order. In the fierce hand-to-hand fighting Apollonius himself was killed, which further demoralized his troops. They started streaming in disarray down

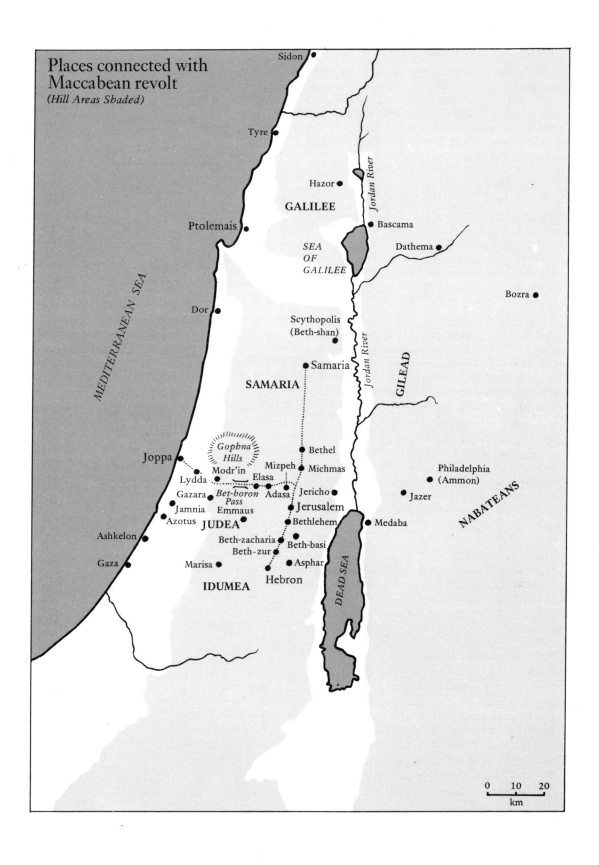

Places connected with
Maccabean revolt
*(Hill Areas Shaded)*

Sidon

Tyre

Hazor

**GALILEE**

Bascama

Ptolemais

Dathema

*SEA
OF
GALILEE*

*Jordan River*

Bozra

*MEDITERRANEAN SEA*

Dor

Scythopolis
(Beth-shan)

Samaria

**SAMARIA**

*Jordan River*

**GILEAD**

*Gophna
Hills*

Bethel

Joppa

Modr'in     Mizpeh     Michmas

Philadelphia
(Ammon)

Lydda          Elasa

Gazara     *Bet-horon*     Adasa     Jericho

Jazer

**NABATEANS**

Jamnia     *Pass*     Emmaus              **Jerusalem**

Azotus     **JUDEA**

Bethlehem

Ashkelon                                        Medaba

Beth-zacharia     Beth-basi

Beth-zur

Gaza                Marisa              Asphar

**IDUMEA**          **Hebron**

*DEAD SEA*

0     10     20

km

the mountainside, leaving the pass strewn with their dead and wounded and their baggage. At the foot of the pass their line of retreat had been cut by another Maccabean detachment that inflicted more heavy casualties. The retreat turned into a rout. A great pile of arms was collected by the Maccabees. Judah took for himself the sword of Apollonius, and was to use it for the rest of his life.

The blow inflicted on a regular army formation, commanded by an experienced Seleucid general, raised the prestige of the guerilla movement and rallied fresh support for it. The Seleucid garrison in the Jerusalem citadel, and the Jewish Hellenist group led by the high priest Menelaus, were now virtually isolated. General Seron, the commander of all the Seleucid forces in Syria, mounted a large military expedition to crush the Judean rebels. He advanced down the coastal plain, turned inland at Lydda (near the present international airport), and proceeded along the road that led over the Beth-horon pass to Jerusalem. The intention was to reassert full control over Jerusalem and to use it as the base for 'pacification' of the Judean countryside.

The Seleucid force camped for the night near the foot of the pass, and started the long ascent at first light. Judah used similar tactics to those that had succeeded against Apollonius. As the vanguard of the column neared the top of the pass, and was at its most vulnerable, it came under sudden surprise attack from the front and from the sides of the ravine. The column retreated in disorder and was pursued by the Maccabeans down to the plain below; 'some eight hundred of the enemy fell, and the rest fled into the land of the Philistines' (1 Macc. 3:24). In his Antiquities, Josephus, the first-century AD Jewish historian, states that Seron himself was killed.

*Early Battles* *(165 BC)* This fresh reverse caused consternation in the palace at Antioch. For the first time the king and his advisers took a grave view of the troubles in Judea. They had come at a bad time. The Seleucid empire was facing a crisis in the east. Persia and Media were in a mutinous mood, and had withheld payment of the annual tribute. Behind them was the rising challenge of Parthia. Antiochus had drained his exchequer to amass a large army, and was about to lead it eastward. He had appointed Lysias, a senior member of the royal family, as regent in Antioch during the king's absence, and as temporary guardian of the

nine-year-old crown prince (the future Antiochus V Eupator).

Yet the Judean situation could not be ignored until the king's return from his eastern campaign. For one thing, there was the looming shadow of Rome. It would be tempting for Rome to take advantage of turbulence in Judea, and to move in either through Egypt or by sea. The king instructed Lysias to take strong action against the Judeans. As the First Book of Maccabees puts it: 'Lysias was to send a force against them to wipe out and destroy the strength of Israel and the remnant of Jerusalem; he was to banish the memory of them from the place, settle aliens in all their territory, and distribute their land' (1 Macc. 3:35–36).

Lysias appointed a triumvirate of generals to take charge of the Judean operation. They were Ptolemy the son of Dorymenes (probably the governor of Syria at the time), Nicanor and Georgias, the latter to be the commander in the field. The size of the army at their disposal is given in the First Book of Maccabees as forty thousand infantry and seven thousand cavalry, but these figures seem much inflated.

The Seleucid force moved along the coastal plain and set up a base camp in the foothills at Emmaus in the valley of Aijalon (near the present Latrun). There they were reinforced by local auxiliaries. Merchants came to the camp carrying gold, silver and a quantity of fetters, to buy the expected Jewish captives as slaves.

Judah mustered his followers, estimated at some three thousand men, at Mizpeh, seven miles northwest of Jerusalem. Georgias, an able and aggressive general, determined to seize the initiative and keep the Maccabees off-balance. Regular armies did not as a rule operate at night, but Georgias made an unexpected thrust under cover of darkness. With a division of five thousand foot-soldiers and a thousand horsemen he advanced into the hills, guided by men from the citadel in Jerusalem who were familiar with the terrain. His plan was to encircle the Maccabean encampment during the night and storm it at first light.

On learning that the enemy had split its forces, Judah made a swift counter-thrust. That same night he and his men slipped away, leaving their camp-fires burning to deceive the Seleucid scouts. Picking their way down the mountain tracks, the Maccabees assembled before dawn just south of the base camp at Emmaus. In the fierce hand-to-hand engagement that followed, the Seleucid rearguard troops were routed and fled towards the coast. Judah ordered his men to break off the pursuit and deploy themselves to meet the enemy force returning from the hills.

When Georgias found the Maccabean camp at Mizpeh deserted, he at first concluded that the guerillas had heard his army approach and had fled into the hills. But the detachments he sent out found no sign of them. His exhausted soldiers had to turn round and march back towards the Emmaus base camp. To his dismay, reconnaissance patrols reported back that the camp was burning, the plain around it was littered with dead bodies and the Maccabees were drawn up in battle array. Georgias retreated, and the expedition was abandoned.

*The First Campaign of Lysias (164 BC)* In Antioch, the regent Lysias was 'perplexed and discouraged, for things had not happened to Israel as he had intended, nor had they turned out as the king had commanded him' (1 Macc. 4:27). He prepared to renew the campaign the following year, this time under his personal charge. In the late summer or the autumn of 164 BC he advanced southward into Judea at the head of a fresh army.

Lysias and his military staff had carefully studied the lessons of the previous encounters with Judah and his men. The Seleucid troops had on each occasion ventured into difficult hill country where the insurgents could exploit the weapons of ambush and surprise, and could operate within a rural population sympathetic to them. Lysias accordingly planned to make a lengthy detour and reach Jerusalem from the south, through territory inhabited by Idumeans loyal to the regime. He marched down the coastal plain as far as the town of Marisa in the foothills. Here he swung eastward, and by an easy gradient reached the Hebron-Jerusalem road close to the Judean border fortress of Beth-zur, twenty miles south of the capital. Lysias reckoned that once the isolated garrison in Jerusalem had been relieved and reinforced the city would be a firm base from which to subdue the countryside district by district, before closing in on the rebel hideouts.

Following Lysias' line of march through their intelligence network, Judah and his brothers grasped its strategic implications. They resolved to meet the challenge head-on, with all the risks involved. Rallying his forces, Judah moved them

southward to Beth-zur in a last-ditch effort to block the Seleucid army before it could reach Jerusalem. No details are given of the battle that followed. It is probable that the Seleucid forward units came under attack by fierce Maccabean charges, and were sent reeling back.

Though the main body of his troops was still intact, Lysias made a sober assessment of the situation. The hope of a quick and unimpeded march to Jerusalem had gone. The Maccabean adversary was clearly bold and willing to fight to the death. To continue the push would mean a drawn-out operation with heavy casualties, for which his mercenary auxiliaries would have little stomach. There was a danger that the approaching winter would find his army still out in the open in the Hebron hills, exposed to the cold and rain and bogged down in the mud. Lysias himself was no doubt under pressure to return to Antioch, the Seleucid capital, and attend to urgent matters, since he was responsible for administering the ailing empire while King Antiochus was away campaigning in the east. Lysias decided to suspend his campaign for the time being.

The Second Book of Maccabees states that before his withdrawal Lysias negotiated a truce with Judah guaranteeing freedom of worship, but that is unreliable. Whether a pact was made or not, the withdrawal of Lysias' army left the way clear for Judah to lead his men into Jerusalem. In addressing them he declared the immediate war aim: 'Let us go up to cleanse the sanctuary and dedicate it' (1 Macc. 4-36).

*The Temple Rededicated* In Jerusalem the Seleucid garrison stayed behind the stout walls of the Acra fortress. They did not try to halt the jubilant Maccabean entry into the city, beyond loosing showers of arrows at those who came within range. Also pent up in the Acra were leaders of the pro-Hellenist Jewish faction, headed by the high priest Menelaus. Judah posted part of his force to contain the fortress, while he led the rest of his men across the Tyropean valley and on to the Temple Mount.

The Temple had remained unused and neglected since it had been profaned three years earlier. The Maccabees were overcome with grief at the sight that met their eyes on the sacred Mount: 'And they saw the sanctuary desolate, the altar profaned, and the gates burned. In the courts they saw bushes sprung up as in a thicket, or as on one of the mountains. They saw also the chambers of the priests in ruins' (1 Macc. 4:38).

Judah soon stopped the mourning rites for the Temple and put his followers to work. He chose 'blameless priests devoted to the law' to cleanse and purify the sanctuary, and to build a new altar of unhewn stones. The buildings and courtyards were repaired and the furnishings and holy vessels restored. The joyful dedication ceremony took place in December 164 BC, on the twenty-fifth day of the month of Chislev by the Jewish calendar. The celebrations lasted for eight days. It was decided that 'every year at that season the days of the dedication of the altar should be observed with gladness and joy for eight days' (1 Macc. 4:59).

Thus was inaugurated the festival of Hanukkah, named after the Hebrew word for dedication. It is also known as the Feast of Lights, marked by the kindling in each Jewish home of an eight-branched candelabrum called a *hanukkiah*. By tradition, one light is kindled on the first evening and an additional one each evening after. At the beginning of the annual festival in modern Israel a lighted torch is carried by relays of runners from the village of Modi'in to Jerusalem.

There is an old talmudic legend that when the Maccabees regained the Temple all the holy oil for the lamps had been defiled except for one small cruse, just enough for a single night. Miraculously it kept the Temple candelabrum burning for eight full days.

*The Rescue of Jews (163 BC)* With the Temple restored, Judah's first concern was the military security of the Maccabean position in Jerusalem. The Temple Mount was fortified with a wall and towers. He also strengthened Beth-zur, commanding the southern approach to Jerusalem 'so that the people might have a stronghold that faced Idumea' (1 Macc. 4:61).

The Maccabees next turned their attention to hostile peoples around Judea who were persecuting local Jews and harassing Jewish travellers. For some time, these neighbouring provinces of the Seleucid empire had been taking advantage of the weakness of Judea. Their antagonism was fanned by the success of the Maccabees in regaining Jerusalem and the Temple. As the national resistance leader, Judah received heart-rending appeals for help from isolated Jewish communities across the border, who were being made scapegoats.

One letter came from a number of Jews who were holding out in the fortified town of Dathema, in northern Gilead east of the Sea of Galilee. The letter read: '... The Gentiles around us have gathered together against us to destroy us. They are preparing to come and capture the stronghold to which we have fled, and Timothy is leading their forces. Now then come and rescue us from their hands, for many of us have fallen' (1 Macc. 5:10–12).

A similar letter came from the Jews in western Galilee, who wrote that they were under dire pressure from the three coastal cities of Ptolemais (Acre), Tyre and Sidon.

The Maccabean brothers conferred earnestly over these frantic messages. Relief expeditions would have to face difficulties that seemed insurmountable. Substantial forces would be required, and they would have to travel at a fast pace over long distances, much of it through hostile territory. But appeals from fellow-Jews in distress could not be disregarded. Judah called a general assembly that endorsed the bold decision to act, however heavy the odds. (More than two thousand years later the same moral imperative would send the Israeli descendants of the Maccabees on perilous rescue missions into Nazi Europe, or flying thousands of miles to bring out kidnapped Jewish hostages held captive by terrorists at Entebbe in Uganda.)

Judah's brother Simon advanced up the coastal plain to western Galilee with three thousand troops under his command. He routed the garrison troops stationed in the area and pursued them to the gates of Ptolemais, The Jews were evacuated from that part of the country with their families and possessions, and brought to Judea with great rejoicing.

Judah and his brother Jonathan led a force of eight thousand men to the relief of the Jews in Gilead. The direct route was avoided, as it might have meant fighting on the way. In a three-day journey they crossed the Jordan and made a wide detour along the fringe of the desert, through the territory of the friendly Nabatean people. They captured the town of Bozrah fifty miles east of the Jordan, and released its Jewish residents. A forced march through the night brought them next morning to the outskirts of the Dathema stronghold, just as the government troops were about to storm the walls. Suddenly attacked from the rear by the redoubtable Maccabeans, the enemy panicked and fled.

After the release of the Jews in Dathema, other fortified towns in the vicinity were taken one by one. The enemy commander Timothy re-grouped his forces and reinforced them with locally recruited auxiliaries, but was defeated in a pitched battle.

Judah assembled the rescued Jews in Gilead, and set out with them on the long, slow trip to Jerusalem. 'And Judah kept rallying the laggards and encouraging the people all the way till he came to the land of Judah. So they went up to Mount Zion with gladness and joy, and offered burnt offerings, because not one of them had fallen before they returned in safety' (1 Macc. 5:53,54).

While Judah, Jonathan and Simon were away campaigning, two senior commanders, Joseph and Azariah, were left in charge in Jerusalem, with orders not to take any military initiative. In spite of that, they sought to emulate the successes of their leaders and sallied out against the city of Jamnia on the coastal plain, in the territory of the Idumeans. The military governor of Idumea at the time was Georgias, who had been the general commanding the Seleucid forces at the battle of Emmaus, where Judah had won an early victory. Georgias routed the forces from Jerusalem and pursued the remnants back to the Judean border.

On his return with the Jewish evacuees, Judah carried out a punitive strike against the Idumeans, the biblical Edomites. Traditional foes of the Hebrews, they had occupied the Hebron hill region of Judea after the fall of Jerusalem in the sixth century BC. Later, they had spread into the adjacent foothills and coastal plain. In the period of the Maccabees the Idumeans constantly harassed the Judean border district and the roads leading to it from the south. They also collaborated with the efforts of the Seleucid authorities to suppress the Maccabean revolt, notably in the abortive offensive of Lysias. Judah attacked southward though Beth-zur, captured Hebron and the villages around it, and swept into the coastal plain as far as Azotus (Ashdod), where he destroyed a pagan temple.

In another thrust, Judah led his men westward across the coastal plain to Joppa (Jaffa). The local inhabitants had taken the Jewish community of two hundred souls out to sea in boats and drowned them. In their retaliation raid, the Maccabees destroyed the Joppa port and set the vessels in it alight. They repeated this action at the port of Jamnia south of Joppa, and saved its tiny Jewish community.

One expedition was directed against the marauding Bedouin tribe of the Beonites, east of the Dead Sea. At the town of Jazer, near Philadelphia (modern Amman), there was another victory over the forces commanded by Timothy, who was killed in the battle.

By the end of the year 163 BC, the Maccabees were in firm control of Judea, except for the Seleucid garrison in the Acra fortress in Jerusalem. The Temple had been restored, and with it the free observance of the Jewish faith. The hostility of neighbouring peoples had been neutralized by the military actions to the north, south, east and west. Outlying Jewish settlements had been evacuated and their inhabitants taken to safety in Judea. These achievements had been brought about by the bravery and inspired leadership of the Maccabees. They were helped also by the inability of the Seleucid regime to intervene in full force. The bulk of the army, led by the king himself, remained committed to the inconclusive campaign in Persia and Media.

In 163 BC, King Antiochus succumbed to illness in the Persian city of Gabae (now Isfahan). On his deathbed he appointed a kinsman called Philip as regent and as guardian of his young son and heir, a boy of nine. In theory that meant that Lysias was stripped of these functions. However, as Philip remained in the east to continue the campaign there, Lysias refused to abdicate his position. He enthroned the boy prince as King Antiochus v Eupator, with himself as regent. An internal power struggle between the rival regents had become inevitable.

Judah decided that the time was ripe for an attack on the Acra fortress in Jerusalem, the key to continued Seleucid rule over Judea. In Antioch Lysias received urgent messages from the besieged defenders, begging him to come to their aid. He decided to respond, in spite of the potential threat from Philip. Lysias reckoned that a swift and victorious campaign in Judea would restore the waning Seleucid prestige throughout the area, and would at the same time entrench his own position as regent. Taking the young king with him he marched south again with a stronger army than before, numbering about thirty thousand men. It included a fearsome weapon previously unknown in Judea: a score or more of

*The Second Campaign of Lysias (162 BC)*

war elephants. In the treaty Antiochus III had been forced to sign with Rome a quarter of a century earlier, the use of elephants by the Seleucid kingdom was expressly prohibited. Lysias ignored the ban, hoping that the devastating impact of the huge beasts would help to gain the decisive result he sought.

Lysias followed his previous line of advance, down the coastal plain and into the hills towards Beth-zur. Judah was left with little room for manoeuvre. He was compelled to have a direct collision with the powerful Seleucid army moving on Jerusalem, its flanks well protected by cavalry units. Some of Judah's men were stationed in the Beth-zur fortress to hold up the enemy advance, but they had to surrender for lack of food. (The supply problem was a difficult one for the Maccabees, since it was a 'sabbatical year' when Jews were obliged by religious law to leave their fields fallow.)

The main battle took place at Beth-zechariah, six miles north of Beth-zur on the highway to the capital. The Seleucid onslaught on the Maccabean positions was spearheaded by the elephants. Each animal had an Indian mahout (driver), carried a turret with four fighting men in it and moved in a protective screen of foot soldiers in chain-mail, in turn protected by horsemen. Behind them came the infantry in their tight phalanx formations. The Maccabees were unable to halt this moving wall, and were pushed back.

Judah's younger brother Eleazar tried to rally them by a desperate act of courage. One of the elephants was larger and more richly caparisoned than the others, and might have been carrying the young king. In a fierce rush Eleazar hacked his way through to the elephant, got underneath it and plunged his sword into its belly. The elephant keeled over and Eleazar was crushed to death. He was the first of Mattathias' sons to lose his life.

The sacrifice was of no avail. With his positions overrun, Judah gave the order to break off the fight and save what was left of his force. Scattering through the hills, they made their way back to Jerusalem. Since the defence of the city was hopeless, Judah left one contingent to make a last-ditch stand on the Temple Mount. He and his brothers led the rest, weary and dispirited, back to their hideouts in the Gophna hills. The wheel had come full circle. The years of unremitting struggle since Modi'in had brought them mastery of Judea. Suddenly they were once more outlaws in their own land, clinging to what seemed a lost cause.

The Jews on the Temple Mount held on stubbornly, beating off one attack after another. Lysias fretted at the delay. Then he received word that Philip was marching back from the eastern campaign and making his bid to take power. Lysias had to disengage from the Judean campaign and lead his army northward for the crucial showdown over the regency. He reflected that the Maccabean revolt had been sparked off by religious coercion and would subside again if religious freedom was restored. He put his views before a council meeting attended by the boy king and his top commanders:

> We daily grow weaker, our food supply is scant, the place against which we are fighting is strong, and the affairs of the kingdom press urgently upon us. Now then let us come to terms with these men, and make peace with them and with all their nation, and agree to let them live by their laws as they did before; for it was on account of their laws which we abolished that they became angry and did all these things.
>
> The speech pleased the king and the commanders, and he sent to the Jews an offer of peace, and they accepted it. So the king and the commanders gave them their oath. On these conditions the Jews evacuated the stronghold. (1 Macc. 6:57–61)

As a further sop to the orthodox, the pro-Hellenist high priest Menelaus was removed from office and taken to Syria, where he was tried and executed.

Lysias' calculations were shrewd. Most of the popular support for the Maccabean revolt receded with the military defeat of Judah, followed by the switch to a policy of religious tolerance. For the Hassidim, the religious zealots who had joined forces with the Maccabees earlier on, the struggle had been won. Not so for the Maccabees. The protest movement against persecution of the faith had developed into a movement for political independence. Judah and his brothers did not believe that their future could be built on the shifting sands of Seleucid promises, or that freedom of worship could be assured unless they were masters in their own

'Death of Eleazar.' An engraving from the Doré Bible (1865).

*Demetrius Seizes the Throne*

house. However bleak the prospect, the fight had to continue. Judah steadily built up and trained his forces, and imbued them afresh with his own martial spirit.

At this time the Seleucid regime in Antioch was plunged into a dynastic struggle that was to tear the kingdom apart.

When Seleucus IV had died in 175 BC, he had been succeeded not by his own son Demetrius, but by his younger brother Antiochus IV Epiphanes. Demetrius was at the time eleven years old and being reared in Rome, where he was kept as a hostage for the good conduct of his father. On the death of Antiochus IV his young son succeeded him as Antiochus V. Demetrius was by then a dashing and ambitious young man of twenty-three. He petitioned the Roman senate to support his legitimate claim to the Seleucid throne, but he was turned down. The senators considered that Roman self-interest would best be served by leaving the Seleucid kingdom under weak and divided rule, with a nine-year-old boy on the throne, and two of his senior kinsmen, Lysias and Philip, contending for the regency.

Demetrius refused to submit to this rebuff. He left Rome secretly and made a dramatic appearance at Tripoli, on the Syrian coast south of Antioch. The local population rallied to his cause. What was more important, the army went over to him. The boy king Antiochus V and the regent Lysias were seized by the troops and brought to Demetrius, who had them put to death. He then had himself crowned as Demetrius I Soter. (The rival regent, Philip, seems to have retired from the scene, for no more is heard of him.)

Demetrius was challenged by a rebellious eastern vassal called Timarchus. Rome, by no means loth to foment trouble, recognized Timarchus and gave him political support. Demetrius was thus involved from the outset in a struggle for the control of the vital eastern provinces: Babylonia, Persia and Media.

In these circumstances Demetrius had an obvious interest in keeping Judea pacified. He filled the vacant post of high priest in Jerusalem by appointing Alcimus (the Greek form of the Hebrew name Eliakim), a member of a priestly family of Aharonic descent. Bacchides, the commander-in-chief of the region west of the Euphrates, was despatched to Jerusalem with a contingent of troops to supervise the installation of Alcimus. The garrison stationed in the Acra fortress was reinforced as a prop to the new high priest's authority.

Alcimus was at first well received by both the pro-Hellenist and the orthodox factions. However, he had difficulties with a group of the Hassidim, the religious zealots. In an ill-advised show of force, he had sixty of them executed. This harsh act provoked popular resentment. Before long, Alcimus came to be despised in orthodox circles as a puppet of the Seleucid regime, kept in office by foreign mercenaries.

The atmosphere in Judea had become propitious for the Maccabees to take the offensive again. From their base in the Gophna hills they revived the resistance movement in the countryside, and resumed hit-and-run raids on military objectives and road traffic.

Alienated from his own people, Alcimus found himself unable to control the unrest that had sprung up. He appealed to Antioch for assistance. More troops were sent to Judea under the command of the Seleucid general Nicanor. (He had, with Georgias, been involved in the campaign that had ended in the debacle at Emmaus three years before.)

Nicanor's first priority was to open and secure the road that led northwest from Jerusalem over the Beth-horon pass to the main Seleucid base in the coastal plain at Gazara. Maccabean raiding parties had been harassing the road and the pass from the adjacent Gophna hills. Moving along the road, Nicanor's force was ambushed and attacked at the village of Capharsalama (Kfar Shalom), and forced to beat an undignified retreat back to Jerusalem.

Smarting under this reverse, Nicanor asked for reinforcements to be sent up from the coastal plain. He arranged to meet the additional troops at the Beth-horon pass and escort them along the vulnerable stretch of road back to the capital. For this purpose Nicanor sallied out again with the strongest force he could muster. The meeting at the pass took place as planned. Nicanor marched back without incident as far as Adasa, about half-way to Jerusalem. Judah's men had slipped across the road the previous night and concealed themselves on the south side. Their attack from that unexpected direction achieved complete surprise. Nicanor was killed in the first rush. His troops were routed and fled in disorder back along the way they had just come. They were pursued all the way down the pass to Gazara.

*The Day of Nicanor (161 B*

Once more the Maccabees moved into Jerusalem. Soon they had reasserted their control of Judea, except for the Acra fortress. For a long time observant Jews would celebrate this resounding success in the annual 'Day of Nicanor'.

*Judah's Last Stand*

For some time King Demetrius was unable to react to the fresh defeat in Judea, as he was fully engaged in Mesopotamia. Judah used this respite from military pressure to take a bold political initiative. The conduct of the Roman senate over the accession of Demetrius had been revealing to the Maccabean leaders. It was apparent that Rome would take every chance to weaken and disrupt the Seleucid empire from within, while avoiding direct military involvement. The implication was that Rome would favour any armed insurrection or national liberation movement with which the regime in Antioch had to cope. (In the 20th century AD, the Soviet Union would exploit the same policy of indirect aggression in its conflict with 'western imperialism'). In a bid for Roman protection, Judah sent two trusted supporters, Eupolemus and Jason, on a special mission to Rome. Judah's expectations were justified. The Maccabean ambassadors were received by the senate and permitted to address that august body. Their opening words were: 'Judas, who is also called Maccabeus, and his brothers and the people of the Jews have sent us to you to establish alliance and peace with you, that we may be enrolled as your allies and friends' (1 Macc. 8:20).

In spite of the fact that Judah was not a head of state but an insurgent leader within the territory of a foreign power, the senate agreed to conclude with him a treaty of friendship and of mutual support in war. According to the text given in the First Book of Maccabees, if either side found itself at war the other side 'shall act as their allies wholeheartedly, as the occasion may indicate to them' (1 Macc. 8:25). Moreover, an economic blockade would be imposed on the enemy by withholding from it grain, arms, money or ships. As was customary, the treaty was inscribed on bronze tablets.

The Maccabees could have had few illusions about the practical value of this pact in time of stress. The Romans were unlikely to intervene unless and until it suited them to do so. But Judah hoped the treaty would have a useful psychological impact. His own people might be readier to believe that political independence was a feasible

aim. At the same time, it might have a deterrent effect on the Seleucid regime.

Unfortunately, the effect on Demetrius was contrary to what Judah had assumed. Antioch had been presented with a challenge it dared not evade. It would be a crippling blow to the Seleucid empire if Judea were to secede, place itself under the umbrella of Roman power and maybe align itself with Ptolemaic Egypt. There was also a prestige factor involved, for Demetrius could not afford to seem frightened of the Roman senate. He decided on a major offensive without delay to subdue the troublesome Judean province.

General Bacchides moved again into Judea at the head of a large and heavily equipped army that included crack regiments from the Seleucid forces. He advanced by the shortest route, straight through the Samarian hills, and reached Jerusalem unopposed. Judah mustered three thousand men. But when they saw the overwhelming strength deployed by the enemy, defeatism spread through the force and most of it melted away. Judah was left with a nucleus of only eight hundred fighting men.

Bacchides planned systematic 'search and destroy' operations against the insurgents. Following the military logic of Nicanor before him, he first led his army out of Jerusalem towards Beth-horon, in order to establish a firm hold on the vital road and pass. Against all the odds, Judah decided to attack the Seleucid troops on the march. He picked a place for the purpose at Elasa, some six miles from Beth-horon. His comrades tried to dissuade him: 'We are not able. Let us rather save our own lives now, and let us come back with our brethren and fight them; we are too few' (1 Macc. 9:9). Judah replied firmly: 'Far be it from us to do such a thing as to flee from them. If our time has come, let us die bravely for our brethren, and leave no cause to question our honour' (1 Macc. 9:10).

Bacchides grouped his cavalry, infantry, archers and slingmen in two groups. Judah left the smaller part of his men to contain the enemy's southern wing. He and the main body flung themselves ferociously against the northern wing, sending it reeling back towards the pass. But the southern wing broke through and counter-attacked the Maccabees from the rear. Hand-to-hand fighting swirled over the hills for hours, and ended only when Judah was struck down. He

OVERLEAF LEFT 'Susannah and the Elders', a painting by the nineteenth-century French artist Theodore Chassériau (1856).

died still clutching the sword he had taken from the Seleucid commander Apollonius in the early days of the Revolt. The surviving Maccabees scattered.

After darkness had fallen, Judah's brothers retrieved his body from the battlefield, carried it to the deserted village of Modi'in, and wept as they buried it in the family tomb.

Judah the Maccabee has remained for the Jews one of the great heroes of their national saga, and a symbol of their never-ending struggle for freedom.

## Jonathan and Simon (161–134 BC)

THE THREE REMAINING MACCABEAN BROTHERS and their followers met secretly in the Gophna hideout. Jonathan was chosen as their new leader. He was the youngest of the sons of Mattathias, and the ablest after Judah. It was plain that they could no longer remain where they were. The group disbanded and reassembled at a pre-arranged place, the well of Asphar in the Wilderness of Judea, about eight miles south-east of Bethlehem. Their new home was a barren expanse of canyons and caves that dropped steeply from the crest of the Hebron hills to the Dead Sea, four thousand feet below. From time immemorial, fugitives had gone to ground in this inhospitable terrain, including David and his band of outlaws eight centuries before the Maccabees.

In the course of his mopping-up operations, Bacchides sent a detachment of troops to hunt down Jonathan and his men. On a Sabbath day the Maccabean remnant was cut off in the marshy ground where the Jordan river flows into the northern end of the Dead Sea. The trapped men fought their way out and escaped by leaping into the river and swimming across it.

John, the eldest Maccabean brother, was in charge of a party taking their baggage into Transjordan for safekeeping by the friendly Nabateans. They were waylaid and killed, and the baggage plundered, by marauding Bedouin of the Beni Jambri tribe from Madeba, east of the Dead Sea. Jonathan and Simon, the two surviving brothers, took swift revenge. They ambushed a wedding procession of the offending tribe, killing some of the tribesmen and taking a great deal of booty.

Having crushed the rebellion, Bacchides took a series of measures to consolidate the Seleucid

hold on Judea. Official positions were filled with those who had proved themselves loyal to the regime. These 'king's men' collaborated in rounding-up Maccabean sympathizers: 'They sought and searched for the friends of Judas, and brought them to Bacchides, and he took vengeance on them and made sport of them. Thus there was great distress in Israel, such as had not been since the time that prophets ceased to appear among them' (1 Macc. 9:26,27). Youths from distinguished Judean families were taken into the Acra fortress and kept there as hostages. On the other hand, nothing was done to interfere with worship in the Temple or to offend Jewish religious susceptibilities. The lesson of Antiochus IV Epiphanes had not been forgotten. *Pacification Measures*

Bacchides ensured the military control of the country by establishing a system of strongholds and garrisons at strategic points commanding the centres of population and the main roads. The royal fortresses of Acra in Jerusalem, Gazara on the coastal plain and Beth-zur in the Hebron hills were strengthened and provided with ample reserve supplies. A ring of new forts was constructed at seven more places within a radius of twenty miles from Jerusalem.

The success of Bacchides' programme was almost marred by another provocative action by the high priest Alcimus. The internal courts of the Temple were closed off by a lattice beyond which Gentiles were forbidden to pass. Presumably wanting to show his Seleucid masters how broadminded he was, Alcimus ordered the lattice to be demolished and pagans to be given access to the enclosures beyond it. The orthodox community was outraged by the intended sacrilege. Alcimus suffered a stroke before the work was started, and died soon after. The Seleucid authorities did not appoint another high priest in his place, and the office remained vacant for the following seven years. By a strange twist of irony its next incumbent would be that self-same Jonathan the Maccabee who at that time was hiding out in the caves of the Judean desert.

The Maccabean Revolt appeared to be over, and the situation in Judea stabilized. The occupation forces were in full military control, basing themselves on the network of fortresses. With his mission accomplished, Bacchides returned to Syria with part of his army.

Two years later he was brought back to deal

PREVIOUS PAGE 'Judas Maccabeus', a wall painting by the fifteenth-century Italian artist Taddeo di Bartolo.

with renewed unrest. He found that Jonathan had occupied and rebuilt the ruined fortress of Beth-basi, at the edge of the Judean desert near Bethlehem. From this base the Maccabees had quietly moved around the countryside, renewing old contacts, gaining recruits and stirring up resistance. Once more they had become a focus for patriotic sentiment at the grass-roots level. They were helped by the inertia of the bored Seleucid garrison troops, and by the lack of leadership in the loyalist camp in Jerusalem since the death of the high priest.

Bacchides set out to eliminate the trouble at its source by capturing the remaining Maccabean leaders, and laid siege to their stronghold at Beth-basi. Jonathan managed to slip away, leaving Simon in charge of the defence. Enlisting the help of two desert sheikhs attracted by the chance of loot, Jonathan harried the besieging troops and their supply lines. Simon made a surprise sortie from the fortress and set the heavy siege machinery on fire. Bacchides became tired of this futile mini-war. Further fighting against the small but unquenchable foe did not seem worth the cost in men, money and effort, at a time when the regime of his royal master Demetrius was in danger from plots and intrigues nearer home. Bacchides negotiated a truce. Jonathan and his fellow-rebels were granted an amnesty, and their captured comrades were released. They were permitted to return unmolested to normal civilian life, provided they gave up armed activities and kept out of Jerusalem. With that arrangement concluded, Bacchides went back to Syria. The date was about 155 BC.

*The Contest for the Throne*

Jonathan and his group settled down at Michmash, eight miles north-east of Jerusalem. For the next few years Judea was at peace, and the occupation forces reduced. Jonathan worked patiently to gain the allegiance of his people, and became accepted as the unofficial national leader. 'And Jonathan began to judge the people, and he destroyed the ungodly out of Israel' (1 Macc. 9:73). Meanwhile, he waited for an opportunity to move closer to the ultimate goal of Judean independence. Events on the larger Seleucid stage took a turn favourable to him.

In 152 BC a new claimant to the Seleucid throne appeared on the scene. He was a handsome young man called Alexander Balas, who maintained that he was a son of Antiochus IV Epiphanes, and he did indeed have a strong physi-

cal resemblance to that departed monarch. In all probability he was an imposter, produced by the enemies of Demetrius in a plot to overthrow him. Powerful forces antagonistic to Demetrius were ranged behind Balas. He was actively supported by the Egyptian ruler Ptolemy VI Philometor and by the kings of Cappadocia and Pergamum in Asia Minor. The Roman senate extended recognition to the claimant. The threat to Demetrius became very real when Balas landed at Ptolemais (Acre) and proclaimed himself ruler of the Seleucid empire. The ensuing struggle gave scope to Jonathan's innate political sagacity. He promoted the Judean cause by getting the contenders to bid against each other for his allegiance.

Demetrius perceived that Judea had become the 'soft under-belly' of his kingdom and that the Maccabees were the dominant party in it. He sent Jonathan a letter in peaceable words to honour him; for he said, 'Let us act first to make peace with him before he makes peace with Alexander against us, for he will remember all the wrongs which we did to him and to his brothers and his nation' (1 Macc. 10:4,5). Jonathan was given the status of an ally, with authority to raise and equip armed forces. The young hostages held in the Acra citadel were released and returned to their families.

Jonathan promptly moved back to Jerusalem, called together the citizens and read out the royal letter. He then began to rebuild the fortifications of the Temple Mount. The outlying fortresses that had been constructed by Bacchides were abandoned, and the Seleucid presence in Judea was limited to the Acra in Jerusalem and to Beth-zur. Except for these two fortified positions, Jonathan was now in effective command of Judea. He proceeded to reorganize its administration and expand its military forces, while remaining uncommitted in the dynastic struggle.

Alexander Balas made his counter-offer for Maccabean support in a message which read: 'King Alexander to his brother Jonathan, greeting. We have heard about you, that you are a mighty warrior and worthy to be our friend. And so we have appointed you today to be the high priest of your nation; you are to be called the king's friend . . . and you are to take our side and keep friendship with us' (1 Macc. 10:18–20). With the letter came a gift of a purple robe and a gold crown for Jonathan to wear as high priest. Soon after, at the Feast of Tabernacles (Succoth) Jonathan appeared at the Temple service in the vestments of the high priest, thereby assuming the office that had remained empty for seven years. The importance of the appointment was not just religious; it gave formal endorsement to the political and military authority Jonathan had gained.

Alexander's overtures to Jonathan drove Demetrius to promise sweeping concessions. They included the return of three Judean districts that had previously been transferred to the province of Samaria; evacuation of the Acra citadel; general exemption from taxes; and an annual grant from the royal treasury. Jonathan and his colleagues received this lavish offer with scepticism. They regarded it as an insincere gesture from a king who was fighting desperately to retain his throne, and would withdraw the concessions if he came out on top. The Maccabean leaders decided to back Alexander Balas.

At the decisive battle in 150 BC, Demetrius was defeated and killed. Alexander Balas entered Antioch in triumph and was enthroned as Alexander I. The Egyptian ruler Ptolemy gave his daughter Cleopatra Thea in marriage to the new king. At the insistence of Ptolemy, the marriage ceremony was held not in Antioch but at Ptolemais, because it was closer to Egypt. Jonathan was among the guests invited to the wedding. He returned with an additional appointment as the governor and military commander of the Judean province. For the next three years Judea enjoyed a peaceful local autonomy.

In 147 BC the struggle for the Seleucid throne broke out afresh. A youthful son of Demetrius I, also called Demetrius, landed on the north Syrian coast with a formation of mercenary soldiers from Crete. Alexander led his troops from Antioch to meet the thrust. An experienced general, Apollonius, was sent by Demetrius to gain control of southern Syria. He occupied the coastal plain and sent Jonathan a contemptuous command to surrender. Jonathan went on to the offensive. Heading a well-trained army of ten thousand men, he crossed the coastal plain and captured the port-city of Joppa (Jaffa). Apollonius withdrew southward, leading the Judeans into an ambush. They were hard pressed, but the tide turned when Simon arrived with fresh auxiliary contingents. The enemy was routed. Alexander was grateful for this unexpected victory over his rival's forces; Jonathan was rewarded with the golden buckle denoting the high title of 'king's kinsman', and with the transfer to Judea of the city and district of Ekron on the coastal plain.

At this stage Ptolemy projected Egypt into the Seleucid civil war. He led an army northward and occupied the coastal cities. Jonathan met him in Joppa and escorted him for some distance. Ostensibly Ptolemy was marching to the aid of his son-in-law, and Jonathan's friend, Alexander Balas. In actual fact Ptolemy was taking cynical advantage of the conflict to extend Egyptian influence. On arrival in Antioch, he turned against Alexander and joined forces with the rival claimant, whom he helped to put on the throne as Demetrius II Nicator. To mark the switch, Ptolemy remarried his daughter Cleopatra Thea to Demetrius II. (This lady was to have an extraordinary marital career. In due course she was again wed to Demetrius' brother Antiochus VII Sidetes. Her son by Alexander Balas, and two sons by Demetrius II, would all reach the throne. She thus became the wife of three emperors and the mother of three more – surely an unbroken world record!)

The combined army of Demetrius II and Ptolemy defeated Alexander I in battle. Alexander fled, and sought protection with an Arab sheikh, who cut off his head and sent it with his compliments to Ptolemy. A little later, the Egyptian ruler himself died of wounds sustained in the battle.

Jonathan was summoned to appear before King Demetrius II at Ptolemais. He went with great foreboding, as he had been a supporter of the previous ruler Alexander Balas. He had also incurred Seleucid displeasure by laying siege to the Acra fortress. But the new ruler seemed eager to gain his allegiance, and received him cordially. He was confirmed as high priest. The three districts in Samaria that Demetrius I had previously offered were now incorporated in Judea. The province was relieved of tax burdens. Jonathan paid three hundred talents of silver for these far-reaching concessions. The siege of the Acra fortress was quietly dropped.

The reign of Demetrius II soon ran into trouble. Disaffected elements in the army, led by an ambitious general called Tryphon, stirred up a popular rising. Demetrius sent an urgent appeal to Jonathan for help, offering to evacuate the Acra fortress as an inducement. Three thousand Judean troops were sent to Antioch, and arrived in time to save the king just as the mob was about to storm his palace. With the danger passed, Demetrius II failed to carry out his promise about the Acra, a fact that he would regret when his empire was again torn by civil war.

Before Alexander Balas was killed, he had secretly entrusted his infant son to the care of a friendly Arab chieftain. Tryphon found the boy and proclaimed him emperor as Antiochus VI Dionysos, with himself as regent. Tryphon occupied Antioch. Demetrius fled to the port-city of Seleucia, further to the north, where he set up his capital. Months of confused fighting led to a stalemate, with the empire divided between the two factions. Demetrius retained control of the eastern provinces and Tryphon of the western.

Tryphon sent a friendly message to Jonathan in Jerusalem, seeking his allegiance. He offered to recognize Jonathan as high priest, appoint Simon as the military commander of the coastal region and confirm all the territories acquired by Judea, including the Perea district of Trans-jordan. The offer was accepted. The two Maccabean brothers had gained *de facto* control of an area stretching from the Mediterranean coast to Trans-jordan, and comprising most of the biblical Land of Israel. Within its expanded borders Judea had virtual home rule, though not yet independence. Jonathan and Simon commanded the strongest army between Syria and Egypt.

Demetrius II was not as yet prepared to acquiesce in the loss of Judea. He sent a military expedition to regain the province. Jonathan marched north to meet it and repulsed it in a battle near Hazor in the Huleh valley. When he learned that a larger Seleucid force was on its way, Jonathan intercepted it at Hamath in the valley of Lebanon, before it reached the Judean border. Faced with the tough Maccabean army, Demetrius' force withdrew without giving battle. On his journey back Jonathan swung through Damascus, rescuing a persecuted Jewish community along the way. Simon meanwhile had retaken Joppa and captured the fortress of Beth-zur, where he installed a Judean garrison.

Jonathan sent emissaries to Rome to renew the pact made by Judah. This was a measure of political reassurance, even though Rome had not lifted a finger to help Judah when he was defeated. On their way back, the Judean envoys visited Sparta in Greece, and delivered a friendly message from Jonathan to his Spartan 'brothers'.

Jonathan assembled 'the elders of the people' and explained that they had to step up their defence preparations, 'to build the walls of Jerusalem still higher, and to erect a high barrier between the citadel and the city to separate it from the city, in order to isolate it so that its garrison could neither buy nor sell' (1 Macc. 12:36). *The Death of Jonathan*

Judea was next threatened from an unexpected quarter. Intelligence reports reached Jonathan that Tryphon was leading an army from Syria towards Judea, along the Jordan valley route. The motive behind this action can only be surmised. Tryphon was preparing the ground to depose his royal ward, Antiochus VI, and to seize the throne in Antioch for himself. The growing strength and independence of Judea under Jonathan's leadership made it a doubtful accomplice in such a move. Without Judea, the southern flank of the Seleucid kingdom would lie exposed to Egypt and possibly to Rome. Tryphon was determined to gain firm control over Judea.

Jonathan was puzzled and disturbed by this military move, since he had aligned himself with Tryphon against Demetrius II. Unwilling to take a chance on the intention behind the move, he mobilized his forces. Tryphon reached the Beth-shan plain to find Jonathan there with a Judean army of forty thousand men. The onus was on Tryphon to show his hand. He knew that bluster and threats would have not the slightest effect on the seasoned and resolute Maccabees. Tryphon resorted to guile. He invited Jonathan to his camp, showered gifts and honours on him and in a rhetorical flourish told his officers to obey Jonathan as they would himself. Turning to Jonathan, he said: 'Why have you wearied all these people when we are not at war? Dismiss them now to their homes and choose for yourself a few men to stay with you, and come with me to Ptolemais. I will hand it over to you as well as the other strongholds and the remaining troops and all the officials, and will turn round and go home. For that is why I am here' (1 Macc. 12:44–45).

Jonathan stifled his doubts, and thought it prudent to show that he had confidence in Tryphon. He was also tempted by the prospect of acquiring, through Tryphon, Ptolemais and other coastal cities, thereby adding much to the size and regional importance of Judea. He sent his army back, keeping only three thousand men with him. Two thousand of them were left in western Galilee and the rest accompanied Jonathan into Ptolemais as his bodyguard.

Having lured the Maccabean leader within the gates of the heavily fortified city, Tryphon had him seized, while the men with him were attacked and slaughtered by the garrison troops and the population. Cavalry units were sent from Ptolemais to round up the contingent Jonathan had left in the nearby Galilee hills. It was assumed that these men had either run away or would surrender, especially since the story had been put out that Jonathan had been killed. When the cavalry found the Judeans drawn up and ready to fight to the last man, they left them alone and returned to Ptolemais. The Judean contingent brought the shattering news to Jerusalem 'and all Israel mourned deeply'.

Simon immediately took charge. Before he could prepare to withstand the impending invasion by Tryphon, he had first to dispel the mood of gloom and fear that had seized the people. He called together a public gathering in Jerusalem and addressed it as follows:

> You yourselves know what great things I and my brothers and the house of my father have done for the laws and the sanctuary; you know also the wars and the difficulties which we have seen. By reason of this all my brothers have perished for the sake of Israel, and I alone am left. And now, far be it from me to spare my life in any time of distress, for I am not better than my brothers. But I will avenge my nation and the sanctuary and your wives and children, for all the nations have gathered together out of hatred to destroy us (1 Macc. 13:3–6).

Simon's courageous words inspired the gathering. They acclaimed him as their new leader and pledged themselves to carry out his orders. Simon had them finish the work of repair on the defence walls of Jerusalem. An army unit was sent to seize and hold Joppa. Simon personally led the main part of the army down to the coastal plain and took up positions round the newly-constructed fortress of Adida. He did not anticipate much danger from the Seleucid garrison in the Acra citadel. They were cut off behind the blockade wall Jonathan had constructed round the fortress, and their supplies were running out.

Marching down the coast from Ptolemais, Tryphon had to accept the fact that the Judean people had not collapsed with the loss of their leader Jonathan. On the contrary, they had rallied behind Simon, and stood ready to fight. Tryphon sent officers to parley with Simon. They disclosed that Jonathan was alive in their camp. Tryphon maintained that Jonathan was being detained for failure to pay the tribute due to the royal treasury. He offered to release him on payment of a hundred talents of silver and the handing over of two sons of Jonathan as hostages for his good conduct.

Simon was in an agonizing dilemma. He felt that the offer was another piece of trickery. On the other hand, if he rejected it, it would be said afterwards that he had failed to save Jonathan's life while it was still possible. Simon complied with the blackmail demands. But his premonition proved correct, for Jonathan was not freed.

Tryphon resumed his advance. He outflanked the Judean force and continued down the coast, swinging inland towards Hebron. He was following the strategy of Lysias, and trying to reach Jerusalem by the southern back door. Near Hebron, Tryphon received desperate messages from the Acra garrison. They were starving and would not be able to hold out unless relief came at once. Tryphon ordered his cavalry to break through to Jerusalem by making a sweep to the north-east through the Judean desert. But winter had already closed in. A snowstorm made it impossible for the horses to get through the mountain tracks. At this point Tryphon decided to abandon the campaign. He moved his troops down into the warmth of the Jordan valley, and turned northward on the long march back to Damascus. When he reached Baskama on the north-east shore of the Sea of Galilee, he had the captive Jonathan executed and buried.

Simon retrieved the body and had it reburied in the family tomb at Modi'in. He built an impressive monument of polished stone over the tomb, in memory of his parents and his four dead brothers.

The year was 142 BC. Almost a quarter-century *Simon the* had passed since the fateful morning when *Standard-* Mattathias had raised the flag of revolt in *Bearer* Modi'in. Judah had been the Maccabean leader for five years, then Jonathan for nearly twenty. Simon, the second son of Mattathias, was the only one left alive. He assumed the family mission and carried on as the standard-bearer of Jewish freedom.

Simon's first move was a political one. Turning against the treacherous Tryphon, he sent envoys to restore relations with the emperor Demetrius II. It was a well-timed initiative. Demetrius had every reason to welcome a Judean switch to his side. Tryphon had carried out his plan to depose the child Antiochus VI and proclaim himself emperor. Demetrius was unable to throw himself fully into the bitter struggle against the usurper. He was fighting off a Parthian invasion of Babylonia, the last of the eastern provinces that had remained loyal to him. Demetrius accepted Simon's conditions. His reply stated that 'we are ready to make a general peace with you and to write to our officials to grant you release from tribute ... and let the strongholds that you have built be your possession' (1 Macc. 13:37,38). This letter was a striking diplomatic victory. In effect, it acknowledged the independence of Judea. The people understood that a new era had dawned, for they began to date their documents and contracts: 'In the first year of Simon the great high priest and commander and leader of the Jews.'

Simon now had a free hand to eliminate the last bastions of Seleucid power left in Judea. He besieged and took Gazara, the fortress and military base that commanded the road from the coast to Jerusalem. The city was settled with Judeans and placed under the command of Simon's eldest son, John Hyrcanus. Simon built himself a residence in Gazara.

The most resounding event was the surrender of the garrison in the Acra citadel in Jerusalem – the symbol of Seleucid rule for about thirty-seven years, since the days of Antiochus IV Epiphanes. A procession of Jews entered the citadel, joyfully singing psalms of praise and playing musical instruments, 'because a great enemy had been crushed and removed from Israel' (1 Macc. 13:51).

Simon's status, and the succession to it, were given a constitutional basis in a popular mandate. In 140 BC there met in Jerusalem 'the great assembly of the priests and the people and the rulers of the nation and the elders of the country' (1 Macc. 14:28). This representative body

solemnly conferred on Simon the offices of high priest, commander and ethnarch (governor). The religious, civil and military authority was thus combined in the person of the high priest. It was vested in Simon 'for ever', which meant that it would remain a hereditary position in the Hasmonean house to which he belonged.

Under Simon's leadership Judea enjoyed freedom from external pressure for five years, until 137 BC. The country was then once more sucked into the maelstrom of Seleucid politics. In his eastern campaign, Demetrius II had been taken captive by the Parthian king Mithridates. (He was well treated and regained his throne twelve years later.) His rival Tryphon was left as an unopposed Seleucid ruler – but not for long. Antiochus, a younger brother of Demetrius II, raised a mercenary army and sailed from the island of Rhodes to regain the Seleucid realm for his house. He declared himself emperor as Antiochus VII Euergetes (better known by his nickname of Sidetes). In a bid for Simon's support, Antiochus wrote to him pledging friendship and undertaking to respect all the concessions granted to Judea by previous rulers.

When Antiochus Sidetes landed on the coast most of Tryphon's troops and supporters defected to him. Tryphon fled and reached the port-town of Dor, between Caesarea and Haifa. Antiochus' troops cut off the town and his warships blockaded it from the sea. Simon sent two thousand men to assist Antiochus, but the gesture was rebuffed. It was an ominous sign that the new emperor, with victory in his grasp, had lost interest in conciliating the Maccabean leader. Tryphon escaped by ship.

A trusted counsellor of Antiochus Sidetes soon came to call on Simon in Jerusalem, carrying a stiff ultimatum. Simon was to hand back Joppa, Gazara and the Acra citadel in Jerusalem, together with all the monies obtained as tribute from places conquered by the Maccabeans outside the original borders of Judea. Failing that, he was to pay a thousand talents of silver as compensation; 'Otherwise we will come and conquer you' (1 Macc. 15:31).

Simon's reply invoked the historic rights of the Jews in the Land of Israel:

We have neither taken foreign land nor seized foreign property, but only the inheritance of our fathers, which at one time had been

OVERLEAF LEFT A page from the world's first printed Bible, with hand-painted illuminations, produced by Gutenberg at Mainz, Germany, in 1453–55. It took two years to complete the first edition of one hundred and fifty copies.

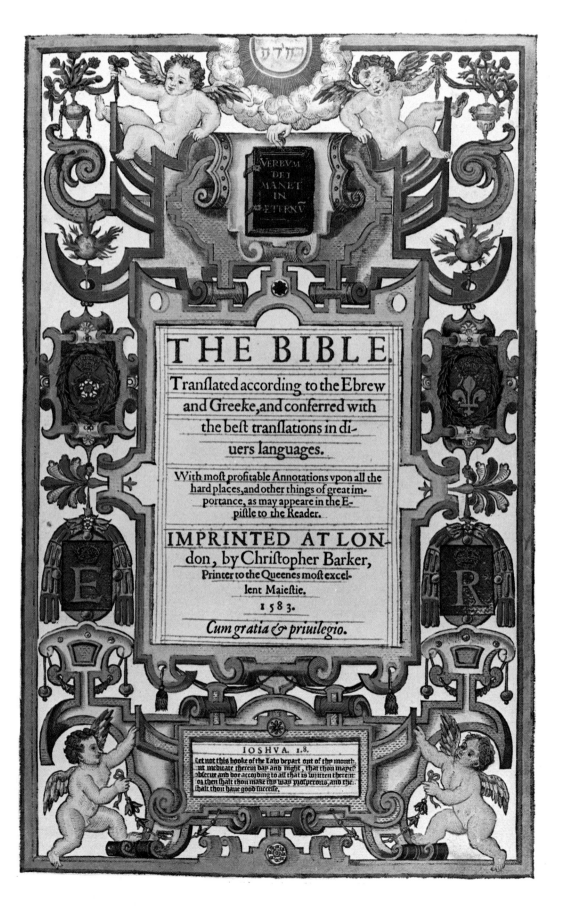

VERBVM
DEI
MANET
IN
ÆTERNŨ

# THE BIBLE.

Translated according to the Ebrew
and Greeke, and conferred with
the beſt tranſlations in di-
uers languages.

With moſt profitable Annotations vpon all the
hard places, and other things of great importance, as may appeare in the E-
piſtle to the Reader.

**IMPRINTED AT LON-**
don, by Chriſtopher Barker,
Printer to the Queenes moſt excellent Maieſtie.
1 5 8 3.

*Cum gratia & priuilegio.*

IOSHVA. 1.8.
Let not this booke of the Law depart out of thy mouth,
but meditate therein day and night, that thou mayeſt
obſerue and doe according to all that is written therein:
for then ſhalt thou make thy way proſperous, and thou
ſhalt thou haue good ſucceſſe.

unjustly taken by our enemies. Now that we have the opportunity, we are firmly holding the inheritance of our fathers. As for Joppa and Gazara, which you demand, they were causing great damage among the people and to our land; for them we will give a hundred talents (1 Macc. 15:33–35).

Without another word the angry envoy rose and departed. In reporting to the emperor on his mission, he added a touch of malice by describing how Simon lived in state, with gold and silver plate displayed on his sideboard.

The emperor was determined that at a suitable time Judea would have to be subdued by force. Meanwhile, he set out in pursuit of Tryphon, who was later caught and forced to commit suicide. The general Cendebeus was left in command of the coastal area. Cendebeus established his headquarters at Jamnia and constructed an advance fortified position at Kedron (near modern Gedera). They carried out penetration raids across the border, harassing the local population and cutting the roads. Plans were drawn up to regain full control of the coastal plain by the recapture of Gazara and Joppa, two key cities in Maccabean hands.

Simon reacted vigorously. A Judean army of twenty thousand men was mobilized, and placed under the command of Simon's two elder sons, John Hyrcanus and Judah. They advanced into the coastal plain and bivouacked for the night at Modi'in. At dawn next morning they launched a massive assault across the Sorek river. The enemy was routed and the Kedron stronghold taken. Judah was wounded in the fighting, but Hyrcanus continued the pursuit as far as Azotus (Ashdod), where the fortifications were destroyed.

For the next three years, Judea was left undisturbed. Simon was able to develop what was an independent Jewish state in all but name.

Simon's period of leadership later seemed a relaxed and idyllic interlude in the turbulent Jewish history of the period. The First Book of Maccabees contains a nostalgic poem in praise of Simon:

> They tilled their land in peace;
>     the ground gave its increase,
>     and the trees of the plains their fruit.
> Old men sat in the streets;
>     they all talked together of good things;

> and the youths donned the glories
>     and garments of war.
> He supplied the cities with food,
>     and furnished them with the means
>     of defence,
>     till his renown spread to the ends of
>     the earth.
> He established peace in the land,
>     and Israel rejoiced with great joy.
> Each man sat under his vine and his
>     fig tree,
> and there was none to make them afraid.
> No one was left in the land to fight them,
> and the kings were crushed in those days.
> He strengthened all the humble of his
>     people;
>     he sought out the law,
>     and did away with every lawless
>     and wicked man.
> He made the sanctuary glorious,
>     and added to the vessels of the
>     sanctuary.
>                         (1 Macc. 14:8–15)

Like all his brothers before him, Simon was *Simon* destined to come to a violent and untimely end. *Murdered* His son-in-law, whose name was Ptolemy (unrelated to the ruling dynasty in Egypt), had been appointed military governor in Jericho. A vain and ambitious man, he secretly plotted with the adherents of Antiochus VII Sidetes to restore Seleucid rule over Judea, with himself as governor. The unsuspecting Simon came on a visit to Jericho, accompanied by two of his sons, Judah and Mattathias. Ptolemy gave a banquet in their honour. When they were drowsy with food and wine, Ptolemy's men rushed in and killed them and their attendants.

John Hyrcanus, Simon's eldest son, was at his post in Gazara at that time. Ptolemy sent a squad of soldiers to surprise and murder him as well. Another detachment of troops was despatched to seize control in Jerusalem. One of Simon's party had managed to escape and reached John Hyrcanus. Forewarned, he was able to waylay and wipe out the men sent against him, and to reach Jerusalem before Ptolemy. The conspiracy had been aborted.

The First Book of Maccabees ends with the death of Simon, and the election of John Hyrcanus to succeed his father as high priest, military commander and political leader. The

PREVIOUS PAGE Title page of a Bible presented to Elizabeth I of England in 1583. By a royal proclamation of 1589, the exclusive privilege to print bibles in England was conferred on the Queen's Printer and the Universities of Oxford and Cambridge.

heroic deeds of the five Maccabean brothers had given birth to a Hasmonean state that was to last for another two-thirds of a century.

## Epilogue: The Hasmonean State

THE THIRTY-YEAR PERIOD OF JOHN HYRCANUS' rule (134–104 BC) was to be rich in accomplishment, but it started badly.

Shortly after Simon's death, the emperor Antiochus VII Sidetes forcefully reasserted Seleucid suzerainty over Judea. He invaded the country and laid siege to Jerusalem. The city held out for two years, till John Hyrcanus was forced to submit. He agreed to pay tribute for Joppa and other cities occupied by Judea, and to supply a body of troops for the renewed Seleucid campaign against the Parthians in the east. The conditions might have been harsher but for the emperor's fear of provoking the intervention of Rome, the external power with whom Judah, Jonathan and Simon had cultivated their ties.

In 129 BC Antiochus Sidetes was killed in the Parthian war. He was the last strong ruler of the Seleucid empire, and his death ended its role as a great power. For the next sixty years it would flounder through a morass of dynastic intrigue and civil strife, until its existence ended in Roman occupation.

*Expansion and Decline* Against this background of Seleucid weakness, John Hyrcanus consolidated and expanded the Hasmonean state. His conquests pushed out the borders to include the coastline north and south of Joppa; Idumea in the south, as far as Beersheba; and the Samarian hill region of Shechem (Nablus). The Idumeans were converted to Judaism. The Samaritans in Shechem clung to their own identity as a separate Jewish sect.

In the latter years of his reign John Hyrcanus moved against three fortified Hellenist cities that cut Judea off from the Galilee. They were Strato's Tower (later Caesarea) on the coast, Samaria north of Shechem, and Scythopolis (Beth-shan) in the Jezreel valley. The siege of Samaria was protracted and difficult. Two sons of John Hyrcanus, in command of the Judean forces, had to beat back a Seleucid relief force. When the city fell, Hyrcanus expelled its inhabitants and destroyed it. With the capture of the other two Greek cities, the way was open to Galilee.

John Hyrcanus' elder son and successor, Judah Aristobolus I, ruled for only one year (104–103 BC). He was the first of the Hasmonean dynasty to assume the title of king. Galilee was annexed at this time. The Itureans, an Arab people that had spread into the Galilee highlands, were also converted to Judaism.

Under Alexander Jannai (103–76 BC), a younger son of John Hyrcanus, the Jewish state reached the zenith of its power. He completed the conquest of practically the whole biblical Land of Israel, from the Egyptian border below Gaza in the south-west to the sources of the Jordan in the north-east, including most of Trans-jordan.

Alexander Jannai's rule was followed by that of his widow Salome Alexandra (76–67 BC) and his son Aristobolus II (67–63 BC). In 63 BC Judea was occupied by Pompey's Roman legions, who brought the Seleucid empire to an end. Hyrcanus II (63–40 BC), the brother of Aristobolus II, remained the nominal ruler, but was deprived of the title of king. A shrunken Judea became in fact a Roman protectorate.

There was a last brief flicker of independence under Mattathias Antigonus (40–37 BC), who was supported by Parthia against Rome. Then the Hasmonean dynasty was swept aside by Herod the Great, who was of Idumean stock. With Roman help he seized power in Judea and founded a new dynasty. Herod's marriage to the Hasmonean princess Mariamne, granddaughter of Hyrcanus II, was designed to make his regime more acceptable to the Judean people. But Herod remained so jealous of the popularity and legendary prestige of the Hasmonean house that he had Mariamne executed on dubious charges of conspiracy, and later arranged for the murder of the two sons he had by her.

*The Internal Schism* As the Hasmonean state grew outwardly stronger, its internal cohesion weakened. Two parties had emerged in the rule of John Hyrcanus, the Sadducees and the Pharisees. The Sadducees, in Hebrew *zadukim*, took their name from Zadok, high priest in the reign of King David. They represented the priesthood and an upper-class elite, loyal to the throne and conservative in Temple worship. The Pharisees, in Hebrew *perushim* ('dissenters'), were closer to the common people and critical of the establishment. In religious matters they based themselves on the Bible rather than the Temple, and became expert at adapting the scriptural laws to daily life by a process of interpretation and precedent.

'The Worship of the Golden Calf.' From a Passover
Haggadah illustrated by the American artist Ben Shahn.

The Jordan Valley near the confluence of the Jordan and Yarmuk Rivers. In the background are the Golan Heights, left, and the Gilead plateau, right. The Naharaim hydroelectric station is on the river in the middle distance. The valley here is over seven hundred feet below sea level, and about four miles wide.

The differences between Sadducees and Pharisees were thus political and social as well as theological. Alexander Jannai, an oriental despot in character, regarded the influence of the Pharisees as subversive and persecuted them with great cruelty. However, the two divergent trends persisted through the Hasmonean and Herodian periods until both the State and the Temple were wiped out by the Roman legions in 70 AD.

While it lasted, the Hasmonean state embodied the ideals of Jewish freedom and independence that the Maccabean brothers had fought for with such tenacity and selflessness. In other respects, the state did not always live up to the Maccabean legacy, particularly concerning the moral calibre of its leaders.

Seen in historical perspective, the Hasmonean period left an indelible mark on Jewish history. It preserved and carried forward the biblical heritage of the Jewish people, and its distinctive identity, faith and culture. Without the Maccabean Revolt and the religious and national liberation it achieved, Judaism might have withered away in the Hellenist world. The other great monotheistic faiths, Christianity and Islam, might then never have come to birth, and world history would have taken a different turn.

## The Sources for the Maccabean Story

THE PRIMARY SOURCE FOR THE STORY OF THE Maccabean Revolt is the First Book of Maccabees. Starting with a brief historical introduction from the time of Alexander the Great, the work covers a period of forty-one years from the beginning of the reign of Antiochus IV Epiphanes in 175 BC, to the death of Simon, the last of the five Maccabean brothers, in 134 BC. The dates given in the text are according to a calendar that begins with the establishment *The First* of the Seleucid empire in the year corresponding *Book of* to 311 BC. *Maccabees*

It is surmised that the bulk of the book may have been written in Judea about 140 BC, when the Revolt was still fresh in men's minds; and that the two final chapters were added about 100 BC, after the reign of John Hyrcanus I. The Hebrew original was lost, and the work was preserved only in Greek translation. The style is on the whole straightforward and factual. However, the unknown author was not a detached historian but a Jew who was fully

identified with the independence struggle of his people, and probably lived through the events he described.

The Second Book of Maccabees is an abridged *The Second* version of a lost five-volume history by a certain *Book of* Jason of Cyrene. (Jason is the Greek form of the *Maccabees* Hebrew name Joshua; Cyrene, the main centre of Cyrenaica, was on the North African coast that is now part of Libya.) The summary, like Jason's original work, was written in Greek. It covers a period of nearly twenty years from about 180 BC, during the reign of the Seleucid monarch Seleucus IV, to 161 BC, shortly before the death of Judah the Maccabee. The work supplements the First Book of Maccabees, though there are a number of factual discrepancies between the two, and a marked difference in style and purpose. The Second Book of Maccabees has a definite theological slant. Its tone is one of religious fervour, and it stresses the role of divine miracles and angelic interventions in the story. It also injects an element absent from the First Book of Maccabees: martyrdom for the faith. The date of Jason's work has been the subject of scholarly controversy. One conjecture is that it was composed within a decade after the death of Judah the Maccabee, which would make Jason a contemporary of Judah. The summary that survives was probably written about the middle of the first century BC. It starts with the texts of two letters sent by the Jews of Jerusalem to their brethren in Alexandria, stressing the importance of the Festival of Hanukkah.

There is a Third Book of Maccabees, but this title is a misnomer, since the work has no reference to the Maccabean Revolt. Apparently written in Alexandria about 25 BC, it describes how the Egyptian Jews were miraculously saved from persecution and death in the reign of Ptolemy IV Philopator (221–204 BC). There is no historical corroboration for the episode described in the work. It is not included in the Apocrypha, though it does appear in one of the early versions of the Septuagint.

The Fourth Book of Maccabees is a religious- *The Fourth* philosophic work in the form of a sermon or *Book of* lecture delivered in Greek on a Jewish religious *Maccabees* occasion, probably in Antioch in Syria about 40 AD. The unknown author must have been a man learned in both the Jewish scriptures and Greek philosophy. His theme is the control of human passions and fears by the power of pious reason,

'Thus said the Lord: "Heaven is my throne And the earth is my footstool."' Pen and ink illustration for the Book of Isaiah by contemporary Jewish artist Chaim Gross.

# Seleucid Rulers in the Books of Maccabees
*(With Dates of reigns - all BC)*

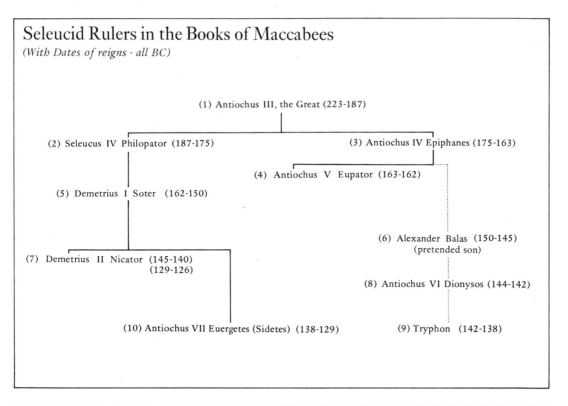

(1) Antiochus III, the Great (223-187)

(2) Seleucus IV Philopator (187-175)    (3) Antiochus IV Epiphanes (175-163)

(4) Antiochus V Eupator (163-162)

(5) Demetrius I Soter (162-150)

(6) Alexander Balas (150-145)
(pretended son)

(7) Demetrius II Nicator (145-140)
(129-126)

(8) Antiochus VI Dionysos (144-142)

(10) Antiochus VII Euergetes (Sidetes) (138-129)    (9) Tryphon (142-138)

# The Hasmonean Dynasty
*(With Dates of leadership or rule - all BC)*

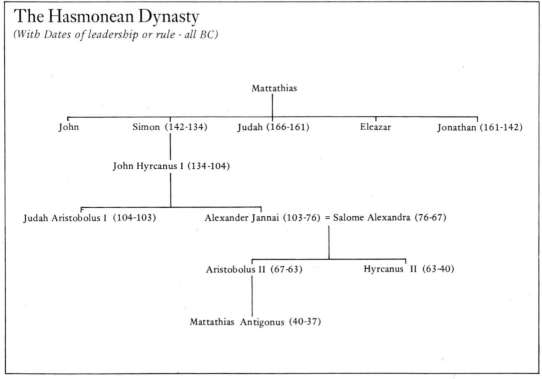

Mattathias

John    Simon (142-134)    Judah (166-161)    Eleazar    Jonathan (161-142)

John Hyrcanus I (134-104)

Judah Aristobolus I (104-103)    Alexander Jannai (103-76) = Salome Alexandra (76-67)

Aristobolus II (67-63)    Hyrcanus II (63-40)

Mattathias Antigonus (40-37)

and the original title appears to have been 'On the Sovereignty of Reason'. This theme is illustrated by an extended and embellished account of two episodes taken from the Second Book of Maccabees, and dealing with Jewish martyrdom at the hands of Antiochus IV Epiphanes. One of these stories concerns the aged sage Eleazar, and the other Hannah and her seven sons. Though this work does not figure among the Apocrypha, it is included in two of the most important surviving manuscripts of the Septuagint, the fourth-century Codex Sinaiticus and the fifth-century Codex Alexandrinus.

*The Book of*    The apocalyptic visions in the second half of
*Daniel* the Book of Daniel are a thinly veiled attack on Antiochus IV. Probably written between 167 and 165 BC, these chapters reflect the persecution in Judea that gave rise to the Maccabean Revolt. A passage in Chapter Eleven of Daniel has been interpreted as a reference to the resistance movement and the beginning of the revolt. It reads:

> He shall seduce with flattery those who violate the covenant; but the people who know their God shall stand firm and take action. And those among the people who are wise shall make many understand, though they shall fall by sword and flame, by captivity and plunder, for some days. When they fall, they shall receive a little help (Dan. 11:32,33,34).

The unknown author of the Book of Daniel predicted that after an age of tribulation a messianic kingdom would arise. This hope helped to maintain the courage of his persecuted fellow-Jews.

*The Classical*    The Classical historians of the second and first
*Historians* centuries BC, such as Polybius, Diodorus Siculus and Livy, do not refer directly to the Maccabean Revolt. The trouble the Seleucid regime was having with its Judean subjects must have seemed to them a marginal matter, compared to the great events they chronicled – the turbulent transition of Rome from republic to empire, and its rise to domination of the Mediterranean world. Nevertheless, what has survived of their historical works fills in the broad background to the developments in Judea. It was a period in which Rome had a growing impact on the affairs of the Near East, until in the first century BC it swept away the Seleucid and Ptolemaic dynasties and occupied their realms.

*The Antiquities of the Jews*, the monumental twenty-book work by the first-century AD Jewish historian Josephus Flavius, contains a detailed and straightforward account of the Maccabean *Josephus* Revolt, the events leading up to it and the *Flavius* subsequent history of the Hasmonean dynasty. Writing about two-and-a-half centuries after the beginning of the Revolt, Josephus generally follows the First Book of Maccabees for the period covered by that work – that is, up to the death of Simon in 134 BC. The *Antiquities* is the major source for Hasmonean history after that date. The term 'Hasmonean' first occurs in this work, and became standard usage in later Jewish literature.

Josephus Flavius was the Latin name acquired by Joseph ben Mattathias, a well-born and gifted young Jerusalem priest. At the outbreak of the Jewish revolt against Rome in 66 AD, he was sent to take charge of the Jewish insurgent groups in Galilee. Captured when a Roman army subdued that district, Josephus was convinced that the rebellion had become a lost cause, and went over to the Roman side. He gained the confidence of the Roman commander Vespasian, and then of his son Titus, who remained in charge of the campaign when Vespasian returned to become emperor in Rome. After the fall of Jerusalem in 70 AD, Josephus settled in Rome, where his imperial patrons granted him citizenship and an annual pension. Here he wrote *The Jewish War*, a detailed account of the conflict. In it Josephus exonerated the Roman command and placed the blame for the calamity on the Jewish extremists, and on the disunity and bickering among the factions defending Jerusalem.

Josephus then devoted his outstanding intellectual and literary talents to compiling *The Antiquities of the Jews* in an effort to acquaint the Roman world with the story of his own small and defeated people. The first half of the work is a resumé of the Old Testament. The second part is a history of Judea up to 66 AD, on the eve of the Jewish War.

Josephus followed the *Antiquities* with an autobiographical work, *The Life of Josephus Flavius*. Its purpose was to justify himself against the criticisms of his fellow-Jews for his role in the defence of Galilee and his defection to the Roman side. His last work was the polemic *Against Apion*, a defence of the Jewish people against the anti-semitic smears of a Greek–Egyptian historian in Alexandria. Apion's writings, incidentally, contained the first known version of the 'blood libel' – the charge that the Jewish religion required the ritual drinking of Gentile blood. The story was to play a grisly part in Jewish history, up to modern times.

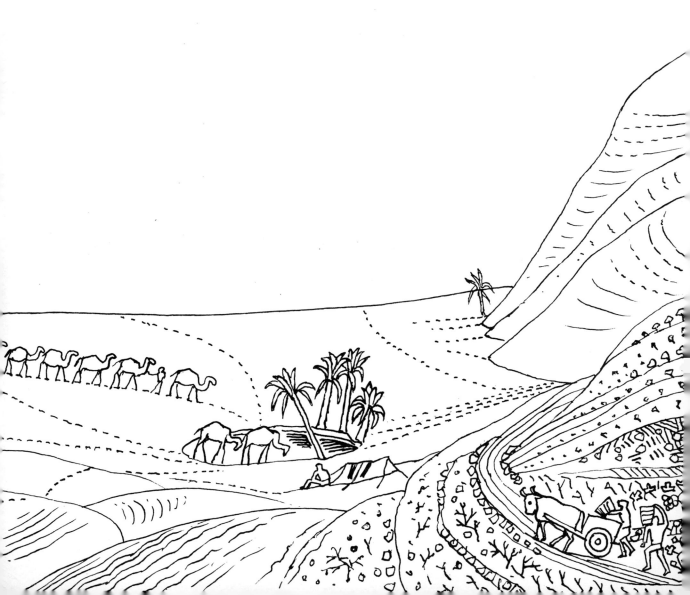

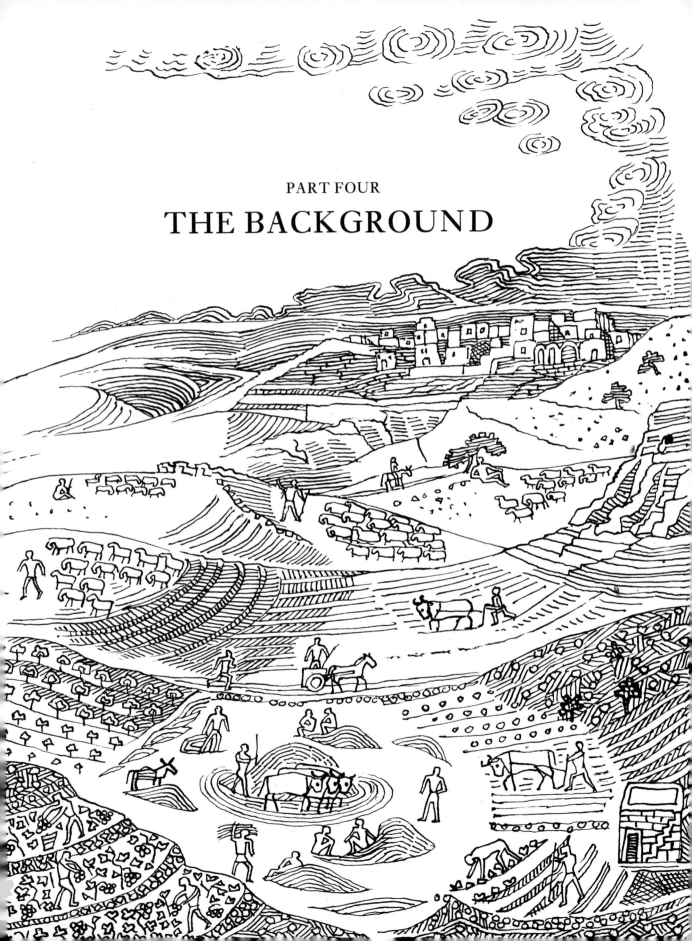

PART FOUR

# THE BACKGROUND

# THE LAND

### *The Name*

THE OLD TESTAMENT HAS NO GENERAL name for the land of the Bible. As a rule, it simply refers to 'the land', as in these two examples:

So Joshua took the whole land, according to all that the Lord had spoken to Moses; and Joshua gave it for an inheritance to Israel according to their tribal allotments. And the land had rest from war (Josh. 11:23).

When you allot the land as a possession, you shall set apart for the Lord a portion of the land as a holy district . . . (Ezek. 45:1).

Egyptian texts before the Israelite conquest used the name Land of Canaan for the area between the Jordan River and the coast. It extended up to what is now Lebanon and southern Syria, but did not include Transjordan. The word Canaan probably means 'Land of the Purple', a reference to the celebrated purple dye extracted from a type of mollusc on the shore.

The united kingdom of Saul, David and Solomon may have carried the name of Israel, but

that is nowhere explicitly stated. After the split in the monarchy that followed the death of Solomon, the southern Hebrew kingdom was called Judah and the northern kingdom Israel.

Under Persian, Hellenist and Hasmonean rule, from the sixth to the first centuries BC, Jerusalem and the territory round it retained the name of Judah – in Hebrew, Yehudah. An inhabitant was a Yehudi – the origin of the word Jew. Judea was the Latinized form of the name, used under the Roman occupation.

Eretz Yisrael (the Land of Israel) was not a biblical term for the whole country. It is used once in the historical books to indicate the area actually occupied by the Israelite tribes (1 Sam. 13:19) and once for the northern kingdom of Israel (2 Kings 5:2). The name has been regularly used by Jews in the post-biblical period from the time of the Mishnah, the compilation of Jewish laws produced in the second century AD.

The name of Palestine was derived from Philistia (in Hebrew, *Peleshet*), the territory of the Philistines, who had settled in the coastal plain in the twelfth century BC. After the emperor Hadrian crushed the revolt of his Jewish subjects under Bar-Kokhba, in 132–135 AD, he officially called the country Palestina in order to eradicate the name of Judea – in the same way as he gave Jerusalem the Latin name of Aelia Capitolina. The word Palestine remained in use in the West as a name for the Holy Land. But after Roman times there was no political or territorial entity officially called by that name, until it was revived under the British Mandate at the end of World War I. The name disappeared again from the map at the end of the Mandate in 1948, when the State of Israel was established.

## The Biblical Landscape

THE LAND OF THE BIBLE LIES BETWEEN THE Mediterranean coast and the desert. In its relatively small expanse – about three hundred miles long and with a maximum width of a hundred miles – the territory contains a remarkable variety of landscape and climate.

*The Coastal Plain* The coastal plain is sandy, well-watered and fertile. In all periods it has been the most populous part of the land. The northern end of the coastal plain contained the port-cities of Phoenicia. The Philistines settled in the wide southern part of the plain. They were part of the waves of Sea Peoples who swept across from the Aegean region in the twelfth century BC, and raided the eastern Mediterranean coast from Asia Minor to Egypt. In their new home they established a strong league of five cities: Gaza, Ashdod, Ashkelon, Ekron and Gath. From this territory they exerted pressure on the Israelites in the hill areas. Although they were non-Semitic newcomers from the west – and, as the Bible points out, uncircumcised – the Philistines quickly assimilated the local Canaanite language and religion. For instance, the god Dagon, whom the blind Samson brought crashing down in Gaza, was the Canaanite deity of grain.

*The Shephelah* Between the coastal plain and the Judean hills lies a belt of undulating foothills known as the Shephelah. During the period of the Judges it formed a disputed borderland between the Israelites in the hills and the Philistines on the plain. This was the scene for the exploits of Samson. His tribe, Dan, came under such Philistine pressure that it was eventually forced to leave the foothills and migrate to the northeastern corner of the land.

The central backbone of the country consists of a range of hills two to three thousand feet high, running parallel to the coast. The southern part round Jerusalem and Hebron is known as the Judean hills; further north, they become the hills of Samaria (or Ephraim) with Nablus, the biblical Shechem, as their main centre. After the Conquest, the Israelite tribes settled mainly in the hill areas, which were sparsely populated and had little arable land. *Judea and Samaria*

The western flanks of the range are exposed to the sea winds that bring the winter rains. In biblical times these slopes were covered with dense vegetation and cultivated terraces, but in later centuries they were denuded by erosion and neglect.

The eastern slopes drop sharply down to the Jordan valley and the Dead Sea. This is the Judean Desert, a khaki-coloured wilderness of canyons and cliffs. It was here that the fugitive David and his outlaw band found refuge from the wrath of Saul.

The central mountain spine of the country is broken by the Valley of Jezreel (or Esdraelon) that crosses from the coastal plain to the Jordan river. The Jezreel valley, like the coastal plain, remained firmly in Canaanite hands after the Conquest. The men of the tribes of Manasseh and Ephraim came and complained to Joshua that there was not enough space for them in the hills. The Canaanites in the valleys, they said, could not be subdued because they were armed with iron chariots. Joshua, unsympathetic, told them to make room for themselves by clearing the hillsides of their trees and bushes. The battles of Deborah and Barak against a Canaanite army at Mount Tabor; of Gideon against the Midianites at the Spring of Harod; and of Saul against the Philistines on Mount Gilboa, all focussed on control of the strategic Jezreel valley. *The Jezreel Valley*

To the north of the Jezreel valley rise the Galilee highlands, with peaks going up to four thousand feet. It is an expanse of ridges and valleys covered with thick scrub and groves of olive trees. At the time of the Israelite settlement, this hill terrain was occupied by the tribes of Asher, Zebulun and Naphtali, later joined by the tribe of Dan. *The Galilee Highlands*

The Jordan valley is part of a deep crack in the earth's surface that continues along the Wadi Araba, the Gulf of Akaba and the Red Sea into the heart of Africa. The valley holds the only two inland lakes in the country: the Sea of Galilee *The Jordan Valley*

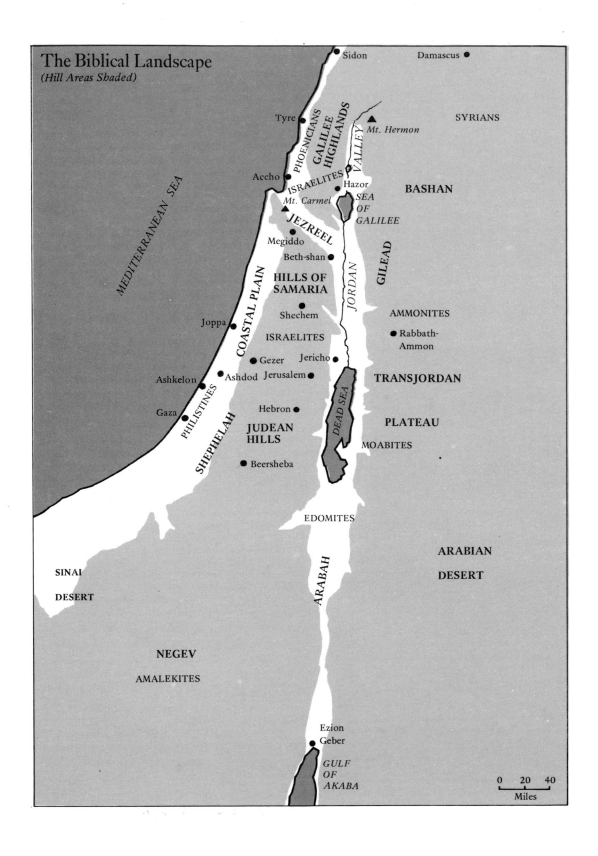

The Biblical Landscape
(Hill Areas Shaded)

Sidon

Damascus

SYRIANS

Tyre

PHOENICIANS

GALILEE HIGHLANDS

VALLEY

Mt. Hermon

Accho

ISRAELITES

Hazor

Mt. Carmel

SEA OF GALILEE

BASHAN

MEDITERRANEAN SEA

JEZREEL

Megiddo

Beth-shan

GILEAD

HILLS OF SAMARIA

COASTAL PLAIN

Shechem

JORDAN

AMMONITES

Joppa

ISRAELITES

Rabbath-Ammon

Gezer

Jericho

Ashkelon

Ashdod

Jerusalem

TRANSJORDAN

Gaza

PHILISTINES

Hebron

DEAD SEA

PLATEAU

SHEPHELAH

JUDEAN HILLS

MOABITES

Beersheba

EDOMITES

SINAI

DESERT

ARABAH

ARABIAN

DESERT

NEGEV

AMALEKITES

Ezion Geber

GULF OF AKABA

0    20    40

Miles

(also called Lake Tiberias, or Lake Kinneret in Hebrew) is seven hundred feet below sea-level; the Dead Sea (or Salt Sea), is thirteen hundred feet below sea-level – the lowest point on earth. The Jordan river rises near Mount Hermon in the north, enters the northern end of the Sea of Galilee, flows out at the southern end and snakes its way down to end in the Dead Sea.

*The Negev*  The southern part of the country is the Negev, an inverted triangle with its point at the head of the Gulf of Akaba. In biblical times the small port of Ezion-geber stood near where modern Eilat is now located. The northern part of the Negev around Beersheba is a flat, semi-arid plain. Through this area Abraham and Isaac moved from well to well, their flocks grazing on the low scrub in the dry water-courses. Further south the Negev becomes more broken, with eroded cliffs and depressions. To the west, it runs into the Sinai desert. Kadesh-barnea, the large oasis in the Wilderness of Zin where the children of Israel remained for over a generation, is in Sinai fifty miles south-west of Beersheba. From Kadesh the Israelites crossed the Negev and made a detour round the Dead Sea to enter the Promised Land from the east, because the report of the spies sent by Moses had discouraged any attempt to invade Canaan directly from the Negev. Solomon used his control of the Negev to open a shipping route from Ezion-geber through the Gulf of Akaba to the Red Sea area. During the divided monarchy the Israelite hold on the Negev was intermittent.

The Amalekites were nomad tribes who roamed the desert region of the Negev and the adjoining Sinai peninsula. Their biblical name was said to have been derived from Amalek, the grandson of Esau. They are depicted in the Bible as fierce marauders, who for centuries were traditional foes of the Israelites. Among the scriptural accounts of armed conflicts with them were the battle of Refidim during the Exodus; Saul's campaign against them, when he captured their king Agag; and the pursuit of the Amalekite band that had plundered Ziklag and carried off the wives and children of David and his men.

*The Trans-jordan Kingdoms*  East of the Jordan valley and the Dead Sea a steep escarpment rises to the Trans-jordan plateau, some two thousand feet above sea-level. Approaching the Promised Land from this direction the Israelites under Moses encountered a line of Trans-jordan kingdoms that had come into existence only a little while before, in the

fourteenth and thirteenth centuries BC. Their inhabitants, originally desert nomads, spoke Semitic tongues akin to Hebrew.

The southernmost of these kingdoms was Edom, in the rugged terrain on both sides of the Wadi Araba below the Dead Sea. This kingdom included the high ground of Mount Seir, a name sometimes used in the Old Testament to denote the whole of Edom. By biblical tradition, the Edomites were descended from Esau, Jacob's twin brother. During the period of the monarchy they were generally involved in strife with the Israelites, and at times Edom was an Israelite vassal. After the fall of Jerusalem in 587 BC, they moved into the Hebron hills. In the Hasmonean period (second to first centuries BC) the Edomites, called Idumeans by the Romans, were converted to Judaism and absorbed into the Jewish people. Herod the Great was of Idumean stock.

The kingdom of Moab occupied the fertile tableland to the east of the Dead Sea and three thousand feet above it. According to the Bible, the Moabites were descended from one of Lot's daughters through her incestuous union with her father. Both Edom and Moab refused passage to Moses and the Children of Israel, and had to be bypassed. Moab became a vassal state of David and Solomon, and later of the northern kingdom of Israel during the reigns of Omri and Ahab. The famous Mesha Stone records how the Moabite king of that name regained his independence.

To the north of Moab lay the nameless Amorite kingdom of King Sihon, in the territory later known as the Land of Gilead. Sihon went out to battle against the Israelites and was defeated, giving them access across his country to the Jordan river fords. The tribes of Reuben and Gad and part of the tribe of Manasseh settled in the territory wrested from Sihon.

Between the Land of Gilead and the eastern desert was the kingdom of Ammon, with its capital at Rabbath-ammon (the modern Amman). The attempts of Ammon to expand towards the Jordan river across Israelite territory in Trans-jordan led to recurrent hostilities. In the period of the Judges, Jephtah led a successful campaign to repulse the Ammonite pressure. Before he became king, Saul relieved the Israelite city of Jabesh-gilead that was being besieged by an Ammonite force. David conquered Ammon and incorporated it in his empire, but it regained

An Arab herdsman grazing his cattle in a field of stubble near ancient Acre in Western Galilee.

its independence after his death.

On the Hauran plateau (the Golan Heights) east of the Sea of Galilee stood the small kingdom of Bashan. It was noted for the stalwart physique of its people, its rich grain fields and its 'strong bulls of Bashan' (Ps. 22:12). The men of Bashan were said to be descended from a legendary race of giants. When the Children of Israel advanced through Trans-jordan, Og the king of Bashan attacked them and was heavily defeated. His territory was allotted to that half of the tribe of Manasseh that settled east of the Jordan.

*The Caravan Routes*  Though small and poor, the Land of Israel gained regional importance because it lay astride the two main trading routes of the ancient Near East. One was the Via Maris (the Way of the Sea) that linked the Nile Valley with Mesopotamia. It came along the Sinai coast through Gaza, up the coastal plain and through a pass behind the Carmel range into the valley of Jezreel at Megiddo. It then ran along the floor of the valley, crossed the upper Jordan river and traversed the Hauran plateau to Damascus. From there it continued eastward to the Mesopotamian plain. Along this route armies and laden merchant caravans had passed since time immemorial.

The King's Highway ran from Arabia to Damascus, passing through the Trans-jordan kingdoms of Edom, Moab, Ammon and Bashan. It was the main road for the lucrative spice trade.

David's conquests gave the Hebrew kingdom control over both the Via Maris and the King's Highway. His son Solomon was thus able to expand the trade of the kingdom and also to derive substantial revenues from the tolls imposed on passing caravans.

*Rainfall*  A passage in the Book of Deuteronomy stresses how dependent the Children of Israel would be in the Promised Land on rain that fell by God's favour:

For the land which you are entering to take possession of it is not like the land of Egypt, from which you have come, where you sowed your seed and watered it with your feet, like a garden of vegetables; but the land which you are going over to possess is a land of hills and valleys, which drinks water by the rain from heaven ... he will give the rain for your land in its season, the early rain and the later rain, that you may gather in your grain and your wine and your oil ... Take heed lest your heart be

deceived, and you turn aside and serve other gods and worship them, and the anger of the Lord be kindled against you, and he shut up the heavens, so that there be no rain, and the land yield no fruit, and you perish quickly off the good land which the Lord gives you. (Deut. 11:10–17).

Rain falls only during the half-year between October to November and April to May. The precipitation from the Mediterranean sea-winds decreases from north to south. It is highest in upper Galilee, up to 44 inches a year, while parts of the southern Negev get only 1 to 2 inches. The amount of cultivable land largely corresponded to the rainfall map.

Poor rains in the winter months could produce disastrous drought and famine. It was in such years that the Hebrew patriarchs were driven to seek grain in Egypt. After the Israelite settlement, the use of plaster-lined rock cisterns for water storage made the Israelites in the hills less vulnerable to lack of rain. The plains had easier sources of water from wells.

## Canaan at the Time of the Conquest

THE PROMISED LAND INTO WHICH JOSHUA LED the Children of Israel was not and never had been a unified country. It was split up among a number of small city-states, each under its own local ruler or 'king'. The early Canaanites were a Semitic *The* people who had settled in the land many centuries *Inhabitants* before the Hebrew patriarchal age. Excavations show that some of their walled cities had a history going back to at least 3000 BC. The Old Testament notes that Abraham received a blessing from Melchizedek, the priest-king of Salem (Jerusalem); and that both Abraham and Isaac had dealings with Abimelech king of Gerar, a little south of Gaza.

The Amorites were another Semitic people with a nomadic background. They infiltrated into Canaan some centuries before the time of Joshua, and assimilated with the older Canaanite population. In the Old Testament the distinction between Canaanites and Amorites is blurred. Sometimes the term Amorite is a synonym for Canaanite, and sometimes it indicates a separate group. Certain passages suggest that the Amorites were mainly concentrated in the hill areas and the Canaanites on the coastal plain. The

Trans-jordan kingdom of King Sihon overrun by the advancing Israelites was termed an Amorite state.

In addition to Canaanites and Amorites, the Old Testament refers to several other peoples inhabiting the country at the time of the Conquest: Hittites, Jebusites, Hivites (or Horites), Perizzites and Girgashites.

The Hittites were presumably groups of settlers in Canaan from the Hittite empire of Asia Minor that expanded as far as northern Syria. Abraham bought the Cave of Machpelah in Hebron from one of the residents of that city, Ephron the Hittite. Uriah the Hittite was Bathsheba's husband and an officer in David's army.

The Jebusites were a Canaanite sub-group who inhabited the city-state of Jebus (another name for Jerusalem); after the capture of the city by David they merged with the Israelites.

It has been conjectured that the Hivites or Horites were an offshoot of the Hurrian people that came from the region east of Asia Minor. Before the fifteenth century BC the Hurrians established the important kingdom of Mitanni in northern Mesopotamia and later ruled the city-state of Nuzi. The Old Testament mentions Hivite communities in the Gibeon area and around Shechem. A delegation from Gibeon and three neighbouring Hivite towns tricked Joshua into making a peace pact with them. At a later stage they became the 'hewers of wood and drawers of water' for the Jerusalem Temple.

The identity of the Perizzites and Girgashites is obscure; they are mentioned in the text but play no distinctive part in the biblical narrative.

The Phoenicians were the most advanced and sophisticated people of Canaanite stock. They were a literate population of merchants, seafarers and craftsmen inhabiting the narrow coastal strip of what is now Lebanon. From their great port-cities of Tyre and Sidon, they sailed the length of the Mediterranean. The Phoenicians were never conquered by the Israelites, but always maintained good-neighbour relations with the Hebrew kings. Hiram, king of Tyre, supplied David and Solomon with timber and skilled craftsmen for their building projects. Ahab, Omri's son and successor in the northern kingdom of Israel, was married to the redoubtable Phoenician princess Jezebel, daughter of the king of Sidon.

At the height of Egypt's imperial power in the fifteenth and fourteenth centuries BC, Egyptian governors and garrisons had kept order among the Canaanite vassal-kings. But since then *The City-* Egypt's control had waned. It had become *States* impotent to defend Canaan against external attack, or to prevent its kings from feuding with each other. This lack of cohesion made it possible for Joshua to subdue a large part of the country piecemeal, in separate campaigns. At best, neighbouring city-states could improvise shaky alliances against him. Joshua defeated such a coalition of five southern kings, led by the king of Jerusalem. In the northern part of the country he overcame a joint force assembled from all the local rulers by Jabin, king of Hazor.

The invading Israelite tribes encountered in Canaan a material culture far more advanced than their own austere nomad way of life. The Canaanite cities were well-built, with solid walls, water systems and drainage. The city defence walls were too formidable for direct assault by Joshua's desert fighters, and he had to lure the defenders into the open. Certain of these cities, like Jerusalem, Gezer, Megiddo and Beth-shan, remained unsubdued for the following two centuries, until the conquests of David.

The religion of the Canaanites was a nature *The Cults* cult, marked by fertility practices that the Israelites regarded as abominable. The Canaanite father-god was El, a somewhat shadowy figure compared to the god of rain and storm, Baal – the Syrian Hadad. The annual death and resurrection of Baal symbolized the cycle of the agricultural year. The wife of Baal was the fertility goddess Asherah – also called Ashteroth and Astarte. The word Asherah is used in the Old Testament to denote both the goddess herself and the tree or pole that served as her sacred symbol. The shrines of the Canaanite gods, especially of Asherah, were centres of sacred prostitution, both male and female, and of orgiastic rites.

At the threshold of the Promised Land, before the death of Moses, the Israelites were already affected by the insidious Canaanite cults. The struggle to preserve the Mosaic faith against pagan encroachment is a major theme of the biblical story in the periods of the Judges and the Hebrew kings. The conflict was dramatized in Elijah's confrontation on Mount Carmel with the priests of Baal and Asherah.

## 2

# THE NEAR EAST SETTING

### *The Cradle of Civilization*

THE OLD TESTAMENT WAS SHAPED mainly by factors special to the Hebrew nation: its unique faith, its collective experience and its superb ethical and literary gifts. But that small nation was part of a wider environment, and was affected by contacts and conflicts with other peoples in the area. The Old Testament can only be fully understood in its regional context.

*The Two River Basins* The ancient Near East has rightly been called the cradle of civilization. Its major centres were two rich alluvial river basins: the Nile valley in Egypt and the Mesopotamian plain between the Tigris and Euphrates rivers. In these lands there developed large-scale irrigation systems, the central administration needed to operate them, the first cities and the revolutionary invention of writing. The land of the Bible was part of the corridor between Egypt and Mesopotamia, and lay in the path of the armies and caravans that passed to and fro.

*The Fertile Crescent* In ethnic origin, language and culture, the links of the Israelites extended northward rather than southward. Their territory lay at the south-western end of a great arch of cultivable land that curves round the top of the Arabian desert, from the head of the Persian gulf to the border of Egypt. In the biblical period of the Hebrew kings, this Fertile Crescent (as it is now called) included Assyria and Babylonia; the Aramean (Syrian) states from Haran to Damascus; Phoenicia; the Israelite kingdoms of Israel and Judah; and the Trans-jordan kingdoms of Ammon, Moab and Edom. The area today comprises Iraq, Syria, Lebanon, Israel and Jordan.

From time to time waves of Semitic nomads would emerge from the desert and erupt into the settled countries of the Fertile Crescent, producing upheaval and change. These nomads would in due course blend with the indigenous population. The Israelites under Joshua were in a sense such nomad invaders; the difference was that they did not disappear, but retained their distinctive identity and faith.

The mingling of nations and cultures in the Fertile Crescent over three millennia formed the matrix from which the Old Testament emerged. Abraham's journeys illustrate the basic unity of the area. He and his family started out from the

Sumerian city of Ur in southern Mesopotamia and moved up the Euphrates valley to the Haran region of northern Syria. Here they lived as sheep-farmers, watering their flocks at the local wells. Abraham then travelled south-west to the land of Canaan. At that point he had migrated from one end of the Fertile Crescent to the other.

*The Arameans* The Arameans were one of the Semitic nomad peoples that moved into the Fertile Crescent. They spread over Mesopotamia and Syria, at a time that is uncertain. The trading city of Haran, where Abraham's family settled, was the centre of an Aramean area called Paddan-aram (the field of Aram).

The Book of Genesis stresses the family ties between the Hebrew patriarchs and the Aramean inhabitants. The Table of the Nations in Genesis makes Aram one of the children of Noah's son Shem. Several names in Abraham's family line actually corresponded to place-names in Paddan-aram – his ancestors Peleg and Serug, his grandfather Nahor, his father Terah, and his brothers Nahor and Haran.

When Abraham sent his servant to find a wife for Isaac among his kinsmen in the Haran locality, the servant returned with Rebekah, who is described as 'the daughter of Bethuel the Aramean of Paddan-aram, the sister of Laban the Aramean' (Gen. 25:20). Bethuel was Abraham's nephew, so Rebekah was his great-niece. In due course Jacob married his first cousins Leah and Rachel, the daughters of Laban, who is repeatedly referred to as an Aramean. A verse in Deuteronomy calls Jacob himself 'a wandering Aramean' (Deut. 26:5).

By the time of King David, eight centuries or so after Abraham, the centre of Aramean influence had become the city-state of Aram-Damascus, north-east of the Israelite territory. David captured Damascus and made it part of his empire, but it broke away again before Solomon's death. Aram-Damascus then became the chronic antagonist of the northern kingdom of Israel, and periodic wars were waged between them. Both kingdoms were wiped out at the same time, by an Assyrian invasion in 732 BC.

Other neighbouring Aramean states at the time of David were Zobah to the north of Damascus; Hamath, further north on the Orontes river; Maacah, east of the Jordan near Mount Hermon; and Geshur, east of the Sea of Galilee.

Aramaic, a Semitic language with close affinities to Hebrew, became the *lingua franca* of the whole Fertile Crescent. At the beginning of the Christian era the common spoken tongue in Judea was Aramaic, while Hebrew was the language of religion and literature. Jesus must have preached, and conversed with his disciples, in Aramaic. There are passages in the Hebrew Bible and Prayer Book that have survived in Aramaic to this day – including the Kaddish, the Jewish prayer for the dead.

## The Clash of Empires

IT WAS THE STRUGGLE FOR MASTERY AMONG THE imperial powers that decided the fate of the small nations in the Near East, including the Hebrew people.

In Mesopotamia the civilizations of Sumer and Akkad were followed by two dynamic powers, the Babylonians and the Assyrians, who vied with each other for domination. In its periods of expansion, Egypt exerted its sway across the Sinai desert into the Canaanite-Syrian area. Up to the twelfth century BC, the Hittite horsemen pushed down from Asia Minor. From the sixth to the fourth centuries BC, the vast Persian empire included the whole Near East. Then Alexander the Great of Macedonia swept eastward and ushered in the Hellenist (Greek) period. It was replaced within three centuries by the might of Rome. Each of these ancient empires had its impact, direct or indirect, on the events recorded in the Bible.

*Sumer* From about 4000 BC a group of Sumerian city-states developed in the southern part of the Mesopotamian plain. They evolved extensive irrigation, urban architecture, epic literature, cuneiform writing, pottery, astronomy and mathematics. There was a Sumerian renaissance in the twenty-first century BC when Abraham's home-city of Ur under its Third Dynasty became the leading centre in Mesopotamia, with a population estimated at over half-a-million. The earliest Flood story was a fragment of a Sumerian epic.

*Akkad* The Akkadians were a Semitic people that established itself in the Mesopotamian plain to the north of Sumer, with its capital at Akkad (or Agade). In the twenty-fourth century BC the great Akkadian leader Sargon I carved out the world's first empire, with control over most of the Fertile Crescent. The Akkadian language came into general use in the region, and was the forerunner of a group of Semitic tongues that included Aramaic, Hebrew and Arabic.

*The Old Babylonian Empire* Babylonia was a small and unimportant kingdom in southern Mesopotamia until the rise of the illustrious Hammurabi (1728–1686 BC). He conquered Sumer and Akkad and merged them into what scholars today call the Old Babylonian Empire. In his reign Babylon grew from an obscure townlet into a great city and centre of learning. The most important of Hammurabi's achievements was a systematic law code engraved on an eight-foot stele of black stone, now kept in the Louvre in Paris. It has certain points of affinity with the Mosaic Code. The Old Babylonian Empire declined after Hammurabi and was extinguished by the Hittites in the sixteenth century BC. It revived a thousand years later, after the fall of Assyria.

*Egypt* The Greek historian Herodotus aptly wrote in the fifth century BC that 'Egypt is the gift of the Nile'. The annual flooding of the river deposited along its banks and in its delta a layer of fertile silt that was the source of its wealth and grandeur. Its development went back to about 5000 BC. When Abraham journeyed to Egypt to buy food, about the eighteenth century BC, the twelfth Egyptian dynasty was already on the throne, and the Great Pyramid, which covers thirteen acres (the largest single structure ever erected by man), was already nine centuries old.

In the seventeenth century BC Egypt was conquered by the Hyksos, a Semitic people who invaded through Canaan, equipped with horse-chariots. It was under one of these Hyksos 'shepherd kings' that Joseph (also a non-Egyptian Semite) rose to power at court, and that Jacob and his clan were encouraged to settle in the Land of Goshen in the Eastern Delta, near to Avaris, the Hyksos capital. In 1567 BC the Hyksos were overthrown and expelled by the Egyptians. In the New Kingdom that followed, the vigorous Eighteenth Dynasty brought Egyptian power to its greatest height. A series of campaigns regained control of the Canaanite-Syrian area. But Egyptian strength waned again during the religious schisms precipitated by the young reformer, King Amenhotep IV (Akhnathon), married to the beautiful Nefertiti. The fifteenth-century BC Amarna Letters, discovered in the royal archives at the site of Akhnathon's palace, include hundreds of clay tablets with com-

munications from Egypt's local vassals in Canaan. They give a picture of general unrest and strife at that time, and a slackening of Egyptian control.

The Nineteenth Dynasty restored Egyptian authority for a short while. Its second ruler, Seti I (1305–1290 BC), was probably the pharaoh 'who did not know Joseph' and started to oppress the Israelites. His son and successor Rameses II (1290–1223 BC) put them to work as slave labour on the construction of two new cities in the Eastern Delta, Raamases and Pithon. Most scholars accept that Rameses II was the unnamed pharaoh of the Exodus.

From the time of Joshua's Conquest, the role of Egypt in biblical history was marginal. During the centuries of the Hebrew kingdoms, Egypt was for the most part an important bystander in the Near Eastern power-struggle. The pharaohs incited Judah and its neighbours to revolt against their Assyrian or Babylonian overlords, usually with disastrous results. Isaiah warned King Hezekiah against relying on promises of Egyptian support; so did Jeremiah with King Zedekiah, a century later.

*The Hittites* Hatti, the land of the Hittites, lay in the mountainous region of Asia Minor that is now the Anatolian province of Turkey. From about 1400 BC the Hittite kingdom expanded southwards into Syria. But this advance was halted by the army of the Egyptian Pharaoh Rameses II in 1286 BC, in the battle of Kadesh on the Orontes river. During the rest of the thirteenth century BC the Hittite empire disintegrated under the blows of the raiding Sea Peoples from the Aegean. The Hittites thus never conquered Israelite territory, though there were Hittite elements in the population.

The Hittites were noted horse-breeders. King Solomon's agents developed a lucrative trade in horses from the Hittite state of Cilicia in Asia Minor (the biblical Kue). The Hittites were also pioneers of iron-smelting and at first held a monopoly of this skill. It was acquired and jealously guarded by the Philistines.

Scholars have shown that in its formal aspect the Sinai Covenant between God and the Children of Israel had some affinity with the treaties between Hittite monarchs and their vassals. This is a striking example of the influence on the People of the Book of other Near Eastern peoples and cultures, even those like the Hittites

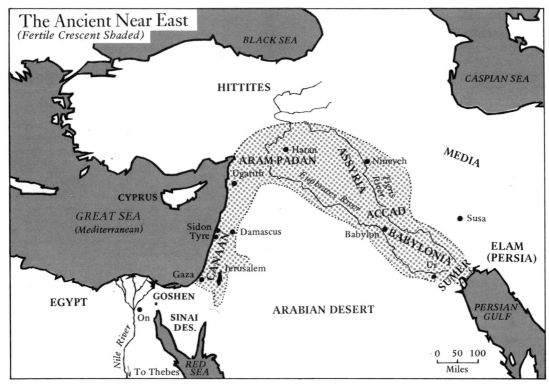

## The Ancient Near East
### (Fertile Crescent Shaded)

BLACK SEA

CASPIAN SEA

HITTITES

MEDIA

Haran

ARAM-PADAN

ASSYRIA

Nineveh

Uganth

Tigris River

CYPRUS

GREAT SEA
(Mediterranean)

Euphrates River

ACCAD

Susa

Sidon
Tyre

Damascus

Babylon

BABYLONIA

ELAM
(PERSIA)

Gaza

Jerusalem

Ur

SUMER

CANAAN

EGYPT

GOSHEN

ARABIAN DESERT

PERSIAN
GULF

On

SINAI
DES.

Nile River

RED
SEA

To Thebes

0   50   100
Miles

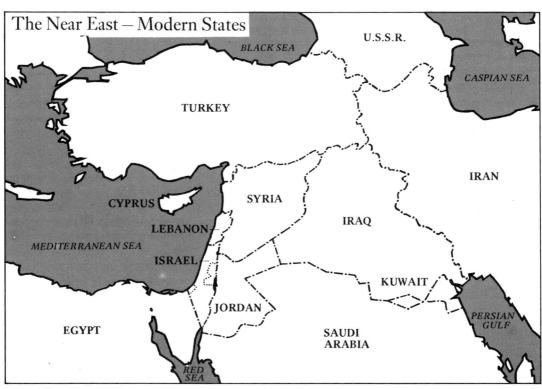

## The Near East — Modern States

BLACK SEA

U.S.S.R.

CASPIAN SEA

TURKEY

IRAN

CYPRUS

SYRIA

MEDITERRANEAN SEA

LEBANON

IRAQ

ISRAEL

KUWAIT

JORDAN

EGYPT

SAUDI
ARABIA

PERSIAN
GULF

RED
SEA

who did not play a direct role of importance in the biblical story.

*Assyria*   Assyria was situated on the Upper Tigris river, in the north-eastern part of Mesopotamia. The country took its name from its early capital Assur, later succeeded by Nineveh. In the ninth century BC Assyria became the leading power in Mesopotamia and started pushing westward towards the Mediterranean. The inconclusive battle of Karkar in northern Syria in 853 BC was fought by a coalition of twelve local kings to stem the advance of the Assyrian monarch Shalmanezer III. King Ahab of Israel was a prominent member of the coalition.

Later, a series of Assyrian campaigns culminated in the destruction of the kingdom of Israel in 722 BC. A number of the inhabitants were removed into captivity – the origin of the Lost Ten Tribes of Israel. A weak and shrunken kingdom of Judah remained a tribute-paying vassal of Assyria. In 701 BC King Sennacherib invaded Judah and sacked a number of towns. Assyrian power reached its zenith with the occupation of Egypt in the seventh century BC.

With their arrogant, bearded faces, their winged bull-images and their obsession with war and conquest, the Assyrians were the 'herrenvolk' of the ancient Near East, and the strongest military power the world had seen till then. But in the latter part of the seventh century BC their empire began to crumble. It finally collapsed when Nineveh fell in 612 BC to the combined forces of two neighbouring countries, Media and Babylonia.

*The Neo-Babylonian (Chaldean) Empire*   After the fall of Assyria, the power-vacuum in the Near East was filled by the Neo-Babylonian empire. Its greatest ruler was Nebuchadnezzar (605–562 BC), who emerged as the dominant figure in the region. During his reign Babylon became the largest and most luxurious city in the known world. Among its notable features were the 'hanging gardens' on the roof-tops of the palace complex, and the huge ziggurat or stepped pyramid that appears in Genesis as the Tower of Babel.

The Old Testament frequently uses the name of Chaldeans instead of Babylonians. The Chaldeans were a Semitic people who gained control of Babylonia by the seventh century BC. Nebuchadnezzar was the second king of the Chaldean dynasty. The statement in Genesis that Abraham came from 'Ur of the Chaldees' is an anachronism, since the Chaldeans only appeared in Mesopotamia about 1000 BC – that is, at least seven centuries after Abraham.

Persia was a kingdom inhabited by a people of *Persia* Indo-European or Aryan stock (its modern name, Iran, is derived from the word Aryan). It lay to the east of Babylonia along the shore of the Persian Gulf, with its capital at Susa (Shushan). Its northern neighbour was the larger kingdom of Media. The Medes were a mountain people also of Indo-European race, and famous for their horses. In the middle of the sixth century BC Cyrus the Great of Persia (559–529 BC) conquered Media and established the dual kingdom of the Medes and the Persians. In 539 BC Cyrus captured Babylon. By the time of Darius the Great (522–486 BC), the Persian empire covered the entire Near East.

In 538 BC, the year after he had occupied Babylonia, Cyrus issued the famous edict that started the movement of the return of the Jewish exiles to Jerusalem. Judea became a tiny sub-province in the Fifth Satrapy of the vast Persian empire. In the reign of Darius the Great the Second Temple was rebuilt in Jerusalem. Xerxes I (486–465 BC), the son of Darius, was probably Ahasuerus, the king who appears in the Book of Esther, and his palace at Susa was the setting for the story. The mission of Nehemiah took place in the reign of the next monarch, Artaxerxes I Longimanus (465–424 BC). It is uncertain whether Ezra's mission was in the same reign or in the next one, that of Artaxerxes II (404–358 BC).

The Persian empire came to an abrupt end *The Hellenist* with its conquest by Alexander the Great in 333 *Period* BC. After his death the Near East was divided between dynasties founded by two of his Macedonian generals, Ptolemy and Seleucus. The Ptolemies ruled in Egypt and the Seleucids over the northern area from Asia Minor to Persia. Judea came under Egypt for a century, until in 198 BC it was incorporated into the Seleucid empire. The reign of Antiochus IV Epiphanes (175–163 BC) was the background for the Maccabean Revolt and the apocalyptic visions in the Book of Daniel. The declining Seleucid empire was taken over piecemeal by the Romans. It ended when a Roman army under Pompey occupied Syria and Judea in 64–63 BC and turned them into a Roman province. The same fate befell Ptolemaic Egypt in 30 BC, after the defeat and suicide of Cleopatra. The Roman world was the background to the New Testament.

## The Origin of the Hebrew Alphabet

THE WORD BIBLE COMES FROM 'BIBLIA', THE Greek or Latin word for books. The word scriptures is from the Latin for writing. These derivations emphasize that there would have been no Bible and no Scriptures – that is, no Old Testament – unless the ancient Hebrews had been able to write down their traditions and thus preserve them for all time.

*The Invention of Writing* The use of written signs to communicate or store information and ideas was one of the key inventions in human history. A written language first appeared in the Mesopotamian land of Sumer about five thousand years ago, at the beginning of the Bronze Age. It was soon followed by Egypt – whether independently or not is uncertain.

The earliest writing was in the form of pictographs. They were simple line drawings of familiar objects: human figures; bodily parts such as the head, eye, mouth, hand or foot; houses; animals and birds; trees, hills or ripples of water. In the Sumerian city-states the pictographs evolved into a system of wedge-shaped marks known to-day as cuneiform, from the Latin word for a wedge, *cuneus*. This script was adopted by the Akkadians and then the Babylonians, and came into general use in the Near East. It was incised on the walls of palaces and temples and on stone monuments, and for more portable purposes was inscribed with a blunt-ended stylus on small, damp clay tablets that were then dried, and became practically indestructible.

In Egypt the pictographs were stylized, and formed the basis of a complex system of writing called hieroglyphs. Here too, in addition to the walls of public buildings and monuments, a cheap and portable writing surface was available – scrolls of rough paper, made from the fibres of the papyrus reeds that grew in profusion along the banks of the Nile.

The cuneiform and hieroglyphic scripts were difficult to master. Each had many hundreds of symbols representing words or syllables. They were not a true phonetic alphabet, which may be defined as a fixed set of written signs each standing for a single spoken sound. Such an alphabet, composed of twenty-two consonants, evolved before 1000 BC in Phoenicia. The

Phoenician alphabet was adapted to the languages of other Near Eastern peoples, including the Hebrews, close neighbours of the Phoenicians and fellow-Semites. Phoenician traders carried their alphabet with them on their voyages around the Mediterranean. The Greeks amplified it by adding five vowel signs. From the Greek came the Latin alphabet used for most modern languages. A later offshoot of the Greek alphabet was Cyrillic, still in use for Russian and other Slav languages.

The word 'alphabet' comes from the first two letters: 'aleph' and 'beth' in Phoenician or Hebrew, or 'alpha' and 'beta' in Greek. 'Aleph' meant an oxhead, and 'beth' a house; these derivations bear out that alphabetic letters can be traced back to pictures of physical objects.

Scholars still cannot clearly mark the development from cuneiform or hieroglyphic script to the Phoenician alphabet. Three Canaanite scripts have been discovered – each in one place only – that may possibly have been intermediate stages or prototypes in the process.

The oldest of the three is a 'pseudo-hieroglyphic' script found on stone and bronze tablets in the ancient port-city of Byblos, on the Phoenician coast. Their date cannot be determined, and may be anywhere between 2100 and 1300 BC. There are just eighty characters, which suggest that they represented syllables, since there are too few signs for words and too many for single letters.

In the Sinai Peninsula, at a place called Serabit, the Egyptians worked turquoise mines with Semitic-speaking Canaanite labourers. These miners left some fifty inscriptions on the quarry walls, dating from about the fifteenth century BC. The script has not been deciphered, but since it used only twenty-seven hieroglyph-type characters, it may well have represented the beginnings of a crude alphabet.

A third mysterious script was discovered in the ruins of the ancient North Canaanite city-state of Ugarit (Ras Shamra), on what is now the Syrian coast. The clay tablets found here go back to the fifteenth and fourteen centuries BC. They are in a cuneiform script, but use only thirty signs.

The Phoenician alphabet made the art of writing immeasurably easier and more widespread. One result was to stimulate the urge among nations to record their traditions and legends. When the Hebrews in the Land of Israel were producing the earliest versions of the Pentateuch, Homer in Greece was writing the Odyssey and the Iliad.

The oldest inscription in Hebrew to have been discovered is the calendar of Gezer, dating from the tenth century BC. Its seven lines, engraved on a slab of limestone, set out an annual cycle of farming activities: fruit picking, grain sowing, late sowing, flax harvest, barley harvest, wheat harvest, vintage and wine pruning, and the picking and drying of figs.

*The Hebrew Language* Hebrew is one of a group of Near Eastern Semitic languages that originated with the early nomad influx from the desert. From the original Semitic tongue were derived Akkadian, Babylonian, and Assyrian in the Mesopotamian plain; Aramaic in the Syrian area; Phoenician and Hebrew in Canaan; Edomite, Moabite and Ammonite in Trans-jordan; the different dialects of Arabic and Ethiopic. The vocabulary and grammar of early biblical Hebrew was strongly influenced by both Phoenician and Aramaic.

# 3

# DIGGING UP THE PAST

## The Methods of Biblical Archaeology

THE ARCHAEOLOGIST'S TASK IS TO discover and interpret the physical remains of the human past. These remains do not always need to be excavated: many ruins and ancient occupation sites stay exposed on the surface.

The Holy Land may seem relatively poor soil for such efforts. It has no great architectural monuments from antiquity comparable to the Pyramids, the Parthenon, or the sumptuous palaces of Nineveh and Babylon. No glittering treasure hoards, massive carved masterpieces, or rich royal archives have come to light here. Yet this small land offers a unique challenge to the archaeologist, for its landscape was the setting for the world's greatest story. The patient sifting of its dust and stones and the survey of its topography have for the last century and a half thrown new light on the Bible.

*The Pioneers*     Down the ages there have been many travellers and pilgrims to the land of the Bible, each bringing back his own impressions of its scenes, people and sacred sites. But systematic research on its ancient past started only in the nineteenth century.

The man who pioneered the geographical approach to Bible study was an American theologian, Edward Robinson, who held a Chair in Biblical Literature at New York College. In 1838 Robinson travelled all over Palestine on horseback with a companion, Eli Smith, who had been a missionary in Beirut and knew Arabic well. Robinson was able to relate many local Arab place-names to those occurring in the scriptural text.

Forty years later, between 1872 and 1878, an accurate survey of Western Palestine, on a scale of one inch to the mile, was compiled by two English experts, C. R. Conder and H. H. Kitchener (later Lord Kitchener of Khartoum). The outstanding literary product of the topographical school was the classic *Historical Geography of the Holy Land* by the Reverend Adam Smith of Edinburgh, first published in 1894.

The nineteenth-century British interest in the Holy Land led to the establishment in 1865 of the Palestine Exploration Fund, under the patronage of Queen Victoria. For the next century it sponsored biblical exploration and excavation in

357

# Main Old Testament Archaeological Sites

1967 Cease Fire Line —·—·—·—
Israel occupied Areas ·············

LEBANON

*MEDITERRANEAN SEA*

Tyre

Dan

GOLAN HTS.

Achzib

Hazor

SYRIA

Acre

**GALILEE**

*SEA OF GALILEE*

CARMEL

JORDAN

Megiddo

Beth-shan

*RIVER JORDAN*

Samaria

Shechem
(Nablus)

Joppa

**SAMARIA**

Bethel

Jericho

Gezer

Ashdod

Beit
Shemesh

Jerusalem

Ashkelon

**JUDEA**

Ein-
gedi

*DEAD SEA*

Gaza

Lachish

Hebron

Beersheba

Arad

Sodom

**ISRAEL**

**NEGEV**

0        20

miles

*MEDITERRANEAN SEA*

Jerusalem

*DEAD SEA*

Beersheba

Kadesh-
barnea

Wilderness
of Zin

**NEGEV**

**SINAI**

Ezion-geber
(Eilat)

*GULF OF SUEZ*

St. Catherine

▲
*Mt. Sinai*

*GULF OF AKABA*

**SAUDI
ARABIA**

**EGYPT**

*RED SEA*

the country. The first project was a survey of Jerusalem, under the direction of Captain Charles Wilson of the Royal Engineers. His name was given to Wilson's Arch, the remains of the bridge that connected the Temple Mount with the Upper City in the Second Temple period. Another Royal Engineers officer, Captain Charles Warren, then carried out a hazardous exploration of the walls enclosing the Temple Mount, by digging a series of deep shafts and underground galleries through the accumulated debris of centuries.

During this period a brilliant young Frenchman, Charles Clermont-Ganneau, made a number of discoveries of the highest importance, while serving as French Consul in Jerusalem. It was he who acquired from the Arabs the famous Mesha stone from ancient Moab (now in the Louvre), and who discovered the inscription prohibiting the admission of Gentiles into the inner courts of the Second Temple.

*Biblical Tels*     The salient feature of Palestinian archaeology is the artificial flat-topped mound known by the Arabic word *tel*. The buildings of a town may crumble or be destroyed, and another town later be built on top of the debris. Horizontal layers or strata of occupation are thus created one above the other, steadily raising the level of the site. Hundreds of such tels are dotted about Israel and other Near Eastern countries. Outwardly, a tel may appear to be just another hillock covered with earth, grass and bushes, though a trained eye would notice its characteristic shape. Enclosed within it may be the record of anything up to twenty periods of occupation, covering thousands of years.

The significance of the tel was first brought out by an English archaeologist of genius, Flinders Petrie. His career was mainly devoted to Egypt, but in 1890 he spent six weeks excavating Tel el-Hesi in the south-western part of Palestine. This pioneering dig established two factors that were basic to later biblical archaeology: the lessons of stratification in tels, and the use of pottery as a dating tool.

Since Petrie's day the techniques of tel digging have become far more elaborate and controlled. A tel is not as a rule constructed in neat, horizontal strata, like a layer cake. Later occupants of the site use the building stones of earlier ones. Pits and hollow spaces fill up with rubble from upper layers. Parts of the tel may subside from natural

causes. Indiscriminate digging causes confusion and error, and unfortunately the archaeologist can destroy the evidence by the very act of excavating it.

In a modern dig, the site is divided by grids into small squares, marked by letters and numbers. Every foot of earth is sifted. An exact record is kept of the location of each object found – walls, household artefacts, potsherds, coins or anything else that can add a clue, however trivial it may seem. Written notes are supplemented by photographs, sketches and architectural plans. Baskets of potsherds are taken to sorting tables, and where possible pottery vessels are reconstructed from fragments. The services are enlisted of specialists in architecture, surveying, geology, ceramics and other fields. An important dig, spread over several seasons, will accumulate a mass of data that may take years to classify, analyse and compile for publication.

Among the biblical cities that have been dug out of tels are Hazor, Megiddo, Samaria, Bethel, Ai, Gibeon, Gezer and Lachish.

Up to the turn of the century archaeologists   *Dating the* lacked any means for dating their finds, except for   *Finds* the occasional inscription that could be linked to a particular event or reign. Petrie's 'sequence-dating' of pottery developed into the most effective means to this end. Each period and each area had its own typical pottery, distinctive in shape and in decorative design. At the beginning hardly anything was known about the types and periods of Palestinian pottery. This knowledge was gradually built up through the scientific excavation of tels. It would be assumed, unless shown otherwise, that a piece of pottery belonged to the same period as a datable object found in the same stratum. This principle was useful when local pottery was found together with vessels imported from other countries like Egypt or Greece, where the dates were already known. By the late 1930s practically any fragment of pottery found in a dig could be assigned to its period by an expert.

The earliest examples of pottery found in the land of the Bible were in neolithic Jericho, and date back to about 5000 BC. The potter's wheel first came into use in Egypt about 3000 BC and was introduced into Canaan a millennium later.

An additional dating technique provided by science is that known as radio carbon dating. It was developed at the Institute of Nuclear Studies in the University of Chicago. From the carbon dioxide in the atmosphere living matter absorbs carbon both in the regular form, Carbon-12, and in the form of a radioactive isotope, Carbon-14. When the organism is no longer alive, the unstable Carbon-14 diminishes at an infinitesimal but regular rate. Nearly half of it will have disappeared after five thousand years. By measuring the loss of Carbon-14, the age of the substance can be determined with a margin of error of about five per cent. This test is now regularly used where an archaeological find of unknown age contains organic matter, such as bones, wood, leather, linen and other fabrics, or basketware woven from reeds or rushes.

The most sensational example in modern archaeological history concerned the Dead Sea Scrolls discovered in 1947. There was fierce controversy over their authenticity and their age. Fragments from the cloth wrappers of the scrolls, made of linen flax, were sent for Carbon-14 analysis to Professor W. F. Libby of Chicago University, one of the two scientists who developed the test. The result put the date at 33 AD. Allowing for the margin of error either way, the age had to be between the second century BC and the second century AD. That fitted in with evidence from other sources, such as comparative analysis of the textual script and style.

Another example of much greater antiquity concerned charcoal embers found at the lowest level of the Jericho excavations. The Carbon-14 test showed that camp-fires had been made next to the spring of water about 8600 BC.

*Archaeological Periods*

Archaeologists mark the stages of man's early history by technological advances – in much the same way as one talks to-day about the Space Age or the Atomic Age. The criterion in ancient times was the material used for making tools and weapons – whether stone, copper, bronze (an alloy of copper and tin), or iron. In the following table, which has become standard for biblical archaeology, it must be borne in mind that the dates are approximate, and that the periods overlap with each other:

| | |
|---|---|
| 8000–4000 BC | Neolithic (New Stone) Age |
| 4000–3200 BC | Chalcolithic (Copper-Stone) Age |
| 3200–1200 BC | Bronze Age |
| | Early Bronze: 3200–2100 BC |
| | Middle Bronze: 2100–1550 BC |
| | Late Bronze: 1550–1200 BC |

| | | |
|---|---|---|
| 1200–300 BC | Iron Age | |
| | Iron I: | 1200–900 BC |
| | Iron II: | 900–600 BC |
| | Iron III: | 600–300 BC |

The end of the Old Testament period corresponds roughly to the end of the Iron Age. From then, the archaeological periods relevant to the Bible take their names from the successive masters of Judea. They are:

| | |
|---|---|
| Hellenist period: | 300–142 BC |
| Hasmonean period: | 142–63 BC |
| Roman Occupation: | 63 BC–323 AD |
| Herodian Period: | 37 BC–44 AD |

In Old Testament chronology, the age of the Patriarchs would be Middle Bronze; the Exodus and the Conquest at the end of Late Bronze; the Judges and the United Monarchy in Iron I; the two Kingdoms in Iron II; and the Exile and Return in Iron III.

## Archaeology and the Old Testament

SINCE ITS BEGINNINGS IN THE NINETEENTH century, biblical archaeology has steadily broadened its scope. The territory it covers includes not only the land of the Bible but also other Near Eastern lands that influenced the history of the ancient Hebrew nation. The time-span is not confined to the period of the biblical narrative, but extends backwards to the beginnings of civilization in the region. As for the subject-matter, the archaeologist does not just seek to verify specific scriptural events and places. He also tries to recreate the daily life of the Israelites in different periods – their dwellings, tools and weapons, occupations, trade, laws and customs, religious beliefs, literature, legends and language. In all these respects, there were points of contact between the Israelites and other peoples and cultures in the Near East, and discoveries about them add to the understanding of the Old Testament. These other peoples include close neighbours like the Canaanites, Moabites or Arameans, and imperial powers like Egypt, Assyria, Babylonia or Persia.

It is nevertheless of primary importance when archaeological finds directly corroborate the scriptural text. Here are a few examples.

About Hazor, the Bible tells us that it was the *Hazor* leading Canaanite city in the north of the country; that Joshua destroyed it by fire; that

The necropolis of Silwan is situated opposite the original city of David on Ophel Hill and became a cemetery for the Jerusalem nobility of the Monarchy. The tombs have been excavated by Gabriel Barkai of the Institute of Archaeology in Tel Aviv.

Solomon constructed one of his three 'chariot cities' there; and that Tiglath-pileser, the king of Assyria, invaded eastern Galilee, sacked a number of cities, including Hazor, and carried off their inhabitants into exile. The excavations carried out by Professor Yigael Yadin on the Hazor tel in 1955–59 established that there had been an extensive and well-developed Canaanite city; that it had been destroyed and burnt in the second half of the thirteenth century BC (the period of Joshua); that at the raised southern end of the site, Solomon had built a citadel; and that the last Israelite town at Hazor was sacked in the late eighth century BC, about the time of Tiglath-pileser.

*Shishak's Invasion*    The Book of Kings states that in the fifth year of the reign of Rehoboam, Solomon's son, Judah was invaded by the Egyptian pharaoh Shishak, who carried away treasures from Jerusalem. Shishak (or Sheshonk) was the founder of the Twenty-Second Dynasty. On the wall of a temple at Karnak in Egypt, he left a carved relief celebrating the campaign to which the Bible refers, and listing towns in Judah and Israel plundered by him.

*The Moabite Stone*    The Bible recounts an Israelite campaign against Mesha, a ninth-century ruler of Moab, which was abandoned when he sacrificed his own son to their national god Chemosh. In 1868 a missionary travelling through Trans-jordan reported coming across a black basalt stele on which Mesha had inscribed the exploits of his reign. The stele confirmed that Moab had been under subjection to kings Omri and Ahab of Israel, and Mesha claimed to have regained his independence with the help of Chemosh.

*Lachish*    In the year 701 BC, in the reign of Hezekiah, Judah was invaded by the Assyrian monarch Sennacherib. It appears from the Book of Kings that he set up his main camp outside Lachish, a strongly fortified Israelite city in the foothills west of Hebron. The Book of Chronicles adds that Sennacherib 'was besieging Lachish with all his forces' (2 Chr. 32:9). Archaeologists have found confirmation of the siege both in Sennacherib's palace and on the Lachish site.

In 1849 the Englishman A. H. Layard exca-vated the palaces of the ancient Assyrian capital of Nineveh – one of the milestones of Near Eastern archaeology. In the royal annals disco-vered there, Sennacherib gave an account of his invasion of Judah, boasting that he had captured forty-six towns, taken 200,150 captives and shut Hezekiah up in Jerusalem 'like a caged bird'. On a palace wall Layard found a series of thirteen stone bas-relief panels on which Sennacherib had pictured the siege and capture of Lachish. Now in the British Museum, these panels are one of the most dramatic illustrations ever found of military siege techniques in the ancient world.

From 1932 on, the Lachish tel was excavated under the direction of J. L. Starkey, a British archaeologist who had been a young assistant to Sir Flinders Petrie, and was murdered by Arab bandits in 1938. The dig revealed the ramps of earth constructed for Sennacherib's assault on the bastion of the city gates, the burnt debris of the destroyed walls, and the bones of fifteen hundred corpses flung haphazard into a huge pit.

A little more than a century after Sennacherib, in 587 BC, the kingdom of Judah was invaded and wiped out by another Mesopotamian conqueror, King Nebuchadnezzar of Babylonia. According to the Book of Jeremiah (34:7) the last two places outside Jerusalem to keep up resistance were Lachish and Azekah, a town in the foothills twelve miles further to the north-east. Starkey's excavation at Lachish revealed that it was again demolished and burnt about that time. The most sensational find was a group of twenty-one ostraca (inscribed potsherds), most of them buried in the debris of the guard-house at the gate. They were addressed to a certain Yoash, apparently the military commander in Lachish, by a subordinate officer called Hoshaiah, com-manding an outlying post somewhere between the two cities. One of these Lachish Letters must have been written in the last days before the end. It reports that '. . . we are watching for the signals of Lachish, according to all the indications which my lord hath given, for we cannot see Azekah'. The communications between these unknown Judean officers, unearthed twenty-five centuries later, give a striking endorsement to the Bible.

*Hezekiah's Tunnel*    Anticipating the Assyrian invasion under Sennacherib, Hezekiah strengthened the fortified walls of Jerusalem and took steps to safeguard its vital water supply in case of a siege. It is recorded that '. . . he made the pool and the conduit and brought water into the city' (2 Kgs. 20:20). The Book of Chronicles adds that Hezekiah closed the upper outlet of the Gihon spring and diverted its water along the side of the Kidron valley into the city, to deny it to the enemy – 'Why should the kings of Assyria come and find much water?' (2 Chr. 32:4) The preparations proved justified when Sennacherib sent his top officials from his Lachish camp to demand the surrender of Jerusalem – a demand Hezekiah was persuaded by the prophet Isaiah to reject.

Nineteenth-century explorers found that Hezekiah's workmen had cut a tunnel that zigzagged through the solid rock of the Ophel hill and connected the Gihon spring with the Pool of Siloam, a reservoir constructed inside the walls of David's city. In 1838 Edward Robinson and his companion Eli Smith crawled through the tunnel and estimated that it was 1750 feet long – one-third of a mile. Captain Charles Warren, sent to Jerusalem by the Palestine Exploration Society of London, surveyed it in December 1867. He spent four hours submerged in the water, which in places was only a few inches below the ceiling.

In 1880, some boys were playing inside the tunnel near its lower end. One of them slipped and fell into the water. In scrambling up he noticed an inscription cut into the wall, three feet above the floor. The inscription, part of which was missing, was found to be written in the classical biblical Hebrew of Hezekiah's time. It commemorated the completion of the tunnel, and described how it was carved out by two teams of miners working from opposite ends and meeting in the middle – an astonishing engineering feat for the biblical world of the eighth century BC.

*Jericho and Ai* Archaeological discoveries do not always conform with the scriptures as neatly as in the above examples. The excavations at the site of ancient Jericho show that the history of its walls goes back six thousand years before Joshua, which makes it the oldest fortified town ever found. Unfortunately, the latest wall appears to have been destroyed at least a century-and-a-half before the date now attributed to Joshua's Conquest. The discrepancy remains a perplexing problem for biblical scholars.

According to the biblical account, Joshua proceeded from Jericho to capture the Canaanite city of Ai on the Judean uplands. The dig at what is thought to be the site of Ai indicates that the city was abandoned a thousand years before Joshua. It is surmised that the biblical traditions may have confused Ai with Bethel, two miles away. By the archaeological evidence, Bethel was destroyed by fire about the time of the Israelite invasion.

On occasion the archaeologist may fill a gap in the biblical record. In 853 BC Shalmaneser III of Assyria fought a crucial battle at Karkar on the Orontes river in northern Syria. His own account *The Battle of* is inscribed on a monolith now in the British *Karkar* Museum. Shalmaneser claims he won a great victory over a coalition of Syrian and Canaanite kings, whom he lists. One of them was 'Ahab of Israel' who is credited with contributing two thousand chariots and ten thousand foot-soldiers to the allied army. The battle was no doubt more inconclusive than Shalmaneser made out, for he did not resume his westward expansion for many years. The Bible makes no reference to this battle, which saw the kingdom of Israel aligned with its chronic enemy Aram-Damascus against the dreaded Assyrians. The interest of the biblical writers in the reign of Ahab focussed on the internal religious struggle that involved the king, his queen Jezebel and the prophet Elijah.

Where direct evidence is lacking, archaeology *Near Eastern* can help to interpret the Old Testament by *Analogies* finding among surrounding nations similarities with the life and thought of the biblical Israelites. It can now be seen how much they were an integral part of their environment. The accounts of the Creation and the Flood in Genesis are related to Sumerian and Babylonian legends, like the Epic of Gilgamesh. Biblical Hebrew was one of a group of Semitic languages that included Akkadian, Babylonian, Assyrian, Aramaic, Phoenician, Ugaritic, Moabitic and Arabic. The alphabetic script used in the Old Testament evolved over three thousand years, from the birth of writing in Mesopotamia. Scholars have pointed to certain affinities between the Mosaic Code and the Code of Hammurabi, the great eighteenth-century BC Babylonian ruler – though the differences between the two are more significant than the points of similarity. Light may be thrown on aspects of Old Testament religion and literature by studying the libraries of clay tablets unearthed in buried cities like Nuzi, Ugarit and Ebla, that are not even mentioned in the Bible.

The ancient city-state of Nuzi was situated a *Nuzi* little to the east of Haran, where Abraham and his kinsmen settled before he trekked on to Canaan. (The site of Nuzi is south of Kirkuk in modern Iraq.) Excavations between 1929 and 1931 unearthed over twenty thousand clay tablets written in cuneiform in the Akkadian language.

They show that in the fifteenth and fourteenth centuries BC Nuzi was an important centre of the Hurrian people, who moved into Upper Mesopotamia and Syria from the mountainous region that later became Armenia. A study of the Nuzi documents has shown some striking parallels with early Hebrew patriarchal customs depicted in the Book of Genesis.

Sarah, Rachel and Leah each arranged for her husband to have offspring by a slave-maid, when she believed herself barren or unable to have more children. This concept of a wife's duty was so accepted in Nuzi that it was even written into marriage contracts.

When Jacob left Haran to return to Canaan, his wife Rachel stole the *teraphim* or household god-images belonging to her father Laban. Her motive for this strange action has remained obscure. In Nuzi, when the head of the family died the household gods passed together with the bulk of his property into the possession of his heir. If a man had no natural sons he might adopt his son-in-law, who would then be his heir and his potential successor as the family head. From the biblical text it seems that Laban's sons may have been born some time after Jacob became his son-in-law. The Nuzi analogy suggests that Jacob may originally have been designated as Laban's heir, and that Rachel may have taken the household gods in order to maintain her husband's status in the family and his future property claim.

There are also Nuzi references to the biblical institution of levirate marriage, whereby a dead man's brother is obliged to marry his widow if she is left childless.

*Ugarit (Ras Shamra)* The ancient North Canaanite port-city of Ugarit was buried in a mound known by the Arabic name of Ras Shamra, on the coast of northern Syria. In 1928 a peasant ploughing his field at this spot accidentally found an opening to an underground passage that led to a burial chamber. Excavations of the mound revealed the remains of the city. The most important find was a library of clay tablets, the majority of them written in a Semitic language and a cuneiform script, neither of them previously known. When they were deciphered, it appeared that Ugarit had flourished in the fifteenth to fourteenth centuries BC as the main port of entry for copper ore from the island of Cyprus, sixty miles away. The city's trading hinterland stretched from Mesopotamia

to Egypt. It seems to have been destroyed about 1200 BC by raiding Sea Peoples from the Aegean.

The Ugaritic literature caused a wave of excitement in academic circles. Apart from the linguistic challenges, the lengthy epic poems found at Ugarit had affinities in style, language and metaphor with poetic passages in the Old Testament. They also for the first time shed light on the Canaanite pantheon of gods and goddesses against whose fertility cults the Israelites struggled so long and so fiercely. If there were a bible of the Canaanite religion, the bulk of it would come from Ugarit.

The many poetic expressions that are similar in the Ugarit texts and the Bible can be illustrated by one example. The Baal Epic of Ugarit relates how Baal, the god of storm and rain, fought against the mythical sea-monster Lothan (the biblical Leviathan): '... when thou smotest Lothan the slippery serpent and madest an end of the wriggling serpent'. Isaiah echoes this verse: 'In that day the Lord with his hard and great and strong sword will punish Leviathan the fleeing serpent, Leviathan the twisting serpent' (Isa. 27:1). Like the Ugaritic Lothan the biblical Leviathan is described as having a number of heads.

A Canaanite practice of special interest to the Jewish religion is referred to in one of the Ugarit poems. A magic rite used to bring rain was to seethe a goat-kid in its mother's milk. That no doubt explains why this act was prohibited by the Mosaic Law, in the context of the battle against infiltration of pagan practices among the Hebrews. In later Judaism, all the elaborate rules about keeping meat and milk separate evolved from this single scriptural ban against seething a kid in its mother's milk.

*Ebla* In 1973 a team of Italian archaeologists started excavating the 140-acre mound of Tel Mardikh, south of the modern Syrian city of Aleppo. Under one wing of a destroyed palace, archives containing some fifteen thousand clay tablets came to light. They were written in an early Canaanite language, using Sumerian cuneiform symbols. From these records it appeared that a great city-state called Ebla flourished here between 2400 and 2250 BC, during the period of the Akkadian empire in Mesopotamia. The influence of Ebla extended southward as far as the Egyptian border, and the archives refer to dealings with such ancient Canaanite cities as Hazor, Megiddo,

Jerusalem, Akko (Acre), Lachish and Gaza. Far-reaching claims have been made concerning the possible ties between Ebla and the Hebrew patriarchs, and the impact of the discoveries on the dating of the patriarchal period. But it is premature to draw any conclusions.

*Conclusion* The current Ebla dig demonstrates that biblical archaeology is far from being a closed book. Striking advances have already been made; yet only a small part of the ancient cities buried in Near Eastern tels have as yet been excavated. Future discoveries will add to the understanding of the Bible, and perhaps revise some existing interpretations.

At the same time, analogies between the ancient Hebrews and their regional neighbours must be treated with caution. There were undoubtedly traditions and customs of common origin. But whatever the People of the Book derived from other sources, it transmuted into the spirit of its own religion and outlook. The distinction was basic. The pagan gods of other peoples in the region were identified with heavenly bodies, physical forces, the cycle of the seasons, the rhythmic but unchanging pattern of nature. In all the societies of the time there was no analogy with the single and invisible Hebrew God, without consort, progeny, pantheon or graven image.

The small Hebrew nation and its faith have uniquely lasted through forty turbulent centuries to the present day. The other civilizations of the ancient Near East have long vanished, the mighty with the humble. Their stories can be resurrected only by the labours of the archaeologists and the references in the Bible.

# CHRONOLOGY

| DATE (BC) | ISRAELITE | NEAR EAST |
|---|---|---|
| | *From the Creation to the Flood*<br>(Gen. 1–11) | MESOPOTAMIA<br>Sumerian City-States: 29th–24th century<br>Akkadian Empire: 24th–21st century<br>Third Ur Dynasty: 21st–18th century<br><br>EGYPT<br>Old Kingdom: 29th–23rd century<br>Middle Kingdom: 23rd–18th century<br>EGYPTIAN DOMINATION OF CANAAN |
| | *From the Patriarchs to the Exodus*<br>*c.* 1800–*c.* 1250<br>(Gen. 12 – Exod. 1) | Old Babylonian Empire: 1830–1530<br>    Hammurabi: 1728–1686 |
| 1800 | The Patriarchs in Canaan: *c.* 1800–1700 | Hyksos Regime in Egypt: 1720–1560 |
| 1700 | The sojourn in Egypt: *c.* 1700–1250 | Egyptian New Kingdom (Empire):<br>    1560–1100 |
| 1400 | | Rise of Hittite Empire: 1400–1300<br>Egypt loses control over Canaan |
| 1300 | Israelites forced labour in Egypt | Pharaoh Rameses II (1290–1224) |
| | *From the Exodus to the Monarchy*<br>*c.* 1250–1020<br>(Exod. Lev. Num. Deut. Josh. Judg. 1 Sam.) | End of the Hittite Empire |
| 1250 | The Exodus: *c.* 1250<br>The Law at Sinai<br>Joshua's Conquest *c.* 1220–1200 | |
| 1200 | Settlement of Israelite tribal areas<br>    from *c.* 1200 | Eclipse of Egyptian Empire<br>Rise of Aramean kingdoms: Damascus,<br>    Zobah, Hamath<br>Philistine settlement on coast |

| DATE (BC) | ISRAELITE | NEAR EAST |
|---|---|---|

*From the Exodus to the Monarchy*—continued

THE JUDGES

| | | |
|---|---|---|
| 1150 | Ehud | |
| 1100 | Shamgar | |
| | Deborah | |
| | Gideon | |
| | Jephtha | Assyrian domination in Mesopotamia |
| | Samson | |
| 1050 | Philistines defeat Israelites at Aphek and capture Ark | |
| | Samuel's leadership: *c.* 1040–*c.* 1020 | |

## The United Monarchy

1020–922

(1, 2 Sam. 1 Kgs. 1, 2 Chr.)

| | | |
|---|---|---|
| | SAUL (1020–1000) | Period without external pressure from Near Eastern imperial powers. |
| | Campaigns against Philistines, Ammonites, Amalekites. | |
| | Defeat and death at Mount Gilboa | |
| 1000 | DAVID (1000–961) | |
| | Capture of Jerusalem | |
| | Expansion of Israelite Empire | |
| | Ark of the Law brought to Jerusalem | |
| | Revolt of Ansalom | |
| 950 | SOLOMON (961–922) | |
| | Building of the Temple | |
| | Red Sea Trade Route | |
| | Visit of the Queen of Sheba | |
| | Death of Solomon and division of Kingdom: 922 | |

## The Two Kingdoms

922–587

(1, 2 Kgs. 2 Chr. Amos. Hos. Isa. Mic. Jer.)

| | JUDAH | ISRAEL | |
|---|---|---|---|
| | Rehoboam (922–915) | Jeroboam (922–901) | Pharaoh Shishak's Campaign |
| | Abijah (915–913) | Nadab (901–900) | |
| | Asa (913–873) | Basha (900–877) | |
| 900 | Jehoshaphat (873–849) | Elah (877–876) | |
| | | Zimri (876) | |
| | | Omri (876–869) | |
| | | Founding of Samaria | |
| | | Ahab (869–850) | Mesha, King of Moab |
| | | Elijah | ASSYRIAN DOMINATION |
| | | Ahaziah (850–849) | Campaigns of Shalmaneser III (859–824) |

| DATE (BC) | ISRAELITE | | NEAR EAST |
|---|---|---|---|

*The Two Kingdoms*—continued

| 850 | Jehoram (849–842) | Jehoram (849–842) Elisha | Battle of Karkar: 853 |
| | Ahaziah (842) | Jehu (842–815) | |
| | Athaliah (842–837) | | Hazael, King of Aram-Damascus |
| | Joash (837–800) | Jehoahaz (815–801) | |
| 800 | Amaziah (800–783) | Jehoash (801–786) | Adad-nirari III (811–783) |
| | Uzziah (783–742) | Jeroboam II (786–746) Amos Hosea | Ben-hadad II, King of Aram-Damascus |
| 750 | | Zechariah (746–745) | |
| | Jotham (742–735) | Shallum (745) Menahem (745–738) | Tiglath-pileser III (745–727) |
| | Ahaz (735–715) | Pekahiah (738–737) | |
| | Isaiah | Pekah (737–732) | Shalmaneser V (727–722) |
| | Micah | Hoshea (732–724) | |
| | | FALL OF SAMARIA: 722 Deportations | Sargon II (722–705) |
| | Hezekiah (715–687) | | Sennacherib (705–681) |
| 700 | | | Invasion of Judah: 701 |
| | Manasseh (687–642) | | Esarhaddon (681–669) |
| 650 | | | Asshurbanipal (669–633) |
| | Amon (642–640) | | |
| | Josiah (640–609) | | Fall of Nineveh: 612 |
| | Religious reforms | | Battle of Megiddo: 609 |
| | Jehoahaz (609) | | BABYLONIAN DOMINATION |
| | Jehoiakim (609–598) Jeremiah | | |
| 600 | Jehoiachin (598) Jerusalem surrenders First deportations to Babylonia Ezekiel | | |
| | Zedekiah (598–587) FALL OF JERUSALEM: 587 Deportations to Babylonia Judah a Babylonian province Gedaliah assassinated Babylonian Exile Second Isaiah | | |

| DATE (BC) | ISRAELITE | NEAR EAST |
|---|---|---|
| | *The Return* | |
| | (Ezra, Neh. Hag. Zech. Esther) | PERSIAN DOMINATION |
| 550 | Edict of Cyrus and beginning of the Return: 538 | Cyrus the Great (550–530) |
| | | Fall of Babylon: 539 |
| | Zerubbabel governor | |
| | Temple rebuilt: 520–515 | Darius the Great (522–486) |
| | Haggai | |
| 500 | Zechariah | |
| | | Xerxes I (Ahasuerus) (486–465) |
| | Ezra's mission (if under Artaxerxes I): 458 | Artaxerxes I (465–423) |
| 450 | Mission of Nehemiah: 445–425 | |
| | Walls of Jerusalem rebuilt | Artaxerxes II (404–358) |
| 400 | Ezra's mission (if under Artaxerxes II): 398 | |
| | Religious reforms | |
| 350 | | Alexander the Great (356–323) |
| | | Defeat of Darius III of Persia at Issus: 333 |
| | *The Hellenist Period* | |
| | 331–63 | |
| | (1, 2 Macc, Dan 11) | |
| 300 | Judea under Ptolemaic (Egyptian) rule: 301–198 | |
| 250 | | SELEUCID DYNASTY |
| | | Antiochus III, the Great (223–187) |
| 200 | Judea under Seleucid (Syrian) rule: 198–142 | Defeats Egyptians at Panias: 198 |
| | | Defeated by Romans at Magnesia: 188 |
| | | Seleucus IV (187–175) |
| | | Antiochus IV Epiphanes (175–163) |
| | Temple profaned: 167 | |
| | Start of Maccabean Revolt: 166 | |
| | Judah's leadership: 166–161 | Antiochus V (163–162) |
| | Temple re-dedicated: Dec. 164 | Demetrius I (162–150) |
| 150 | Jonathan's leadership: 161–142 | Alexander Balas (150–145) |
| | Jonathan high priest: 152–142 | Demetrius II (145–144) |
| | Judea autonomous: 142 | Antiochus VI (144–142) |
| | Simon leader and high priest: 142–134 | Tryphon (142–138) |
| | The Hasmonean State: 134–37 | |
| 100 | Pompey takes Jerusalem: 63 | Pompey occupies Syria – end of Seleucid Empire: 64–63 |

NOTE: Where dates are uncertain, the author has followed the chronology of Professor W. F. Albright

# ACKNOWLEDGMENTS

Photographs and illustrations are supplied by kind permission of the following:

The Barber Institute of Fine Arts, University of Birmingham: *166–7*
Bibliothèque Nationale, Paris: 121
Bildarchiv Photo Marburg: 20, 33, 41, 64 (above and below), 73, 217, 299
Bodleian Library, Oxford: *331*
Yaakov Boussidan: 27
British and Foreign Bible Society: 337
British Library: 15 (right), 121, 211 (right), *330*
Camera Press (photograph by Yael Braun): 361
Cooper Bridgeman Library: *162*
Deutsche Museum, Munich: 211 (left)
Douglas Dickens: *39*, *335*, *346–7*
Arnold Fawkus and the executors of Ben Shahn: *334*
Fotomas Index (courtesy of the British Library): 147, 287
Giraudon: *38*
Felix Gluck Archives: 54, 109, 129, 176, 186 (above and below)
Guildhall Library: *70–1*
Sonia Halliday: 89, 171
André Held: *31*, *159*, *222–3*, *263*, *322*, *323*
Historia Photo: 23, 81
Michael Holford: *75* (courtesy of the British Library)
Patricia Mandel: 229 (below)

Mansell Collection: 205, 319
Mary Evans Picture Library: 229 (above right)
Netherlands Bible Society: from the series *What the Bible Tells*: *219*
Oxford Scientific Films: 42 (© Dr. J. A. L. Cooke), *218*
Picturepoint, London: *30*, *66*, *67* (courtesy of the British Library), *74*, *78* (courtesy of the British Library), 156, *163*, 180, 189, 208 (above left, right and below), *262* and 308 (courtesy of the Bibliotheque Nationale)
Pierpont Morgan Library, New York: 229 (above left)
Staatsbibliothek Bamberg: 255
Staats und Universitätsbibliothek, Hamburg: 26
Tate Gallery: 58–9, *158*, 198, 260, © Mrs. Lilian Bomberg) *270–1*
University Library, Cambridge: 15 (left) from *Graphic zur Bibel* published by Verlag Ernst Kaufmann: 97, 107, 138, 274, 311
Victoria and Albert Museum: *34–5*, *258–9*
The Walker Art Gallery, Liverpool: 29, 47, *154–5*

*Numerals in italics indicate colour illustrations*

Picture research by Patricia Mandel
Maps by John Payne

# INDEX